The Lower and Middle Palaeolithic Periods in Britain

Archaeology of Britain

Edited by

Barry Cunliffe

*Professor of European Archaeology in
the University of Oxford*

The Lower and Middle Palaeolithic Periods in Britain

Derek A. Roe

*Donald Baden-Powell Quaternary Research Centre,
University of Oxford*

Routledge & Kegan Paul
London, Boston and Henley

First published in 1981
by Routledge & Kegan Paul Ltd
39 Store Street, London WC1E 7DD,
9 Park Street, Boston, Mass. 02108, USA and
Broadway House, Newtown Road,
Henley-on-Thames, Oxon RG9 1EN
Set in 10pt Press Roman by
Columns, Reading
and printed in Great Britain by
Lowe & Brydone Printers Ltd, Thetford, Norfolk
Plates printed by
Headley Brothers Ltd, Ashford, Kent
© Derek A. Roe 1981

British Library Cataloguing in Publication Data

Roe, Derek Arthur

The lower and middle Palaeolithic periods in
Britain. – (Archaeology of Britain).
1. Palaeolithic period – Great Britain
I. Title   II. Series
936.1'01   GN772.22.G7   80-41098

ISBN 0-7100-0600-4

Contents

Plates

Figures

Tables

Preface

This book has been written in the period 1975-9, much too slowly, in time salvaged from that demanded by the hundreds of other duties that somehow arise in an allegedly tranquil academic life, which is officially merely divided between teaching, advanced study and research. Perhaps it is easy to be a flint implement and wait for hundreds of thousands of years, with a heart that registers 7 on the Mohs scale; mine, confronted with the pressing needs and the imminent triumphs or disasters of colleagues and students, seems to register about 2, or 3 on really ruthless days.

The text of the book has been written consecutively in the order in which it is presented; this is worth mentioning only because in setting out a British Palaeolithic sequence I have followed a careful thread of argument that is not simply chronological. If the geochronological evidence in Britain were better and more abundant, one could simply proceed to describe the material in order of Quaternary time, divided into periods of convenient length; as it is, all manner of other evidence needs to be consulted, and for clarity's sake the Palaeolithic industries cannot necessarily be described in the order in which they were made. But if it is an author's privilege to write and present a text book in any order he wishes, he must not forget that the reader has a corresponding freedom of choice in making use of it. I hope those who have time will read from beginning to end, but I also hope that the index will enable those who think they know the outline well enough already to consult points of detail more easily than that.

If the preparation of this book has been essentially a solo effort, that has not prevented my receiving some very kind and welcome help from generous colleagues. Those who have read the whole of the text and corrected errors, added information or offered helpful suggestions, include Dr L.H. Keeley, Mrs G.M. Cook, Mr S.N. Collcutt and Dr R.M. Jacobi. Professor R.G. West kindly read Chapter 2 and gave much invaluable advice. Mr John Wymer did the same for Chapters 3 to 5, and Mr J.N. Carreck for parts of Chapter 5 and Chapter 6. Many others have given help on specific points. I am most grateful to them all; any inaccuracies which may survive in the text are certainly my own responsibility. I also thank Prof. H. Müller-Beck for the German translation of my English summary, and Mr and Mrs Collcutt for the French translation. I have stressed in the book the need for the British Palaeolithic to be seen in its European context, and perhaps colleagues in Continental Europe will find it directly useful to understand in some detail the material of that period from 'the British peninsula'. I hope the French and German summaries will encourage them to wrestle with the long English text: Continental authors have been providing us with English summaries for many years, and we reciprocate too infrequently.

Many of the figures in this book will be familiar to those well versed in the subject's literature, but their gathering together from otherwise scattered sources should prove useful. Those sources are acknowledged in the captions or elsewhere, and I am very grateful to all whose help or permission has enabled such illustrations to be reproduced here. Some of the line-drawings are new, and I would like particularly to thank Mr M.H.R. Cook and Mrs D. Timms for their skill and for all the trouble they have taken. The sources of the photographs, old and new, are acknowledged in the list of plates and I repeat my gratitude here to all those who took the pictures, provided prints, loaned negatives or gave permission for use. Photographs taken by V.P. Narracott of the Pitt Rivers Museum, Oxford, B.W. Conway and J.J. Wymer together make up a large proportion of the plates: I simply could not have managed without them. The maps have been drawn from my rough versions by Oxford Illustrators to

whose staff I offer my thanks for undertaking this.

Lower Palaeolithic archaeology and Quaternary studies in general have made enormous strides in the past decade, and many spectacular finds have been made, not least in several different African countries. The attention of many may have wandered from Britain, as the directions and emphases of research have changed. Perhaps as the 1980s begin it is no bad moment to offer an assessment of the British material, with an eye on its general context, and to suggest reasons for thinking that in Britain too there remains much to be done and much of importance still to be found.

Donald Baden-Powell Quaternary Research Centre,
University of Oxford

Derek A. Roe

Background to a Study of the Old Stone Age in Britain

Chapter 1

It's a good thing that archaeologists are inclined to
be optimists. If some level-headed realist from
another discipline were to be confronted with the
task of presenting a factual account of what
actually happened, in human terms, during the
Lower and Middle Palaeolithic periods in the area
now known as Britain, would he not decline the
task as soon as he had taken stock of the evidence?
He would note, for example, that something like a
hundred thousand stone artefacts of the period
were available to him, but that only a tiny proportion of these had been found *in situ* – that is
to say, in approximately the places where their
makers or users left them. He would observe that
it is not really possible to assign a date in years to
the manufacture of any one of them, knowing on
unimpeachable evidence that it is certainly accurate
within ten thousand years either way. He would
consider the almost total lack of artefacts of
perishable materials like wood and bone to offset
the abundance of stone, though it is reasonable to
suppose by analogy with recent primitive stone-
tool-using peoples that stone implements would
not have been the most numerous material posses-
sions of the British Palaeolithic populations, and in
many day-to-day situations would not have been
the most important, either. He would take account
of the fact that no certain trace of a habitation
structure has been properly recorded from any
British Lower or Middle Palaeolithic site – a
situation that can be contrasted with the rather

fleeting British Mesolithic period, let alone with
the remainder of British prehistory which is
documented by a rich variety of field monuments
including domestic, defensive, ceremonial and
sacred sites. And, as regards the Lower and Middle
Palaeolithic population itself, the human beings
with whom he is seeking to make historical contact, *they* are represented by about enough fragments of skeletal material in all to fill a medium-
sized paper bag. Even those survive by pure
chance; deliberate burial of the dead does begin in
the Middle Palaeolithic, but no British example is
known.

In parallel to these grave shortcomings of the
archaeological evidence, the British Pleistocene
sequence, which should ideally provide not merely
the evidence for the succession of natural back-
grounds to human activity in Britain during
the Palaeolithic period, but also a finely calibrated
time-scale, presents major interpretive problems of
its own in many parts of the country. The highly
important matter of establishing both archaeological and geological correlations between Britain
and adjacent areas of Continental Europe, let
alone further afield, is again notoriously difficult.

One way and another, then, the meandering
byways and infrequent highways of the British
Lower and Middle Palaeolithic certainly seem to
have been laid out with the optimist in mind, and
our level-headed realist might well feel inclined to
advise his readers to go straight to the science-
fiction shelves instead while he directed his efforts
as an archaeological author into some period not
older than the spread of early agriculture. Would

he do that? If he is really worthy of the title assigned to him here, he ought actually to conclude that he is needed as never before in his academic life: it requires an optimist to undertake this task, but a realist to carry it out successfully. When the evidence is in such a sad state, tentative or even firm conclusions may still be perfectly possible, but a careful watch must be kept upon them. The present writer gladly aspires to the title of optimist in this and everything else; his attainment as a realist must remain for the reader to judge.

The fact is clear enough, that there was human occupation in Britain during the Lower and Middle Palaeolithic periods over at least a quarter of a million years, and perhaps nearly twice as long, though probably not continuously. That is to say, the period with which we are here concerned is fifty or even a hundred times the length of the time which has elapsed between the start of the British Neolithic, remote as that may seem, and the present day. Inevitably, much that was vital to human physical and cultural development took place during that long span, and every item of information that can be salvaged from so remote a period is of value. Small wonder if we discern the events of that time somewhat hazily, for in searching for evidence of them we enter a world utterly different from the one we know. The name Britain becomes meaningless: we are concerned with a small area of land which lay right at the north-west extremity of the world so far as early Palaeolithic man knew it (Fig. 1:1). Sometimes it was a peninsula of the main land-mass, substantial tracts of what are now the southern North Sea and the English Channel being dry land; at other times it was an island (Fig. 1:2). Sometimes ice-sheets covered most of the land, and periglacial conditions gripped the rest; at other times animals and plants which we should not today seek outside the mediterranean or sub-tropical climatic zones of the world could thrive as far north as the English Midlands and occasionally further. Some areas of Britain were also as different from the present in their relief and drainage patterns as they were in their fauna and flora.

As regards man himself, it is not merely a question of shedding modern attitudes and the accumulated experience of the whole historic and later prehistoric periods, but, for the earlier Palaeolithic stages at least, even of trying to penetrate the physical and psychological make-up and properties of men of other species, all now extinct, within the genus *Homo*. All living men today belong to the same sub-species, *Homo sapiens sapiens*, and differences of race and colour, not to mention creed, are genuinely superficial: it is simply not possible to go elsewhere in the world and observe men of other sub-species, let alone species, in the way that one can go out and study, say, processes of erosion or deposition under glacial conditions. This then must be a real barrier to knowledge and one would suppose it to be an increasingly serious one the further back in time one goes: neither primate behaviour studies nor the ethnography of modern primitive peoples can provide complete answers.

It is then surely fair to say that there is a bigger gap of comprehension, as well as of time, between the prehistorian and his archaeological objectives in the earlier Palaeolithic than there is between his colleagues and the archaeology of whatever other period they may be studying. It is also true that in Britain the Palaeolithic material has been subjected to far greater disturbance and destruction than that belonging to more recent periods. This is not merely a matter of passing time: when one considers the destructive power of the forces at work in the glaciation and deglaciation of northern and midland Britain, and even in the more southerly periglacial zone (forces which in many parts were unleashed on several separate occasions), then it seems remarkable that anything has survived at all. As we have already noted, a great deal that would have been immensely informative has not been preserved. This is the main reason why so much of this book has to do with stone implements, because they have a very high survival capacity. It is an interesting and perhaps sobering reflection, in passing, that when the great ice sheets extend again, as there is every reason to suppose they eventually will, the Lower Palaeolithic stone handaxes, cores and flakes, stored in their thousands in the dusty basements of our museums, will come through it, all over again, with much less damage than the beautiful and sophisticated arte-

1:1 World map, with some conservative estimates
for the earliest occupation of important areas.
Note the position of Britain at the north-western
edge of Lower Palaeolithic settlement

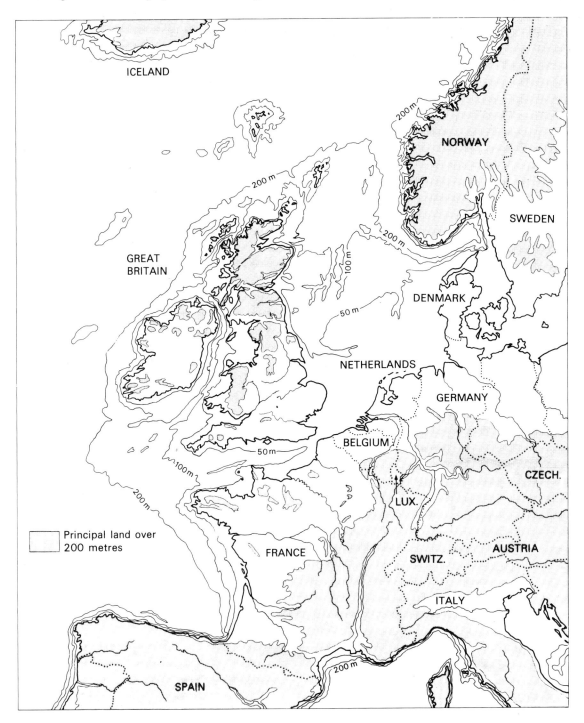

1:2 Britain in relation to the north-west of
Continental Europe. The modern marine contours
give some idea of the shape of a former 'British
peninsula'

facts on show in the galleries upstairs where they have been placed to represent the summit of artistic or technological achievement in the various stages of our own culture. And how will subsequent archaeologists judge us then? By other peoples' handaxes, redeposited in glaci-fluvial or fluviatile gravels? If so, a certain amount of rough justice may well be done.

If the preceding paragraphs have stressed the difficulties attendant on a study of the British Lower and Middle Palaeolithic, it has not been the author's intention to put the reader off the subject altogether so much as to warn him, if he is perhaps used to the study of more recent periods, that he may find the conclusions reached in this book few in number, imprecise and tentative in quality, and resting on evidence that is often painfully weak. Only rarely can cause and effect, and the more dynamic aspects of human existence, be brought into sharp focus. This is certainly no green pasture for the New Archaeologists (as they used to be called): they must either tread the steep and rugged pathway rejoicingly, as some may care to do, to the subject's profit, or go elsewhere muttering about low-density evidential catchment situations inevitably productive of low-resolution culture-historical syntheses poorly time-calibrated. Indeed, it is not merely legitimate but quite essential when examining the British Palaeolithic material, to keep an eye firmly on other parts of the world, where sometimes the evidence for similar situations is altogether better preserved: missing data can on occasion be fairly borrowed from elsewhere. But there is another compelling reason for proceeding in this way. It has already been observed that Britain lay at the extreme edge of the Palaeolithic world, and was subject to marked fluctuations of climate and temperature. It follows from this that Britain is essentially an area to which human groups came intermittently when conditions were favourable, rather than one which they occupied permanently. So, from the outset, we can hardly expect to find in the British Palaeolithic continuous 'cultural evolution' so much as a discontinuous record of changes for which the explanations may often lie elsewhere. On the other hand, at times when the peninsula became an island, it would clearly be possible for

human groups in Britain to become isolated from external influences and to develop along their own lines for a while. For all these reasons it is important that the British Palaeolithic should be studied in its proper context rather than on its own, and its immediate context is western Continental Europe, especially France and the western end of the North European plain.

SCOPE OF THE ENQUIRY: A PREVIEW

The formal limits of the period with which this book is concerned can be stated quite simply, at the cost of delving briefly into the history of archaeology.[1] The name 'Palaeolithic' implies 'Old Stone' Age and is a nineteenth-century off-shoot of the original Three Age System defined and pioneered by C.J. Thomsen, J.J.A. Worsaae and several others (Daniel 1962, 1967, 1975). This division of the prehistoric period into a Stone Age, followed by a Bronze Age, followed by an Iron Age, was a theoretical step of no small importance which occurred early in the nineteenth century, and over 150 years later it still retains a strong hold on the more popular section of the archaeological literature (cf. Roe 1970). Such terminology is however wholly out of keeping with the spirit of current research, much of which is directed towards elucidating the totality of any human group's existence, including the intricate relationships between it and all the diverse elements of the contemporary natural background; it is scarcely appropriate therefore to name major periods of prehistory after raw materials which were exploited by some human groups in certain areas for making a small proportion of their customary artefacts. But one can't get rid of the Three Ages terminology just like that, for whatever good reasons: the various names have by now become shorthand labels whose use generally implies a whole mass of technological, economic and social information, without actually spelling it out.

Even by the middle of the nineteenth century 'Stone Age' had been found too restricted a term to cope adequately with all the different kinds of archaeological material that could be seen to precede the first occurrences of metal artefacts, and so it became divided first into the 'Age of

Chipped Stone' followed by the 'Age of Polished Stone', with 'Old Stone Age' and 'New Stone Age' or the Greek-derived 'Palaeolithic' and 'Neolithic' coming in later as alternatives. In due course a 'Mesolithic' (Middle Stone Age) or 'Age of Pygmy Flints' was found to be necessary as well, interposed between the other two. These names clearly reflect various attitudes of the times. Fine implements were collected and studied individually for their own sake, from the points of view of typology and technology; what one observed in one's own area would doubtless be the case in other lands, so that the 'ages' were regarded as being of general validity; age succeeded age by a kind of evolutionary process. With luck there might be stratigraphic evidence to demonstrate the order in which the different kinds of stone tool occurred through time, but it did not greatly matter, since one had only to decide their evolutionary status to place them in their correct sequence.

These broad subdivisions of the Stone Age naturally attracted their own specialists amongst the collector-antiquaries, and gradually each became known in greater detail, the new information being accommodated by further subdivision. The Palaeolithic was seen to begin with a Drift Period or Age of Drift Implements, which was followed by a Cave Period: that is to say, it was reckoned, and in due course demonstrated, that the implements which could be found deep in the gravel deposits of river valleys like those of the Thames and the Somme, were older than those which occurred in the fillings of the caves in south-west France, or in Belgium or elsewhere. Were not their typology and the technology of their manufacture far cruder? To be fair, there was other evidence too, of a more reliable kind, notably the different faunal assemblages accompanying the artefacts — some chronological schemes of the period used designations like 'Reindeer Age' or 'Age of the Mammoth'. As the pace of discovery quickened over the second half of the nineteenth century, the Cave Period had to be divided again, because it was clear that in an ideal sequence the lower levels would produce artefacts more like those of the Drift Period, though better made and including some new types, while the upper levels yielded finely made tools

worked on narrow blade-like flakes, accompanied by frequent artefacts of bone and antler, many of which were beautifully decorated. Different human types, too, were associated with these two parts of the Cave Period — the suitably more primitive-looking Neanderthal man with the earlier, and essentially modern types with the later.

Thus, by the late nineteenth century, there already existed a three-fold division within the Old Stone Age, which forms the basis of Lower, Middle and Upper Palaeolithic as we know them, much refined, today. By then it had also become customary to distinguish cultural periods and call them after type-sites (the sites where material belonging to each was first found): the majority of the names were French, since most of the relevant early work was done in France. The main culture names for the Drift Period were Acheulian and Chellean, called after Saint-Acheul and Chelles in the Somme Valley, though others were also used. The older division of the Cave period became Mousterian, or the Age of Le Moustier, after the *abri supérieur* at Le Moustier in the Dordogne, while the principal subdivisions of the later Cave Period at this time were Aurignacian, after Aurignac (Haute-Garonne), Solutrean after Le Roc de Solutré (Saône et Loire) and Magdalenian after the shelter of La Madeleine, near Cursac, Dordogne. Most of these terms remain in use today, although their precise meaning has altered somewhat in some cases.

In the archaic terminology of the foregoing, therefore, this book is concerned with the representation in Britain of the Drift Period and the earlier division of the Cave Period, and use can reasonably be made of the names Acheulian and Mousterian, out of those mentioned above. In more modern language, but still for the moment in terms of material culture, we are considering the period from the earliest appearance of man-made tools in Britain, down to the almost explosive spread of distinctive Upper Palaeolithic technology, which took place over most of Europe, in parts of North Africa, and in parts of Asia, notably South-West Asia and certain areas of the USSR; between about 45,000 and 30,000 years ago.

In human terms, the period to be studied ends

at the spread of *Homo sapiens sapiens* to Western Europe, he being traditionally regarded as the bearer of the Upper Palaeolithic cultures and indeed of all those which followed, including our own, though whether the beginning of the Upper Palaeolithic and the first appearance of *Homo sapiens sapiens* always coincide exactly in every area is becoming increasingly open to doubt. Some Middle Palaeolithic populations may have crossed a technological frontier before the new human type reached their area; this is a point of great interest, but regrettably it is not one on which the British evidence can cast any useful light at present. As regards what earlier human types[2] we are actually concerned with in Britain, much doubt

must remain until new fossil hominid finds are made (Fig. 1:3). The only substantial British discovery has been the fragments of the famous Swanscombe skull (Plate 14), classified as belonging to *Homo sapiens* — that is, to an early form of our own species apparently ancestral both to our own subspecies *Homo sapiens sapiens*, and also to the extinct Neanderthal Man, who is properly called *Homo sapiens neanderthalensis*. In so far as there is a small amount of classic Mousterian archaeological material present in Britain, it may seem safe enough to suppose that Neanderthal man too was here for a while, since, so far as Western Europe is concerned, there are plenty of good associations between Neanderthal man and

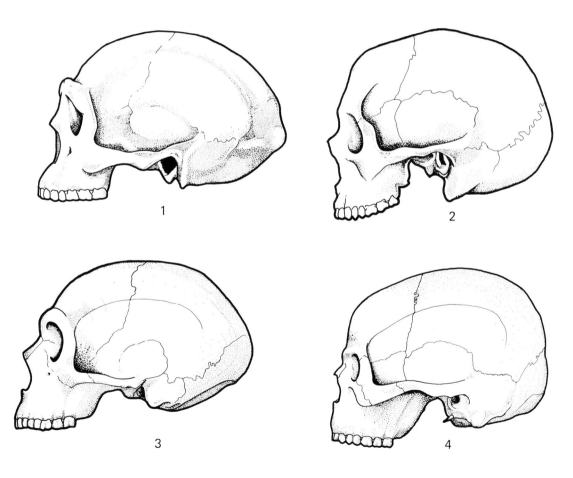

1:3 Skulls of some important hominid types (generalized): 1 *Homo erectus*; 2 *Homo sapiens* (early undifferentiated form); 3 *H. sapiens neanderthalensis*; 4 *H. sapiens sapiens*. Drawn by M.ᴴ.R. Cook

the Mousterian, while it has yet to be demonstrated that any other hominid type made Mousterian industries there. (In fact, this is a good example of a tentative conclusion resting on inadequate evidence, as forecast and regretted in the previous section: the truth is that there are *no* Neanderthal remains from Britain proper, while the question of the authorship of some of the Continental variants of Mousterian should more correctly be left open.) Beyond this, it is simply not known whether all our British Lower Palaeolithic industries, amongst which there is considerable variety, were made by hominids of the Swanscombe type or not, or even what precisely the alternative might be. It has recently been shown, thanks to finds in East Germany (DDR), that the earlier occurrences of artefacts in Britain do fall within the time range of *Homo erectus*, who is represented in Europe by the famous Heidelberg (Mauer) jaw, and by new material from Bilzingsleben (Mania 1976), but that is far from being an assertion that *Homo erectus* was in fact their maker and speculation on this point seems futile. On the negative side, it may be observed here for completeness' sake that there is no trace whatsoever in Britain of the hominid types which in certain parts of sub-Saharan Africa are contemporary with the earliest stone tool industries: various species of *Australopithecus*, and of early *Homo*, the latter as yet unnamed specifically, except *Homo habilis*, whose status at the time of writing seems in fact to have become somewhat uncertain once more.[3] These earliest Pleistocene human types are absent also from Continental Europe. Present indications are that they were current in Africa at least 1½ million years and in some cases perhaps more than 2 million years before the first human arrivals in Western Europe.

Pleistocene geology and the British Pleistocene sequence are subjects that must be dealt with at greater extent later on. By way of preview, it is sufficient to say that the British Lower and Middle Palaeolithic seem at present to fall within the Middle and Upper Pleistocene (see Table 1, p. 38). Whether the very earliest industries occur just the early side of the Lower/Middle Pleistocene boundary is an open question, but certainly the vast majority of the British Palaeolithic sites are

of Middle and Upper Pleistocene age. Elsewhere in the world the Lower Palaeolithic can sometimes be seen to begin much earlier, notably in East Africa where on the longest chronology proposed the first industries might even be regarded as of final Pliocene age (Oakley 1970). Even so, we are still dealing in this book with a large slice of time, from a beginning probably in the time range 250,000 to 500,000 years ago (depending on how one views the dating of the sparse earliest occurrences), perhaps shortly before the first time ice sheets actually reached Britain, to an ending which should be between 40,000 and 30,000 years ago in a relatively mild phase about halfway through the last of the Pleistocene glaciations. Such an expanse of time would be meaningless were it not broken up into convenient shorter segments by the major climatic fluctuations of the Pleistocene, which it is convenient to see in terms of periods very substantially warmer or colder than those to which we ourselves are accustomed.

PROBLEMS, APPROACHES AND SOURCES
OF EVIDENCE

In the simplest terms the author's tasks are: to describe the main archaeological occurrences which lie within the period limits referred to in the previous section; to use the evidence of Pleistocene geology and biology to date them and place them in their correct order against the changing natural background; to distinguish any significant clusterings of the sites, whether through resemblances in their stone industries or any other similarities, which might suggest that 'cultures' or 'periods' can reasonably be recognized; to consider the affinities of the British Palaeolithic material in other areas and thus to assess the importance of the British sequence and its relationship to the rest of the Old World; and in all of this, to look especially for items of evidence which may make it possible to write the prehistory of these long-vanished hunter-gatherer populations rather than a mere assessment of some aspects of their material culture. This last is the most daunting task, given the state of the evidence. Meanwhile, some of these aims and the resources for achieving them are considered in this section.

Sites

So far as the basic description and recording of sites and of artefacts is concerned, there is already some useful literature (e.g. Wymer 1968; Roe 1968b) which, while it can be added to and brought up-to-date, does not require repetition or reworking here. It would be quite ridiculous to set out to mention in this book all the British Lower and Middle Palaeolithic find-spots, because a high proportion of them, even including some which have yielded artefacts by the hundred, are sterile sources when it comes to useful information. Even the find of a single stone tool in an unstratified context may have a certain importance — for example, from the point of view of the British distribution of sites, or because the artefact happens to be a clear example of some implement type which is known to have been current only for a restricted period. Conversely, a couple of hundred heavily worn and generally nondescript artefacts in a gravel may be able to tell us little, if they are likely to have come from different sources and to have been redeposited, perhaps more than once, in the course of reaching their present situation. The author has therefore been very selective as regards the sites mentioned, the criteria for selection merely being that the site has produced worthwhile information, whether archaeological of any sort, geological or biological. Many of the sites which are included have been published before, some in great detail, and the major literature is quoted here: the bulk of it will be found to occur in national or local archaeological or geological journals. Other sites mentioned however have remained to all intents and purposes unpublished, although the finds may have been made a very long while ago. Here the essential source of information is the survival of the archaeological material itself in a museum or even in a private collection (of which many remain) — or, in some cases, scattered in several museums and private collections.

Britain can boast well over 3,000 find-spots of Palaeolithic implements (Roe 1968b), but relatively few of these really deserve the term 'site' in the sense of yielding useful evidence relating to Palaeolithic settlement beyond the presence of stone implements. Perhaps about a dozen in all were, or might have been, substantial *in situ* finds of importance by world standards — 'might have been', because some of the discoveries were made long before modern archaeological techniques and scientific aids existed to enable the best to be made of them, and they were therefore wasted. Even the better of these sites are incomplete. Others, still a small proportion of the total, were 'slightly disturbed' occurrences, perhaps representing the artefact output of single working sites, transported only a short way in stream channels. The rest, the overwhelming majority, either comprise single finds or just a few artefacts, as opposed to complete industries, or else they are in greatly disturbed contexts or in no recorded context at all, so that nothing whatsoever can be said of the nature of the original site.

Lower and Middle Palaeolithic sites in general, including those with which we shall be concerned in the following chapters, are either 'open' or 'cave' sites. Open sites are almost always situated close to a contemporary water source: on or near the shore of a lake, or beside a stream channel. Indeed, it seems likely from finds in various parts of the world that some sites, notably those of the handaxe-makers, were situated actually *in* stream channels during the drier times of the year. This is not so unreasonable as it might sound: pools of water probably survived here and there, or water might be obtainable by shallow digging; boulders and other rock fragments suitable as raw material for tool-making would be ready to hand; trees and bushes along the stream banks might offer shade (and wood as another raw material), while in some types of vegetation the dry stream bed might be the easiest route across country; where actual pools were to be found, they would attract the game animals. This situation then probably suited early man well, but it is less satisfactory from the archaeological point of view since, when the stream bed became active again, the remains of the Palaeolithic occupation were bound to be disturbed and material from separate sites along the stream course was liable to be mixed together. The lakeside settlements are often far better archaeologically. Some of the floors at Kalambo Falls, Zambia (Clark, J.D. 1969), offer good examples of virtually undisturbed stone industries in lake margin sediments. Hoxne, Suffolk, is the best British site of this kind, and recent excavations have shown the high quality of the evidence there, though only fragments of the occupation floors now remain (Wymer 1974, pp. 400-4). Hitchin (Hertfordshire), Caddington (Bedfordshire) and Foxhall Road, Ipswich (Suffolk) are other examples, but all are old finds whose potential was not realized. Cave sites (which include rock-shelters) of Lower or Middle Palaeolithic age are rather rare in Britain, but Kent's Cavern, Torquay, Devon and the Hyaena Den, Wookey, Somerset, will serve here as examples of occupied caves, and others will be mentioned later. The survival of archaeological evidence in caves, even from these early periods, can be excellent: the work by H. de Lumley at Lazeret (1969c) and other sites in southern France (1969a, 1971) illustrates this well.

Where sites are well-preserved and little disturbed it should often be possible to decide the nature of the occupation. Archaeological discovery and ethnographic observation in various parts of the world have shown that both ancient and recent hunter-gatherer peoples have seasonal patterns of movement within their over-all territories, and tend to operate at different times of the year in larger or smaller groups according to the nature, location and relative abundance of the plant and animal food resources on which they are principally dependent at the time (see, for example, Lee and DeVore 1968; Higgs and Vita-Finzi 1970). They use 'home-base' camps where at certain times the whole tribe may congregate, though at others only the women and children and the elderly may reside there. There are also different kinds of 'exploitation' camps, where smaller groups may go to hunt or to gather raw materials (which would include the obtaining of stone for making tools). And where important resources lie more than a few hours' journey from the main base there will be a need for 'transit camps' of some kind — a conveniently placed cave or rock-shelter perhaps. It is against this now well-established background that the archaeologist may be able to distinguish 'kill' or 'butchery' sites and 'stone-working' or 'quarry' sites, and the locations

with signs of dense and more or less continuous occupation over a long period which are likely to be the home bases. Clearly much can be done as regards interpretation if there is any evidence to help show at what time of the year a site was occupied. Some animal species are particularly useful in this way: the bones, teeth and antlers of several kinds of deer, for instance, offer good evidence of this kind, since the young deer are all born at the same time of year and the annual growth and shedding of antlers is also a regular cycle. Plant remains, and known patterns of the seasonal migrations of various animals and birds can also sometimes be used in a similar way by the archaeologists if the evidence is there, and this is important because these were just the kind of factors which controlled human movements and activities at the time. At Terra Amata, Nice, evidence has been claimed (de Lumley, 1969b, 1975) for some 15 successive annual occupations of the same Lower Palaeolithic site in late spring or early summer.[4] Regrettably, nothing of this kind has come to light in Britain yet.

Quaternary studies

As regards Pleistocene geology and biology, it is fortunate that British specialists on the Quaternary period have produced some useful and up-to-date general accounts in the past five or ten years (Sparks and West 1972; Mitchell *et al.* 1973; Shotton (ed.) 1977; West 1977) to add to the sections devoted to Britain in wider-ranging books (e.g. Charlesworth 1957; Zeuner 1958, 1959; Butzer 1964, revised 1971; Flint 1971; Bowen 1978) and to the older works, notably that of Wright (1937). There are also very many area or site studies and other shorter reports in the major geological and geographical, or general scientific periodicals, in regional field conference hand-books, and in the Pleistocene sections of the various official regional geological publications of the Geological Survey, though the state of revision of these latter is somewhat patchy.

Gone, or almost gone, are the days when a Palaeolithic archaeologist could be his own geological specialist, though he certainly requires a working knowledge of the erosional and depositional processes of the Quaternary period, and he needs to be able to understand and evaluate the reports of his geologist colleagues and to ask them the right questions. Nor are Quaternary deposits merely a matter of geology, and the various aspects of them and their contents are now so diverse that they no longer lie within the scope of any single expert: glacial and periglacial geomorphology, terrestrial sediments and soils, marine sediments and beaches, mammalian remains, microfauna, bird remains, fish remains, plant remains and pollen, insects, shells and the rest, are fast becoming separate fields of study, as witness the large numbers of contributors to the definitive publication of any fruitful Pleistocene site (e.g. de Lumley's Lazeret report (1969c) or, for a British example, the volume on Swanscombe, edited by C.D. Ovey 1964). On the one hand it is excellent that so much more can now be done with good quality evidence in the various laboratories, but on the other the need to consult so many specialists — who are few and busy — can act as a serious brake on publication. The various chronometric dating methods applicable to finds of Pleistocene age are also the work of specialists in various fields, and archaeological samples must again wait their turn. Once more, it is highly desirable that the Palaeolithic archaeologist should be as far acquainted with the techniques as possible, so that he can take samples in the field correctly and evaluate the probable accuracy and meaning of the results he finally receives.

The present writer cannot fairly claim more than a working knowledge of broad aspects of some of the fields of Quaternary studies mentioned above, so that the second chapter of this book is a respectful short synthesis based mainly on the sources already quoted. Archaeologists are quite naturally far more concerned with the solid results of their Quaternary colleagues' research than with the methods used, and they clamour for answers to questions like: how old is a given site in Pleistocene terms, what was the climate at the time of occupation, what can be said about the environment, how long a period separates two distinct archaeological horizons, what was the nature of the contemporary topography, or what is the place of the site in the whole local sequence?

Those who have little or no knowledge of the problems faced by the Pleistocene experts are inclined not to appreciate the guarded answers they may be given.

For the Palaeolithic archaeologist, a great deal does indeed turn on being able to place his major sites in their correct order and know the time interval between them. If firm stratigraphic evidence or other means of relative dating for the various deposits which contain the industries cannot be obtained, then there will be a strong temptation or even a positive need to date the artefacts by their appearance and by comparison with similar looking industries elsewhere whose age is known. This can be extremely dangerous. Must tool-kits be of the same age merely because they look alike? At a simple level of technology, may not human responses to similar situations produce almost identical artefacts, regardless of how far apart in time the similar situations arose? One should never lose sight of the fact that Palaeolithic tools were made for day-to-day use rather than to help prehistorians order their impressions of the remote past. For reasons of this kind, then, the importance of the contribution to Palaeolithic archaeology of experts in other aspects of Quaternary studies can hardly be overstated, and it would be true to say that the fulfilment of the various tasks mentioned at the beginning of this section, except that of purely archaeological description, depends at least as much on the other Quaternary evidence as it does on the archaeological material.

What then is the proper province of the Palaeolithic archaeologists themselves as technical experts? Collectively, they are concerned first with bringing the evidence for ancient human activities to light, by discovering sites and by excavating them (a highly technical process), and second with interpreting that evidence. In the latter capacity, they are both the co-ordinators of the many different specialist contributions already mentioned, and also specialist contributors in their own right, since it is they who must undertake the detailed study of the artefacts and of whatever traces of settlement can be recognized, including actual structures if they are present.

Artefacts in Palaeolithic archaeology

In the case of Britain, no habitation structures have in fact been preserved, and traces of settlements are vague in the extreme, so even more emphasis than usual falls upon the artefacts, and of those all but the barest handful are made of stone. It cannot be denied that stone artefacts are very much a stock in trade of the Palaeolithic archaeologist, whatever aspect of his whole work he may himself prefer. It is the occurrence of stone artefacts which reveals the existence of almost every new site. Their nature and morphology is always a major guide to the kind of human activities carried out at any site in Palaeolithic times, and theirs may indeed be the only evidence for this if animal and plant remains are not preserved. Stone artefacts still yield the main basis for the sequence of Lower and Middle Palaeolithic 'cultural' stages, even if we now use their evidence with more insight than formerly, and even though the computer-based methods of analytical study now available are so formidable that there is a risk of their being regarded as genuine archaeological evidence in themselves. Certainly, then, the Palaeolithic archaeologist must know his stone artefacts: if he cannot distinguish a naturally fractured surface of stone from an artificially flaked one, or if he cannot infallibly recognize the different technological devices employed by various Palaeolithic groups, his interpretations of Prehistory may be highly inaccurate, even though he himself be both a brilliant exponent of excavation techniques and one of those people who can make computers give the right answer first time.

When stone is worked by man in the manufacture of tools, the process yields various characteristic products, all of which count as *artefacts*. At the broadest level of classification, these are either tools or waste products. First, there are the successfully finished stone tools themselves, which may be called *implements*. They are highly diverse in type, the morphology of some – like a knife or an awl – proclaiming their function quite clearly, while others remain enigmatic. They do not, of course, often survive in pristine condition and the archaeologist frequently has to accept them (and the other classes of artefacts too) somewhat water-worn or weathered, scratched and abraded by soil movement or cracked and shattered by repeated freeze-thaw conditions, patinated from exposure on the surface or stained from inclusion in iron-rich deposits, damaged by use or, much more likely, broken by one of the natural processes which brought them to the place where they were found.

The second broad category of artefacts consists of knapping *waste* or *débitage*. In the manufacture of any implement a surprisingly large number of sizeable waste flakes, and an extremely large quantity of minor chips, may be struck off (Plate 1). They are the equivalent of the sawn-off ends, wood shavings, splinters and even sawdust on the floor of a carpenter's workshop, but they have a higher survival capacity. Mark Newcomer (1971), in a recent careful experiment, recorded that in the manufacture of a single handaxe, representative of good quality later Acheulian workmanship, the waste products amounted to 51 major flakes and over 4,600 minor flakes and chips. It is not surprising therefore to find that at a properly excavated prolific working site, waste products account for the overwhelming majority of the artefacts, finished implements often subsiding to a single-figure or even fractional percentage of the whole aggregate. On the other hand, since waste flakes are less attractive to collectors of artefacts (as opposed to archaeologists), in assemblages which were recovered by collection rather than excavation a long while ago the waste products are usually gravely under-represented and sometimes were simply not collected at all. Many British Lower Palaeolithic assemblages are incomplete in this way.

The proper recovery of the knapping waste is in fact important, because it may reveal the kinds of implement that were being made even when some of them are not themselves directly represented on the site, having been taken away by their makers for use elsewhere. The distinctive 'tranchet' axe-sharpening flakes of the Mesolithic period are the classic example of this, but Lower Palaeolithic handaxe trimming flakes are also very characteristic. Study of the waste may also reveal important information about the particular technological devices the knappers were employing, which is often helpful in deciding a site's affinities. Waste does not only consist of flakes. Many implements are made on flake 'blanks' rather than being shaped directly from whole nodules or pebbles. When a nodule is used to obtain flakes intended as the blanks for implements, or even for use without modification, then it is the eventual residue of the nodule, a chunk of stone bearing various flake-removal scars and often subspherical in shape, which is the main waste product.[5] It is called a *core*.

The two major artefact categories thus far considered, implements and waste, are susceptible of almost infinite subdivision in the classification of artefact assemblages and many different schemes have been put forward, either for general use or to meet particular needs (for example, Bordes 1961; Kleindienst 1961, 1962; Wymer 1968). At this stage we need not go too deeply into the subject of classification, and in fact few of the British assemblages are of sufficient quality to warrant really exhaustive treatment — in the sense that most are demonstrably either mixed or incomplete or both. But it is certainly worth noting how the task of classification is approached and the general nature of the subdivisions. Thus the implements can usually be divided into 'heavy duty' and 'light duty' categories, within which they are further classified according to type, morphology and technique of manufacture. Types are often very arbitrary: names like 'handaxe', 'cleaver' and 'scraper' imply specific functions, usually quite unproved, which have been tacitly accepted by generations of archaeologists on no better basis than that of general superficial similarity between Palaeolithic implements and modern or recent forms. Morphology can at least be quantified by measurement, though this is a comparatively recent innovation in the analysis of artefact assemblages; it is more common to find individual artefacts described morphologically without measurement, for example 'a flat ovate handaxe', 'a thick scraper with convex working edge' or 'a narrow leaf-shaped point'. These are all descriptive classifications of implements, incorporating typology and morphology, and often some technological information may be added at the same low level of precision, thus: 'a narrow

lanceolate handaxe worked bifacially from a flint nodule', or 'a rectangular cleaver made from a side-struck flake of fine-grained lava', or 'a double convergent side-scraper made on a Levallois flake.'

Within the broad category of waste, descriptive classification along similar lines is easy enough, involving the different kinds of cores and waste flakes; fewer classes are needed and the potential information, though important as we have seen, is usually less in quantity. One particular artefact class is worth mentioning here — waste, but waste of a somewhat special kind: the various sorts of *unfinished implements*. Some will have been broken during manufacture, while others were perhaps roughed out successfully but for some reason did not undergo the final stages of manufacture. Others will have been abandoned as failed attempts without actually having been broken, perhaps through the maker's incompetence or perhaps because the preliminary stages of flaking revealed a flaw in the raw material. It is important that artefacts of these kinds should be recognized for what they are: for one thing, if they were assumed to be finished implements, they would take on a false appearance of crudeness (which often tends to be regarded, not always justifiably, as a sign of high antiquity), and for another, their presence in quantity amongst other artefacts is a reliable sign that the site was one where stone tool manufacture actually took place, rather than one where tools made elsewhere were being used.

Many classificatory schemes also include a category of *utilized waste*, by which is meant casual flakes or other fragments which, while they have not been shaped into formal implements by *secondary flaking* (also called *retouch*) seem nevertheless from their chipped or worn edges to have been used on an *ad hoc* basis. There is nothing surprising about the existence of such pieces. No cutting edge in the world, unless perhaps some of the super-sharp machine-made hard metal edges of our own times, is sharper or more effective than that on a thin freshly-struck flake of flint or some similar siliceous material. Such an edge cannot be sharpened further: retouch may perhaps strengthen it by making the edge angle less acute while leaving it still usefully sharp, but for simple cutting tasks it is far more effective when entirely unmodified.

Palaeolithic man may therefore be assumed to have made frequent use of what we might take to be waste flakes, picking up and throwing down suitable ones at need. Some would bear no definite trace of his having done so, but others, used repeatedly or with some force, may show clear 'utilization traces' on the cutting edge, in the form of polish or minute damage to its original sharpness. They are not formal, regular shaped implements of classifiable types; hence the term 'utilized waste' and the category offers one more salutary reminder of the humanity of Palaeolithic man and his complete unconsciousness of the needs of future prehistorians. It is worth noting, however, that even slight soil movement can cause minute damage to sharp flake edges, which might well be taken for utilization damage if due caution is not exercised. Really the category 'utilized waste' should be reserved for the classification of assemblages in mint condition from primary context sites, i.e. sites where the artefacts lie in contemporary deposits, wholly undisturbed; indeed, the diagnoses should ideally be verified under a high-power microscope, for a sample at least, though in practice few people will be prepared to go to such trouble, or will have the necessary equipment.

Other categories which will sometimes be found include *manuports* and *modified cobbles*. Neither of these is an artefact class, properly speaking. Manuports are objects (almost always natural boulders or pieces of rock) which could not occur naturally on the site or have been brought there by any natural process, so must have been picked up and brought by man, whether for some use such as forming part of a structure or as objects of curiosity; they do not show traces of working. Modified cobbles, though not worked into an artificial shape, show some form of battering, polish or abrasion which cannot be the work of nature: most were probably used as knappers' hammerstones, or as anvils, or for pounding or crushing tasks in food preparation.

The kinds of classification mentioned above are essentially descriptive and obviously provide a sound enough framework when it is merely necessary to describe and classify an individual artefact or a handful of finds. More important, however, is the matter of comparing and contrasting different stone artefact assemblages and here a firmly quantitative approach is needed. Each item in the assemblages concerned must be identified according to a single scheme of classification, preferably by the same observer or else by observers who are in close agreement about typological and morphological definitions and will not therefore classify similar artefacts quite differently. Raw totals of the pieces falling into each major or minor category will not suffice: they must be converted to percentages of the whole assemblage, or percentages of the implements total, or percentages of a major tool category, or whatever is appropriate to that stage of the whole analysis. This makes possible a direct comparison when the assemblages themselves contain substantially different totals of artefacts, as is often the case. Thus 100 handaxes would constitute 50 per cent of an assemblage containing only 200 artefacts, but a mere 1 per cent of one containing 10,000. These results can be tabulated, or presented as frequency graphs or histograms or cumulative graphs, or in any of a number of ways which give an easy visual impression in a single diagram of how the essential features of the assemblages being studied compare (Fig. 1:4). However, a great deal more than this is likely to be necessary, including detailed analyses of morphology and technology within each major tool class, and here detailed measurement of each piece and the calculation of various metrical indices may be necessary (cf. Chapter 5). This kind of comparison between assemblages certainly cannot be left solely to visual inspection of diagrams, and various mathematical and statistical methods of formal comparison may be needed. Here again the archaeologist needs to enlist the help of specialists from other disciplines (Clarke, D.L. 1968; Doran and Hodson 1975; Hodder and Orton 1976).

When this is the general nature of artefact analysis and of the detailed comparison of Palaeolithic stone tool assemblages, it can readily be appreciated that much depends on the integrity of the assemblages themselves. They should be as complete as possible and they should also be single-period artefact groups rather than a palimpsest of occupations of various ages, brought together by natural processes. They also need to be large

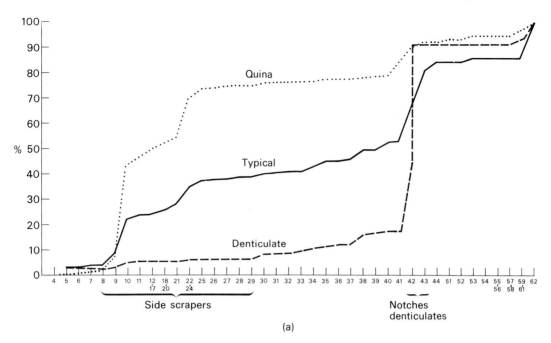

(a)

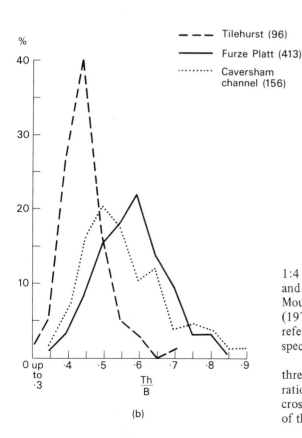

(b)

1:4 (a) Cumulative graphs of Quina, Typical and Denticulate variants of the south-west French Mousterian, after Bordes and de Sonneville-Bordes (1970). The numbers along the horizontal axis refer to carefully defined tool-types listed in a specific order

(b) Frequency curves used to compare three sets of Acheulian handaxes in respect of the ratio thickness/breadth — a test of thickness of cross-section (from Roe 1964:256). For details of the three sites, see Chapter 5

assemblages, if the percentage figures are not to be meaningless and if the statistical comparisons are to give worthwhile 'significant' results. Regrettably, it is just such large and reliable assemblages that are hardest to come by in the British Palaeolithic, so that it is often a case of making do with what there is and endeavouring to be rigorously objective about both the analyses and the results they yield. The integrity of the artefact assemblages in Britain which the archaeologists seek to use as 'statistical samples' is poor enough to give a professional statistician nightmares, especially considering the kind of conclusions they hope to draw from the results. But there is not much that can be done about it, beyond a constant search for new sites with rich industries in primary contexts. Either the existing evidence must be accepted for the meanwhile and the best possible job done with it, or else the whole study of the British Lower and Middle Palaeolithic must be abandoned as technically impossible to achieve at a worthwhile level at present. The writer for his part prefers the first alternative.

There are of course various other aspects of the study of artefacts, and some of them are a little less arid than the business of classification may seem to some readers. For example, sometimes the raw material from which the implements have been fashioned may be of particular interest — not just 'flint', but flint of some distinctive kind, traceable to a specific source. To be honest, however, not much productive work has been done along these lines for the Palaeolithic period in Britain, mainly because the rock used for implement manufacture almost always came from a secondary position — that is, it was not rock quarried from its *in situ* source at an outcrop, but pebbles, nodules or other fragments distributed widely over Britain by glacial or fluviatile action. Actual movements of people in the exploitation of known rock sources are therefore not clearly documented in the way that they can be in the case of Neolithic (and later) stone axe manufacture in Britain, or even in the case of some important Lower Palaeolithic sites elsewhere, of which Olduvai Gorge, Tanzania, is a good example (Leakey 1971).

Another highly important aspect of artefact study, relatively recent in its development, is the examination of actual utilization traces surviving on the working edges of the implements themselves, and also on the pieces classifiable as 'utilized waste' as already mentioned. Various kinds of minute edge-damage, polish and striation commonly result when stone artefacts are used to process such substances as wood, meat or hide (Plate 2). These traces are usually quite invisible to the naked eye, and many will remain so even at low magnification, but a high-power microscope may not only reveal them but also enable specific wear patterns to be distinguished which are characteristic both of different use-actions (chopping, sawing, cutting, scraping, piercing and so forth), and also of the different materials on which the tools were used (cf. Semenov 1964, 1970; Keeley 1974, summarizing earlier work, 1970; Keeley and Newcomer 1977; Tringham *et al*. 1974). It is obvious that for this kind of study the artefacts must be in exceptionally fresh condition, since most kinds of natural abrasion or weathering or even heavy patination or staining can wholly obliterate the 'microwear' traces. Britain therefore has few suitable artefact groups to offer, but happily some work has proved possible, notably the very promising efforts of L.H. Keeley at Oxford, mostly with artefacts from the recent excavations of J.J. Wymer at Clacton and Hoxne, and of J. d'A. Waechter at Swanscombe (see Chapter 7).

These then are some of the major approaches of the Palaeolithic archaeologist to artefacts, his largest single potential source of prehistoric information. Detailed examples and the discussion of further aspects of artefact study may be left to the main chapters describing the British sequence. It is almost entirely on the basis of the comparison of stone artefact assemblages that such close resemblances between sites as can be seen in Britain depend, and when 'cultural stages' are claimed, it is almost inevitably on the same basis. The observed similarities of the stone industries certainly need to be supported by geochronological evidence for closeness of age before there is talk of contemporaneity or of cultural stages, but where no geochronological evidence at all is available, it is hard to resist the temptation to interpret the similarity in such a way as a working hypothesis.

On the other hand, it is also becoming clear that during certain periods of time — say during a given interglacial or interstadial — industries were being made more or less contemporaneously which were strikingly dissimilar. To discover that quite different industrial traditions were actually contemporary is clearly not something that can be done by a mere classification process, which would simply express and quantify the differences. In this case, the geochronological evidence is essential; provided it is reliable, it should *always* override conclusions based on artefact analysis, whether it is similar or different industries which are being assessed. The existence at the same time of strikingly different industries need not of course imply the coexistence of different cultural traditions. The variation may be purely 'functional' — i.e. the different industries could have been made by the same people for the performance of quite different tasks (cf. Binford 1973 and the literature to which he refers in his article: a classic controversy is involved here). If this were so, one would hope that the evidence of microwear analysis might help to elucidate what the different tasks were in each case.

Britain and other areas

Lower and Middle Palaeolithic occupation is widely, if in places patchily, distributed over a great deal of the Old World, important areas at various periods being East, southern and North Africa, the Indian sub-continent and South-East Asia, the Middle East, parts of the USSR and almost the whole of Europe except the north. We have already noted that Britain constitutes the north-west extremity of this distribution, and it would therefore be unrealistic to expect close comparisons between the British material and, say, that from sub-Saharan Africa or India, though at these fairly unsophisticated levels of prehistoric culture broad similarities can be found more or less anywhere. The major Lower Palaeolithic movements into Western Europe are likely to have been both from north-west Africa via Iberia, the present Straits of Gibraltar probably having become a negligible barrier more than once during times of marine regression, and also from Western Asia via

Eastern Europe and the lowlands of Central Europe north of the Alps (Fig. 1:5). Both routes would readily continue to reach Britain at times of low sea level, the former via western and northern France and the latter through the Low Countries and across what is now the southern North Sea. The nearer these routes approached to Britain, the closer would the conditions of geography and climate become to those of southern Britain itself, and the Palaeolithic material from the nearer parts of the Continent should accordingly bear the closest resemblance to that found in Britain, since all Palaeolithic industries must in part reflect local conditions — the nature of the available raw materials, for example, and the kind of animal and vegetable food resources. Theoretically also the chronological gap should be at its narrowest: it would be narrow indeed if one could be sure of recovering the last traces left in what is now Continental Europe by particular human groups and also the first signs of their arrival in Britain, but Palaeolithic archaeologists have long learned not to expect such precision. However, it is clear that the more work that can be done on comparing British assemblages with those from north-west Continental Europe, the better. Not much has been achieved in the past, but work by P. Callow (1976) and others currently in progress should prove to be of considerable interest.

In the Middle Palaeolithic there was altogether less occupation of Britain than in the Lower Palaeolithic, partly no doubt because the period is shorter but also partly because the most intensive Middle Palaeolithic activity in Western Europe seems to have occurred during the earlier part of the Last Glacial, when Britain, while intermittently perfectly well habitable, was probably a less attractive area than southern and western France where so many sites are known. It is not by any means clear how far, in the Middle Palaeolithic, we need to envisage major movements of people into Europe from outside, rather than internal developments and local population movements within the continent itself. In any case, there are only slight signs of activity on the earlier route from north-west Africa to Iberia at this time. The trans-European lowland route may well have continued to be important, though not necessarily only in an

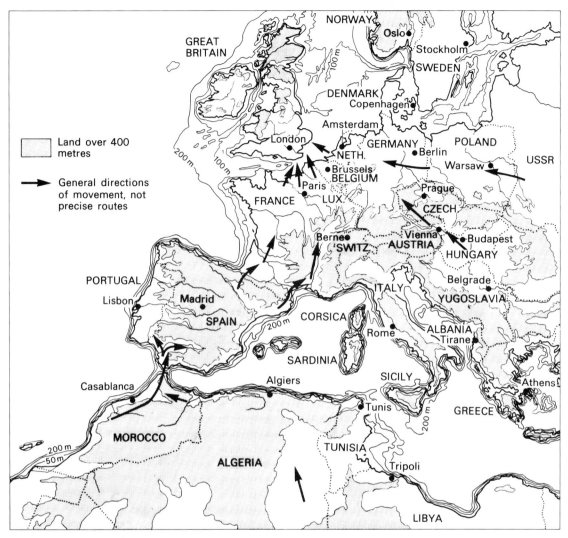

1:5 Probable routes of approach to Britain for
Lower Palaeolithic groups

east to west direction. But so far as the sparse
British Middle Palaeolithic is concerned, there
seems no reason to look beyond France, the Low
Countries and perhaps Western Germany for its
archaeological affinities.

PALAEOLITHIC RESEARCH IN BRITAIN

Finally, in the present chapter, it seems to be
worth devoting a section to the development of
Palaeolithic studies in Britain, partly to set the
present work in its historical context and partly

because we shall necessarily be closely concerned
in the following chapters with observations made
and assemblages recovered over a period of about a
century. Some reference has already been made to
the history of archaeology, when the original
concept of a Palaeolithic period was discussed
earlier in the chapter, and there are various books
at various levels which the reader can profitably
consult to follow this up, for example Daniel
1943, 1950 (revised and enlarged 1975), 1962;
Evans, J. 1956; Bibby 1957; Jessup 1964.

So far as the British Palaeolithic is concerned,

there is very little to note prior to the first half of the nineteenth century. Certainly stone implements, including handaxes, were occasionally collected before then, and they were not uncommonly regarded as thunderbolts or meteorites — it is interesting that these notions occasionally persist even today, though the writer has unfortunately never heard them put forward in such sonorous language as the mid seventeenth century assertions of Aldrovandus that such objects were 'due to an admixture of a certain exhalation of thunder and lightning with metallic matter, chiefly in dark clouds, which is coagulated by the circumfused moisture and conglutinated into a mass (like flour with water) and subsequently indurated by heat, like a brick'; or of Tollius that they were 'generated in the sky by a fulgurous exhalation conglobed in a cloud by the circumposed humour' (both quoted in Daniel 1950, pp. 25-6).

A slight improvement on these opinions, archaeologically speaking, is to be found in connection with the famous Grays Inn Lane handaxe, now in the British Museum (Daniel 1962: 32-3; Wymer 1968: 289-90), which was found by John Conyers about 1690 in some sort of association with elephant bones (though whether it was a true archaeological association of contemporary and connected objects is not clear). In this case the handaxe (a classic Acheulian 'ficron' not at all unlike some of the Swanscombe Middle Gravels specimens) was recognized as an implement or weapon of human manufacture, but the elephant was less fortunate, being ascribed by John Bagford, writing in 1715 for the first volume of Hearne's five volume edition of Leland's *Collectanea*, to the invading Romans under Claudius: the artefact was therefore reckoned to be of similar age. That error of course was wholly in the spirit of the times: that the Romans reached Britain was well known from their own writings, as was the fact that they encountered there some sort of Celtic or Ancient British population, but there was little curiosity about the latter (with the exception of the Druids, who attracted much attention) and no knowledge of how long the pre-Roman period might have lasted. Had not Archbishop James Ussher (1581-1656) established to his own satisfaction on biblical evidence that the world had been created in 4004 BC? That was certainly good enough for those who bothered to consider the matter at all, and there seemed no way of finding out more. There was accordingly only a short length of time available for a 'prehistoric' period in Europe — whatever remained between 4004 BC and the start of the classical world.

The same lack of interest confronted John Frere on another famous occasion (Evans, J. 1956: 202-3), often quoted but worth mentioning once more for the light it throws on contemporary attitudes. In 1797 he found stone artefacts, including handaxes, deeply buried in Pleistocene deposits which were undisturbed and contained bones of extinct animals, at Hoxne in Suffolk, a site of which much will be said in later chapters. Not only did he recognize them as artefacts, but he clearly realized and accepted the implications of his discovery. He sent specimens of his finds to the Society of Antiquaries of London, already an institution of some seniority, and read a paper there in which he said that the flints 'if not particularly objects of curiosity in themselves, must, I think, be considered in that light from the situation in which they were found.' He regarded them as

> weapons of war, fabricated and used by a people who had not the use of metals . . . the situation in which these weapons were found may tempt us to refer them to a very remote period indeed; even beyond that of the present world.

Frere even argued in the language of the times that his finds were in what would now be called 'primary context': 'The manner in which they lie would lead to the persuasion that it was a place of their manufacture and not of their accidental deposit.' The recent excavations have confirmed his opinion. But the scientific world was not ready for this burst of enlightenment, and although the paper (Fig. 1:6) was published (Frere 1800), his finds were put quietly away and forgotten, and his interpretation of them was ignored. Nor was there any general change of attitude during the next quarter century. In 1823 Rev. William Buckland (1784-1856), writing as *inter alia* Professor of Mineralogy and Geology in the University of

[204]

XVIII. *Account of Flint Weapons discovered at Hoxne in* Suffolk. *By John Frere, Esq* F.R.S. *and* F.A.S. *In a Letter to the Rev.* John Brand, *Secretary.*

Read June 22, 1797.

Sir,

I TAKE the liberty to request you to lay before the Society some flints found in the parish of Hoxne, in the county of Suffolk, which, if not particularly objects of curiosity in themselves, must, I think, be considered in that light, from the situation in which they were found. See Pl. XIV, XV.

They are, I think, evidently weapons of war, fabricated and used by a people who had not the use of metals. They lay in great numbers at the depth of about twelve feet, in a stratified soil, which was dug into for the purpose of raising clay for bricks.

The strata are as follows:

1. Vegetable earth 1½ feet.
2. Argill 7½ feet.
3. Sand mixed with shells and other marine substances 1 foot.
4. A gravelly soil, in which the flints are found, generally at the rate of five or six in a square yard, 2 feet.

In the same stratum are frequently found small fragments of wood, very perfect when first dug up, but which soon decompose on being exposed to the air; and in the stratum of sand, (No. 3,) were found some extraordinary bones, particularly a jaw-bone of enormous size, of some unknown animal, with the teeth remaining in it. I was very eager to obtain a sight of this; and finding it had been carried to a neighbouring gentleman, I inquired of him, but learned that he had presented it, together with a huge thigh-bone, found

in

1:6 Part of John Frere's report to the Society of Antiquaries of London of his discoveries at Hoxne, Suffolk

Oxford, published a major work entitled *Reliquiae Diluvianae, or Observations on the Organic Remains contained in Caves, Fissures and Diluvial Gravel, and on other Geological Phenomena attesting the action of an Universal Deluge*. In it he surveyed a very considerable quantity of records in England and abroad of the finds of animal bones and other evidence in deposits of the kind referred to in the title, and explained them as having been deposited at the same time by a world-wide Flood (Buckland, *Reliquiae Diluvianae*, 2nd edition, 1824: 228):

All these facts, whether considered collectively or separately, present such a conformity of proofs, tending to establish the universality of a recent inundation of the earth, as no difficulties or objections that have hitherto arisen are in any way sufficient to overrule.

In the full confidence that these difficulties will at length be removed by the further extension of physical observations, we may for the present rest satisfied with the argument that numberless phenomena have already been ascertained, which without the admission of an universal deluge, it seems not easy, nay, utterly impossible to explain.

Some authors believed in one such Flood, either explicitly or implicitly equated with Noah's flood of the Old Testament account, but most seem to have thought that there had been several such events, of which Noah's was merely the last. Man was not thought to have spread to Western Europe before the flood or floods — in other words, in this area he was 'postdiluvian', not 'antediluvian'. Buckland restated his views without significant change in these respects in 1833 in his contribution to the *Bridgewater Treatises* and again in 1836 in his *Geology and Mineralogy considered in relation to Natural Theology*. But perhaps even more revealing than these interpretive statements, so far as contemporary attitudes are concerned, are some instances of Buckland's own reactions when confronted with the evidence in the field. Best known is his misinterpretation of the famous 'Red Lady of Paviland', an ochre-stained Upper Palaeolithic ceremonial burial (actually male), which he himself uncovered in the Goat's Hole Cave at Paviland, Gower — the only one of its particular kind and age ever to come to light in Britain yet. He concluded that it belonged to the Romano-British period and must be connected with a nearby 'British camp', because he would not believe the stratigraphic evidence before him for its much greater age and its broad contemporaneity with the animal bones, including elephant, rhinoceros and bear, which the cave also yielded. Included in his list of the 'most remarkable of the animal remains' from Paviland we find the entry 'Man . . . Portion of a female skeleton, clearly postdiluvian'.

No less striking were Buckland's dealings with Father J. MacEnery over the latter's finds at Kent's Cavern, Torquay (Plate 3), an important British site (see Chapters 4 and 6). MacEnery dug at Kent's Cavern between 1825 and 1829 and found what appeared to him (quite rightly, as we now know) to be the association of flint artefacts with the bones of extinct animals, sealed below a stalagmite floor and necessarily of great age. He wrote to Buckland for advice on how he should interpret this discovery. Buckland seems to have made no attempt to assess the finds *in situ* for himself, but merely replied that the flints must have fallen into the lower deposit through 'cooking holes' in the stalagmite layer. When MacEnery protested that there were no such cooking holes, he was simply told to look and he would find them. In fairness to Buckland, we should here note that, arch-supporter though he was at this stage of his life of the 'Diluvial Theory' and even of the biblical account of the Creation, he did become converted shortly afterwards (1838-40) to acceptance of the new 'Fluvial' and 'Glacial' theories, which had begun to make headway by the middle of the century in spite of the grave handicap of not being clearly referred to in the Old Testament. Indeed, he devoted just as much energy to supporting the new theory as he had expended on behalf of the old. Considering the period at which he was working, Buckland's positive achievements and useful observations far outweigh his errors, and he was immensely influential in the development of geological studies at this time, fully deserving the appreciation of him written half a century after his death by W.J. Sollas, a successor of his in the Chair of Geology at Oxford (1905: 243-8).

That a more reasonable appreciation of the length, scope and nature of the prehistoric period had begun to spread by the end of the 1830s, in spite of the deeply rooted attitudes referred to above, was largely thanks to certain more open-minded geologists, like James Hutton, William Smith and especially Charles Lyell (1797-1875), who showed that there was no need to believe in supernatural catastrophes like Noah's flood to explain the observable fossil and stratigraphic record: all past geological processes were essentially the same as those which could be seen at work in different parts of the world at the present time and they must necessarily have proceeded over an immensely long period, since they could be seen to be operating so slowly now. Ussher's

date for the Creation was therefore a piece of nonsense. (Perhaps the Diluvialists, if they had to use the Old Testament as a major source, should not have concentrated so heavily on Genesis. What of the Psalmist's perceptive observations: 'For a thousand ages in thy sight are but as yesterday, seeing that is past as a watch in the night' or 'He giveth snow like wool and scattereth the hoar frost like ashes : he casteth forth his ice like morsels : who is able to abide his frost?'). L. Agassiz (1807-73) was another geologist whose support of the Glacial Theory in particular was influential in Britain,[6] but these ideas took hold only slowly and it was well into the second half of the nineteenth century before they had gained general acceptance and before it was widely recognized that actual glaciation on a wide scale had occurred on a number of occasions in Britain, and that the distribution of far-travelled erratic rocks including some of Scandinavian origin was due to the spread of major ice-sheets overland rather than to the grounding of icebergs during periods of land submergence as had been argued in the early days of the Glacial Theory.

Meanwhile, quite independently, the contribution of biologists like Charles Darwin, Alfred Wallace and Thomas Huxley, who developed and preached the doctrine of animal evolution, including human evolution, by processes including those often referred to as 'natural selection' and 'survival of the fittest', was another body blow to both the Genesis account of the Creation and the traditional ideas of chronology. The theory of evolution both showed the true mechanisms of 'creation', which became a continuous process rather than a seven day affair, and also demanded, like the new ideas of the geologists, an immensely long time for the past. In a sense too, when it had gained acceptance, it made the crude implements of the earlier Palaeolithic not merely plausible but essential as evidence that man too had passed through a long process of evolution which had cultural as well as physical aspects.

So it came about that, as finds of stone implements along with the bones of extinct animals continued to be made from time to time, they were received more favourably. Plenty of sceptics remained, but now there were also champions to defend the validity of the 'Drift implements'.[7] Better still, investigating committees or delegations of senior and respected scientists began to be appointed or sent to examine some of the claims made, considering the field evidence carefully. It was such a delegation that examined the discoveries made over more than twenty years from 1837 by Jacques Boucher de Perthes in gravels of the River Somme near Abbeville and Amiens in northern France — finds which had been ridiculed in France, but which the visiting British scientists, Joseph Prestwich and John Evans, now accepted (1859) with all their implications, in reports to the Royal Society and the Society of Antiquaries. Others soon followed their lead, and the opportunity was taken to recall that similar finds had also been made in Britain, notably at Hoxne. Evans (Plate 4a), later to become Sir John Evans and to write a classic work, *The Ancient Stone Implements, Weapons and Ornaments, of Great Britain* (first edition 1872), published his report in *Archaeologia* (Evans, J. 1860). In it he argued carefully that the flints found by de Perthes were humanly worked and he discussed carefully the evidence for their being truly *in situ* in the 'drift' deposits in which they were claimed to have been found. He described sections and recorded his own and Prestwich's observations of the positions in which individual flints were found during their visit, painstakingly refuting various possible arguments that might be brought to suggest that the artefacts were not contemporary with the fossil animal bones found in the same deposits. It is a scholarly paper, with the relevant evidence marshalled and used skilfully: there are no unsupported assertions. He concluded that (*op. cit.*, p. 19):

the chain of evidence adduced must I think be sufficient to convince others, as I confess it did me, that the conclusions at which Mons. de Perthes had arrived upon this subject were correct, and that these worked flints were as much original component parts of the gravel, as any of the other stones of which it consists.

He then goes on to tell how, on his return to England, he found John Frere's Hoxne report in *Archaeologia* XIII and realized its significance in the light of the very similar flints and deposits he

had just seen in France. He and Prestwich went to Hoxne at the earliest opportunity and were able to confirm Frere's observations and recover further implements. Evans also recalled Conyers's find near Grays Inn Lane in his report. These occurrences, manifestly quite independent of Boucher de Perthes' work and long preceding it, seemed to him to afford strong confirmatory evidence of the genuineness of the French discoveries (*op. cit.*, p. 27):

Thus much appears to be established without a doubt; that in a period of antiquity, remote beyond any of which we have hitherto found traces, this portion of the globe was peopled by man; and that mankind has here witnessed some of those geological changes by which the so-called diluvial beds were deposited. Whether they were the result of some violent rush of waters such as may have taken place when 'the fountains of the great deep were broken up, and the windows of heaven were opened', or whether of a more gradual action, similar in character to some of those now in operation along the course of our brooks, streams and rivers, may be a matter of dispute. Under any circumstances this great fact remains indisputable, that at Amiens land which is now one hundred and sixty feet above the sea and ninety feet above the Somme, has since the existence of man been submerged under fresh water, and an aqueous deposit from twenty to thirty feet in thickness, a portion of which must at all events have subsided from tranquil water, has been formed upon it; and this too has taken place in a country the level of which is now stationary, and the face of which has been but little altered since the days when the Gauls and the Romans constructed their sepulchres in the soil overlying the drift which contains these relics of a far earlier race of men.

Even while Evans and Prestwich were visiting France, another site was being treated as a test case in Britain itself, and they were already aware of the first results (preliminary reports were made to the British Association in 1858 and the Geological Society in June 1859). MacEnery's operations at Kent's Cavern, referred to above, had been continued sporadically by others, notably R.A.C. Godwin-Austen and then William Pengelly (1812-94). They had obtained convincing evidence that artefacts were associated with extinct animal bones in undisturbed deposits, and Hugh Falconer, especially, amongst other influential geologists had been impressed with Pengelly's finds. Since the deposits had by now been much dug into, it was decided that when a promising new site next turned up in Britain it should be excavated under the careful scrutiny of a committee of scientists. The Windmill Cave at Brixham, Devon, was discovered in January 1858, and it was thus that Pengelly came to excavate there as a member of a very eminent committee: his colleagues, appointed by the Geological Society with financial aid from the Royal Society and other sources included Falconer (chairman and secretary), Prestwich (treasurer), Lyell, Godwin-Austen, R. Owen, A.C. Ramsey and several others. The work at the site quite quickly produced 'worked flints, apparently arrow-heads and spear-heads . . . in juxtaposition with the bones of the *Rhinoceros tichorhinus*, *Ursus spelaeus*, *Hyaena spelaea* and other extinct animals' (Evans, J. 1860: 3). The finds were clearly of great antiquity and the Committee duly accepted the evidence, though it was not until 1872 that the final report (delayed by the death of Falconer) was read to the Royal Society by Prestwich, who published it later the same year (1872). From 1859 Pengelly continued his work at Kent's Cavern under the auspices of another Committee, this time of the British Association, and his efforts were again extremely successful and continued over a long period. But already by 1860 there could no longer be reasonable doubt that man had lived in Britain for an immensely long period, that he had been the contemporary of animals long extinct, and that he had made implements of stone. The latter could be seen to include some very characteristic forms, which were now beginning to come to light quite frequently not merely in cave fillings but also in the ancient gravel deposits of river valleys all over southern England.

The foregoing is an abbreviated, selective and somewhat superficial account of the recognition of the antiquity of man in Britain, mentioning only a few of the leading figures involved. The next stage in the development of British Palaeolithic studies was one of consolidation followed by expansion, in which the work of the professional scientists continued, but was matched in importance by the efforts of many amateur collectors, some of whom were content to acquire artefacts uncritically, often in great numbers, while others took a deep interest in the implications of their finds and sought not only to interpret them using any available evidence, but also to reconstruct other aspects of the life of early man.

The recognition of the great antiquity of man made an impact which lasted throughout the second half of the nineteenth century, and any collector with a general interest in antiquities was naturally keen to acquire specimens of the newly vindicated ancient stone implements. It was not hard to do so, as indeed Evans had foreseen at the close of his 1860 paper (*op. cit.*, p. 28):

> As to the localities in England where mammaliferous drift, of a character likely to contain these worked flints, exists, it would occupy too much time and space to attempt any list of them. Along the banks of the Thames, the eastern coast of England, the coast of western Sussex, the valleys of the Avon, Severn and Ouse, and of many other rivers, in fact in nearly every part of England, have remains of the *Elephas primigenius* [more properly, *Mammuthus primigenius*] and its contemporaries been found. Almost everyone must be acquainted with some such locality: there let him search also for flint implements such as these I have described, and assist in determining the important question of their date. A new field is opened for antiquarian research, and those who work in it will doubtless find their labours amply repaid.

This was in the heyday of gravel-digging by hand and the gravels which were being worked by shovel and pick were mainly the high and middle terrace gravels of the major river valleys, where so many implements were to be found. The workmen, poorly enough paid, were glad to earn a few extra shillings by putting aside flint implements for the collectors as they came across them. It is also true enough that skilled forgers like the notorious Flint Jack (Jessup 1964: 139-43) began to be active as soon as the implements had acquired a certain commercial value (cf. Smith, W.G. 1894: 294-8), and for this same reason it is only too likely that genuine artefacts were translated from pits where they were common and therefore cheap to others where they were very rare and correspondingly expensive. Only the most serious and far-sighted of the collectors took much trouble over checking exact provenances or gathering information about the depth and nature of the levels at a pit where implements were found. Section drawings and photographs remained very rare until after the end of the century.

There is no space here to mention more than a few of the great nineteenth-century and early twentieth-century collectors, to whom we owe so much of the extant British Lower and Middle Palaeolithic collections of our national and local museums. At their best, they were very good indeed, and some of their observations would even do credit to their successors among the amateur archaeologists of our own time who have the benefit of many more decades' accumulated knowledge of the Palaeolithic period. An outstanding example of the best of these early amateurs was certainly Worthington George Smith (1835-1917) of Dunstable (Dyer 1959, 1978), whose book *Man the Primeval Savage* (1894) may be read and re-read with profit today. Smith (Plate 4b), in the 1880s and early 1890s, was already saving every fragment he could of worked flint rather than selecting the fine specimens, recording every detail he could about the provenance of each specimen, drawing sections in the gravel pits he observed and even causing photographs to be taken of interesting exposures, rejoining anciently struck flakes or refitting original trimming flakes to completed or partially finished implements, and drawing artefacts with a skill and precision that has only rarely been surpassed. His book makes a serious attempt to reconstruct many aspects of Palaeolithic life in a readable way, and it shows wide knowledge of many sites and finds beside his 'own' ones in Bedfordshire and north-east London. All this work he achieved on his own slender resources in the spare time left over from other activities and

interests; even after he reached the age of 70 he would sometimes walk twenty or even thirty miles in a day between his home and the gravel and brick-earth pits where his most important finds were made.

Other amateur collectors who approached or reached these standards include F.C.J. Spurrell (mainly in north Kent), J. Allen Brown (in Middlesex) and S. Hazzledine Warren (mainly in Essex) — the latter's first finds were made early enough for him to be mentioned in the second edition of Sir John Evans's *Ancient Stone Implements*, published in 1897, and he was still writing papers of considerable importance on his discoveries in the Clacton area in the 1950s (e.g. 1951, 1955, 1958). J.P.T. Burchell was essentially an amateur collector, who wrote important papers on the palaeolithic of north Kent, on occasion seen in a much wider context (e.g. 1931). Henry Stopes also collected many thousands of artefacts from north Kent, especially the Swanscombe pits (Plate 15), and they are now mostly in the reserve collections of the National Museum of Wales; he entered the field from geology. A.T. Marston, a London dentist, made important discoveries in the same region, including parts of the famous Swanscombe fossil hominid skull (Plate 14). Many other distinguished amateurs were also active in the Swanscombe region at one time or another. There was also a long line of important collectors who operated in East Anglia, though not all of them lived there, going right back to the 1860s: W.A. Sturge, J.W. Flower, H.H. Halls, W.G. Clarke, F.N. Haward and J.E. Sainty are merely a few of them, and they have several active successors in the same region today. Almost any area in southern England had its own leading collectors (cf. Evans 1897). Then there were others with a major professional interest in archaeology or geology, more often the latter, since there were few professional archaeological posts (excluding museum curatorships) until well into the twentieth century: men like Evans himself, Henry Bury, A.S. Kennard, Henry Dewey, M.A.C. Hinton, O.A. Shrubsole and many others amassed substantial collections, and between them contributed important articles or longer works of local or national scope. So too did A.D. Lacaille (1894-

1975; Plate 4c), though his post at the Wellcome Historical Medical Museum was scarcely a professional archaeological post, and he always preferred to regard himself as an amateur.

Some collectors were more successful in acquiring implements than in publishing or causing to be published accounts of their finds. The superb Llewellyn Treacher collection from Middle Thames sites, now in the Oxford University Museum, was only sparsely written up by its owner, though what he did write was useful, and he kept manuscript records some at least of which have survived. G.W. Smith, an important collector in the Reading area, also left a journal which is preserved, but published little or nothing himself. Anyone who cares to check through the hundreds of palaeoliths from various pits in the Yiewsley-West Drayton area of Hillingdon (Middlesex) acquired by R. Garraway Rice and now in the reserve collections of the London Museum, will learn from almost every one of the laboriously hand-written paper labels that the owner was a Fellow of the Society of Antiquaries, but will look in vain for more useful archaeological information beyond the name of the pit, although there was an important stratified sequence of deposits. Devious too may be the ways of collectors when the fever is on them to outdo their rivals in the number or quality of their acquisitions, or when their collection gets too large for the space they have available. For example, Dr Armstrong Bowes of Herne Bay, Kent, sought to protect his favourite sites from the attentions of other collectors by labelling his specimens with single letter abbreviations for each word of the site name; but it would have been too simple to use the initial letters, so he used the second letter in each case. Thus Fordwich was abbreviated to O and the site known to him as Canterbury West became A E. If it were not such a disaster, one might see a pleasing element of poetic justice in the fact that after his death his notebooks were destroyed and many of the labels washed off the implements by flood water in the 1950s; many of his treasured specimens subsequently spent an inglorious period in a chicken house. The truth is that such information as does survive in this case has done so by tenuous chance, and we are left to wish that he had expended the energy he devoted

to his private recording system on proper publication instead and outshone his rivals that way. The present writer recalls a visit in the early 1960s to Mr C.E. Bean of Sherborne, Dorset, a knowledgeable and brilliantly successful collector of all things archaeological by his own efforts in his own area, who was living in the last two or three rooms in his house which the assembled artefacts had not taken over, and was apparently still collecting as energetically as ever. Amongst his material were more than a thousand Lower Palaeolithic artefacts from the famous Broom Pit at Hawkchurch near Axminster: he decided that it would be actually physically impossible for him to extract them and make them available for study, and he showed the writer the place in his garden where he had stacked the boxes of lesser flakes and worked fragments, but now grass and weeds had grown over them and there was nothing to be seen on the surface. These are perhaps extreme cases of collectors' mania, but there are only too many cases of individuals who amassed large numbers of superb artefacts and died leaving little or no detailed record of their sources beyond the site names: H. Dale, for example (south Hampshire material now at Winchester Museum), or H. Druitt (Bournemouth area material now mainly at the Red House Museum, Christchurch). Some collectors were also dealers in implements: G.F. Lawrence is the best known example, though he did also hold a curatorial post at the London Museum for some while.

It would be misleading to give the impression that the only work done by amateurs was collecting and occasional recording: some made highly important discoveries of sites, and, more recently, several have directed important excavations. The work of the late J.B. Calkin, a schoolmaster, at the important site of Slindon in west Sussex is an example and so is that of P.J. Tester, another schoolmaster, at several very interesting Kent sites, notably Bowman's Lodge and Cuxton. J.C. Draper of Fareham, too, has a number of important finds to his credit in south Hampshire over the past thirty years, including the Rainbow Bar and Red Barns sites, and L.W. Carpenter discovered some small but important sites in Surrey. Long before any of these, Worthington Smith was a great discoverer of sites, as already noted, in both north-east London and Bedfordshire, and even did what he could in the way of excavation, more or less single-handed. Some dozens more names could well be mentioned if space allowed and indeed injustice has been done to many distinguished workers by their omission.

The work of the amateur collector continues today, with many gifted observers doing their best to save and record artefacts torn out of Pleistocene deposits during commercial excavations. R.J. MacRae, now living near Oxford, has collected many thousands of artefacts in this way, for example. Such men are now fewer, however, and do not usually operate on the grand scale of the past, for two main reasons: first, gravel extraction has become a high-speed mechanized operation, in which any palaeoliths included among the stones are whisked along a fast conveyor belt to be crushed or loaded into transport before anyone can see them, let alone save them — to stop such machinery for a moment is to cost the operating company many pounds of income. The occasional dexterous driver of a mechanical excavator, like Mr R.C. Benham at Romsey, may sometimes be able to extract visible handaxes from a scooped load of gravel without bringing his employers to ruin, but generally speaking the chances of finding much are greatly reduced. Second, the majority of the gravel workings today are situated on the lower terraces or even the flood-plains in the river valleys, where Lower Palaeolithic material *in situ* is very unlikely to be found: implements are scarce accordingly, and usually much battered and worn, their derived state making them of marginal archaeological importance. However, there are other kinds of commercial digging which may be well worth watching — road construction, for example, which may cut through important Pleistocene deposits — and it is satisfactory to report that finds are still being made and new sites recorded.

It should not be thought that after 1860 all interest was concentrated on the gravel sites. Many caves were dug into over the next sixty or seventy years, too often without much care: few of those responsible reached Pengelly's standards, and their operations have left only fragments of the cave fillings available for modern research in most cases.

W. Boyd Dawkins (1837-1929) was one of the most active of the early cave diggers and his books *Cave Hunting* (1874) and *Early Man in Britain* (1880) contain much information, including section drawings and even advice on digging procedure so that the work should be done 'with sufficient accuracy to be of scientific value' (1874: 438). Alas, more than one excavator in recent years has found the spoil heaps left by Boyd Dawkins to be almost as rich in artefacts, missed by his workmen, as the undisturbed levels. The long career of A.L. Armstrong (1879-1958) included many seasons' work at caves, especially at Creswell Crags (Derbyshire). Armstrong was a more skilful and imaginative excavator than many of his predecessors and contemporaries, and published various accounts of his work in local and national journals, but those who have followed him have found both his detailed recording and his interpretation of the evidence wanting in various ways on occasion. It is probably fair as a general comment to say that all the best and most useful work on British Palaeolithic cave sites postdates the Second World War, though there are certainly a few exceptions. The Spelaeological Society of the University of Bristol has a record of cave excavation going as far back as 1919 and including some distinguished work (cf. ApSimon 1969). Many of the excavations in British caves have naturally been concerned with occupations of Upper Palaeolithic age (cf. Garrod 1926; Campbell 1973, 1977), which do not directly concern us here.

After the turn of the century it became less uncommon for formal excavation to be added to the work of collection and observation at the open sites. Experts in various fields would join together to report on sites of particular interest — for example, the work of R.A. Smith and H. Dewey at Swanscombe (1913, 1914) and Rickmansworth (1915) in the Thames Valley. More often, however, existing sections were studied and reported on rather than new ones being dug. The name of R.A. Smith (1874-1940) of the British Museum is frequently found as author or co-author of such reports at this time, often as the authority consulted to pronounce upon the flint artefacts in particular, as well as on the general archaeology of the site in question. This was the zenith period of typological classification of artefacts, when they could be attributed on morphological grounds to particular stages (or even sub-stages) of general 'cultures' like Clactonian, Acheulian or Levalloisian. L'Abbé H. Breuil (1877-1961) in France was the high priest of this particular religion, but there were British experts too, with R.A. Smith, M.C. Burkitt and J. Reid Moir amongst them. R.A. Smith's reports on the Tilehurst, Berkshire (1915a) and Fordwich, Kent (1933) sites will serve to illustrate contemporary approaches well enough; see also his detailed catalogue of the British implements in the Sturge Collection produced for the British Museum (1931). Excavation was becoming more frequent and of better quality by the time the Second World War broke out: see for example the work of K.P. Oakley and M.D. Leakey at Clacton (1937) and of the Swanscombe Committee (1938) at Barnfield Pit after the discovery of the first skull fragments.

The general acceptance of the great antiquity of man from about 1860 onwards, and the gradual development of Palaeolithic studies in Britain along the lines indicated, did not of course mean that all scholarly controversy was ended. It remained, for example, to be settled (indeed it still remains to be settled) just how old the first artefacts were. Inevitably some workers got a little carried away and overstretched one or another part of the evidence, usually by failing to distinguish what was probably the work of nature from what was quite certainly the work of man, or else by applying less than rigorous standards of judgement about what was or was not *in situ* in early Pleistocene or late Pliocene deposits. Hence several entertaining but in the event unproductive controversies about 'eoliths', 'pre-Crag man', 'Pliocene man', and the like, which we need not discuss in detail here. A couple of examples will suffice. The first of these is taken from the work of Benjamin Harrison (1837-1921; Plate 4d) of Ightham, Kent; see the biography of him by his son, Sir Edward Harrison (1928). He collected large numbers of what became known as 'eoliths' (literally, 'dawn-stones') from Tertiary (pre-Pleistocene) deposits on the high ground of North Kent, believing them to be artefacts of pre-palaeolithic age, the work of 'Plateau Man'. Their edges certainly show many scars which are the result of 'mechanical' fracture, and the forms are rudimentary in the extreme (Plate 5). On an 'evolutionary' and strictly typological view of stone artefacts, the eoliths were certainly ideally suited to occupy an early place in the time scale. Similarly, the recent recognition of the great antiquity of man was bound to encourage searchers to push the dating as far back as they could. How should one, anyhow, distinguish the very earliest genuine artefacts from the products of natural flaking, if they were as simple in character as one might expect? The 'Harrisonian eoliths' are now generally regarded as the work of nature, the simple chipping of their edges, mainly in one direction, being most likely to have been caused by pressure during soil movement (cf. Warren 1923). But for more than a decade either side of 1900, those who supported them and those who did not fought out many a battle, in print, in correspondence or at the meetings of the learned Societies (Harrison, E. 1928). Prestwich was firmly in their favour, and presented the case on Harrison's behalf (e.g. 1889, 1892). J. Evans, who died in 1908, remained opposed to them; Worthington Smith (died 1917) was also unconvinced by all he saw, though ready to keep an open mind. Sir John Lubbock (Lord Avebury) was another who accepted them in the end. Other famous names were disposed on either side. All the most eminent figures of the archaeological and geological worlds beat a pathway to the door of Benjamin Harrison's grocery and general store at Ightham, and his specimens can still be seen preserved in many museum collections, notably the British Museum and Maidstone Museum in Kent. Five came into the writer's possession a few years ago, together with a charming watercolour sketch of them, signed, dated 1903 and inscribed on the back with comments by Harrison himself: a delightful memento of what now seems a rather unimportant and protracted debate, though it was far from that at the time. It is a little sad that Harrison's association with the eoliths controversy has since rather obscured the fact that he collected many hundreds of genuine palaeoliths in north

Kent and discovered many sites of considerable interest by his own painstaking field work, all carried out on foot from his own home. These artefacts too are to be seen now in museum collections all over Britain — a testimony to his generosity in giving away his finds to his learned visitors. Harrison was indeed one of the great nineteenth century local natural historians, in many respects comparable to Worthington Smith with whom he long maintained a correspondence full of humour. But he himself published very little indeed, being content to leave the exposition of his finds to his eminent friends; see however his note (1892) published in conjunction with one of Prestwich's papers.

Very different indeed from Harrison was J. Reid Moir of Ipswich — a senior member or fellow and in some cases president of several of the learned societies, and the author of a great number of papers on palaeolithic subjects, especially, but by no means solely, dealing with East Anglian sites. Read today they are inclined to make him sound somewhat pompous and dogmatic and a little too persistent in his endeavours to prove the existence of 'Pliocene Man' or 'Pre-Crag Man' in Britain — see for example his presidential address to the Prehistoric Society of East Anglia in 1932, or parts of his *The Antiquity of Man in East Anglia* (1927). Again, the material he studied in this connection was sometimes of natural origin, but sometimes it is his arguments that genuine artefacts were *in situ* in very early deposits which have failed to stand the test of time. Moir, however, also produced a number of useful and uncontroversial papers, and studied many of the leading British sites at important stages of their history, for example Hoxne (1926, 1935), Broom in Dorset (1936) and Brundon in Essex (Moir and Hopwood 1939). A similar comment could be made of other figures of importance during the earlier part of the present century: that amongst a good quantity of useful papers they would suddenly produce what seems to us now a bee-in-the-bonnet affair, like the work of Burchell with Moir on supposed Lower Palaeolithic artefacts from Northern Ireland (Burchell *et al.* 1929; Burchell and Moir 1932) which would find few supporters today, or A.L. Armstrong's identification as Lower Palaeolithic of certain objects from Lancashire which are so many lumps of stone. To be fair, it is mainly through hindsight that we now perceive the fallacies so clearly. Others however seem to have specialized in pure moonshine without the compensating useful papers, for example Rev. Frederick Smith, with his books on *The Stone Ages in North Britain and Ireland* (1909) and *Palaeolithic Man and the Cambridge Gravels* (1926), not uncommonly to be found on the shelves of dealers in secondhand archaeological books, in both of which a great number of non-artefacts are minutely, lovingly and fancifully described, though the author seems to have realized in the second work that his views commanded less than total acceptance in some quarters.

But these are byways in the history of British Palaeolithic research and it does not do to spend too much time exploring them, though they are by no means wholly irrelevant, for they reflect contemporary thought in various ways both directly and through the reactions they provoked; at least the views referred to were sincerely held by their various protagonists. No doubt some of us studying the British Palaeolithic today will be regarded by posterity as unintentionally purveying a certain amount of moonshine amongst the other kinds of illumination, and posterity itself will be similarly guilty in its turn. To conclude this selective review, however, it is worth saying something of how matters have proceeded in the period since the Second World War.

There are plenty of weighty reasons, connected with the development of general archaeological thinking, to account for why interests should have changed in Palaeolithic research over the last thirty years to assume their present directions, but one important practical consideration should not be overlooked: the ending of gravel extraction by hand. It simply ceased to be possible to go and purchase quantities of handaxes from gravel-pit workers and watch the slow development of a section. Also the archaeologically more productive higher terrace gravels were becoming exhausted. At the same time, partly for these reasons and partly independently, Palaeolithic research in Britain, from having rather dominated the scene in local prehistoric archaeology for many years, declined in popularity.[8] Very interesting work on the Neolithic in the Middle East and in Europe was being done, and the later prehistoric periods were also enjoying something of a boom. For the Palaeolithic itself, areas other than Britain, notably sub-Saharan Africa, were beginning to produce exciting finds of far greater antiquity, with the evidence better preserved; there was a growing feeling of disenchantment with derived implements coming from gravel contexts which could merely be classified and reclassified typologically. Seventy or eighty years' work on the British Palaeolithic had amassed huge quantities of such artefacts, but there was little general agreement on a detailed British Palaeolithic and Pleistocene sequence, and the work of publication lagged far behind that of collection. It was clearly a time to take stock, to analyse and to make what order could be made out of chaos. No doubt that was why, in the early 1950s, the Council for British Archaeology set up 'period' Research Committees and the one concerned with the Palaeolithic and Mesolithic periods (lumped together as so often) set itself to collect information for a 'Palaeolithic Gazetteer'. Predictably, the project got off to an enthusiastic start and then soon lost momentum as circular letters remained unanswered by harassed curators who had neither the time nor the specialist knowledge to deal with them, and no one had the energy to complete the task. The present writer was later able to absorb this lapsed project into his own doctoral research from 1961 onwards, and to complete the intended Gazetteer, but it was 1968 before it was finally in print. This in any case was merely a stocktaking operation, not an analytical one, though it certainly helped to clear the way for work of the latter kind.

Meanwhile the archaeological world was becoming aware, dimly at first and then eagerly, of the possibilities offered in the study of artefacts by the development of certain techniques of statistical analysis. In the first instance, their most obvious use was for the objective assessment and comparison of artefact assemblages by very simple methods, and Palaeolithic stone tools were an obvious class of material on which such techniques could be tried out. Professor Françis Bordes in France was one of those showing what could be done as early as 1950. Charles McBurney (see West and McBurney 1954) used simple methods of metrical analysis to compare and contrast some of the handaxes from Hoxne with those belonging to Mousterian industries.[9] A much more sophisticated computer-based statistical approach (matrix analysis) was used by David Clarke (1962) on material of a different archaeological period, when he was a Cambridge research student studying British Beaker pottery; his work, and that of F.R. Hodson on Iron Age brooches from the Münsingen (Switzerland) cemetery, were both very influential in Britain on the methodological side in the early and middle 1960s, and many others were working on similar lines elsewhere. From that time progress has been headlong all over the world, if a little erratic here and there, while the technical aids now available for such work are a formidable array. It is indeed rare in the late 1970s to find a major work of archaeological analysis which does not employ statistical methods. Some idea of the variety and complexity of the experiments tried over the past decade, and even a certain glimpse into the nearer future, can be gained from such works as David Clarke's *Analytical Archaeology* (1968) and the volume *Models in Archaeology* edited by him a few years later (1972), or from L.R. Binford's collected papers published under the title *An Archaeological Perspective* (1972), or from the recent book by J.E. Doran and F.R. Hodson *Mathematics and Computers in Archaeology* (1975), to name only a few sources. These between them contain abundant references for those who wish to explore the methods themselves further, while those who are appalled by the whole thing may find a little solace here and there in the pages of the journal *Antiquity* over the past decade: they could start with Mrs Jacquetta Hawkes's paper on 'The proper study of mankind' (1968) and they should also keep an eye on the editorial colums. For there has indeed been some reaction against what has been seen as a massive invasion by statisticians and computer scientists of the proper territory of 'traditional' archaeological methods, and against what has been regarded as the needless and unjustifiable reduction of beautiful and expertly made artefacts to mere computer-fodder — an ugly string of figures and symbols. And where does the present writer stand? He is wholly in favour of the study of artefacts by rigorously objective methods, but sees no reason why this should prevent appreciation of them at the same time from other points of view; he has used only the simplest kinds of statistical techniques in his own metrical analyses of handaxe assemblages (1964, 1968a and cf. Chapter 5 in this book), hoping to keep the treatment of them within his own limited understanding of such things, and being well aware of the poor quality of the assemblages as statistical 'samples'; however, he is always delighted when those competent to do so make more ambitious use of his data (Graham and Roe 1970; Hodson 1971; Isaac 1972b).

If such methods are going to be used, the whole value of the results must indeed turn on the quality of the sample, and the mere desirability of discovering undisturbed sites becomes a prime essential. Enough has already been said to indicate that the existing British collections make very poor subjects for such analytical work, and this has been one of the main reasons why the excavation of new sites or the re-excavation of old ones has played an important part in British Palaeolithic studies lately. However, there have been other equally important reasons, including the renewal of interest in the social, economic and environmental sides of earlier prehistory, beginning in the middle and late 1960s – nothing new in itself (cf. Clark, J.G.D. 1952, and earlier works by the same author), but a great re-discovery by some of the so-called 'New Archaeologists'. It is of course true that increased knowledge and many improvements in laboratory techniques have made advances possible in this field. But the point is that disturbed sites and derived assemblages offer little or no useful data of this kind: undisturbed *in situ* occurrences in deposits preserving organic material are required for worthwhile attempts to reconstruct ancient environments and ancient economies. All the language – and the jargon – of such studies, like 'symbiotic relationship', 'ecological niche', 'economic strategy' and so forth imply that sites can be examined with the evidence in a complete state. Approaches like 'site catchment analysis' (Higgs and Vita-Finzi 1970) may in ideal

circumstances go far towards reconstructing how ancient human groups supported life and obtained their various resources, but they can make very little progress unless well-preserved sites are available on which to work.

For these reasons, then, excavation of Palaeolithic sites in Britain has continued in recent years, and there have been other aims too, notably the continual need to check geological contexts in the light of new and more detailed knowledge, and to obtain dating evidence – mainly dating in Pleistocene terms that is – since opportunities for chronometric dating in Britain are extremely rare still, although the development of some of the uranium series methods that can be applied to bone has offered a little new hope lately (cf. Szabo and Collins 1975). In the post-war period successful excavations have been conducted on varying scales at several of the classic sites, notably Barnfield Pit, Swanscombe (Ovey 1964; Wymer 1968: 334-46; Waechter 1968; Conway 1968; Waechter *et al.* 1969, 1970, 1971); Hoxne (West and McBurney 1954; Wymer 1974); Clacton-on-Sea (Wymer and Singer 1970; Singer *et al.* 1973); Baker's Hole, Northfleet (Sieveking, work in preparation); High Lodge, Mildenhall (Sieveking 1968 and work in preparation); Slindon (A. Woodcock, work in progress) and La Cotte de Saint-Brelade, Jersey, C.I. (McBurney and Callow 1971). Other sites which were previously unknown or little regarded have also been dug, for example, Cuxton near Rochester (Tester 1965), Highlands Farm Pit near Henley-on-Thames (Wymer 1961, 1968: 191-8), Red Barns, Portchester (A. ApSimon and C. Gamble, report in preparation), Coygan Cave (McBurney, unpublished), Westbury-sub-Mendip (Bishop, M.J. 1974, 1975) or the Rhinoceros Hole at Wookey, Somerset (E.K. Tratman, report in preparation). These are only examples, not a complete list: more information will be found about all these sites in later chapters, and others where post-war excavation has taken place will be mentioned. In view of the present necessary bias in British archaeology in general towards rescue excavation, it is worth mentioning that the work at several of the sites named was indeed a rescue operation for one reason or another – quarrying at Westbury, housing development at Red Barns, gravel extraction at Highlands Farm, and so forth.

In short, then, the study of the British Lower and Middle Palaeolithic is actively continuing, both in the field and in the laboratory, and a number of major reports are being prepared for publication, several of them arising out of the recent work referred to in the previous paragraph. The growth of student numbers at University archaeological departments, and indeed the increase in the number of the teaching departments themselves, has led to the undertaking of more post-graduate research on Palaeolithic subjects; the absolute number of research students in this field in Britain is still small, but the increase seems a big one to the writer when he recalls that when he began his own research in 1961 at Cambridge he was the first to choose a pure British Palaeolithic subject for some years.

Yet with all the activity, past and present, referred to in this section, it is still true to say that there is no full-scale book available which attempts to give comprehensive and even coverage to the British Lower and Middle Palaeolithic. This is not to say that there have been no major analytical accounts of this period of British archaeology at all: there is, for example, John Wymer's admirable account (1968) of the Thames Valley material, which deals with general aspects of the Lower Palaeolithic as well as giving a site-by-site account of the Thames Valley artefacts and stratigraphy, though its author could pay only lip service to the sites outside his area. Long before there was John Evans's famous *Ancient Stone Implements*, first published as early as 1872, with a second revised edition in 1897, but this ranged far beyond the Lower and Middle Palaeolithic and, for all its excellent qualities, it came too early to achieve much more than speculation about those aspects of the material it described which chiefly concern students of the period today. Worthington Smith's *Man the Primeval Savage* is still a remarkable book by any standards, but 1894 was again too early for an overview of the British earlier Palaeolithic that could meet today's requirements: many of the key sites were still undiscovered. Smith wrote meticulously and in many ways brilliantly about what he knew, and the present value of his work lies in his perceptive and highly intelligent observation of some very remarkable Lower Palaeolithic sites. Indeed, he would probably be the best possible author of the present book, had his whole career run its course eighty or ninety years later than was in fact the case. His own valuation of *Man the Primeval Savage* was altogether lower: in a letter to Benjamin Harrison written from Dunstable in November 1893 (quoted in Harrison, E.R. 1928: 345) he mentions in passing:

> I am just writing a brief readable account of the geology and implements of this place, which Mr. Stanford will publish. I have many times asked you to do something of the sort but I think you never will . . . .

These books by Evans and Smith seem to the writer to be clearly the best of their period, though there are other important ones such as Boyd Dawkins' *Early Man in Britain* (1880), or W.J. Sollas's *Ancient Hunters* (first edition 1911). Between 1900 and about 1930, many books were written with titles which vary the theme 'Our Prehistoric Ancestors' and they make frequent reference to British sites, though most are of wider scope, and it is rare to find no chapter on the French Upper Palaeolithic and the cave art (still a recent discovery at that time). Examples of such books, many of which were excellent, are Burkitt's *Prehistory* (1921), Vulliamy's *Our Prehistoric Forerunners* (1925) or *Remains of the Prehistoric Age in England* by Windle (1904). None of these or their contemporaries, however, can be regarded as giving a broad and deep account of the British Lower and Middle Palaeolithic, and the same is true of the next generation of books, which perhaps starts with Burkitt's *The Old Stone Age* (1933, revised 1955) and L.S.B. Leakey's *Adam's Ancestors* (1934, revised 1953) and continues right up to Oakley's *Frameworks for dating Fossil Man* (first published 1964) and his highly successful little handbook *Man the Toolmaker*, first published in 1949, with many subsequent editions. This group might also include the English translation in 1965 of Breuil and Lantier's *Les Hommes de la Pierre Ancienne*, published first in 1951. No adverse criticism of these works is intended here, for they never set out to provide such an account, being altogether wider in scope; they merely underline the need for a specialist work. On the other hand one might feel that recent books by some of the Continental authors, such as Bordes (1968) or Müller-Karpe (1965) are a little *too* sketchy in their references to the British Palaeolithic. Some of this lost ground is made up by Paul Mellars's excellent chapter in *British Prehistory: a New Outline* (A.C. Renfrew, ed. 1974), by the archaeological information in J.G. Evans's *The Environment of Early Man in the British Isles* (1975) and by Desmond Collins's chapter in *Background to Archaeology* (Collins *et al.* 1973), but these contributions are sections or extended chapters rather than whole books, and their treatment of the material is therefore necessarily brief.

As for the present writer's *Gazetteer of British Lower and Middle Palaeolithic Sites* (1968b), that is perhaps as comprehensive as anyone has tried to be, so far as the recording of the existence of find-spots and artefacts goes, but it is merely a list of them and to seek answers to questions of prehistory from it would be hardly more practicable than to try and learn modern British History from the index to an atlas. All things considered, then, the writing of the present book seems to be a necessary exercise, and it is accordingly high time to close this long chapter of preliminaries and get down to the main business in hand. Yet even now there is the British Pleistocene sequence to be considered before we can pass on to the archaeology of the British Palaeolithic.

NOTES

1 In this chapter attention is confined to aspects of the history of Palaeolithic research rather than the history of archaeology in general. A discipline describable as archaeology can be traced back perhaps as far as the first half of the nineteenth century, but beyond that it merges into a misty background better called antiquarianism. The course of the development of archaeology is of sufficient interest to have prompted various studies, the work of G.E. Daniel on this subject being perhaps best known and most readily accessible (see especially Daniel, 1950, 1962, 1967 and 1975, which are all entertaining as well as informative accounts; some other references, general and specific, are quoted later on in this chapter). Some might think it a fair comment that only an author who had been educated archaeologically at Cambridge and had enjoyed Professor Daniel's lectures would think it worth devoting so much space in the present chapter to historical aspects of the British Palaeolithic.

2 The study of hominid fossils as a branch of physical anthropology or human biology is a rapidly developing field which is becoming ever more complicated. The main reason for this is the vastly increased amount of material to study, produced by archaeological expeditions which had the recovery of such evidence as one of their main objectives rather than merely hoping to strike lucky. The Rift valleys in East Africa, especially, have been systematically searched in this way, and the East Turkana (formerly known as East Rudolf) study area alone has produced finds since 1969 amongst

which over 150 individual hominids are fragmentarily represented: contrast this with Britain. It takes a long while even for one scientist to study one find comprehensively: to get several to agree on a general scheme of hominid evolution within the earlier Pleistocene, based on them all, will require many years (during which fresh finds will be made). So it is not surprising if no major up-to-the-minute textbook exists to be recommended here. Amongst many useful smaller handbooks, those who wish to follow up the subject further might try the accounts given by Day (1965; new and revised edition 1977), Napier (1971), Howells (1972), Pilbeam (1972) or Leakey and Lewin (1977), but others may soon be available.

3 See the works quoted in the previous note, plus Tobias (1967), M.D. Leakey (1971: 272-81) and relevant papers in Zuckerman (1973), Butzer and Isaac (1975), Coppens *et al.* (1976), Hay (1976), Isaac and McCown (1976), etc. Watch also for new reports of work in the East Turkana basin, the Olduvai area and the Afar Depression in northern Ethiopia, some of which may be available by the time this book is published.

4 A monograph on Terra Amata is in preparation, and meanwhile only short accounts are available by de Lumley (1969a, 1969b: 140-3), who reports that oval huts were erected in successive years on almost precisely the same spot, where structural traces from the previous occasion probably showed through the accumulation of blown sand. Evidence for the time of

year was provided by the nature of the food debris and by the pollen, which was obtained from human coprolites. Some of the stratigraphic conclusions may require modification following the work of P. Villa (1977).

5 The basic data about flint fracture and artefact manufacture and their terminology, clearly and simply set out, can be found in various little books, notably those of Oakley (1949), Watson (1950; various later editions), Bordaz (1970) and Timms (1974). A more detailed study of flint as a raw material will be found in Shepherd (1972).

6 Agassiz was the principal agent of Buckland's conversion. An entertaining contemporary report of Agassiz's important lecture on 'Glaciers and the Evidence of their having once existed in Scotland and Ireland' to the Geological Society on 4 November 1840, and of Buckland's supporting remarks on the same day and at another meeting a fortnight later, and of the discussion on both occasions, is quoted by H.B. Woodward (1907: 136-44).

7 The term 'drift' which has stuck firmly in the geological and to some extent also archaeological literature, and is still used today, originated in the idea of deposits 'rafted in' by drifting icebergs at a time of land submergence; the icebergs grounded, dropping the loads of morainic material attached to their bases (cf. West 1977: 2-3). All Pleistocene deposits of a morainic or even merely gravelly character seem to have been lumped together by some authors as 'drift', much as they were previously lumped together as 'diluvial', while the main body of the Pleistocene could similarly be referred to as 'the Drift period' and Lower Palaeolithic handaxes could be called 'drift implements'.

8 In fact it is the number of professional Palaeolithic archaeologists in Britain that has dwindled more strikingly; although there are currently far more holders of professional archaeological posts of one sort or another than ever before, only a handful of them specialize in Palaeolithic teaching or research. The main reason for this is that there are now so many other archaeological problems demanding urgent attention — demands which are being well matched by the supply of specialized knowledge and research expertise. For reasons referred to in this section, significant new Palaeolithic sites are at present rather rare in Britain, while sites belonging to later periods, always much more numerous in aggregate, are being discovered or threatened with destruction every day.

9 Though he was not by any means the first to do so: cf. for example J.D. Solomon's metrical treatment of handaxes from Warren Hill, Mildenhall, Suffolk, some twenty years earlier (Solomon 1933).

The Pleistocene Background   *Chapter 2*

The sequence of stages in the British Pleistocene may seem complicated enough to the uninitiated even in Table 1: how much more so when discussed in the specialist books. As set out in the present chapter, however, it is likely eventually to prove much too simplified, and there may well be serious errors or omissions which only future work can reveal and correct. Fortunately, since our principal concern is with the archaeological rather than the geological record, we need not get too deeply involved with all the difficulties and possible pitfalls. The Palaeolithic period in Britain, unlike that in certain other parts of the world, is much shorter than the length of the Pleistocene, and a nodding acquaintance with the local earlier Pleistocene stages will suffice. Our main interest in the British Pleistocene sequence is in the first instance unashamedly concerned with relative and absolute chronology, since it is the assigning of archaeological occurrences to particular stadials, interstadials or interglacials, or better still to specific parts of them, which enables such occurrences to be placed in their true order and which may sometimes offer at least a hint regarding their absolute age. Thus an industry of Hoxnian age is demonstrably older than one belonging to some part of the Ipswichian, whatever a mere techno-typological approach to the artefacts might have encouraged one to think. But it would be narrow-minded indeed to seek no more information than this from the Pleistocene deposits in which implements are found, because they may be capable of yielding much valuable data concerning the contemporary environment and landscape, and hence the food supplies and the resources of all kinds available at that time to Palaeolithic man.

It would of course be quite wrong to imagine the various named Pleistocene stages in simple terms of 'cold' or 'warm', though that is how Table 1 necessarily presents them for the sake of brevity. Glaciations and interglacials are neither uniform nor static events: they do not come into existence or disappear like heat or cold in the modern home at the flick of a switch. Any of the palaeotemperature curves calculated for a major segment of the Pleistocene[1] shows major peaks and troughs and minor oscillations (Figs. 2:11, 2:15, 2:16). The pronounced fluctuations of temperature and climate which have so far occurred in Britain during what we are pleased to call the 'postglacial period' are an important reminder of what variations there will have been during past interglacials, for which the evidence is a great deal less well preserved. Yet whenever slow-forming and essentially undisturbed Pleistocene deposits are available for study, like the Middle Pleistocene interglacial lake sediments of Hoxne, Suffolk, or Marks Tey, Essex, discussed below, something of the complexity of such Pleistocene periods can readily be seen. It is the same with the glacials: the fluctuations of the last glaciation (Würm/Weichsel/Devensian) are best known (cf. Fig. 2:11) mainly because they are best preserved, and they will serve to illustrate the point, as described in many recent papers (e.g.

van der Hammen *et al.* 1967; Vogel and van der Hammen 1967; van der Hammen *et al.* 1971).

It is essential then to remember that any Pleistocene stage, labelled by some misleadingly simple name like 'Cromerian' or 'Wolstonian' is in fact a succession of many varying units, and that in some cases we may well be acting arbitrarily when we define a precise beginning or end to it. It is also important not to lose sight of what actual mechanisms are implied by such easy phrases as 'extension of the ice-sheets' or 'shift of the climatic and vegetational zones' or 'colonization by a fauna indicative of warmer conditions'. All such effects were vast on a horizontal scale, yet so often we must view the scraps of evidence for them in vertical terms – that is to say, in the succession of Pleistocene deposits at some single locality where they happen to be exposed. It is considerations of this kind that may be suppressed by the facile presentation of Table 1 or anyone else's Pleistocene table in any other book.

The evidence for the British Pleistocene sequence comes principally from deposits and geomorphological features which may be variously classified as 'pre-glacial', 'glacial', 'interglacial' or 'interstadial'; these terms and a few others must be explained briefly by way of introduction.

Pre-glacial refers to the earlier part of the sequence, during which warmer or colder phases can clearly be distinguished, but in which there is as yet no record of actual glacial deposits in Britain. That is not to say, of course, that there was not glaciation elsewhere in the northern hemisphere at this time, and 'pre-glacial' should therefore be regarded as a local term.

Glacial refers to any one of the major cold phases in which actual glaciation did take place in Britain. A glacial deposit, properly, should be one such as a ground moraine (till) or end moraine, formed as a result of the actual presence of the ice-sheet. Outwash deposits, formed when an ice-sheet melts, are certainly of glacial origin, but the meltwater can carry its load of sediment well beyond the limits which the ice itself previously reached. One complete glaciation (or glacial complex) may be made up of several colder and less cold periods. The colder phases, during which the ice-sheets were extended, are referred to as *stadials* of that particular glaciation, while any substantially milder period between two such stadials is an *interstadial*. Interstadials may last a few hundred or even a few thousand years, according to our present knowledge, and conditions during them were mild enough for a considerable withdrawal of the ice-sheets from their stadial maxima, and for the establishment of characteristic animal and plant communities over much of the previously glaciated areas; the vegetation of an interstadial includes a certain amount of forest growth, but not to the level of fully temperate mixed oak forest.

An *interglacial*, on the other hand, is an altogether longer and more intense period of relative warmth, whose duration may be as much as some tens of thousands of years. It is the warm interval between two separate glaciations, as opposed to that between two stadials. During an interglacial, so far as Britain is concerned, fully temperate conditions became established over a long period of time, up to at least today's level and sometimes beyond, as the faunal and floral remains clearly show.

Periglacial is another important and useful term, best applied to an area of land, as in 'periglacial zone' or to certain types of cold climatic conditions ('periglacial conditions') with permafrost but without full glaciation; it is less correct to refer to a 'periglacial period' although one can certainly say 'a period of periglacial climate'. The *periglacial zone* is the area of arctic to sub-arctic tundra beyond the extremities of an actual ice-sheet. Palaeolithic man might well enter parts of it during the warmer months of the year, while the fully glaciated areas themselves would have little to offer him. Periglacial conditions are especially important to the British Pleistocene and Palaeolithic, because the limits of actual glaciation only rarely and locally extended south of the Midlands (Fig. 2:12), while the periglacial zone quite frequently extended all the way to our present south coast in many places. The periglacial deposits in the famous cliff section at Black Rock, Brighton, in what some advertisements today like to call the 'Sussex Riviera', will serve as an example (Plate 6). It follows that the great majority of 'cold' deposits of Middle and Upper Pleistocene age in the southern part of Britain are of periglacial rather than glacial origin; this naturally does not prevent the periods they represent being referred to as glacial periods, since the condition of glaciation in Britain at the time is fulfilled. Similarly, it is perfectly proper to refer to periglacial conditions in certain parts of Britain during the 'pre-glacial' phase of the Lower Pleistocene: the contemporary climate was cold enough to produce permafrost, and there is no doubt that snow lines were lowered and ice margins advanced in other regions, though no ice sheet reached Britain. It has also always to be remembered that the periglacial zone was not static. As the ice-sheets expanded, so the periglacial zone advanced before them. Thus, in an ideal sequence representing one of the Pleistocene glaciations, one would expect to see evidence of periglacial conditions preceding the deposition of an actual glacial moraine, and also overlying the moraine too, because when the ice-sheets withdrew, the periglacial zone necessarily followed them back. Indeed, if the sequence were really ideal, the observable section at the notional site concerned should record all the fluctuations of that glaciation and one might look to find a succession of the following kind, or perhaps an even more complicated one, depending on the number of stadials and interstadials:

9 Pretemperate and then temperate deposits of the following interglacial
8 Periglacial conditions (ice withdrawal)
7 Till (moraine) of Stadial II
6 Periglacial conditions (readvance of ice)
5 Interstadial deposits
4 Periglacial conditions (ice withdrawal)
3 Till (moraine) of Stadial I
2 Periglacial conditions (initial ice advance)
1 Sediments of the previous interglacial

Actual sections, of course, are seldom ideal, but it is worth comparing the records of Corton, Hoxne and Marks Tey, given later in this chapter, with the theoretical sequence above.

It is not a function of the present chapter to describe exhaustively the different kinds of Pleistocene deposits which represent the glacials, interglacials and interstadials in Britain. Excellent accounts of them are readily available in works by West (1977, previous editions in 1972 and 1968),

Sparks and West (1972), Flint (1971), Zeuner (1959), Butzer (1971), Bowen (1978) and several others, and the reader should certainly consult these books. Some of the main kinds of evidence with which we shall later be concerned can, however, be listed:

Glaciations

Former ground moraines of glaciers or ice-sheets (usually called *till* or *boulder clay*), being accumulations of material resulting from contact between the base of an extending ice-sheet and whatever rock or superficial deposits it passed over (Plate 7); *end moraines*, material pushed ahead of the advancing ice and eventually left behind at withdrawal, marking the maximum extent of that advance; various *subglacial features*, both depositional and erosional; *meltwater lakes* and *outwash gravels*, formed when an ice-sheet 'withdraws' by melting; *ice-dammed lakes*, which are water-bodies trapped between one or more ice-fronts and high ground; *kettle-hole lakes*, formed in depressions created (usually in old moraines) where stranded blocks of ice melted in place; *topography characteristically shaped* by the passage of ice (Plate 8), and *glacially striated or polished rocks* (whether as outcrops in place or removed and redeposited); ice-transported erratic rocks (*glacial erratics*).

Periglacial conditions

Solifluction, cryoturbation and related effects (movements within the seasonally thawed upper levels of ground which remained permanently frozen below, causing characteristic convolutions and disturbance to the pre-existing stratification (Plate 6)); *loess*, a wind-blown fine dust, originating in the glaciated zone but deposited in the periglacial zone; *ice-wedges* (Plate 9), *frost-polygons* and other kinds of *patterned ground*, all of which are formations typical of permafrost conditions; *thermoclastic scree* in caves.

Cold conditions generally (i.e. effects of glaciation which may occur beyond the actual glaciated or periglacial zones).

2:1 Location map for English sites mentioned
in Chapter 2 (Pleistocene)

with occasional support from pollen and plant remains. The series of so-called 'Crag' deposits of eastern and northern Norfolk, eastern Suffolk and eastern Essex are by far the best known. We need not concern ourselves very closely with them here, because no traces of Palaeolithic settlement can be clearly associated with them or seen to occur before them, notwithstanding the views of J. Reid Moir (e.g. 1927) and others. These Crag deposits were mostly formed in a marine basin

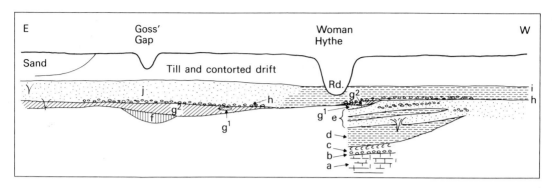

2:2 Sketch section at West Runton, Norfolk, about 450m long (not to scale vertically), after Sparks and West (1972). For explanation, see Table 2

(the 'Crag Basin'), whose western edge now forms the fairly low-lying parts of eastern East Anglia, though just a few Crag deposits further west are known. The sequence is described in some detail in works by West and others (Funnell 1961; West 1977: 281-7; Sparks and West 1972: 122-46; Mitchell *et al.* 1973: 3-4, 8-18; all quote earlier references). The Coralline Crag, the oldest of the series, best known near Aldeburgh, Suffolk, is of Pliocene age and was deposited in a temperate sea. The succeeding Red Crag (with various facies), well exposed near Walton-on-the-Naze and in south-east Suffolk, contains the initial Pleistocene deposits, with evidence of climatic deterioration. Our main knowledge of the succeeding stages of the British Lower Pleistocene comes from bore-holes, notably one put down at Ludham in Norfolk by the Royal Society (West 1961b) and another at Stradbroke Priory in Suffolk (Lord 1969; Beck *et al.* 1972), supplemented by the examination of foreshore deposits and cliff sections in various parts of East Anglia. Exposures of the latter kind become crucial when we reach the transition from Lower to Middle Pleistocene and from the pre-glacial to the glacial part of the sequence. We can turn straight to this interface by looking next at the famous localities of West Runton, near Cromer, Norfolk and Corton, near Lowestoft, Suffolk. (Figs. 2:2, 2:3; Plates 10, 11; Tables 2, 3).

At West Runton (Plate 10), and indeed at other exposures in northern Norfolk, the Cromerian mud and peat have produced abundant biological evidence for temperate conditions — to call them 'interglacial' is possibly a little misleading since the underlying cold phase (Beestonian) does not apparently pass beyond a periglacial stage in East Anglia.[2] However, there would hardly be true and evidently quite prolonged periglacial conditions in East Anglia if the ice-sheets of the northern hemisphere had not been substantially extended during our Beestonian stage, even if no ice front actually reached Britain, so in a wider context 'interglacial' is perfectly correct. The Cromerian mud and peat of 4 (the classic 'Cromer Forest Bed' of many authors) are overlain by clear evidence of continuing temperate conditions and an actual marine transgression, to which the continued melting of ice must surely have contributed, before cold conditions returned, represented by the overlying fluviatile sands (deposited during marine regression). This time the lowering of temperature proceeded to full glaciation, for which the presence of some 30m of true till is unequivocal evidence. This till at West Runton is considerably contorted by ice pressure doubtless belonging to a later cold phase of the Anglian (Banham 1975).

The section in the cliff at Corton (Plate 11) affords much better details of the Anglian than does that at West Runton. It has long been quoted in the literature that at Corton two separate Anglian tills could be seen, separated by the marine Corton Sands, though the latter were perhaps too 'cold' in character (see Table 3) to constitute evidence for the 'Corton Interstadial'

TABLE 2 : *West Runton, Norfolk: essentials of the Lower and Middle Pleistocene sequence revealed in the cliff face and on the foreshore* (details mainly from West 1977 and West and Wilson 1966)

Deposits	Interpretation
7 Contorted till some 30m thick (above j in Fig. 2:2)	Till representing the first period of glaciation in northern Norfolk. *Anglian (Cromer Stadial)*
6 Fluviatile sand, and disturbance to top of 5, including cast of an ice-wedge (Fig. 2:2, j)	Periglacial conditions. At Mundesley, in another well-known section further east along the Norfolk coast, there are freshwater sands and silts with plant remains of 'Arctic' character, and again, evidence for permafrost conditions following Cromerian transgression deposits. *Early Glacial (Anglian)*
5 Estuarine and beach deposits up to 5m thick (Fig. 2:2, h, i)	Marine transgression under interglacial conditions. *Cromerian maximum*
4 Channel cut into the Beestonian deposits of 3, filled with organic freshwater mud and peat; some sands with temperate (non-marine) mollusca also	Temperate terrestrial deposits, with excellent faunal and floral evidence: a major 'warm' phase, for which this is the type locality.

occur. These deposits are capped by a soil (Fig. 2:2, g)	*Cromerian*
3 Various sands, gravels, silts and marls, with clear evidence for permafrost conditions, ending with a marl of 'Late Glacial' character. One of the freshwater silt units has good 'Arctic' plant remains (Fig. 2:2, e, f)	Mainly terrestrial and fluviatile deposits formed in very cold (periglacial) conditions. *Beestonian*
2 Tidal silts and sands with some peat (Fig. 2:2, d)	Mainly estuarine deposits, with good evidence for 'temperate forest' flora. *Pastonian temperate period*
1 Weybourne Crag (Fig. 2:2, c), overlying the chalk bedrock and a stone bed (a, b).	Marine sediments with shells indicating mainly cold conditions. *Baventian cold period and early Pastonian*

Note

In this simplified table the label 'Cromerian' is used, as so many authors have used it, for the organic deposits of 4 (often called the Cromer Forest Bed) and the marine transgression of 5 following them. More properly, on the basis of recent work, one should use the term Cromer Forest Bed Series (cf. West and Wilson 1966; West 1977, table 12.2) which includes everything between the Weybourne Crag and the Anglian Till, i.e. 2 to 6 inclusive above. This certainly helps to bring the British Cromerian more into line with the longer and more varied Cromerian complex recognized on the Continent.

which is not infrequently referred to. Recent work at Corton by P. Banham (1971) has shown however that *three* separate Anglian tills can be seen in the cliff section in places, so that there are two intervals of deglaciation, represented by the Corton Sands and the Oulton Beds. In northern Norfolk at Happisburgh, and in the area of Bacton, Mundesley and Trimingham (Banham 1968) there are also complex records of the Anglian, with three separate deposits or stages of 'Cromer Till' *and* a later Chalky Boulder Clay (Lowestoft Till)

as well. What we know of later glaciations certainly makes it reasonable to suppose that the Anglian would comprise more definable sub-stages than the West Runton section would suggest; it is no use pretending, however, that we know much yet about Anglian interstadials in Britain, which is a pity because this is certainly likely to be a period of critical importance as regards the earlier appearances of man in our area. But it is hard to be sure that any of the intervals of deglaciation seen in the coastal sections referred to above was a true

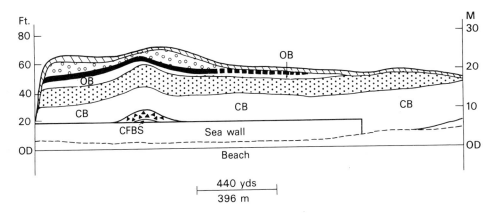

2:3 Section of the cliffs near Corton, Suffolk, after Banham (1971). CFBS, Cromer Forest Bed Series; CB Corton Sands (Corton Beds); OB, Oulton Beds; black triangles, Cromer Till/Norwich Brickearth; black circles, Lowestoft Till; open circles, Plateau Gravels; solid black, Pleasure Gardens Till; oblique lines, soil and blown sand. For further details, see Table 3

TABLE 3 : *Corton, Suffolk: the essentials of the Middle Pleistocene sequence exposed in the cliff face* (details from Banham 1971)

Deposits	Interpretation
8 Soil and blown sand	Recent
7 'Plateau gravels' (4m+)	? Upper Pleistocene
6 Pleasure Gardens Till (3m)	Till, lying generally conformably on the Oulton Beds: chalky, and generally similar to the Lowestoft Till. *Readvance within the Lowestoft Stadial (Anglian)*
5 Oulton Beds (4m)	Grey clay, overlain by sand, with no clear evidence for contemporary plant life: reworked till and/or outwash. *Period of deglaciation within the Lowestoft Stadial (Anglian)*
4 Lowestoft Till (7m)	Typical chalky boulder clay of the later Anglian advance, for which this is the type locality. *Ice advance, Lowestoft Stadial (Anglian)*
3 Corton Sands (also called Corton Beds) (7m)	Marine sands, with shells and foraminifera which some regard as *in situ* and others as derived; the latter seems more likely, and the sands cannot be regarded as representing interstadial conditions unless the shells really are contemporary with the deposit. *Period of deglaciation (Anglian)*
2 Cromer Till (also referred to as Norwich Brickearth)	Till, representing the first ice advance of this glaciation. *Ice advance, Cromer Stadial*, also called *Gunton Stadial (Anglian)*
1 Cromer Forest Bed series	Traces at the base of the cliff section of organic deposits of the preceding temperate period. *Cromerian*

interstadial: the evidence may in part merely be showing us minor fluctuations of the ice sheet at times when its margin lay close to what is now the coast of Norfolk and Suffolk.

The lower Anglian till is most often called the Cromer Till, but a more weathered and somewhat different facies of it elsewhere in East Anglia is known as the Norwich Brickearth. A more general name than either of these, still used occasionally, is North Sea Drift, arising from the fact that these early Anglian tills frequently contain erratics of Scandinavian origin, which was taken to suggest that the ice arrived from across the North Sea bearing a load of such material. In fact the preferred stone orientation of the till seems at least as much in favour of a north-westerly origin so far as East Anglia is concerned (cf. West 1977: fig. 12.9a). The upper Anglian till sheet by contrast has erratics derived mainly from the English Midlands, including Jurassic rocks and also much chalk, the latter giving rise to the names (Great) Chalky Boulder Clay or Chalky-Jurassic Boulder Clay in some of the literature, though 'Lowestoft Till' is now more common. Its stone orientation suggests the arrival of ice in East Anglia, this time from a mainly westerly direction (Sparks and West 1972: fig. 5.12), which agrees with the erratic content. The stratigraphic difference between the Cromer and Lowestoft tills is thus borne out by the nature of the deposits themselves, whether or not there was a true interstadial between them.

We ought not to leave the Lower and Earlier Middle Pleistocene without noting that it is at present impossible to effect a satisfactory correlation between the sequence in East Anglia as outlined above and that in the nearest part of Continental Europe, the Low Countries, where a fine pollen and sedimentary record offers a much fuller and more satisfactory picture of the whole period, and where a Cromerian Complex much longer than the British Cromerian (even in the full sense of Cromer Forest Bed Series – cf. note to Table 3 above) can be discerned, including apparently no less than three separate temperate phases with colder periods between them (cf. van der Hammen *et al.* 1971; Zagwijn *et al.* 1971). There is also the presence of an important palaeomagnetic reversal[3] between the oldest and second

oldest of these three Cromerian warm peaks in the Netherlands. That particular polarity change cannot be other than the one which divides the Matuyama (Reversed) Epoch from the succeeding Brunhes (Normal) Epoch (which includes our own time); it is well known in many parts of the world and is reliably dated by the potassium-argon method to about 0.7 million years ago (cf. Emiliani and Shackleton 1974). It has not been detected in the British Pleistocene sequence up to the time of writing, from which one is left to conclude either that the British deposits are younger than that date, or that they preserve inadequate information so far as the palaeomagnetic record is concerned, or else – which is the likeliest – that there is a gap in the British sequence.[4] The Netherlands evidence, and that obtained from Philippi in Eastern Macedonia in a quite extraordinary pollen record covering at least half a million years (extracted from lake sediments and reported in van der Hammen *et al.* 1971), both suggest the likelihood of one or more major gaps in the East Anglian sequence – some hitherto unperceived disconformity, perhaps, in the tentative linking of the top of the sequence at one site with the base of that at another. Time alone will reveal what is wrong, or will show how our sketchy sequence is to be correlated with the more detailed Continental ones. For the moment it certainly seems that any such gaps should lie in the period of time before the first arrival of Palaeolithic man in Britain, and on that assumption we can here decently refrain from exploring the issue further; one might speculate that the most likely places in the East Anglian sequence for major disconformities to occur seem to be at the apparent Plio-Pleistocene boundary itself, i.e. between the Coralline Crag and the Red Crag, and between the Baventian and Antian (cf. Evans, P. 1971: 278, 303).

To pick up the Middle Pleistocene sequence following the Anglian glaciation, we need to leave the coastal exposures and consider some sites further inland. Interglacial lake sediments are known from several sites in East Anglia, filling hollows which either lie in an Anglian till or else were gouged out as subglacial features below the Anglian ice sheets. Hoxne, Suffolk, type site of this 'Hoxnian interglacial' is an example of the former kind and Marks Tey, Essex, is an instance of the latter.

As has already been observed, there is a long history of research at Hoxne, going back to John Frere in the closing years of the eighteenth century. Not surprisingly, the interpretation of the geological succession has passed through various stages, but two major studies during the past twenty or so years have greatly clarified our knowledge: that by R.G. West (with C.B.M. McBurney to study the archaeology) in 1954 (West and McBurney 1954; West 1956) and that sponsored by the University of Chicago from 1971 onwards, directed by R. Singer and J.J. Wymer, with B.G. Gladfelter as principal geologist (brief reports in Wymer 1974: 400-4; Gladfelter 1975; Singer and Wymer 1976; further work in preparation). West (1956: 267-9, 293-302) has summarized

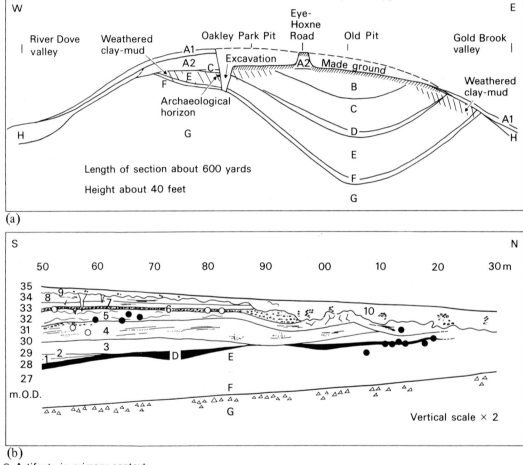

(a)

(b)

○ Artifacts in primary context
● Derived artifacts

2:4 Sections through the Hoxne deposits, (a) after West and McBurney (1954): the letters A – G follow West's (1956) subdivisions of the sequence and are explained in Table 4; (b) after Wymer (1974), based on the University of Chicago excavations and on previous work: the letters D-G follow West (1956), while the numbers 1-10 include West's stratum C and various subdivisions within the Upper Series (A and B of West) – not explained here in detail, since only preliminary information is yet available.

the earlier work at Hoxne.

There is no doubt that the Hoxne lake sediments rest upon an actual till, and most authorities agree that this is the chalky Lowestoft boulder clay of the Anglian glaciation (but cf. Bristow and Cox 1973). It had better be an Anglian till, too, if Hoxne is to remain the type site of the interglacial which immediately followed the Anglian, and the present writer will regard it as such for the pur-poses of this book. How satisfactory it would be to be able to report further, as many passing references suggest, that the lake sediments at Hoxne are overlain by a further till, of Wolstonian age; but the current view is that none of the rather varied deposits above the lake beds at Hoxne (Plate 13) is of true glacial rather than periglacial origin. Erratics brought to East Anglia by what we may loosely call Wolstonian ice do indeed occur in the

TABLE 4 : *The Pleistocene sequence at Hoxne*

	Deposits	Zone, vegetation, etc.
A, B:	the Upper Series	*Upper Pleistocene* See note 2 below
C	Silt and brecciated mud, lying unconformably on D: reworking of D and some solifluction, but also some silt deposited in water	*Post-temperate and/or Early Glacial* (*Wolstonian I*) following a break in the sequence with the end of Hoxnian Zone III and the whole of Zone IV missing. Periglacial conditions at least in part, with the water level fluctuating. Variable vegetation, with some 'park-tundra'; birch, arctic willow, etc. A mainly cold period
D	Peaty detritus mud, with wood remains; upper part removed or reworked	*Late-temperate, Hoxnian Zone III* (*truncated*) Decline of mixed oak forest in favour of boreal types including pine. The lake reduced in size and partly overgrown with alder carr at the edges
E	Temperate lacustrine clay-mud; sediments forming in the lake in interglacial conditions	*Early-temperate, Hoxnian Zone II*; *subdivisible into stages a-d* Birch and pine forest giving way to temperate mixed oak forest. There is a notable phase of (temporary) deforestation in sub-zone c
F	Postglacial lacustrine clay-mud and marl: the first accumulation of sediments in the kettle-hole lake. At the base of F is a thin band of sediment with remains of late-glacial flora (see note 3 below)	*Pre-temperate, Hoxnian Zone I.* Open scrub, with some scattered birch, developing to birch parkland. The base of F represents arctic tundra, freshly deglaciated, with pioneer vegetation only (*Late Glacial, Anglian*)
G	Till (boulder clay)	Glaciated arctic desert (*Anglian*)

Notes

1 The letters A-G follow West (1956), but A and B are better replaced for the moment with the term Upper Series.

2 Much detail has been added to West's (1956) account of the deposits younger than C in subsequent work, but only brief interim reports are yet available (Wymer 1974: 400-4; Gladfelter 1975; Singer and Wymer 1976). In principle, the lacustrine sequence comes to a final end and the lake sediments are covered by various deposits of fluviatile and periglacial origin, including a gravel with some 'Wolstonian' erratics and a flood-plain silt. The analysis of pollen, fauna and microfauna from various parts of this Upper Series, now in progress, should clarify the nature and age of the various levels and indicate the successive environments; it appears that both cold and milder periods are involved.

3 This stratum was first reported in West's (1956) account and was studied in detail by C. Turner (1968) in work carried out much later on samples taken at the time of West and McBurney's work. It contains plant and insect remains but fossil pollen is not preserved.

'upper series' of deposits, in a gravel formerly interpreted as the remains of a till, but it now seems that they have reached their present position by fluviatile and perhaps outwash action, and that no actual ice-sheet reached Hoxne later than the Anglian one which deposited the till at the base of the section. It therefore appears that the type-site Hoxnian sediments lie between Anglian glacial deposits and Wolstonian periglacial ones, rather than actually between two tills. Plenty of information, both geological and archaeological, has come from the interglacial deposits themselves; the archaeological discoveries are considered in a later chapter. The essentials of the Pleistocene sequence at Hoxne are summarized in Table 4 and Fig. 2:4; see also Plates 12, 13.

At Hoxne, then, we see the first half of the interglacial, so to speak, notably Zones I and II, in considerable detail and much information about the plant and forest growth is available (West 1956; Turner 1968). But we lose the continuity after the start of Zone III, at the disconformity between C and D, and the details of what follows are not yet clear. At Marks Tey in Essex (Turner 1970) an altogether better Pleistocene sequence from late Anglian to early Wolstonian is available, though in this case only bare traces of Palaeolithic man's presence occur.

The Marks Tey deposits (Fig. 2:5), like those of Hoxne, include lake sediments which can be seen to overlie an Anglian till: the lake filled a deep trough which seems to have been gouged out subglacially during Anglian times. The sediments

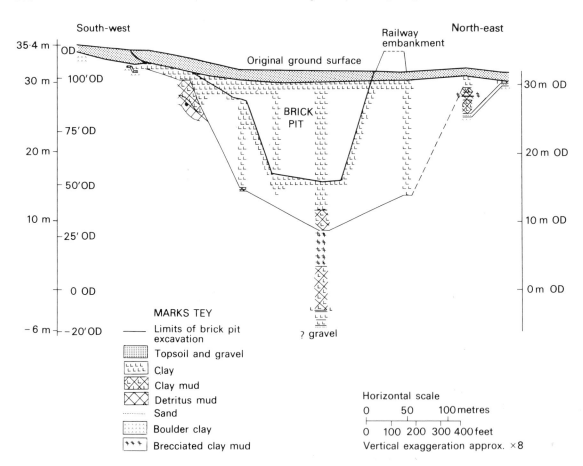

2:5 Section across the lake deposits at Marks Tey, Essex, after Turner (1970)

represent the gradual silting up of this lake throughout the Hoxnian interglacial and latterly during a distinctly cold period which directly followed it and may therefore be regarded as of early Wolstonian age. There is no break of any importance during the deposition of these sediments and a continuous succession is therefore offered from the Anglian late glacial period through the classic four zones of the Hoxnian (subdivisible to some extent) to the Wolstonian early glacial stage, very much like the ideal sequence set out on page 37. Pollen recovered from the lake sediments provides the main basis for this sequence, supported principally by the presence of macroscopic plant remains and the study of the sediments themselves. The essential sequence is given in Table 5; while there is rather more detail than in the comparable Table for

TABLE 5 : *The Pleistocene sequence at Marks Tey* (based on Turner 1970)

Deposits	Zones, vegetation, etc.
Grey clay and some reworked material from earlier deposits	*Early Glacial (Wolstonian I)* Non-arboreal dominant over arboreal pollen; pine and birch the main trees, but declining in quantity as the climate became increasingly severe. Periglacial conditions eventually set in, giving an open sub-arctic environment by the end of this zone, with the lake basin finally filled in
Organic clay mud, disturbed by later slumping, etc.; some brecciation	*Post-temperate (Hoxnian Zone IV)* Cooling of the climate led to gradual reduction in tree cover and corresponding expansion of open grassland country. Pine and birch became dominant in the arboreal pollen record at the expense of the leading types of Zones II-III
The same continued from below (laminated organic clay mud)	*Late Temperate (Hoxnian Zone III)* Expansion of late arrivals among the temperate trees, notably hornbeam (*Carpinus*) and fir (*Abies*) at the expense of the mixed oak forest
	types. A few exotic plant types indicative of warmth occur, notably grapevine (*Vitis*) and wingnut (*Pterocarya*)
Laminated organic clay mud	*Early Temperate (Hoxnian Zone II)* Temperate mixed oak forest developed with little open grassland remaining. Hazel (*Corylus*) became very common. Winters were mild and summers moist and warm. In sub-zone IIc there was a phase of temporary deforestation (cf. Table 4)
Clay mud, often with laminations	*Pre-temperate (Hoxnian Zone I)* Birch forest including some open areas; pine also present and increasing. Late in Zone I there was a temporary spread of oak and other temperate trees, but this was followed by a climatic setback before Zone II began.
Sand, fine gravel and clay: the initial lake sediments	*Late Glacial (Anglian)* Sub-arctic scrub land, giving way to open grassland with a few birch copses (birch parkland). The margins of the lake were marshy, with willow (*Salix*) and sedges
Boulder clay (till)	*Full glacial (Anglian)* Glaciated arctic desert

Hoxne, it will be noted that the general agreement between the two sites is close.

It will not have escaped notice that at both Hoxne and Marks Tye there is an interesting phase of temporary deforestation, or at least of drastic reduction in the tree cover, in Zone IIc of the interglacial. This has sometimes been viewed as a climatic phenomenon – a sharp cold spell in the middle of the interglacial. Turner (1970: 426-30) suggests that the cause was more likely to have been a forest fire or fires – perhaps even a single major conflagration which swept across much of East Anglia and affected both sites (they are just under 40 miles apart). Charcoal is certainly present in the relevant levels at both sites. Such a fire could have had purely natural causes, but since man is known to have been in the area at the time in question it is open to us to reflect on the habitual carelessness of *Homo sapiens sapiens* with regard to fire and view his predecessors' presence with dark suspicion.

Also of interest at Marks Tey is the lamination of much of the lake sediments (Turner 1970: see especially 391-5). The distinct bands in the deposits are thought likely to correspond to an annual sedimentation cycle somewhat after the manner of the well-known 'varves' of the terminal Pleistocene and early Holocene meltwater lakes of northern Europe (see for example Zeuner 1958: 20-43). This assumption is not absolutely proved, but on the basis of it a duration for the Hoxnian inter-glacial of about 30,000-50,000 years was suggested (Shackleton and Turner 1967), later revised to a maximum of 25,000 (Turner 1975). This is well worth keeping in mind when European Pleistocene chronometric dating is being discussed.

The observations made at Hoxne and Marks Tey will suffice to establish the Hoxnian for the purposes of this chapter. In passing, it is worth noting that there are several other Hoxnian sites in eastern England (Fig. 2:1) broadly similar in nature to Hoxne and Marks Tey, but less complete. Some have already been well studied, such as Hatfield and Stanborough (Sparks *et al.* 1969), while others are unpublished or await investigation (Mitchell *et al.* 1973: 8-18). There are also Hoxnian deposits in East Anglia and elsewhere of quite other kinds, some of which will be discussed in

some detail in later chapters: raised beaches or other evidence for marine transgression, for example, or aggradation phases of certain kinds in the terrace sequences of river valleys. Actual raised beaches are particularly well known in West Sussex, notably around Slindon, and the highest of them has been widely regarded as representing the maximum transgression of the Hoxnian sea. Other kinds of deposit resulting from marine transgression are known in the Nar Valley of Norfolk (Stevens 1960) and at Clacton, Essex (the latest account is that of Singer *et al.* (1973), quoting the extensive earlier literature). Fluviatile deposits attributed to the Hoxnian are fairly widespread in southern England, those in the Lower Thames Valley being perhaps the most famous; some of the attributions are beginning to look a little shaky here and there.

It should not be thought that Hoxnian sites are confined to eastern and southern England, even if the best exposures are certainly there (Fig. 2:1). There are important occurrences in the Midlands, notably the Nechells and Quinton lake sediments (Kelly 1964; see also Mitchell *et al.* 1973: 19 and Shotton (ed.) 1977: 276-7), which are crucial to correlation between the East Anglian and Midlands Pleistocene sequences. There are Hoxnian raised beaches or shorelines in various parts of Devon and Cornwall. Ireland has produced good organic deposits of Hoxnian age, the local name for this interglacial being Gortian after a type site in County Galway (Jessen *et al.* 1959). There is even an interglacial peat as far north as Fugla Ness in Shetland for which a Hoxnian age has been suggested (Birks and Ransom 1969). Nevertheless, our main interest must remain with the Hoxnian sites in the south-east of Britain, because it is with the Palaeolithic archaeology that we are mainly concerned, and in the more northerly and westerly areas artefacts are not intimately associated with Hoxnian deposits if indeed they can be related to them at all.

We have already seen that the Hoxnian deposits at the type-site and at Marks Tey were followed by clear traces of periglacial conditions and the latter may be expected to belong to the Wolstonian glaciation; there was no suggestion at Marks Tey of any substantial break between the post-temperate stage of the interglacial series and the following early glacial horizon. Formerly it was thought that the Wolstonian ice-sheets extended almost as far over East Anglia as those of the Anglian (Fig. 2:12); indeed, the type-site, when the name Gipping was used for this glaciation, was the Gipping valley in Suffolk near Ipswich. Reinterpretation over the past ten years or more strongly suggests, however, in the first place that some of the deposits once regarded as tills are not of a morainic nature (we have seen an example of this already at Hoxne in the gravel with erratics in the Upper Series), and in the second place that there is only one major stage of chalky boulder clay in southern East Anglia, rather than two as previously thought: i.e., all the chalky boulder clay is of Anglian age. The older literature refers to a Lowestoft (= Anglian) Great or Lower Chalky Boulder Clay. Since the Devensian ice sheets are known only just to have reached East Anglia in the north of Norfolk (see below), it seems clear that only one glaciation left true till deposits in

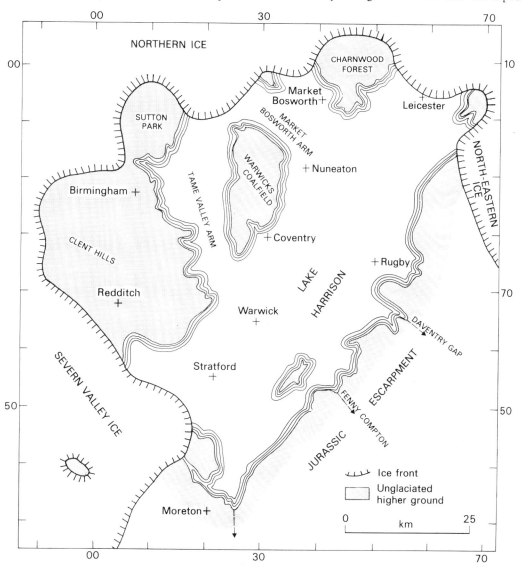

2:6 Approximate maximum extent of proglacial Lake Harrison (after Shotton)

Suffolk, Essex and Hertfordshire: the Anglian (*pace* Bristow and Cox 1973).

It is equally clear however that there *was* a Wolstonian glaciation in Britain, and the argument is therefore merely about its extent; we can be sure in any case that southern England suffered periglacial conditions at this time in the areas that lay beyond the ice limits themselves. Wolstonian tills or other glacial deposits are still claimed further north in East Anglia: at High Lodge near Mildenhall, in the Breckland, an important but so far poorly published site with very interesting Palaeolithic artefacts, at least one and possibly two tills attributed to this glaciation are present, apparently with interstadial lake sediments between the deposits in question (Turner in Mitchell *et al.* 1973: 13; a full report on the site is being prepared under the direction of G. de G. Sieveking). There are also outwash gravels and possible ice-contact or subglacial features in northern Norfolk, arguably of Wolstonian age (Mitchell *et al.* 1973: 14; Straw 1973; West 1977: 290). But the type-site for the Wolstonian is in Warwickshire, near Birmingham, and in this area the Wolstonian glacial complex can be seen in some detail, with tills and outwash gravels present, and good evidence for the existence in Wolstonian times of a large proglacial lake, Lake Harrison (Fig. 2:6), over 50 miles long at its maximum, impounded between the various ice-fronts which affected the Midlands and the higher ground to the south (Shotton 1953, 1968; Bishop, W.W. 1958; Kelly 1964, 1968; Mitchell *et al.* 1973: 18-22, listing other references). Eventually the waters of the lake reached a sufficient height to overflow into the Upper Thames drainage system, though their main dispersal took place later westwards, via what is now the Avon. The sediments deposited in this lake, and the history of its fluctuations, are vital to an understanding of the early Upper Pleistocene of the Midlands. Some points of correlation can certainly be established in the Midlands between the glacial and outwash deposits on the one hand and the terrace sequences of the Avon and the Severn and even the Upper Thames on the other, but direct correlations with eastern England are less easy to achieve.

Tills and other deposits of Wolstonian age are

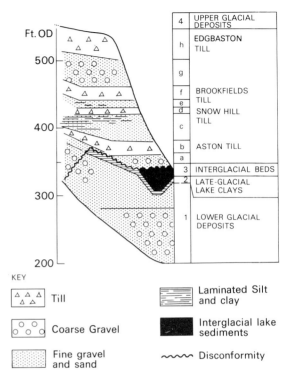

2:7 Pleistocene succession in the north Birmingham area, after Kelly (1964), showing several distinct Wolstonian tills. The Lower Glacial Series (1) is Anglian, consisting mainly of fluvio-glacial (outwash) deposition. Initial lake sedimentation of Anglian Late Glacial age (2) is followed by interglacial lacustrine sediments of Hoxnian age (3), best recorded at Nechells. The Upper Glacial series (4 a-h) is Wolstonian: the four named till deposits are separated by relatively coarse fluvio-glacial sediments or by finer sediments mainly deposited in ponded meltwater.

also well seen elsewhere in Britain — in north Lincolnshire and east Yorkshire, for example (cf. Plate 7) — but they do not have much direct bearing on the British Palaeolithic sequence and will not be discussed further here. The south Midlands area around Birmingham and Coventry received ice advances from the west, north and east during the Wolstonian, and it is not yet clear how many separate stadials one should envisage: three or even four separate Wolstonian tills (Fig. 2:7) can be seen in some sections (Pickering 1957;

Kelly 1964; Shotton 1976). There was deglaciation of the immediate area at least between the
ice advances, and this is represented by outwash
deposits and meltwater lake sediments, but there
may not have been ice withdrawal to the extent
of an interstadial each time, or indeed on any of
the occasions.

For the succeeding interglacial, the Ipswichian,
a fair number of reasonably satisfactory sites are
known. The very fact that Sparks and West (1972)
could include a chapter (which the reader should
certainly consult) on the physical geography of

the Last Interglacial in Britain reflects this happier
situation. The main criteria for the recognition of
Ipswichian deposits are botanical and faunal, with
supplementary data from mollusca and insect
remains: that is to say, the Ipswichian deposits
contain biological evidence reflecting fully interglacial conditions and temperatures, and the plant
and animal communities differ in various important
respects from those which characterize the
Hoxnian. For example, it is frequently quoted that
Hippopotamus occurs in the Ipswichian in Britain
but not in the Hoxnian, so much so that there

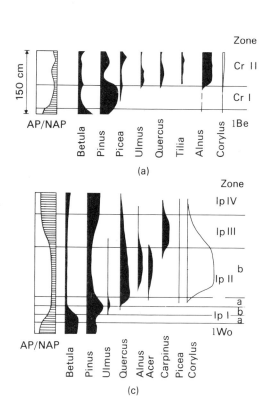

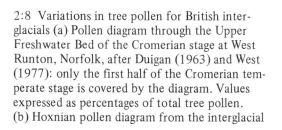

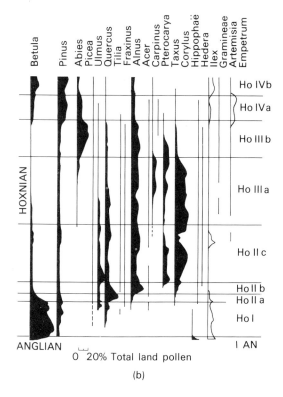

2:8 Variations in tree pollen for British interglacials (a) Pollen diagram through the Upper
Freshwater Bed of the Cromerian stage at West
Runton, Norfolk, after Duigan (1963) and West
(1977): only the first half of the Cromerian temperate stage is covered by the diagram. Values
expressed as percentages of total tree pollen.
(b) Hoxnian pollen diagram from the interglacial
lake deposit at Marks Tey, Essex, after Turner
(1970). Values expressed as percentages of total
land pollen. (c) Composite pollen diagram for the
Ipswichian, based on a number of sites, after
West (1977). Values expressed as percentages
of total tree pollen. AP: arboreal pollen; NAP
non-arboreal pollen.

seems a real risk that finds of *Hippopotamus* may be regarded as definitive 'dating' evidence for any deposit in which they occur, or even that Ipswichian faunal assemblages without *Hippopotamus* may be regarded with suspicion! This is ridiculous, especially the latter notion, which ignores the ecological and environmental requirements of the hippo. The truth behind all this is merely that where good *in situ* faunal assemblages are available for study, an Ipswichian one will usually differ sufficiently from a Hoxnian or a Cromerian one to be diagnostic, and the difference will be in terms not only of the presence or absence of individual genera or species but also of the evolutionary status of some of those which are represented, since fair periods of time separate the three interglacial maxima. The same is broadly true of the pollen and plant remains (Fig. 2:8): there are few if any plants or trees whose mere presence or absence can be relied upon as completely diagnostic of one specific warm stage, though quantity may be a different matter. Thus the supposed absence or extreme rarity of alder (*Alnus*) in Ipswichian deposits has now been shown to have important exceptions (Sparks and West 1970).

The difference between the pollen spectra of the different interglacials is best shown by the distinctive patterns of behaviour of certain genera through the zones I-IV and in some cases by the relative abundance of particular kinds of pollen (Fig. 2:8). Thus, in the arboreal record, hazel (*Corylus*) reaches its peak earlier in a typical Ipswichian sequence than it does in a typical Hoxnian one, and the quantities of it at its maximum are inclined to be higher. Lime (*Tilia*) is commoner in the Hoxnian, and so is alder (*Alnus*); fir (*Picea*) is scarce in the Ipswichian. Hornbeam (*Carpinus*) reaches a larger peak in the late temperate zone (III) of the Ipswichian than in the corresponding Hoxnian phase, and so forth. Similarly, such Cromerian pollen spectra as are known have their own differences of emphasis over what is essentially much the same range of tree types: e.g. hazel is always scarce. Lower Pleistocene pollen spectra are poorly known in Britain, and need not concern us closely, but they do have some distinctive features like the occurrence of hemlock spruce (*Tsuga*) which is absent in Britain from the Middle Pleistocene onwards. The non-arboreal pollen is capable of giving useful supporting evidence, though in the warmer parts of an interglacial the tree pollen greatly exceeds it in quantity. Of the Ipswichian pollen record in general, we may say by way of conclusion that there is some suggestion of slightly higher temperatures at the maximum than those of either the Hoxnian or today, and also of a somewhat more 'continental' type of climate – impressions which the faunal, molluscan and insect evidence would all tend to confirm.

Stress has been laid on the faunal and floral evidence for the Ipswichian, because the purely stratigraphic evidence for the age of the deposits concerned is less satisfactory, in the sense that the levels containing the organic remains are not seen filling hollows that obviously formed in the moraines of the previous glaciation, like the sediments filling the kettle-hole lake at Hoxne. Most are deposits of fluviatile origin: terrace gravels with 'warm' faunas, or organic horizons within such gravels, or finer sediments of one sort or another (often given the general name 'brickearth'), formed usually in the lower reaches of rivers, with the occasional trace of brackish water molluscs to confirm the proximity of the sea. Some more obviously estuarine deposits are also known, for example on the foreshore at Selsey in Sussex and Stone in Hampshire (West and Sparks 1960), where they directly represent a marine transgression and where raised beaches are also to be seen in the cliff faces, interpreted as marking the maximum of the same transgression (Fig. 2:9). Beaches associated with this Ipswichian high sea-level occur elsewhere in Sussex, including the well-known example at Black Rock, Brighton (Plate 6), which lay at the foot of a contemporary chalk cliff buried beneath later Coombe Rock (soliflucted chalk). Another important estuarine or brackish water deposit of Ipswichian age occurred at Stutton, Suffolk (Sparks and West 1964). Other sites have been studied at Histon Road, Cambridge (Sparks and West 1959), Trafalgar Square, London (Franks 1960), Aveley and Ilford in Essex (West *et al.* 1964; West 1969) and Wretton and Wortwell in Norfolk (Sparks and West 1968, 1970). In East Anglia the Ipswichian

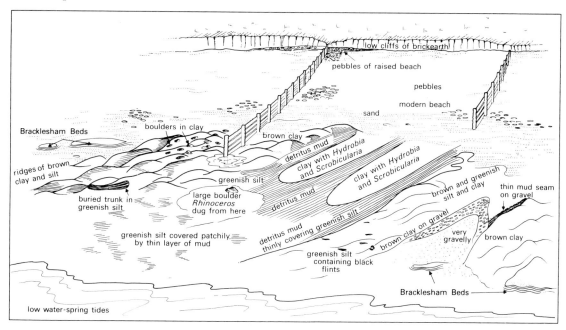

2:9 Sketch of the Selsey interglacial channel from seaward, after West and Sparks (1960).

2:10 Some of the principal Ipswichian sites in south and east England: location, and time-span covered within the interglacial, after Sparks and West (1972)

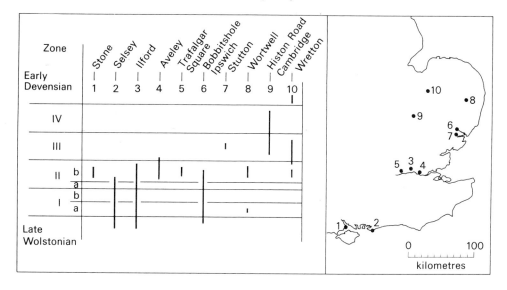

marine transgression would have brought sea water to much of what is now the Fenland.

The type-site for the Ipswichian is Bobbit's Hole near Ipswich (West 1957; Sparks and West 1967), where there were freshwater sediments

with Ipswichian fauna and pollen; at the base of the section, the preceding late glacial stage was well represented, as indeed it is also at Selsey and at Ilford, but at none of these three sites does the Ipswichian interglacial record go beyond Zone II

(Fig. 2:10). There is, in fact, no site in Britain which gives a complete profile of the Ipswichian, or records in detail and without a break the transition from the Ipswichian to the early stages of the last glaciation, the Devensian. No doubt such sites will be discovered eventually, but it has to be admitted meanwhile that the record of the Ipswichian remains patchy in Britain, even if the patches are of high quality, and we shall see later that much the same is true of the archaeology of the period. At Wretton important Devensian levels overlie those of the Ipswichian (West *et al.* 1974), but there is a break between the two series. Several of the other sites mentioned also show clear evidence of cold conditions overlying the Ipswichian levels, but always a break intervenes. On the Continent, the Eemian Interglacial is usually regarded as equivalent to the British Ipswichian, and is known in reasonable detail in certain areas, notably in the Netherlands (cf. van der Hammen *et al.* 1971).

In Britain the last glaciation is quite well known by comparison with its predecessors, since the evidence remains mostly fresh: classic features of glaciated topography can be readily examined over much of the Highland Zone — in various parts of Scotland, Wales and the Lake District, for example, and in Ireland too. Also the second half (roughly speaking) of the Devensian falls within the range of the radiocarbon chronometric dating method, which is helpful both in assigning deposits to the various phases of the middle or late Devensian in the first place, and also in establishing correlations between such occurrences in different parts of Britain and between British and Continental climatic oscillations. Even so, the many fluctuations of the equivalent glaciation in Continental Europe, Weichsel/Würm, are known in far more detail (Fig. 2:11) and there are definite gaps in the British Last Glacial record.

It seems clear enough that the margins of the Devensian ice-sheets at their maximum did not encroach so far on southern and midland Britain as had those of the Anglian and perhaps the Wolstonian — even allowing for considerable disagreement as to what precisely the southern Devensian limits were in England and Wales. In Ireland too the last glaciation was clearly of lesser extent than its predecessors. The Devensian ice-sheets did, however, reach as far south as the most northern part of Norfolk (West 1961a) and south Staffordshire in the Midlands (Morgan 1973), and they certainly covered at least parts of South Wales (John 1970; Bowen 1970). These however were all areas reached by projecting lobes of a very irregular ice margin, and much of Lincolnshire, the southern Pennines, and south Yorkshire as far north as York, seem to have remained clear of ice (Fig. 2:12). Nevertheless, the Devensian stadials caused acutely cold conditions over the whole of Britain and contemporary periglacial phenomena are widespread in the unglaciated areas.

The pattern of this last glaciation in north-west Europe seems clear from Fig. 2:11. The early phase was comparatively mild in aggregate, because of its interstadials: three of them, Amersfoort, Brørup and Odderade, are distinguished on the Continent, with the Chelford Interstadial widely accepted as likely to be the British equivalent of Brørup (Simpson and West 1958; Coope 1959). Then follows a long 'pleniglacial' period, apparently lasting at least 40,000 years, though periods of amelioration of climate can again be detected in some areas. In the Netherlands the Lower Pleniglacial is a period of arctic desert conditions, but in the Middle Pleniglacial three separate interstadials, Moershoofd, Hengelo and Denekamp, can be recognized (Kolstrup and Wijmstra 1977). The Upper Pleniglacial, from about 26,000 to about 13,000 years ago, is again intensely cold. So far in Britain only one interstadial during this main part of the Devensian is clearly known: that named after Upton Warren (Coope *et al.* 1961; see also West *et al.* 1974), for which radiocarbon readings in the region of 41,000-42,000 years ago have been obtained.[5] These figures are closest to those for the Continental Hengelo, though not in exact agreement; however, the Upton Warren Interstadial clearly falls within the Middle Pleniglacial.

It seems that in Britain the Upper Pleniglacial period was the coldest part of the Devensian, and presumably it was at this stage that the ice-sheets actually reached their maxima — for example in south Staffordshire (Morgan 1973), where the till deposit occurs correspondingly late in the sequence.

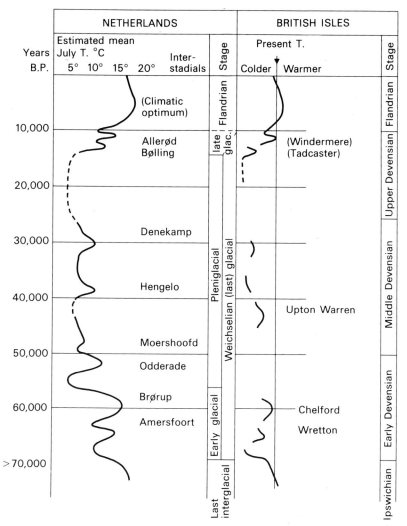

2:11 Temperature fluctuations during the Last Glacial in Britain and the Netherlands, based on the work of van der Hammen *et al.* (1967, 1971) and West (1977) and various British colleagues. Names of interstadials/warm oscillations are given; 'Windermere' is a proposed name, while 'Tadcaster' (Bartley 1962) refers to an oscillation observed only at that site

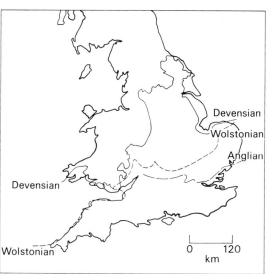

2:12 Approximate southern limits of the principal glaciations in England and Wales, based on West (1977)

The remainder of the Devensian is a story of gradual ice retreat punctuated by temporary readvances in certain areas (the best evidence is seen in Scotland) and it corresponds to the Late Glacial sequence long established and well attested in several parts of north-western Europe, with many radiocarbon dates from different sites, often set out as follows:

Late Glacial Zone	Period	Cold/ Warm	Starting date (radiocarbon years BP)
III	Younger Dryas	Cold	10,900
II	Allerød Interstadial	Warm	11,800
I (c)	Older Dryas	Cold	12,000
(b)	Bølling Interstadial	Warm	12,400
(a)	Oldest Dryas	Cold	c. 13,000

The Younger Dryas cold phase ended by 10,000 years ago or a little earlier in some areas, and it marks the formal end of the last glaciation, since there is no subsequent ice advance, and also the end of the Pleistocene. The Zone numbers continue directly into the Holocene, in the postglacial Flandrian, beginning with a Pre-Boreal period (which is Zone IV) and continuing with the well known sequence of Early Boreal, Late Boreal, Atlantic and so forth, past the climatic optimum of some 5,000-6,000 years ago through to the present day.

The Last Glacial in north-west Europe therefore runs from the end of the Continental Eemian or British Ipswichian Interglacial, through to the close of the Younger Dryas, Late Glacial Zone III, and as many as eight interstadials can be counted in the exceptionally clear pollen records available in places on the Continent, notably in those from the Netherlands and from Macedonia (van der Hammen *et al.* 1971; Kolstrup and Wijmstra 1977), though some are events of short duration (Fig. 2:16). Indeed, if we add in further mild oscillations which have been recorded elsewhere, notably those named after Tursac and Lascaux in France which occur during the Upper Pleniglacial, then the total reaches at least 10 and the picture begins to look very complicated, especially to British eyes.

Most works of even a few years ago hesitate to allow more British Devensian interstadials than those already mentioned, namely the mild oscillations named after Chelford (Cheshire) and Upton Warren (Worcestershire), plus the mild Zone II of the late glacial sequence, which is usually referred to by its Continental name, Allerød, since the radiocarbon dates and the stratigraphy at various sites clearly show it to be a direct equivalent. However, the recent work at Wretton, Norfolk (West *et al.* 1974), has shown two periods of interstadial status within the early Devensian, represented by organic horizons contained in a river terrace; the younger is regarded as equivalent to Chelford, and thus probably to the Continental Brørup (though Odderade would not be an impossible correlation), while the older one has been given the name Wretton Interstadial and is tentatively correlated with the Continental Amersfoort. There are also beginning to be signs elsewhere that some of the other Last Glacial oscillations may be represented in Britain too — for example, in south Staffordshire, where the Four Ashes Gravel Pit is the type locality (Fig. 2:13) for the Devensian (Mitchell *et al.* 1973: 19; Morgan 1973; see also discussion in West *et al.* 1974). Here several organic levels have been noted in a deposit of Middle Devensian age. A weak oscillation possibly equivalent to the Continental Bølling (Late Glacial Zone I b) has also been claimed at Tadcaster, Yorkshire (Bartley 1962), but it may be that in Britain Bølling and Allerød have sometimes

2:13 Devensian stratigraphy (diagrammatic) at the type-site, Four Ashes Gravel Pit, Staffordshire (after A.V. and A. Morgan in the Guidebook for Excursion A2 of the Inqua Xth Congress, 1977). Only one actual till is present, but there are several different periods of periglacial activity, represented by cryoturbation and ice-wedge casts. The site also produced horizons with organic material, representing periods of milder conditions

2:14 Coleopteran evidence in the study of Devensian sites. (a) Modern British distribution of two species found at Upton Warren: *Elaphyrus lapponicus* (black) and *Otiorrhyncus arcticus* (hatching). The maximum extent of the Devensian ice-sheet is also shown (after Shotton, 1965). (b) Some British occurrences of *Diachila arctica* Gyll, and the modern distribution of this species in Europe, after Coope (1970)

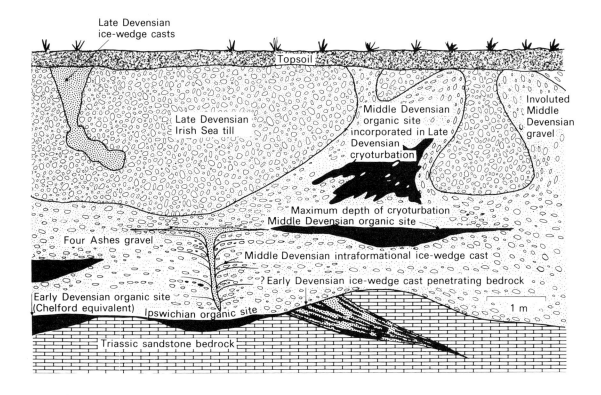

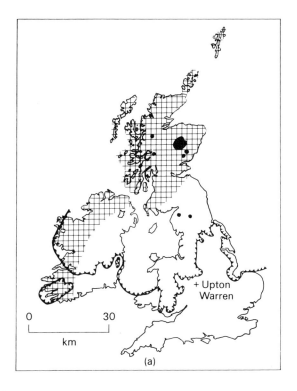

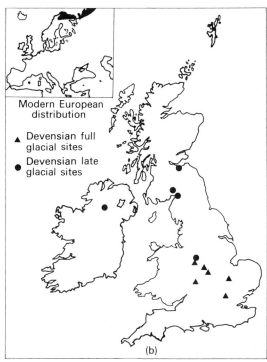

(a)   (b)

merged into one generalized rather uneven interstadial period, for which the name Windermere has been suggested (R.G. West, pers. com.). For all such occurrences, the main evidence is the pollen and plant remains plus any insect or molluscan evidence that can be recovered from organic horizons, the latter often but not invariably being contained within fluviatile deposits. Examples of work on the insect remains (Fig. 2:14) – mainly coleoptera – can be found in studies by Coope and others (e.g. Coope 1961, 1962, 1965; Shotton 1965; Coope and Sands 1966; Coope *et al.* 1971). Molluscan evidence is often of interest (Sparks 1961, 1969; Kerney 1963; Sparks and West 1972: 207-18; Evans, J.G. 1972). Pollen is always important, as should be abundantly clear already from this chapter,

and radiocarbon dating of good quality samples can be crucial.

So far as the closing stages of the Devensian are concerned, our interest in them is a passing one under the title of this book, and they have been mentioned mainly for the sake of completeness. The Middle Palaeolithic of Britain is not well dated, but by analogy with other parts of western Europe it is unlikely to have been present later than the Upton Warren Interstadial and might even not have been current so late. The small number of radiocarbon readings which go with the rather sparse 'Earlier Upper Palaeolithic' episode in Britain may indeed extend back to the later part of the Middle Pleniglacial, while the severely cold Upper Pleniglacial almost certainly saw Britain depopulated (Campbell 1977; see also Campbell

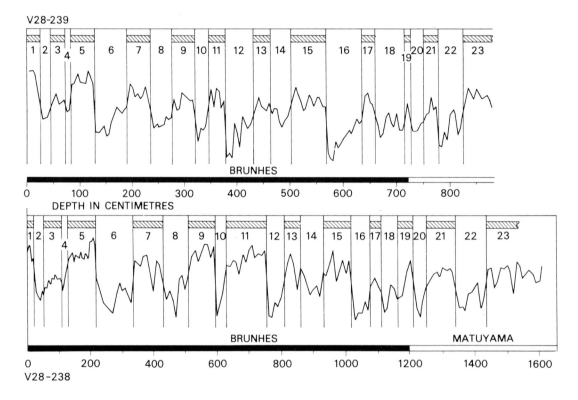

2:15　Oxygen isotope records of two important deep-sea cores from the Equatorial Pacific, V28-238 and V28-239, representing the whole of the Brunhes (normal) epoch and part of the Matuyama (reversed) epoch, after Shackleton and Opdyke (1973, 1976). Note the great number of temperature fluctuations, shown by peaks (warmer) and troughs (colder) in the curves. There are 19 numbered stages back to the polarity change, which occurred at about 0.7 m.y.a. The warmer stages are denoted by shading above the number

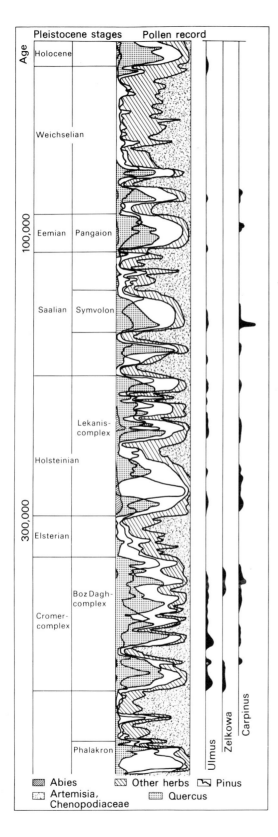

and Sampson 1971: 24-34). Occurrences younger than 30,000 bp would in any case be unlikely to be classifiable as Middle Palaeolithic, since Upper Palaeolithic groups had spread widely over western Continental Europe well before this date.

The foregoing sketch of the Devensian necessarily suggests that the Last Glacial may have had a somewhat simpler structure in Britain than it did in Continental Europe, and it can fairly be asked whether this is really likely to be true. Partly, we may suppose that we do not yet have sites with long enough unbroken records of the Devensian to give a full picture, but it has also to be borne in mind that not every interstadial may have been substantial enough to leave a clear record in all areas. Midland and northern Britain are a considerable distance north of some of the regions (Macedonia or southern France, for example) where interstadials have been detected in the faunal or floral record of the Last Glaciation. A weak interstadial of only a few hundred years, or perhaps even a thousand, might not always have offered time enough in Britain for some of the warmth-loving plants and trees to have achieved more than a marginal recolonization, if the preceding cold phase had been long and severe and their 'refuge areas' were correspondingly far removed. That this was actually so is certainly suggested by the disagreement in some cases between the insect evidence and that of the pollen, the former suggesting much less cold conditions than the latter (cf. Coope 1970; Coope *et al.* 1971), presumably because the beetle population was quicker to move than the flora. Thus the coleopteran remains show the close of the Older Dryas (Late Glacial Zone Ic) actually to have been a warmer period in Britain than the succeeding Allerød (Zone II), while the floral record insists that it was still very cold. There could well be 'latent interstadials' in parts of the Devensian for which only a pollen record is so far available.

2:16 Pollen diagram of a 120 metre section at Tenaghion Philippi, eastern Macedonia, from the Cromerian Complex to Recent, after van der Hammen *et al.* (1971). Note the numerous fluctuations, including the substantial warm event (locally named Symvolon), within the Saalian. The British equivalent of the Saalian may be the Wolstonian

Time and further research may well close some of the gaps of agreement between the British and Continental Last Glacial sequences, but it may yet remain true in the end that there were less definable interstadials, and weaker ameliorations of climate and temperature, in Britain during this period. The general scarcity of archaeological sites of Devensian age, by comparison with those in, say, the southern half of France during the same period, is suggestive that Britain did not often have much to offer late Middle Palaeolithic and Upper Palaeolithic settlers.

Chronometric dating

Two things remain in this account of the British Pleistocene: the not-so-small matter of the absolute time-scale, and a final note of caution.

Britain is badly off as regards long-range chronometric dating (for a summary of the main methods available, see Brothwell and Higgs 1969: 35-108; West 1977: 180-207; updating comments on some of the methods will be found in *World Archaeology*, vol. 7, no. 2, October 1975). There is no British Pleistocene volcanic activity yielding 'marker' horizons which could be dated by the potassium-argon or fission track methods, or which might help to pinpoint important palaeomagnetic polarity changes. Of the chronometric methods based on the decay of radioactive uranium isotopes, little has yet been heard in Britain in the way of local results: only those obtained by Szabo and Collins (1975), using animal bones from interglacial sites, have so far been published. Amino-acid racemization (Bada 1972; Bada and Helfman 1975, quoting earlier references) is still new, and for Britain is at present only a future hope. Radiocarbon dating is generally agreed to give uncertain results at present beyond about 40,000 years ago, except on rare occasions. So far as the 'borrowing' of well-established dates from other countries goes, its effectiveness must depend on one's ability to correlate the British sequence precisely with that of the area yielding the good dates, and enough has already been said in this chapter to indicate how much doubt is likely to remain on that score. Let us then indulge unashamedly in informed guesswork to construct a provisional chronometric table (Table 6) for the Pleistocene

divisions and subdivisions mentioned in the foregoing pages of this chapter. We must scrabble desperately among the dust and rubble of previous edifices of a similar kind, hoping to find the odd nut or bolt that may serve once more, and from time to time we must go cap in hand to the expert architects in more fortunate lands to beg a little building material.

TABLE 6 : *Provisional dating of the British Pleistocene sequence*

Period	Stage		Suggested starting date (BP)	Notes (see below)
Holocene	Flandrian		10,000	1
Upper Pleistocene	Devensian	Late	26,000	1
		Middle	*c.* 50,000	2
		Early	75-90,000	3
	Ipswichian		*c.* 130,000	4
	Wolstonian		? 190,000	5
Middle Pleistocene	Hoxnian		? 250,000	6
	Anglian		? 300-350,000	7
	Cromerian		? 400,000	8
	Beestonian		? 450,000	9
	Pastonian		? < 700,000	10
Lower Pleistocene	Baventian		?	
	Antian		> 700,000	10
	Thurnian		?	
	Ludhamian		≥ 1,600,000	10
	Waltonian (Red Crag)		? > 2,000,000	11

Notes to Table 6

1 According to Mitchell *et al.* (1973), the Late Devensian begins *c.* 26,000. The Devensian 'Late Glacial' Stage (base of pollen Zone I) may be taken as beginning *c.* 13,000, and the postglacial period (Flandrian) at *c.* 10,000; these are useful 'round figure' dates, and there would naturally be local differences.

2 'Middle Devensian' includes the whole of the period referred to above as the 'Pleniglacial' — see Fig. 2:11. Radiocarbon again provides the basis of its internal chronology, with various dates from Britain and Continental Europe; they are reliable to 40,000 bp at least, and the older readings, on which the figure given here is based, can be checked to some extent against apparently constant sedimentation rates at certain sites (van der Hammen *et al.* 1971).

3 Here we pass beyond the reliable reach of radiocarbon, though a constant sedimentation rate at any site with a long record may make 'extrapolated radiocarbon readings' possible. Uranium series dates (using the decay products Protractinium and Thorium) in deep sea cores are helpful, again allied to a constant sedimentation rate (see Shackleton and Opdyke 1973; Emiliani and Shackleton 1974; earlier references are quoted in both these sources). The timing of the onset of this glacial phase must have differed substantially in different areas. It had probably begun recognizably almost everywhere by 75,000 bp, but could have started appreciably earlier further north (which includes parts of Britain): hence the time-range given.

4 Oxygen isotope analyses in the deep sea cores, notably those from the Equatorial Pacific (references in note 3, plus Shackleton 1967), suggest a warm period and a high sea level, with its peak best dated at about 120,000 bp, correlated by most observers with the Eemian/Ipswichian interglacial. If this is correct, the peak seems to have come early in the interglacial; in Britain the evidence for Ipswichian marine transgression seems to belong to Zone IIb (cf. Sparks and West 1972: 279-83), which is in agreement.

5 Here we start to encounter more serious difficulties and the need to settle for a short, long or medium chronology. Which peaks and troughs on the clear palaeotemperature curve from the deep sea cores – notably core V28-238 from the Equatorial Pacific (see Fig. 2:15; references as in note 3 above) – are we to equate with our Wolstonian, Hoxnian and the rest? Undoubtedly there are more warm and cold events shown in the deep sea sediment record than we have British period names to cover. Which 'warm' peaks are interglacials and which interstadials? Are the reasonably clear stage boundaries in the palaeotemperature curve always echoed in the terrestrial record? The date given here for the start of the Wolstonian equates it with Stage 6 of Emiliani's scheme (see Fig. 2:15) based on the oxygen isotope readings from the deep sea cores (Emiliani 1955, 1966; Emiliani and Shackleton 1974), and the next few dates are estimated accordingly (a medium chronology).

6 Is our Hoxnian really equivalent to the deep sea cores' Stage 7? (cf. Shackleton and Opdyke 1973: 50-1). We have only allowed in this chapter for one major warm period in Britain between the Anglian and the Wolstonian, and we cannot point to much convincing evidence for a really substantial warm interval *within* what we have called the Wolstonian, such as would make it into two glaciations rather than a single one with various stadials. So we must stick to 250,000 for the start of our Hoxnian, for the sake of the Table, but with a nasty feeling that we may be missing something (see also comments below, pages 62-3). Certainly *some* warm period seems to have begun at that time. The uranium series readings of Szabo and Collins (1975) from Clacton and Swanscombe could be argued as fitting in with our choice, for what their evidence is worth.

7 The duration of our Anglian, and hence its starting date, is not at all clear. This figure is simply determined by those either side of it. We could be more precise if we knew how long was the warm phase represented by the Cromerian of the type site.

8 It has already been remarked that the British Cromerian is only the latter part of the 'Cromerian Complex' of the Continent; the latter seems to be longer than the whole of the British Cromer Forest Bed Series, and much longer than the time represented by the classic 'Forest Bed' organic mud and the following marine transgression at the type site. The date given here however is thought appropriate to the interface between the Beestonian and classic Cromerian at the type site; in Continental terms it would date the base of the 'Cromerian III' (West and Wilson 1966; van der Hammen *et al.* 1971: 405-10; Shackleton and Opdyke 1973: 50-2).

9 See remarks in note 8: the Beestonian forms part of the Cromer Forest Bed Series of West and Wilson (op. cit.), and it might be guessed that it corresponds to Stage 10 or 12 of the deep sea core record, or to some part of one of them; but there could be a substantial time-lag between the Equatorial Pacific and more northerly latitudes for the start of such a phase. The figure here is merely an estimate, having in mind the 'Cromerian' date of 400,000 and the extrapolated dates suggested for the long Macedonian pollen record (Fig. 2:16; cf. van der Hammen *et al.* 1971: 410) and also assuming the Beestonian to correspond to the cold interval between the 'Cromerian II and III' stages of the Continent.

10 Where is the Matuyama/Brunhes polarity change in the British sequence? – a rhetorical question, alas, for the present, but an important one to answer, since we could then mark in '700,000 years bp' at the appropriate point on the time scale with fair confidence. It seems safest to assume meanwhile that the whole of

the Pastonian is younger than this polarity change, but there seems no solid evidence on which to suggest a definitive date for its start. On the other hand, it seems impossible that the Antian can be *younger* than the 'Lower part of the Cromerian Complex' in which this same polarity change is said to have been recognized on the Continent (van der Hammen *et al.* 1971: 405-9; van Montfrans and Hospers 1969). It should in fact be older, but even if it were the equivalent of the 'Cromerian I' itself we could still safely write in > 700,000 for its base. The real figure may be quite a bit greater. Fortunately, these British stages seem to be pre-Palaeolithic (in a local sense), but dating them would certainly help with various problems of long distance Pleistocene correlation. See also note 4 at the end of this chapter. In the Stradbroke borehole the base of a Ludhamian horizon appears to be at least 1.6 million years old.

11 *If* the base of the Red Crag really marks the Plio-Pleistocene boundary, then we have a choice of dates determined by various authors for that event to assign to it: they range from a little under 2 million years BP to about 3 million. It seems fair to settle here for > 2 million and to regard it as a hypothetical date anyhow, since there seems very likely to be a disconformity between the Red Crag and the Coralline Crag.

A final note of caution

The more one considers the British Pleistocene sequence outlined above, and the more one compares it with the climatic fluctuations revealed in the best of the deep sea cores (Hays *et al.* 1969; Shackleton and Opdyke 1973; Emiliani and Shackleton 1974), the more uncertain it looks. We need not, as archaeologists, shed too many tears over the shortcomings of the British Lower Pleistocene record, but there is a real possibility, even perhaps already a certainty, of major upheavals to come as research proceeds on the Middle Pleistocene and even the Upper Pleistocene. The deep sea core record looks much more reliable than most terrestrial sequences. What then are we to think when it shows up to 19 identifiable stages (alternating colder and warmer periods) since the Brunhes Normal Polarity Epoch began 700,000 years ago? This record is shown in Fig. 2:15, together with stage boundary dates as suggested by

Shackleton and Opdyke (*op. cit.*, 48-9); the core producing it was 16 metres long, and in fact extended well back into the preceding (Matuyama) reversed polarity epoch, showing twenty-two stages in all through some 870,000 years' worth of continuous and undisturbed marine sedimentation. Other cores that cover the whole of the Pleistocene have been raised. Fig. 2:15 should be compared and contrasted with our Table 6, where 10 named stages, or 11 at most, are shown for the Brunhes epoch.

It is not hard, then, to see that there are more distinct cold and warm events in the Pleistocene than we have allowed for in describing the British sequence, as already indicated in the notes to Table 6. Yet the exposures available in the field today, or recorded in the past, do not seem disposed lightly to surrender the secret of where the error or errors may lie. It seems probable that another glacial and another interglacial may eventually have to be inserted between the Hoxnian and the Wolstonian, or an interglacial and a glacial between the Wolstonian and the Ipswichian. But which are the deposits that really belong to them?

If our sequence does have to be expanded in this way, there is certainly already supporting evidence in Continental Europe as well as in the deep sea core record, since the existence has long been recognized there of a major warm interval, probably of full interglacial status, intermediate between the Holsteinian (equivalent of our Hoxnian) and the Eemian (equivalent of our Ipswichian): it has been referred to under various different local names, of which the most persistent are the German ones Treene, Gerdau and Dömnitz. In Denmark, there are even two mild periods, separated by a rather minor cool phase, at this same time; they are known as Vejlby I and II. Further south the two might well have merged into one and the intervening cool phase have disappeared. The Macedonian pollen record, already referred to several times, also shows a clear warm interval (Symvolon) in the same place. But where is the evidence in Britain? And have we got to move back some of our projected chronometric dates in Table 6, and if so, which ones and how far? Only the classic site of Barnfield Pit, Swanscombe, in the Lower Thames Valley (Kent), comes readily to mind as offering a well known stratigraphy which could be interpreted as including this extra cold and warm cycle;[6] perhaps detailed work on the Upper Series at Hoxne, or on High Lodge, Mildenhall, may also in due course pick it out. K.W. Butzer (1971: 22-3) has allowed for it by assigning the 'Ilford beds', usually regarded as Ipswichian, to a pre-Ipswichian/post-Hoxnian warm phase and placing the Hunstanton till between them and the Ipswichian itself, but this suggestion does not seem to have been widely accepted by British Pleistocene geologists (cf. however Zeuner's views (1958) on the 'Last Interglacial').

There may well be other important sorting out of the sequence to be done — outstanding claims exist for example of true glacial deposits older than the Anglian here and there in southern Britain, and one or more English Channel glaciations have recently been proposed (Kellaway *et al.* 1975). Certainly there is a great deal of detail to be filled in almost everywhere, especially as regards interstadials from the Anglian onwards: the almost Alpine outline of the palaeotemperature curve suggests how much we are missing in that direction. Some of the information will doubtless never be forthcoming, having been wholly destroyed by subsequent Pleistocene events. Even so, the author cannot suppress a shudder at the thought of what drastic revision the present chapter will need as the years pass, if indeed it doesn't need it already. Meanwhile there seems no point in worrying too much at present over absolute chronology or stage names or points of fine detail, except as aspects of the working hypothesis which is always needed. We are clearly still some way short of having established a complete basic sequence and an infallible understanding of the whole order of known deposits and their relationship to each other; these must be the really important aims. New sites are urgently needed and doubtless also some reconsideration of old ones. Archaeologists can help with these problems to some extent, but the basic solution of them is a matter for geologists and their other colleagues in Pleistocene studies; as the succeeding chapters will show, there are plenty of gaps and specialist tangles in the archaeological sequence too — enough to keep the archaeologists' own hands full for some while. But all the problems, geological and archaeological, Palaeolithic and Pleistocene, are ultimately bound up together as aspects of Quaternary Research. A more complete and detailed knowledge of the British Pleistocene sequence will be a most powerful weapon to aid the conquest of many of them. The great advances made over the past two decades by the exponents of Pleistocene studies in Britain, and their colleagues abroad, offer a fair sign of hope for the future.

NOTES

1 Some references for palaeotemperature and isotopic studies of deep sea cores are: Emiliani 1955, 1961, 1966, 1969; Emiliani and Shackleton 1974; Shackleton 1967, 1968, 1975, 1977; Shackleton and Opdyke 1973, 1976. Other sources are quoted by these authors.
2 But the temperate deposits of g, h and i in Fig. 2:2 have been widely used as the type deposits for the 'First Interglacial' of Western Europe, on the assumption that there was a glaciation before the one which in Britain is called Anglian or before the one which is named Elsterian in northern and west-central Europe; the Anglian and the Elsterian are probably but not yet certainly the same. In terms of the original Alpine sequence, there were 4 major glaciations, Günz, Mindel, Riss and Würm, and the 'Cromerian' would be the interglacial between Günz and Mindel. Alas for simple original sequences! There would be few now who would defend that one as an accurate and sufficient scheme for the Alpine glaciations (though the names are still in use, notably in France), or who would dare to propose an exact correlation between it and the cold phases of the British sequence with any hope of general acceptance. As indicated in the note to Table 2, the term 'Cromerian' or 'Cromerian Complex' is now used with much greater scope in the Netherlands.
3 At various times during the Earth's history complete reversals of direction of the magnetic

field have taken place, and have lasted for differing but substantial amounts of time. 'Normal' and 'Reversed' polarity epochs are thus distinguished, though they may contain various shorter 'events' of reversal or normality respectively. Evidence for past polarity changes may be preserved in certain contemporary rocks or sediments, of which volcanic lavas and ocean-floor fine-ooze sediments are the most important. The lavas are more often than not datable chronometrically by the potassium-argon method, with the result that all the individual polarity changes now carry chronometric values in their own right, which is of great importance. Studies of past variations in magnetic declination and intensity are also beginning to yield promising results. Some useful references to studies of the palaeo-magnetic reversals are: Cox *et al.* 1967; Glass *et al.* 1967; Cox 1969, 1972; Hays *et al.* 1969; Dalrymple 1972; Opdyke 1972; Shackleton and Opdyke 1953; Brock and Isaac 1974.

4   A little light is perhaps cast on this situation by the results so far published from the Stradbroke borehole (van Montfrans 1971; Beck *et al.* 1972). A 'pre-Ludhamian' zone (with some useful pollen) gave a 'normal' polarity reading which perhaps represents one of the normal events within the Matuyama reversed epoch implying an age of at least 1.6 m.y., but it could easily be older, and might represent part of the previous normal epoch. Ludhamian deposits overlay this, and their lower part also showed normal polarity, presumably the same normal event.

5   The precise figures are: 41,900 bp ± 800 (Gro-1245) and 41,500 bp ± 1200 (Gro-595).

6   Recent palynological work by R.N.L.B. Hubbard, so far only briefly reported by him (1977), looks likely to cast much light on the number of separate temperate stages represented in the Barnfield Pit sequence and on their attributions in terms of the wider north-west European Pleistocene sequence. Watch for reports on the continuation of this work, and hope, as the writer does, that the present chapter can soon be revised and some of the problems solved.

The Search for a Basic Lower Palaeolithic Sequence

Chapter 3

APPROACHES

With the long but necessary preliminaries of the two preceding chapters concluded, it would be possible to adopt various approaches to the Palaeolithic archaeology itself of Britain. For example, one might take the country by regions, study the local sequences, and then add up the sum of information afterwards. Or one could simply proceed through the Pleistocene sequence, describing all the sites, regardless of area, which certainly or possibly belonged to each succeeding phase.

In the writer's view neither of these approaches would be wholly satisfactory. The regional sequences are too unequal and direct correlation between them is always hard to effect. Besides, modern regions do not necessarily reflect the salient features of Middle and Upper Pleistocene geography. The parts of Britain inhabited by Palaeolithic man comprise only a limited span of latitude and longitude and the environmental variation accordingly is not on the scale of that in, say, Continental Europe. The Palaeolithic population would have been much more concerned with environmental variation on a purely local scale, in the sense of what food resources were available from hillside or waterside, woodland or open grassland, or where the raw materials for tool-making were to be found. Such detailed information we at present lack from almost all our sites. In other words, Britain for present purposes is best regarded as a single unit. And as for trying to give an account in pure chronological order, so many

of the British sites are undated or undatable that one could use only a tiny proportion of the whole material without qualification, and alternative hypotheses would be necessary at every stage.

For these reasons the writer has adopted what may seem a rather roundabout approach, firmly believing it to be the most productive, given the nature of the material and the erratic quality of the documentation. There is one area in Britain, north Kent, in which one can see a reasonably long succession of occurrences of Palaeolithic artefacts contained in a stratified series of Pleistocene deposits and therefore able to be placed in their correct order: this sequence will be considered first and used as a basis for the examination of other occurrences elsewhere. Since the north Kent sequence happens not to include the oldest industries in Britain, we shall *not* be starting at the beginning, and we shall also find that certain stages at the younger end are missing. But it still provides a most useful central frame-work, to which quite independent items of information can afterwards be attached.

The workings of this strategy must be clearly understood before the battle begins. At this stage, we are not particularly concerned with the absolute age of the north Kent occurrences, but only with their relative age, to make of them an initial archaeological sequence. No claim is made that the sequence is a continuous one; indeed, we can readily observe from the accompanying geological evidence that there are certainly gaps in it. In accordance with various precepts in the foregoing chapters, it is also important to avoid making the assumption (which has not infrequently been made in the past) that this observable sequence in north Kent *must* be valid elsewhere in Britain. There are many reasons which have nothing to do with passing time why lithic industries should exhibit marked variation: that they were made to accomplish different tasks is merely one of the more obvious. The north Kent sequence *may* be valid generally for at least some other areas of Britain, but to enquire (having studied it) whether this is so is something quite different from setting out with a closed mind to demonstrate that it is. In the same way, since it is palpably a discontinuous sequence, we must be prepared to encounter elsewhere in Britain industries or even Lower Palaeolithic stages which are not seen in north Kent.

The procedure, then, will be to begin with an account of this basic sequence, noting the nature and order of the Palaeolithic industries in it, and after that to seek answers to the questions it poses, using all kinds of available evidence. Thus we can ask: what industries are there in Britain which can

certainly be fitted on at the beginning of the basic sequence, extending it backwards in time, because they are earlier on clear geological evidence? What industries might also be *tentatively* added at the beginning on archaeological grounds — that is to say, what industries appear to be early by reason of the morphology and technology of their artefacts? This is a less certain kind of argument, and it is to be hoped that at least a hint of supporting geological evidence here and there can be found. We can also ask whether there are any British industries which are geologically or archaeologically *later* than the range of the basic sequence. Finally, we can examine those which appear to be contemporary with one or another part of it, and this may be expected to cast any light that is forthcoming on the question of contemporary variation of Palaeolithic industries in Britain.

All of this, however, relates mainly to the typology, morphology and technology of Palaeolithic stone artefacts, so far as the archaeological side of the arguments is concerned. We must therefore return separately in a later chapter

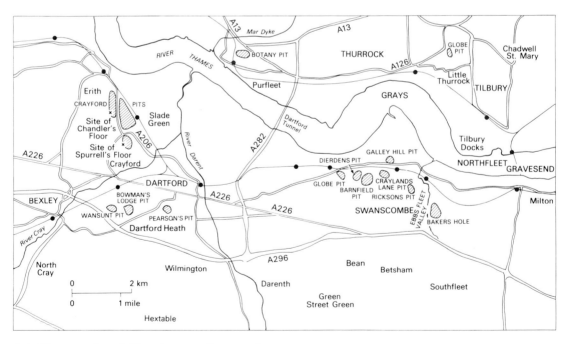

3:1 The area of north Kent between Gravesend
and Bexley, to show the locations of the main
sites mentioned in the text

to matters of prehistoric settlement and the life of Palaeolithic man, devoting further attention to the rather small number of British sites which have furnished relevant evidence.

THE BASIC SEQUENCE

The name of Swanscombe (Kent) is one of the few amongst British Palaeolithic site names that is known all over the world. Its fame is mainly due to the discovery at Barnfield Pit of the Swanscombe Skull (Plate 14), belonging to an early form of *Homo sapiens*, of which the first fragments were found in 1935 and 1936 by A.T. Marston, with another part coming to light in 1955. John Wymer (1968: 332-61) has given a useful account of the various pits in the Swanscombe area (Fig. 3:1), including Barnfield Pit, where he himself excavated in 1955-60. Many other books and papers refer to the Swanscombe sites, and to Barnfield Pit especially (Plate 15), too many to list here in full: among the more important accounts, besides that

of Wymer already quoted, are those of Smith, R.A. and Dewey (1913, 1914); the Swanscombe Committee (1938); Ovey (ed. 1964); and, more recently, Waechter (1968); Conway (1968); Waechter *et al.* (1969, 1970, 1971). The results of actual excavations are presented in all these works, and the authors between them give a comprehensive bibliography of other references to the Swanscombe sites.

So far as the basic sequence is concerned, we shall refer here mainly to Barnfield Pit and to Rickson's Pit at Swanscombe, and to the pit known as Baker's Hole at Northfleet nearby and to exposures in the Ebbsfleet Valley. But these were by no means the only sites in the Swanscombe area to produce palaeolithic artefacts: Wymer (1968: 332-54) gives a useful summary of the rest, and there are some famous names among them, notably the Globe Pit at Greenhithe, Dierden's Pit at Ingress Vale and the Galley Hill and Craylands Lane pits at Swanscombe itself (Fig. 3:1).

Fig. 3:2 combines the classic accounts of the

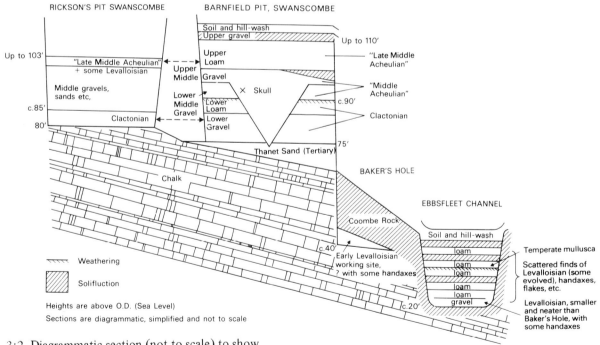

3:2 Diagrammatic section (not to scale) to show the relationships of key sites and deposits in the Swanscombe area, Kent. Drawn for the author by M.H.R. Cook

archaeological and geological sequences of the key sites to provide most of our own basic sequence, and the following pages discuss the sites in turn, explaining the order of the deposits and commenting on the nature of the archaeological material. Whether or not the classic accounts suffice in all respects is also briefly considered. It should be noted that the sections shown in Fig. 3:2 are diagrammatic, i.e. they are summaries and interpretations of the observations of various workers over several decades, not measured drawings of the working faces of gravel pits or actual sections from individual archaeological excavation trenches.

Barnfield Pit, Swanscombe

(a) *The base of the sequence*   At the base of the Pleistocene deposits in this pit a bench has been cut at about 75 feet O.D. into the Thanet Sand, which itself is of Tertiary age and does not concern us directly. Since we appear at Swanscombe to be dealing with the lower reaches of a major

river (the Thames), it may not be too naïve to equate this bench with a period of downcutting in response to a falling sea-level during cold conditions, and this is borne out to some extent by clear traces of solifluction at the very base of the Lower Gravel which lies directly on this bench (Conway 1968 and in Waechter *et al.* 1969 etc.). There are not, however, higher Thames terrace deposits in the Swanscombe area to provide evidence of the previous floodplain of that river, for the good reason that the Lower Thames previously flowed to the sea by a more northerly route, probably through the Finchley Vale and across Essex (Wooldridge 1957, 1960) and was only diverted to approximately its present course by a major ice advance, presumed to be of Anglian age, of which one of the protruding lobes extended as far south as Finchley itself and another reached to Upminster in Essex[1] (Fig. 3:3).

(b) *The Lower Gravel, and Clactonian artefacts*
On the 75-foot bench at Barnfield Pit lies the

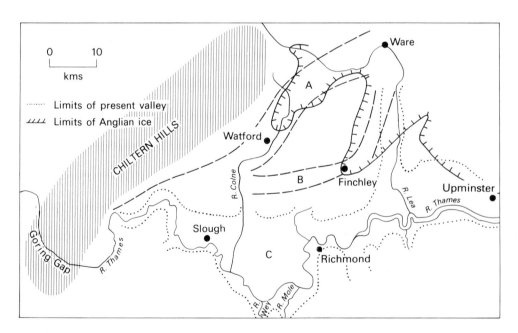

3:3 Successive courses of the River Thames, resulting from diversion by advancing ice, after Wooldridge (1957, 1960). A: Late Pliocene/ Lower Pleistocene course through the Watford Gap; B: Through the Finchley Gap, after diversion by first ice advance from the Chilterns; C: Present course, after advance of main Anglian ice sheet, whose maximum local extension is shown. The limits of the present valley are indicated

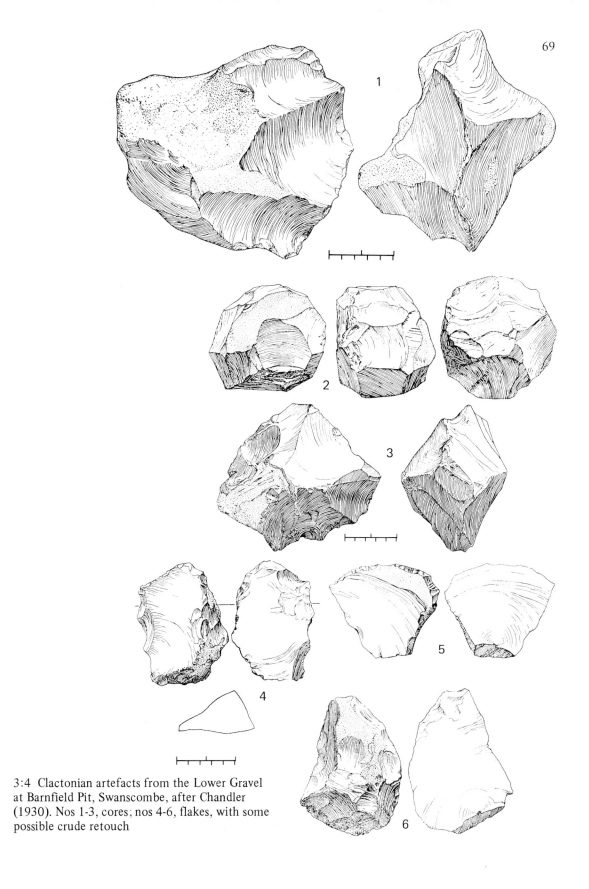

3:4 Clactonian artefacts from the Lower Gravel
at Barnfield Pit, Swanscombe, after Chandler
(1930). Nos 1-3, cores; nos 4-6, flakes, with some
possible crude retouch

Lower Gravel (Plate 16), with a maximum observed thickness of a little over 3 metres, the major part of which is clearly a fluviatile aggradation. Faunal remains contained in it suggest an interglacial climate,[2] and the gravels have long been known as a rich source of *Clactonian* artefacts. The Clactonian is a division of the British Lower Palaeolithic in which the industries are characterized by rather crude and heavy flakes, some of which are roughly retouched, and the cores from which they have been struck (Fig. 3:4). Many of these cores have been so flaked that jagged and sharp edges have been left on them between the large and deep flake-removal scars (cf. Fig. 3:4): it has often been suggested that such cores, which by definition are essentially waste products, may on occasion have had a secondary use as choppers. The Clactonian includes very few formally repeated tool-types, and the flaking technology is of a somewhat rudimentary character, with only hard hammer-stones used to produce and retouch the flakes, except where the 'block on block' technique of smashing one nodule against another may have been used. More specifically, formal bifacially flaked handaxes, so characteristic of most British Lower Palaeolithic industries, appear to be completely absent from the Clactonian, though many thousands of artefacts in aggregate have been recovered from the various Clactonian sites in Britain. Most authorities seem agreed that the Clactonian is something genuinely distinct from the series of industries with handaxes, rather than being an alternative industry made at specific times for some specific function by essentially the same population which was responsible for the handaxe industries (cf. for example Collins 1969; Singer *et al.* 1973; however, see also Ohel 1977a, b; 1979).

If we accept at face value all the reports of collection and excavation in the Lower Gravel, we must conclude that Clactonian material is scattered through the whole thickness of the deposit, though perhaps with concentrations at certain depths. The most recent excavations, as reported by Waechter and others in the sources already quoted, revealed a particularly important concentration of artefacts and accompanying animal bones (Plate 17) on or close to the surface of the gravel, and belonging to

it rather than to the overlying deposit (Lower Loam). The preliminary reports suggest that the finds here represent the outer scatter of an occupation site which has suffered only slight disturbance, though whether its central areas may survive for future excavation is not clear. The presence of Clactonian material within the Lower Gravel proper was also confirmed — not that it was in doubt — without any major new horizons coming to light. The probability is that within the whole area of Barnfield Pit, during more than 60 years' work, localized concentrations of artefacts were indeed found at differing depths in the gravel; Waechter's important floor on the gravel surface is doubtless also a local feature. Two other points remain to be noted: first, that no-one has demonstrated beyond question the presence of any artefacts that are certainly characteristic of anything other than the Clactonian in the Lower Gravel, and second, that some of the material found near the base of the deposit appears to be derived. This may well mean that it is older than the deposition of the gravel, but it could merely reflect the fact that the artefacts in question had travelled further than the rest, without necessarily being older, at the time the gravel was being aggraded.

(c) *The Lower Loam*   This is a fine-grained, silty deposit, with some lenses of shelly sand, which overlies the coarser Lower Gravel without evidence for a major gap in time between the two (Plates 16, 18). It certainly seems however that the surface of the gravel was occupied at least briefly, as we have seen, by makers of Clactonian artefacts before deposition of the Loam began in earnest, and the junction is marked by an erosion surface between the two deposits and a change in the nature of deposition: the loam may be regarded as having accumulated in still fresh water — a lake, perhaps, or very watery fenland or marshland; these conclusions are supported by the sedimentological and molluscan evidence. The loam also contains pollen, on which some preliminary comments have been published (in Waechter *et al.* 1971 and Wymer 1974), suggesting that most of the deposit is certainly of Hoxnian age. A surprising concentration of pine pollen towards the top, and a corresponding drop in alder, may indicate a rather abrupt change to colder conditions, not matched by any change or break in the sedimentation, but other explanations are possible and the present writer prefers to reserve judgement for the moment. The top of the Lower Loam appears to be quite strongly weathered to a variable depth which may on occasion reach a metre (Plate 18). If this alteration of the Loam has indeed been brought about by weathering and soil formation, which is not yet fully established, then there must certainly be a break of some kind in the sequence after the deposition of the Lower Loam: the water-table must have fallen, and the top of the loam must have been exposed as dry land, perhaps for quite a long period.

The earlier accounts of the Swanscombe sequence mostly refer to the Lower Loam as being empty of artefacts or at least extremely poor in them. Only A.T. Marston (1937, 1942) claimed the finding of flakes within it and also on its surface, and he never gave a detailed account of them. The recent work directed by Waechter, however, has clearly established that there are horizons within the deposit on which artefacts occur, so whatever the water-body was in which the Loam formed, it must have undergone fluctuations which left temporary land-surfaces available. The most interesting of this material incorporated several conjoinable flakes in very fresh condition (Fig. 3:5) and represented fragments of one or more actual knapping areas, to which disturbance had been minimal (Waechter *et al.* 1970). In so far as the Lower Loam artefacts in aggregate consist of various flakes and a few cores not too dissimilar from those of the Lower Gravel, it might be thought that they represent intermittently continuing 'Clactonian' occupation, but in fact they

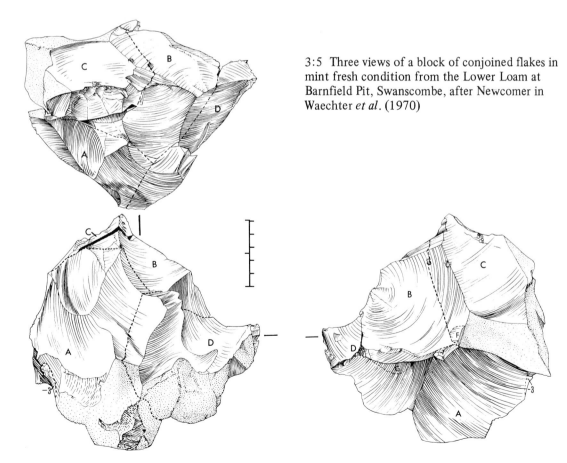

3:5 Three views of a block of conjoined flakes in mint fresh condition from the Lower Loam at Barnfield Pit, Swanscombe, after Newcomer in Waechter *et al.* (1970)

are rather too sparse and scattered yet to deserve any firm 'cultural' designation (Waechter, pers. com.); the non-specialized knapping debris of many industries may look pretty similar in small quantities. If typical handaxes had been manufactured on the spot, however, at least some of the highly diagnostic trimming flakes should be present to betray the fact, but they appear to be completely absent. This is not of course the same as saying that handaxe manufacture was unknown in Britain at the time. The only fair conclusion, then, is that the Lower Loam continues the archaeological sequence but does not clearly introduce any new industry. Some faunal remains also occur in the Lower Loam, mostly in rather poor condition, but they are not abundant. The species represented are much the same as those found in the Lower Gravel (see note 2).

(d) *The Lower Middle Gravel, and Acheulian artefacts*   The weathering or chemical alteration of the top of the Lower Loam surely marks a break in the Pleistocene sequence of deposition at Barnfield Pit, and this is confirmed by the nature of the succeeding deposit, a relatively coarse gravel (Plate 19). In short, fluviatile aggradation seems to have been resumed, at a higher base level (about 90 feet O.D.) than that of the Lower Gravel, which, it will be recalled, rests on a bench at about 75 feet. Gravels with a base at around 90 feet O.D. are fairly common in north Kent (Wymer 1968: 360), both in the immediate Swanscombe area and further west, and in Essex across the river. Whether or not any phase of down-cutting may have intervened between the end of the deposition of the Lower Loam and the start of the Middle Gravel aggradation is not entirely clear, but one might feel that a cold phase sharp enough to have lowered the sea-level would have left the Lower Loam cryoturbated rather than weathered at the top. It depends somewhat on exactly where we have reached in the Middle Pleistocene or earliest Upper Pleistocene; if we are still in the Hoxnian, as the faunal remains from the Middle Gravels might suggest (see note 2), then the clear evidence of Marks Tey discussed in the previous chapter would stand out against the existence of any major cold oscillation within the interglacial. The tradi-

tional view places the Lower Gravel, the Lower Loam and both parts of the Middle Gravel all in the Hoxnian, and some would include the Upper Loam as well. M.P. Kerney (1971), on the basis of molluscan evidence, attributed the Middle Gravels to a period beginning in Hoxnian Zone III (late temperate) and probably extending into the Early Glacial (Zone I) phase of the Wolstonian; cf. also note 6 to the preceding chapter.

Leaving these issues for the moment, and returning to the geological and archaeological sequence, we must next note that the Lower Middle Gravel contains artefacts in considerable abundance, and that although there may be some Clactonian material present, perhaps derived (Waechter *et al.* 1971: 77), the majority can be safely ascribed not to the Clactonian but to the *Acheulian*, on the grounds that the material contains abundant and typical handaxes (Fig. 3:6) and plenty of the characteristic by-products (flaking debris) of their manufacture.

The name Acheulian, still firmly in use, comes from a French type site, Saint-Acheul, near Amiens in the Somme Valley. Industries that have been called Acheulian are very widespread in the Old World, unlike those of the Clactonian, ranging from peninsular India in the east to West Africa in the west, and from southernmost Africa in the south to north Germany and the English Midlands in the north. Within these extremes, the distribution includes the large majority of the African continent, much of South-West Asia as far north as the Caucasus, large parts of Western Europe and much of Central Europe too. Scarcely less impressive is the distribution of the Acheulian in time, since there is good evidence that handaxe industries were current in parts of East Africa well over a million years ago and perhaps as much as one and a half million (Isaac 1972a; Hay 1976:113), while on the other hand handaxe industries that can be regarded as belonging to the final stages of the Acheulian rather than to the Mousterian seem to be demonstrable in France and Germany at least as late as the early part of the last glaciation, say a mere 60,000-70,000 years ago (Bosinski 1967; Bordes 1968: 60, etc.). To suppose that all these scattered industries can really be attributed to a single unified archaeological 'culture' is unrealistic

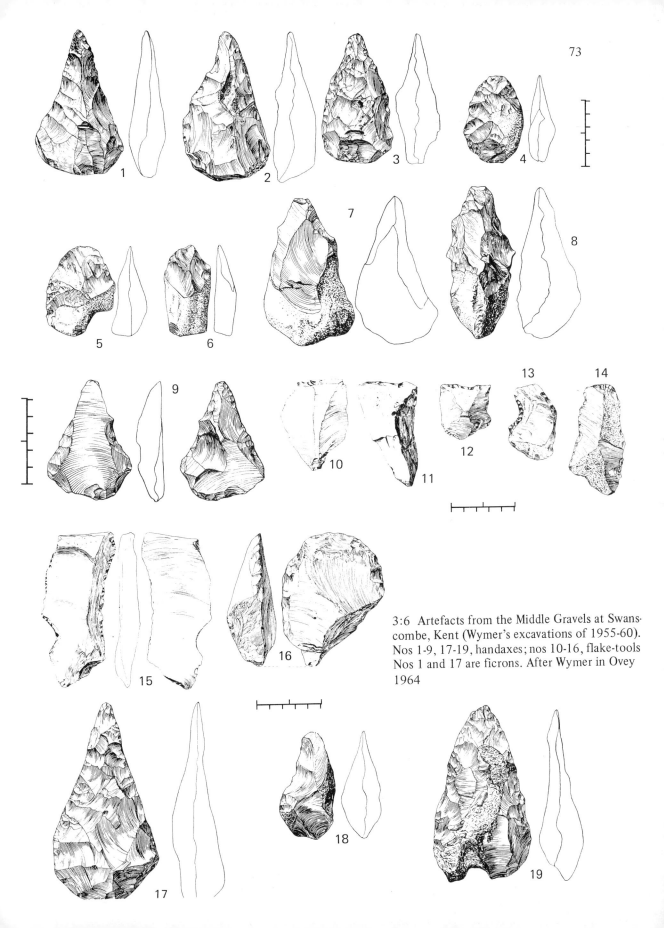

73

3:6 Artefacts from the Middle Gravels at Swanscombe, Kent (Wymer's excavations of 1955-60). Nos 1-9, 17-19, handaxes; nos 10-16, flake-tools Nos 1 and 17 are ficrons. After Wymer in Ovey 1964

if not ridiculous, and if the title 'Acheulian' gives such an impression then it should cease to be used or at the very least be modified to 'Acheulian Tradition': the term 'techno-complex' (Clarke 1968: 321-57) will probably satisfy those who can bring themselves to use it, but it seems to be being employed a little variably at present. The point is that the handaxe industries of the whole Lower Palaeolithic exhibit wide regional variation in the first place and span a considerable technological range in the second; such variability would hardly be implied by the finds made at Saint-Acheul if it be treated as the type-site for them all. Even so, there are undeniably certain common factors, at the level of generalization, and these will serve to introduce the artefacts from the Swanscombe Middle Gravels as 'an Acheulian industry' and as the next stage of our basic sequence.

'Acheulian' industries, then, have the tools known as *handaxes* (Fig. 3:6) as their most striking feature:[3] handaxes are shaped tools, usually of medium to large size by the standards of flint artefacts in general, characterized by the presence of a cutting edge which normally extends around most of the circumference. So far as Britain and north-west Europe are concerned, the vast majority of handaxes are fashioned by bifacial flaking, though this does not mean that the whole of each face is necessarily worked: cortex patches may be left, or, where the implement has been made from a large flake rather than from a nodule, areas of the flake's bulbar surface may survive. Handaxes as a class include a considerable variety of shapes (in the sense of plan-forms). These shapes usually tend towards regularity and symmetry, but only rarely are they so symmetrical in all respects that a distinct 'tip' and 'butt' cannot be defined. Handaxe tips may be more or less pointed, or tongue-like, or rounded, but occasionally a squared transverse cutting edge may be found at the tip end. Butts may be anything from fully and delicately worked with complete cutting edges to wholly unworked or just roughly shaped here and there to provide a hand-hold. In profile handaxes vary from thick and irregular to flat and symmetrically lenticular, according to the nature of their flaking. In so far as technological skills tended slowly but per-

sistently to increase during the Lower Palaeolithic, it is by no means unreasonable to expect earlier handaxe industries to include many rather thick and crudely made implements, and later ones to show a majority of flatter and more symmetrical examples, but to deduce from this that any crude handaxe *must* be 'early' and any well-made one 'late' would be quite unsound; any handaxe-maker at any period of the Lower Palaeolithic had to have a first shot, and in addition to that manual skill was doubtless as variable between individuals then as it is today.

Exactly what function handaxes served is one of the more basic problems of Lower Palaeolithic archaeology, but not one of the more easily answered.[4] They are often described vaguely as 'all-purpose tools' with cutting as one main function. However, they were not so comprehensively effective that Acheulian man needed nothing else: his industries also regularly include neatly made flake tools (Fig. 3:6), amongst which are scrapers of various kinds, points, and knives. These may sometimes have been made from flakes originally struck off in the process of handaxe manufacture, since cores (in the sense of flaked nodules classifiable as waste products) are rather rare in most Acheulian industries, another contrast with the Clactonian. It is also clear from such microwear studies of British Acheulian industries as have so far been attempted that flakes which had not been formally retouched as flake tools were nevertheless quite frequently used for cutting and scraping tasks. Apart from all of this, any major Acheulian occurrence usually includes very large numbers of waste and trimming flakes which are merely knapping debris. Some of these waste flakes, as already indicated, notably those which were struck off with a 'soft' hammer at a late stage of the manufacture of handaxes ('handaxe trimming flakes'), are especially characteristic in such features as the pattern of scars on their dorsal surfaces, their thin and often carefully prepared striking platforms and diffuse bulbs of percussion, their over-all flatness and their curved profiles; they are diagnostically 'Acheulian' even when no actual handaxe is present.

Such then is the general nature of the assemblage of artefacts from the Lower Middle Gravels at Barnfield Pit. This is not material in place on a completely excavated living floor, but consists rather of artefacts recovered from various depths in the gravel on many different occasions. Its generally fresh condition certainly suggests that most of it has not moved very far from the original site or sites where it was made or used, but there is still little point in attempting classification in minute detail since we can never know how much of the material really belongs together. One thing at least is clear, and it is an important point for our basic sequence: the handaxes, of which certainly hundreds and probably thousands have come from this deposit at Barnfield Pit, show a strong preference for pointed types (Fig. 3:6). Their tips are carefully and sometimes finely made, while their butts are often left rough or only casually shaped. Flat ovate handaxe forms, so dominant in some British Acheulian industries, are here notably rare though certainly not completely absent. In a sample of handaxes from the Barnfield Pit Middle Gravels studied by metrical and statistical analysis, the present writer (1968a) found almost 80 per cent of the implements to be pointed forms. Amongst them are several good examples of the *ficron* shape, which has incurving sides in the plan view and a narrow acutely pointed tip (Fig. 3:6).

(e) *Upper Middle Gravel*   According to the classic view of the Barnfield Pit sequence, a deep channel was cut through the Lower Middle Gravels, and indeed through the underlying deposits, its base descending even to the top of the Thanet Sand below. This channel was then filled up again quite quickly with fine gravel and sand during a phase of renewed aggradation which continued until the Lower Middle Gravels were covered by some metres of the new deposit, to which the name of Upper Middle Gravel is given. At the junction between the Lower Middle and Upper Middle Gravels (Plate 19), i.e. at the edge and base of the supposed channel, artefacts were abundant and it was apparently at this level too that the original fragments of the Swanscombe Skull were found in 1935-6 (Marston 1937; Swanscombe Committee 1938; Wymer 1964, 1968: 338). It was A.T. Marston who observed and recorded (more or less in passing) the presence of this channel, and its existence has been generally accepted ever since, though it can only have been a temporary feature so far as the sections in the gravel pit were concerned and no proper drawing or photograph of it exists. More recently J. d'A. Waechter's work has failed to find any trace of it (Waechter 1973: 73) and B.W. Conway (in Waechter *et al.* 1971: 83) has suggested that what Marston saw may have resulted from the collapse of the deposits into a solution cavity rather than from an extra cycle of fluviatile erosion and aggradation. The present writer has no new evidence to offer and can merely report the different views. If the Middle Gravels are to be regarded as of Hoxnian age, then it would be very convenient to be able to forget the supposed deep channel within them which would seem to call for a climatic explanation which would be hard to supply on the basis of confirmatory evidence from other sites. On the other hand, if the complexities of the deep-sea cores' record of the Brunhes epoch are kept in mind, along with the likelihood of a missing interglacial between the Hoxnian and the Ipswichian (see the preceding chapter), one could take the view that the Middle Gravels Channel may well have existed and might have been just the sort of elusive evidence for an extra cold-warm cycle that sorely needs to be produced. It seems however that the critical area of the gravel may have gone for ever.

As regards the Palaeolithic content of the Upper Middle Gravel, most accounts seem agreed that it does not substantially differ from that of the Lower Middle Gravel, i.e. it is another Acheulian industry in which pointed handaxes are particularly frequent. Such certainly seems to be indicated by the excavations of John Wymer (1964, 1968: 339). Unfortunately, in many of the old collections no distinction has been made between the two parts of the Middle Gravels in the marking of the artefacts, so it is not possible to make a formal comparison of the two assemblages based on large and well-provenanced samples. One might also reflect that if a channel did exist in the Middle Gravels, or perhaps even in the alternative case of a collapse of the deposits, implements which were found near the junction but actually in the Upper Middle Gravel might well have been redeposited there directly from the Lower Middle Gravel, having been moved only a few feet in the process. Exactly what belongs where within the Middle Gravels is clearly open to some doubt, but at least we can say that there is no clear evidence of any new archaeological stage in the Upper Middle Gravel.

(f) *Upper Loam*   Some observers have reported solifluction at the top of the Upper Middle Gravels (Marston 1937; Dines *et al*. 1938) and the recent excavations have confirmed this (Waechter 1973: 69, 73), so there is clear evidence for periglacial conditions following the completion of the aggradation of the Middle Gravels. The Upper Loam itself (Plate 20) has the character of sediments accumulated by intermittent flooding in rather cold conditions (see Conway in Waechter *et al*. 1971, but according to Hubbard (1977) the pollen in it is fully temperate and he ascribes it tentatively to the Ipswichian); and it is certainly not to be regarded as a true continuation of the Middle Gravels aggradation (see also Wymer 1968: 343-4). There are persistent reports of minor land surfaces within it at various levels,

suggesting pauses in its accumulation, and it is generally believed that some at least of these surfaces contained occurrences of artefacts, though none has been located in the more recent campaigns of excavation. Wymer (1968: 343-4) and Waechter (1973: 70-4) are among those who have discussed the artefacts in question, originally recorded by Smith, R.A. and Dewey (1914) and by Marston (1937). The artefacts were white-patinated and included as the dominant implement type well-made flat ovate handaxes (Fig. 3:7), some of them showing advanced technological devices like the *tranchet finish* and the deliberately *twisted cutting edge*[5] (see Fig. 3:7 and Plate 21). The old collections, notably the Stopes Collection now in the National Museum of Wales at Cardiff, do indeed contain a certain number of white-patinated handaxes answering this description and some have certainly been marked as coming from the Upper Loam. On the basis of those he has seen, including a small sample studied metrically (Roe 1968a), the writer can confirm the shift to flat refined ovates as the preferred handaxe type, though pointed forms are not completely absent. There seems no reason to doubt the old reports, but it is regrettable that they are wholly uncon-

3:7 Finely made ovate handaxes from the Upper Loam at Barnfield Pit (nos 1-4), from Rickson's Pit (nos 5-9) and from Pearsons's Pit, Dartford (nos 10-12). Note the shallow 'soft hammer' flaking, and the occurrence of *tranchet* finish

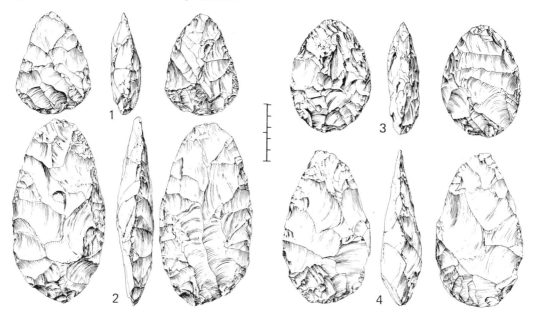

firmed by more recent controlled excavation. Evidently the floors were small and localized within the Loam.

So far as the basic sequence is concerned we might feel somewhat hesitant about accepting the Upper Loam artefacts on their own as convincing and sufficient evidence for a further stage. However, the case is a good deal strengthened by other finds (Fig. 3:7) in north Kent between Northfleet and Dartford (Wymer 1968: 320-361; Waechter 1973). Notably, at Rickson's Pit, Swanscombe (also known as Barracks Pit), not much more than half a mile away from Barnfield Pit, well-made ovates were found by J.P.T. Burchell (1931, 1934b), some of them actually in what may well have been a specific continuation of the Barnfield Pit Upper Loam deposit (see also Wymer 1961: 6). Other sites in the area where similar ovate industries occur, sometimes in deposits which clearly should not be far removed in age from the Barnfield Pit Upper Loam, include Craylands Lane Pit (Swanscombe), and Bowman's Lodge Pit, Pearson's Pit and the Wansunt Pit (all at Dartford). Another similar series comes from the Globe Pit at Greenhithe (Smith, R.A. and Dewey 1913: 192-4; Dewey 1932: 48-9), but their context there is

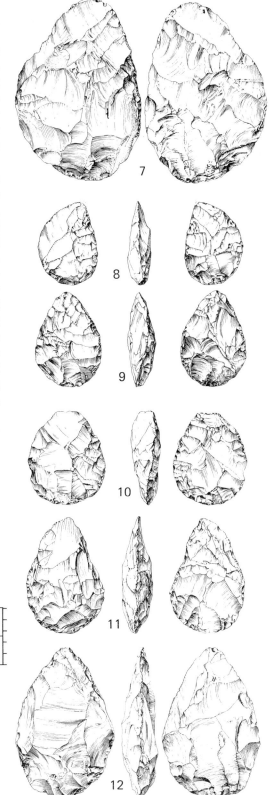

(e.g. nos 7, 8, etc.) and twisted profile (nos 5, 6 etc.). After Waechter (1973)

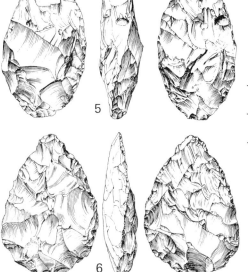

rather uncertain. None of these sites however can show such a full sequence of deposits and industries as Barnfield Pit; even at Rickson's Pit the Middle Gravels stage is only poorly represented if at all, although there was a Lower Gravel rich in Clactonian artefacts. But, taking the various occurrences together, and considering their positions in their own sequences, though we cannot discuss all the details here, it does seem justifiable to regard them as tending to confirm the existence of the industry reported as occurring in the Barnfield Pit Upper Loam. This view is in accordance with the conclusions of Wymer (1968) and Waechter (1973), who have discussed such details as are available of the stratigraphy at the sites just mentioned.

We can therefore take the basic sequence further by adding to it an Acheulian industry characterized by relatively frequent flat ovate handaxes, whose manufacture commonly shows evidence of advanced flaking technology. This stage in north Kent apparently follows the Acheulian dominated by pointed handaxes: a few pointed types occur in it, but the ovate forms are dominant. None of the sites mentioned in the preceding paragraph, unfortunately, offers us a clear picture of the other artefacts accompanying the handaxes, except perhaps Bowman's Lodge (Tester 1951, 1976), where many flakes, some of them retouched as tools, were found. There were also several cores at this site, suggesting that here at least the ordinary waste flakes from handaxe manufacture were not always adequate as flake-tool blanks, but this is a rare situation in the British Acheulian (if the old collections are not giving us a completely false impression). Bowman's Lodge was an interesting site in many ways, casually revealed during commercial digging; the artefacts, or what was left of them after mechanical diggers had stripped off the upper levels, were rescued thanks to the keen observation and resourcefulness of Mr P.J. Tester. They lay on top of a gravel and had been gently covered by loam, evidently with minimal disturbance (as suggested by the occurrence of a pair of conjoinable waste-flakes).

(g) *The Upper Gravel*   The final Pleistocene horizon in the Barnfield Pit sequence is a soli-

fluted gravel (the Upper Gravel). It indicates renewed periglacial conditions and it contains artefacts, but the latter seem to have been gathered from earlier deposits over which the gravelly mass slid when the solifluction was active. In particular in certain parts of the pit ovate handaxes from the surface of the Upper Loam seem to have been caught up in it. The Upper Gravel does not therefore add any fresh stage to our basic archaeological sequence, to continue which we shall need to consider other sites in the immediate neighbourhood.

Levalloisian technique   At Bowman's Lodge, and to a lesser extent in the upper deposits of Rickson's Pit, there are some signs that the *Levalloisian* flaking technique may have been known to the makers of the ovate handaxes (Fig. 3:8). This technique is important in the later part of the Lower Palaeolithic and throughout the Middle Palaeolithic in various parts of the Old World; closely related techniques occur sporadically in the Upper Palaeolithic too, and survive or are reborn later still, in the post-Pleistocene period. Levalloisian technique is usually concerned with the production from a given nodule of a single substantial flat flake of predetermined size and shape, which was either directly usable as a tool or else required only minor retouch to bring it to completeness. The technique (Fig. 3:9) involves a clear order of stages of work and leaves characteristic end-products in both the flake itself and the core. First, the nodule is given its basic shape, according as a flake of oval, elongated, triangular or other plan-form is required. Second, the top of the basically shaped nodule is prepared by flat flake removals in order to form the dorsal face of the flake-to-be, creating a well-domed surface or else leaving long ridges, since this is necessary if a large and relatively long flake of regular shape is to be obtained. Thirdly, a striking platform is carefully prepared at one end of the core, and lastly a hard blow is directed on to it at precisely the right angle to detach the flake as intended, leaving the 'struck' core as a waste product.

The 'Levalloisian' flake thus produced is characteristic (Fig. 3:9) in the pattern of scars on its dorsal face: most or all of them will be incomplete, since their proximal (bulbar) ends were left

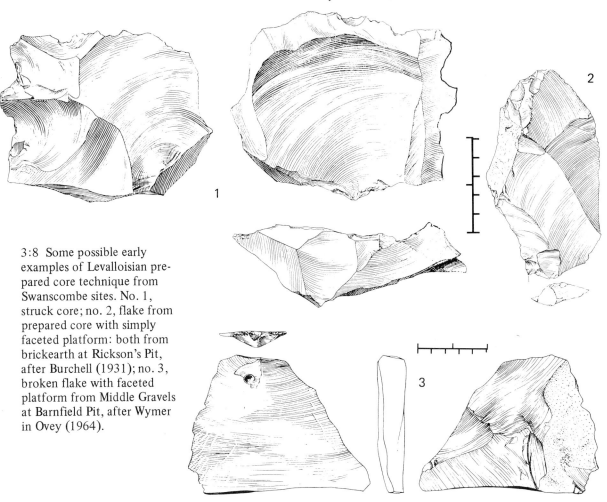

3:8 Some possible early examples of Levalloisian prepared core technique from Swanscombe sites. No. 1, struck core; no. 2, flake from prepared core with simply faceted platform: both from brickearth at Rickson's Pit, after Burchell (1931); no. 3, broken flake with faceted platform from Middle Gravels at Barnfield Pit, after Wymer in Ovey (1964).

3:9 Production of a Levalloisian flake from a 'tortoise core' (diagrammatic). I, basic shaping of nodule; II, preparation of domed dorsal surface; III, preparation of faceted striking platform on core; IV, the flake and the struck core, with their characteristic features (see pages 78, 80). Drawn for the author by M.H.R. Cook

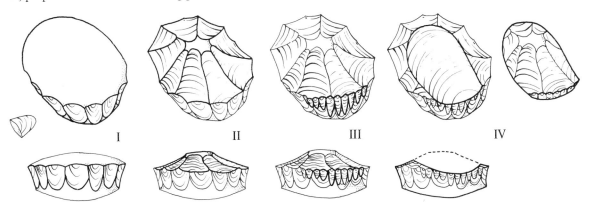

behind on the core. The flake's striking platform is also characteristic, having usually a 'faceted' appearance, caused by the removal of various small flakes in its preparation. The distal ends of some at least of these facet scars will remain on the core. As for the Levalloisian core, it retains on its upper surface the proximal ends of the flake's dorsal scars, clearly truncated by the large removal scar where the flake itself was detached. It also bears at one end traces of the preparation of the striking platform, i.e. the distal ends of the facet scars referred to above, again truncated by the main flake removal. Finally, its sides will show evidence for the original rough shaping, and indeed its over-all shape will be far more regular (like that of the flake it yielded) than any unprepared core of, for example, Clactonian type. Large oval Levalloisian cores are not infrequently referred to as 'tortoise cores' and any fancied resemblance to a tortoise's shell reflects this regularity of shape and a surface bearing large even scars.

In typical form, these end-products of the Levalloisian 'prepared core technique' are unmistakable, and they clearly represent a co-ordinated sequence of ideas with a definite end-product in view — a relatively sophisticated technological process by earlier Palaeolithic standards. It is however possible for the more elaborate handaxe trimming flakes, whose striking platforms may also be prepared, to be confused with small Levalloisian flakes, though they will be seen to be different if examined carefully enough; this potential confusion should be kept in mind when the presence of Levalloisian technique is claimed on the basis of a few small flakes alone.

A case in point is the Middle Gravels at Barnfield Pit, where several authors have claimed the occurrence of Levalloisian technique (e.g. Tester 1952a; Wymer 1968: 243). Typical struck Levalloisian cores are not clearly present in the Middle Gravels, and not all the flakes which have been claimed as Levalloisian are outside the handaxe trimmer range. The present writer's own opinion is that one or two of them *are* true Levalloisian flakes, but the technique is only very sparsely represented, and it would be stretching the evidence too far, given the nature of the deposit, to say that it certainly forms an integral part of the Middle Gravels

Acheulian industry.

Baker's Hole, Northfleet

This superb site, unfortunately, was discovered far too early in the history of Palaeolithic research for its potential to be realized, and although the pit remained active long afterwards and indeed still exists today, the crucial area of it was destroyed by chalk quarrying long ago. The site lay on a spur between two arms of the Ebbsfleet Valley. Reduced to its barest essentials, the section showed that a mass of Coombe Rock (soliflucted chalk mixed with flints, clay and sand, mainly derived Tertiary material, formed under periglacial conditions; cf. Plate 6a) had slid over an exceptionally rich Palaeolithic working site, many of the artefacts being caught up and carried down the valley sides. The industry is based upon a bold use of the Levalloisian technique to exploit the large nodules of good quality flint which occur here abundantly in the chalk: it is almost classifiable as a quarry site or factory site, the product being large Levalloisian flakes and the waste including classic tortoise cores (Fig. 3:10; Plate 22) and the various flakes struck off during their preparation. Whether the Levalloisian flakes made at Baker's Hole were all produced as tools in themselves, or whether some at least were blanks designed for further modification, is a point to which we must return in a later chapter. Meanwhile, the industry carries the basic sequence a stage further: we saw the Levalloisian technique first beginning to be used perhaps already in the Middle Gravels stage of the Barnfield Pit sequence, or, if not, at the time when deposits of slightly younger age were forming at Rickson's Pit and Bowman's Lodge — that is to say, either back in the Interglacial which the Middle Gravels represent, or else in the following cooler phase. But at Baker's Hole we see a great flowering of Levalloisian technique which completely dominates a whole industry.

It would seem logical perhaps to regard these as two successive 'Levalloisian stages' — a somewhat tentative beginning followed by a massive development — and this indeed has often been done, and even regarded as an argument sufficient in itself

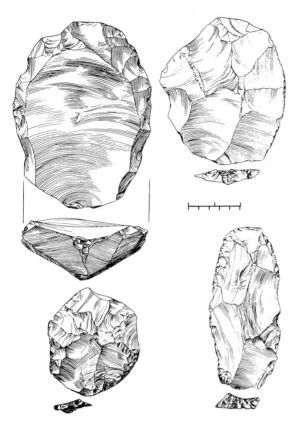

3:10 A struck core (top left) and three Levalloisian flakes, from Baker's Hole, after Wymer (1968)

for making Baker's Hole younger than the Upper Loam or equivalent deposits. Must it necessarily be so? The Levalloisian is a *technique*, not a *culture*: we have already noted its wide and discontinuous occurrence in the Palaeolithic and even afterwards. As a technique, it is one that is essentially wasteful of flint, in the sense that only a single usable flake is normally produced from a given block of raw material: more than 90 per cent of the original nodule may be wasted. It follows therefore that only when large nodules are available in abundance can Levalloisian technique be used on the scale seen at Baker's Hole. The elegant typological sequence of the prehistorian can hardly be expected to take precedence over such practical considerations of the Palaeolithic. What artefacts should we have seen in the Upper Loam

at Swanscombe, if that deposit had been forming at the base of a chalk cliff where large fresh nodules of flint were easily obtainable?

These are important considerations. We cannot re-excavate the Baker's Hole Levalloisian site to determine its age, so must reach conclusions about the latter from the contemporary accounts and an overview of the Pleistocene sequence of north Kent. Wymer (1968: 354-6) gives a useful account of what is known of Baker's Hole and lists the main references, amongst which the reports by Spurrell (1883), Smith, R.A. (1911, 1926), Burchell (1931) and Dewey (1932) are the most important. Most of the sections recorded by these various authors refer only to Coombe Rock directly overlying an eroded chalk surface, though Spurrell, if what he found was a part of the same site,[6] as seems highly likely, stated that the artefacts lay in enormous quantities on a river-beach, and some have suggested that aggradation of the 50-foot terrace had already begun, though Burchell has argued strongly against this in various papers. Spurrell may have seen an exposure of the main area of the original Palaeolithic site, while the sections observed by the others were perhaps at or just beyond its periphery. There is at least general agreement that aggradation at the so-called 'hundred-foot level' (i.e. on the 90-foot bench) had ceased and that major downcutting had already taken place: indeed, it was this downcutting which established the Ebbsfleet Valley in which the site was located, producing the bare chalk slopes which underlay the Coombe Rock. It was recognized from the start by R.A. Smith (1911) that the Coombe Rock contained, as well as the Levalloisian artefacts, some derived handaxes which seem to have come from gravels of the 90-foot terrace nearby (the base level of the Barnfield Pit Middle Gravels is at about 90 feet, it will be recalled). This observation merely confirms that the Coombe Rock is younger than the 90-foot terrace gravels, and does not offer a definitive date for the Levalloisian material, though the remarkably fresh and sometimes even unpatinated condition of a fair proportion of the Levalloisian artefacts suggests that the working floor did not lie exposed for very long before the Coombe Rock covered it. Indeed, the geologists who studied the exposures described by Smith seem agreed that the working site immediately antedates the Coombe Rock. There seems little evidence for any major build-up of deposits between the eroded chalk surface, representing the post 90-foot terrace downcutting, and the Coombe Rock. The most likely reading seems to be that the erosion of the chalk, in cold conditions, produced the abundant supplies of flint, which were exploited more or less immediately by Palaeolithic man; he was eventually driven from the site by the increasing cold which caused the massive solifluction represented by the Coombe Rock itself.

The Baker's Hole industry would on this view fall into place very soon after the end of the aggradation on the 90-foot terrace, with no substantial warm phase intervening: if so, it should be of specifically early Wolstonian age. But exactly when, in terms of the Barnfield Pit sequence considered in the foregoing pages, did the erosion and downcutting take place? This must depend on what interpretation is placed on the Upper Loam, and the traces of solifluction beneath it must not be ignored. They imply periglacial conditions, and the downcutting could accordingly have taken place *before* the loam was deposited, in which case the Levalloisian of Baker's Hole would be closely similar in age to the ovate hand-axe industries of the Upper Loam. If, however, the Upper Loam were regarded as an integral part of the fluviatile aggradation which took place on the 90-foot bench, following the Middle Gravels much as the Lower Loam followed the Lower Gravel in the previous cycle, then it must be only *after* the Upper Loam that the downcutting phase occurred. In that case the Upper Gravel at Barnfield Pit would no doubt represent the same periglacial phase as the main Coombe Rock, and the Baker's Hole Levalloisian would come immediately after the ovate handaxe industries of the Upper Loam and its local equivalents. Both of these interpretations have been suggested, though the present writer regards the first as the most likely. It is important to remember, however, that the Baker's Hole industry should be viewed in technological and functional terms rather than as a link in a chain of typological evolution.

One other point about the industry itself needs discussion: were there handaxes properly associated with the Levalloisian artefacts or not? The occurrence of the derived handaxes in the Coombe Rock, referred to above, has somewhat confused the issue because, although Smith clearly indicated that they were extraneous, they have sometimes been lumped together with the Levalloisian cores and flakes and used accordingly in various typological arguments from which chronological conclusions have unwisely been drawn. But if we disregard those implements, there still remain a few handaxes much closer in condition and raw material to the Levalloisian artefacts, and these *may* have belonged with them (cf. Wymer 1968: 355-6). Spurrell's early account of the site (1883) could also be interpreted as suggesting that hand-axes and the Levalloisian cores and flakes lay together *in situ*. But there seems to be no conclusive evidence, and it is fair to conclude that in any case handaxes cannot have formed a very large percentage of the assemblage if they were present at all. It would even be arguable too (with little chance of proof or disproof) that any handaxes present might represent a separate exploitation of the same raw material source by a different but contemporary human group. These things are imponderable, since there never was a scientific excavation of the original Palaeolithic site to guide us. Most of the extant Baker's Hole material, and there is a great deal of it (Roe 1968b: 168-9), was collected from the Coombe Rock. For further discussion of the possible significance of Baker's Hole, see below pages 275-6.

A minimal view of the Baker's Hole occurrence, then, is to take it as indicating for the purposes of our basic sequence an expansion of the use of Levalloisian technique, or at least a demonstration of the lengths to which use of this relatively new flaking method could be taken on occasion (i.e. in favourable circumstances with abundant raw material ready to hand). The industry certainly dates from after the end of the aggradation on the terrace we have been considering in the previous sections, and the Coombe Rock is clear evidence that the episode was quickly followed by a major periglacial phase; indeed, the Palaeolithic occupation itself probably took place in relatively cold conditions. Some faunal remains[7] were collected with the flints, including mammoth (*Mammuthus primigenius*), and horse (*Equus caballus*), though the 'steppe' rhinoceros (*Dicerorhinus hemitoechus*) was also present, as opposed to the cold-specialized variety *Coelodonta antiquitatis*, and so was red deer (*Cervus elaphus*). The bones, however, were poorly preserved and their presence in the Coombe Rock hardly constitutes a proper archaeological association with the artefacts.

The Ebbsfleet Channel

If the precise relationship of the Coombe Rock to the upper levels at Barnfield Pit is open to more than one interpretation, at least it is certain that the next series of deposits in the Ebbsfleet Valley is younger than the Coombe Rock itself, for the deposits in question fill channels which are cut into it, both at Baker's Hole itself and further along the valley (Dewey 1932; Burchell 1933, 1934a, 1936a, b, 1954; Zeuner 1958: 193-4, 1959: 163-7; Wymer 1968: 356-9). Burchell recorded various sections through a major channel, which has usually been referred to in the literature as the Ebbsfleet Channel. It was cut into the Coombe Rock and in places right through the latter into the chalk. The basal deposit in it, overlying the chalk and Coombe Rock, was a coarse gravel formed in cold conditions (local meltwater could well have been the main agent of its deposition), containing traces of a cold fauna including mammoth. There follows a long series of loams, between some of which are solifluction deposits; the principal constituent of the loams is certainly loess, even if in some cases it has been redeposited by water. The sections are described in the references quoted, and all the details need not be repeated here, but Table 7 offers a summary of the composite sequence as given by Burchell (composite, because not all of the deposits are present in all of the sections).

There is plenty of evidence for cold conditions in this sequence, and also reasonably clear indications of one major warm phase, in the weathering of the loess and the occurrence of temperate molluscan species directly above it in a water-laid deposit which may reflect aggradation at a time of

TABLE 7 : *The Ebbsfleet Channel deposits*
(after Burchell)

Suggested correlation	Sequence of deposits	Artefacts as described by Burchell
Recent	Hill-wash and recent soil	
Cold: Devensian	Solifluction / Loessic loam deposited in water ('Uppermost Loam' of Burchell) / Solifluction	
Warm: Ipswichian	Loessic loam deposited in water, with temperate shells mainly in its lower half ('Upper Loam' of Burchell) Weathered surface of the underlying loess	'Micoquian' (pointed handaxes)
Cold: Wolstonian	Loess ('Upper Middle Loam' of Burchell) Solifluction Loess ('Lower Middle Loam' of Burchell) Loess ('Lower Loam' of Burchell) Fluviatile gravel Occasional band of loessic material ('Lowermost Loam' of Burchell) Coarse gravel with mammoth, etc. Coombe Rock	Handaxes and flakes in fresh condition 'Middle Levalloisian' Levalloisian at Baker's Hole
	Chalk	

high sea-level. The usual interpretation of the whole Ebbsfleet Channel series places the deposits up to the weathered horizon in the Wolstonian, the weathering and the loam with temperate mollusca in the Ipswichian, and the remainder of the Pleistocene levels in the Devensian. In so far as those named stages constitute a sufficient Pleistocene sequence, there seems no reason to argue with the correlation of the deposits with them at present, and the whole picture is perfectly consistent with the specifically early Wolstonian age suggested above for the Baker's Hole industry.

As indicated in Table 7, some of the Ebbsfleet Valley deposits have yielded artefacts, mainly collected by Burchell himself over many years' painstaking observation of the exposures. It is sad that though a few hundred artefacts in all exist (mainly in the British Museum's reserve collections), no large and well-characterized assemblage can be assigned to any one of the several different strata. It is also not completely clear in every case what came from which level, since Burchell's naming of the levels and industries not surprisingly underwent some development and variation over the years. The table shows those attributions which seem beyond doubt, though there may well have been a few pieces from some of the other levels. Some deductions at least can be made.

First, use of the Levalloisian technique remained current in the area after the Coombe Rock periglacial phase, and the cores and flakes (Fig. 3:11) are typically smaller and neater than those of Baker's Hole. The striking platforms are often markedly convex (a device which increased accuracy in delivering the final blow that removed the flake from the prepared core), and the preparatory scars on the dorsal surfaces often (though not always) run longitudinally from the ends rather than convergently from the whole circumference. Some of the flakes are quite blade-like — 'flakeblades' is a useful term for them — and some of the cores tend towards a 'prismatic' form and have sometimes been designed to yield more than one Levalloisian flake-blade. All these features may be counted as 'advanced' or 'developed', in that they suggest considerable mastery of the principles of the Levalloisian technique. Flakes and cores of this kind were probably scattered through several of the deposits which fill the Ebbsfleet Channel,

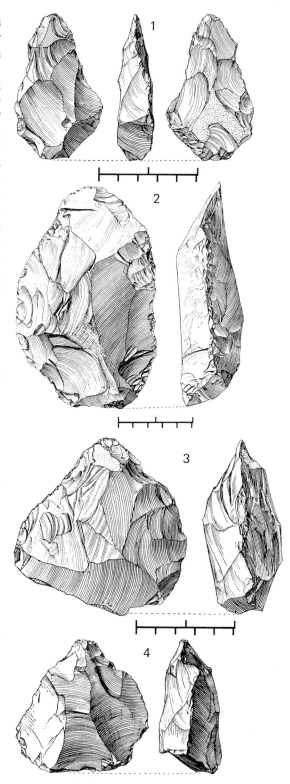

3:11 Artefacts from the Ebbsfleet Channel, after Burchell (1933, 1936b). Four handaxes (nos 1-4), from gravel between the lower and lowermost loams; struck Levalloisian core (no. 5) and four Levalloisian flakes (nos 6-9), from the basal gravel below the lowermost loam (cf. Table 7)

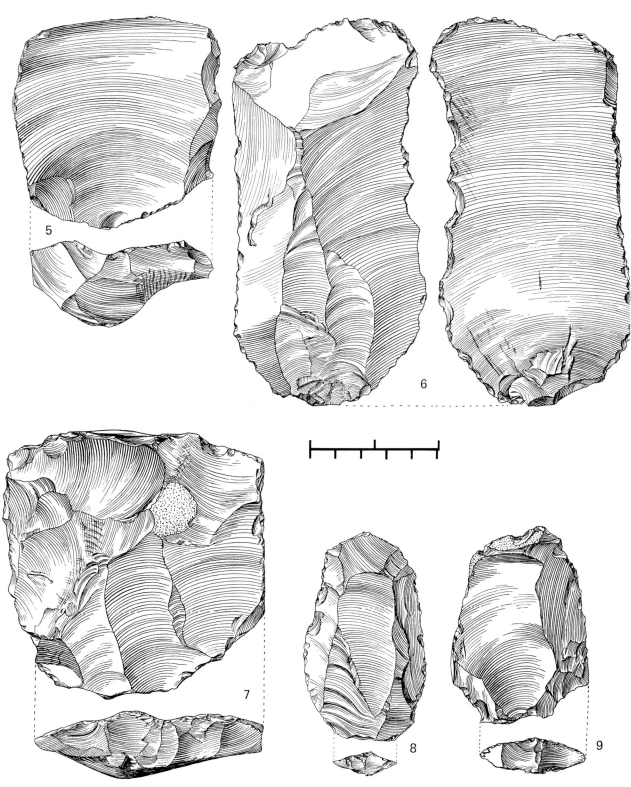

but they can already be seen in the gravels towards the base. Though Burchell often referred to 'floors' at this level, true primary context occurrences do not seem to have been present, though many of the artefacts are fresh and they are probably to be regarded as contemporary with the deposits which contained them. Burchell initially called these artefacts 'Middle Mousterian', just as he called Baker's Hole an 'Early Mousterian' site, but he eventually settled on 'Middle Levalloisian', and this name certainly conveys the part played by the material in our basic sequence well enough. Most of Burchell's cultural attributions should not be taken too seriously in the light of improved knowledge, though they were entirely appropriate at the time when he was writing.

The other thing to note about the artefact collections from the Ebbsfleet Channel is their clear demonstration that handaxe manufacture also survives the Coombe Rock cold phase: several handaxes (Fig. 3:11) are known from the Channel filling (cf. Wymer 1968: 357-9). Amongst them are some pointed types: Burchell called them Micoquian, but there is no solid reason to connect them specifically with the very late stage of hand-axe manufacture represented in level VI of the site of La Micoque, Dordogne, France (the 'Micoquian' type-site). Again, they are likely to be contemporary with the containing deposits, and they

apparently occurred at various levels, notably in the temperate Upper Loam.

The Crayford Brickearths

Crayford, a few miles west of the Ebbsfleet area just discussed, is the last port of call in the search for a basic sequence. The sites there offer a fair degree of confirmation of the observations made by Burchell, and there are tantalizing indications that undisturbed floors of exceptional quality were present, notably when F.C.J. Spurrell[8] collected artefacts there in the 1880's (Spurrell 1880, 1884; Chandler 1916; Kennard 1944; Wymer 1968: 322-6).

At Crayford the sequence[9] begins with a phase of deep erosion which clearly extended down to well below the present level of the Thames, represented by a buried cliff of Thanet Sand and chalk (Fig. 3:12). It was the view of Burchell and others that this downcutting reflects the same major cold phase as was responsible for the deep erosion and the cold deposits that underlie the Ebbsfleet channel series described above. There seems no reason why this correlation should not be correct, even if it is not positively proved. Against the base of the cliff is banked a coarse gravel of uncertain depth, from which just a few derived artefacts have come. The gravel appears

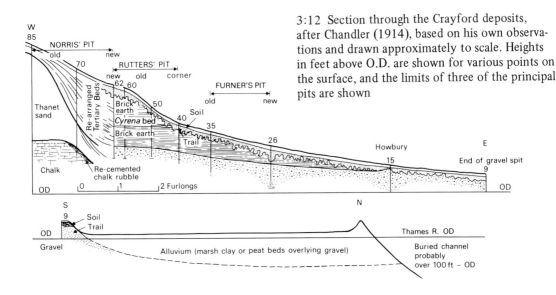

3:12 Section through the Crayford deposits, after Chandler (1914), based on his own observations and drawn approximately to scale. Heights in feet above O.D. are shown for various points on the surface, and the limits of three of the principal pits are shown

to have been deposited by torrential water, perhaps flood-water from the melting of local ice or snow. Overlying the gravel is the famous brickearth series, which comprises a Lower Brickearth, a shell bed and an Upper Brickearth. There is solifluction at the top of the Upper Brickearth.

The Lower Brickearth appears to be a loam, deposited by a slowly moving stream as aggradation probably in response to rising sea-level; the nature and contents of the shell bed suggest a more freely flowing river, while the Upper Brickearth appears to be not so much a fluviatile deposit as an accumulation caused mainly by hill-wash and sludging, probably including material of loessic origin although apparently none of the deposit can be regarded as a true wind-blown loess *in situ*.

It seems clear that a land-surface existed at the top of the gravel, perhaps even for a long period, before the Lower Brickearth began to be deposited.

It was with this land-surface that the principal occurrences of artefacts were associated: Spurrell (see note 8) found numerous flakes, many of which could be conjoined to reconstitute large parts of the original nodules flaked by Palaeolithic man (Plates 23-4 and Fig. 3:13). The industry included the production of 'evolved Levalloisian' flake-blades, which are not at all unlike some of those from the Ebbsfleet Channel. The main floor at Crayford was clearly in primary context, and faunal remains were associated with the artefacts, including the occurrence of a jaw of woolly rhinoceros (*Coelodonta antiquitatis*), lying just above a heap of flint flakes (Plate 24). A few handaxes are also known from Crayford, and at least one fine ovate is claimed as coming from the brickearth, but to the present writer this does not seem an adequate demonstration that it was directly associated with the Levalloisian artefacts, as is sometimes claimed (cf. Kennard 1944:

3:13 Two cores (nos 1, 2) and five flake-blades (nos 3-7) from the Crayford Levalloisian industry, redrawn by M.H.R. Cook (no. 7 after Waterhouse in Watson 1950, the rest after the very poor illustrations in Chandler 1916). The arrows in nos 1, 2 and 3 indicate the directions of major flake removals so far as these can be made out from the original drawings

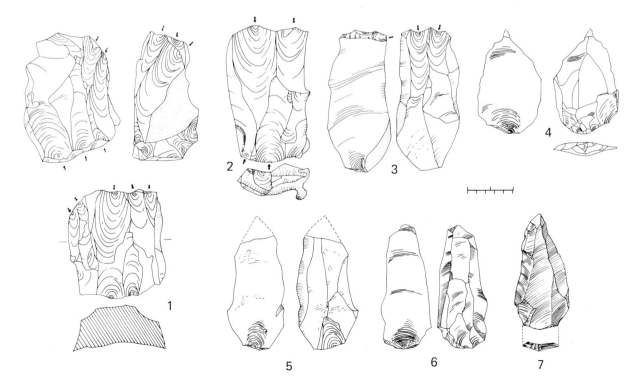

139-40), any more than the handaxes incorporated in the Ebbsfleet Channel fill are properly associated with the Levalloisian artefacts there.

R.H. Chandler (1916) also found conjoinable flakes like those recovered by Spurrell, and at much the same level. It is also certain that isolated artefacts of similar type have been found at higher levels in the Lower Brickearth proper (Kennard, *op. cit.*, 140-2). The Lower Brickearth has produced an immensely rich fauna (see note 7); the area was famous for its faunal remains by the mid-nineteenth century. It is a somewhat curious assemblage, amongst which can be noted frequent mammoth (*Mammuthus primigenius*) but also rare straight-tusked elephant (*Elephas (Palaeoloxodon) antiquus*), frequent woolly rhinoceros (*Coelodonta antiquitatis*) but also occasional steppe rhino (*Dicerorhinus hemitoechus*), horse (*Equus caballus*), steppe wisent, a form of bison (*Bison priscus*), wolf (*Canis lupus*), musk ox (*Ovibos moschatus*), red deer (*Cervus elaphus*), giant deer (called *Cervus euryceros* — an obsolete taxon, referring either to *Megaloceros giganteus* or to a large sub-species of *Cervus elaphus*), ox (*Bos primigenius*) and many others, including several microfaunal species. The full list seems to mix open country and woodland types, quite certainly, and also apparently specialized 'cold' and 'warm' forms. To Kennard[10] there seemed no reason for not regarding it as a reasonable group which represented 'warm temperate conditions, probably warmer than to-day' (*op. cit.*, p. 138); others may find this judgement rather hard to accept, for all Kennard's careful arguments to accommodate such classically 'cold' species as the mammoth, musk ox, woolly rhino and various rodents which we would now regard as distinctively 'northern' types. However, the Lower Brickearth certainly seems to represent a substantial aggradation phase, and the shell bed which crowns it and is generally treated as forming part of it, undoubtedly contains abundant temperate mollusca, including for example *Corbicula fluminalis* and *Belgrandia marginata*, which suggest fully interglacial conditions, presumably those of the Ipswichian. Bones of lemming and other northern rodent types were found in this bed, but they are fragmentary and appear to be derived, while the shells are not

(Kennard, *op. cit.*, p. 127). As regards the mixed appearance of the Lower Brickearth mammalian fauna, it is not by any means clear exactly where each specimen came from, so one could envisage for example deposition starting in cool conditions and proceeding through increasing warmth up to an interglacial maximum in the temperate shell bed: the fauna would span a considerable period during which important changes took place, rather than the less compatible species' having existed at exactly the same time.

The overlying 'Upper Brickearth' contains little or no archaeological material, and faunal remains and shells are also rather sparse there: no clear picture of contemporary conditions emerges, but the convolutions which affected the upper parts of the deposit (called 'trail' in most of the literature) indicate a return to periglacial conditions with solifluction, at some relatively late stage of the deposition, or perhaps subsequently.

It seems fair to suggest that the sequence at Crayford is comparable to that in the Ebbsfleet Valley, if a little less detailed, and that the respective temperate horizons represent the same climatic phase, presumably the Ipswichian maximum. If so, both sequences are also comparable in their archaeology. Both show the use of 'evolved' Levalloisian technique to produce flake-blades; this technique appears sometime after the initial major downcutting, but well before the warm maximum, though its use continues sporadically through the loamy deposits which seem to represent fluviatile aggradation. At both sites well-made handaxes are also occasionally present, not necessarily as part of the 'Levalloisian' industries. There is no sign in the Crayford area, however, of the distinctive 'early Levalloisian' so richly represented at Baker's Hole. This may merely be because there was no particular abundance at Crayford of large nodules of high quality flint to be exploited in such a way.

The basic sequence: summary and conclusions

In the area of north Kent considered in this chapter we can feel reasonably satisfied that the following Palaeolithic industries occur in the following order (the sites named are those already discussed, though there are various other occurrences of similar material in the area at sites where the stratigraphy is less well known):

Industry	Site details
1 *Clactonian*: flakes and cores, without handaxes	Lower Gravels of Barnfield and Rickson's Pits, Swanscombe
2 Flakes and cores, again without evidence for handaxe manufacture, perhaps a continuation of *Clactonian*	Lower Loam at Barnfield Pit, Swanscombe
3 *Acheulian*: a handaxe industry, in this case specializing in pointed handaxes, often with rough butts. Use of Levalloisian technique extremely rare if present at all	Middle Gravels (both parts) at Barnfield Pit, Swanscombe
4 *Acheulian*: a handaxe industry with a preference for flat, well-made ovate handaxes; Levalloisian technique occasionally used, but still rare	Upper Loam at Barnfield Pit, Swanscombe; deposits arguably of similar age at Rickson's Pit, Swanscombe; Bowman's Lodge, Dartford; Pearson's Pit, Dartford and Wansunt Pit, Dartford
5 An industry dominated by use of Levalloisian technique, with large bold flakes and cores in great abundance; a few handaxes possibly, but not certainly, associated	Baker's Hole, Northfleet, on bare freshly-eroded chalk surface, covered and disturbed by Coombe Rock
6 Industries in which an advanced form of Levalloisian technique is employed for the production of neat elongated flakes and flake-blades. Occasional handaxes are present in the same deposits, but whether or not they are associated with the Levalloisian material remains uncertain	Ebbsfleet Channel: sporadic occurrences in the basal gravel overlying the Coombe Rock, and in the succeeding deposits up to the temperate horizon. Also at Crayford: floors on a land surface at the base of the Lower Brickearth, and sporadic occurrences in the Lower Brickearth itself

So far as the period of Pleistocene time which contains this north Kent archaeological sequence is concerned, some uncertainties remain. The Barnfield Pit Lower Gravel lies on a bench at about 75 feet O.D., established presumably before the end of the Anglian, but the Lower Gravel and Lower Loam themselves seem to represent fluviatile aggradation during an interglacial, traditionally regarded as the Hoxnian. However, they are directly overlain at this site by a new cycle of aggradation, the Middle Gravels, on a bench at about 90 feet O.D. which is a far commoner feature in the area; the Middle Gravels fauna is also traditionally regarded as Hoxnian. Yet why should there be two separate cycles in the same interglacial, when the good Hoxnian palaeobotanical sequences in East Anglia suggest an interglacial of no particular complexity and no extra length? Then there is the occurrence of solifluction to be considered, between the top of the Middle Gravels and the base of the succeeding Upper Loam, although the Upper Loam itself has been regarded by some authorities at least as a continuation of the aggradation represented by the Middle Gravels. If one considers this whole rather complicated sequence dispassionately, forgetting the traditional interpretation, it seems inconceivable that everything from the base of the Lower Gravel to the top of the Upper Loam can fall within the same interglacial, namely the Hoxnian. Maybe one or more of the 'extra' climatic events shown in the deep sea core records is to be fitted in here, to expand the British version of the much less complete terrestrial sequence.

There can hardly be a major overlap between the main part of the Barnfield Pit sequence and that of the Ebbsfleet Valley sites, because downcutting from the higher terrace (to which the Middle Gravels at least properly belong, if not some of the other deposits too) had apparently taken place before the Ebbsfleet Valley sequence began. At the new lower level, we see cold conditions giving way to the warmth of a full interglacial: traditionally, this means the Wolstonian followed by the Ipswichian. There is also some evidence at least after the temperate levels for the subsequent Devensian glacial, though without fine detail.

If there is indeed only a single glacial cycle to be fitted in between the warm conditions of the Swanscombe Middle Gravels and the temperate loam of the Ebbsfleet Channel series, then it appears to be one with several definable episodes, though having said that we cannot point to horizons which clearly represent interstadials.[11] Evidently, the geological record needs clarification, and fresh faunal and botanical evidence from some of the key deposits will be required to achieve this. Some of the necessary information will doubtless be forthcoming as work proceeds on the samples taken during the recent excavations at Swanscombe, and a report is also awaited on work carried out by G. de G. Sieveking a few years ago at Baker's Hole and in the Ebbsfleet Valley.

The archaeological sequence derived from the sites considered in this chapter is certainly the best area sequence available in Britain and there is, not surprisingly, a tendency for authors not familiar with the rest of the British Palaeolithic material to treat it as if it comprised the whole, or almost the whole, of the British Lower Palaeolithic. This is far from being the case, as we must now pass on to see in subsequent chapters. The north Kent sequence is a highly important one, but purely local, and the best use we can make of it is to note its contents and ask the following questions:

1 Are there important Lower Palaeolithic stages represented elsewhere in Britain, for which there is no evidence in north Kent?
2 Are there sites in other parts of Britain, demonstrably contemporary with the north Kent ones, which offer good confirmatory evidence for the observations made there?
3 What evidence is there from contemporary sites elsewhere in Britain for industries which differ in minor ways from the north Kent ones — in ways, that is, which do not suggest the presence of entirely different Lower Palaeolithic technological traditions, but indicate shifts of emphasis or particular specializations? In other words, can we say anything about *contemporary* variations amongst the industries of the British Lower Palaeolithic, as opposed to variations which succeed one another as time passes — 'horizontal' as opposed to 'vertical' variability?

By seeking answers to these questions, we may hope to build up the basic sequence established in this chapter into a complete outline of the British Lower Palaeolithic sequence, to which an account of the rather brief Middle Palaeolithic episode can be added separately. Discussion of the palaeo-anthropology of the sites can also be kept as a separate operation from the business of establishing the order of broad stages, which is necessarily mainly concerned with aspects of artefact technology and morphology, and with stratigraphic correlations.

NOTES

1 Wooldridge (1960) has summarized the evidence for earlier courses of the Thames. It is important to note that at Upminster, Essex, Thames gravel on a bench at about 90 feet O.D. actually overlies a deposit of boulder clay laid down by this ice advance (cf. Wymer 1968: 312, 366). Near Finchley the glacial deposits can be shown to be younger than the Winter Hill terrace of the Middle Thames, and the Winter Hill gravels should certainly be a whole stage older than those of the 90-foot terrace of the Swanscombe area.
2 Full lists of the fauna identified from various levels at Barnfield Pit will be found in the sources quoted earlier in this chapter. Among species common in the Lower Gravel which are regarded as typical of the Hoxnian inter-

glacial may be mentioned the straight-tusked elephant *Elephas (Palaeoloxodon) antiquus*, the 'Clacton' fallow deer *Dama clactoniana*, and a particular form of rhinoceros *Dicerorhinus kirchbergensis*, Merck's rhinoceros. These species of elephant and rhino are not absolutely confined to the Hoxnian, but one would not expect to find them so strongly represented in, say, the early Ipswichian, if one found them at all; besides, earlier and later forms can sometimes be distinguished within such species. *Dama clactoniana* apparently does not occur after the Hoxnian at all. Many other mammals are represented in the Lower Gravel, but most of them have an altogether wider distribution in time, for example the ox, *Bos primigenius* and the red deer, *Cervus elaphus*, or the horse *Equus cf. caballus*. All the species mentioned are also reported from the Middle Gravels at Barnfield Pit, though their relative frequency varies. One interesting detail of the Middle Gravels fauna concerns the mollusca: the presence of certain specifically Rhenish forms has been noted, and it has been suggested that the Thames and Rhine may have been directly connected for a while, perhaps during the time interval represented by the weathering of the Lower Loam, or else during the Middle Gravels stage (though this latter alternative would be less easy to imagine, if there were a high sea level at the time). No Rhenish elements were detected in the Lower Gravels molluscan assemblage (Ovey 1964: 75-83; see also Kerney 1971, including a reasoned account of the mollusca right through the sequence).

3 This phrase is carefully chosen: handaxes are not at all the most numerous artefact type in the Acheulian, since vast numbers of waste flakes (all of which count as artefacts, though not as implements) were produced when handaxes were made (cf: Newcomer 1971). Thanks partly to the selectivity of collectors (as opposed to excavators), who did not always think the flakes worth saving, one might get the impression from extant collections that handaxes *were* more numerous than flakes. Also, Acheulian sites where handaxes were merely being used and abandoned, rather than actually being *made*, might on occasion give the same impression.

4 What, indeed, were handaxes *for*? The writer has recently discussed this question (1976), and indicated that there is no easy answer. Analysis of microwear traces is just beginning to provide some evidence in individual cases (cf. Chapter 7), but it is necessary for the artefacts to be in absolutely fresh condition, unweathered and unpatinated: such specimens are extremely rare in Britain. Microwear studies are not effective for all rock types. English flint is certainly a good subject, but the freshness is all important.

5 The 'tranchet finish' technique involves the removal at a late stage of manufacture of a large flat flake from the tip end of a handaxe: the outer edge of the resulting scar provides the implement's cutting edge, which is straight and sharp, and has a bevelled appearance when seen in section. Some handaxes have a *tranchet* flake removed from one face, which gives a single-bevelled edge, while others show a *tranchet* scar on each face and a double-

bevelled edge formed by the intersection of the two *tranchet* scars. A *tranchet* flake needed to be detached with considerable precision, and its striking platform usually needed to be carefully prepared by the maker. The whole technique is very similar to that used by the makers of Mesolithic axes in northern and north-western Europe in the early Holocene to create the original cutting edges of the axes and to re-sharpen them when they became blunt. Indeed, axe-sharpening flakes or re-sharpening flakes are frequent finds on sites of the earlier Mesolithic, including in Britain (cf. Clark, J.G.D. 1954: 114, and Fig. 43). Fig. 5:41 shows a flake of *tranchet* type, refitted to the Lower Palaeolithic handaxe from which it was struck during manufacture at Caddington, Bedfordshire.

The twisted cutting edge feature which is also common in industries of the kind under discussion is puzzling. It is easy enough to reproduce experimentally, but the reason for it is not at all clear, or at least not to the present author. In some evolved Acheulian industries it is found very frequently: towards half the handaxes present may have it (cf. Roe 1968a: 64-7). In other industries of similar age and otherwise similar appearance, it may be totally absent. This suggests that it had some specific function, which is what one would expect, but there is no light on what that function was (cf. note 4). The twist may take the form of an S or a Z when the implement is viewed in profile, but no systematic study of the distribution of each kind seems to have been made. And beware: an S-twist in the side-view may become a Z-twist in an end-on view of the same implement, so a consistent view-point is needed!

6 The following quotation may suggest the quality of the evidence Spurrell observed (1883: 102-3):

> about 20' above O.D. or less, I found a kind of beach, on which lay several *hâches*; they lay, according to the slope, from 5 to 25 feet below the surface . . . Mammoth remains of great size, also those of Rhinoceros, Bos, Bison, Horse, Deer, etc., are found on this spot. Here perfect *hâches* of five distinct kinds and make were obtained, and some unfinished and spoilt examples. I have examined many thousand flakes, and discovered numerous flint hammers, and knapping tools, with which the *hâches* were made, also some elegant slicks or scrapers of peculiar form, oval,

flat on one side and rounded on the other. Of the hammers some were pointed, and some flat headed, being 'used' at the edges of the 'face'. A number of flakes, mostly flat, and thin, and hollow on one side, varying in weight from 1 oz. to 8 lbs., were also found; the method of using them resembled that of the bricklayer's trowel.

Spurrell goes on to describe and give the dimensions of a few implements, though he does not, unfortunately, illustrate any of them. In describing the final item, he gives a fascinating early appreciation of Levalloisian technique, and implies that some of the Levalloisian flakes were being worked into bifacial handaxes, since this is what he appears to mean by *hâche* (the term handaxe was not in common use as early as 1883, and he specifically refers to handaxes illustrated by J. Evans as *hâches*) (*op. cit.*, p. 103):

4.0 x 2.8 x 0.9. This *hâche* was thus made: a mass of flint was trimmed from the sides, and worked roughly into a rounded form at the top. This worked part was then detached at a single blow (by the pointed hammers mentioned above), leaving a turtle-back flake; when trimmed on one side only, such a flake was used as a scraper or slick; when trimmed on both sides, and worked to a point, it became a *hâche*.

7   There is inevitably some confusion about translating the early attributions of the faunal remains to species into modern terminology, not least with mammoth and rhinoceros, for which terms like *Elephas primigenius* and *Rhinoceros antiquitatis* were used, which are not now regarded as correct. For the mammoth, for example, it is important to distinguish between the steppe form *Mammuthus trogontherii* and the woolly mammoth *Mammuthus primigenius*, and there were early and late forms of each of these. So a reference in the earlier literature to *Elephas primigenius* ought not to be thought of as necessarily implying the kind of woolly mammoth known during the last glaciation. Exactly which species, in what stage of its internal evolution, was present at some of these sites may be of critical importance in connection with chronology, and this information is not necessarily available. In this book the old names have been translated where possible into the correct modern forms, but the accuracy of the old identifications is not thereby guaranteed. The writer is grateful

to Mr S.N. Collcutt for expert advice on the correct nomenclature.

8   Spurrell gave various brief accounts of his discoveries at Crayford (see annotated bibliography in Kennard 1944), and the following quotations are taken from the paper he read to the Geological Society of London on June 23, 1880 when exhibiting some of his finds to a distinguished audience (Spurrell 1880: 544-6):

at the base of this section is a step in the chalk cliff, and a sort of foreshore seems to have been formed, consisting here of hard sand, and there of small heaps of flint stones brought down from the cliff above by aerial action. It is on one of these small slopes of sand that the layer of flakes was found. The uppermost edge of the area covered by them is about thirty-six feet from the present surface, the lowest nearly six feet lower. This area is thickly covered with chips for the space of about ten feet north and south, and, as far as I know at present, fifteen feet east and west, or parallel to the cliff: but I expect that it will be found to extend further.

The fragments of flint lay touching each other, in parts to a thickness of several inches, and had fallen so lightly that in several places there were minute cavities underneath the mass of larger and flatter flakes. . . .

Though the workman had abundance of material to work on, he seems to have found the flints very obstinate, as may be seen from the difficulty he had in procuring good heart pieces of flint and the patient way he chipped away the outside.

That he worked on the spot is evident. As I noticed before, the flakes lie lightly on each other; they are perfectly free from the slightest abrasion such as must have occurred had the edges rubbed over each other by the action of water; they did not fall from the cliff into the water, for occasionally long flakes broken in two have been seen, which could not have occurred had water intervened; and notably one large flake was found by me, the broken ends facing each other as at the moment it fell and broke! A few small concretions remain on the opposed faces to show that the fracture was previous to the discovery and not due to accident since. . . .

The bones with which these traces of man are associated are those of the brickearth of Crayford in general . . . but one specimen, which was found a few inches over the flints, is worthy of notice, being part of the distal end of the lower jaw of *Rhinoceros tichorhinus* [more properly, *Coelodonta antiquitatis*], with four milk teeth and the thin alveolar edges of the recently shed outer incisors uncrushed. The rest of that row of teeth were afterwards found about 18 inches off the first, the ends of the jaw having been rounded. From the body of the jaw had been extracted one uncut tooth of the coming series, which lay about a foot from the last; numerous splinters of the large bones lay around, and suggested their having been broken for food.

These extracts may suggest the archaeological potential of Spurrell's discovery in modern terms, though none of the site, alas, remains. They also show how acute an observer Spurrell was, bearing in mind the date at which he was working.

9   It is generally agreed that the sequence of Pleistocene deposits was uniform over the area, though exposed at various times in several different brick-pits. The exact location of the earlier finds in terms of the later pit names is by no means clear (cf. Kennard 1944: 122-5). Stoneham's Pit, at the Crayford end rather than the Erith end of the deposits, was probably the major source of artefacts, with the westernmost of Rutter's pits the next most important.

10   Kennard first observed the sections at Crayford as early as 1892. His account written and published over fifty years later (1944) is a contribution of the highest quality to the literature of the sites. It includes a long bibliography with comments on the value and content of many of the works cited.

11   Some of the problems may well relate to what we at present call the Ipswichian interglacial. A.J. Sutcliffe has recently (1975, 1976) expressed the opinion that there are too many distinct mammalian assemblages attributed to the Ipswichian to be accommodated within a single interglacial. Various authors at various times, including Zeuner, have argued for two distinct temperate phases with a cool interval between them, and the Lower Thames terrace sequence has also been interpreted as showing two separate terraces ('Taplow' and 'Upper Floodplain') at different heights but both of Ipswichian age. The palaeobotanical evidence however does not at present seem easy to reconcile with the idea of two distinct warm phases. Further research is clearly needed.

Expanding the Basic Sequence

Chapter 4

The purpose of this chapter is to consider whether there are important Lower Palaeolithic episodes or stages which are not represented in the basic north Kent sequence already described. We are not here concerned with the existence of marginally different industries that may have been current elsewhere in Britain while the Acheulian of Swanscombe or the Levalloisian of the Ebbsfleet Valley and Crayford were being made — that will be considered later on. At present we are simply enquiring whether, by concentrating on north Kent, we may have missed important evidence that might enable us to extend the sequence backwards or forwards in time.

It will be recalled that the basic Lower Palaeolithic sequence outlined in the previous chapter appeared to begin at the close of the Anglian glaciation, with a Clactonian industry. The first stages of handaxe manufacture came later (Middle Gravels at Barnfield Pit) in an industry which was not particularly archaic in appearance since the handaxes, especially their fine pointed tips, were often made with considerable skill. From these facts certain obvious questions immediately arise for discussion. First, are there any British industries demonstrably older than those at the base of the Swanscombe sequence? Second, is the Clactonian indeed the earliest Lower Palaeolithic tradition to reach Britain, as the Swanscombe evidence suggests? Third, are there Acheulian industries in Britain which are older than the first occurrence of handaxes at Barnfield

Pit, or does the Acheulian in Britain really begin at a relatively advanced stage, technologically speaking? These questions are considered together in the first part of this chapter: in simple terms, we are looking in the first instance for Lower Palaeolithic occurrences with any evidence for a date older than the close of the Anglian, and for handaxe industries of initial Hoxnian or pre-Hoxnian age. A map of the sites mentioned in the present chapter is given in Fig. 4:1.

After the base of the sequence has been discussed from these points of view, attention must be turned to the other end of it. We saw that the Barnfield Pit Middle Gravels Acheulian was followed by industries with finely made ovate handaxes, and we noted from sporadic finds that handaxes remained current in north Kent later still. In the second part of this chapter we must ask whether there are any major Acheulian sites elsewhere in Britain that can offer a clearer picture of the nature and age of the youngest British Lower Palaeolithic handaxe industries.

EARLY INDUSTRIES, ACTUAL AND POSSIBLE

(a) *Westbury sub Mendip, Somerset*

This site is a comparatively recent addition to the British Lower Palaeolithic (Bishop, M.J. 1974, 1975), and an important one. Most unfortunately the deposits were revealed in a dangerous working face of a limestone quarry, and large amounts of them, almost certainly including the most crucial

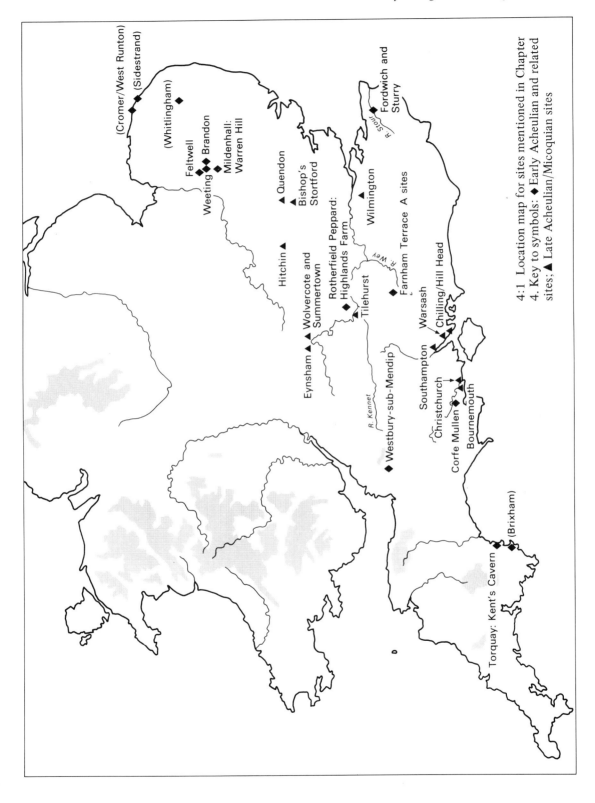

4:1 Location map for sites mentioned in Chapter
4. Key to symbols: ◆ Early Acheulian and related
sites; ▲ Late Acheulian/Micoquian sites

areas, have been destroyed. The conditions of the find made full-scale scientific excavation virtually impossible (Plate 25).

The deposits (Fig. 4:2 and Plate 25) fill a large fissure in the Carboniferous Limestone, which seems to have been part of a cavern system. The fissure filling has been divided into a lower 'Siliceous Group' and an upper 'Calcareous Group' of sediments. The former apparently consists of waterlaid material (sands, silts and gravels), while the latter includes breccias and conglomerates, well stratified in places, which must have formed under cave conditions. Faunal remains occur throughout the sequence; they are sparse and fragmentary in the Siliceous Group, but in the Calcareous Group they are abundant and well preserved. The fauna is clearly of late lower Pleistocene (Siliceous Group) to early Middle Pleistocene (Calcareous Group) age, in terms of Table 1. The fauna of the Calcareous Group includes such characteristic Cromerian or epi-Cromerian species as the bear *Ursus deningeri*, the wolf *Canis lupus mosbachensis*, the rhinoceros *Dicerorhinus etruscus*, the horse *Equus mosbachensis* and the dhole *Xenocyon lycaonides*. *Homotherium latidens* (a scimitar-tooth cat) is also present. Among the microfauna, the vole *Pliomys episcopalis* and the desman *Desmana moschata* are examples of species which should be pre-Hoxnian in Britain. *Pitymys gregaloides* and *Arvicola cantiana* are also present. The micro-faunal remains are abundant and in good condition, notably from the Rodent Earth, a dark red-brown earthy deposit in the Calcareous Group, rich in small mammal and rodent remains. While such a faunal assemblage, viewed overall, need not belong unequivocally to the full Cromerian interglacial, it must certainly be pre-Hoxnian, so we can call it 'inter-Anglian or earlier'. In due course, there may be other lines of evidence to help fix its age more precisely — radiometric dating of stalagmite, or pollen analysis, for example.

We are surely, however, dealing at Westbury with a site that is earlier than the base of the Swanscombe sequence. Several of the layers of the Calcareous Group produced pieces of flint, and there are undoubtedly a few artefacts among

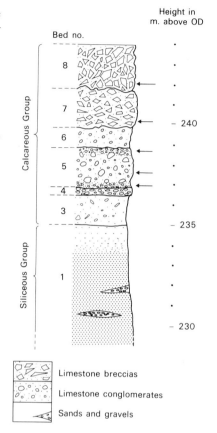

4:2 Section through the Pleistocene deposits at Westbury-sub-Mendip as exposed up to 1974, after M.J. Bishop (1975). The arrows indicate the vertical position of finds of flints

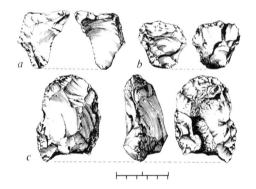

4:3 Three flints from the Westbury-sub-Mendip Calcareous Group with probable artificial flaking, after M.J. Bishop (1975): (a) possible trimming flake, from Bed 5; (b) and (c) bifacially flaked pieces from Beds 5 and 8 respectively

them, including two which are bifacially worked and at least one good flake which is most unlikely to be the work of nature (Fig. 4:3). There may well be more artefacts than these, because most of the flint is in a thoroughly rotted and crumbly state, and though the existence of scars on the surfaces can be detected, their nature cannot be assessed. Flint does not occur naturally in the local limestone rock. It is also worth nothing that the sediment samples taken for pollen analysis proved to contain abundant flecks of charcoal (Bishop, M.J. 1975: 96); this could be explained in various ways, of which the nearby presence of a human occupation site at which fire was used, perhaps near the cave mouth, would certainly be one.

The artefacts are too few in number, and in too poor condition, to be clearly diagnostic. That two of them are bifacially worked might incline one to think of Acheulian as opposed to Clactonian technology, but the present writer could not feel when he examined them that either was necessarily a complete or typical handaxe, or even a fragment of one, as opposed to, say, some kind of bifacially worked chopper. It can only be hoped that more flints may turn up as the remains of the site continue to be explored. The deposits do apparently continue beyond the quarry area, but the extension probably runs away from the direction of the vanished cave mouth, and hence, one would suspect, away from the occupied area.

(b) *Kent's Cavern, Torquay, Devonshire*

This cave (Plate 3) has already been referred to for its historical importance as one of the earliest examples of excavation at a British Palaeolithic site (see pages 20-3). It has long been appreciated that more than one Palaeolithic stage was represented there, since typical Upper Palaeolithic flints and bone work, as well as handaxes, were found by Pengelly and others. A fine series of woodcut illustrations of them was published by Sir John Evans in the first edition (1872) of his *Ancient Stone Implements* (cf. his figures 386-408): his commentary on the finds (*op. cit.*, pp. 442-66) allows for the artefacts' belonging to various different Palaeolithic 'ages'. Confusion has certainly existed, however, about the relationship of the handaxes to the deposits, masking the presence at the cave of what may well be one of the earliest handaxe industries in Europe, to which attention has recently been drawn by J.B. Campbell (Campbell and Sampson, 1971). It is only fair to remark that this confusion was not of Pengelly's making, except in so far as fuller publication of his own extremely careful work at the site might perhaps have avoided it.[1]

The main elements of the stratigraphy at Kent's Cavern can be summarized as shown in Table 8 (mainly using Pengelly's original names for the layers).

TABLE 8 : *Main components of the sequence at Kent's Cavern*

Black Mould, capped by broken limestone blocks and smaller fragments, up to 1 foot thick: Holocene, recent, disturbed

Granular stalagmite, 1 to 5 feet thick, containing limestone fragments: early Holocene

Cave Earth, reddish in colour, divisible (following Campbell and Sampson) into an upper stony part (0 to 6 feet thick, with frequent angular fragments of limestone in a sand/clay matrix) and a lower loamy part (0 to 30 feet thick, with much less frequent limestone fragments which are sometimes rounded, the matrix being similar). In the upper (stony) part of the Cave Earth, a *Black Band* was noted in one part of the cave: it seems to have consisted of a concentration of hearths and occupation debris, and some soil, and was up to 6 inches thick in places. The whole of the Cave Earth seems to be of Upper Pleistocene age

Deposits below the Cave Earth (?Middle Pleistocene and perhaps earlier). These vary considerably in different parts of the cave, and the underlying bedrock — Devonian Limestone — clearly has a most uneven surface. In places the Cave Earth rests directly on it, while elsewhere a considerable depth of other deposits intervenes. In these areas, the deposits below the Cave Earth include some or all of the following:

Crystalline Stalagmite (flowstone), only localized patches, immediately beneath the Cave Earth, but up to 12 feet thick in places where it fills hollows

Breccia, consisting of some angular and some rounded limestone fragments, cemented into

a dark red matrix of sand and silt; up to
9 feet thick in places

Red Sand (uncemented), apparently washed
into the cave from outside; up to 10 feet
thick in places, but usually much less

(Older) Crystalline Stalagmite, localized
occurrences, represented mainly by derived
fragments incorporated into the breccia or by
traces adhering to the cave walls; original
thickness not known

Sands and Silts, laminated in places, localized
occurrences, only rarely seen. Thickness
not known

Note

It will be apparent from the above list that the
stratigraphy at Kent's Cavern is extremely
variable: it must be recalled that the cavern is not
a simple cave, but a substantial cavern system in
the limestone, with several chambers connected by
passages and galleries. The artefacts came from
several parts of the system.

So far as the archaeological material is concerned, the 'Black Mould' produced various later
prehistoric and recent artefacts, from Mesolithic
to Medieval, and some Mesolithic and Neolithic
material is recorded from the granular stalagmite,
but these upper levels do not concern us. Buckland,
as we saw earlier, had refused to believe MacEnery's
reports of artefacts *in situ* in the Cave Earth under
the stalagmite, but their presence there had been
amply proved by Pengelly even before 1860 and
his later work at the site showed that they were
not merely present but abundant, especially in the
'Black Band' area; this information J. Evans
accepted without question in his 1872 account
already referred to, also making it clear (in the
terminology of the time) that the Cave Earth
included both blade-tools of Upper Palaeolithic
type, and characteristic Mousterian handaxes
and flake-tools of Middle Palaeolithic age. Evans
did not refer in this work to the deposits below
the Cave Earth, of which little was then known,
and comparatively few writers in more recent
years seem to have understood that artefacts also
occurred *in situ* in these older deposits, or to have
realized their significance. This is curious, since
Pengelly in his manuscript notes (1865-80) made
it abundantly clear that artefacts were certainly
found in the breccia, and he faithfully recorded
their positions in considerable detail (Campbell

and Sampson 1971: 6-7). He did also publish the
fact that the breccia contained artefacts (e.g.
Pengelly 1873a, b) and Evans quoted him accordingly in the second edition of *Ancient Stone
Implements* (1897: 495); so did Boyd Dawkins in
his *Cave Hunting* and *Early Man in Britain* (1874:
328-9; 1880: 194-5).

One source of confusion therefore about the
age of the Kent's Cavern artefacts is the unjustifiable assumption, which has passed into some of
the literature with the status of a fact, that all the
Palaeolithic material occurred in the Cave Earth
of Upper Pleistocene age. But confusion has also
arisen from a second source, namely misunderstanding of the breccia itself and of its place in
the sequence. Derived blocks of the breccia were
found *within* the lower parts of the Cave Earth,
and this has caused some writers to suppose that
the breccia was brought into the cave from outside
(Campbell and Sampson 1971: 19), presumably
through swallow holes or lost entrances, rather
than having formed inside the cave. Campbell and
Sampson point out what actually happened (*op.
cit.*, p. 10): there was an important period of
erosion after the formation of the stalagmite that
locally overlies the *in situ* breccia, and this erosion
cut deeply into the breccia itself, breaking up and
removing a fair amount of it. In places the hard
stalagmite resisted the erosive agent – doubtless
rushing water – which therefore passed beneath it,
with the striking result that in those places the
thick stalagmite floor has sometimes been left in
place suspended over a substantial air gap where
the deposits below had been eroded away.[2] But,
as the stalagmite was breached in places, and may
anyhow never have completely sealed in the
underlying deposits, the way was open for detached
blocks of the breccia to be redeposited above it
and thus to become incorporated in the base of
the Cave Earth, which began to form sometime
after the phase of erosion has ceased. Other pieces
seem to have fallen into it from the cave walls
during deposition. These blocks of breccia contained both animal bones and a few artefacts,
which were of course much older than the Cave
Earth itself, but found their way into it in this
way.

So far as the artefacts belonging to the breccia

are concerned, there is yet a third source of confusion in their physical condition (Campbell and Sampson, *op. cit.*, p. 19). Their surfaces have undergone profound chemical alteration which past writers have sometimes mistaken for physical abrasion during transport and have used as evidence to support the notion that these artefacts were brought into the cave by natural means (e.g. Smith, R.A. 1926: 71). But since they are not actually abraded, there is no reason to suppose that they reached the cave other than by the hand of man.[3]

The contribution of Campbell and Sampson thus gives overdue support in modern terms to Pengelly's forgotten original observation that some of the Kent's Cavern Lower Palaeolithic artefacts came from the breccia, which means of course that they were contemporary with the deposit of sand and scree that became brecciated. It should be emphasized that Pengelly's diary and publications (1865-80, 1873a, b) confirm that artefacts were found *in situ* in undisturbed breccia in several areas of the cavern, as well as in the redeposited breccia masses; traces of breccia, incidentally, still adhere to some of the surviving artefacts. Campbell also indicates that a few artefacts may have come from the Red Sand, which underlies the breccia itself.

It seems therefore entirely reasonable for us to accept here that, at Kent's Cavern, Palaeolithic artefacts occurred in the breccia below the Cave Earth; noting accordingly that they are stratigraphically older than the Upper Palaeolithic and Mousterian occurrences at the site, we must next consider their nature and then such evidence as there is for the age of the breccia itself.

A selection of the artefacts in question, from the collections at the Museum of the Torquay Natural History Society, is shown in Fig. 4:4. A few others of generally similar character are at the British Museum and the Natural History Museum. Campbell (*op. cit.*, pp. 17-23), using information in the Pengelly manuscripts, was able to identify twenty-seven surviving artefacts in all,[4] which he was satisfied came from the breccia, though Pengelly recorded the finding of no less than 116 in that deposit between 1872 and 1880. Among Campbell's twenty-seven were fourteen handaxes,

a chopper, a possible crude cleaver, a unifacial chopping tool, a core and nine miscellaneous flakes. These are a small enough number of artefacts upon which to pronounce, but the handaxes undeniably have an archaic look about them, in their rather asymmetrical shapes, in the thickness of their sections, and in the general crudeness of their flaking, with few scars and no clear evidence of 'soft hammer' work. In these respects the Kent's Cavern industry would appear rougher than any of the handaxe industries of the Swanscombe area discussed in the previous chapter. The chopper (Fig. 4:4 no. 1) is an interesting piece, though one must not make too much of a single specimen: simple choppers of this kind are not common in the English Lower Palaeolithic, though they are a regular part of 'Early Acheulian' industries in other parts of the world, such as Biberson's 'Acheulian I' and 'Acheulian II' from the marine conglomerates of Maarifian age at the Sidi Abderrahman Quarry original and extension sites, Casablanca, Morocco (Biberson 1961: 120-55), or the Acheulian of Early Middle Pleistocene age from 'Ubeidiya, Israel (Stekelis 1966; Stekelis *et al.* 1969; Bar-Yosef 1975), or at some of the Early Acheulian sites in Middle Bed II of Olduvai Gorge, of which EF-HR is the best (M.D. Leakey 1971, 1976). Somewhat nearer at hand, at Terra Amata, Nice, industries dated by their excavator, H. de Lumley, as of Mindel age also include a few handaxes and cleavers as well as choppers: only brief accounts of them have yet been published (de Lumley 1969a, 1969b: 140-3; 1975: 761-70).

In short, if the Kent's Cavern artefacts from the breccia are indeed the remnants of an Early Acheulian industry, then their typology and technology are very much what one would be led to expect, not merely by making a facile equation between crudeness of the handaxes and high antiquity on purely theoretical grounds, but by observing that those handaxe industries which are known on geological evidence to be early – like the occurrences cited in the preceding paragraph, which are by no means a complete list – are undoubtedly dominated by thick, heavy, rather irregular implements, flaked in an unsophisticated manner, while the numerous demonstrably younger

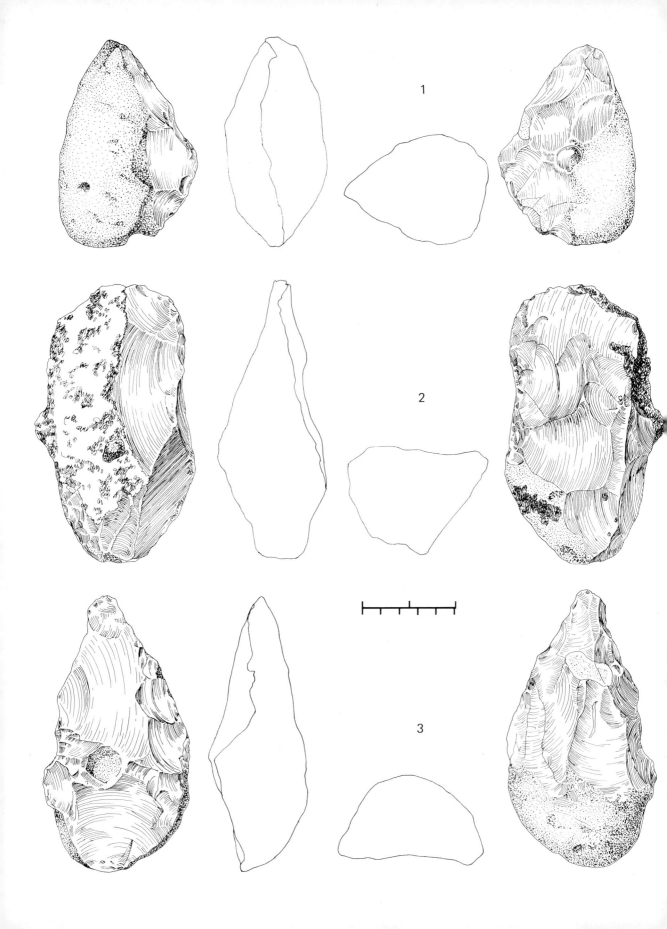

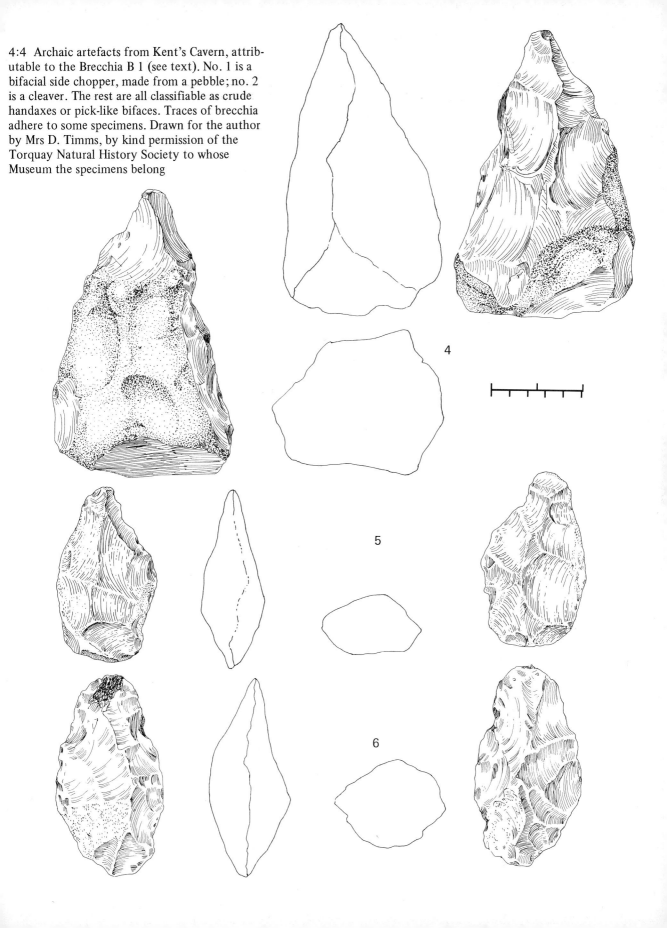

4:4 Archaic artefacts from Kent's Cavern, attributable to the Brecchia B 1 (see text). No. 1 is a bifacial side chopper, made from a pebble; no. 2 is a cleaver. The rest are all classifiable as crude handaxes or pick-like bifaces. Traces of brecchia adhere to some specimens. Drawn for the author by Mrs D. Timms, by kind permission of the Torquay Natural History Society to whose Museum the specimens belong

4

5

6

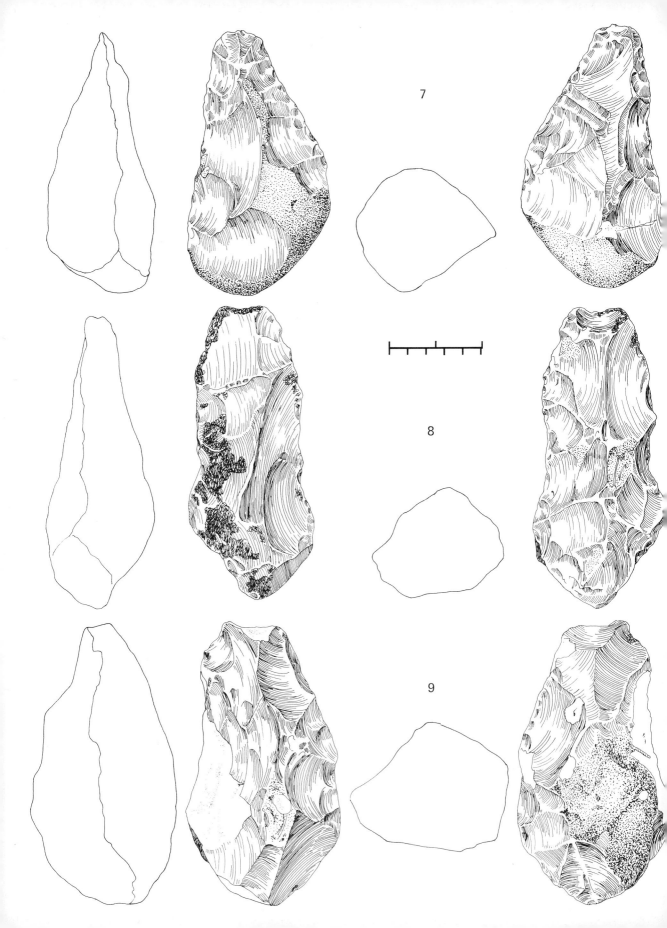

7

8

9

industries from the same areas show a majority of flatter, symmetrical, finely-flaked handaxes.

In addition to these considerations, there is at least some independent suggestion that the Kent's Cavern breccia itself is a deposit of — by the standards of British caves — high antiquity. The nature of the strata at the site, and the geological sequence, suggest that the breccia should be a good deal older than the Cave Earth, and the physical condition of the implements from the breccia perhaps supports this, being very different from that of the Middle and Upper Palaeolithic artefacts. The fauna of the breccia is dominated by bear, *Ursus deningeri* (thought it has often been described as *Ursus spelaeus*). Campbell (*op. cit.*, pp. 13-16, 22) was able to attribute to the breccia a few other examples of archaic species: the scimitar tooth cat *Homotherium latidens*, and the rodents *Pitymys gregaloides* and *Arvicola greeni*, synonymous with *A. cantiana*. Most, if not all, of the archaic specimens were unfortunately found at the base of the Cave Earth where, as we have already noted, detached blocks of the breccia occurred in a secondary position, but those three species can hardly belong to the Cave Earth itself. The misunderstanding of the stratigraphy which caused confusion over the artefacts discovered at this level also affected the interpretation of the fauna, so that several writers have concluded that in Britain *Homotherium latidens* survived into the Early Devensian — a most unlikely situation, since elsewhere in Europe it is rarely found after the Cromerian.[5] On this somewhat slender basis of the stratigraphic succession and the faunal attributions, a late Cromerian or inter-Anglian date might tentatively be suggested for the Kent's Cavern breccia and hence for the archaic-looking handaxes found in it: if this were correct, they would be of broadly the same age as the finds at Westbury, and substantially older than the Swanscombe Middle Gravels Acheulian of our basic sequence. Indeed, the existence of the Westbury occurrence makes this reading of the Kent's Cavern evidence somewhat more acceptable. It will be noted that all the faunal species named in this paragraph also occurred at Westbury. Both sites, by reason of the very different circumstances of their discovery and

exploration, leave much to be desired. At Kent's Cavern it seems likely, however, that much of the breccia may remain in place, and it is to be hoped that this crucial deposit can one day be re-examined. But the cave to-day is a highly lucrative tourist attraction, visited mainly for its stalactite formations, and at the time of writing it is not available for excavation.

(c) *The Windmill Cave, Brixham, Devonshire*

In passing, at this point, we may briefly take note of another famous cave explored by Pengelly (cf. page 23), which produced much less in the way of artefacts[6] than Kent's Cavern, and of which little has been written: the Windmill Cave at Brixham, a few miles along the coast from Kent's Cavern itself. It is just worth mentioning the presence there of at least one crude bifacial implement, pretty comparable to those from the Kent's Cavern breccia (Sir John Evans 1897: 512-6; see his fig. 409. Evans lists the other early references). In the Brixham cave the excavated strata consisted of stalagmite, overlying Cave Earth, which itself overlay gravel, with bedrock below; but there were signs of a more complex stratigraphy than this, since the apparent roof of the cave was found to consist in fact of a suspended stalagmite sheet like that noted at Kent's Cavern (see above): clearly there had been erosion of former deposits, followed by partial refilling of the cave, and a long period of time in all may have been involved. The present writer would not wish to make much of the one archaic-looking Brixham implement, and it would certainly be difficult to produce good evidence to show that it was actually of high antiquity. However, since the opinions of Pengelly and his distinguished contemporaries seem to have been largely vindicated at Kent's Cavern, it is worth quoting Boyd Dawkins' opinion of it (1880: 197):

An implement of the River-drift type . . . has been discovered in the famous cave at Brixham, explored also under the superintendence of Mr. Pengelly. And it may most probably be referred to the same early stage as those from the breccia in Kent's Hole.

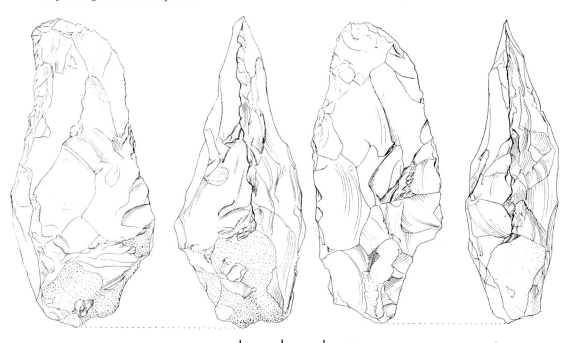

4:5 Three crude handaxes from Fordwich, Kent,
after R.A. Smith (1933)

(d) *Fordwich, Kent*

We now leave the caves and fissures of south-west
England for three sites in the gravels of the south
and east which have produced handaxe industries
of archaic appearance. The first is at Fordwich
near Canterbury in the valley of the Kentish Stour.
The relevant points about this occurrence can be
summarized quite simply:

1 The containing deposit is a high terrace gravel
   of the Kentish Stour: there are various Stour
   terraces, and this is the earliest one of the
   series to yield artefacts, which it did at both
   the Fordwich and Stonerocks pits (Dewey
   and Smith 1924: 134).

2 There were several hundred artefacts (Smith,
   R.A. 1933), though various misfortunes have
   reduced the surviving material to around 200
   handaxes and a few flakes (Roe 1968a: 7,
   14-15). Even so, this is a fair quantity of
   extant artefacts, which gives some weight to
   the observation that the series is
   overwhelmingly dominated by thick, crude
   archaic implements with little trace of
   advanced flaking techniques (Fig. 4:5).

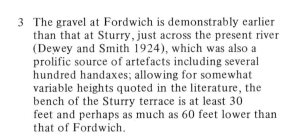

3 The gravel at Fordwich is demonstrably earlier
   than that at Sturry, just across the present river
   (Dewey and Smith 1924), which was also a
   prolific source of artefacts including several
   hundred handaxes; allowing for somewhat
   variable heights quoted in the literature, the
   bench of the Sturry terrace is at least 30
   feet and perhaps as much as 60 feet lower than
   that of Fordwich.

4   The Sturry implements are also of quite a different character: they include a mixture of industries, with some evidence, summarized by Dewey and Smith (*op. cit.*), that the different types occurred at different levels in the deposits. Well made ovates, with abundant soft hammer work and sometimes with twisted cutting edges are common (*op. cit.*, figs 5, 6, 9, 15-20); ficrons occur, not at all unlike those of the Swanscombe Middle Gravels (*op. cit.*, fig. 26). There are various other types of handaxe present, but it is notable that those which resemble the archaic Fordwich handaxes just described are almost always abraded, while the other material is generally fresh.

So far as the contents of the Sturry gravels are concerned, Dewey and Smith regarded the abraded archaic handaxes, which they attributed in the terminology of the time to the (pre-Acheulian) Chelles period, as derived from older deposits, while they considered the other material to be generally contemporary with the formation of the Sturry deposits, or only slightly earlier. According to the careful and systematic observations of Dr A.G. Ince, who lived close to the pits and watched the sections, especially those in Homersham's West Pit, over several years, the 'derived Chelles hand-axes' came mainly from near the top of the main gravels and sands, below the overlying brickearth (see Fig. 4:6). Dewey and Smith described clear indications of disturbance to the deposits at this level, including the incorporation into the main mass of the gravel of 'rafts' of earlier deposits. From their now soft nature, and the odd angles at which they sometimes occurred, it was clear that these masses must have been transported and injected into the gravel in a frozen state during periglacial conditions (*op. cit.*, pp. 120-1).

There is thus clearly a mechanism by which archaic artefacts from the Fordwich high terrace could have found their way down the slope of the valley side to become incorporated in the top of the gravel on the lower and younger Sturry terrace, which already contained implements of its own. Exactly when this mechanism operated does not greatly matter. We can only say that the redeposition of these artefacts from the higher terrace, reflected in their abraded condition (except those found actually within the rafted masses, which had remained pretty fresh), must have taken place

in a period of periglacial activity later than the aggradation of gravel on the Sturry terrace — the lowest metre at least of the Sturry gravel is certainly an aggraded fluviatile deposit. The periglacial phase in question could have belonged within the Wolstonian or even the Devensian.

A case can thus certainly be made out from the foregoing information for supposing that the high terrace at Fordwich contained an assemblage of handaxes dominated by archaic forms, which at Sturry were only found in a derived state, and that the archaic assemblage is indeed a whole stage earlier than gravels whose artefacts include hand-axes generally similar to those of the Middle Gravels and Upper Loam at Swanscombe. The unfortunate thing is that there seems to be no other direct dating evidence for the Fordwich gravels in the way of faunal or floral remains. Can these perhaps be obtained in future exposures? Meanwhile we have only the archaic appearance of the implements, and the substantially higher altitude of the gravels (130 to 150 feet above O.D., with the Stour here only a few feet above present sea level) than the Sturry terrace to guide us — suggestive circumstantial evidence, but *not* conclusive, in a situation where firm proof is particularly important.

That the Fordwich handaxes appear archaic is not merely an empty assertion repeated by the present writer. In a comparison of 38 British handaxe assemblages by metrical and statistical methods (1968a) he was able to demonstrate in fairly precise quantitative terms how thick, narrow and crudely made these implements were, and how scarce amongst them were the elegant and regular specialized forms of the later stages of the Acheulian. For example, the ratio thickness/breadth gives some idea of the thickness or flatness of a handaxe viewed in cross-section (Roe 1964: fig. 9), higher values indicating thicker implements. Table 9 shows the figures obtained for some of the sites.

Drawings of three handaxes from Fordwich are shown in Fig. 4:5, and may give some idea of the archaic appearance of the industry: they are by no means the crudest from the site. The thickness of section should be noted, and so should the rather low number of flake scars, the lack of typical

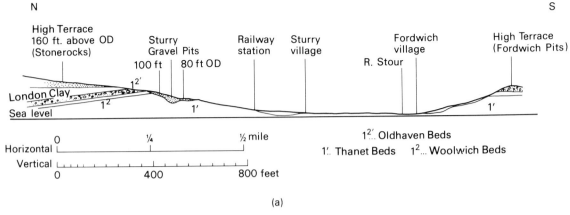

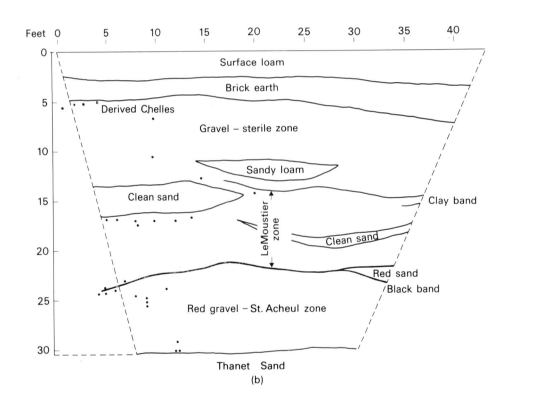

4:6 Sturry, Kent: sections, after Dewey and
Smith (1924). (a) Section across the Stour Valley,
showing heights of deposits and locations of pits;
(b) section at Homersham's West Pit, Sturry, the
dots showing positions of implements as noted
by Dr Ince

TABLE 9 : *Mean values for the ratio thickness/breadth: selected British handaxe assemblages*

Site	Sample size	Classification	Mean	Standard deviation
Oldbury	31	Mousterian of Acheulian Tradition, probably of Devensian age, see pp. 182-3	0.41	0.07
Corfe Mullen	45	Refined ovate handaxes, evolved Acheulian, see pp. 189-90	0.42	0.08
Swanscombe Upper Loam	18	Acheulian dominated by ovate forms, see pp. 76-8	0.47	0.11
Bowman's Lodge	30	Acheulian ovate handaxes, similar to last, see pp. 78, 178	0.48	0.09
Swanscombe Middle Gravels	159	'Middle Acheulian' pointed handaxes, see pp. 72-6	0.55	0.12
Wolvercote	47	Evolved Acheulian industry of plano-convex pointed handaxes, see pp. 118-27	0.56	0.12
Baker's Farm	239	'Middle Acheulian' with large pointed handaxes and cleavers, see pp. 164-8	0.58	0.11
Fordwich	194	Proposed as Early Acheulian	0.69	0.17

Note

A table with figures for all the 38 assemblages will be found in Roe 1968a: 27-8, but the full range is in fact indicated here in that Oldbury gave the lowest mean value of all and Fordwich the highest. 'T-tests' were also carried out to enable the various figures to be compared, and these showed that the Fordwich figures differed 'significantly' from all the rest, the t-values obtained ranging from 4.2 to 20.9.

'soft-hammer' flake removals, and the meandering nature of the cutting edges in the section view, especially in Fig. 4:5, no. 1. R.A. Smith, in his analysis of the collections formed by Dr Ince, Dr Willock and Dr Bowes divided the material into 267 fresh examples of the 'Fordwich' type ('pear-shaped handaxes of rough workmanship') plus 21 rolled, and 67 'St. Acheul ovates and pointed implements' (1933: 165-9). Much less than this quantity of handaxes survives today, and the present writer encountered less than a dozen which could be regarded as technologically or morphologically refined[7] during a thorough search for Fordwich material in the museums of Britain. Smith could obtain no stratigraphic information about the level or levels within the gravel at which the artefacts occurred, and he felt that more than one industry might be represented. He referred to material in the Bowes collection clearly classifiable as Clactonian, but did not illustrate any of it or give clear details. The present writer has seen no Clactonian material from Fordwich. There seems no doubt that even if there were more than one horizon yielding artefacts at Fordwich, the overwhelming majority of the implements from the pit is made up of crude handaxes.

Of the gravel, Smith (1933: 165) reports that its depth varied from about seven to about twenty feet. It rested on Eocene sands and, while not well bedded, was clearly water-laid. The lower parts were interstratified with sand, while the main mass of gravel was almost structureless; above came current-bedded sand and then a further thin layer of gravel. The upper part of the section showed 'trail' (i.e. convolutions or cryoturbation of some kind, doubtless representing periglacial conditions). There is one scrap of evidence that the artefacts were horizontally localized in the pit, though it does not bear on their vertical distribution. A letter from Dr Willock, preserved with flints from his collection in the British Museum mentions that:

the flints only seem to occur when they are working on the extreme western portion of the surface. The grab works from West to East, and as it moves Eastwards the chance of finding anything diminishes.

It is also worth noting that another exposure of gravel at the same height as that of Fordwich, on the opposite side of the present valley but apparently belonging to the same high terrace, at Stonerocks, produced a few similarly archaic handaxes according to Dewey and Smith (1924: 134-6), though the present writer knows of only two extant examples, both in the British Museum.

The sum of the available information about Fordwich is sadly deficient in many important respects. The present writer has little doubt himself that the site did produce an Early Acheulian assemblage and the containing gravel might well be older than any of the deposits in the Swanscombe area considered in the last chapter. But it is one thing to have little doubt and quite another to have positive proof. There are few references to the site and even fewer accounts of it in the literature of the British Palaeolithic. Little attempt seems to have been made to re-examine the stratigraphy or to obtain dating evidence in a modern controlled excavation. Few Palaeolithic specialists outside Britain seem to have heard of Fordwich at all, though it could be one of the few substantial Early Acheulian sites of Europe. R.A. Smith referred to the implements as Chellean (= Abbevillian) or Acheulian. The single one illustrated in the British Museum's *Flint Implements* handbook is classified as Abbevillian. The present writer will settle for 'Early Acheulian', while 'Archaic Acheulian' may better suit those who are anxious to play safe.

(e) *Farnham, Surrey (Terrace A)*

In the valley of the River Wey near Farnham, on the Surrey/Hampshire border, a situation appears to exist not dissimilar to that just described for the Sturry-Fordwich area of the Kentish Stour: that is to say, there is a sequence of river terrace deposits of which the highest has yielded an archaic-looking handaxe industry and the next an industry comparable to that of the Swanscombe Middle Gravels and Upper Loam. The crudeness of the Terrace A implements can again be demonstrated in quantitative terms by metrical analysis (Roe 1968a): it is a little less extreme than that of Fordwich, but striking enough when considered in the full context of British Lower Palaeolithic industries. Like the Fordwich handaxes, those from Farnham Terrace A had a clear tendency to narrowness as well as thickness, and advanced flaking techniques were absent. The similarity of the two situations, unfortunately, also includes the absence of clear dating evidence for the key deposits and a lack of detailed stratigraphic information about the occurrence of the implements in them.

The Farnham terraces have been described by several authors, notably Henry Bury (1913, 1916, 1935) and Kenneth Oakley (1939). There are five terraces in all, A to E (Fig. 4:7), but we are here directly concerned only with the top two, A and B. Bury and Oakley were able to expound in considerable detail the successive stages of river development in what is now the Wey Valley, and all their arguments tend to the conclusion that the first aggradation of gravel at the Terrace A level (on the Alice Holt Plateau, with a base level some 145-150 feet above the present river) took place relatively early in the Pleistocene. However, it is equally clear that gravel was deposited at this height several times, with intervals of downcutting, before Terrace B was formed. Also, the upper levels of Terrace A suffered solifluction at some later stage, so that a certain number of younger artefacts have become incorporated in the periglacially disturbed top few feet of Terrace A gravel, while some Terrace A material has spread out over the top of Terrace B. The difficulties inherent in this somewhat complex geological record are rendered far worse from the archaeologists' point of view by the deplorable state of the Terrace A artefact collections. It is clear from the literature that large numbers of handaxes and other artefacts were collected from Terrace A gravels at several different sites, but even by the mid 1930s some of these collections had been dispersed (cf. Oakley, *op. cit.*, 29-30). Worse, most of the artefacts were never marked, or else were

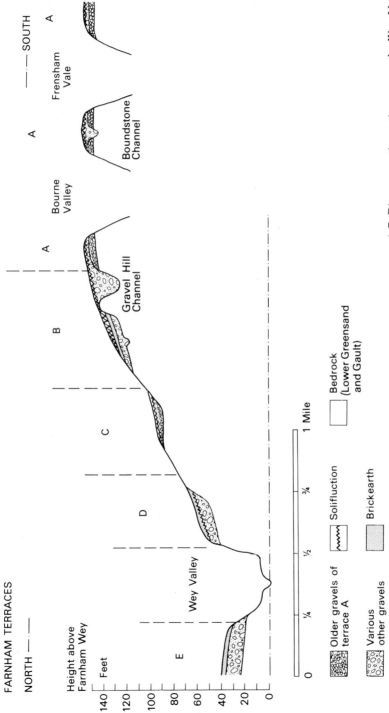

4:7 Diagrammatic section across the Wey Valley and adjacent areas to the south, to show the relationships of Terraces A-E of the Farnham sequence. The main deposits are indicated in simplified form; see pages 108-11 for commentary. Drawn for the author by M.H.R. Cook, on the basis of information in Oakley (1939)

marked only 'Farnham'. It seems impossible now even to put together a satisfactory sample of Terrace A artefacts, let alone to examine the whole assemblage. In these circumstances we must rely heavily on the literature from 1910-40 and be grateful for the carefulness of Bury's observations and for the fact that he lived near the pits in question for many years. Such provenanced material as does survive seems to accord well with the published accounts of it.

There were both fresh and rolled archaic-looking handaxes from Terrace A at Farnham. The fresh ones came from two deep channel fillings within the terrace deposits, which are *not* the oldest of the Terrace A gravels, but which seem certainly to be older than the establishment of the Terrace B bench or the deposition of any Terrace B deposits. These two features are the 'Gravel Hill Channel' and 'Boundstone Gravels' of Bury (1935: 60-3). The Gravel Hill channel exposures showed at least 25 feet of gravel in the channel fill, and the two features are believed to be of the same age; the fresh implements are apparently more or less contemporary with the channel fillings in which they occurred. The present writer, using all the surviving implements he could find from the two sites, plus some drawings made by Bury of others which cannot now be traced, was able to get a patchy set of data, including measurements, for a mere thirty-nine handaxes to represent the original assemblages, though probably more than a hundred once existed.

Apart from this series of more or less fresh implements, which is usually classed as 'Early Acheulian' in the literature of Farnham, both Bury and Oakley referred to rolled archaic handaxes, which they called 'Chellean' or 'Abbevillian', from Terrace A deposits which they regarded as earlier than the two channels just mentioned (Oakley, *op. cit.*, pp. 24-30). Such artefacts were not found very frequently, but were evidently older than the Boundstone and Gravel Hill assemblages and perhaps even as old as the first aggradation on Terrace A. Oakley suggested that a whole glacial phase might separate these two series of Terrace A implements. Various rolled archaic-looking handaxes from Farnham certainly exist today, and may well have come from Terrace A, but none

is clearly marked with a full provenance, so we are in no position to supplement what the literature tells us about them, which amounts to little more than the fact of their existence. Both authors also referred to Clactonian flakes from the Gravel Hill Channel, but the present writer has seen no flakes himself from there which are necessarily outside the Acheulian range, and no typical Clactonian cores seem to be known. Apart from all of this material, there is a certain amount from Terrace A which is of less archaic aspect, but almost all of it was white patinated and Bury and Oakley attributed it, with some justification, one would think, to the 'trailed' (soliflucted) gravels at the top of Terrace A, which are above the true fluviatile gravels (e.g. Bury 1935: 63); some of these white patinated artefacts are actually known to have been surface finds.

It seems clear that even if the various artefacts from Terrace A are not all of exactly the same age, they must all (except the white patinated ones) be older than Terrace B. The gravels of Terrace B reach virtually to the height of those of Terrace A in several places and the solifluction already referred to has left a slope in which there is little visible break between the two features. However, the sections in the gravel pits dug into Terrace B gravel showed the true state of affairs: Terrace B is aggraded on its own bench, which lies 20 to 30 feet below the base of Terrace A, and a river cliff of Greensand separated the two terraces before it became buried under the Terrace B gravels banked against it.

Abundant artefacts were recovered from various Terrace B sites at Farnham, and more survive today with a proper record of their provenance than was the case with the Terrace A material. The Terrace B handaxes are quite different in character from those of Terrace A: they are smaller and flatter and show plenty of 'soft-hammer' flaking. Pointed, straight-sided or convex-sided shapes are commonest, and there are also plenty of good, flat, broad ovates with cutting edges extending right round their circumferences; there are a few twisted ovates among them. Some well-made flake-tools were also present. Oakley compared the Terrace B artefacts specifically with those from 'the Middle Gravel of the 100 foot terrace at

Swanscombe' and regarded the handaxes as Middle Acheulian (*op. cit.*, pp. 34-7). The present writer's impression when examining the material was certainly that the range of sizes and shapes of the handaxes was similar to that of the Middle Gravels plus the Upper Loam of Barnfield Pit at Swanscombe, and the general standards of technology also appeared comparable, but it would require a detailed metrical and statistical comparison to determine whether the various individual handaxe types were of approximately equal importance at Farnham and Swanscombe, or whether there are major latent differences within the general similarity. Oakley and Bury also noted that Levalloisian flakes make their first appearance in Terrace C, while handaxes which they regarded as Mousterian appeared to be contemporary with Terrace D.

There is no record of any faunal or floral evidence from either Terrace A or Terrace B. Terrace D contained some good faunal remains, including mammoth and woolly rhino, and also some organic lenses and rafts of peat with mollusca, plants and mosses, all indicative of a rather cold climate. Terrace D certainly seems to be of full Devensian age; Terrace E is a very late Pleistocene feature. These facts do not greatly assist us in the present discussion, though we can note that Terrace B is at least two stages, and Terrace A three stages, older than the Devensian Terrace D — whatever may be implied by 'stages' in this case. Bury and Oakley, as one would expect considering the time at which they were writing, relied heavily on implement typology to 'date' the terraces: in these terms, Terrace B was equivalent to the Swanscombe Middle Gravels, and Terrace A was older. It is sad that there is no new and stronger evidence to adduce: we cannot accept implement typology as a valid form of chronology, but the writer strongly suspects that Bury's and Oakley's assessments of the age of the various Farnham artefacts may be right. The rolled archaic handaxes of Terrace A seem highly likely, in the light of what has been said, to be genuinely ancient and probably pre-Hoxnian in age. The fresher material from Boundstone and Gravel Hill would be a little younger; whether it is actually pre-Hoxnian does not clearly appear. The downcutting that created

the Boundstone and Gravel Hill channels appears to be earlier than that which established the cliff and bench of Terrace B, and the channels were apparently filled by a major phase of aggradation (as opposed to being choked by soliflucted material). There might perhaps be an echo here of the double cycle of river activity that seems to have been responsible for the Lower Gravel and Lower Loam followed by the Middle Gravels at Barnfield Pit, Swanscombe (see the previous chapter). Could the fillings of the deep channels in Farnham Terrace A be equivalent in age to the Swanscombe Lower Gravels and Loam? If so, it is important to note that they contained archaic handaxes rather than a pure Clactonian industry. But this is mere speculation, with no clear evidence to support it.

In summary, then, there seems to be a strong likelihood of genuine 'Early Acheulian' in Terrace A at Farnham, but we cannot give precision to this observation or assign a reliable date to the industry. Oakley's description of the handaxes as showing a majority of 'massive pear-shaped or long ovate' types is well borne out by the present writer's poor sample (Roe 1968a). The outline shapes of some of the Boundstone and Gravel Hill handaxes were rather more regular than was usual at Fordwich, though others were magnificently irregular in shape. Several of the large narrow ovates had fully worked edges. The over-all mean value for the ratio thickness/breadth (see above and cf. Table 9) was 0.57 for the thirty-nine implements for which these measurements could be obtained, with a standard deviation of 0.09. This is not as extreme as Fordwich, but is still higher than most of the sites in Table 9. However, the sample is so unsatisfactory that one hesitates to regard it as certainly properly representative of its parent assemblage, or to take the mean figure very seriously. The distribution of handaxe shapes did however resemble that of Fordwich rather strikingly (Roe 1968a, figs 23 and 24).

(f) *Warren Hill, Mildenhall, Suffolk (also called Three Hills)*

This site is of a somewhat different nature from the two preceding ones, and in the aggregate of

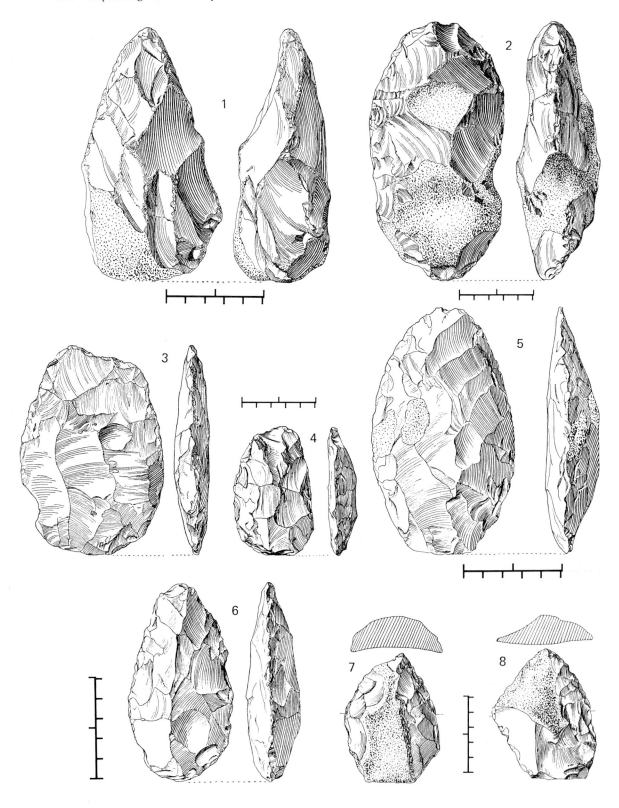

artefacts, or at least of handaxes, from it, it is probably the richest in Britain. Rather surprisingly, the supporting literature is sparse in the extreme. The most informative papers are those by J.D. Solomon (1932, 1933); R.A. Smith gave a passing account in his publication of the Sturge Collection (1931: 20-6); Dr W.A. Sturge himself described the site and provided a map of the area in the Early Man (Palaeolithic) section of the *Victoria County History of Suffolk* (1911); a not particularly useful section was published, with little comment, by J.E. Marr *et al.* in a paper (1921) principally concerned with the important nearby site of High Lodge. At the time of these various publications only a rough outline sequence of the British Pleistocene had been established and the relationship of the principal Palaeolithic stages to it was only poorly understood.

Solomon's main arguments, which are succinctly expressed, can be summarized quite briefly. He showed clearly that the Warren Hill gravel was not a fluviatile deposit but an unstratified glaci-fluvial mass; this conclusion was based on observation of the sections and analysis of the composition of the deposit in which flint, much of it unabraded, chalk pebbles and Midlands quartzite pebbles were the main elements. He argued that the glaciation responsible for its deposition must be the one subsequent to that which deposited the (Anglian) Great Chalky Boulder Clay, and separated from it by an interglacial period: that is, the Warren Hill glaci-fluvial gravels were of what we should now call Wolstonian age. He further showed that the artefacts were a mixture, caught up and contained in the gravel mass without any stratigraphic order, but he argued that different groups of them could be picked out according to their condition (Fig. 4:8). His study of the artefacts was based on the Sturge Collection: Dr Allen Sturge lived for many years at Icklingham, only a few miles from Warren Hill, and he assembled the largest and best collec-

tion of handaxes and flakes from the site, mainly by purchase, and bequeathed it to the British Museum along with the rest of his material in 1919. Solomon's classification of the complete handaxes from Warren Hill in the Sturge Collection was as follows:

Group I	Much rolled	109
Group II	Slightly rolled	90
Group III	Unrolled, but bleached and sometimes patinated	330
Group IV	Unrolled and unbleached	174
Total		703

He also noted a fair quantity of flake-tools, most of which he regarded as belonging to (or contemporary with) Groups II and III, on grounds of their condition.

Solomon regarded his Group I as 'a generation (probably a glaciation) older than the rest' (1933: 102), and these are the artefacts with which we are concerned here, since if Solomon was right they should constitute an Early Acheulian assemblage. They are, as he recorded, an archaic-looking series of mainly pear-shaped handaxes, with edges 'anything but straight', and their rough flaking was carried out with a stone hammer. A few flake implements were present. Since so much of the flint in the Warren Hill gravels was unabraded, it followed that these heavily worn implements had acquired their abrasion *before* they were incorporated in the glaci-fluvial gravel.

Solomon classed his Groups II to IV as Middle and Late Acheulian, not far removed in age from the formation of the gravel. The vast majority of the handaxes were flat and finely made ovates, in all three of these groups. Interestingly, he then checked his predicted results by some simple metrical analyses, giving frequency curves for length and the ratio thickness/breadth. The curves showed satisfactorily different modes, occurring in the 'correct' order (fig. 4:9). The archaic Group I implements stood out as larger and thicker than the rest, in these terms, though Solomon did not calculate means or standard deviations to assist him in interpreting his distributions. He also used one other argument to support the supposed substantially greater antiquity of the Group I implements, an argument which may not be

4:8 Artefacts from Warren Hill, Mildenhall, Suffolk, after R.A. Smith (1931). Nos 1 and 2 are handaxes from the heavily worn series: note their archaic technology. The remainder are all fresh: four handaxes (nos 3-6) and two flake implements (nos 7, 8)

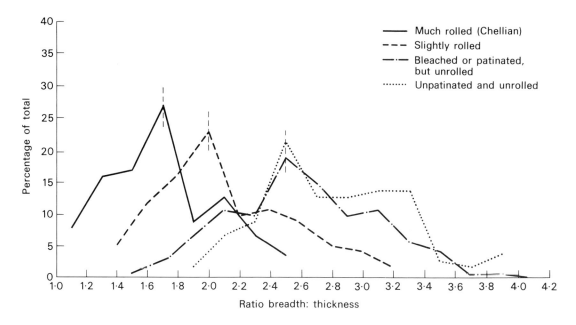

4:9 Redrawn version of the frequency curves for the ratio breadth/thickness produced by J.D. Solomon in 1933 for groups of handaxes from Warren Hill. He distinguished the four series as follows: — much rolled (Chellian); - - - slightly rolled; ·-·- bleached or patinated, but unrolled; ···· unpatinated and unrolled

conclusive but is certainly suggestive when placed alongside the other evidence. He observed that all the 'Chellian' implements, as he called his Group I, were made of dark flint, i.e. the local East Anglian chalk flint, whereas for some of the later ones grey flint of Lincolnshire origin had been used. Could this be chance? If not, Solomon's conclusion was that the archaic implements ante-dated the arrival of Lincolnshire flint in the area by glacial transport. This would be highly signifi-cant if true, because it was the glaciation which produced the Great Chalky Boulder Clay, that is to say the Anglian, which transported the Lincolnshire flint to the Breckland area. The Group I artefacts would be pre-Anglian accordingly, or at least older than an Anglian stage.

While no one of Solomon's arguments by itself proves beyond all doubt that the archaic imple-ments from Warren Hill are necessarily of high antiquity or necessarily pre-Anglian, it is hard to shrug off their cumulative effect altogether. The present writer had begun to make metrical analyses

of handaxes before he encountered Solomon's work, but in due course found himself applying his own metrical tests and statistical analyses to the very same material in the Sturge Collection which Solomon had studied thirty years earlier. Being a little suspicious of patination as a criterion, and also of the finer distinctions in estimating rolling by eye, he extracted only two groups from Sturge's Warren Hill material: one consisting of very worn handaxes, and one of completely or almost completely unworn ones. Handaxes whose condition lay between these two extremes were omitted. This gave the following samples:

Worn sample	116
Fresh sample	642
Omitted	58
Total	816

On the basis of a somewhat more elaborate series of tests than those of Solomon (Roe 1968a), the present writer can confirm that there are abundant morphological   and   technological   differences between the heavily worn and the fresh implements. Probably the most striking single example is a comparison of the ratio thickness/breadth, referred to earlier in this chapter, which gave the following result:

	Sample size	Mean	Standard deviation
Worn series	116	0.60	0.13
Fresh series	642	0.43	0.09

These figures should be compared with those in Table 9. The 't-value' for the comparison was 13.4, which indicates a highly significant difference at any level of probability.

Warren Hill, then, may be added to the sites previously discussed in this chapter as possibly Early Acheulian, though once again the picture lacks clarity and the evidence leaves much to be desired. In passing, though it does not affect the real issue, we may note the existence of similar worn archaic handaxes in what may well be further occurrences of the same fluvio-glacial gravels in the same area of central East Anglia. These gravels are distinctive in various ways, including the suite of heavy minerals they contain, as Solomon showed (1932), but the most obvious feature when they are exposed is the abundance of Midlands quartzite pebbles in their composition. Their distribution occupies a narrow and now discontinuous band running roughly north-north-west to south-south-east from near Downham Market in Norfolk to near Bury St Edmunds in Suffolk (unpublished information from R.W. Hey and G. Ll. Isaac); Warren Hill is towards the south-eastern end. Several of the main exposures were known in the late nineteenth century to Sir John Evans and his contemporaries, who recognized their distinctive character (cf. Evans 1897: 534-71). Several of the gravel pits proved prolific in implements, notably at Lakenheath, Brandon, Weeting and Feltwell. Some indeed produced artefacts in hundreds, though none was anywhere near so rich as Warren Hill itself and the old collections are now scattered. The early literature is somewhat confused on the relationship of the gravels to the boulder clays of central East Anglia, but it seems likely (though it is certainly not proved) that Solomon's analysis

of the geological situation at Warren Hill would apply to several of the other exposures. Certainly there still survive from these other pits a substantial number in aggregate of worn archaic handaxes much like those from Warren Hill discussed above – notably from Shrub Hill (Feltwell), Gravel Hill (Brandon) and Broomhill (Weeting). There is however no clear indication that any of the sites ever contained early assemblages *in situ* in early deposits and one may guess that most of the archaic implements were redeposited in Wolstonian times, mixed with younger material. Evans illustrated a couple of archaic specimens (1897, figs 439, 444) and commented on the relative abundance of these 'rude' forms at Gravel Hill: he thought it hardly worthwhile to figure them by comparison with the finer pieces.

(g) *Other sites*

It would be possible to suggest the presence of early Acheulian material in other parts of Britain too, but the evidence is even less clear than the foregoing. For example, it is worth mentioning the area of west Hampshire and east Dorset (Roe 1975), where near Corfe Mullen J.B. Calkin and J.F.N. Green (1949) were able to demonstrate the presence of heavy rather crude pointed handaxes in an earlier stratigraphic context than an assemblage of refined ovates very much like those of the fresh series at Warren Hill. The age of the crude pointed implements in Pleistocene terms did not clearly appear, but it could hardly have been later than Hoxnian according to Green's interpretation of the local terrace sequence, and could have been earlier. The implements showed little in the way of advanced flaking technology, even if they looked less impressively archaic than those of Fordwich or Kent's Cavern. Other arguably (though not demonstrably) early assemblages may be represented at Highlands Farm, Rotherfield Peppard, Oxfordshire (Wymer 1961, 1968: 191-8) and in the Kennet Valley in Berkshire and Wiltshire (see below, pp. 151-2).

THE EARLY ACHEULIAN QUESTION:
SUMMARY AND CONCLUSIONS

The sites mentioned in the preceding paragraph represent the scrapings from the bottom of the barrel: the writer would be happy to rest his case for the existence of an Early Acheulian stage in Britain on those discussed earlier in the chapter. Of those, Westbury seems certainly early, but the 'cultural' affinities of the artefacts are obscure. The crude Kent's Cavern handaxes are undoubtedly Acheulian, but a little harder to date with certainty, and the same is true of the Fordwich, Farnham Terrace A and Warren Hill assemblages. There is a degree of variety in the arguments used to suggest early dating, and at least we are not relying solely on typological criteria — though, to be fair, the consistently archaic morphology and technology of the handaxes has been a starting point in each case.

Anyone who is prepared to swallow the various arguments whole may by now feel that in Britain there is convincing evidence for an Early Acheulian stage, based on several sites; that such sites antedate the Clactonian of Swanscombe, some at least being of pre- or inter-Anglian age; even that more Early Acheulian artefacts survive in Britain than Mousterian ones. Those of a more cautious turn of mind may prefer to conclude that nothing of the sort is provable: they might allow that Westbury suggests hominid activity of an uncertain kind which could be earlier than the base of the Barnfield Pit archaeological sequence, but the other sites they might regard as suggestive at most and deserving to be set aside till proper proof is forthcoming through re-excavation. The present writer takes his stand between these extremes, finding the cumulative effect of the evidence impressive: he offers the *hypothesis* that the Barnfield Pit Middle Gravels Acheulian is *not* the earliest in Britain, but is preceded by a stage in which the handaxes were heavy, thick, narrow and rather large, and made by 'hard hammer' technique only. For such material, 'British Earlier Acheulian' is perhaps the most appropriate name, for if we have regard to the well-dated African sequence (at Peninj, or in Bed II of Olduvai Gorge, for example — Isaac 1972a), we must admit the existence of

handaxe industries at least a million years older. This suggested British Earlier Acheulian appears to be at least as old as the Clactonian, on present evidence, and may well turn out to be older — but we know little yet of the earliest Clactonian and its antecedents (if any). The Earlier Acheulian also appears to have been present before the Hoxnian, but how much earlier is not yet known. Of the palaeoanthropology of the Earlier Acheulian population, and even of the full range of their stone artefacts, we can say nothing with certainty.

Here then is an hypothesis which differs from that of Wymer (1968, 1974), though it would probably not have seemed extraordinary to many workers earlier this century. Like all hypotheses, it is liable to be unceremoniously upended in due course. But if it is to be replaced, it can only be replaced by contrary views based on superior evidence.

Finally, it should not have escaped notice that this discussion of potentially early material in Britain has proceeded without reference to the 'eoliths' of Benjamin Harrison and others, or to the 'Crag' and 'pre-Crag' material claimed by Reid Moir and his supporters (Fig. 4:10a). These and other occurrences have been ably summarized and discussed by John Coles (1968; Coles and Higgs 1969: 201-2), with whose comments the present writer is in agreement. Some of the material is inherently impossible; some can be shown to have a very likely natural cause; some pieces are artefacts, but were not *in situ* as claimed in the Pliocene or Early Pleistocene deposits concerned. When all that has been said, just a few remain which are individually not unconvincing, but there is none which ultimately defies being explained away. Any which are handaxe-like and attributable to Cromerian deposits or Anglian till (e.g. Moir 1923) would of course fit in with the hypothesis just proposed (Fig. 4:10b), but the writer does not wish to invoke support of such dubious value. It is a curious twist of fate that while (by East African standards at least) the notion of artefacts at about the Plio-Pleistocene boundary has become readily acceptable, even the cream of Reid Moir's Crag material looks less and less convincing in itself. 'Not proven' is the kindest possible verdict; many may feel compelled to pass it also on the

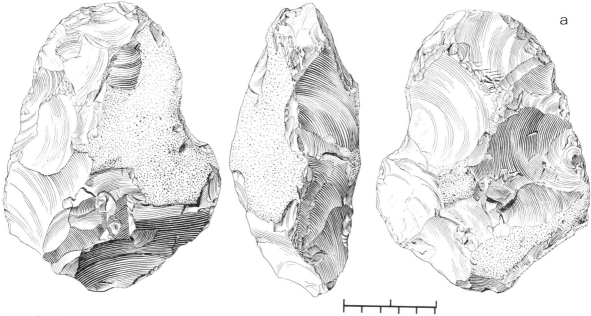

4:10 (a) Three views of the 'Norwich Test Specimen', after J.R. Moir in *Proc. Prehist. Soc. East Anglia*, 6:223-4. This large naturally flaked flint came from below the Norwich Crag at Whitlingham, Norfolk, and is not to be confused with artefacts from the Whitlingham Acheulian site (pages 170-2). It was one of Moir's prime pieces of evidence for the presence of Pliocene or 'Pre-Crag' Man in East Anglia and was much debated in the 1930s. (b) Possible crude handaxe found by J.E. Sainty, apparently *in situ* in Anglian till at Sidestrand, Norfolk, after Moir (1923). It is more likely than (a) to be artificially flaked, but is perhaps still open to doubt

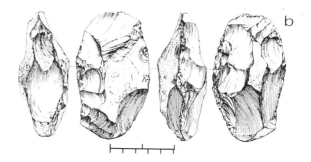

writer's suggested Earlier British Acheulian, but at least there the artificial nature of the pieces is not open to doubt.

THE QUESTION OF A 'FINAL ACHEULIAN' STAGE

We may now turn to the other end of the 'basic sequence' of Chapter 3 to enquire whether it too can be expanded. It will be recalled that the Barnfield Pit Upper Loam and certain other sites in the area yielded fine ovate handaxe industries, but thereafter the story was mainly concerned with industries characterized by use of the Levalloisian technique: the bold flakes and 'tortoise cores' of Baker's Hole, or the flake-blades of the Ebbsfleet Channel series or Crayford. It was clear, however, that handaxes continued to be made after the end of the Wolstonian, though we saw no major handaxe site of that age in north Kent. Are there any substantial sites elsewhere in Britain that might fill the gap? Once again, in considering such occurrences, it is necessary to combine the evidence of handaxe technology and typology with geological evidence that is susceptible of more than one interpretation; once again, we can obtain a little guidance by looking at the situation outside Britain, this time no further away than France and Germany.

The Wolvercote Channel, Oxford

An important feature of the Thames Valley is the Goring Gap, the somewhat narrow route some seven miles long by which the river passes through the barrier of the chalk hills. This gorge-like feature divides the Upper Thames from the Middle Thames, and has proved, incidentally, a formidable barrier to the correlation of their respective terrace sequences. Downstream, Lower Palaeolithic sites are relatively frequent and rich in artefacts (Wymer 1968); upstream, finds are much fewer and more scattered, consisting for the most part of single handaxes, with only occasionally a site producing the remains of a Lower Palaeolithic industry. One reason for this contrast is evidently the scarcity of good flint, in Palaeolithic times as now, in the Upper Thames Basin: what there is occurs in the form of pebbles in some of the gravels, most of them quite unusable for tool manufacture. Upstream of the chalk the gravels consist largely of limestone pebbles and fragments derived from what are now the Cotswolds and the neighbouring hills north-east of them, together with a fair amount of Midlands material, including the characteristic Bunter quartzite pebbles. Downstream from the Goring Gap and its approaches, the whole character of the gravel lithology changes, with flint becoming extremely abundant. Whether or not the scarcity of good flint in the Upper

Thames Basin was the main controlling factor — and there must have been others of a geographical nature — it is undeniably the case that north of the Goring Gap one comes relatively quickly to the edge of known Lower Palaeolithic settlement, not merely in Britain but in the Old World. Amongst what artefacts there are it is not uncommon to encounter handaxes and other tools made from Midlands quartzite pebbles.

Amongst the scatter of Upper Thames find-spots one is outstanding: the Wolvercote Channel site on the northern edge of Oxford. One need hardly trouble to observe, in this particular chapter, that the best finds were made more than fifty years ago, that the brick-pit which contained the site has long been abandoned and the area mainly built over, and that no exposure of the crucial part of the deposits has been seen for thirty or more years. This is the story of all too many British sites, as we have seen. It is, however, well worth the effort to extract what information one can from the Wolvercote occurrence, because of the strikingly individual character of the industry. The literature of the site is rather sparse (Bell 1904; Sandford 1924, 1926, 1939; Bishop, W.W. 1958: 279-91; Wymer 1968: 87-90).

In the various museum collections at Oxford nearly 200 artefacts from the Wolvercote site survive, including seventy-five handaxes; another eight handaxes were recovered from drainage trenches dug close to the old brick-pit, from what is believed to have been an extension of the same occurrence. Other implements probably passed

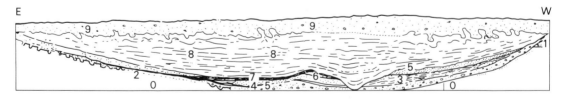

Scale as shown: vertical,
1 cm = 9 feet; horizontal, 1 cm = 13′ 6″

4:11 K.S. Sandford's (1924) section of the deposits filling the Wolvercote Channel, Oxford: for key, see Table 10. The industry came from level 2, the basal gravel of the channel, with swirl-holes cut into the Oxford Clay. Note especially level 1,

interpreted by Sandford as a tiny fragment of the Wolvercote Terrace, with the channel cutting through it: this is crucial to Sandford's reading of the age of the channel in terms of the local sequence and the British Pleistocene succession

into private collections. A few of the artefacts are abraded, but most are in a remarkably fresh state, and many are unpatinated. Where detailed provenances have been recorded, it is clear that the pieces came from the very base of the deposits. A section is shown in Fig. 4:11, and the sequence is given in Table 10.

It seems reasonably clear on faunal grounds that the basal deposits of the Wolvercote Channel were laid down in temperate conditions and the fresh, often unpatinated, condition of the artefacts suggests that they belong to whatever warm phase it is that is represented. The evidence to solve the latter problem is inconclusive. The bedded fluviatile gravels (1 in Fig. 4:11) are crucial, because Sandford regarded them as part of the Wolvercote Terrace of the Cherwell valley and there seems to be general agreement, backed by a fair body of evidence (Bishop, W.W. 1958; Tomlinson 1963), that the Wolvercote Terrace contains Midlands material derived from Wolstonian tills and brought into the Cherwell Valley by the spilling over of the pro-glacial Lake Harrison (cf. pages 49-50): i.e., the terrace is a Wolstonian feature. If Sandford were right, then the Channel must belong to a post-Wolstonian temperate phase, which must mean the Ipswichian. Bishop, however (1958: 290-1) did not believe that the gravel through which the Channel was cut did (or could) belong to the Wolvercote Terrace and, while not ruling out an Ipswichian date for the Channel, argued that a later Hoxnian one seemed more probable, a conclusion which Wymer (1968: 90) found acceptable.

The problem cannot be explored in full detail here, since to examine it properly would require the exposition of much data on the Upper Thames and Cherwell sequences; this information can be found by those who are interested, in the literature already quoted. One important but unknown

---

TABLE 10 : *The Wolvercote Channel sequence*
(after Sandford)

(a)	*Pre-Channel deposits*
0	Oxford Clay (Jurassic)
1	Fluviatile gravel, said by Sandford to belong to the Wolvercote Terrace of the Cherwell, though other authors have disputed this
(b)	*Lower Channel filling*
2	Calcareous gravel: the basal deposit of an old river channel, with its original river beaches. In places swirl-holes occur in the underlying Oxford clay, created by eddying water on the outside of a bend in the channel: these holes are also filled by the calcareous gravel. This basal deposit was the source of those implements which are properly provenanced, and there are good reasons for thinking that the whole of the industry belongs here (Sandford 1926, 1939). Important faunal remains also occurred at this level, including *Elephas (Palaeoloxodon) antiquus*, *Dicerorhinus hemitoechus, Bos primigenius, Cervus elaphus* and *Equus caballus*
3	False-bedded fine sandy gravel, over part of the channel bed (eroded away elsewhere)
4	(Lower) iron pan: hard oolitic gravel mainly replaced by iron compounds, capping 3 and in places 2 where 3 is absent. Not surprisingly, several of the artefacts bear traces of iron encrustation
5	Shelly sands, with temperate mollusca, incorporating a small channel filling
6	Fine gravel (localized)
7	(Upper) iron pan
(c)	*Upper Channel filling* There was a break in deposition after 7, represented by an erosion surface followed by:
8	Silt and clay, apparently deposited in still water, filling the remains of the old channel depression. At the base of this silt a thin layer of peat was recorded by Bell (1904) and the contents studied much later by Duigan (1956). It contained flowering plants, mosses and beetles of 'cool-temperate' character. The main body of the silt (maximum thickness 15 feet) had scattered faunal remains including horse, deer and possibly one antler of reindeer.[8] A few rather undiagnostic artefacts have also been recorded from the silt. The upper two feet or so of the silt showed cryoturbation and contortion
(d)	*Post-Channel deposit*
9	'Warp Sand': a solifluction spread, covering and sealing in the underlying series of Channel deposits, and not forming a part of them. Represents periglacial conditions.

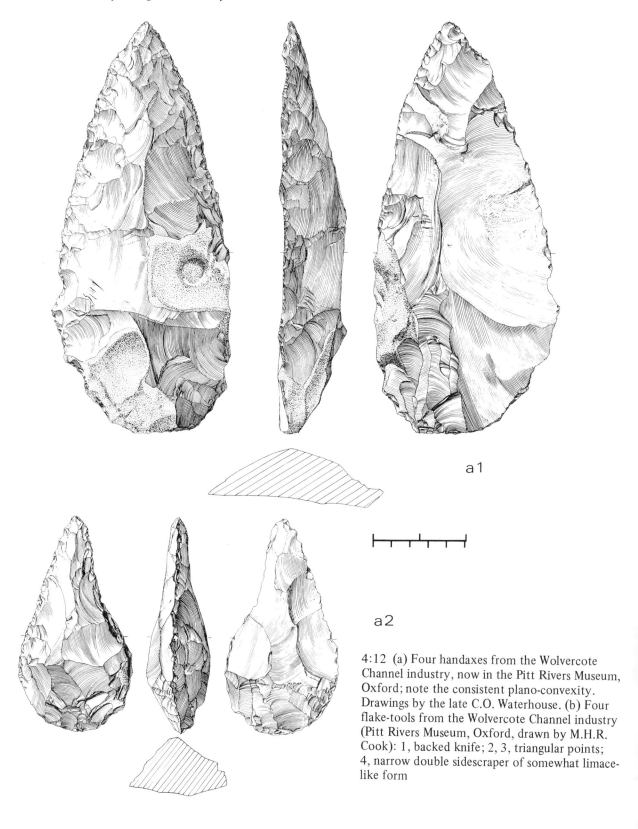

a1

a2

4:12 (a) Four handaxes from the Wolvercote
Channel industry, now in the Pitt Rivers Museum,
Oxford; note the consistent plano-convexity.
Drawings by the late C.O. Waterhouse. (b) Four
flake-tools from the Wolvercote Channel industry
(Pitt Rivers Museum, Oxford, drawn by M.H.R.
Cook): 1, backed knife; 2, 3, triangular points;
4, narrow double sidescraper of somewhat limace-
like form

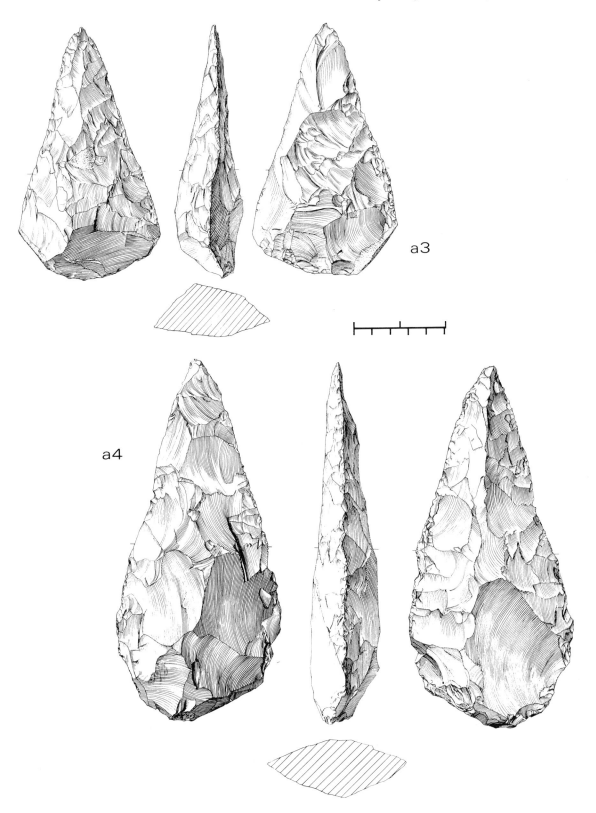

a3

a4

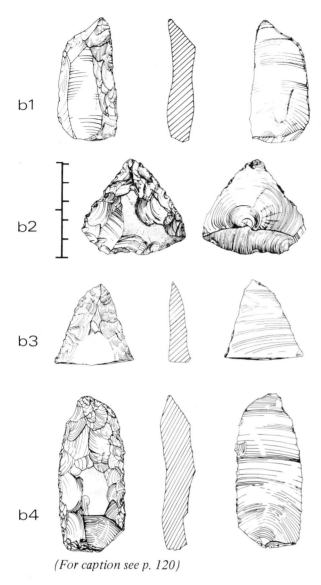

b1

b2

b3

b4

(For caption see p. 120)

assemblage is generally regarded as Ipswichian. *Hippopotamus* and *Corbicula fluminalis* were both absent at Wolvercote; Sandford attributed the Wolvercote Channel accordingly to a later part of the Ipswichian than that in which they were current, noting that the Channel filling as a whole became progressively cooler. In Bishop's view, however, the Wolvercote Channel fauna would be a whole cycle *older* than the Ipswichian fauna of the upper division of the Summertown-Radley terrace.[9] It does not help the situation that all current and recent exposures of the Summertown-Radley gravels have been in the lower 'cold' section of it.

Without fresh exposures of the Wolvercote Channel, which seem unlikely to occur in the foreseeable future, the recorded disagreement must remain and we may perhaps feel entitled accordingly to express an opinion on the archaeological side. After all, the two suggested datings, late Hoxnian and late Ipswichian, stand about 100,000 years apart in Table 6: notwithstanding all the vagaries of implement typology, and without prejudice to the priority of geological dating in ordinary circumstances, may we not say which of the two readings we would expect to see prevail if and when clear evidence becomes available?

A glance at the Wolvercote handaxes illustrated in Fig. 4:12a and Plate 26 shows this side of the industry to be dominated by elegant pointed forms, convex or straight sided, or sometimes with one slightly concave side, though there are no true ficrons. The scar patterns show abundant 'soft-hammer' work, and the edges are often minutely finished. But a more detailed look will suggest that there are technological points which we have not met before. The cross-sections of the handaxes are often markedly plano-convex, especially towards the tip end (Plate 26b). In a few cases this reflects the fact that the implements concerned were made from big flakes, which left them naturally flatter on one face. But on several other occasions the handaxes are demonstrably made from nodules, and the plano-convexity of section undoubtedly reflects the maker's intention and a distinctive manufacturing technique. It is the flatter face which is worked first, leaving a comparatively small number of shallow scars. There are

relationship is that between the Wolvercote Channel and the Summertown-Radley Terrace, the next younger terrace after the Wolvercote Terrace. There are Summertown-Radley gravels within half a mile of the Wolvercote site, but the relationship of the Wolvercote Channel to them remains problematic. The Summertown-Radley terrace apparently has a 'cold' lower part, whose fauna includes mammoth and woolly rhinoceros, and a 'warm' upper part with *Elephas (Palaeoloxodon) antiquus*, *Hippopotamus*, and even the warmth-loving mollusc *Corbicula fluminalis*. This latter

typically far more scars on the domed side of the handaxe, and they tend to truncate the proximal ends of the scars on the flatter face. The finer finishing scars, too, are almost always struck on to the domed face. Thus treated, the handaxes have a markedly D-shaped or flat triangular cross-section, which, combined with the strong preference for pointed shapes, mostly rather narrow, gives them a very distinctive character; they have sometimes been described as 'slipper-shaped' (cf. for example Sandford 1926: 138). It is notable that, while one or two plano-convex handaxes may turn up anywhere in the Lower Palaeolithic, the Wolvercote implements as a group are quite unlike any series we have encountered thus far. Examined in detail they do not closely resemble, for example, the Swanscombe Middle Gravels pointed handaxe industry. In fairness it must be added that this assertion does not correspond with the views of Wymer (1968: 90), though the present writer's own metrical analyses (1968a) seem to show various quantifiable differences between the Wolvercote and Swanscombe handaxe industries.

Can we then find elsewhere dated industries of a similar nature to guide us in assessing the Wolvercote occurrence? The present writer believes that we can, on the Continent, and suggests that a relevant comparison can be made with La Micoque level VI (Dordogne), Bockstein III (Rammingen, near Ulm) and Klausennische (Essing, near Lekheim), and with certain other German and French occurrences of broadly similar character. A selection of handaxes from these Continental sites is illustrated in Fig. 4:13, to show the general similarity to those previously illustrated from Wolvercote, and it can be observed that the resemblances include technological as well as morphological features. It would be a useful and interesting exercise to carry out a full-scale metrical and statistical comparison between the Wolvercote industry and the relevant Continental ones, which has never been done; meanwhile, the present writer feels justified, on the basis of the published accounts and illustrations, in suggesting that interesting similarities exist. These Continental industries are all of late date, by the standards of the whole Acheulian Tradition. There is good

literature for some of them at least, and the reader should consult *inter alia* the works of G. Bosinski (1967, 1968), R. Wetzel and G. Bosinski (1969), F. Bordes (1968: 51-146), H.J. Müller-Beck (1957), G. Freund (1952), D. Peyrony (1931, 1938) and M. Gábori (1976).

At La Micoque (Peyrony 1938; Bourgon 1957), the handaxe industry in question came from level VI (Layer N), the youngest of the six levels at that site yielding Lower Palaeolithic artefacts, and it *overlay* a fossil soil attributed to the Riss-Würm (Last Interglacial), making the industry presumably of early Würmian age, or Early Devensian in British terms. The industry of La Micoque VI is the type industry, in fact, for the 'Micoquian' phase, usually viewed as a terminal event within the handaxe tradition,[10] setting aside the sporadic occurrence of handaxes in certain late Mousterian industries.

At Bocksteinschmiede,[11] the 'Bockstein III' industry can be dated on several lines of evidence (fauna, pollen, sediments) to the Last Interglacial (Wetzel and Bosinski 1969). Bosinski classified this industry as belonging to the Central European Micoquian (Fig. 4:14), which he distinguishes from the *Spät-Jungacheuléen* (Late Upper Acheulian) on techno-typological grounds (Bosinski 1967; see also note 10 to this chapter). Within the Central European Micoquian, he defines four *Inventartypen*, named respectively after Bockstein, Klausennische, Schambach and Rorshain. Amongst these, the Bockstein *Inventartyp*, named after the Bockstein III industry, includes the oldest sites. The second (Klausennische) *Inventartyp* is perhaps a little younger: the dating at Klausennische itself is not quite so well documented as that of Bocksteinschmiede, but even so it seems established that the Micoquian industry there belongs either to a final stage of the Last Interglacial or else to an early and mild episode within the Last Glacial. The Schambach *Inventartyp* sites are perhaps slightly younger than those of the Klausennische group, while the age of the Rorshain group is somewhat uncertain. So far as the existing evidence goes, the Wolvercote industry seems to have more in common with the Bockstein *Inventartyp* than the others, but this opinion could be disproved by a proper analysis.

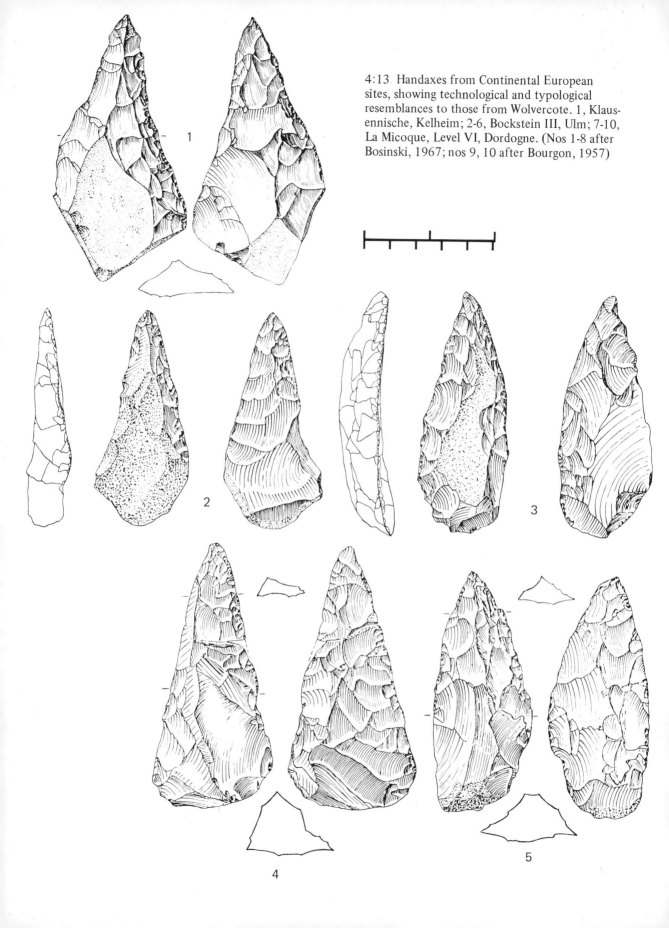

4:13 Handaxes from Continental European sites, showing technological and typological resemblances to those from Wolvercote. 1, Klaus-ennische, Kelheim; 2-6, Bockstein III, Ulm; 7-10, La Micoque, Level VI, Dordogne. (Nos 1-8 after Bosinski, 1967; nos 9, 10 after Bourgon, 1957)

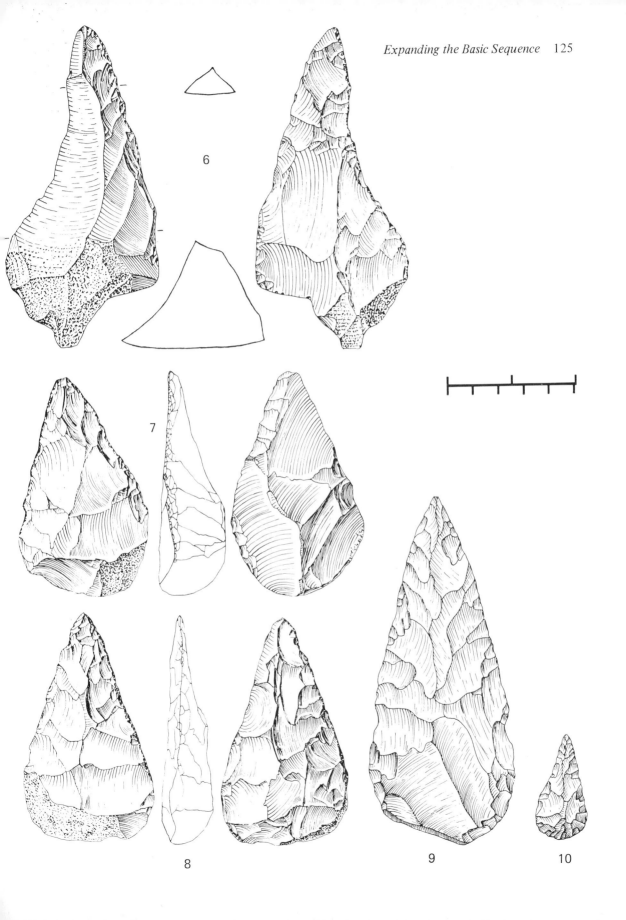

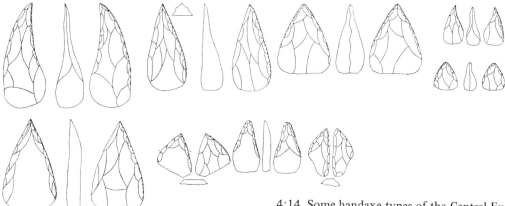

4:14 Some handaxe types of the Central European Micoquian, shown diagrammatically, after Bosinski (1967)

Space does not permit a fuller examination of these important Continental sites, or mention of others like them. Also, if we explored in detail the nature of other Central, East European and Russian industries of the late Lower Palaeolithic and initial Middle Palaeolithic, we should encounter in some of them various tool types, notably leaf-shaped forms but also some pointed ones, which are worked in a plano-convex bifacial style not unlike that of the German Micoquian handaxes — and indeed of the Wolvercote handaxes which were our starting point. What, if any, direct connection there may be between such tool types — the 'pradnik' knives of the Polish Kultura Mikocko-Pradnicka (Chmielewski *et al.* 1975: 64-91) for example, or the 'East Mousterian' plano-convex points (McBurney 1950) — and the handaxes of Bocksteinschmiede, Klausennische or Wolvercote, must remain uncertain. Nor does the present writer wish to imply that the Continental Micoquian industries mentioned are *precisely* similar to each other or to Wolvercote. But, given the technological peculiarities of the Wolvercote artefacts viewed only in a British context, the nature and dating of these Continental occurrences surely offer us a strong hint that the Wolvercote industry is a late one, that an Ipswichian date would suit it very well, and that it may have affinities in France and Germany.

We should not of course leave the Wolvercote occurrence without a few words about the arte-facts other than handaxes which were found there, though the haphazard nature of their recovery naturally means that we cannot give a formal and complete account of the industry's flake-tool element. It is likely that only the more obvious flake tools were saved, even though a few good handaxe-trimmers and other waste flakes have been preserved. There is no trace of Levalloisian technique, and this too corresponds with the Continental Micoquian industries. Several well-made flake-tools (Fig. 4:12b) are included in the collection of Wolvercote material in the Pitt Rivers Museum at Oxford: for example, two unifacial broad triangular flake points, with broad plain striking platforms, and a narrow double side-scraper, unifacial, of almost limace-like form occur amongst them, and there are also some other well-made scrapers and at least one backed knife with a canted top. All these seem more elaborately worked and regularly shaped than, say, the flake-tools from the Swanscombe Middle Gravels. They offer no kind of dating evidence in themselves, but it is fair to observe that they would certainly not look out of place in various Continental industries of Last Interglacial or Early Last Glacial age, including, according to the writer's impressions of the published literature, the Continental Micoquian.

In short, then, the writer suggests that Sandford's reading of the age of the Wolvercote Channel is more likely to prove correct; that the

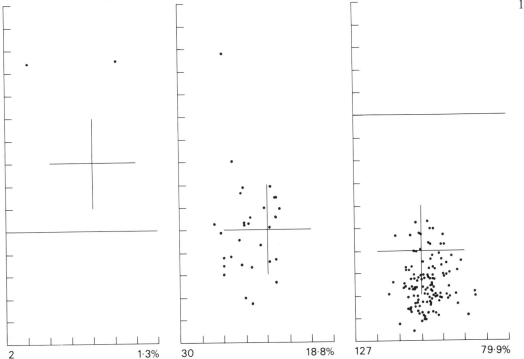

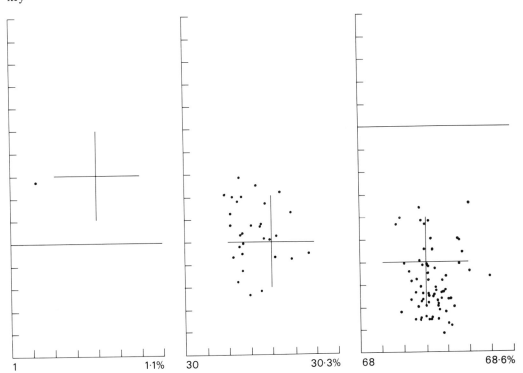

Wolvercote industry occupies a very late position in the British Lower Palaeolithic sequence; that the industry adds a new stage to our basic sequence of the preceding chapter; and that this assessment of it need not occasion surprise to those who are prepared to look outwards, as it is so essential to do, given the geographical situation of Britain, since the affinities of the Wolvercote industry are likely to lie with the final Acheulian/Micoquian (cf. note 10 to this chapter) of Continental Europe.[12]

Is the Wolvercote Channel industry then unique within Britain? In fact there very probably are other occurrences of the distinctive 'Wolvercote type' handaxes, but too often they take the form of stray finds with little or no dating evidence. Three isolated handaxes of this kind, found separately not far from Wolvercote itself (two at Summertown and one at Eynsham) may have come from the Summertown-Radley terrace gravel, but their actual relationship to it is not really established. Isolated occurrences from Tilehurst (Berkshire), Quendon (Essex), Bishop's Stortford (Hertfordshire) and a few other scattered places are also known (Roe 1967: 219-22), but yielded no useful chronological data. A few of the distinctive handaxes have been found at Wilmington in Kent (Dartford Museum), and a number rather reminiscent of Wolvercote came from Hitchin in Bedfordshire. Hitchin is a fairly prolific source of handaxes in the older collections; it is best known

for its 'lake beds' of Hoxnian age (Oakley 1947, quoting earlier literature), but the stratigraphic position of the plano-convex handaxes is not known, and there is no clear indication that they are of Hoxnian age, which would conflict with the reading of Wolvercote suggested above (cf. the account of Hitchin in the next chapter).

However, the area of Britain in which finds of the plano-convex handaxes of Wolvercote type are commonest is in fact south Hampshire, in the areas of Bournemouth, Christchurch and Southampton, notably the latter. For example, several came from an old pit adjacent to Shirley Church, Southampton (the best examples are now in the Dale Collection at Winchester Museum). All that is known of their provenance is that they came from a gravel about 70 feet above sea level, but the surviving artefacts from the pit do not necessarily all belong together and there is a typical twisted ovate among them — a type not known at Wolvercote. At Warsash, a few miles south-east of Southampton, several more plano-convex handaxes were found (Fig. 4:15), including both bifacially and unifacially worked examples — the unifacial ones resemble the *Halbkeile* of Bosinski's German Micoquian. Although the Warsash deposits contain no undisturbed industries firmly *in situ*, much Lower Palaeolithic material has come from them and attempts have been made to establish some kind of archaeological sequence. M.C. Burkitt, T.T.

4:15 Three plano-convex handaxes from Warsash, Hampshire, after Burkitt *et al.* (1939)

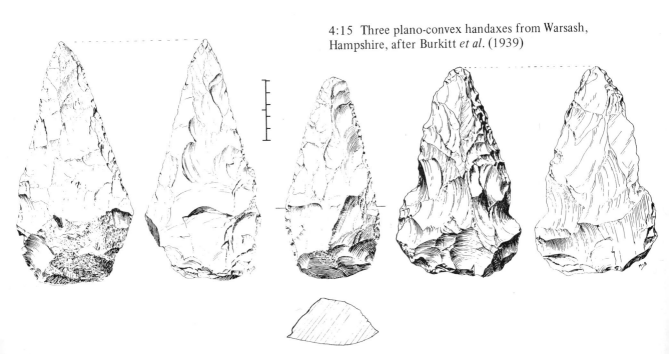

Paterson and C.J. Mogridge published a brief account of the pits and the finds from them (1939) in which Burkitt, on grounds of the condition, typology and technology of the artefacts, distinguished four series: Early Acheulian, Middle Acheulian, 'very late Acheulian (Micoque)' and Levalloisian. Paterson described and figured a section and interpreted the age of the deposits as extending from 'Mindel' to 'Würm I' and later. Burkitt argued from the condition of the 'Micoque' handaxes, which are the ones which concern us here, that they were younger than the 'Middle Acheulian series', and this is probably true, but his dating of them as 'just prior to the last glaciation' is unfortunately only an assertion based on a comparison of them with dated Continental industries, and is not supported by any independent stratigraphic evidence or faunal associations from the Warsash deposits: the main trouble is that there is no proper record of the stratigraphic provenance of the individual implements, and only rarely is so much as an estimate of depth below the surface available. At Wolvercote there was at least Sandford's carefully argued interpretation of the position of the Channel in the local sequence, and a record of the finding of the implements and fauna at the extreme base, to assist the discussion. Burkitt's conclusions about the Warsash 'Micoquian' are absolutely ideal so far as the present writer's view of the Wolvercote industry is concerned, but, considered coldly, they in fact offer no substantial support whatsoever.[13] However, the reader may care to compare the Warsash artefacts shown here (Fig. 4:15) with those previously figured from Wolvercote and the Continental sites, and may find himself reflecting that Burkitt's unprovable conclusions may well be correct!

It will be seen that there is little good supporting evidence from within Britain for the suggested age of the Wolvercote industry, but that the Wolvercote occurrence does not seem to be unique. As ever, new finds are badly needed. On the other hand, the *absence* of 'Wolvercote type' plano-convex pointed handaxes from our prolific British Acheulian of known Hoxnian to Wolstonian age seems surprising, if the type is *not* restricted in time, and the Continental evidence is highly suggestive.

CONCLUSION

On the basis of the discussion in this whole chapter, then, we can now amend and expand the 'basic sequence' of Chapter 3 to read as follows:

1 (a) *British Earlier Acheulian*: industries with heavy, crude handaxes
   (b) *Clactonian*: industries lacking handaxes, with flakes and cores

   These are apparently separate entities, perhaps overlapping in time, with absolute priority not yet firmly established

   Age: Pre-Hoxnian to Hoxnian

2 *Middle Acheulian*: variable industries, tending to specialize in 'pointed' or 'ovate' handaxe types, and sometimes incorporating sporadic use of Levalloisian technique.
   Age: Hoxnian and later

3 *Late Acheulian/Micoquian*: a rather sparsely represented phase, with industries which include technologically distinctive plano-convex pointed handaxes.
   Age: Ipswichian (?)

4 Industries specializing in artefacts made by the *Levalloisian* technique, which sometimes at least may be separate from the Acheulian sequence.
   Age: Wolstonian and later

The numbers 1 to 4 should not be taken to imply a rigid chronological succession, since there is a clear possibility of overlap between 1 (b) and 2, 2 and 4, and 3 and 4. How far the Middle Acheulian of 2 is subdivisible remains to be considered in the next chapter. In considering north Kent, we merely recorded Acheulian industries of two kinds, which in that area appeared to be stratigraphically distinct, but now that we have also documented an Earlier Acheulian and a Late Acheulian/Micoquian, it seems more appropriate to bring these industries together for the moment into a general Middle Acheulian stage.

The handaxe tradition does not finally expire in Britain with the Wolvercote industry and those like it, since there are Middle Palaeolithic (Mousterian) examples to be noted in due course, but, as we shall see, the morphological contrast between them and the handaxes of Wolvercote is very great, and there may well be an important gap in time between the two series.

NOTES

1 It may perhaps seem a bit unfair to regret lack of publication by Pengelly when he produced a good quota of annual reports and summaries of the continuing work at the cave in the *Reports of the British Association for the Advancement of Science*, between 1865 and 1871, and in the *Transactions of the Devonshire Association*, between 1868 and 1874, plus a few other short papers and published lectures, but these references count as rather obscure by modern standards and he never put all his work together into a major site monograph with a complete analytical account of the finds.

2 Boyd Dawkins clearly understood what had occurred, and so did Pengelly himself (cf. Boyd Dawkins, 1874: 328-30; 1880: 196-7). They also appreciated that a long interval of time separated the Cave Earth from the Breccia.

3 Whether they were made there or merely carried in for use is another matter. The extant collections do not contain much obvious manufacturing debris, but Pengelly in 1875 reported that such material did occur in the breccia (quoted by Boyd Dawkins, 1880: 194-5).

4 He lists 29 pieces, but regards two of them as of natural origin.

5 It is worth commenting that Boyd Dawkins argued strongly (1874: 330-5) that the teeth of *Homotherium latidens* (or *Machairodus latidens* according to the then current classification) belonged to an earlier rather than a later position in the Kent's Cavern sequence, although he knew that they had actually been found in the Cave Earth. The writer owes the information given here about *U. deningeri* and *A. greeni* to Mr S.N. Collcutt, who has examined the Kent's Cavern and Westbury faunal remains in connection with his doctoral research at Oxford.

6 Thirty-six were said to have come from the cave (Pengelly 1873a, b; Boyd Dawkins 1874: 319), but they have not all survived and the present writer has seen less than half a dozen.

7 Of the four handaxes illustrated by R.A. Smith (1933: 167-8), one is certainly a fine ovate (his figure 3).

8 Sandford 1926: 140. Note — as not all authors seem to have noted — that Sandford merely remarks that the antler's condition and the adhering sand and clay 'give some grounds for referring it to the silt bed'. It does not seem to have been found *in situ*.

9 We might pertinently recall at this point the real possibility, referred to in Chapter 2, that there is actually more than one interglacial between the close of the Hoxnian and the start of the Devensian. If this is shown to be so, there may be more room for manoeuvre in establishing the relationship between the Wolvercote Channel and the Summertown-Radley Terrace, but for the present we cannot usefully construct such a scheme.

10 Use of the term 'Micoquian' has been rather variable over the past fifty years, and on occasion highly misleading. Some current authors, notably F. Bordes in France, define 'Micoquian handaxes' in a way which makes it perfectly reasonable for them to occur in what we have called Middle Acheulian industries. D.A.E. Garrod applied the term Micoquian to certain Lower Palaeolithic industries of the Middle East, notably those of level E at the Tabun Cave, Mount Carmel (Garrod and Bate 1937: 78-87), in which exaggeratedly pointed handaxes occurred, accompanied by numerous specialized flake-tools, but these industries are now usually called Jabrudian, following the work of A. Rust (1950) at the Jabrud Cave in Syria, and few people would wish to press a close comparison between Tabun E and La Micoque VI. L'Abbé Breuil referred to some of the bifacial tools of certain East European Mousterian industries as Micoquian handaxes, and others have used the term in yet further ways. The present writer would prefer to see the name Micoquian reserved for industries rather than individual implements: such industries should be specifically and demonstrably late in the handaxe tradition, as is La Micoque level VI itself, and should contain a strong element of finely made pointed handaxes whose technological range includes the plano-convex style of working described and stressed in this chapter. There is of course no reason at all why there should not be other handaxe industries contemporary with them but differing morphologically and technologically and indeed functionally; these can be referred to as Late Acheulian or Final Acheulian as appropriate, but should not be given the more specific designation Micoquian, which indicates a special tradition within the final stages of the Acheulian, whatever may be the reasons for its existence. The conclusions reached by G. Bosinski (1967) in Germany seem to the writer to be interesting and

important in this connection, but they appear to have been less well studied in Britain than should be the case. However, since the writer's first-hand experience of the Continental material is limited, and since no detailed formal comparison has been made between the British and Continental industries, it seemed best to settle on 'Late Acheulian/ Micoquian' as a designation for the British sites discussed in this section; this should fix their general position and affinities without begging detailed questions, though the writer has indicated his own more specific impressions.

11 Bocksteinschmiede is the name of one of a group of Bockstein sites: the full list of names, and details of what came from where, can be found in the reports by Wetzel (1958) and Wetzel and Bosinski (1969). The two most important in the present context were Bocksteinloch, a small cave some eight metres deep by eight metres broad, and Bocksteinschmiede, which is the open area immediately in front of this cave. Wetzel and Bosinski (1969: 15-20) have given a summary of the stratigraphy, including a section diagram. Their level *h*, which contained the Bockstein III Micoquian industry, occurs both in the cave and in front of it: IIIa, from Bocksteinschmiede, yielded 2791 artefacts and IIIb, from Bocksteinloch yielded 41. Eleven more artefacts came from the junction between IIIa and IIIb, where the two sites merge. The whole lot are thought to belong together.

12 As a final comment on these suggested affinities of the Wolvercote industry, the writer would just like to record that in September 1976 he took a few characteristic Wolvercote handaxes, and some of the flake-tools, to the IXth UISPP Congress in France, and showed them, inviting comments, during Colloque X (the Evolution of the Acheulian in Europe), which was directed by M. Jean Combier and took place at Orgnac, Provence. The attendance at Colloque X included several specialists who were familiar with the German and French handaxe industries. *All* those who offered informal comments were agreed that from the techno-typological point of view the Wolvercote implements certainly ought

to be of later rather than earlier date; some even expressed the opinion that a Holsteinian (Hoxnian) date would be 'unthinkable'. A few other colleagues expressed similar opinions during the main Congress at Nice. All these comments were informal, so the writer will not attach specific names to them.

13 However, Dr M. Shackley (pers. com.), during work for her Southampton University Ph.D. thesis (1975) was able to make some direct observations in the Warsash areas which are well worth quoting in this connection. She recorded several exposures of a raised beach in the present cliff sections between Chilling and Hill Head; the base of the beach shingle in each case was close to +8m O.D. and the marine deposits were several metres thick, showing cryoturbation and occasional ice-wedge casts at the top. They were capped in several places by brickearth. Dr Shackley was able to trace seventy-six artefacts in various collections, which certainly came from these raised beach deposits and to find some herself *in situ*: they were all in a physical condition fresh enough to suggest that they were contemporary with the beach and had not merely been redeposited by marine action during its formation, though there is no suggestion that they constitute a single unmixed industry. Amongst them she recognized several classic 'Wolvercote' handaxes, and also some typical 'Mousterian of Acheulian Tradition' material. The age of the 7.5/8m beach in this part of the south coast is generally regarded as late Ipswichian (cf. West and Sparks 1960), and the artefacts described by Dr Shackley match such a date well. Her observations, then, tend to confirm our preferred reading of the chronology of Wolvercote, and to illuminate the conclusions of Burkitt *et al.* (1939) — always provided, of course, that one accepts the 'Wolvercote' implements as being so distinctive technologically as to represent a handaxe type which was current for one relatively brief period only. That is certainly the present writer's view of them. He is grateful to Dr Shackley for permission to include this brief account of her findings.

More Sites, and the Question of Variation

Chapter 5

The two preceding chapters have sought to establish an outline sequence for the British Lower Palaeolithic, using only a few sites to do so. It is now time to cast the net wider and to see what other British sites can be fitted into the suggested general stages. It may be expected that some further occurrences will fit easily into the framework, matching well with those already described, but it may equally be anticipated that others will show less close similarities, and this leads to the important question of what may be termed 'horizontal variation'. The latter term refers to differences between industries which are precisely or approximately contemporary, as opposed to 'vertical' variation, which denotes differences between industries which demonstrably occur in succession through a substantial period of time — not necessarily in a continuous sequence, of course, but at least in a known order. We look for 'vertical' variation between, for example, Early, Middle and Late Acheulian industries, though not necessarily for continuous evolution or clear 'time trends'. But *within* each of those stages, provided there are enough sites of good quality, we must also look for 'horizontal' variations between the industries. And may we not look in expectation of finding it? It is inconceivable that an identical toolkit would have suited Acheulian man for each of his different activities wherever he set up camp through all the different seasons of the year. If he had not been adaptable and inventive, should we even be here to speculate about his activities or to criticize other prehistorians' views on typology? This chapter's wider review of the British Lower Palaeolithic

begins with some general comments on the distribution of sites, and then considers each of the main units previously defined, in the following order of convenience:

Clactonian
Acheulian: Early
                 Middle
                 Late/Micoquian
Levalloisian

THE LOWER PALAEOLITHIC IN BRITAIN

Modern geography is only partially relevant to earlier Palaeolithic distributions in Britain, since coastlines, drainage and even relief have changed profoundly during the Pleistocene, and indeed during the Holocene. However, it is mainly in modern geographical terms that we are bound to speak. The present writer (1968b) has listed the locations of over 3,000 British Lower and Middle Palaeolithic find-spots, to which basic corpus of information a few dozen new finds made since 1968 could be added; it is only necessary here to give a working summary.[1]

Some amplification of the general comments which follow is forthcoming from Figs. 5:1 to 5:4, which are taken from an earlier publication (Roe 1964: plate XXVII). This distribution map was made by the present writer at ¼ inch scale, and showed the first 2,000 sites recorded by him during the process of data collection, plotted in relation to modern coastline and drainage, but even ¼ inch scale did not provide sufficient space to set out in full the concentrations of sites in

132

5:1 Distribution map of some 2,000 British Lower and Middle Palaeolithic find-spots, as published by the author in 1964 (see page 131): North-west section, almost empty of finds. The key also applies to Figs 5:2 to 5:4

5:2 North-east section (for key, see Fig. 5:1)

5:3 South-east section, the most densely populated (for key, see Fig. 5:1)

5:4 South-west section (for key, see Fig. 5:1)

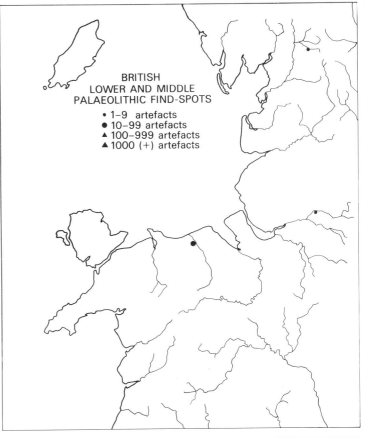

BRITISH
LOWER AND MIDDLE
PALAEOLITHIC FIND-SPOTS
• 1–9 artefacts
● 10–99 artefacts
▲ 100–999 artefacts
▲ 1000 (+) artefacts

1

2

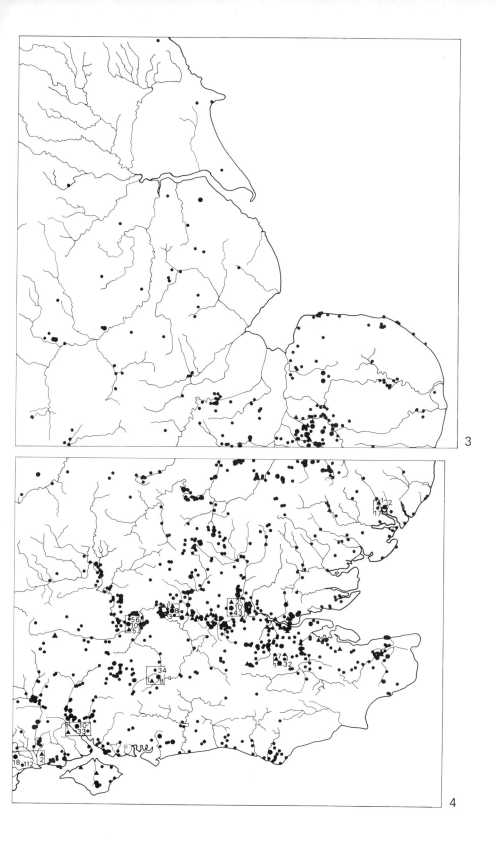

3

4

certain areas. Attempts to reproduce the map on a single page have not been satisfactory, so it is here split into sections to give a clearer result. The remaining 1,100 or so find-spots have not been added, because the map is already overcrowded and because they merely make denser the existing distribution pattern without essentially changing it.

Distribution maps are generally regarded as essential to archaeological publication, and quite rightly, but in many ways maps of this particular kind represent a somewhat empty exercise. Very few of the recorded find-spots are true occupation sites rather than mere places where gravel was dug and found to contain derived implements. There is no sorting by period within the Lower and Middle Palaeolithic: the map covers the full range of time from pre-Hoxnian to Ipswichian and indeed later, and does so blindly because the precise dating of the vast majority of the sites is unknown and unknowable. The light it casts on the life and movements of actual people is thus obscure at best. For example, the strong lowland bias of the distribution positively indicates a preference for settlement by rivers and lakes and clearly implies man's ability to construct such artificial shelters as must certainly have been necessary (caves and rockshelters being extremely rare in most areas) — but we cannot give any examples of such structures, or even say whether our recorded sites were seasonal camps and, if so, where the other seasons were spent; nor do we see evidence for individual communities or for regional variation of a cultural kind, such as one might seek in distribution maps drawn for later prehistoric periods.

On the positive side, the sheer density of the find-spots is perhaps impressive, especially when one recalls that Britain is a remote and peripheral area of Palaeolithic settlement. Again, the scarcity of finds in the north Midlands and their total absence in the north seems likely to have a basis in Palaeolithic fact rather than Pleistocene process. It is true enough that the north bore the brunt of glaciation and that any evidence for settlement there accordingly runs a far higher risk of destruction by geological forces. But can we really believe that *all* the evidence was destroyed or swept down and re-deposited from the south Midlands south-wards, and that none of it escaped movement or was merely re-deposited locally? Plenty of people have looked for sites in the north and artefacts have even been claimed (e.g. F. Smith 1909; Asher 1922), but none is really convincing and most are frankly of natural origin so far as the writer's experience of them goes. A few genuine Lower Palaeolithic finds from northern England or even from Scotland may well one day come to light, suggesting occasional hunting or prospecting forays northwards from the Midlands; this would not be surprising. But for the moment there is no definite Lower or Middle Palaeolithic of these areas, although there are important Pleistocene sequences and deposits containing evidence of conditions in every way suitable for Palaeolithic settlement (Mitchell *et al.* 1973: 22-36, 53-9).

And what of Ireland? The claims made by Reid Moir, Burchell and others (e.g. F. Smith 1909; Burchell *et al.* 1929; Burchell and Moir 1932) for Lower and Middle Palaeolithic artefacts near Sligo and in certain other localities do not amount to a convincing body of evidence for genuine artefacts of unequivocally Middle or Upper Pleistocene date (see also Movius 1942: 105-17). However, one typical handaxe at least has been found in Ireland (Murphy n.d.); but the implement, which is abraded, turned up (in 1974) in a crevice among the *chevaux de frise* at the side of the late prehistoric fort of Dun Aenghus at Inishmore in the Aran Islands, County Galway. Such a provenance scarcely constitutes a clear demonstration that earlier Palaeolithic man reached Ireland — any more than does the existence of a single typical enough handaxe marked 'Antrim', which the present writer once noted at the British Museum. That one occurred in a drawer of miscellaneous Lower Palaeolithic artefacts from Kent, and there was no documentation: 'Antrim' is as likely to be a house name in Kent, or the name of the finder, as it is to refer to Antrim in Ireland. The orthodox view is that during the Pleistocene there may always have been a sufficient deep-water barrier between England, Wales and south-west Scotland on the one hand, and Ireland on the other, to inhibit human movement, however reduced in width the barrier might have been during times of low sea-level. The shortest access route, setting deep-water barriers aside, would have been from south-west Scotland to north-east Ireland – but as we have seen, there is no clear indication that Lower or Middle Palaeolithic man ever reached south-west Scotland. Nor in fact do we know that he ever reached what is now the west-facing coast of Wales, let alone passed beyond it to lands now submerged below the Irish Sea. As for possible land-bridges at times of low sea-level, was man present in Britain at all, let alone in the western fringes, when sea-levels were at their lowest during the cold maxima? Yet if he only reached the coasts that faced Ireland during the milder spells of climate, presumably he would have had no more sight of land over the water than one gets today. Nor does any single feature of the Old World earlier Palaeolithic distribution, not even the peopling of Britain itself, at present demand the use of sea-going craft, or suggest that speculative crossing of open sea took place. So there is no Palaeolithic of Ireland to write about either.

So far as the actual British Lower Palaeolithic distribution is concerned (the Middle Palaeolithic will be considered in the next chapter), we see a broad coverage of England south of a line from the Bristol Channel to the Humber, with a scatter of sites a little way further north. There is only the most marginal penetration of Wales, represented by a fine quartzite handaxe from Pen-y-Lan, Cardiff (Lacaille 1954b) and possibly by the very poorly known industry with handaxes from the Pontnewydd Cave, Cefn, near St Asaph (Hughes and Thomas 1874; Hughes 1887; Molleson 1976), though this is usually regarded as a Middle Palaeolithic occurrence (see Chapter 6). In southern England there are major concentrations of finds in the Middle and Lower Thames Valley, in East Anglia, and in south Hampshire. It is true enough that these are areas where sedimentary deposits of Middle and Upper Pleistocene age have been widely exploited commercially over many decades, and it is also true that they are regions which have always been keenly watched by knowledgeable collectors, but nevertheless their relative richness does seem to reflect a greater density of Palaeolithic settlement, since there has been no shortage of either exposures or competent observers in the less

densely populated areas on the map – the Upper Thames Valley, say, or the south Midlands, or the south-western peninsula. In all these latter areas sites have been found; however, not only are the sites themselves fewer, but also, with very few exceptions, the quantities of artefacts they have yielded are low. The density of finds thus tails off as one goes north or west from south-east England: the distribution is not suddenly truncated, which would make one suspect destruction of the evidence rather than genuine absence of material, but simply peters out. Thus, in the large counties of Yorkshire and Lincolnshire we see almost exclusively single finds of artefacts, and prolific sites are rare all over the Midlands proper; only Hilton and Willington in Derbyshire (Posnansky 1963: 364-78) have yielded over a hundred artefacts, and that between them and including waste-flakes. Gloucestershire, Worcestershire and Shropshire can muster only a handful of Lower Palaeolithic artefacts between them: a comparison of the respective distributions in the Thames and Severn Valleys makes the point strikingly enough. Cornwall and Devon, too, are poor in material: from the extreme south-west, one must go eastwards as far as the Exe Valley on the Devon/ Dorset border before encountering a really prolific site, the famous Broom Pit at Hawkchurch (Moir 1936; Roe 1968a: 11), where an admirable raw material, the Axminster Greensand chert, was abundantly exploited by handaxe makers. Another prolific western site, which yielded artefacts in hundreds, was Chapel Pill Farm at Abbots Leigh on the outskirts of Bristol (Lacaille 1954a; Roe 1974), but the map shows that such rich find-spots remain rare until one has proceeded as far east as the Bournemouth region. It is the writer's belief that the distribution he has here summarized is a fair indication that Lower Palaeolithic man only rarely passed beyond the limits of southern and eastern Britain as broadly defined by the Bristol Channel – Humber line; contrast however the view expressed by John Wymer (Wymer and Straw 1977).

CLACTONIAN SITES

We encountered the Clactonian in the north Kent

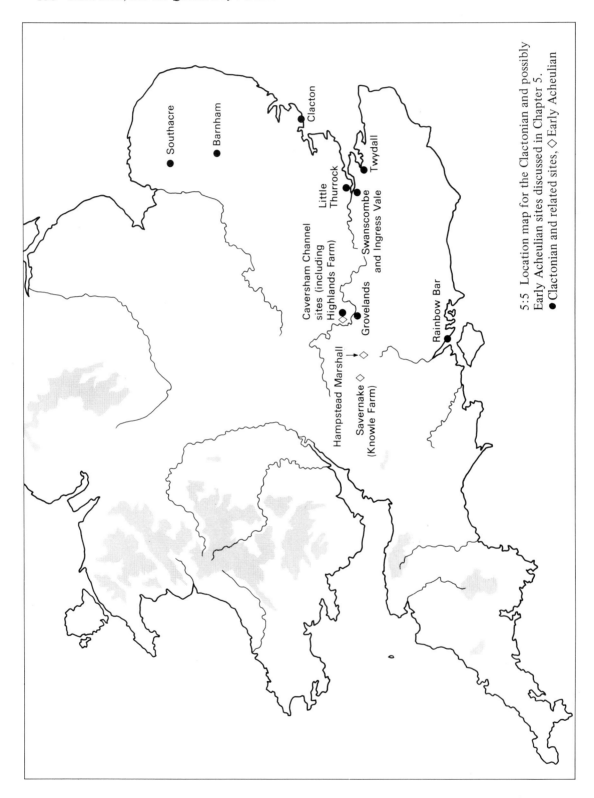

5:5 Location map for the Clactonian and possibly Early Acheulian sites discussed in Chapter 5. ● Clactonian and related sites, ◇ Early Acheulian

Southacre

Barnham

Clacton

Twydall

Little Thurrock

Swanscombe and Ingress Vale

Caversham Channel sites (including Highlands Farm)

Grovelands

Hampstead Marshall

Savernake (Knowle Farm)

Rainbow Bar

sequence, in the Barnfield Pit Lower Gravels and Lower Loam, and also at Rickson's Pit. From these occurrences, which are rich in artefacts, it appeared (cf. Chapter 3) that Clactonian industries contain no handaxes at all, nor the *débitage* of their manufacture, but they include somewhat informal and haphazardly retouched tools made on thick heavy flakes; cores also commonly occur as waste products of Clactonian flake production and sometimes, according to some authorities, these cores may have had a secondary use as choppers, even if they were not fashioned as such. Rough choppers and chopping tools, unifacially or bifacially worked, which are certainly *not* cores, also occur. The dating seemed most likely to be earlier Hoxnian, with some suggestion that older Clactonian occurrences might exist (see pages 68-70).

Certain other sites in Britain (Fig. 5:5) have yielded similar finds to those made in the lower levels at Swanscombe, though the dating is not always clear and where there is dating evidence the chronological position indicated is not always as early as that just mentioned. One must beware of some authors' use of the term 'Clactonian technique', which may merely denote the production of large heavy flakes with broad plain striking platforms, pronounced bulbs or cones of percussion and a high figure (say 110 to 140 degrees) for the angle between the general plane of the striking platform and the general plane of the bulbar surface. But these are all common features of the production of large flakes by use of a hard hammerstone, and can clearly occur at any stage of the Palaeolithic or even of Prehistory in general; more specifically, flakes showing these characteristics are certainly not outside the range of Acheulian industries, where they may occur for example as the initial hard-hammer removals from a large nodule as a first stage of shaping it into a handaxe, or even as blanks for handaxes themselves, since it is by no means uncommon for handaxes to be made on large flakes as well as from nodules. If one must seek a single hallmark, as it were, of the Clactonian, it might be better to regard the Clactonian 'chopper-cores' as providing it (cf. Wymer 1961: 3, 22-3, 1968: 34-44), since they are in fact very uncommon in other Palaeolithic industries, though not totally absent in every case, while in the Clactonian they are relatively frequent. However, it is far better not to rely on a single characteristic feature at all, but to reserve the name Clactonian for unmixed industries which consist wholly of the cores, flake implements and flakes of the kinds described, lack all sign of handaxe manufacture or Levalloisian technique, and, where dated, belong to the earlier stages of the Lower Palaeolithic (cf. Singer *et al.* 1973). This would not of course preclude the possibility of developments of somewhat younger date from the Clactonian thus rigidly defined; nor would it prevent one from suggesting, when dealing with mixed assemblages from gravels, that true Clactonian material is involved in the mixture on the grounds that very characteristic-looking cores and flakes were present in quantity.

If we confine ourselves to a rigid definition of Clactonian, then there are very few British sites indeed to set alongside the Swanscombe occurrences. Of what there is, pride of place must go to the sites in the type area, Clacton-on-Sea, Essex. Artefacts have been collected here since before the beginning of the present century, and faunal remains since as long ago as the 1830s. Whatever future work may be done, the sites will always be closely associated with the name of S. Hazzledine Warren, a gifted archaeologist and geologist and a most dedicated collector, who devoted much of his life to the Palaeolithic of Essex. He watched the main Clacton exposures for more than forty years from about 1910, and published an important series of papers about them (e.g. Warren 1922, 1924, 1933, 1951, 1955, 1958; Warren *et al.* 1923). He did not himself carry out formal excavations at Clacton, but excavations have taken place there: by Kenneth Oakley and Mary Leakey at Jaywick Sands in 1934 (Oakley and Leakey, 1937), and more recently by the University of Chicago under the direction of Ronald Singer and John Wymer on land belonging to the Golf Club, in 1969-70. The principal report on the latter excavations (Singer *et al.* 1973) effectively summarizes previous work at Clacton and offers a useful bibliography as well as reporting the latest finds.

The Pleistocene deposits in the Clacton region

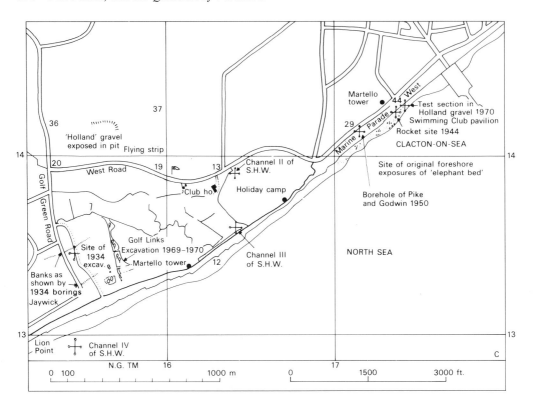

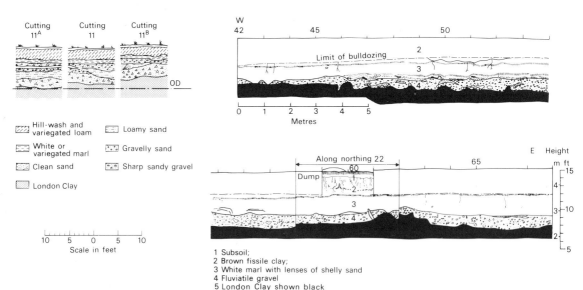

1 Subsoil;
2 Brown fissile clay;
3 White marl with lenses of shelly sand;
4 Fluviatile gravel
5 London Clay shown black

5:6 (a) map to show important archaeological locations in the Clacton area, after Singer *et al.* 1973; (b) sections in three cuttings through the Clacton Channel deposits at Jaywick Sands in the 1934 excavations, after Oakley and Leakey (1937); (c) section along north face of the main cutting of the excavations by Singer, Wymer and others in 1970 at the Golf Course site at Clacton, after Singer *et al.* (1973): key to numbers (see also Table 12): 1, Subsoil; 2, Brown fissile clay; 3, white marl with lenses of shelly sand; 4, fluviatile gravel

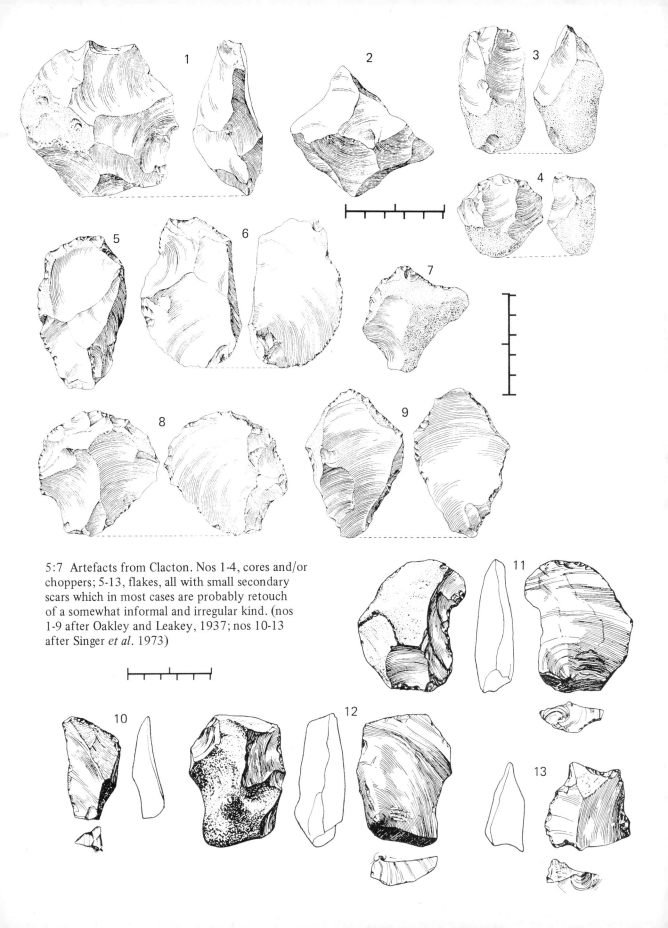

5:7 Artefacts from Clacton. Nos 1-4, cores and/or choppers; 5-13, flakes, all with small secondary scars which in most cases are probably retouch of a somewhat informal and irregular kind. (nos 1-9 after Oakley and Leakey, 1937; nos 10-13 after Singer *et al*. 1973)

(Fig. 5:6), which have yielded the Clactonian artefacts, are often referred to as 'the Clacton Channel', but there seems no doubt that several distinct channels are involved and that their fillings may between them span a longer period of time than used to be thought; some at least of these channels may be closely related to each other, forming part of a braided stream complex (Singer *et al.*, *op. cit.*). Some of the Pleistocene deposits have been exposed inland in the Jaywick area, and this is where the excavations have taken place, but others have been revealed by marine erosion on the foreshore below present high tide level. Warren and others recovered artefacts and faunal remains at several foreshore localities between Lion Point and Clacton Pier. Building work (e.g. at the Butlin's Holiday Camp site) and other modern disturbances have also exposed the channel deposits and have sometimes yielded artefacts. The Lion Point foreshore was especially rich, and Warren alone collected some thousands of artefacts there at times of low tide. The material from the proper archaeological excavations, on the other hand, is less prolific: rather less than 200 artefacts were obtained by Oakley and Leakey in 1934, and rather more than 1,200 by Singer and Wymer in 1969-70. Apart from the stone artefacts (Fig. 5:7), there is one other exceptional find, the famous Clacton spear tip, made of sharpened yew wood and 15¼ inches (38.8cm) long (Fig. 5:8). A new study of it by K.P. Oakley *et al.* (1977) has recently been made. This is the only surviving Lower Palaeolithic wooden artefact from Britain, though a few other possible ones have been recorded from Stoke Newington in East London (W.G. Smith 1894: 268-70, and see also the account of Stoke Newington later in this chapter). Such artefacts of comparable age are extremely rare all over the world, and the Clacton spear tip is best compared with the wooden spear of Eemian age, some 240 cm or 7 feet 10 inches long, found broken in 10 pieces at Lehringen, near Verden, Lower Saxony, about 1948 (Movius 1950). Unfortunately the Clacton find did not come from an excavation, but was discovered by Warren (1911) in a casual exposure of the Channel deposits on the Clacton foreshore.

On grounds of the lithology of the deposits, it seems reasonably certain that the complex of channels at Clacton belonged to a river which was a predecessor of the present Thames or was at least a part of the Thames-Medway drainage system; it flowed in a generally north-easterly direction, and was here evidently approaching its estuary, since some of the deposits are estuarine in character. It will be recalled from Chapter 3 that it was apparently an Anglian ice-advance which pushed the course of the Thames south from its former routes through the Vale of St Albans and the Finchley Gap, and that a terrace gravel on a 90 foot bench is banked against a chalky boulder clay near Upminster. What may have happened further east in the river's course at this time is perhaps less clear. The main filling of the Clacton channels has usually been regarded

5:8 The wooden spear
point from Clacton, after
Oakley (1949)

as of Hoxnian age on faunal grounds (with *Elephas (Palaeoloxodon) antiquus*, *Trogontherium boisvilletti*, *Cervus elaphus*, *Bos primigenius*, *Dama clactoniana*, *Dicerorhinus hemitoechus* and *Dicerorhinus kirchbergensis* all among the species present) and by virtue of the pollen analyses published by Pike and Godwin (1953) and Turner (Turner and Kerney 1971).

The various sections observed by Warren and others between 1911 and the mid 1950s suggested the generalized sequence at Clacton as shown in Table 11.

The results obtained in recent work by Singer and Wymer do not correlate precisely with the foregoing, and suggest that an extension of the time range envisaged above may be necessary. At the Golf Course site, their excavations gave the sequence (Table 12, Plate 27) here summarized and stated in general terms (for fuller details see Singer *et al.* 1973).

There is no suggestion that the whitish marl is an estuarine deposit as found in the previously studied Clacton exposures. The authors believe that there is a depositional break in the sequence between the top of the marl and the base of the sterile brown clay, and that the estuarine part of the sequence, for which no actual evidence survives at the Golf Club site, belongs there.

There are further complexities, too, which make correlation difficult. Examination of the stratigraphy at the Golf Course site indicates that the basal gravel was subjected to very cold conditions, probably periglacial, before the marl was deposited over it. There are also signs of at least intermittent cold conditions during the deposition of the marl itself and again during deposition of the brown fissile clay. The gravel and the marl both contained pollen, on which only a preliminary report is yet available, but the results so far suggest, very tentatively, that the marl contains a cool flora which may represent the pre-temperate zone (Zone I) of an interglacial, presumably the Hoxnian, while the gravel which underlies it was deposited during a period of rather variable conditions of temperature and climate, which may lie within the Anglian complex. The cold episode between the deposition of the gravel and the marl would thus presumably represent the final Anglian

TABLE 11 : *The Clacton Channel sequence*
(after Warren and others)

4 Hill wash and modern soil
3 An upper 'estuarine' series, consisting of various loams, marls and clays, with lenses of shelly sand and occasional estuarine peat. Mammalian fauna was rare in most exposures and artefacts were rare or absent. There are estuarine mollusca, and the pollen was attributed by Turner to Hoxnian Zone III
2 A lower series of freshwater (fluviatile) deposits, consisting of gravels and sands, with occasional lenses of peat. This freshwater series was rich in mammalian faunal remains, especially elephant bones and teeth, and has sometimes been called the 'Elephant Bed'. Clactonian artefacts were also abundant. Pollen from these levels was attributed by Pike and Godwin (*op. cit.*) to Hoxnian Zone II
1 At the base, London Clay (Tertiary), into which the channel or channels were cut

TABLE 12 : *The Clacton Channel sequence*
(after Singer and Wymer)

1 London Clay, into which the channel complex was cut
2 Fluviatile gravel (Layer 4 of Singer *et al.* 1973): a thin bed, defining one particular channel within a 'channel complex'. Mammalian fauna, of generally temperate character, and freshwater mollusca, were found and artefacts were also present. The gravel was capped locally by shelly sand in an area adjacent to the excavation trenches
3 Whitish marl (Layer 3 of Singer *et al.* 1973), with lenses of shelly sand. Faunal remains were very scarce (*op. cit.*, p. 23 and Fig. 8). Artefacts were present at all levels, though less common than in the gravel
4 A small localized gravel spread capped the marl in one part of the excavation. Scattered faunal remains and artefacts were associated with it. It may well represent redeposition of material from near the edges of the channel, rather than being a new land surface *in situ*
5 Brown fissile clay, archaeologically sterile (Layer 2 of Singer *et al.* 1973). Its precise age and origin remain obscure, but it is evidently younger than the channel fill proper
6 Subsoil (sandy loam, Layer 1 of Singer *et al.* 1973), with a little late Prehistoric material, capped by ploughsoil

advance. If these provisional conclusions prove to be correct, it must follow: (a) that the whole of the channel fill at the Golf Course site is older than any part of the freshwater and estuarine deposits observed by Warren and his contemporaries, since these were not earlier than Hoxnian Zone II; (b) that, as regards the general sequence in the Clacton area, more is missing at the Golf Course site in the supposed hiatus between the marl and the fissile clay than the estuarine deposits, since they were of Hoxnian Zone III age and the marl is taken to be Hoxnian Zone I; (c) that the Clactonian is present in Britain before Zone I of the Hoxnian and indeed before the final advance of the Anglian ice; (d) that the Clactonian of Clacton begins somewhat earlier than that of Swanscombe, if the Barnfield Pit Lower Gravels are of Hoxnian age, as is usually supposed.

It does however appear from the reports on the work at the Clacton Golf Course site that there may be some room left for manoeuvre with the pollen analyses, so perhaps it is best to reserve judgement on the dating for the moment.[2]

With regard to (d) above, if we return to the views of Warren, Oakley and others, based on the earlier work at Clacton, we find the Clactonian of Clacton regarded as specifically *younger* than that of the Swanscombe Lower Gravels. Typology played a part in this: the industries of the type area were considered to be smaller, neater and better made than those of Swanscombe. It was customary to refer to the Clactonian of Swanscombe as 'Clactonian IIa' and to that of Clacton as 'Clactonian IIb'. The 'Clactonian I' stage was thought to be represented by certain crude derived Clactonian flakes and cores from the Swanscombe Lower Gravels, which were thought to be older than the deposit itself and its contemporary 'Clactonian IIa'. Some authors also applied the term Clactonian I to some of the supposed artefacts from the 'Crag' and 'Cromerian' deposits mentioned briefly in Chapter 4. There was also a 'Clactonian III' stage, of which the chief occurrence was thought to be a fine flake industry (made on plain-platform flakes), discovered at High Lodge, near Mildenhall, Suffolk. The real affinities of the High Lodge find will be discussed in the next chapter. These numbered Clactonian

stages have persisted in the literature until comparatively recently, but none now retains any usefulness.

However, it was not only on typological grounds that the Clactonian of Clacton was held to be younger than that of the Swanscombe Lower Gravels. A correlation of the two sequences was proposed, as follows. At Swanscombe, the Lower Gravels lie, as we saw, on a bench at about 75 feet O.D., being capped by the Lower Loam, whose surface is markedly weathered, indicating a break in aggradation before the overlying Middle Gravels were deposited. But the lower part of the Clacton Channel filling exposed on the foreshore is mainly a few feet *below* modern sea-level, in spite of being a fluviatile deposit and containing an interglacial fauna and flora. It was therefore supposed that after the deposition of the Lower Loam, the sea level had fallen and the river had cut down, possibly aided by tectonic disturbance or movement, but probably in some kind of short colder spell within the interglacial. Thus the Clacton Channel was formed, at a curiously low level for a Hoxnian deposit,[3] and thus the basal deposit was a freshwater one in a channel still some way from the river's mouth. Then the sea-level rose again, drowning the freshwater series at Clacton, which is covered by estuarine deposits. It was thought that this rising sea-level was also responsible for the aggradation at Swanscombe of the Middle Gravels, later in the same interglacial, by which time the Clactonian had been replaced or joined in the Lower Thames Valley by the Middle Acheulian, though while the Clacton freshwater beds were forming a Clactonian industry had still been current — the so-called Clactonian IIb, as we have seen. This is a rather attractive argument, and some truth at least may lie in it, but the question now is whether the work of Singer and Wymer indicates an earlier Clactonian stage, current before any of that sequence of events would have taken place.

As regards the artefacts from the Golf Course site, much of the material recovered by Singer and Wymer consists of flaking *débitage*. It is probably mainly debris scattered from immediately adjacent living sites and has for the most part undergone minimal disturbance. Lawrence Keeley, who studied the artefacts at Oxford for microwear traces, was able to conjoin no less than twenty pieces, which had been scattered over several square metres of the excavated area. The industry seems typically enough Clactonian, as defined above, with no trace of handaxe manufacture. No structure or hearth was found, but if such existed they would probably have been placed a little back from the channel banks. Keeley's conclusions about the activities carried on at this site are mentioned in the final chapter of this book.

As regards other Clactonian sites in Britain (Map, Fig. 5:5), John Wymer has summarized them (in Singer *et al.* 1973: 43-60; see also Wymer 1968) and the present writer is in general agreement with his conclusions. We have already noted the occurrences in the Swanscombe area at Barnfield and Rickson's Pits. At Dierden's Pit, Ingress Vale, less than two miles away, Clactonian artefacts are recorded as occurring in a gravel which features an important shell bed, and is believed on the basis of old reports to be approximately equivalent in age to the Swanscombe Lower Gravels. The records of this occurrence are none too clear, however, leaving doubt about the relationship of the Clactonian artefacts to various handaxes found at the same pit (Smith, R.A. and Dewey 1914; Wymer 1968: 333-4, quoting earlier references). Across the present river, in the area of Grays Thurrock, there are more Clactonian find-spots, of which the most important is certainly the Globe Pit at Little Thurrock. Here Wymer himself (1957; 1968: 314-17; Singer *et al.* 1973: 51) was able to carry out a small-scale excavation in 1954, to check and amplify discoveries first made nearly fifty years earlier. He obtained 294 artefacts (5 cores and 289 flakes and fragments), from a rather thin bed of sandy gravel overlying the Tertiary Thanet Sand on a bench at about 49 feet O.D. This gravel appeared to be a remnant of a terrace and was formerly of greater thickness; it is covered by another gravel (without artefacts) and both are truncated by a channel containing brickearth. The 49 foot bench height is too low to correspond with that of the Swanscombe Lower Gravels, since the sites are only about three miles apart, and the Little Thurrock gravel unfortunately contained no faunal remains or other dating evidence. One

suggested interpretation was that the deposit corresponded to a period of lower sea-level, later than the Swanscombe Lower Gravels and Lower Loam, which might suit the classic interpretation of the Clacton Channel's low altitude, outlined above, but there seems no clear proof of this. The brickearth in the channel at the Globe Pit was part of the famous Grays Brickearth, which has a rich fauna and is thought most likely to be of Ipswichian age (West 1969). Wymer illustrates some cores and flakes from his excavations in the gravel, which certainly look typically Clactonian (Fig. 5:9; see also Wymer 1957: figs 5-10), and there was no clear trace of handaxe manufacture. The artefacts were in fresh condition. There are also extant old collections with considerable quantities of artefacts from Little Thurrock which correspond technologically and typologically to the Clactonian assemblages described in this chapter – for example, the Worthington Smith collection at Luton Museum – though whether they came from earlier exposures at this same site, or from other find-spots, is not clear.

At East Farm, Barnham, Suffolk, T.T. Paterson (1937) excavated a site at which he distinguished several levels of artefacts and proposed a sequence (Fig. 5:10) with a local facies of Clactonian (his Industries A-E) underlying Acheulian (Industry F). There are certainly some typical and well-made ovate handaxes from the top level, but the material lower down in the series is pretty generalized and not wholly convincing as a series of Clactonian industries, although there are certainly some cores and flakes in the Clactonian manner amongst it. None of Paterson's Industries A-E is in primary context, and it is not clear to the present writer that his Industries B-E do in reality constitute four separate occurrences. We must remember the profound influence of typological considerations at the time when the paper was written: Paterson envisaged gradual technological advances made by the local 'flake people' of Barnham, before the first appearance of handaxe makers in Industry F. The site, however, remains of some importance because the gravel series containing Industry A, the oldest, is underlain by a chalky (Anglian) boulder clay, and the main body of the gravel itself appears to be an Anglian outwash deposit,

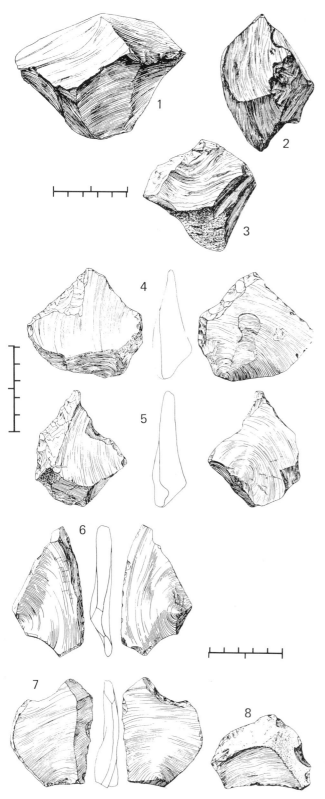

within the upper part of which the artefacts of Paterson's Industry A are incorporated in an abraded condition. They are all flakes, with some possible crude retouch in some cases; no cores were found, but some at least of the pieces do seem to be artefacts. Industries B-E, substantially less abraded than A, occur at the top of this gravel and evidently postdate the outwash period itself; the typical Acheulian artefacts of F are in a brick-earth overlying the gravel. According to Paterson, this brickearth is capped by an Upper Chalky Boulder Clay (of presumably Wolstonian age), and there are other Pleistocene levels above that. If nothing else, then, the Barnham site suggests that flake manufacture of loosely 'Clactonian' character (Industry A) may have been current locally before the Anglian ice-sheets had fully withdrawn – a conclusion not inconsistent with Wymer's opinions of the age of the earliest Clactonian in Britain, as Wymer himself has noted (in Singer *et al.* 1973: 51). M.Y. Ohel, however, has recently expressed important reservations about the 'Clactonian' nature of the Barnham artefacts (1977a).

There do not seem to be any further undoubted examples of pure Clactonian industries from British sites, though there are several instances where one can point to heavy cores, and crude flakes in the Clactonian style amongst mixed assemblages in which typical Acheulian or even Levalloisian material is also present. A mixed assemblage, collected over many years from the Barnham Heath Gravel Pit, not far from Paterson's East Farm site just discussed, is a good example. We have seen that Clacton-style cores are *not* a common feature of handaxe industries, and it may well be that some of these confused sites do indeed contain true Clactonian artefacts in a derived state, but we cannot take serious account of them all. A few, however, are worth a brief mention for one reason or another.

5:9 Artefacts from the gravel at the Globe Pit, Little Thurrock. Nos 1-3, cores; 5-8, flakes, of which nos 4 and 5 show clear retouch. After Wymer, 1957

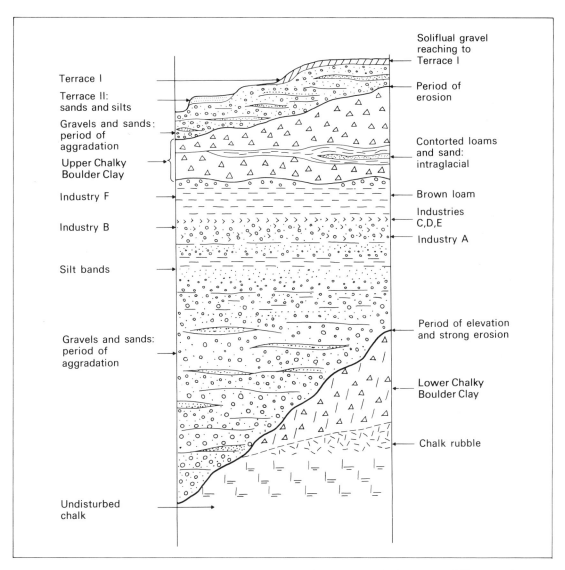

Terrace I

Terrace II: sands and silts

Gravels and sands: period of aggradation

Upper Chalky Boulder Clay

Industry F

Industry B

Silt bands

Gravels and sands: period of aggradation

Undisturbed chalk

Soliflual gravel reaching to Terrace I

Period of erosion

Contorted loams and sand: intraglacial

Brown loam

Industries C,D,E

Industry A

Period of elevation and strong erosion

Lower Chalky Boulder Clay

Chalk rubble

5:10 T.T. Paterson's composite section showing the sequence in the Barnham area and the strati- graphic position of the various different industries he distinguished, after Paterson (1937)

Of such occurrences, the famous 'Caversham Ancient Channel' may be considered first (Treacher *et al.* 1948; Wymer 1961, 1968). This feature cuts across a loop of the present Thames course between Caversham, near Reading and Henley-on-Thames (Fig. 5:11), at a level much above that of the present river (+45 metres approximately). Its height in fact corresponds to that of the Winter Hill Terrace of the Middle Thames, which is now usually regarded as of Anglian age. The account given in 1948 by Treacher, Arkell and Oakley suggested that this gravel, which was exploited commercially for many years at several pits, was a true Thames deposit, of Winter Hill age, containing an assemblage of artefacts dominated by 'Early Acheulian' or 'Abbevillian' forms. This assessment of the artefacts was based on an analysis of the material gathered by Llewellyn Treacher, a well-

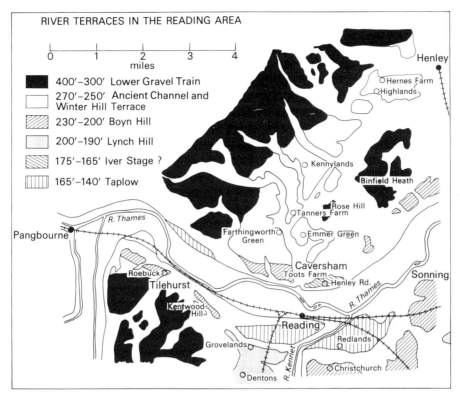

RIVER TERRACES IN THE READING AREA

0 1 2 3 4
miles

■ 400'–300' Lower Gravel Train
□ 270'–250' Ancient Channel and Winter Hill Terrace
▨ 230'–200' Boyn Hill
▨ 200'–190' Lynch Hill
▨ 175'–165' Iver Stage ?
▥ 165'–140' Taplow

Henley
○ Hernes Farm
○ Highlands
○ Kennylands
Binfield Heath
R. Thames
Rose Hill
○ Tanners Farm
Pangbourne
○ Farthingworth Green
○ Emmer Green
Caversham
Toots Farm
○ Henley Rd.
Sonning
Roebuck○
Tilehurst
R. Thames
Kentwood Hill
Reading
Redlands
Grovelands○
R. Kennet
○ Christchurch
○ Dentons

5:11 Map to show location of the 'Ancient Channel' gravels between Caversham and Henley, and their relationship to other gravel deposits in the area. Pits from which large numbers of artefacts have come are shown by small circles. After Wymer (1968)

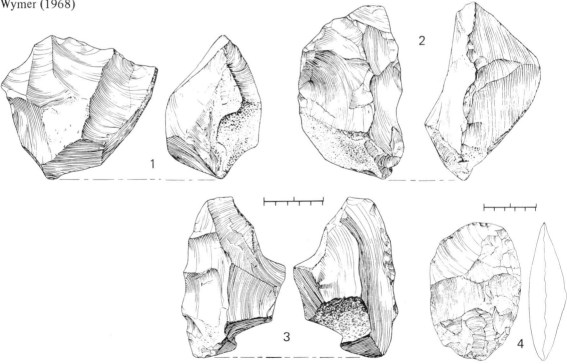

1

2

3

4

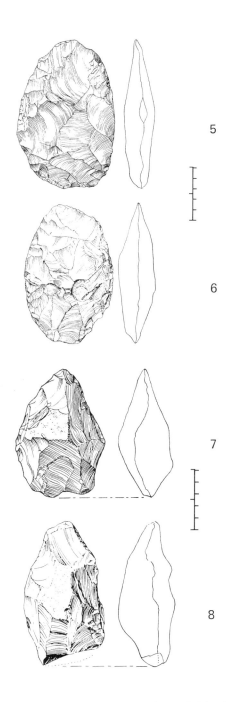

5:12 Principal artefact types from Highlands Farm Pit, after Wymer (1961). Nos 1, 2, chopper cores of Clactonian type; no. 3, side chopper on heavy Clacton-style flake; nos 4-6, well-made Acheulian ovate handaxes (note tranchet finish scars); nos 7, 8, crude handaxes, possibly Early Acheulian

known local collector, from such sites as Farthingworth Green, Kennylands (Tar Pit), Hernes Farm Pit and others. The conclusions of these authors were disputed by John Wymer (1961) on the basis of his own observations and excavations at Highlands Farm Pit, Rotherfield Peppard, the last of the Ancient Channel pits to be active. Wymer found that the gravel at this site was very much disturbed by collapses into solution hollows in the chalk, and that its character suggested deposition by fluvio-periglacial processes rather than by fluviatile aggradation, though it was possible that a pre-existing true Thames deposit had been drastically resorted when the main mass of material was laid down. Wymer concluded that the artefacts from the Highlands Farm Pit, which incidentally run into thousands if one includes the amounts amassed by private collectors (notably Mr R.J. MacRae) as well as Wymer's own excavated series, by no means constituted an Early Acheulian industry (Fig. 5:12). The two most striking elements present were, in his view, (a) evolved Middle Acheulian with fine, flat, ovate handaxes, in pretty fresh condition: Wymer's actual excavation trenches appear to have coincided with an important concentration of these, possibly transported together from a single site not far away, though similar implements have also come from other parts of the pit; (b) Clactonian, represented by large numbers of cores, choppers, flake-tools and unretouched flakes of the classic kind, mostly appreciably more abraded and patinated than the ovate handaxes. In addition, Wymer noted the presence of a relatively small quantity of crude, thick, archaic-looking handaxes, made by hard-hammer technique, which he felt more likely to be the remnant of a true Early Acheulian industry than the 'rough' and 'unfinished' element of the handaxe industry to which the fine ovates belonged. The classic pointed Middle Acheulian forms, so common at Swanscombe in the Middle Gravels, appear to be quite absent at Highlands Farm. Re-examination of the original Treacher Collection, now at the University Museum in Oxford, and a metrical analysis of the handaxes in it, and of those from the Highlands Farm Pit, suggested to the present writer (1964, 1968a) that Wymer's assessment of the Ancient Channel artefacts was nearer the mark than that of Treacher *et al.*, though to be fair there is very little obvious Clactonian material in the Treacher Collection; there may have been a particular concentration of Clactonian artefacts in the area of the Ancient Channel into which the Highlands Farm Pit happens to have been dug. It is also worth noting that Kenneth Oakley, the surviving author of the 1948 paper, is in full agreement with this revised view of the archaeology of the Ancient Channel.

While the exact nature and dating[4] of the Ancient Channel gravel itself must remain uncertain, it does look as if the deposit caught up at the time of its formation various artefacts of various different ages, spanning perhaps a whole interglacial or even longer. Some may have lain on the contemporary surface of the valley and hill sides; some may have been *in situ* in pre-existing fluviatile deposits which became completely resorted. Certainly there is no stratigraphic order to the different sets of implements as they now lie in the gravel. But one can see that 'true' Clactonian material of potentially early age may well be involved, though this is scarcely proved; the same may be said of the archaic-looking handaxes, that they could indeed be 'true' Early Acheulian.

Brief mention must also be made of two other sites which have often been called Clactonian: Grovelands Pit (Reading, Berkshire) and Southacre (Norfolk). In both cases the artefacts include 'chopper' cores and large flakes with broad, plain high-angle platforms and pronounced conchoidal fracture features, in sufficient quantity to suggest the presence of some distinctive industry of which these are characteristic products. In both cases, however, the flakes include a fair proportion of formal flake-tools, regularly and even elegantly shaped and retouched with flat secondary work right outside the normal quality of retouch found on the irregular flake-tools of the Clactonian of Clacton or Swanscombe (Fig. 5:13). In both cases, too, the deposits containing these artefacts also contain substantial quantities of implements which we would regard from the basic sequence of Chapter 3 as typically younger than the true Clactonian — fine ovates at Grovelands and well-made handaxes and Levalloisian cores and flakes at Southacre.

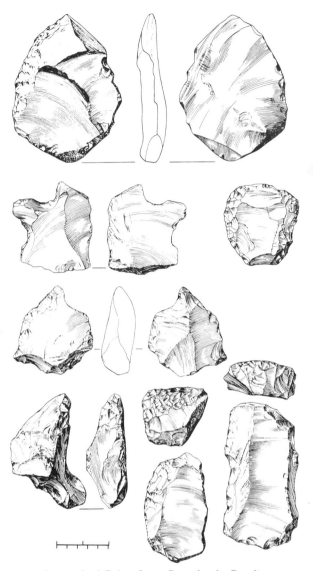

5:13 Retouched flakes from Grovelands, Reading, after Wymer (1968). Note the relative regularity of the retouch, and the presence of carefully shaped flake-tools

At Grovelands (Wymer 1968: 152-8, including a good list of early references) the artefacts occur mainly in a bluff gravel between the Lynch Hill and Taplow terraces of the Middle Thames — that is to say, in the confused area where material from the higher (Lynch Hill) terrace has slumped down at its eroded edge, immediately prior to, during, and to some extent also after, the formation of the lower one. However, it is very likely that the majority of the material belongs properly to the gravels of the Lynch Hill terrace; the finds were mostly made before the end of the nineteenth century, and there is no detailed account of their stratigraphy. Some faunal remains were also found, apparently including *Elephas (Palaeoloxodon) antiquus* and mammoth. The curious thing is that the well-made handaxes are much more heavily worn than the big cores and flakes. One cannot justifiably conclude that the cores and flakes are younger than the handaxes without knowing more about the formation of the containing deposit, which may well be composite and has certainly undergone disturbance when the bluff was formed, but the situation does reverse that encountered in the Caversham Ancient Channel a few miles away across the present river, where the Clactonian material was the more worn. The consistent difference in condition at Grovelands between the cores and flakes on the one hand, and the hand-axes on the other, certainly suggests that they do belong to different series. Technologically, the cores and flakes (cf. Fig. 5:13) of Grovelands look a more advanced series than the Clactonian of Clacton or Swanscombe, and the circumstances of the site at least do not contradict such a notion. As for the deposit, the most likely origins for the Lynch Hill Terrace gravels in this part of the valley would be either Hoxnian fluviatile aggradation, or fluvio-periglacial accumulation during some cold period after the Hoxnian maximum and before the Ipswichian, but we cannot safely judge between these alternatives on the basis of the old accounts of the Grovelands site. The Middle Thames terraces are discussed further in the 'Middle Acheulian' section of this chapter.

The Southacre site is very poorly known and there is not much literature dealing directly with it (see however Sainty 1935: 100; Sainty and Watson 1944). The deposit containing the artefacts seems to be an outwash gravel, presumably belonging to some phase of the Wolstonian, but that would merely provide an upper limit for the age of the artefacts, which are not much water-worn but deeply patinated and in some cases well weathered. There was no faunal evidence with them, and they

occurred at all depths in the gravel from 2 to 15 feet, apparently without stratigraphic distinction. It is not clear how many separate industries are represented, but the heavy cores and flakes and rather well-made flake-tools are generally speaking like those of Grovelands (cf. Singer *et al.* 1973: 59).[5]

Finally in this section, passing mention should be made of the discoveries made by J.C. Draper (1951) at Rainbow Bar, Hill Head, Hampshire. Here, there is a spread of gravel on the foreshore, uncovered only at low tide, from the surface of which large numbers of artefacts have been picked up over the past thirty years. No serious excavation has been attempted, and indeed it is difficult to see what could be done. Some Mesolithic artefacts and later prehistoric material have been found, but the vast majority of the pieces (several thousand) are flint flakes, with some cores and occasional choppers, which seem very similar to those of the true Clactonian of the type-site. There is no dating evidence; the presence amongst the material just mentioned of undeniably later implements in similar condition renders it perfectly possible that this may be flint-working debris of relatively late Prehistoric age – post Palaeolithic. But we may note on the other hand that a similar situation prevailed on the foreshore at Lion Point, Clacton, where not only the Clacton Channel deposits were being eroded by the sea, but also a postglacial land surface (the so-called 'Lyonesse' surface), with Neolithic and Bronze Age artefacts, some of which had become mixed in by wave action with the scatter of Lower Palaeolithic material (Warren *et al.* 1936). It seems perfectly possible that the Rainbow Bar gravel might represent the surface of a buried Pleistocene channel, capped by traces of a much younger land surface; it would at least be desirable to learn whether this were so, and to establish if possible the relationship of the gravel spread to the Pleistocene gravels which cap the low sea cliffs nearby, since at many points along the south Hampshire coast the cliff-top gravels contain undoubted Lower Palaeolithic artefacts, mostly Acheulian handaxes. Indeed, a prolific occurrence of such a kind existed (and has been known since last century) in the cliff-top gravels at Hill Head, only a very short distance from the Rainbow Bar site, even if many of the handaxes are in a somewhat abraded state and there is no question of a site in primary context.

The present writer, rightly or wrongly, is rather impressed with the 'Clactonian' affinities of the Rainbow Bar artefacts, as are several of his colleagues who have seen the material. We can reach no firm conclusion whatsoever in the present state of affairs, but there is a clear possibility that the Rainbow Bar assemblage may prove to include one of the more prolific Clactonian occurrences in Britain, in a situation comparable to that observed at Lion Point. Regrettably, no inland extension of the gravel has yet been located, and no faunal remains or other dating evidence have yet been recovered from the foreshore site. One may also be reminded of a not entirely dissimilar occurrence just across the Channel in north-west France, at La Pointe-aux-Oies, Wimereux (Pas-de-Calais), where unifacially and bifacially worked pebble tools and choppers were recovered from the fore-shore, exposed by marine erosion, in a gravel which was probably continuous with deposits at the base of the cliff (Tuffreau 1971a, b, 1972; Sommé and Tuffreau 1976). Some of the Wimereux artefacts have been specifically compared to the industry of Clacton itself, and the site is thought likely to be of early Pleistocene age, perhaps Cromerian. A few flakes were also present in the Wimereux assemblage, but it is not clear whether all of them are artefacts, or whether all belong with the pebble tools, though some of them are thought to be associated.

To summarize this account of the Clactonian, we may stress that there is good evidence in Britain for occurrences of the typical rather crude cores, choppers and flakes, lacking any firm indication of associated handaxe manufacture, dating to the earlier half of the Hoxnian interglacial and perhaps also the later part of the Anglian complex. Sealed and well-dated sites are rare, and the evidence of the mixed assemblages clearly needs careful handling. Some indication of broadly similar but technologically more advanced industries of younger age may be afforded by Grovelands and Southacre, but this needs confirmation by the discovery of new sealed sites. However, we can usefully refer again to Grovelands and Southacre

when considering the industries of High Lodge in the next chapter. Setting them aside for the moment, there is little that we can say of the fate of the Clactonian population after the mid-Hoxnian. The Clactonian may be a brief episode in Britain, appearing and disappearing rather mysteriously. But if these British industries are viewed in a broad European context (cf. Collins 1969), we can perhaps attempt a wider interpretation. The evidence has filled out somewhat since it was customary to speak of a 'flake-tool province' and a 'core tool province' in the European Lower Palaeolithic, meeting at a frontier roughly where the Rhine now flows, with handaxes very scarce east of that river and early flake industries correspondingly rare to the west (McBurney 1950). The German Acheulian, for instance, is now numerically a much stronger phenomenon. Yet, for the earlier part of the Middle Pleistocene at least, the hypothesis can still be defended, and, accordingly it may be that our Clactonian of south-eastern England *is* the westernmost extremity of a tool-making tradition of essentially eastern origin. Finds of early industries which have no sign of handaxe manufacture are increasing in Central and Eastern Europe (Valoch (ed.) 1976), and there are still no handaxe industries in the USSR except where movements of people from the south have reached just north of the Caucasus. By contrast, the Acheulian distribution in Atlantic and Western Europe is massive. Britain may well have received separate influences from the south and from the east as her first palaeolithic arrivals, and here may lie the wider significance of our 'true' Clactonian. There is nothing new about this idea, but it is important that one can review it at the present time and find it still supportable. What was the culture history of Central and Eastern Europe later in the Middle Pleistocene and in the early Upper Pleistocene, and what technological traditions accompanied it, are not matters which we can justifiably explore at length here. But it is fair to remark that there are still plenty of prehistorians who do not think that the early flake-tool and pebble tool industries of Europe vanished leaving no descendants: rather, they believe that this technological tradition survived and advanced to make an important contribution to the technology of the Middle Palaeolithic, or at least to some of the facies of it. Is it against that background that we should perhaps be thinking of the fine flake-tools of Grovelands and perhaps Southacre, if those sites had yielded closed primary context assemblages instead of derived mixtures?

THE EARLY ACHEULIAN

There is not much to be added here to the account given in the previous chapter. But it should be noted that there are a few more sites worth mentioning, if the hypothesis of an Early Acheulian stage be accepted on the basis of Kent's Cavern, Fordwich, and the other sites already discussed (Map, Fig. 5:5). For example, there is the possibility of Early Acheulian handaxes in the Caversham Ancient Channel gravels, mixed with Clactonian and evolved Acheulian, as we have just seen in discussing the Clactonian of Highlands Farm Pit, and the argument need not be repeated. There is also the possibility of rather similar material at certain sites in the Kennet Valley; the Kennet is an eastward-flowing tributary of the present Middle Thames, which joins the main river at Reading.

The most interesting of the Kennet Valley sites is far up the valley, at Knowle Farm, Savernake, a little east of Marlborough, Wiltshire. The gravels here were extremely rich in artefacts, including handaxes, though the site was never properly excavated or published (Cunnington and Cunnington 1903; Dixon 1903; Kendall 1906). Rev. H.G.O. Kendall, an enthusiastic amateur archaeologist and collector, whose work is of somewhat variable quality, watched the site for some years and described a section with ochreous gravel covered by river silt, which was in turn overlain by two further separate fluviatile strata. Both the gravel and the silt were rich in Palaeolithic artefacts, around 2,000 of which survive in widely scattered museum collections, the best single series being now at Devizes Museum. Other accounts of the site attribute the Knowle deposits to what we would now call fluvio-periglacial processes: they envisage solifluction, floods and slope processes bringing large quantities of material, including the artefacts, down the hillsides to choke the existing

valleys and there to be partially resorted by local streams. Dixon comments particularly (1903: 139) that the gravel is mainly angular and unrolled. The Knowle Farm gravel deposits are thus probably unrelated to the main Kennet terrace sequence, and no fauna seems to have been recovered from them. Kendall reported a concentration of fresher handaxes in his 'river silt', but artefacts seem to have occurred at all levels. They are in a variety of conditions, and are presumably mixed and derived from different sources. Within the mixture, one can note large numbers of very crudely made archaic handaxes of all sizes, and a strong component of well-made ovates, which do show signs of soft-hammer technique. If these are two distinct series, they are now inextricably mixed and cannot be separated (as was done in the case of Warren Hill) on grounds of condition and differences in raw material. The present writer analysed a large sample of the undifferentiated assemblage (1968a), and found that the archaic features were strongly enough represented to have a dominant effect on the over-all picture of the morphology and technology, thus marking off the Knowle Farm handaxes from the other British handaxe industries studied in which ovate shapes were in the majority. There is thus certainly a strong archaic element amongst the Knowle Farm handaxes, but we lack any definite evidence that it is actually of early age. It is merely open to us to *guess* that the assemblage is a mixture much of the kind seen at Warren Hill and probably also in the Caversham Ancient Channel, incorporating ancient and younger Acheulian material. Knowle Farm is not a good site, but the situation there seems worth recording, in the light of the basic British sequence derived from occurrences of somewhat better quality.

Mention was made above of the main Kennet terrace sequence. There are good terrace gravel deposits along much of the valley, attributable to at least five different stages (Wymer 1968: 108-27; Thomas 1961; Cheetham 1975; Chartres 1975). One such terrace, called the Hampstead Marshall terrace by some authors, is at about 47 metres above the Kennet and may represent an equivalent of the Winter Hill feature of the Middle Thames; it could be of inter-Anglian or immediately post-Anglian age, though this is certainly not proved.

The gravels of this terrace have produced a few implements here and there – at the Hampstead Marshall gravel pit itself, for example. Some of the implements are rolled and deeply stained, and should be at least as old as the gravel, in that they are actually an element of it. Those which the writer has seen are archaic-looking implements, thick and narrow, though there are only a few of them (collection of Mr F.R. Froom). A few rolled flakes are also known. On the other hand, finely made ovate handaxes of advanced technology have come from the same terrace. Some of these are in sharp condition, and in few cases is the provenance known in detail: some may have been *on* the gravel rather than in it. Wymer (1968: 124-7) takes the view that the artefacts of this class are likely to be younger in age than the terrace and to have become incorporated in it during resorting of the gravel. Cryoturbation of the top few feet could certainly bring artefacts lying on the surface down into the underlying gravel.[6] If the small number of crude rolled hand-axes properly belonging to these gravels *are* of Winter Hill age, this would accord with Wymer's reading of the Caversham Ancient Channel, and with the other arguments for the existence of an Early Acheulian stage in Britain set out in the previous chapter, and might also assist a little (though only circumstantially) the suggestion of an Early Acheulian contribution to the mixture at Knowle Farm a few miles up the valley. But the Kennet Valley evidence as a whole is suggestive rather than substantial.

MIDDLE ACHEULIAN

The question of explaining the observable variation in the middle phase of the British Acheulian is a major one, and entirely crucial to any understanding of the palaeoanthropology of the Lower Palaeolithic. Why did the Acheulians make different patterns of handaxe – not merely different-looking individual implements, but whole industries showing strong preferences for one pattern or another? That they did do so is abundantly clear from even a superficial study of the artefact output at our least disturbed sites, and such preferences were observed far back in the

history of British Palaeolithic research, for example by Sir John Evans (1872: 477-559). If one takes formal study of the assemblages further, the preferences or specializations become more striking rather than less; the metrical analyses, including 'shape diagrams', produced by the present writer (1968a) should bear out this assertion. Why then does this situation exist? Is it a case of 'time-trends', with all the industries of one pattern broadly contemporary and followed by all the industries of another style? Or do the different types of industry reflect only functional considerations – pointed handaxes for one kind of task, ovate ones for another, and so forth? Or are there local traditions, or influences of different lithic raw materials to be taken into account? The problem is not unlike the classic one of interpreting the variations which may readily be seen amongst the Mousterian industries of south-western France (Bordes 1961; Bordes and de Sonneville-Bordes 1970; Mellars 1969, 1970; Binford 1973; Binford and Binford 1966), but the evidence is more diffuse and the time-span involved is a great deal longer. We must first discuss the nature of the variability, however, before attempting to decide what it means.

Barnfield Pit, Swanscombe, as so often, will serve as a suitable starting point. We saw there a Middle Acheulian industry in the Middle Gravels, very strongly specialized in pointed types of handaxe, followed by another handaxe industry in the Upper Loam, in which the emphasis had shifted to ovate types of handaxe; while the Upper Loam industry itself was numerically weak and stratigraphically rather unsatisfactory, confirmatory evidence for its nature was forthcoming from other sites in the Swanscombe-Dartford region.

The present writer's general study of British handaxe groups (1967, 1968a) involved samples from 38 sites, widely distributed (Fig. 5:14) over southern and eastern England, by no means all of a Middle Acheulian nature: with one or two specific exceptions, they were chosen as being the best Britain could provide in the way of unmixed assemblages of handaxes where the contamination should be no more than slight. The evidence relating to this was discussed in each case. It is of course no use studying mixed assemblages if it is

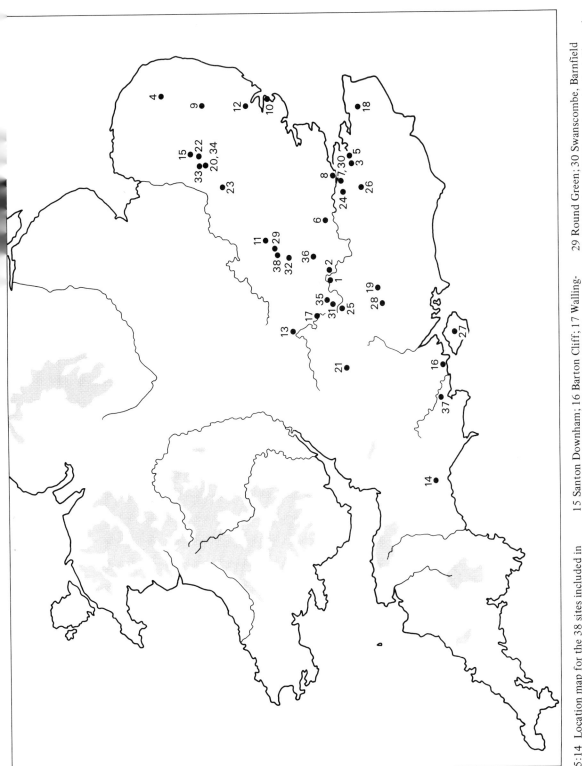

5:14 Location map for the 38 sites included in Table 13. Key to numbers: 1 Furze Platt; 2 Baker's Farm; 3 Cuxton; 4 Whitlingham; 5 Twydall; 6 Stoke Newington; 7 Swanscombe, Barnfield Pit, Middle Gravels; 8 Chadwell St Mary; 9 Hoxne; 10 Dovercourt; 11 Hitchin; 12 Foxhall; 13. Key to numbers: 15 Santon Downham; 16 Barton Cliff; 17 Wallingford Fan Gravels; 18 Fordwich; 19 Farnham (Terrace A); 20 Warren Hill, Mildenhall (worn series); 21 Knowle Farm, Savernake; 22 Elveden; 23 Allington Hill; 24 Bowman's Lodge; 25 Tilehurst; 26 Oldbury Rock Shelter; 27 Great Pan

29 Round Green; 30 Swanscombe, Barnfield Pit, Upper Loam; 31 Caversham Ancient Channel; 32 Gaddesden Row; 33 High Lodge, Mildenhall; 34 Warren Hill, Mildenhall (fresh series); 35 Highlands Farm; 36 Croxley Green; 37 Corfe Mullen, Cogdean Pit; 38 Caddington

type preferences with which one is concerned: one must be as sure as possible that one is studying the output of a single people over a short period of time. The study concerned various aspects of the size, shape, and refinement of the handaxes. 'Refinement' was seen principally in terms of the over-all thickness or flatness of the implements, and the thickness or flatness of their tips in particular, together with the presence or absence of certain advanced features of technology. The general conclusions reached about the relationships of the 38 sites may be summarized here by the following 'family tree' style diagram, though the Groups and the site names are not to be thought of as being displayed in chronological order as would be the case if this were really a genealogical table (Table 13).

This table contains much information of interest. The first thing to note is that 34 of the 38 sites fall (and fall very clearly, if the detailed evidence is studied) into one or other of the two main 'Traditions', one dominated by 'pointed' handaxe types and the other by 'ovate' handaxe types. There are just four sites, those listed as Group IV, in which the samples showed no clear preference of this kind. But – and this is most interesting – in not one case of those four are the arguments for the integrity or purity of the sample at all strong. That from the Wallingford Fan Gravels was known to be drawn from several different pits, and was included to test its general comparability or otherwise to the Caversham Ancient Channel series; the other three are all old and poorly published occurrences, and the samples were included to see what might emerge, their low quality being acknowledged in advance. In fact, therefore, the possible existence of Group IV between the two Traditions does nothing whatsoever to weaken the two Traditions themselves, nor is there the slightest indication that it provides an 'evolutionary link' between them. Group IV may in fact legitimately be ignored. The existence of the two Traditions, however, bears out the evidence of Barnfield Pit, Swanscombe, amplifies

TABLE 13 : *Relationships of the 38 handaxe assemblages* (after Roe 1968a)

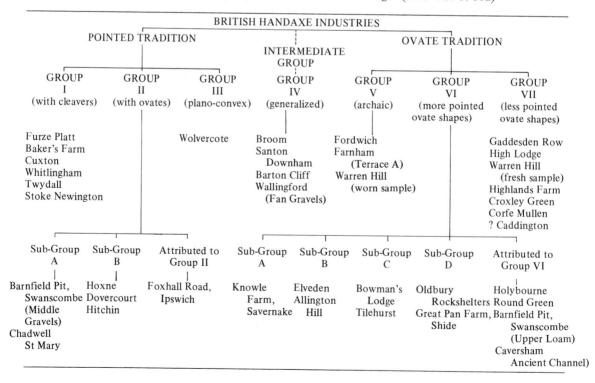

it considerably and suggests that the observation of variability in the Acheulian industries there does reflect a much wider pattern and is not purely local.

For the purposes of our discussion in this section, we shall be concerned with Groups I, II, VI and VII only. Group III contains only the Wolvercote site, discussed in Chapter 4 and believed by the writer with increasing conviction to be a Late Acheulian/Micoquian industry, younger than the general Middle Acheulian stage here being considered. Group IV we have just dealt with. Group V contains those of the proposed 'Early Acheulian' industries considered in Chapter 4 which were involved in this particular exercise, and it is encouraging to see them thus neatly thrown together in the outcome.

Some adjustments to the lists in Table 13 are in fact necessary, as a result of work done since they were drawn up in 1967 — happily, not very many. The most important is that the *Hoxne* sample should be dropped for the present. Hoxne remains a superb Palaeolithic and Pleistocene site, but the recent work of Wymer and Singer there has shown clearly that there are *two* separate *in situ* handaxe industries from different parts of the sequence (Wymer 1974; Singer and Wymer 1976), not to mention derived artefacts at other levels, whereas the present writer (1968a) used every available handaxe from the old Hoxne collections, before Wymer and Singer began their work, in the belief (following West and McBurney 1954) that only one level was present.[7] It is possible, since there appears to be a consistent difference in patination between the artefacts from the two Acheulian levels at Hoxne (Wymer, pers. com.) that two appropriate samples could actually be made up from the old material, but the latter is now so scattered in museums all over Britain that it would be a formidable task to reassemble and sort it. The situation at Hoxne is actually crucial to the discussion in this section, as will be explained later, but the fact remains that the present writer's Hoxne sample used in his 1967 and 1968a publications is misleading and valueless.

For the rest, the writer is now also somewhat disenchanted with the samples from Twydall and Caddington, though perhaps not to the extent of striking their names from the list for present purposes. The recent observations at *Twydall* referred to in note 5 to this chapter suggest that there was far more of a mixture there than he appreciated in 1968. It *may* be that there was still only one handaxe industry involved, but we simply don't know and can't find out. The gravel which originally contained the artefacts was about 100 feet above sea-level, but we have no information about its nature or age. *Caddington* was a superb Lower Palaeolithic site — or series of sites — discovered by Worthington G. Smith, and watched by him over more than two decades from about 1890 (Smith 1894; Roe 1968a: 9). It produced some hundreds of examples of conjoinable waste flakes, as well as handaxes, in sharp condition, along with flake-tools, cores, other artefacts and manuports; clearly, the Caddington occurrences included virtually undisturbed working sites. In 1971-2, the writer, with C.G. Sampson and J.B. Campbell, attempted to rediscover by excavation at least a remnant of one of the Caddington floors, but without success (Sampson 1978) and he now believes that the original floors were relatively small and discontinuous. They were evidently associated with limited and localized pockets of high-level brickearth rather than with a continuous brickearth cover (further discussion below). Those brickearth pockets which Smith watched so fruitfully seem to have been completely dug away by the old brickmakers during and after his time, though it may well be that others, with artefacts associated, remain untouched somewhere beneath the surface of the arable or grazing land around Caddington village. Given however that the brickearth pockets *are* localized, and that Smith's material certainly came from more than one of them, there is a clear risk that the Caddington artefacts which the writer placed together in his sample are actually of more than one age. The 1971-2 work regrettably cast no light on this, except to show up the problem.

To return, however, to the discussion of variability amongst the Middle Acheulian occurrences in Groups I, II, VI and VII: it will be useful first to give a visual impression of it, concentrating on handaxe shapes (in the sense of plan-forms). In the course of his metrical study of handaxes the writer devised (1964, 1967, 1968a) a fairly simple means of representing handaxe shapes in a two-dimensional diagram (Figs 5:15a, b). Exactly how these 'shape diagrams' are made is set out in the works just quoted, and there is no complicated arithmetic involved. The two 'key' diagrams, Figs 5:15 a and b, give sufficient information for present purposes, with the following brief commentary.

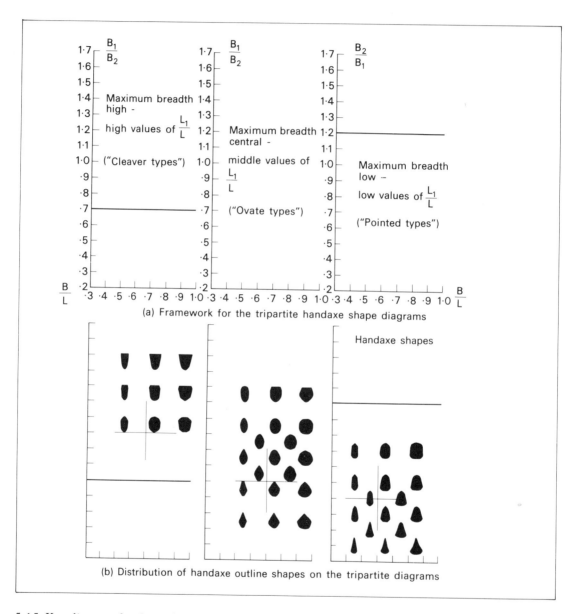

(a) Framework for the tripartite handaxe shape diagrams

(b) Distribution of handaxe outline shapes on the tripartite diagrams

5:15 Key diagrams for the author's method of studying the shapes (plan-forms) of handaxes, as published in 1964: for explanation, see pages 156-7

Each diagram is divided into three complementary parts. In the actual site diagrams, Figs 5:16 to 5:23, each individual handaxe is represented by a dot, and the precise location of each dot is very closely related to the outline shape of that particular handaxe, in the following ways.

(a) If the maximum breadth of the handaxe falls near to the butt end (as it would for example in the case of a roughly triangular or pear-shaped implement), then the dot is plotted on the right-hand section of the three-part diagram; if the maximum breadth is centrally placed (as for oval shapes), the dot goes on the middle section; if the maximum breadth falls high, as it may for an implement with a broad transverse cutting edge at its tip end, then the dot goes on the left hand section. (Whether the position of the maximum breadth counts as low, central or high is of course a matter of precise measurement, not subjective estimation.)

(b) Within each of the three sections, the horizontal scale shows values for the ratio breadth/length, increasing from left to right. That is, relatively *narrow* implements (low values for breadth/length) fall towards the left, and relatively *broad* ones towards the right.

(c) Again for each section, the vertical scale is a measure of relative pointedness of the implement, expressed by a ratio B_1/B_2. (B_1 is a measurement of breadth near to the implement's tip end, taken at a fixed point, and B_2 is a measurement of breadth at a fixed distance from the butt end.) The effect of this index is to throw the more pointed specimens towards the bottom of the appropriate section while the broader-ended shapes rise correspondingly towards the top. Fig. 5:15b shows how these factors operate to produce a logical distribution of possible plan forms, the relationships between which can be followed horizontally, or vertically, or diagonally. The silhouettes are drawn symmetrically, for convenience, and actual handaxes are of course inclined to be rather less regular in their outline shapes. To measure a handaxe and compress the information obtained into a single dot on one of these diagrams is to translate an actual handaxe outline shape into a symmetrical approximation of it. Nevertheless, the distributions of dots on the diagrams remain pretty closely related to the distribution of the silhouette shapes in Fig. 5:15b, which may accordingly be used as a key to interpret the actual shape diagrams which follow. We are, after all, extracting information at a fairly general level, for the sake of comparison or contrast, when we make an assessment of the range of shapes present in a specific handaxe industry, however we set about it. These diagrams aim to summarize the range of shapes objectively and to provide a visual presentation of them. They are naturally no substitute for spreading out all the implements themselves and looking at them all together. But the latter operation, given the often scattered nature of the collections, is not always possible to achieve, and even when it can be achieved it is not always easy to comprehend.

The large crosses on the shape diagrams are merely visual co-ordinates, which are always in the same place, from diagram to diagram: they serve to show just how the different 'swarms of dots' actually do differ from each other. One may ask, for example, whether some of the 'quadrants' thus provided are empty on some diagrams and densely populated on others. Also, as an aid to comparison (since some industries are numerically strong and others very weak), percentages are given as well as totals at the foot of each section of each diagram.

Thus armed, we may proceed to examine actual arrays of handaxe shapes from some of the sites listed in Table 13, choosing a couple of examples from each of Groups I, II, VI and VII. These diagrams (Figs. 5:16 to 5:23) should make two points clear: first, they should show general similarities between assemblages from the same Group, and second, they should reveal important differences when sites from different Groups are looked at together. These things must be so, because handaxe shapes were one of the most influential factors in defining the Groups: indeed, the diagrams came first, and the scheme of Groups was drawn up later. Space does not permit reproduction here of a shape diagram for every site listed in Table 13, but these can be studied in the writer's 1968a paper.

Consideration of Figs 5:16 to 5:23 suggests that the industries in the different Groups have certain characteristic features in the matter of handaxe shapes.

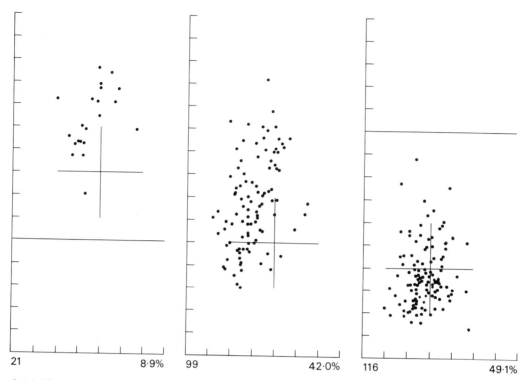

21   8·9%   99   42·0%   116   49·1%

5:16 Shape diagram for 236 implements from
Baker's Farm (Group I), after Roe (1968a); see
Fig. 5:15 for key

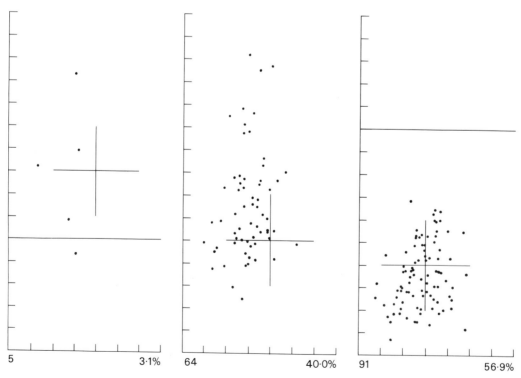

5   3·1%   64   40·0%   91   56·9%

5:17 Shape diagram for 160 implements from
Cuxton (Group I), after Roe (1968a); see Fig.
5:15 for key

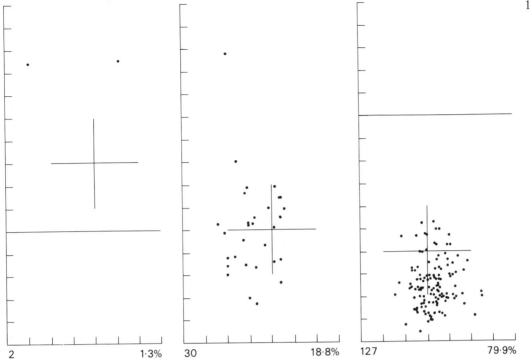

2   1·3%   30   18·8%   127   79·9%

5:18 Shape diagram for 159 implements from
the Middle Gravels at Barnfield Pit, Swanscombe
(Group II), after Roe (1968a); see Fig. 5:15 for
key

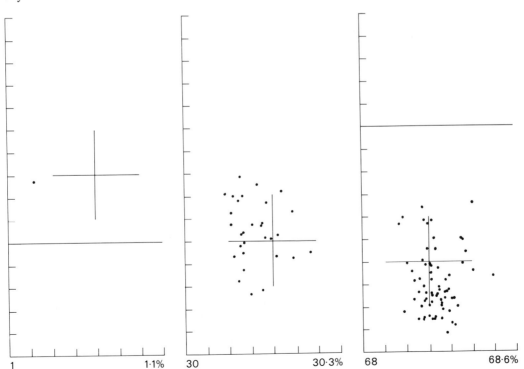

1   1·1%   30   30·3%   68   68·6%

5:19 Shape diagram for 99 implements from
Chadwell St Mary (Group II), after Roe (1968a);
see Fig. 5:15 for key

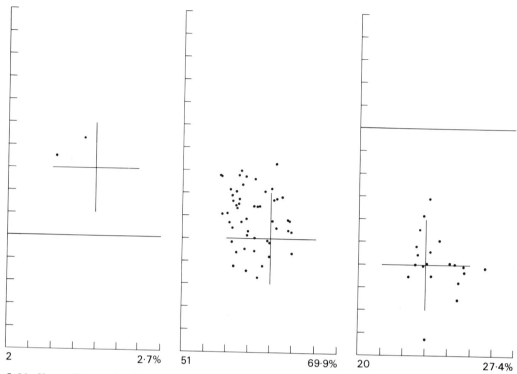

5:20 Shape diagram for 73 implements from
Elveden (Group VIb), after Roe (1968a); see
Fig. 5:15 for key

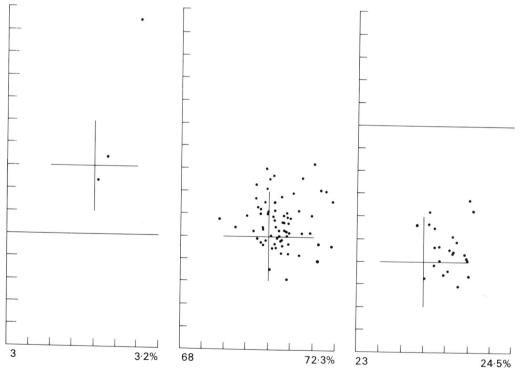

5:21 Shape diagram for 94 implements from
Tilehurst (Group VIc), after Roe (1968a); see
Fig. 5:15 for key

161

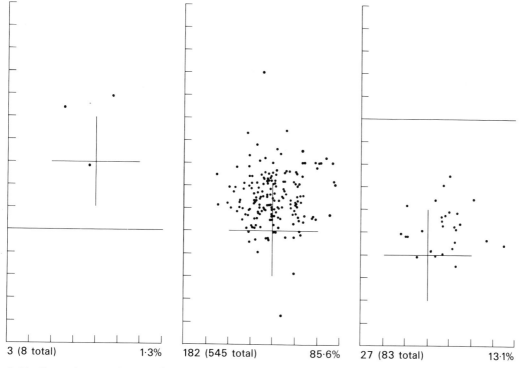

3 (8 total)   1·3%   182 (545 total)   85·6%   27 (83 total)   13·1%

5:22 Shape diagram for 212 (out of 636) implements from the Warren Hill fresh series (Group
VII), after Roe (1968a); see Fig. 5:15 for key

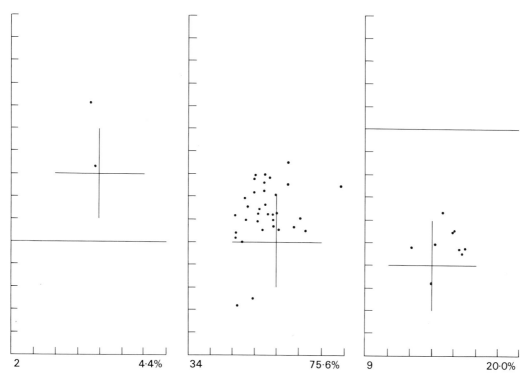

2   4·4%   34   75·6%   9   20·0%

5:23 Shape diagram for 45 implements from
Cogdean Pit, Corfe Mullen (Group VII), after
Roe (1968a); see Fig. 5:15 for key

Group I   There are many pointed handaxes, including the ficron type (which has a long narrow point and sides which are concave rather than straight in the plan view). Ovates tend to be narrow rather than broad. Square-ended handaxes and cleavers are relatively common, which is not true of any other Group: accordingly, in the shape diagrams, appreciable numbers of dots occur on the left hand sections and high up on the centre sections.

Group II   Pointed handaxe forms are always dominant. Cleavers and square-ended ovate forms are rare or absent, though other ovate forms are usually present. Many of the handaxe shapes tend to be broader than those of the Group I industries. The writer divided this Group into Sub-Groups (1967, 1968a), but that was done not only on the basis of plan forms. However, it is worth mentioning that one of the distinguishing criteria was that Sub-Group B had more broad ovate forms than Sub-Group A.

Group VI   Pointed types of handaxe become very rare; it may be suggested that the few which are present in the various industries were tools with particular functions, for which there was only an occasional need. Instead, the bulk of each industry consists of ovate shaped handaxes. Some of these have a tendency towards pointedness (in the shape diagrams there are always some dots in the lower quadrants on the central section), and there are very few classic cleaver shapes anywhere in the Group. Sub-Groups were suggested on the basis of plan-form preferences, combined with various technological features — for example, the shapes in Sub-Group B are characteristically narrower than those of Sub-Groups C and D, and twisted profiles are especially common.

Group VII   Pointed handaxes are extremely rare and the ovates are heavily dominant, as in Group VI. Blunt or even square-ended ovate forms are commoner and pointed ovate shapes rarer than in the previous Group: on the diagrams there are less dots in the lower quadrants of the centre section, more penetration of its upper reaches and occasionally some population of the left hand section, though the heavy-butted divergent sided cleavers of Group I are absent. There are also technological differences between the industries of Groups VI

and VII, but we are not concerned with those at the moment.

It can thus readily be seen that there are major differences between individual Middle Acheulian industries in Britain. Proper statistical tests can of course be used to show the extent and reality of these differences (Roe 1967, 1968a; Graham and Roe 1970), but we need not quote the figures here. It is also clear that there are industries which do resemble each other closely; hence the groupings of sites proposed. All this can confidently be stated simply on the basis of the handaxe shapes; the evidence from the study of aspects of size and refinement of the implements was in broad general agreement with that concerning shape. The same may be said of the study of technology. Indeed, in some cases the technological data provided quite striking confirmation of the similarities already noted in terms of morphology. The table of technological evidence published by the writer in 1968 is worth reproducing here (Table 14), to make this point and because it is highly relevant to the matter of Middle Acheulian variability.

Having thus considered briefly the nature and degree of the variability amongst the handaxe assemblages of the Middle Acheulian stage, we can address the question of what controls it. Is this a simple matter of *chronological* differences — 'time-trends', as they are often called? In areas of the world where it might be possible to demonstrate long unbroken periods of Lower Palaeolithic occupation, one might even dare to speak of 'typological and technological evolution', in referring to the differences between industries ranged in known order over a long period of time. We cannot, however, demonstrate continuous occupation in the British Lower Palaeolithic, and indeed it is not at all likely to have existed, given the geographical and climatic factors previously discussed. Never mind: there could still be time-trends, if one Acheulian occupation of Britain came to an end and was replaced after an interval by a fresh one, whose bearers had elsewhere begun to make new kinds of handaxes. Taking our cue from Swanscombe, as usual, we should expect to have to demonstrate that the occurrences dominated by pointed handaxes (our Groups I and II) were regularly earlier than those

TABLE 14 : *Technological evidence from the 38 handaxe assemblages*

Group	Site	Twisted tips %	Twisted handaxes %	Tranchet finish %
I	Furze Platt	0.8	0.4	5
	Baker's Farm	1.3	Nil	12
	Cuxton	?Nil	Nil	8
	Whitlingham	0.6	Nil	25
	Twydall	?Nil	Nil	10
	Stoke Newington	?Nil	Nil	13
II	Swanscombe M.G.	15	Nil	about 3
	Chadwell St Mary	6 at least	1	2
	Hoxne	11	3.5	13.5
	Dovercourt	8	4	6
	Hitchin	5	10	17.5
	Foxhall Road	2.7	15	27
III	Wolvercote	?Nil	Nil	about 22
IV	Broom	2	12	34
	Santon Downham	4	18	41
	Barton Cliff	1 at least	8 at least	12 at least
	Wallingford	2	9	8
V	Fordwich	3 (coarse)	1 (i.e. 2 handaxes, ? intrusive)	4 (some at least likely to be intrusive)
	Farnham Terrace A	3 handaxes (coarse)	Nil	3 handaxes
	Warren Hill (worn)	Nil	Nil	about 3
VI	Elveden	Nil	36	42
	Allington Hill	Nil	46	31
	Caversham	0.6	3	22
	Knowle Farm	Nil	Nil	2
	Bowman's Lodge	(Nil)	(27)	(47)
	Tilehurst	Nil	6–9*	43
	Shide (Pan Farm)	(Nil)	(7)	(16)
	Oldbury	(3)	(19)	(29)
	Round Green	(Nil)	(7)	(43)
	Holybourne	(Nil)	(3)	(16)
	Swanscombe U.L.	(Nil)	(22)	(39)
VII	Gaddesden Row	(Nil)	(9)	(35)
	High Lodge	Nil	3	38
	Highlands Farm	Nil	Nil	32
	Warren Hill (fresh)	Nil	1.6	27
	Croxley Green	(Nil)	(Nil)	(16)
	Corfe Mullen	(Nil)	(7)	(60)
	Caddington	(Nil)	(3)	(43)

*9 per cent in the sample examined by the present writer, but 6 per cent according to the number of twisted handaxes noted by R.A. Smith in examining a greater quantity of material.
Note: where a sample consists of less than 50 handaxes the percentage figures are placed in brackets as a reminder that they can be misleading: if there are only 20 handaxes in a sample, each single one has a percentage value of 5, and a mere 6 implements account for 30 per cent.

with ovates (Groups VI and VII). To see whether this is in fact so we must next review the assemblages in question, with reference to any dating evidence in each case. Space will not permit an exhaustive account of all of them, but it is worth including as much information as possible because, quite apart from the particular question of relative age, these are certainly some of the very best of the British sites.

Group I

Only one of the sites listed as belonging to this Group has been discussed previously in this book – Twydall – so all the rest will be described in the following pages. It will be most helpful to begin with *Furze Platt* and *Baker's Farm*, which can conveniently be taken together (Figs 5:16, 5:24. 5:25; Plates 28, 29), and this demands a

5:24 Implements from Baker's Farm. Nos 1-3, 5-7, handaxes, including a damaged ficron (no. 1); no. 4, cleaver. After Lacaille (1940, 1960)

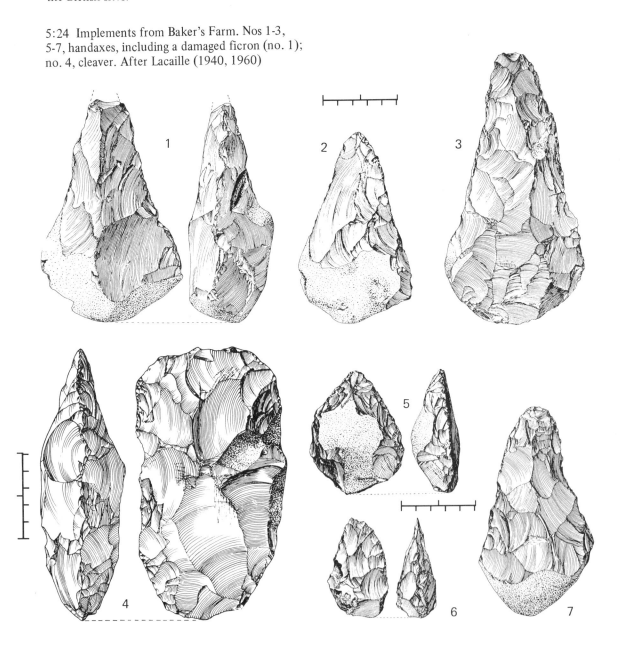

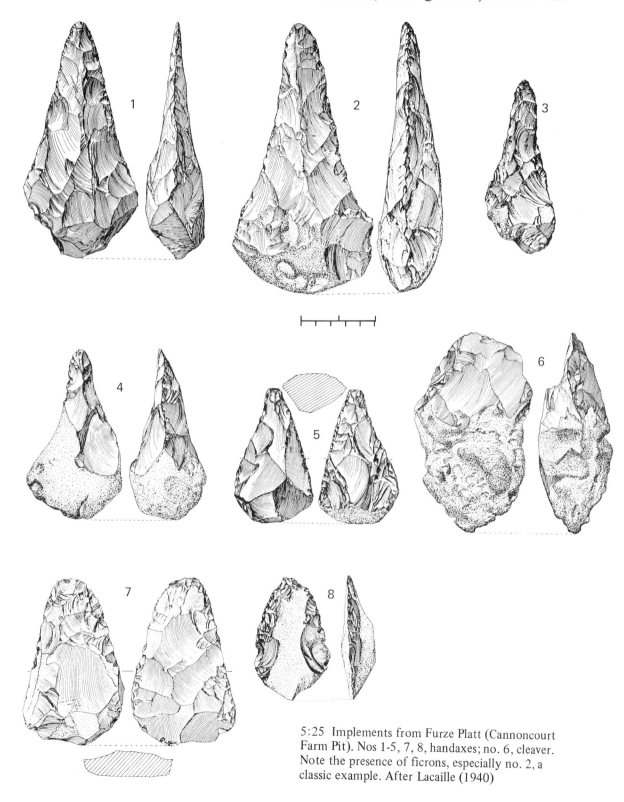

5:25 Implements from Furze Platt (Cannoncourt Farm Pit). Nos 1-5, 7, 8, handaxes; no. 6, cleaver. Note the presence of ficrons, especially no. 2, a classic example. After Lacaille (1940)

summary of the Palaeolithic and Pleistocene sequence in the Middle Thames Valley, which extends from the east end of the Goring Gap to London. Furze Platt, Maidenhead (Lacaille 1940, 1961; Wymer 1968: 217-27, 242-3) and Baker's Farm, Farnham Royal (Lacaille 1940; Wymer 1968: 239-43) are both sites belonging to the Lynch Hill Terrace of the Middle Thames. They lie on opposite sides of the modern river, in Berkshire and Buckinghamshire respectively. Whether they are strictly contemporary with the Lynch Hill gravels, or a little older, is not completely clear. The latter would seem more likely, since the artefacts at both sites lay principally at the extreme base of the gravel and had been only slightly disturbed by its deposition. At both sites the sections (Plate 28) are similar, with a few metres of gravel, rather variably bedded but evidently a single deposit, solifluxted and cryoturbated at the top and in places overlain by brickearth. Fuller descriptions are given in the works cited. A few stray artefacts are known from the brickearth at each site, but these pieces are not numerous enough to constitute identifiable industries (see for example Lacaille 1959). The Furze Platt arte-facts from the base of the gravel were very numerous (certainly more than 2,500 of them) and are now very widely dispersed in museums in Britain and abroad; a particularly good series can be seen at the Oxford University Museum (Treacher Collection). The vast majority came from the Cannoncourt Farm Pit, but most are merely marked 'Furze Platt' or even only 'Maidenhead'. From Baker's Farm around 700 artefacts survive, the best of them being now at the Oxford University Museum (Treacher Collection) and at the British Museum.

The Lynch Hill Terrace, or Lower Boyn Hill Terrace as it was formerly called, has sometimes been regarded, by virtue of its height above the river, as the Middle Thames equivalent of the aggradation which produced the Swanscombe Middle Gravels in the Lower Thames Valley. But there now seems to be considerable doubt as to whether it is indeed a true aggraded terrace or mainly a fluvio-periglacial accumulation, though either way the industries found in it should be of later Hoxnian or earlier Wolstonian age.

The named terraces of the Middle Thames are many, and the correlations and distinctions between them are open to much argument in many cases (King and Oakley 1936; Hare 1947; Sealy and Sealy 1956; Wooldridge 1957; Wymer 1968: 210-12, 242-3). We have seen already that the archaeological situation in the Winter Hill Terrace, which is certainly older than Lynch Hill, is far from clear or straightforward, and the same goes for the Caversham Ancient Channel at the Winter Hill height, though the Winter Hill Terrace proper should be of Anglian age. Following it, in order of decreasing height, come: the Upper Boyn Hill Terrace, the Lower Boyn Hill Terrace (better called Lynch Hill) and the Taplow Terrace. Some authors distinguish also an Iver Terrace, between the Lynch Hill and Taplow stages, but others regard it as equivalent to, or a sub-stage of, Lynch Hill. If the main terraces could all be said to be river-aggraded interglacial gravels, we might indeed feel confident that the descending order of heights was also a descending order of age, but it seems that this is not so. In particular, Upper Boyn Hill (or we may simply call it 'Boyn Hill' if we use the name 'Lynch Hill' to replace 'Lower Boyn Hill') seems to be *younger* than Lynch Hill, in spite of its greater height. Some authors have suggested that these two gravels are merely part of one massive aggradation on a bench at the Lynch Hill height, and that the step between them is merely the result of later erosion and is not a true terrace step at all. A more recent view, however, makes the Boyn Hill gravel not a true terrace deposit at all, but an accumulation of coarse gravel mainly under torrential conditions at some date after the Lynch Hill deposit had been formed (Lacaille 1961; Wymer 1968: 242-3). Either way, it looks as if the higher (Boyn Hill) gravel should be younger than the lower (Lynch Hill) one. As for the Taplow Terrace, that is generally agreed to be younger than Lynch Hill, but we are not much interested in it here archaeologically because its gravels contain only scattered derived artefacts and no fresh industries in place.

We thus have no satisfactory check on the actual ages of the Baker's Farm and Furze Platt assemblages, though they should lie in the late Hoxnian to early Wolstonian range. Since both occur at the base of Lynch Hill gravels, with many pieces in a generally unabraded and unweathered state, they may well be of closely similar age. At neither site is there any clear indication of a second industry stratified in relation to the main one, so we do not get in this case any direct information about the order in which the Middle Acheulian variants occur, which is the main theme of this section. It is interesting, however, that if one looks at *all* the artefacts from the Boyn Hill Terrace sites in this part of the Thames Valley, on the one hand, and at *all* those from the Lynch Hill sites on the other, flat broad ovates are much commoner in the Boyn Hill gravels, where the artefacts are also usually much more abraded. To that extent, since the Boyn Hill deposit is the younger of the two, we may reckon that the pointed handaxe industries do tend in this area to come first. The Furze Platt assemblage is pretty typical of the Lynch Hill gravels in general, with its pointed handaxes (including ficrons), heavy narrow ovates and cleavers (Figs 5:24, 5:25; Plate 29). Another assemblage very comparable to those from Furze Platt and Baker's Farm came from Lynch Hill gravel at Burnham, Bucks — from Almond's Pit and the Stomp Road Pit near Lent Rise, but the artefacts there may have been somewhat more disturbed than at the two former sites. There are plenty of good pointed handaxes from Lent Rise, and a few of the typical cleavers, in pretty fresh condition. At Burnham Beeches, on the other hand, the various pits dug into the Boyn Hill gravel produced between them a few hundred handaxes, amongst other artefacts, from various depths and in various states — some fresh, but most substantially worn — presenting a mixture of types and certainly including many fairly refined ovates. Accounts of the sites in the Burnham area have been given by Lacaille (1939, 1940) and Wymer (1968: 229-43).

The Lynch Hill and Boyn Hill gravels thus perhaps yield a little general confirmation of the order of events in the Swanscombe area, but no more, and in any case these Middle Thames Pointed Tradition industries have their own special features, notably the cleaver element. Besides, we can also glean at least one hint tending in the opposite direction, from this area of the Middle Thames,

from the rather poorly known site of Dorney Wood, near Burnham (Lacaille 1959; Wymer 1968: 229-30, 243). Quarrying at this site, early this century, revealed a substantial thickness of brickearth, interstratified with seams of coarser material, perhaps a hill-wash accumulation with a component of redeposited loess, at a height of some 200 feet above sea-level — i.e., above the height of the Boyn Hill gravels. If the Boyn Hill deposit were indeed laid down in torrential conditions (perhaps by local meltwaters representing the close of a Wolstonian stadial) as suggested by Lacaille (1961), then the Dorney Wood brickearth should postdate that event because the torrential water would otherwise have swept it away. It is therefore very interesting that the seventeen handaxes which survive from the site should be heavily dominated by pointed types, finished with a high degree of skill. The artefacts are generally fresh, and are white patinated: they appear to be contemporary with the brickearth. It is not an assemblage consisting exclusively of classic pointed handaxes, since there are at least two twisted ovoid forms (though even these are somewhat pointed); the sample is of course small, but the *dominance* of fine pointed handaxes seems very clear. The big cleavers and heavy narrow ovates of the Lynch Hill industries are not represented amongst what survives. Nor are the Dorney Wood handaxes, with one possible exception, made in the special plano-convex manner of those from Wolvercote discussed in the previous chapter. It is very regrettable that this site is not well dated, but one can certainly make out a case to argue that here is an industry of finely made pointed handaxes which *postdates* the ovate element in the Boyn Hill gravels. The Dorney Wood implements are now divided between the Buckinghamshire County Museum at Aylesbury, Reading Museum and the Oxford University Museum.

It is also worth a passing mention at this point of another old and poorly known Middle Thames site that also produced a small series of pointed handaxes of particularly fine workmanship: McIlroy's Pit, Reading (Wymer 1968: 150 and plate xiv). All the artefacts but one are very fresh; they are stained, but not much patinated. There are fourteen handaxes amongst them, a few being broken. They evidently lay at the base of, or under, Lynch Hill gravel, but at the extreme edge of the terrace, so that they may well have belonged to its bluff and lain under *redeposited* Lynch Hill gravel rather than being at the base of Lynch Hill gravel proper. The old accounts of the site simply do not make this clear. If they did belong to the post-terrace bluff, they might represent another pointed handaxe industry of younger age than usual, and one would be tempted to bracket them with Dorney Wood (without of course implying precise similarity of the two industries). If, however, they really did lie under *in situ* Lynch Hill gravel, then they should be approximately contemporary with Furze Platt and Baker's Farm. Indeed, one could probably match them piece by piece from amongst the finer products of those two sites if one had to, but the *assemblage* from McIlroy's Pit, as it has actually come down to us, is unlike the Furze Platt or Baker's Farm series, comparing group with group, since McIlroy's pit has only fine pointed handaxes (including some classic ficron shapes) and no hint of cleavers or other handaxe types. One could, however, envisage that this was a highly specific toolkit, made by one or more particularly skilled knappers for some specific task in hand. In view of the doubt over dating, we can only set this assemblage aside, pending new information, as does Wymer (*loc. cit.*), but it deserves to be better known and the circumstances will serve to illustrate some of the general points already made about handaxe morphology and function and about the nature of variation. The McIlroy's Pit implements are now all at Reading Museum.

To consider the other Group I sites we must leave the Middle Thames, feeling (as usual) sold a little short as regards information, but not wholly empty-handed. The remaining Group I sites are Cuxton (Kent), Whitlingham (Norfolk) and Stoke Newington (London), and they will be considered in that order.

The *Cuxton* site, which lies in the garden of the Rectory at Cuxton, near Rochester, was the subject of a proper excavation in 1962-3, directed by P.J. Tester (1965). His five small trenches produced a quite extraordinary quantity of Acheulian artefacts (Fig. 5:26), including some

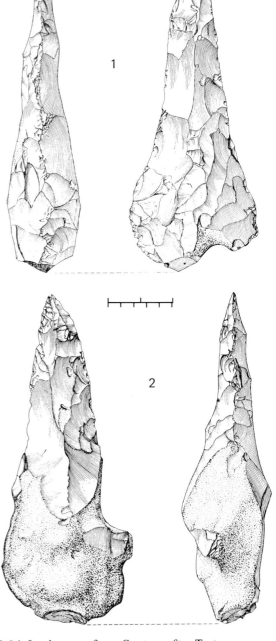

5:26 Implements from Cuxton, after Tester (1965). Nos 1-6, handaxes (note the ficron, no. 1, and the handaxe tip improvised upon a 'handle' consisting of a naturally cylindrical nodule, roughly flaked at the butt end), no. 6 – the site produced several pieces of this nature; cf. also Fig. 5:41, no. 7, from Caddington; nos 7-10, cleavers; nos 11, 12, retouched flakes

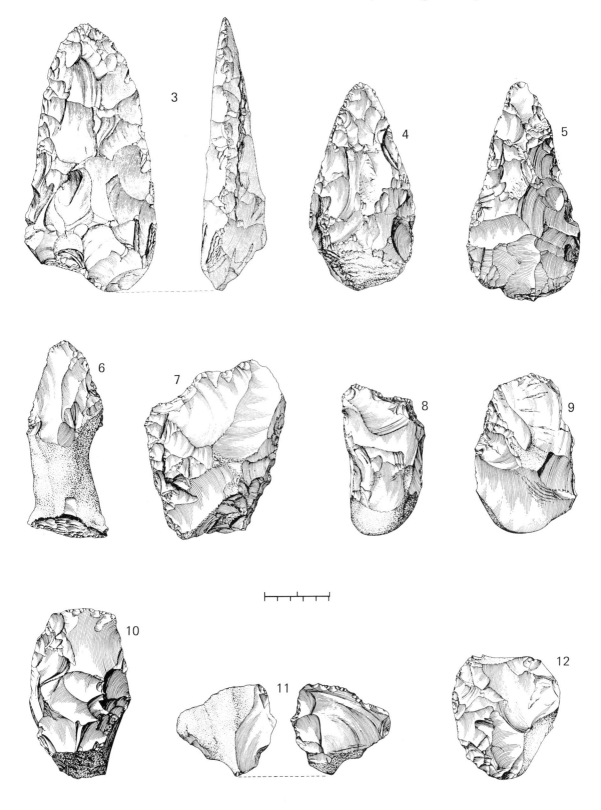

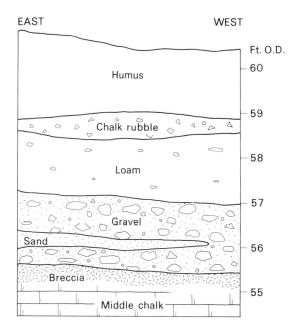

EAST   WEST

Ft. O.D.

Humus

— 60

— 59

Chalk rubble

— 58

Loam

— 57

Gravel

— 56

Sand

Breccia

— 55

Middle chalk

5:27 Section in Trench 2 at Cuxton, after Tester (1965). The industry was mainly in the gravel

210 handaxes and cleavers, 54 flake-tools, 20 cores and 366 waste flakes (Tester's figures). A typical section (Fig. 5:27) showed about 18 inches of rather coarse gravel and sand overlying the chalk (whose top was brecciated) and itself overlain by loam. The vast majority of the artefacts were dispersed throughout the band of gravel (Plate 30), but a few came from the loam. The implements were remarkably fresh (with a few exceptions only) and mostly unpatinated, though some were stained. The gravel has been attributed to the second (50-foot) terrace of the local river, the Medway, though it seems likely to be related to a small and perhaps seasonal tributary stream rather than to the main Medway. Indeed, the circumstances remind one strongly of the classic Acheulian 'stream channel' situations so often encountered in Africa, in which the actual bed of a river or stream seems to have been occupied, during the drier period of the year. There were no useful faunal remains, and no clear dating evidence. Whether the artefacts at Cuxton belong to one single camp in one particular year, is not clear; the material in the loam suggests small-scale visits to the same spot on

later occasions by bearers of a closely similar Acheulian industry. The height of the Cuxton gravel (about 60 feet O.D.) renders correlation on altimetric grounds with the Middle Gravels at Swanscombe (8 miles west) impossible or at least fraught with grave difficulties (cf. Tester's discussion, *op. cit.*, pp. 42-4): it would be necessary to believe firmly in A.T. Marston's channel between the Lower Middle and Upper Middle Gravels, a feature whose existence now seems beyond proof (cf. p. 75 above), and to make the correlation precisely with it, accepting that there was general fluviatile downcutting at this time. It seems easier to accept that the Cuxton deposit is related to drainage to a sea-level lower than that of the Hoxnian maximum and therefore postdating it. If this were so, the Cuxton industry would presumably fall into the same time bracket as was suggested above for the Lynch Hill Terrace industries of our Group I, i.e. Late Hoxnian to Early Wolstonian. How much better it would be to have positive independent evidence that this is indeed the age of the Cuxton gravel and its artefacts. There is, however, at least no obvious reason for supposing them either older or younger than this time range. The large majority of the Cuxton artefacts, including the excavated material, are now in the British Museum.

At the *Whitlingham* site at Kirby Bedon, near Norwich in Norfolk, there are certain resemblances to the Cuxton situation. This site was excavated under the direction of J.E. Sainty and H.H. Halls in 1927, in an operation of at least average quality according to the standards of the day, and a report was published (Sainty 1927). The artefacts lay, mostly in very fresh condition, stained but not much patinated, in a rather thin band of gravel (up to 2 feet thick), which was overlain by a variety of sands and clays, differing in detail from section to section. A few worn and derived pieces seem to have been present among the fresh ones. With the handaxes and cleavers were many waste flakes, unfinished handaxes and items of knapping debris, giving the assemblage a certain 'manufacturing site' character. Some of the cleavers have been made on flakes, which is rather uncommon in Britain (Fig. 5:28). Since the gravel is of a coarse and poorly sorted nature, the very fresh condition of the

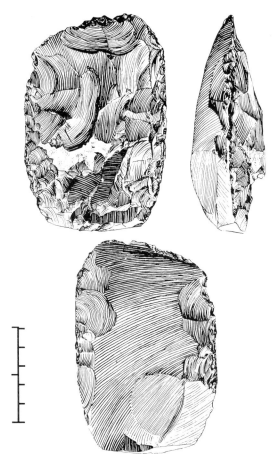

5:28 Three views of a cleaver from Whitlingham, made on a large flake, after Sainty (1927)

majority of the implements is a suggestive argument for their not having been moved far: the nature of the gravel suggests the action of torrential water, and the implements would soon have suffered damage and battering under such conditions. Professor P.G.H. Boswell, who provided a specialist report on the geology (in Sainty, *op. cit.*, pp. 211-13), argued that the conditions under which the gravel had formed involved meltwater flowing in a braided channel system; doubtless, at the Whitlingham site, the makers of the industry occupied the banks and beaches of such a channel and perhaps also its bed when dry, exploited the local chalk flint and left their artefacts on the surface of the gravel to become incorporated in it

as time passed. Boswell attributed the gravel to the 'fifty-foot' terrace of the River Yare.

There are few references to Whitlingham in the later literature, and those which do exist usually ascribe the occurrence to the Hoxnian interglacial, but not on very explicit grounds (e.g. Sainty 1951: 176). It is not at all clear to the present writer that it was Anglian rather than Wolstonian meltwater which coursed through the Whitlingham braided channels not much more than 40 feet above the present Yare. Sainty (1933) attributed a few generally similar artefacts found at Carrow, nearby, to the same interglacial as Whitlingham, but at Carrow a tooth and tusk of mammoth were found with the implements, which seems more likely to imply a younger age. A virtually unpublished site at Keswick — again on a 50-foot terrace, just outside Norwich — yielded to various collectors numerous fresh artefacts, including several large cleavers and ficrons which would count as highly typical in any of our Group I assemblages. This site was never excavated, so it is merely surmise that it is as much a 'pair' to Whitlingham as Baker's Farm is to Furze Platt, though the writer believes this to be true. At Keswick there are clear examples of Levalloisian technique in the collections from the site (Norwich Castle Museum). At Whitlingham several of the handaxe trimming flakes have carefully prepared platforms and the best handaxes are very finely finished (the main material is again at Norwich Castle Museum). These technological points perhaps offer further circumstantial evidence for a younger rather than older age for Whitlingham, by reference to our basic sequence. It is also worth noting that Levalloisian technique seems to have been known to the makers of both the Furze Platt and the Cuxton industries in our Group I list, though only sparingly used by them. On the other hand, Levalloisian technique does appear to be sparsely represented in the Swanscombe Middle Gravels, as we saw (page 80), so the presence of it in these Group I industries is not necessarily a crucial piece of evidence. However, if we are asked to believe that the Whitlingham occurrence is *early* Hoxnian, i.e. that the implements were made soon after Anglian meltwaters ceased to flow, then it would be hard to find supporting evidence elsewhere in Britain for the generally advanced technological status of the industry at so early a date. In summary, the Whitlingham industry is not well dated, but the writer is inclined to think that it is younger than at least one Wolstonian stadial rather than merely 'post-Anglian'.

Stoke Newington, beyond any doubt, was potentially one of the finest British Lower Palaeolithic sites, but it seems unlikely now that its potential can ever be realized. That remarkable observer W.G. Smith was on the scene when many of the mid and late Victorian terraces and other dwellings were being erected around Stoke Newington Common and indeed widely over this part of north-east London. He has recorded (1894: see especially pp. 189-306) the widespread occurrence in this area of an old and undisturbed

Pleistocene landsurface – a 'Palaeolithic floor' as he called it. His observations were made in the late 1870s and early 1880s, especially in the period 1878-83 'by keeping a record of the exposed surface of every drain, house foundation, pit, &c, during these five years'. His best area was the north side of Stoke Newington Common, where the ground rises to Cazenove Road and where he watched houses, many of them with cellars, being built on what had been open fields and market gardens. Alkham Road and Kyverdale Road are still the names of two of the roads which ascend this slope from the Common to Cazenove Road, and Smith published a section through the gardens between them (*op. cit.*, fig. 138, reproduced here as Fig. 5:29). The 'floor' occurred as a distinct gravelly stratum only 2 to 6 inches thick, in fine

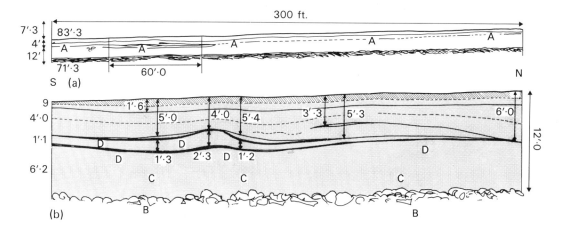

5:29 Scale sections showing the Palaeolithic floor at Stoke Newington, as published by W. G. Smith in 1894. (a) section 300 feet in length through the gardens between Alkham and Kyverdale Roads, from Cazenove Road on the right (north) to Stoke Newington Common on the left. A is the floor. (b) Detail from the above, 60 feet in length. B is gravel about 12 feet below the modern surface, with derived artefacts; C is fine sand with land and fresh-water shells; D is the floor (or floors, since there are two distinct occurrences here, separated by sterile sand). Above the floor is sandy loam and the modern soil. (c) Another exposure of the floor, close to that shown in (b). In this case the floor has been

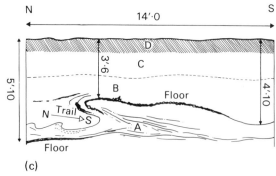

disturbed by 'contorted drift' which also overlies it (B and C); D is the modern soil, and A is an intrusion of London Clay and sand, pushed under the floor by some periglacial process

buff-coloured sand, varying (for topographic reasons) in its depth from the present surface from 4 feet to over 20 feet; in the area just mentioned, it was only 4 to 6 feet down. Above the floor itself comes more sand or loam, and then what Smith called 'contorted drift' — that is, soliflucted material and some disturbance and reworking of the top of the sandy deposits by cryoturbation, evidently representing a periglacial episode, or maybe more than one. Some 12 feet below the present surface, and 6 to 8 feet below the floor, was gravel, which also contained artefacts, though most were derived. The nature of this gravel is somewhat obscure. The Stoke Newington area is close to the confluence of the River Lea and the main Thames, and fluviatile deposits of both rivers seem to be involved, with perhaps a periglacial contribution (solifluction) as well. The gravels are widespread and occur variously between 60 and 100 feet above sea-level.

John Wymer has made a valiant attempt to assess the dating of the various Pleistocene deposits in this area of north-east London and south-west Essex (1968: 293-319), and he is inclined to regard the 60 to 100 feet gravels as a deposit of Wolstonian age and the overlying finer deposits, including the Stoke Newington floor, as Ipswichian. As indicated earlier in this volume, it is no longer necessary or desirable to work within a rigid system limited to Anglian — Hoxnian — Wolstonian — Ipswichian — Devensian for the Middle and Upper Pleistocene of Britain, and the Stoke Newington floor might well prove to belong to a mild period not appropriately described by any current name, younger than the Hoxnian as we at present understand it and older than the early Devensian, but this time bracket is of course much too wide to assist the present discussion greatly.

The present writer, with C.G. Sampson and J.B. Campbell, attempted in 1971 to relocate Worthington Smith's floor, by digging on the northern side of Stoke Newington Common itself, but this operation was little more successful than that mounted at Caddington the previous year and already referred to. The digging was directed by John Campbell, who with Mrs G.M. Cook is preparing a report. A scatter of undiagnostic worked flints, mainly waste flakes, was found which could

have been part of an outer scatter from the main floor, though no definitive dating evidence was obtained. The gravel was also revealed, and found to contain a few derived artefacts, but the upper part of the expected sequence was either missing or badly disturbed in the trenches dug. In 1975, some commercial digging (test pits dug by builders) took place on the north side of Cazenove Road, watched by members of the Inner London Archaeological Unit, and visited by the writer and others; however, no sign of the floor was revealed. It seems that the former site was too low down the slope, and the latter too high. The crucial parts are heavily built over, principally with the houses Smith saw being erected; the digging of their foundations and cellars yielded his best sections and finds, but also removed most of the evidence for ever. Not much undisturbed ground can remain here in places where it is likely to become available for study, but one should watch and wait, not abandoning hope of a future chance to trace a fragment at least of the floor. Meanwhile, we are inevitably thrown back to the old finds and unfortunately very few items of the considerable quantities of artefacts can certainly be attributed to Smith's actual floor, even though many of the surviving pieces very probably did come from it. When one considers the date at which Smith was working, it would indeed be extraordinary if he had recorded their provenances to the standards we now demand, and apart from this it seems that not all his careful notes have survived. One is left to take all the perfectly fresh material and to suppose that all the true 'floor' specimens are among them, but with how much extraneous material one cannot in any way tell. Conversely, some true 'floor' material may actually be somewhat worn, because in some places where the floor was not deeply buried, it is known to have been disturbed or reworked by the 'contorted drift' deposits. Anyhow, the handaxe sample which the writer extracted in this way for metrical analysis did bear a resemblance to the other Group I sites, though it had its own special features. Generally speaking, the artefacts (Fig. 5:30) were smaller (and with no indication that small sizes were forced on the makers by the absence of large nodules of raw material). Also, there were

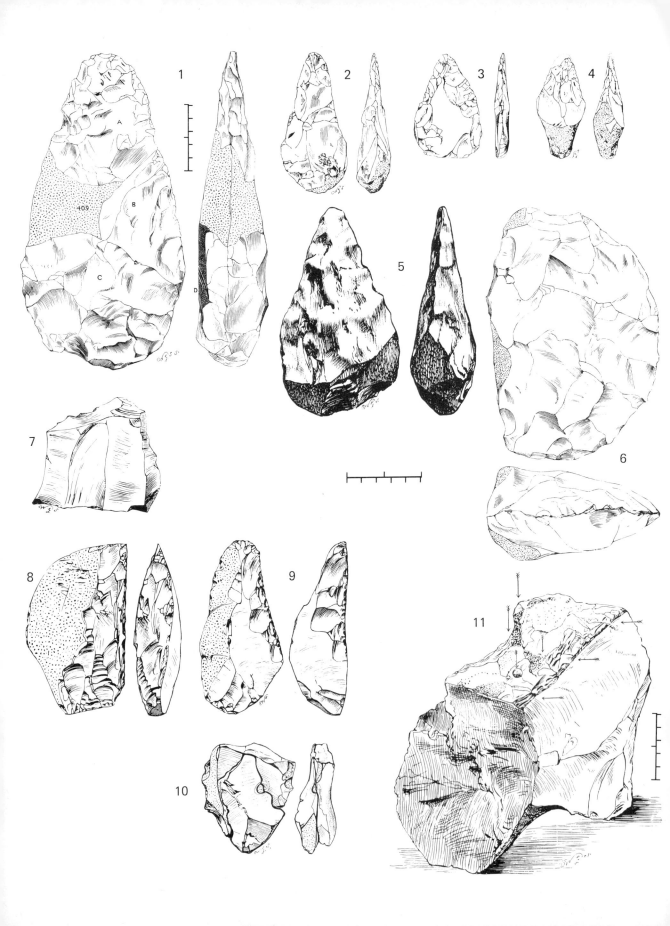

with the handaxes a large number of finely finished flake tools of quite regular patterns, some approaching the typological and technological standards of their counterparts in the Mousterian or 'proto-Mousterian' sites of Western Europe. Such tools appear to be quite absent at the other Group I sites discussed.

Stoke Newington, then, was a fine site, discovered too early for its own archaeological good, notwithstanding the brilliance of Worthington Smith. But indeed, if he had not discovered it, there would have been no later chance to gather the information which he obtained, including hints of possibly a better array of palaeoenvironmental evidence than any other British site has since produced, with much vegetable material and even two birch stakes (Fig. 5:31), apparently artificially pointed.[8] As in the case of Caddington, the floor produced some examples of conjoinable flint flakes, suggesting that knapping took place at the site and that there was little subsequent disturbance to the floor. The small number of examples of conjoined pieces by comparison with Caddington seems mainly due to the fact that numerous collectors descended on the area and took away all the flints they could find or obtain from the workmen, as soon as Smith first made public his discoveries. His more cautious handling of Caddington a few years later, and of Round Green and Gaddesden Row later still, doubtless reflects this experience; at Caddington he had conjoined over 500 flakes in pairs or larger groups by the time he published *Man the Primeval Savage* in 1894. As a final note on Stoke Newington, we may record that S. Hazzledine Warren did independently observe a continuation of Worthington

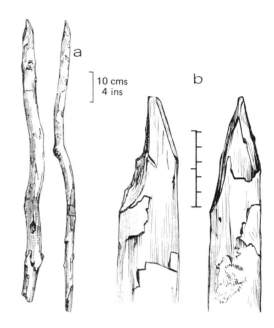

5:31 (a) The two pointed birch stakes found by Worthington Smith at Stoke Newington; (b) detail of their pointed ends. After Smith (1894)

Smith's floor at Geldeston Road, Stoke Newington, and collected fresh artefacts including handaxes from it. These are now in the British Museum, accompanied by a note in Warren's manuscript catalogue, but he did not publish any detailed account of the find. Worthington Smith's Stoke Newington collections have been somewhat dispersed, since he gave his material away quite freely, but large quantities are housed in the British Museum and Luton Museum.

Group II

Of the sites listed in Table 13, we have already discussed *Barnfield Pit, Swanscombe (Middle Gravels)*, and *Hoxne* will be considered separately later in this section, since the sample used by the writer cannot now be regarded as valid for reasons explained above. *Chadwell St Mary*, in Essex, is an old site, virtually unpublished. Over a hundred handaxes and a few other artefacts are preserved from it (at the Colchester and Essex Museum, Colchester, the Sedgwick Museum at

5:30 Artefacts from the Palaeolithic floor at Stoke Newington, found by Worthington Smith, as published by him in 1894. Nos 1-5, handaxes (No. 1 is conjoined from four pieces, A-D, anciently broken; the stippled area is plaster; no. 5 is made from a quartzite pebble; the rest are flint). No. 6, bifacial side-chopper; no. 7, core; nos 8-9, finely worked flake-tools with steep scraper edges; no. 10, pair of trimming flakes, conjoined; no. 11, large stone with percussion marks, interpreted by Smith as an anvil used in knapping

Cambridge and the British Museum). There is a strong unity about them in condition, patination and raw material, quite apart from the morphological unity which the writer's metrical analyses documented. They were found during gravel working 'in the 100-foot terrace gravels' of the Thames, on the opposite side of the modern river to Swanscombe, and a couple of miles downstream — the two sites are about four miles apart in a straight line. It was interesting that the various metrical analyses left the Chadwell St Mary sample closer than any other to the series from the Barnfield Pit Middle Gravels; one would like to have evidence that they were closely contemporary — or it might be even more interesting to have unimpeachable evidence that there was a big gap in time between them. In fact, however, there is no chronological evidence at all, except the vague hint of broad contemporaneity available to those who care to take the apparent altimetric correlation of the respective gravels at face value.

Dovercourt (Gant's Pit) is another rather old discovery, with less literature than one would wish (Underwood 1913; Warren 1933), since the artefacts look from their condition and nature like, as Warren put it, 'the relics of a local living site, all swept up together in a bank of sand and gravel' (*op. cit.*, p. 11). The gravel, in which the implements were found at depths varying from 2 to 9 feet, has a surface height of 87 feet O.D. Patination of the implements, and other surface alteration, decreased as their depth in the deposit increased, suggesting that these effects were post-depositional, caused by percolating water. The gravel was provisionally interpreted as a terrace of the River Stour, in whose valley it lay, though it seemed to have formed very rapidly: hence the supposed contemporaneity of the artefacts from such differing depths. Many delicate handaxe trimming flakes were found with the handaxes, suggesting that flint knapping took place at the site, and some good flake-tools were present. Some faunal remains were recovered by Underwood: elephant, deer (*Cervus aff. Dama*, according to M.A.C. Hinton, quoted by Underwood, *loc. cit.*) and rhinoceros (? *megarhinus*). To these Warren added remains of a large bovid and more traces of elephant (which he believed to be *Elephas (Palaeoloxodon) antiquus*), but his opinion was that these bones were all derived and probably older than the gravel. We are left with no very helpful dating of the Dovercourt site at all. The Stour appears to have cut through a so-called glacial gravel (perhaps Anglian outwash?) before the Dovercourt deposits were laid down, but 'post Anglian' does not assist us much. It does not even seem possible to relate the Dovercourt site to the Pleistocene sequence observed not many miles away at Clacton (cf. Singer *et al.* 1973: 49). No exposures have been available at Dovercourt for over forty years. The best collections from the site are now at the British Museum and Ipswich Museum.

At *Hitchin*, Hertfordshire, situated in a gap through the Chiltern chalk escarpment, the main difficulty is to relate the implements which have been preserved in numerous collections to the stratigraphic details recorded, with some care, by Clement Reid and others, mostly before 1900. The best working summary of research at Hitchin is still that provided by Kenneth Oakley (1947) and it includes a useful list of references. The essential stratigraphic situation is that in the Hitchin Gap a deep channel or trough (with a base estimated to be over 60 feet below sea-level) is filled with boulder clay and glacial deposits, this series being overlain by alluvial deposits capped with brickearth. There seems fairly general agreement that the glacial deposits are of Anglian age; the alluvial series has at various times yielded excellent faunal and floral evidence, which strongly suggests that it should be attributed to the Hoxnian. Further Hoxnian deposits, a mile or so away from the old Hitchin pits, were studied by M.P. Kerney (1959), and included a tufa or travertine with an exceptionally interesting molluscan fauna, but the relationship of these exposures to the artefact-bearing beds has remained obscure. C. Turner has indicated (in Mitchell *et al.* 1973: 18) that the old Hitchin sites are now being reinvestigated. Oakley's summary (*op. cit.*, p. 250) records that the artefacts came mainly from the base of the brickearth which overlies the alluvial deposits, and a few from the marl immediately below the brickearth. The brickearth itself incorporates aeolian and rain-washed material, laid

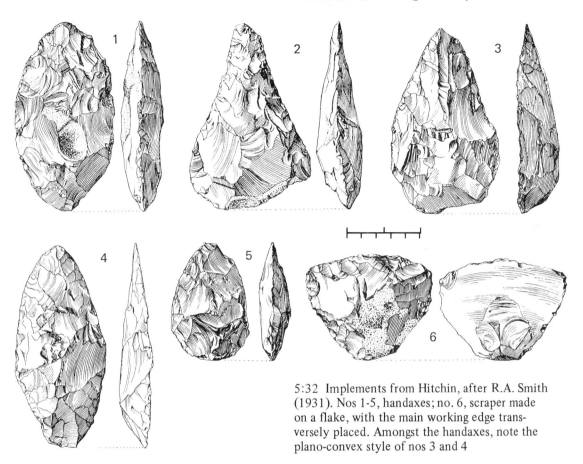

5:32 Implements from Hitchin, after R.A. Smith (1931). Nos 1-5, handaxes; no. 6, scraper made on a flake, with the main working edge transversely placed. Amongst the handaxes, note the plano-convex style of nos 3 and 4

down on a marshy surface either just prior to the Wolstonian or else during a mild interval within it — perhaps, one might think, about the same time that the Upper Loam was forming at Barnfield Pit, or certain parts of the Upper Series at Hoxne. The Hitchin artefacts themselves (Fig. 5:32), of which the best collections are now in the British Museum and at the University Museum, Cambridge, are mostly in fine sharp condition, quite appropriate to a provenance within the brickearth, and Reid was able to confirm the presence of handaxes *in situ* there. But whether all that survive come from the same horizon is not known, since few have any detailed provenance recorded. Though the technology of most is very comparable to that of the other Group II sites, a small number have been flaked in a plano-convex manner not dissimilar to that noted at Wolvercote. The Hitchin

series as a whole does not otherwise strongly resemble that from Wolvercote, and it would be of very great interest to know whether a small group of later handaxes has become mixed in with the main Hitchin material, or whether the plano-convex flaking style appears earlier than the writer suggested in discussing Wolvercote. There are also a few well made flake-tools from Hitchin, in a similar condition to the handaxes.

The *Foxhall Road* site, in Ipswich, Suffolk, is another old find of which there has been no recent exposure. The various researches carried out at the site — originally a brick pit and later built over — have been reported by Miss N.F. Layard (1903, 1904, 1906), R.A. Smith (1921) and P.G.H. Boswell and J.R. Moir (1923). The extant collections of artefacts, including over seventy handaxes, are at Ipswich Museum and the British Museum. The pieces are in fine fresh condition, and the hand-axes are accompanied by flake implements and plenty of examples of trimming flakes, the whole impression being of an assemblage from a living and working site which had been only slightly disturbed. The various accounts of the stratigraphy, taken together, show clearly that the artefacts occurred scattered through a thickness of perhaps 3 metres of brickearth, the top of which was reworked, with at least one major concentration. The brickearth seems to represent the filling of a small lake which had formed in a hollow of the chalky boulder clay which was observed at the base of the section. There were deposits attribut-able to the action of glacial meltwater overlying the boulder clay and underlying the brickearth, and the disturbances to the top of the brickearth seem to be of periglacial origin. The sequence, a classic East Anglian one by the sound of it, is distinctly reminiscent of Hoxne and Marks Tey. The records of the occurrence of the artefacts suggest one major lakeside occupation, and perhaps some shorter visits to the same spot from time to time afterwards, each set of artefacts being covered by sterile lake sediments, perhaps just as the result of seasonal fluctuations of the water-level. The most likely hypothesis would be a middle to late Hoxnian age for the artefacts, the younger of which were somewhat reworked by Wolstonian solifluction and cryoturbation. None of this however has been substantiated by any recent work, the site being no longer available, and it might be — as was the case at Hoxne — that the stratigraphy has complexities which the archaeo-logists of 1900-25 were not in a position to appreciate. As regards the industry, it has a higher proportion of refined ovate handaxes, and a stronger representation of such advanced flaking techniques as 'tranchet finish' and 'twisted profile' than is usual in Group II. On the other hand, it has more of the classic pointed handaxe types than one would find in Group VI of the Ovate Tradition. The writer has listed it as 'attributed to Group II'. It might be that more than one industry has become mixed together by the collectors, and we have indeed envisaged a period of lake-shore visits rather than one single occupation; this was after all what happened in the case of Hoxne.

However, it may genuinely be a more generalized industry after all (i.e., one with a less strong preference than usual for a narrow range of handaxe types), and there is no reason why such should not be the case. At Hoxne, Wymer and Singer were able to re-excavate the site and solve a similar problem. Sadly, at Foxhall Road, there is no present likelihood that this can be done.

Group VI

Of the sites listed in this Group in Table 13, some have already been discussed or mentioned in this or previous chapters. *Knowle Farm*, in Sub-Group A, was the Kennet Valley site near Savernake which produced a large assemblage with an archaic-looking element (see pages 151-2). Dating is unknown and there is a strong likelihood that the assemblage is mixed, but the mode of occurrence of the fresher material in a restricted area of the pit was at least suggestive that much of it might have belonged together originally (cf. Kendall 1906; Cunnington and Cunnington 1903); only the fresh specimens were included by the writer, but no one would claim that the sample is of as high quality as the best of the rest. *Bowman's Lodge* (in Sub-Group C) was one of the Dartford sites (Tester 1951, 1976), mentioned in connec-tion with the Barnfield Pit Upper Loam industry (see pages 78, 107). There were two conjoinable flakes amongst the large amounts of flake material found with the handaxes (Fig. 5:33), and the whole assemblage lay on the surface of a gravel (whose base was at about 90 feet O.D.), having been gently covered with loam, without much disturbance. The dating should be closely compar-able, one would feel, to that of the Barnfield Pit Upper Loam — later than the main Hoxnian, but probably earlier than the Ipswichian. Amongst the sites listed as 'attributed to Group VI', the *Barnfield Pit Upper Loam* has already been exten-sively discussed. The *Caversham Ancient Channel* sample consisted of all the handaxes from several pits in that deposit, collected by Llewellyn Treacher and now housed in the Oxford University Museum. This Caversham sample is quite certainly heterogeneous, but was used by the writer (1964, 1968a) when considering the differing interpreta-

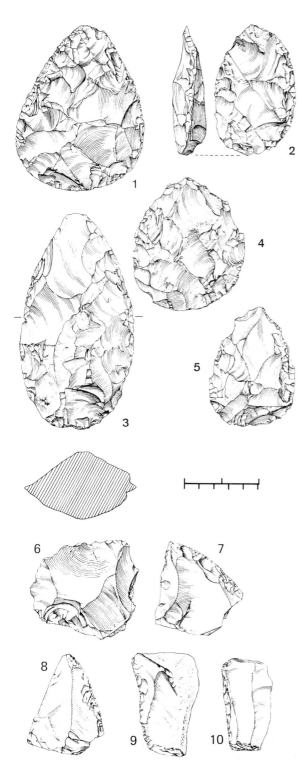

5:33 Implements from Bowman's Lodge, after Tester (1976): nos 1-5, handaxes; no. 6, core; nos. 7-10, flake-tools

tions of the Ancient Channel proposed by Treacher *et al.* (1948) and by Wymer (1961). The remaining Group VI sites require brief discussion.

Elveden, Suffolk, is a Breckland site, not far from Warren Hill and High Lodge; interpretation of its age inevitably encounters the uncertainties regarding the boulder clays of this part of East Anglia. Artefacts were first collected here when a brickpit was active on the Elveden estate, mainly during the first two decades of the present century. Excavations were undertaken at the pit twenty-five years after its closure, under the direction of T.T. Paterson and B.E.B. Fagg, who published a useful account of the results of their work (1940). Some further excavation at the site was carried out by G. de G. Sieveking a few years ago, but the report on this is not yet available. The essentials of the sequence (Fig. 5:34) include a basal boulder clay, overlying the chalk, and a hollow in it filled with finer sediments, representing an old channel or, more probably, a small lake — perhaps a 'kettle-hole' lake like that of Hoxne. The artefacts, mostly in a very fresh condition, appear to come from a typical and very little disturbed waterside occupation, or series of occupations over a fairly short period of time. The upper parts of the probably lacustrine deposits containing the artefacts show pronounced cryo-turbation and other effects of a periglacial climate. Paterson and others thought (*op. cit.*, pp. 5-6) that there were traces here also of an actual boulder clay, much decalcified, but this seems doubtful. In the absence of a definitive pollen diagram or other evidence that might help to identify the precise Pleistocene period at which the lake or channel silted up, much depends on the age of the basal boulder clay, which is chalky (as well it might be, in this part of East Anglia) and not very different from some of the known Anglian tills. Paterson, however, was convinced that it was younger than this — equivalent to the Upper Chalky Boulder Clay which he had claimed capped the brickearth at his Barnham site not far away (see pages 143-4 above), and equivalent also to the lower of the two glacial deposits of High Lodge, Mildenhall, discussed later in this chapter — in a word, Wolstonian, so far as we are concerned. This is a complicated problem which we cannot discuss at

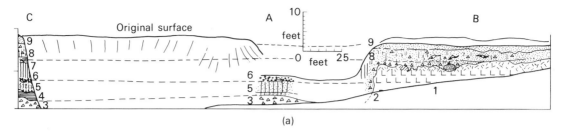

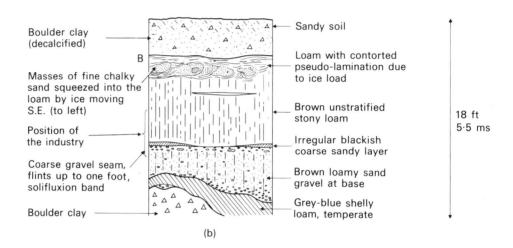

Boulder clay
(decalcified)

Masses of fine chalky
sand squeezed into the
loam by ice moving
S.E. (to left)

Position of
the industry

Coarse gravel seam,
flints up to one foot,
solifluxion band

Boulder clay

Sandy soil

Loam with contorted
pseudo-lamination due
to ice load

Brown unstratified
stony loam

Irregular blackish
coarse sandy layer

Brown loamy sand
gravel at base

Grey-blue shelly
loam, temperate

18 ft
5·5 ms

(b)

length here. Did Wolstonian ice sheets reach as far south as this, or didn't they? Is the boulder clay *in situ* anyhow, or can it be an Anglian till which has been reworked and maybe moved bodily during the Wolstonian cold complex? Geological opinion remains divided on these matters, and we must hope that Mr Sieveking's campaign in the area in the late 1960s and early 1970s will give new evidence when it is finally published. Paterson, not surprisingly, was influenced by artefact typology when it came to interpreting a geological sequence in which some of the deposits contained artefacts. The Elveden industry (Fig. 5:35) is certainly finely made, with much 'soft hammer' work and a high proportion of delicately twisted cutting edges as features of the handaxes. Viewed solely against the archaeological background of all the industries discussed so far in this book, it could only be placed in a later rather than an earlier position, but that is exactly the kind of typological judgement that is resolutely to be avoided. Maybe such technology *was* current in

5:34 Sections in the Elveden brick-pit, after Paterson and Fagg (1940). (a) Longitudinal section; (b) details of the section at C. Key to numbers in (a): 1, solid chalk, passing into chalk rubble at the top; 2, edge of a channel or hollow; 3, boulder clay (till), filling 2; 4, marl with temperate shells, covering eroded surface of 3; 5, fine sand, gravelly at its base; 6, coarser gravel and sand, with remains of land surface; 7, stony loam, deposited in a marshy environment, representing silting up of the lake or channel, contorted and cryoturbated at the top, where it consists mainly of chalky sand; 8, boulder clay (till); 9, sandy soil of Breckland type, developed from decalcified till.

5:35 Handaxes from Elveden, including three with twisted profiles; ovate and pointed ovate forms predominate. After Paterson and Fagg (1940)

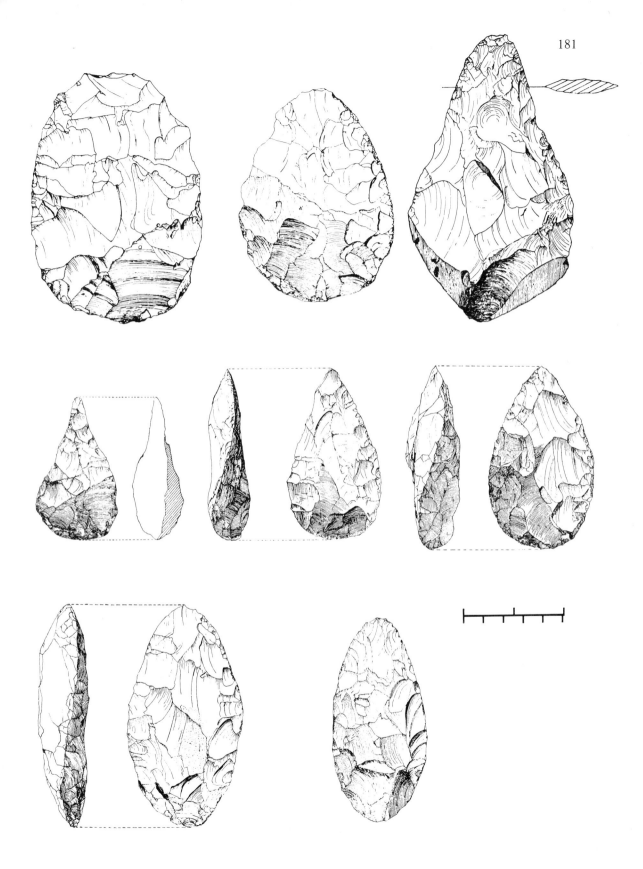

the full Hoxnian and *does* alternate with less advanced-looking styles, rather than occupying a late position; that is what the present section is discussing. On Paterson's reading of the sequence, the Elveden brickearth would have formed during a Wolstonian interstadial or in the Ipswichian, and he may be right, but we can see that there are other possibilities. Clearly this is a crucial site for which to have a definitive date. The best of the artefacts are now at the British Museum, the Cambridge University Museum and the Elveden Estate Office.

Allington Hill, near Bottisham, in Cambridgeshire, is a little west of the Breckland margin. The site is little known and virtually unpublished, though its existence was mentioned by J.G.D. Clark (1938: 251) and J.E. Marr (1926: 114). The artefacts came from a gravel at about 150 feet above sea-level and were collected in the late 1880s mainly by Professor and Mrs T. McKenny Hughes and by H. Keeping. They are now in the Sedgwick Museum, Cambridge, and in Brighton Museum. There is a strong unity about the series in condition, patination, raw material and technology, and the site was not prolific. Regrettably, there is no dating evidence known to the writer. In all the metrical analyses he made, this assemblage compared very closely with that from Elveden; hence their juxtaposition in the table.

The *Tilehurst* site is near Reading and close to the confluence of the modern Middle Thames and Kennet. The artefacts, a fine series of well-made ovates (Fig. 5:36), which resemble each other closely in patination and raw material, and generally in condition, not to mention technology, were recovered at the Roebuck Pit by the dedicated Reading collector, G.W. Smith, who did not publish his observations, unfortunately, though an account of the site was provided by his namesake R.A Smith of the British Museum (1915a). John Wymer has also given a summary of the rather limited amount of information that is available (1968: 148-50, 165). The artefacts are now almost all at Reading Museum, though not as many survive as are implied by the published accounts — about 100 out of the 169 originally found. The artefacts seem to have been dispersed through a gravel capped by remnants of a brick-

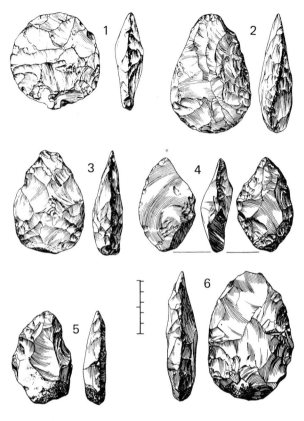

5:36 Implements from Tilehurst, after Wymer (1968): nos 1-3, 5, 6, handaxes (no. 2 with twisted profile and no. 6 with large *tranchet* scar); no. 4, convex sidescraper made on a flake

earth; the gravel is at approximately the height of the Lynch Hill Terrace (see pages 166-8), but it is by no means certain that it was a Lynch Hill gravel and Wymer (*loc. cit.*) seems inclined to favour the view that it is a mass of soliflucted material. In the whole context of the Pleistocene of the Reading area there is a reasonable presumption that the periglacial episode responsible would fall somewhere within the Wolstonian complex, but that is of little use to us here. No faunal remains are recorded from the pit, and there is no effective dating evidence.

In the present writer's view, the next two Group VI assemblages, Oldbury and Pan Farm, are Middle Palaeolithic rather than Lower Palaeolithic — that is to say, Mousterian of Acheulian Tradition rather than Acheulian — and they will accordingly be discussed again in the next chapter. The reasons for this judgement partly involve details of the handaxe morphology, notably presence of a distinctive form to which the name *bout coupé* has been given, which appears to be outside the Acheulian range but is well represented at many Continental Mousterian sites, particularly in France. Apart from that, a strong element of prepared core technique can be distinguished amongst the artefacts accompanying the handaxes at each of the sites, and there are some well-made flake-tools which would not be out of place in a Mousterian industry in France. *Oldbury*, near Ightham in Kent, was a site of Benjamin Harrison's, and he actually excavated there in 1890 on behalf of the British Association, though he never produced a detailed report on his work. Desmond and Ann Collins (1970) carried out research in the area, including excavation in 1965, and have given a useful summary of past work as well as describing their own and listing the relevant literature. They recovered a number of artefacts from a stony deposit overlying the Greensand bedrock and concluded that these were Mousterian and similar to Harrison's material, and that the deposit containing them was probably of earlier Devensian age. The *Great Pan Farm* site, at Shide, near Newport in the Isle of Wight, yielded artefacts from a terrace of the River Medina some 21 feet above O.D. They were collected, with a good deal of care, in the early 1920s, by H.F. Poole (1925), who recorded the provenances of many in detail and believed them all to have been derived together from a nearby working site, although they occurred through a fair thickness of deposit in several distinct strata. They certainly look like an homogeneous group, and the implements are accompanied by much knapping debris. Myra Shackley (1973, 1975: 96-124) reinvestigated the remains of the old pit and re-studied the industry (though both she and the present writer found that less material now survives than Poole originally listed): she was able to confirm Poole's account of the stratigraphy in most respects, though she found no more artefacts herself. She identified a layer of beach sand in the sequence and suggested that it might represent the 'Late Monastirian'

marine transgression at 7 to 8 m O.D. to which various raised beach deposits in south Hampshire have been assigned (cf. note 13 to Chapter 4, above); this would imply a Late Ipswichian date for the industry, which Dr Shackley diagnosed as an early variant of the Mousterian of Acheulian Tradition, wholly comparable to others in Britain and France of Late Last Interglacial to Early Last Glacial age. The chronological side of the argument is inevitably somewhat loose, since few of the sites are unassailably dated, but the conclusions seem to the present writer to be very probably correct or at least to provide the best working hypothesis currently available. These two sites, then, which the metrical tests rather satisfactorily brought together, as well as the typological and technological data, form Sub-Group D of Group VI and are likely to be younger in age than all the rest in Table 13, dating from near the beginning of the Devensian — just before, perhaps, in one case, and just after in the other.

The remaining four samples were 'attributed to Group VI' after the writer's analyses were complete: that is to say, the handaxe morphology and technology strongly suggested the general run of Group VI, but in each case the sample was not wholly satisfactory in one way or another, or else some other factor intervened. The groups from Holybourne, Round Green and the Barnfield Pit Upper Loam were very weak numerically and one could not be sure that if fifty or a hundred handaxes had been present from each of these industries instead of less than twenty, the results would have looked the same in terms of emphasis as they actually do. Percentages become somewhat meaningless when a single implement counts as six or seven per cent of its parent sample. The Caversham Ancient Channel series was known to be a mixture: it merely looks as if a 'Group VI' element might dominate it.

The *Holybourne* site is in north Hampshire, near Alton, and the handaxes were found, with various flakes (including handaxe trimming flakes) on the surface of ploughed ground, concentrated in an area some 40 to 50 yards across. The findspot (Willis 1947) was over 700 feet above sea-level, on a patch of clay-with-flints, overlying the chalk. At first sight the artefacts look somewhat abraded and even water-worn, but this is not in fact the case: their surfaces have merely been altered, and the ridges worn down, by weathering, presumably during long exposure on the surface or just below it. The finders of this site, who also located a number of smaller-scale though otherwise similar occurrences in the same part of north Hampshire, believed that the surface of the patches of clay-with-flints constituted remnants of a land-surface occupied by Palaeolithic man and that the artefacts had lain more or less where he left them, becoming covered gradually by soil and disturbed only by modern ploughing. The present writer regards this hypothesis as perfectly reasonable; no doubt much of the derived Lower Palaeolithic material in the gravels of the Hampshire rivers further south was swept down from sites like these on what is now the high ground, few of which now remain intact (cf. Willis, *op. cit.* 255-6). Myra Shackley (1973: 550; 1976) appears to take the view that the Holybourne industry is Mousterian of Acheulian Tradition rather than Acheulian; it is true that one classic *bout coupé* handaxe was found near the other artefacts, but it is in very different condition from them, being unweathered and almost patinated. In fact there seems to be no independent dating evidence at all for the Holybourne site. The artefacts themselves are now at the Curtis Museum, Alton.

Round Green might have been a superb site if it had been investigated with the aid of modern techniques; the site is now, alas, built over in a suburb of Luton, Bedfordshire. It will probably be clear enough already that the present writer is rather a fan of Worthington Smith, and perhaps therefore inclined to accept his observations somewhat uncritically: Round Green is another of his discoveries. Perhaps because of the upsetting effect which the arrival of keen collectors had had on his work at Stoke Newington, and indeed also at Caddington, Worthington Smith appears to have kept his finds at Round Green and Gaddesden Row (see below) rather more to himself, publishing them retrospectively late in his life (1916), although the principal observations were made in 1906. At Round Green, he evidently found an Acheulian 'floor' *in situ* in brickearth, its virtually undisturbed nature being attested by the presence

of conjoinable flakes which are clearly knapping waste. The brickearth was capped by what Smith called (as elsewhere) 'contorted drift', with festooning and convolutions of presumably periglacial origin (Fig. 5:37a). A few derived or redeposited artefacts came from this deposit. The occurrence appears otherwise, from Smith's description, to have been a single one, and it avoids the confusion of Caddington, where several different brick-pits were involved. Smith recovered '21 well defined sharp edged implements' (the term 'implements' thus used at this period almost always implies handaxes), '9 sharp edged knife forms, mostly thin but a few thick' (almost certainly flake-tools), '261 flakes' (which would be waste), 'and one distinct sharp edged core' (*op. cit.*, p. 68). In Smith's opinion, the artefacts (Fig. 5:38) lay at the edge of a small pond or lake some 350 feet long and 250 feet broad. It may well be that he recovered virtually a complete industry, but we cannot be sure and there is an absence of dating evidence. Animal bones seem to have been found at a pit nearby by the workmen; Smith was unable to recover them, though he did himself find one fragment of antler of *Cervus elaphus* (1894: 167). Most of the lithic material listed by Smith survives, and the majority of it is now at the British Museum.

Group VII

In this Group, we need not devote much further space to *Warren Hill* or *Highlands Farm*. The former sample is made up of fresh implements from the glaci-fluvial gravel of presumed Wolstonian age (Solomon 1933), which contained mixed material apparently including a much worn archaic industry of considerable potential importance (see pages 111-15). The Highlands Farm handaxes all came from a single pit in the Caversham Ancient Channel gravel and include those from John Wymer's own excavations (1961, 1968: 191-7). It looks as if that particular gravel pit happened to coincide with a part of the deposit where one particularly prolific Acheulian site, specializing in ovate handaxes, had been somewhat resorted. This could explain well enough the fact that the diffuse general Caversham Channel series ended up as

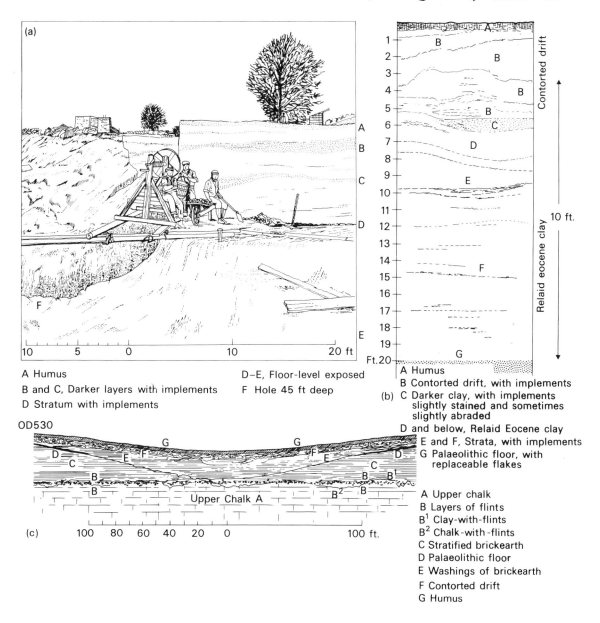

A Humus

B and C, Darker layers with implements

D Stratum with implements

D–E, Floor-level exposed

F Hole 45 ft deep

A Humus

B Contorted drift, with implements

C Darker clay, with implements slightly stained and sometimes slightly abraded

D and below, Relaid Eocene clay

E and F, Strata, with implements

G Palaeolithic floor, with replaceable flakes

A Upper chalk

B Layers of flints

B¹ Clay-with-flints

B² Chalk-with-flints

C Stratified brickearth

D Palaeolithic floor

E Washings of brickearth

F Contorted drift

G Humus

5:37 Sections at Gaddesden Row and Round Green, redrawn after W.G. Smith (1916): (a) drawing of Butterfield's Pit at Gaddesden Row, with stratigraphic information (key below); (b) a more detailed section in the same pit; (c) section at Round Green, showing position of the 'floor' discovered by Smith

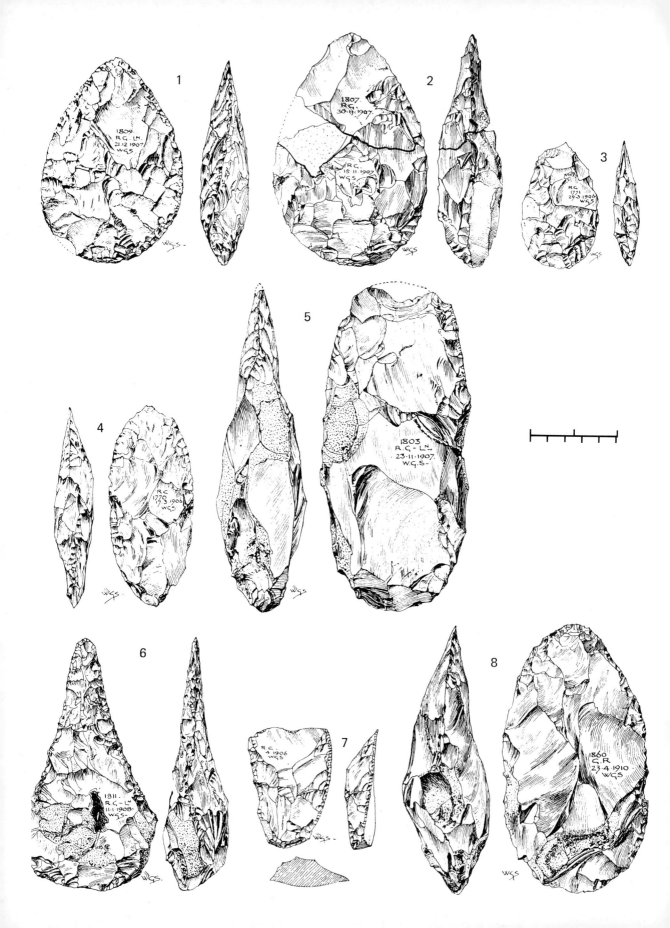

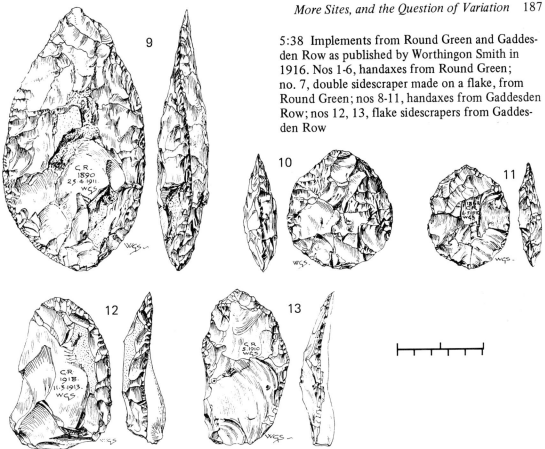

5:38 Implements from Round Green and Gaddesden Row as published by Worthingon Smith in 1916. Nos 1-6, handaxes from Round Green; no. 7, double sidescraper made on a flake, from Round Green; nos 8-11, handaxes from Gaddesden Row; nos 12, 13, flake sidescrapers from Gaddesden Row

'attributed to Group VI', while the Highlands Farm series has a much more individual character, consisting so far as the handaxes are concerned mainly of a rich 'Group VII' industry. There is no reason why 'Group VI' and 'Group VII' industries should not have been current together, since the Groups comprise sets of morphological likes rather than being demonstrable 'chronological units'. The remaining sites in Group VII require brief descriptions.

Gaddesden Row, in Hertfordshire, is another of Worthington Smith's discoveries, published by him along with the Round Green site mentioned in the last section (Smith 1916); there is very little other literature relating to it, and what there is does not add substantially to Smith's account (Oakley 1947: 248-9; R.A. Smith 1926: 49). The site yielded at least one substantial floor, some 20 feet down in brickearth (Fig. 5:37b), with isolated implements, or small quantities of artefacts, occurring at other depths in the same deposit – there may have been as many as eight distinct horizons in all. As at Round Green and Caddington, conjoinable waste flakes were found by Smith, and the artefacts (Fig. 5:38) were mostly in admirably sharp condition; the main floor was probably virtually undisturbed and is likely to have represented occupation by the side of a lake or other water body. The surface of the chalk underlying the brickearth gave evidence of periglacial conditions, and the top of the brickearth was also markedly disturbed by cryoturbation and similar periglacial processes. What we do not know is the age of the brickearth itself: it is an obvious guess that it should be of Ipswichian or inter-Wolstonian age, but we lack guidance in choosing between these alternatives. Recently John Wymer carried out some excavation at the old Gaddesden Row brickpit, long disused but still in existence, which was the scene of Worthington Smith's original finds (pers. com., unpublished), but he found no trace of the major Acheulian floor or floors. The brickearth in this area reaches more than 40 feet in thickness in places, and even if some evidence for its age could be obtained by, for example, pollen analysis, the deposit may have formed slowly over a long period and it would be hard to give a precise date to the main occupation level if all traces of it are indeed gone for ever. Smith's finds included at least fifty handaxes from the floor or floors in the brickearth, and some derived ones from the 'contorted drift' at the top, i.e. the periglacially disturbed top of the brickearth and whatever solifluxed material overlay it. There were also some well-made flake-tools as well as various artefacts representing knapping waste. The material has become somewhat scattered, but there are good series at the British Museum and Luton Museum.

High Lodge is near Mildenhall, Suffolk, in the Breckland area of East Anglia, near the Warren Hill site but on the opposite side of the modern A.11 road. It is a site of the first importance, and of more than purely British significance, one can safely say, which is why many people are awaiting with decreasing patience a definitive report on the major campaign of excavation carried out by G. de G. Sieveking under the auspices of the British Museum over several seasons in the late 1960s and early 1970s. To this document, when available — and the writer understands that it is in active preparation and well advanced — the reader's attention is directed, since it may well overturn the information offered here, which is necessarily based on old literature and a few later hints that may be gleaned here and there. The High Lodge site (occasionally called Warren Lodge) has a long history of research extending well back into the nineteenth century, and it has long been known that the essentials of the sequence comprise lake sediments stratified between two glacial tills (Marr *et al.* 1921; R.A. Smith 1931: 26-30). Controversy has mainly been concerned with the identification of these tills, and, more recently, with the question of whether they are truly *in situ* or whether they and the lacustrine sediments

could possibly have been shifted bodily by the pressure of advancing ice. So far as the writer understands the situation, the most likely interpretation is that the lake sediments formed during an interstadial of the glaciation at present called Wolstonian, and it is accordingly to that glaciation that *both* tills are to be ascribed; we are dealing if so with a mild phase later than the Hoxnian and earlier than the Ipswichian, in the terminology we have followed, and a mild phase, apparently, of interstadial rather than interglacial intensity. Incorporated into the lake sediments near their edge are two separate industries, which are both essentially flake industries and not handaxe industries; whether any trace of handaxe manufacture can certainly be attributed to either must remain to be seen when the report by Sieveking is published. Of these two flake industries, which appear to be *in situ* and therefore to date from the time of the lake itself, the younger is very finely made and includes many flake-tools which approach those of the full Middle Palaeolithic (Mousterian) period in style and in various technological details (further discussion and illustrations in the next chapter); the older industry, however, is of a rather cruder appearance. The implications of these flake industries will be considered in the next chapter, which deals with the Middle Palaeolithic. But there is a third industry at High Lodge, which is a handaxe industry, and it was this that provided the implements studied by the writer and attributed to his Group VII. These artefacts came from a rather thin layer of gravel which appears to have spread out over parts of the lake clays, through the agency of solifluction, after the lake had dried out but before the actual arrival of the ice sheet which deposited the upper till. The handaxes are not much abraded, and the likelihood is that the solifluction brought down the remains of an Acheulian site from the slopes above the former lake. Morphologically these implements resemble very closely those of the Warren Hill fresh sample, and of course they could even have come from the very same gravel ridge which contained the prolific Warren Hill assemblage only a few hundred yards away, if that 'glaci-fluvial' deposit were correlated with the withdrawal of the ice-sheet responsible for the lower till at High Lodge. In any case, since the High Lodge handaxes are in a soliflucted gravel and not *in situ* on the lake shore, we cannot of course say that they really are younger than the two flake industries of the lake clays, even though they overlie them: the solifluction could have brought them down from a deposit which pre-dated the lake. However, if they really are sealed in by a Wolstonian boulder clay, the upper High Lodge till, which is the reading adopted here, then at least they cannot be younger than the later part of the Wolstonian, i.e. they cannot be Ipswichian. We must hope that it will be possible to be more precise when all the information is available, though the reader will be aware by now that in Palaeolithic studies such is not always the case.

The High Lodge artefacts have been collected over a very long period indeed, and have become widely scattered. The best series is certainly that of the British Museum, and there too are housed the finds from the recent excavations, though access to them is restricted until the study of them for publication is complete.

Croxley Green is near Rickmansworth, and the gravels there are related rather to the River Colne than the Thames, though the situation is further complicated by the presence of glacial outwash gravels which the Colne appears to have re-worked. The Rickmansworth area has produced very many Lower Palaeolithic artefacts, including hundreds of handaxes, and the two most prolific pits were at Mill End and at Croxley Green. It proved very hard to isolate from the mass of extant material a group that could usefully be studied metrically, but it seemed to the writer to be worth using some of the artefacts acquired by Sir Hugh Beevor from the workmen at the Croxley Green Pit over a brief period early this century: most of his collection is now at the Geological Museum in South Kensington, and is accompanied by some manu-script notes which suggest that most of the 400 specimens which he obtained had a restricted distribution both vertically and horizontally. All those selected for study are marked as coming from the base of the gravel, just above the surface of the underlying chalk, and the handaxes were certainly accompanied by flaking debris. There is at least a chance that this is a sample from a

slightly disturbed working site, though one cannot put it any more strongly than that. Certainly the artefacts are very consistent in their physical state, including patination and staining, but the latter might well be post-depositional effects and prove nothing in themselves. As for the deposits, some work was carried out by R.A. Smith and H. Dewey (1915) at Rickmansworth, including excavation, and, to judge from their report, the gravels, whose base is approximately 60 feet above the present Colne, are redeposited glacial outwash, with signs of periglacial disturbance at the top. The outwash is apparently Anglian, but the date of its reworking by the river is not at all clear. The base of the deposit, where the handaxes in this sample came from, consisted of an unstratified mass of rubble with many large boulders, representing fallen material where the river had cut into the side of its valley (mantled with glacial outwash) before the main body of the gravel was laid down (*op. cit.*, pp. 217-24; cf. also Wymer 1968: 246-8). Smith and Dewey themselves did not find more than a few dozen artefacts, and most of those were flakes which Smith compared to those he knew from his own work at this same period in the Swanscombe Lower Gravels. The present writer is not however aware of any unequivocally Clactonian artefacts from this site, and the handaxe industry of Croxley Green remains undated. The metrical analyses placed it squarely in Group VII, and there were no pointed handaxe types at all.

Corfe Mullen is near Wimborne Minster in Dorset, in an area of southern England (south Hampshire and east Dorset), which is one of the richest of the whole country in sheer numbers of Lower Palaeolithic artefacts. The present writer has recorded well over a hundred separate find-spots of them in the Bournemouth-Christchurch region alone, some of them prolific (cf. Fig. 5:4). Yet traces of good sealed sites yielding undisturbed industries are extremely rare amongst this wealth, most of the assemblages being mixtures from gravel contexts. In the region of Corfe Mullen the geologist J.F.N. Green and the gifted amateur archaeologist J.B. Calkin studied various gravels exposed at different times from the late 1920s to the 1940s, and were able to deduce an interesting local sequence of Palaeolithic industries (Green

1946, 1947; Calkin and Green 1949; see also Roe 1975). Further relevant work on the gravel terraces of the Avon was carried out by K.R. Sealy (1955). At the Railway Ballast Pit, Corfe Mullen (also known as the Ballast Hole), Calkin and Green demonstrated (1949: 21-8) that an industry with heavy rather crude pointed handaxes underlay scattered occurrences of well-made ovates. At the nearby Cogdean Pit there was an altogether better series of about seventy ovate handaxes, mostly in very fresh condition (Fig. 5:39), which Calkin regarded as belonging together and coming from a single 'camping site' only a short distance away. These were certainly younger than the archaic-looking pointed handaxes from the Railway Ballast Pit, which came from the base of bluff deposits between two terraces, and Calkin thought they were approximately the same age as the younger series from that site, though different in various points of typology and technology. We need not follow the geological arguments of Calkin and Green in detail, but they placed these

ovate industries, which Calkin called 'Upper Acheulian', after a cold phase following the formation of the 100-foot terrace of the Avon. They regarded this terrace as equivalent to the Swanscombe gravels, which, at the time they were writing, is tantamount to assigning a Hoxnian date to it, the term 'Hoxnian' itself not then being current. The Cogdean Pit industry would accordingly be attributable to the Ipswichian or to a Wolstonian interstadial. As for the deposits at the site, the gravel pit appears to have been dug through the filling of a minor valley created by a small tributary of the Avon, a tributary which had ceased to flow at the time when the 100-foot terrace was formed, the valley being later filled in by the movement of debris down its sides through soil creep, solifluction, hill wash and so forth. The handaxes were dispersed throughout the gravelly deposit thus formed, which is up to 11 feet thick, but were still regarded as deriving from a single source on the higher ground above, and this seems perfectly possible. In their 1949 paper, Calkin and

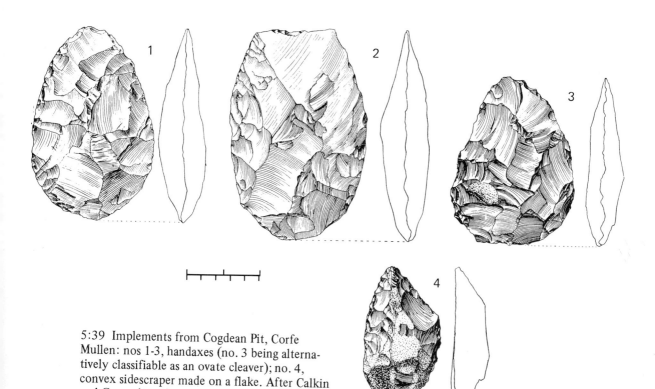

5:39 Implements from Cogdean Pit, Corfe Mullen: nos 1-3, handaxes (no. 3 being alternatively classifiable as an ovate cleaver); no. 4, convex sidescraper made on a flake. After Calkin and Green (1949)

Green also described artefacts from younger terraces in the east Bournemouth and Christchurch regions, but these can more appropriately be considered in the next chapter.

The list of sites under Group VII is concluded by the name of *Caddington*. As briefly indicated earlier in this chapter, the writer's enquiries since his 1968 paper suggest that the handaxes he studied from Caddington came from more than one find-spot, and though the various occurrences *may* very well have been closely contemporary, there is nothing to prove that they were. The results of the metrical analyses suggested that what we may loosely call 'Group VII morphology' was dominant, and so the sample was listed under Group VII with a query. Even so, there are some anomalous features, such as the presence of a few acutely pointed handaxes. What would the shape diagram have looked like if the sample had included a hundred implements or more? Another major difference from the other Group VII sites exists in the abundant presence at Caddington of Levalloisian artefacts, both cores and flakes; indeed, there are more of them than there are handaxes. Partly this reflects the care of Worthington Smith, the discoverer of the Caddington sites, in collecting *débitage* as well as finished tools. Since Smith died before the term 'Levalloisian' came into use, and since large parts of his collection evidently remained virtually unexamined between 1917 and the early 1960s, the present writer was utterly unaware of this important feature of the Caddington industry when he first went to Luton Museum in 1962 to study the specimens. Caddington is undoubtedly an Acheulian industry of Levallois facies, as our Continental colleagues would very reasonably say, assuming that the majority of the artefacts really do belong together, which seems very likely (though cf. Sampson 1978, not published in time to be taken into account here). It is hard to quote a precise British parallel.

The Caddington artefacts (Figs 5:41 to 5:43) include plenty of Levalloisian cores and flakes of classic type, but also some which have been produced by what one might call a 'reduced Levalloisian technique' (Fig. 5:42), in which a nodule was subjected to somewhat rudimentary preparation of its upper surface and a simple striking platform was fashioned at one end, before a single large flake, or in a few cases a couple of sizeable flakes, were removed from it, evidently as end-products of the process or as blanks for subsequent retouch. How should we regard these rather casual-looking prepared cores and the flakes struck from them? To the typologist's eye, they may perhaps look 'proto-Levalloisian' — examples of the 'tortoise-core' technique in a formative stage of its development. Not dissimilar cores and flakes are in fact known from a few other British sites, notably from one at Purfleet discussed below (Wymer 1968: 312-13) and also from Biddenham, near Bedford (examples noted by the present writer but not mentioned in the literature). However, neither of these sites is clearly dated, and at both there are mixtures of artefacts. We should also remember that Levalloisian technique is known as early in our basic sequence as the Swanscombe Middle Gravels, and was fully developed in the Baker's Hole industry; for a proto-Levalloisian industry, one would therefore certainly be looking for a Hoxnian date. Caddington is not well dated — that was something the excavations of 1970-71 (Plate 31) failed to achieve, along with many other aims, since no *in situ* material could be located. But the balance of such palynological and sedimentological evidence as was obtained is in favour of an Ipswichian age for the Caddington brickearths (J. Catt and R.N.L.B. Hubbard, pers. com.; see also Sampson 1978). There is also the presence of classic Levalloisian cores and flakes at Caddington beside the others to be remembered, with clear indications in Smith's published account (1894) and manuscript notes that all the artefacts are of much the same age. In the light of these factors, it seems preferable to regard the 'reduced Levalloisian' material of Caddington not as prototypic for the full technique, but rather as representing reduction of it to the barest essentials by highly competent flint knappers who would sometimes take a flake of planned proportions off the top of a nodule, so to speak, without indulging in needlessly elaborate preliminaries. The flakes thus obtained may have possessed minor irregularities, but if they were blanks for further shaping that would not have

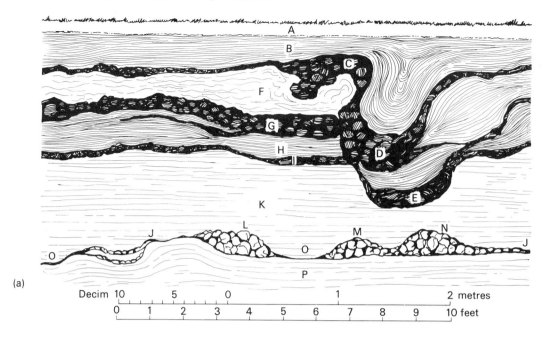

(a)

Decim 10   5   0   1   2 metres

0   1   2   3   4   5   6   7   8   9   10 feet

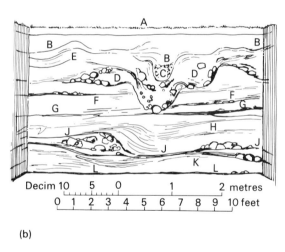

Decim 10   5   0   1   2 metres

0 1 2 3 4 5 6 7 8 9 10 feet

(b)

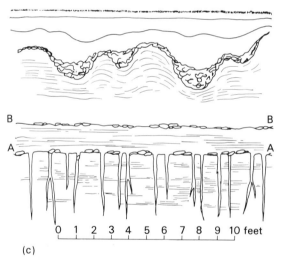

0 1 2 3 4 5 6 7 8 9 10 feet

(c)

5:40 Sections in the Caddington brick-pits show-ing the Palaeolithic floor, as published by Worth-ington Smith in 1894. (a) Key: A, surface soil; B-I, various divisions of 'contorted drift' and subangular gravel, evidently much disturbed by periglacial processes; K, P, undisturbed brick-earth; J, O, the Palaeolithic land surface, with artefacts, including many conjoinable flakes; L. M, N, heaps of flints brought to the site by man as raw material for knapping. (b) Section after a few feet of the pit face shown in (a) had been removed. A, soil; B-D, 'contorted drift', etc.; F, G, H, K, brickearth, more or less hori-zontally stratified; J, land surface with artefacts and imported heaps of flints; L, a lower floor with more artefacts, exposed horizontally when the section was drawn. (c) Another section at Cadding-ton, in which the old land surface A was pene-trated by vertical fissures which Smith inter-preted as sun cracks. There was a second land sur-face at B, and some 18 inches of brickearth separated the two

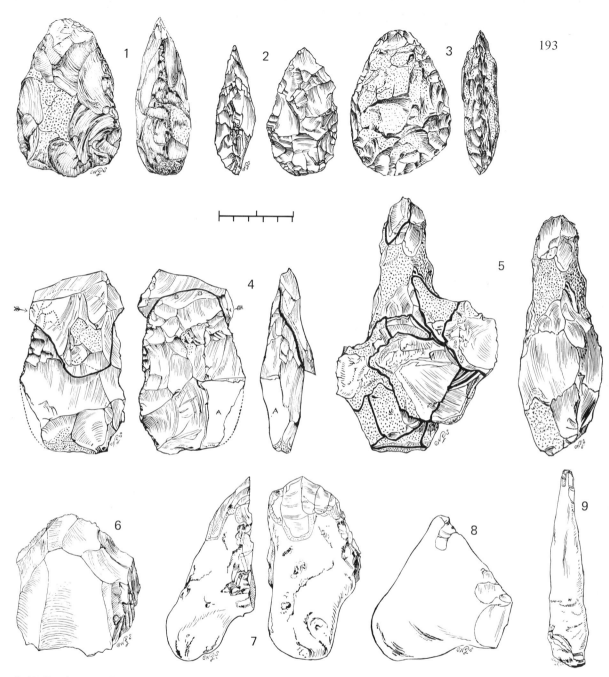

5:41 Implements from Caddington, after W.G. Smith (1894), all from the floors: nos 1-3, hand-axes (the tip of no. 1 apparently anciently re-sharpened); no. 4, handaxe with a flake of 'tran-chet' type replaced: the area at A is a recent break; no. 5, narrow pick-like biface, perhaps unfinished, with various of its trimming flakes re-attached; no. 6 core; no. 7, nodule with end flaked (cf. Fig. 5:26 no. 6, from Cuxton); no. 8, piece interpreted by Smith as a hammer stone; no. 9, possible punch or fabricator, consisting of a narrow more or less cylindrical flint nodule; nos 10, 11, retouched flakes

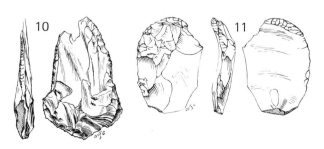

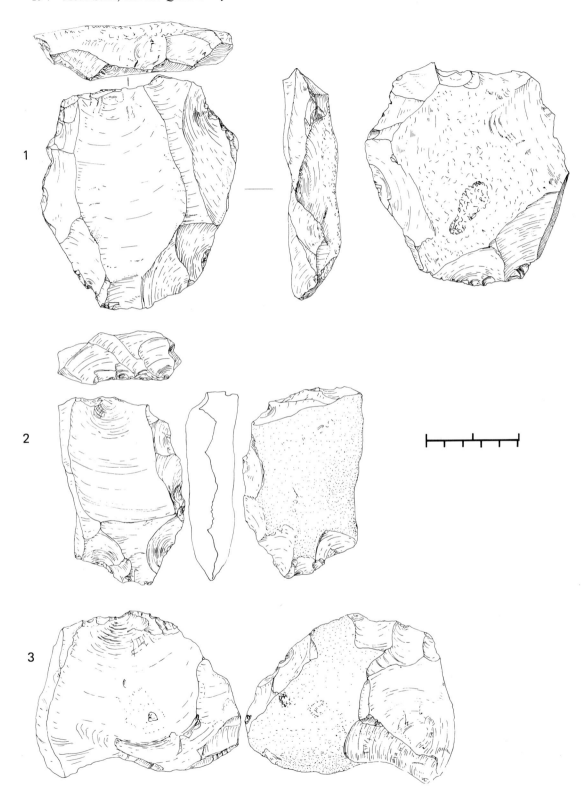

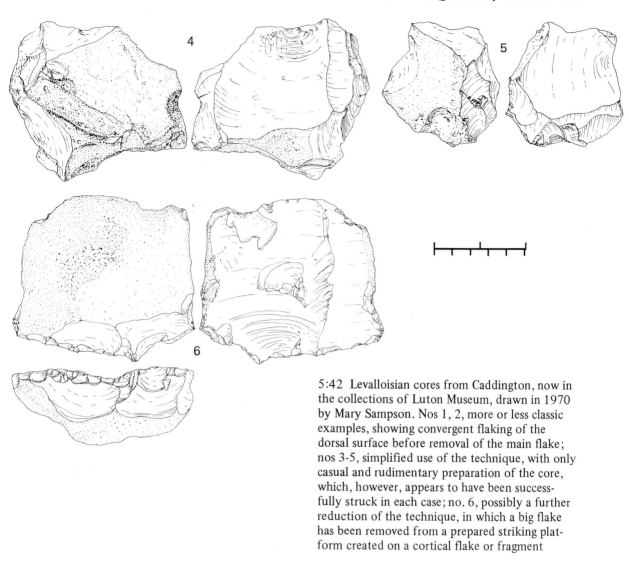

5:42 Levalloisian cores from Caddington, now in the collections of Luton Museum, drawn in 1970 by Mary Sampson. Nos 1, 2, more or less classic examples, showing convergent flaking of the dorsal surface before removal of the main flake; nos 3-5, simplified use of the technique, with only casual and rudimentary preparation of the core, which, however, appears to have been successfully struck in each case; no. 6, possibly a further reduction of the technique, in which a big flake has been removed from a prepared striking platform created on a cortical flake or fragment

mattered greatly. More elegant and regular Levalloisian flakes were evidently available on demand. No one who examines the Caddington handaxes and flake tools, or, better still, the flake debris from the handaxe manufacture, will doubt the competence of the knappers.

It is worth spending a little more space on Caddington, because it must have been a superb site and yet it is very poorly known amongst scholars of the Lower Palaeolithic, because of the shortage of literature; if this summary encourages more people to seek out the collections, it will

have served a useful purpose. The geology of the Caddington Pleistocene deposits resembles that of Round Green and Gaddesden Row, described above. The three sites are not far apart, Caddington itself being just west of Luton, Bedfordshire. At all three there are high-level brickearths, overlying chalk and capped by what Worthington Smith called 'contorted drift' — at Caddington, this takes the form of a strongly convoluted mixture of gravel and stony clay, most of it redeposited from the local Tertiary deposits capping the chalk, and evidently owing its present form to periglacial

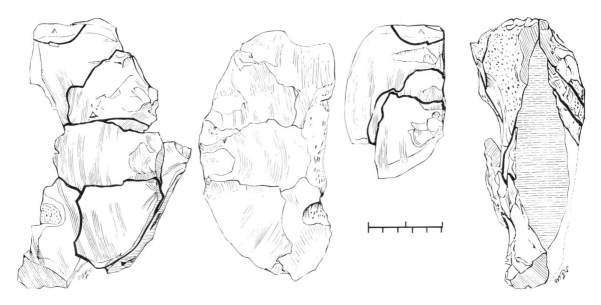

conditions (cf. Fig. 5:40; Plate 31). The buff-coloured brickearth of Caddington occurs intermittently in pockets, apparently filling solution hollows of various sizes in the chalk – doubtless much of it accumulated in still water bodies, ponds or small lakes, as Smith envisaged, though some of the particles of which it is composed can now be seen to be of ultimately loessic origin. The edges of such ponds or lakes would have offered attractive camping sites for Palaeolithic man, especially since flint was abundant in the local chalk. Not all the patches of brickearth produced artefacts, but at least half a dozen separate ones did, over two or three square kilometres (cf. map in Smith 1894: 1). Worthington Smith himself found no faunal remains, in spite of a careful watch, with the exception of one vague report of horse teeth from the workmen (1894: 166). The excavations in 1970 recovered a number of mammal bones in one part of one trench, not in the brickearth proper, but certainly adjacent to a brickearth-filled hollow; this particular brickearth, however, produced no trace of occupation. The bones (Sampson 1978: 55-60) included elephant and deer of indeterminate species, but one can hardly say in the circumstances that they were certainly contemporary with Smith's floors.

Worthington Smith's main floor at Caddington was found at the brick-pit known to him as Pit C,

5:43 Worthington Smith's group of conjoined handaxe trimming flakes from Caddington (see page 197), with the plaster cast of the missing implement. Note that the surfaces marked A also conjoin, as shown in the profile view. After Smith (1894).

and was clearly a rich occurrence. He describes the presence on it of piles of flint nodules (in the otherwise stoneless brickearth), which had been gathered as raw material for implement manufacture by Palaeolithic man. There were also piles of struck flakes, apparently selected. Artefacts, especially knapping debris, were abundant (1894: 114):

My group-find includes broken, unsatisfactory, or unfinished implements, pieces, cores, hammerstones, punches, and a vast number of flakes. With these are beautifully made and perfect implements. Near the tools and flakes were collections of natural flints — many of these were large blocks which had been apparently tested for flaking purposes. Large partially flaked blocks were common, but sometimes so massive and heavy, that they could not conveniently be taken away by hand. Some weighed ten, twenty or even thirty pounds. Certain of the larger blocks had been artificially quartered or crushed in Palaeolithic times.

There is abundant evidence in the surviving material, of which the best collections are at the British Museum and Luton Museum (with some good pieces also at the Ashmolean Museum, Oxford), that this main Caddington occurrence was a manufacturing floor rather than a living or butchery site. It was also virtually undisturbed. In no part of the extant material are these facts so well illustrated as in Worthington Smith's groups of conjoined flakes or of flakes refitted to finished or unfinished implements (Figs. 5:41, 5:43). By the time he published *Man the Primeval Savage* in 1894 — and his work at Caddington continued for many years afterwards — he had already made over 500 such reattachments from amongst the artefacts he had recovered. Most of the conjoinable pieces lay close together, but some were several feet or even yards apart. The patience and perspicacity shown by Smith in achieving these reconstructions were quite extraordinary, especially given the difficulty of retrieving the specimens in the first place, what with the tenacity of the brickearth and the tendency of the pit to flood deeply, not to mention the fact that he was working virtually single handed without any modern technical aids. Perhaps the most eloquent testimony of all is offered in Fig. 5:43: Smith had conjoined one group of ten flat flakes and another of three more, which fitted on to the first group, leaving a curiously shaped gap. Not satisfied, he made a plaster cast of the empty space and it came out as the major part of a square-ended ovate handaxe. The implement itself was never found, and had doubtless been taken away from the site for use, but Smith had recovered and refitted thirteen of the flakes struck off in its making (*op. cit.*, 151-2). These thirteen flakes had come to light in a small area of the pit over the period April-June 1890. They offer in the present writer's view one of those rare and precious moments of contact between the archaeologist and another human being across ages of time, which breathe life into the often arid science of analysing lithic artefacts and remind one of the essential humanity

of prehistory, even in the Lower Palaeolithic. Those flakes were struck off within seconds of each other, and simply remained where they had fallen around the feet of the maker of the implement: the gap in the rejoined block, in its own small way, is symbolic of many of the problems of earlier prehistory — of the kind of evidence which is preserved, and the kind which is not; of the implement made and used for a purpose, not left neatly lying *in situ* to please future typologists. 'Group VII', indeed! — in such a context, the title seems almost sacrilegious. If Caddington were a new discovery now, and could be excavated the way the French Magdalenian open site of Pincevent was dug (Leroi-Gourhan and Brézillon 1972), what might not have been made of it? The failure of the 1971-2 excavations to find anything left, notwithstanding the opening of major areas (Plate 31), some of which must have come within 50 metres of where the best of Smith's finds were made, is deeply disappointing. But the brickpits continued to operate and to be expanded for many years after he finished his work there, and little if any undisturbed ground can remain where Pit C was.

The other Caddington occurrences were evidently much more restricted in their yield of artefacts, though it is not actually possible to say from which pit every surviving piece came. Whether any of these may have been contemporary living sites connected with the factory site of Pit C simply cannot be said, but it is likely enough, and none appears to have been specifically another major working floor. At Pit C, there seems to have been a second and less prolific floor, with white-patinated slightly lustrous artefacts, above the main one (whose artefacts were mostly grey-coloured), separated from it by one to three feet of sterile brickearth. Smith envisaged reoccupation after a period of flooding, and was convinced that the two levels were of virtually the same age. Some of the flakes in the white series proved to be conjoinable, but he saw no actual working place (1894: 109-12). Some fine flake tools occurred amongst the white series, and there are certainly white-patinated Levalloisian artefacts as well as some corresponding in patina to the artefacts from 'the true floor', as Smith called it, below.

The character of the two occupations may well have been different, but the industry does not seem to have changed radically in the probably short space of time between them.

These paragraphs devoted to Caddington have only touched on a few aspects of Smith's finds, illustrating the general comments with a few highlights. Anyone who can get access to a copy of *Man the Primeval Savage* can readily learn more, both about the sites and the artefacts themselves, and also about Worthington Smith, his working methods and his ideas about the objects he found. The book is well illustrated by his own meticulous drawings. A certain amount of his manuscript material survives, mostly at Luton, but it seems that some crucial parts of his records were destroyed in an air raid in London after they had passed into his son's keeping after his death.

This completes the brief description of the sites in the writer's Groups I, II, VI and VII. Returning to the original question (the causes of the observable variability), we may next tabulate the information that relates to the chronology of these industries (Table 15).

TABLE 15 : *Chronological data for the handaxe industries studied*

Site	Date and comments
Group I: pointed handaxes, cleavers, etc.	
Furze Platt (Maidenhead)	Artefacts from base of Middle Thames 'Lynch Hill Terrace', which may be fluvio-periglacial; Late Hoxnian to Early Wolstonian?
Baker's Farm (Farnham Royal)	From similar situation to that at Furze Platt: suggested closely similar in age
Cuxton	From a stream channel in the '50-foot terrace' of the Medway; presumably post-Hoxnian, but exact age uncertain
Whitlingham	From '50-foot terrace' gravels of the Yare, consisting mainly of outwash material? Inter-Wolstonian (younger than at least one Wolstonian stadial)
Twydall	Gravels of uncertain nature; no useful dating evidence and a mixture of industries likely

Site	Date and comments
Stoke Newington	Floor in brickearth overlying gravel of somewhat uncertain origin: ? Ipswichian, or another mild phase post-Hoxnian and pre-Devensian. Unusual fine flake-tools possibly belonging with the other material
Group II: pointed handaxes and some ovates	
Swanscombe, Barnfield Pit (Middle Gravels)	From gravels of the 90 to 100-foot terrace of the Lower Thames. Regarded as Hoxnian here; some think later
Chadwell St Mary	Artefacts attributed to '100-foot gravels of the Thames', but no detailed information or dating evidence. Industry very similar to that of Barnfield Pit Middle Gravels
Dovercourt, Gant's Pit	From a gravel whose surface is at 87 feet above O.D., possibly a terrace of the Stour. No helpful dating evidence
Hitchin	From base of brickearth capping Hoxnian alluvial deposits, and marl immediately below the brickearth: probably late Hoxnian or just post-Hoxnian
Foxhall Road, Ipswich	From brickearth (lake sediment) overlying till attributed to the Anglian. Perhaps Middle to Late Hoxnian, but no conclusive evidence. Technologically the most advanced industry of this Group
Group VI: ovate handaxes, with tendency to more pointed forms within the ovate range	
Knowle Farm, Savernake	In fluvio-periglacial gravels; undated. Assemblage probably mixed, including suspected archaic element
Elveden	In ? kettle-hole lake sediments, overlying a till. Perhaps inter-Wolstonian; new evidence awaited
Allington Hill, Bottisham	In gravel of uncertain origin; undated. Handaxes strikingly

Site	Date and comments
Bowman's Lodge, Dartford	similar to those of Elveden On surface of 90 to 100-foot terrace gravel, covered by loam. Later than the main Hoxnian, but pre-Ipswichian
Tilehurst, Roebuck Pit	In gravel, probably a solifluction deposit. No definite dating evidence
Oldbury (Rockshelters)	Some at least of the artefacts were in a stony deposit on bedrock, perhaps related to former overhang as a rock-shelter. Believed to be Early Devensian. *Bout coupé* handaxes and prepared core technique in the industry, here attributed to the Mousterian of Acheulian Tradition
Great Pan Farm, Shide	In terrace deposits of the River Medina about 21 feet above sea-level. Deposits believed to be contemporary with Late Ipswichian 7 to 8m beach. At least one *bout coupé* handaxe and prepared core technique noted. Attributed to Mousterian of Acheulian Tradition
Holybourne	Brought to the surface by ploughing. No dating evidence
Round Green, Luton	High level brickearth, cryoturbated at top. Undated
Swanscombe, Barnfield Pit (Upper Loam)	At base, and probably also in main body, of loam overlying the gravels of the 90 to 100-foot terrace of the Lower Thames. Certainly later than the Hoxnian maximum and younger than the Middle Gravels Group II industry, but how much younger is uncertain. Inter-Wolstonian ? Hubbard (1977) says Ipswichian
Caversham Ancient Channel	From gravels probably reworked (if not actually deposited) during the Wolstonian. Sample drawn from several pits and representing more than one industry. Youngest artefacts presumably of final Hoxnian or Wolstonian age

Group VII: ovate handaxes, with tendency to blunt-ended plan forms

Gaddesden Row	In high level brickearth, comparable to that of Round Green and Caddington; evidence for periglacial conditions below and above. No clear dating evidence
High Lodge, Mildenhall	From spread of soliflucted gravel capping inter-Wolstonian lake sediments. Artefacts similar to those from nearby Warren Hill (fresh series), and most likely to be of Wolstonian age — not younger, anyhow, as overlain by later Wolstonian glacial deposits. New information awaited
Warren Hill (fresh series) Mildenhall	From a mass of glaci-fluvial gravel, which incorporates abundant artefacts believed to be of more than one age, including an archaic element (not represented in this sample). The fresh implements are unlikely to be much older than the formation of the deposit, i.e. they should be of Final Hoxnian or Early Wolstonian age
Highlands Farm, Rotherfield Peppard	Excavated and collected material from the confused gravels of the Caversham Ancient Channel, at one single pit. Being fresh, the artefacts should not be much older than the suggested reworking of this gravel during the Wolstonian, and therefore of Final Hoxnian or Early Wolstonian age
Croxley Green, Rickmansworth	From the base of a Colne gravel about 60 feet above the present river, consisting mainly of Anglian outwash reworked at a later but unknown date
Corfe Mullen, Cogdean Pit	From gravel (mainly slope deposits) filling a small abandoned stream valley. Inter-Wolstonian or possibly Ipswichian age suggested
Caddington	From various pits dug into high level brickearth, some of

Site	Date and comments
	which is apparently of Ipswichian age. Assemblage dominated by output of one large manufacturing site. Strong element of prepared core technique including 'classic' and 'reduced' Levalloisian

Without making allowance for the undated sites in this list, we can plot the likely ranges in time of the four Groups discussed, as shown in Table 16.

TABLE 16 : *Likely time ranges of Groups I, II, VI and VII*

Pleistocene units	Pointed Tradition		Ovate Tradition	
	Group I	Group II	Group VI	Group VII
Full Hoxnian		X		
Late Hoxnian	?		?	?
Late Hoxnian or Early Wolstonian	X	X	X	X
Early Wolstonian		?		
Inter-Wolstonian	X		X	X
Late Wolstonian			?	
Full Ipswichian	?			?
Late Ipswichian			X*	
Early Devensian			X*	

*Mousterian of Acheulian Tradition

This Table is inevitably somewhat tentative, but what it does indicate is that *in the present state of knowledge* there is very substantial overlapping between all four Groups, even if Group II appears to have the field to itself at the outset. In other words, although individual pointed handaxe industries may antedate individual ovate handaxe industries, as indeed was demonstrably the case at Swanscombe, there is no clear evidence that the whole Ovate Tradition is younger than the whole Pointed Tradition, within the general Middle Acheulian phase. Indeed, on the contrary, it appears that the two are largely contemporary. Passing outside the list of sites in Tables 13 and 14, we might recall the series from the Dorney Wood brickearth, mentioned in the discussion of the Middle Thames sequence in the Burnham area as another likely example of a relatively late pointed handaxe industry, and it would also be

pertinent to mention Burchell's pointed handaxes from the Ebbsfleet Channel filling (see page 86), which were all younger than the Baker's Hole Coombe Rock deposit and some of which were probably of Ipswichian age, being from the loessic loam with temperate mollusca. It is also to be remembered that the Middle Acheulian is followed by a Late Acheulian/Micoquian stage both in Britain and on the Continent, with pointed handaxe shapes generally dominant once more, even if there are new technological features in the industries.

It remains to consider the famous and important site of *Hoxne*, Suffolk, where it is now known, thanks to the recent work of Wymer and Singer and their colleagues, as mentioned earlier, that there are *two* major horizons with handaxe industries in more or less primary context, rather than only one as assumed by West and McBurney in 1954, and by the present writer, following them, in 1968. Clearly, Hoxne now affords us one more chance to check on the order of events in the Middle Acheulian, and to make a comparison with the Acheulian sequence at Swanscombe.

Briefly, it is the opinion of John Wymer, as the principal archaeologist of the University of Chicago research team at Hoxne, that it is the *older* of the two industries there (the 'Lower Industry') which has a dominance of ovates, and the younger one (the 'Upper Industry') in which the pointed handaxes are more frequent (Wymer 1974; Singer and Wymer 1976). In other words, the order of Acheulian industries seen at Barnfield Pit, Swanscombe, appears to be reversed in the case of Hoxne. The Pleistocene geology of the Hoxne site has already been discussed in some detail in Chapter 2, so we need only note here that the Lower Industry was found *in situ* at the top of the highest surviving stratum of the lake sediments (Plate 12) — level D, the peaty detritus mud of Hoxnian Zone III — and also, slightly disturbed, in the overlying chalky brecciated mud which was attributed to the Early Wolstonian, so the industry must be of Late Hoxnian to earliest Wolstonian age. There are good faunal remains associated with it (not yet reported in detail, but including elephant, rhinoceros, horse, deer (Plate 12b), pig and a bovid which may turn out to be ox or

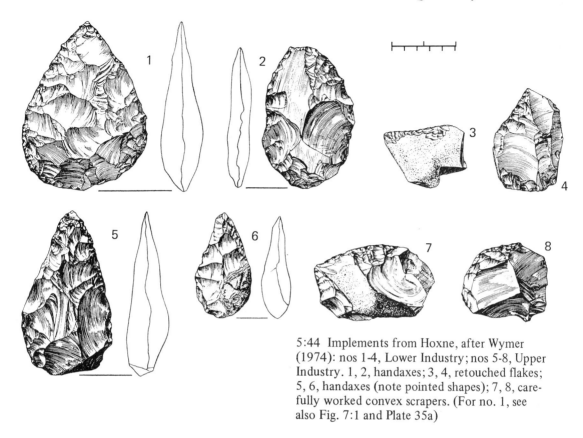

5:44 Implements from Hoxne, after Wymer
(1974): nos 1-4, Lower Industry; nos 5-8, Upper
Industry. 1, 2, handaxes; 3, 4, retouched flakes;
5, 6, handaxes (note pointed shapes); 7, 8, carefully worked convex scrapers. (For no. 1, see
also Fig. 7:1 and Plate 35a)

bison). Pollen and macroscopic floral remains, including abundant wood, were also recovered from this horizon and are being studied.[9] The Upper Industry from Hoxne occurred in the 'flood plain silt' member of the upper series of deposits (Plate 13), younger than the lake beds: this stratum is probably attributable to a mild interval within the Wolstonian complex, and a substantial cold phase certainly intervenes between the two industries. Their stratigraphic order is thus not open to doubt (Fig. 2:4b).

Where doubt may remain, however, is in the small sizes of the two handaxe samples — that is to say, the material actually obtained during the recent excavations from these two levels (Fig. 5:44): Singer and Wymer (1976) list seven hand-axes from the Lower Industry and thirteen from the Upper Industry (of which latter total John Wymer informed the author that four show signs of possibly being derived) and this is really hardly

enough to go by. There are over a hundred more extant handaxes from Hoxne, scattered amongst numerous museums and private collections all over Britain, but the large majority of them lack details of their stratigraphic provenance, and it is uncertain how many could be specifically attributed with an acceptable degree of reliability to either of the two occupation horizons which have now been defined. As we have seen at other British Acheulian sites, there *are* ovates in pointed-dominant handaxe industries and pointed handaxes in ovate-dominant ones. It remains statistically quite possible, though it is perhaps not particularly likely, that if we had a big sample of handaxes from each level we should find that, after all, the Lower Industry had most pointed forms and the Upper Industry most ovates. At the time of writing, there seems little chance of obtaining such larger samples, so we are left with the options of accepting Wymer's interpretation, by act of faith, as a working hypothesis, or passing the more cautious judgement of 'not proven'.

The evidence of the preceding several pages should suggest that Wymer's hypothesis is a perfectly tenable one. Dating near the Hoxnian/ Wolstonian boundary seemed possible for various of the Group VI and Group VII industries — Bowman's Lodge, or Highlands Farm, or the Warren Hill fresh series, for example. Equally, within the Pointed Tradition, there should be no objection to an industry of Inter-Wolstonian age, since it is clearly within the suggested time-span of Group I. It would be less easy to point, on existing evidence, to a Group II occurrence that is firmly within the Wolstonian, but does the Hoxne Upper Industry necessarily belong to Group II? So far, we have only referred to its handaxes. In fact, the most striking and numerically the strongest tool category in the Upper Industry, as excavated, comprised finely made flake-tools, notably elegant convex side-scrapers made on bold plain-platform flakes. Over sixty of these were found (Singer and Wymer 1976: 19-21), and amongst them many are more formally shaped than the usual run of flake-tools found at British Acheulian sites. Isolated well-made flake-tools may turn up in any British Acheulian industry, but a major series like this is more reminiscent of the 'classic flake industry' of the High Lodge lake silts, though that is not clearly an Acheulian occurrence, and it is interesting that the dating there is held to be Wolstonian interstadial. Amongst the British Acheulian industries discussed in this section, the only one that seems reasonably comparable, in that it appears to offer the combination of a dominance of pointed handaxes and a strong flake-tool component, would be Stoke Newington, attributed to Group I but somewhat atypical of the Group in various respects. The Stoke Newington industry included some cleavers as well as pointed handaxes, and the dating was thought likely to be Ipswichian. No typical cleavers appear to be preserved from Hoxne, either amongst the recently excavated material or in the older collections.

It would be easy to point to Acheulian industries with fine flake-tools at various Continental sites, notably in France. We cannot here enter into a detailed account of them, but a couple of examples can at least be given, for which the writer will select the famous *Atelier de Commont* at the Bultel-Tellier quarry at Saint-Acheul itself, near Amiens (Bordes and Fitte 1953), and some of the Acheulian levels at J. Combier's great site of Orgnac III in the Ardèche (Combier 1967: 31-127). Many more examples exist, and all, where dated, appear to be younger than the Hoxnian or its French equivalent (Mindel-Riss Interglacial). From the point of view of Britain, the more northerly occurrences, of which *l'Atelier Commont* is one, are the most relevant. The handaxes at these French sites are of variable shapes, but certainly pointed types are included. At *l'Atelier Commont* there are also one or two cleavers and several well-made ovates. It may well be in fact that the *atelier*, discovered early this century, actually comprises more than one level, but the whole assemblage offers general similarities to the aggregate of the Hoxne implements, or indeed the assemblage from Stoke Newington. One might in fact reflect that it was particularly with *l'Atelier Commont* that C.B.M. McBurney compared the undivided Hoxne material (West and McBurney 1954: 149-54), though his metrical and statistical analyses did not include detailed treatment of plan shapes. As regards the Hoxne Lower Industry, flake-tools were very few in number in the University of Chicago's excavated material, and those that did exist lacked the elegance and regularity of their counterparts in the Upper Industry. It is also worth recording that there is no sign of Levalloisian technique in either industry at Hoxne, and the situation is similar at *l'Atelier Commont* and at Stoke Newington, with only the barest traces of Levalloisian technique possibly associated.[10]

Whether or not Wymer's reading of the Hoxne archaeological sequence be accepted, this long discussion of the Middle Acheulian phase as represented by the principal British sites may be summarized as follows, bearing in mind the general questions posed at the start of this section.

(a) The basic sequence discussed in Chapters 3 and 4, as one would have anticipated, tells us too little about the Middle Acheulian phase to suffice. Its indication of pointed handaxe industries followed by ovate handaxe industries, based on the north Kent finds, reflects a local situation only.

(b) It is more reasonable to speak of 'pointed' and 'ovate' handaxe 'traditions', and there is pattern of groups and even some sub-groups can be proposed. But allowing for this variety, preferences within individual industries for pointed or ovate handaxe shapes remain strong.

(c) We cannot reasonably speak of regional variants. It is true that amongst the sub-groups some 'pairs' of particularly similar sites are located quite close to each other — Barnfield Pit (Middle Gravels) and Chadwell St Mary, Elveden and Allington Hill, Warren Hill (fresh series) and High Lodge — but southern Britain is not a large area, nor does it have formidable natural barriers to divide it into regions. Besides, we unfortunately cannot say certainly that these pairs of sites really are contemporaneous occurrences. In general, the different groups do *not* show significantly restricted distributions. Group II is the most restricted, for what that is worth.

(d) The over-all chronological picture is deplorably out of focus, with far too many sites wholly undated. Yet it is certain that each of the two Traditions spans a substantial period of time and that they overlap considerably — this is so even when for the purposes of the present discussion Group III (Late Acheulian/Micoquian) has been abstracted from the Pointed Tradition and Group V (archaic industries) from the Ovate Tradition, and even if the two Mousterian of Acheulian Tradition industries in Group VI are ignored.

(e) There seems accordingly no justification, when considering Britain as a whole, for referring to a 'Middle Acheulian with pointed handaxes' followed by a 'Late Middle Acheulian with refined ovates', as has sometimes been done in the past. It is better to adopt one long 'Middle Acheulian' phase and allow for variations within it of the kind we have been discussing, whatever such variations may imply. There is no regular linear evolutionary development through time: no simple 'time trends'. The provisional suggestion of a general Middle Acheulian phase put forward at the close of Chapter 4 can therefore now be firmly adopted.

(f) The causes of the observable and quantifiable variability remain obscure. There is no evidence to link the morphological variations to differences in raw material. Since ovate handaxes and pointed handaxes, generally speaking, differ from each other in the shape, nature and even disposition of their functional parts, it seems very likely that the main controlling factors should be concerned with function and type of site — i.e. what the people were doing in that particular place and how they were doing it. Factors of individual manual skill may have operated, and even factors of cultural heritage (if that is not too ponderous a term), but there seems no reason to give them much weight. Sadly, it is the evidence for human activities that is crucially lacking, except in the case of the manufacturing site at Caddington: there are no clearly identifiable kill sites, seasonal resource camps or major home bases. Even the microwear analysis of individual handaxes is only now beginning (Keeley 1977), though it may one day throw much light on such matters using only the stone artefacts themselves.

The foregoing discussion of the Middle Acheulian has been conducted on the basis of the major sites, using the best evidence for the presence of single industries, weak though it often is in absolute terms. There are of course some hundreds if not thousands more British occurrences of material that is likely to be Middle Acheulian or to include Middle Acheulian artefacts, ranging from single finds to prolific assemblages from gravels. With the vast bulk of this, nothing much can be done. But there is at least one approach to it which cannot be omitted in a book of this nature before we pass on. The various morphologically based groups and sub-groups have fairly clear identities: for example, the big transverse cleavers are virtually confined to Group I and the presence of twisted ovates in quantity is highly likely to indicate Group VI. It is therefore sometimes the case that in a derived or mixed or unstratified assemblage of British Lower Palaeolithic artefacts we can feel confident on this basis that a particular Group, perhaps even a particular Sub-Group, is represented. The writer will simply list, with the briefest of comments, cases of this kind known to him. He does not claim that the list is complete or definitive. Middle Palaeolithic attributions are not included (see next chapter). Many of these sites are unpublished, or else their existence is merely recorded without useful details, often in some local periodical. In many cases, the artefacts which survive are now widely dispersed amongst museum collections all over Britain. The writer had occasion to study such collections when compiling his *Gazetteer of British Lower and Middle Palaeolithic Sites* for the Council for British Archaeology (1968b). Visits to museums were made as and when opportunities presented themselves, and consequently different collections from any given site might be seen at quite different times over the whole period of five to six years. Cumulative lists were kept, and it is on the basis of these that the attributions to Groups which follow are made. It must however be stressed that the Groups and Sub-Groups themselves were defined on the basis of the 38 selected assemblages of better quality, as listed in Table 13, and that the following tentative attributions were only made afterwards, as a final stage of the whole research project (cf. Roe 1967: 197-247). Where museum collections are cited in the following pages, the lists are selective, to name the major sources only, and fuller lists are given in Roe 1968b.[11]

Attributions to Group I

Certain areas have produced assemblages characterized by a dominance of pointed handaxes, including ficrons, often large, and by the presence of heavy narrow ovates and a few cleavers. In the Middle Thames Valley, apart from the Baker's Farm and Furze Platt sites which belong to Group I originally, we have already noted that there is similar material from pits in the Lynch Hill gravels in the Burnham area, notably those at Lent Rise. There is more material of Group I character from Cookham, the large majority of it not being marked with specific site names, notably in the collections of Reading Museum and the University Museum at Cambridge. Cookham is not far from Furze Platt itself. Wymer (1968: 214-15) records that the Danefield Pit at Cookham Rise was the most prolific source of Cookham artefacts, and that the main deposits there are Lynch Hill gravels. Material just marked 'Maidenhead' is abundant in

museums: it is in every way similar to that from the Furze Platt site and probably actually came from it. At Ruscombe, further upstream, near Twyford, the Lynch Hill gravel is again well represented, and a good number of classic Group I implements from here are preserved at the British Museum, in the Treacher Collection at the Oxford University Museum, and at Reading Museum.

In Kent, we have already noted the important Cuxton site in the Medway Valley as an original member of Group I, and it is not surprising to find similar occurrences nearby, notably from Aylesford, where several pits yielded between them over 350 handaxes and some other artefacts, though most are not specifically marked (the principal collections are at the British Museum, the Cambridge University Museum, Dartford Museum, Maidstone Museum, Rochester Museum and Manchester Museum). A small assemblage from Ham Hill, Snodland, about midway between Cuxton and Aylesford, produced similar implements, of which the best series is now in the British Museum. Further east in Kent, a quantity of mainly rolled implements of Group I character was collected by Dr Armstrong Bowes at Canterbury, from a site known to him as 'Canterbury West', including two typical cleavers and four good ficrons out of a total of twenty-five large tools (British Museum).

In London, within a few miles of the Stoke Newington Group I site, many finds of similar material have been made, around Clapton (notably Lower Clapton) and Stamford Hill. A few are from specified localities, such as the Northwold Road Nursery at Clapton, but most are attributed merely to the area. The stratigraphy is similar enough to that recorded at Stoke Newington, and Worthington Smith reported the existence of his 'Palaeolithic Floor' widely over this whole area; however, the underlying gravel, in which implements were common, is also present and much of the material here being considered looks as if it came from gravel. Further east, into the edges of Essex, Group I material seems to be fairly common around Leyton and Leytonstone. The main collections of material from these various northeast London find-spots are those at the British Museum, the London Museum, Luton Museum and the Ashmolean Museum at Oxford. There is also material of Group I character from Wandsworth, a few miles away to the west (British Museum, London Museum, and the Pitt Rivers Museum at Farnham, Dorset). Over 500 handaxes and many other artefacts are known from Dawley, towards the west edge of London (Hillingdon Borough) — a mixed lot, many of them much abraded, but it appears to contain some classic Group I artefacts (the British Museum and the London Museum have the main collections, with a scatter elsewhere). It is interesting to note that the Group I implements from Dawley are inclined to be small, as was the case at Stoke Newington itself, but there is no corresponding abundance of fine flake tools.

In the central area of the south coast of England, principally in Hampshire and eastern Dorset, there is more Group I material with some fine large ficrons and cleavers. The Bournemouth and Southampton areas are the main sources; there are few prolific individual findspots, but an impressive number of minor occurrences giving a good cumulative total. These are too numerous to list here in full, but some examples may be given: the Winton area of Bournemouth (scattered museum collections, notably Cambridge University Museum, Liverpool City Museum, and Winchester Museum); Bournemouth Race-course (British Museum, Bournemouth Natural Science Society's Museum); Christchurch, Latch Farm (Red House Museum, Christchurch); Lymington, including Setley Plain (British Museum, Brighton Museum, Cambridge University Museum); Highfield, Southampton, brickfield near the Church (Southampton Museum, Winchester Museum, London University Institute of Archaeology); Netley, including Netley Shoal (British Museum, Southampton Museum, Winchester Museum, Liverpool City Museum); Coxford, unspecified sites (British Museum, Salisbury Museum, Winchester Museum); Warsash, various pits, not usually specified; a mixture of industries, including Group I types (cf. Burkitt *et al.* (1939), who illustrate a few typical pieces), the material being now widely scattered in many museums, including those at Winchester, Portsmouth, Brighton and Bolton. Finally, there are further indications of the presence of Group I industries to be noted in East Anglia. In Norfolk, we have already mentioned the Keswick site, close to Whitlingham itself; this material is at the Norwich Castle Museum, and so is a small series of artefacts from Snarehill, Rushford, which might well belong to Group I although there are no completely typical cleavers present among what survives. In Suffolk, though not far from the Norfolk Border, is Barnham St Gregory, where the Barnham Heath Pit, also called County Hole, produced a remarkable mixture of Lower Palaeolithic material, with virtually something of everything from Clactonian to Levalloisian, regrettably not in a stratified succession. (This site is *not* the same as T.T. Paterson's East Farm Pit at Barnham, discussed in the Clactonian section of this chapter, though the two are sometimes confused.) Amongst the artefacts is a clear Group I element, with large typical cleavers, pointed handaxes and heavy narrow ovate forms (Moyse's Hall Museum, Bury St Edmunds and Ipswich Museum).

Attributions to Group II

Tentative attributions to this Group are made where the dominant element in an assemblage consists of neat pointed handaxes, some of which may have twisted tips, accompanied by a small proportion only of well-made broad ovates, with the heavy cleavers of Group I absent or extremely rare.

In the Middle Thames area, which was rather rich in Group I occurrences, only the fine small assemblage from the Dorney Wood brickearth (see above, page 167) looks to be of Group II character. If this attribution is correct, we should recall the argument that the brickearth in question was likely to be younger than the Boyn Hill gravels, because this would imply a later date for the assemblage than any others in Group II, perhaps even into the Ipswichian.

In the south-east of England, there are first a few other occurrences to be noted not far from Barnfield Pit, Swanscombe, in Kent. Various other Swanscombe pits have produced material which matches that from the Barnfield Pit Middle Gravels, notably Galley Hill, represented in numerous museums amongst which may be mentioned the

British Museum, Plymouth Museum and the Royal Scottish Museum at Edinburgh. Large quantities of typical pointed handaxes from Swanscombe are marked as coming from Milton Street (e.g. in the Stopes Collection at the National Museum of Wales, Cardiff), but it seems likely that this designation was used by some collectors for Barnfield Pit itself (cf. Wymer 1968: 334). A Group II element certainly looks to be present amongst the handaxes from Baker's Hole, Northfleet, which came from exposures of the 90 to 100 feet gravels rather than from the great Levalloisian occurrence (British Museum, and many others, widely dispersed). But in many ways all these occurrences are likely to represent a single Group II area of occupation, of which the principal concentration known to us was discovered in the Middle Gravels of Barnfield Pit. On the other hand, a small occurrence of similar material at Ramsden, Kent, some 10 miles west of Swanscombe, can be regarded as quite separate — a dozen or more handaxes came to light when a new road was being made (Tester 1958) and are now mostly at Maidstone Museum. North of the present Thames, material of Group II character looks to be present in the rather confused and poorly documented collections from the Grays Thurrock area, which lies between the original Group II sites of Swanscombe and Chadwell St Mary. It is perhaps worth mentioning specially one little group of seven handaxes from Grays Thurrock, strikingly similar in their raw material and fresh condition as well as in their general morphology and technology, now in the Colchester and Essex Museum at Colchester. One has a neat twisted tip. It is unfortunate that no details of their precise provenance appear to survive.

West of London, find-spots in the Hillingdon, Hanwell and Southall areas have yielded more Group II material, the majority marked only with those place names but some coming from specified localities such as Seward's Pit in Boston Road and Macklin's Pit in Zion Lane, both in Hanwell, or the Gasworks site in Southall. The totals are not vast — rather less than 200 handaxes of Group II type are extant in aggregate (British Museum, London Museum, Cambridge University Museum).

South Hampshire and east Dorset also have some material probably belonging to this group, though there is less of it here than there was belonging to Group I. In the Bournemouth region, gravels about 100 to 115 feet above the River Stour in the Talbot Woods area (cf. Bury 1923: 23) have produced at least seventy handaxes and a few other artefacts, a mixture, but dominated by artefacts of the Group II kinds. Twenty-five miles or so north-east, in Hampshire, in the Test Valley, the most prolific among the numerous Lower Palaeolithic find-spots was a gravel pit at Dunbridge, not far from Romsey. Perhaps as many as a thousand handaxes from here survive, though very little has ever been published about the site. The material appears to be mixed, and many of the handaxes are well worn, though others are fresh. Pointed handaxes are dominant, though many fine ovates are also present. The majority of the material is patinated and deeply stained ochreous yellow, brown or deep red, but a small proportion is patinated pure white and generally less worn. We have no positive proof that this is a stratigraphically distinct element in the whole mass of material, but it is interesting to note that a large majority of the white handaxes are well-made pointed types, more in the Group II manner than any other, though the writer has seen a few ovates, one cleaver and three or four Levalloisian artefacts belonging to the white series, which includes about 100 pieces in all. The few published references to Dunbridge indicate that there was a layer of white gravel at the top of the section, and deeply ochreous gravel beneath it (Sturge 1912: 144; Smith, R.A. 1926: 64-5) — do we have here a passing hint of another pointed handaxe industry of younger rather than older date?[12] There is not a shred of really solid evidence, but the situation is somewhat suggestive, and such things are worth recording in case future work casts new light on them. The Dunbridge material is widely scattered, but among the more important collections which include some of the white-patinated pieces may be cited those of the Salisbury, Winchester and Bristol City Museums.

Some 60 miles away to the west, in the lower reaches of the Bristol Avon, notably at Abbots Leigh (Chapel Pill Farm), prolific finds (a few hundreds) of Lower Palaeolithic artefacts were made in periglacially disturbed gravels of uncertain age (Lacaille 1954a; Roe 1974). The raw material for their manufacture was mainly pebbles of poor quality chert, some flint and a little quartzite and indurated sandstone: its nature has certainly affected that of the industry, giving it a rough appearance and a bias towards small implements, but when allowance is made for these factors one is left with the impression of a predominance of Group II types and a toolkit which, given better stone to work, might well have resembled that of the Barnfield Pit Middle Gravels rather closely.

Lastly, in an altogether different part of England, Derbyshire, we may mention here the Acheulian material from the Hilton and Willington pits in the Trent Valley — one of the more northerly of our Acheulian occurrences. The artefacts are clearly derived, and there is no evidence that only one assemblage is present (though the area does not in fact appear to have been frequently occupied); the best account will be found in a paper by M. Posnansky (1963), who quotes earlier literature. Pointed handaxe forms, mostly rough-butted, at least one with a twisted tip, are dominant amongst nearly 150 handaxes; ovates are rare, and cleavers absent (Nottingham University Museum, Sheffield City Museum and more material in private hands). It is worth illustrating a few of these artefacts (Fig. 5:45) to show the use of local rocks, notably a fairly fine-grained quartzite occurring as pebbles and boulders, in an area where flint was scarce.

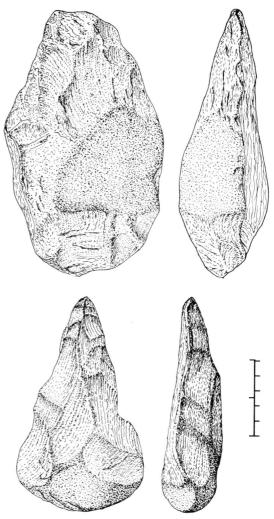

5:45 Four handaxes from Hilton, Derbyshire: note use of local quartzite pebbles in an area where flint is difficult to obtain. After Posnansky (1963)

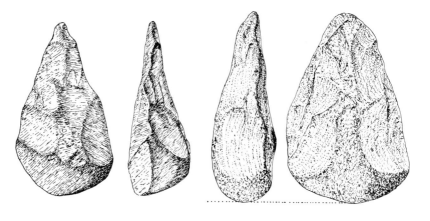

Attributions to Group VI

Within the Ovate Tradition, attributions specifically to Group VI or Group VII are less easy to make on a casual basis than within any Group of the Pointed Tradition. The reason for this is that there is much common ground between Groups VI and VII and the differences concern emphasis in shape when a whole assemblage is considered in detail, plus certain technological preferences such as the much more frequent occurrence of twisted profiles in Group VI. Thus, one may have, say, two or three dozen handaxes from a gravel pit, derived, but clearly enough dominated by ovates for one to be certain that one is dealing with Ovate Tradition material at least in part. But it may well not be possible to get any further using only morphological evidence, whereas in the Pointed Tradition it is not infrequently possible to choose between Groups I and II in a small sample. The exception to this within the Ovate Tradition is the occurrence of the typical *bout coupé* handaxe form, as at Oldbury and Pan Farm amongst the sites already discussed. However, since the assemblages with *bout coupé* handaxes are here taken to be Mousterian rather than Acheulian, consideration of them will be deferred for the moment (see Chapter 6). We are therefore left in the position of being able to make a number of ascriptions to Group VI, discussed in the following paragraphs, but of Group VII there is little more to be said.

There are two areas to be mentioned where Acheulian assemblages of Group VI character seem to be present: north Kent, and central East Anglia. Both of these already have industries in the original Group VI list and we may suppose that we are looking at areas of occupation with several clearly or poorly defined individual concentrations, brought to light according to the chances of modern commercial exposures of gravel, though there is no actual evidence that the occurrences are contemporary.

Thus, in north Kent, we have ovate-dominant assemblages from Rickson's Pit, Swanscombe (British Museum, London University Institute of Archaeology, Ipswich Museum, Rochester Museum), Pearson's Pit, Dartford (British Museum,

London University Institute of Archaeology, Dartford Museum and Ipswich Museum) and the Wansunt Pit, Dartford (British Museum and Dartford Museum). The implements from these sites are generally similar to those from the Upper Loam at Barnfield Pit or from Bowman's Lodge. In each of these three assemblages, there is a strong proportion of twisted-profile handaxes. Waechter (1973) gives some useful details about the sites and industries. The Wansunt Pit assemblage (see also Chandler and Leach 1912; Smith, R.A. and Dewey 1914: 199-212) appears to have been associated with a stream channel, and would have been well worth detailed metrical and statistical analysis if the writer had been able to trace a large enough sample of the handaxes: many seem to have passed into private hands.

In East Anglia, in and around the Breckland area, in east Cambridgeshire and west Suffolk, ovate-dominant industries are common. Group VI handaxes are frequent in the Bottisham area which provided the Allington Hill site, and come in small quantitites from such find-spots as Dullingham, the Heath Farm Gravel Pit at Six Mile Bottom, Swaffham Prior and Newmarket Down. Many of these implements have twisted profiles. They are now scattered amongst various museum collections, notably the British Museum, the University and Sedgwick Museums at Cambridge, the Ashmolean Museum at Oxford and Brighton Museum. A larger quantity of material than all these put together comes from Kennett, Cambridgeshire, principally from the Station Pit and Worlington Road Pit — between two and three hundred handaxes at least survive, though their condition is variable and few precise details of their provenances are known. Many are now in the British Museum, the Sedgwick and University Museums at Cambridge and the Ashmolean Museum at Oxford, with others more widely dispersed. Lastly, there is the Grindle Pit at Bury St Edmunds, which has been known since well back in the nineteenth century (cf. Evans, J. 1872: 487). There may well have been a fine Acheulian site here, to judge from the very fresh condition of some of the artefacts, but there is no record of any floor's having been seen. Evans indicates (*loc. cit.*) that some of the implements at least came from a stiff rather argillaceous gravel of mainly subangular flints, with some material derived from glacial deposits. Many of the ovates are twisted, and the collections include at least two refined pointed handaxes, one at the British Museum and one at the Ashmolean Museum at Oxford; such pieces are by no means unknown in Group VI, though always rare. Other find-spots in and close to Bury St Edmunds and Westley have yielded ovate handaxes much the same as those from the Grindle Pit, singly or in small numbers. The best museum collections in which to find the extant material are the British Museum and the Ashmolean, but several other collections have one or two specimens (Roe 1968b: 263-5).

Attributions to Group VII

All that can usefully be said here is that the out-wash gravels which contained the Warren Hill Group VII industry (i.e., the fresh series) have yielded artefacts in less prolific quantities at various other places (cf. page 115 above). These assemblages are mixed, as indeed is that from Warren Hill itself, but they contain many ovates and it is likely that Group VII material is repre-sented, as at Lakenheath, for example (best material in the British Museum, the University Museum at Cambridge and the Ashmolean Museum at Oxford), or Eriswell (British Museum, Cambridge University Museum, the Elveden Estate Office, and others).

This concludes the list of attributions to the specific Middle Acheulian Groups discussed earlier in the chapter. These second quality attributed sites do not, by the nature of the occurrences, offer much helpful chronological data or cast useful new light on the problem of the nature of Middle Acheulian variability. They may perhaps be thought to strengthen the original Groups a little, though only in the sense of adding a few more site-names to each. Amongst the whole mass of mixed British Lower Palaeolithic assemblages there might of course be latent new Groups, but if so these cannot emerge unless new sites of the first quality are found and yield substantial industries which fall outside the ranges of the seven Groups already defined.

Lest it be thought that the Ovate Tradition is not greatly strengthened by the foregoing attribu-tions, the writer should add that the list of ovate-dominant assemblages which cannot reliably be assigned to Group VI or VII, for the reasons already stated, is a long one. It is worth giving here a list of some of the more important examples. Space does not permit details to be given or a full list of the sources to be provided; a little further information is available in Roe 1967 and 1968b.

Site	Comments	Principal Collections
Limbury, Beds.	A group of four very fresh refined ovates	Luton Museum
Luton: Ramridge End Whipsnade	Further 'floor' sites in Bedfordshire, found by Worthington Smith, but with relatively few artefacts. The handaxes are mainly ovates	Luton Museum; Luton Museum; Bedford Museum
Reading, Grovelands, Berks	Acheulian mixed with ? Clactonian (see pages 148-9); ovates frequent	British Museum; Bedford Museum, etc.
Denham, Bucks	Small ovate-dominant assemblage, including flaking debris	British Museum
Corfe Mullen, Dorset, Railway Ballast Pit	See Calkin and Green 1949: 28; Roe 1975: 4-5. This industry was younger than an archaic one with pointed handaxes, but not quite the same as the Group VII one from Cogdean Pit	British Museum; Dorset County Museum at Dorchester
Walton-on-the-Naze, Essex, including Stone Point	Mixed assemblage from foreshore, with high proportion of ovates (cf. also page 257)	Cambridge University Museum; British Museum; Bolton Museum; Colchester Museum

Site	Comments	Principal Collections	Site	Comments	Principal Collections
Hill Head, Hants	From gravels capping cliffs, and foreshore below. Fine ovates clearly dominant	British Museum; Salisbury Museum and several others	Barton Mills, Suffolk (area) and also adjacent Icklingham area	Ovates common at various find-spots in the Lark Valley, some belonging to Tuddenham and Herringswell	British Museum; Cambridge University Museum; Eldeven Estate Office; Ashmolean Museum, Oxford; Salisbury Museum
Wood Green, Hants	Many ovates in a large (hundreds) mixed series	Salisbury Museum and others			
Dartford, Kent	Many ovates in this area as a whole as well as from sites attributed to Group VI	British Museum; Dartford Museum			
Greenhithe, Kent, area; and Globe Pit	Well made ovates common, some 'from brickearth'	British Museum; National Museum of Wales, Cardiff (Stopes Collection); Dartford Museum and others	Farnham, Surrey	Ovates common, notably in Terrace B sites, e.g. Paine's Field, Broken Back Field, etc. (see Oakley 1939)	Willmer House Museum, Farnham; Geological Museum, London
			Limpsfield, Surrey notably Ridlands Farm	Little material survives but see Evans, Sir John 1897: 609-10. Ovates certainly dominant (cf. however page 266	British Museum; Ashmolean Museum, Oxford; Pitt Rivers Museum, Oxford and others.
Ightham, Kent (area)	Many sites noted by Benjamin Harrison, mostly on high ground, with ovates dominant	British Museum; Maidstone Museum and others			
Wilmington, Kent	Ovates dominant; mainly surface finds. Does not include the Warren Road site which had cf. Group III material (see page 127)	London Museum; Maidstone Museum	Alfriston, Sussex (and area)	Ovates clearly dominant in finds from chalk downland in area of Eastbourne-Beachy Head-Alfriston-East Dean, etc.	British Museum; London Museum; Barbican House Museum, Lewes
			Lavant, Sussex: foot of Trundle Hill	Interesting unpublished old find of 'raised beach' site with many ovate handaxes etc. New study by A.G. Woodcock in progress (report in preparation in his Ph.D. thesis)	Chichester City Museum
Hockwold-cum-Wilton, Norfolk	Small series, ovates dominant	British Museum; Cambridge University Museum; Norwich Castle Museum			
Barnham St Gregory, Suffolk: East Farm	The youngest industry at T.T. Paterson's site (1937) see pages 143-4	Bury St Edmunds (Moyses Hall Museum); Ipswich Museum	Slindon, Sussex (pits in Slindon Park)	Ovate industry not much disturbed (with flake material), overlying raised beach at up to 130 feet O.D. (see Calkin 1935). There are more ovates from Amey's Eartham	British Museum; Barbican House Museum, Lewes; Worthing Museum; Chichester City Museum

	Comments	Principal Collections
	Pit at Boxgrove, a few miles away. Current research by A.G. Woodcock (report in preparation) involves these Sussex sites	(includes the recently excavated material). Not all the old finds appear to survive
Bemerton, Wiltshire	Ovates dominate an abraded series of about 80 handaxes	British Museum; Devizes Museum; Salisbury Museum, etc.

Similarly, we can list sites which have produced mixed assemblages in which it is clear that the Pointed Tradition is well represented, without more specific attributions being possible. This information is perhaps worth recording for future researchers, though we cannot make much use of it here. It may serve, however, to remind those who are unfamiliar with the British Palaeolithic collections of their extent and diversity, and to call attention to sites which are unpublished or less well known than they deserve.

Site	Comments	Principal Collections
Biddenham, Bedfordshire	Some hundreds of artefacts from gravels which also produced shells and fauna; known since mid-nineteenth century (cf. Evans, Sir John 1897: 530-5). Deposits disturbed and assemblage mixed. Some Levalloisian (discussed below) but pointed handaxes predominate	British Museum; Bedford Museum; Pitt Rivers Museum at Oxford; and many others
Kempston, Bedfordshire	Similar to Biddenham and not far away	British Museum; Bedford Museum, etc.
Willington, Bedfordshire	Pointed and pyriform handaxes, mostly very similar in patination	Hunterian Museum, Glasgow, and a few more, scattered

Site	Comments	Principal Collections
Bournemouth, Dorset: (a) King's Park, Boscombe and (b) Moordown area, various findspots	Pointed handaxes dominate in both cases; same gravel probably present at both (cf. Bury 1923: 22)	Birmingham City Museum; Bournemouth Natural Science Society; British Museum; Red House Museum, Christchurch
Poole, Dorset: West Howe, including Council's pit	Pointed types dominate a mixed assemblage	British Museum; Red House Museum, Christchurch; Dorset County Museum, Dorchester
Dunbridge, Hants	See above, page 206; apart from the white series mentioned, pointed types dominate the ochreous implements, which are a mixed series totalling several hundreds	Widely scattered, including Bristol City Museum; Cambridge University Museum; Leicester Museum; Salisbury Museum; Southampton Museum; Winchester Museum
Romsey, Hants: various find-spots	Pointed types dominate most collections though relationship to the stratigraphy is rarely known. Belbin's Pit and Test Road Materials Pit, the most prolific sites, are typical	Birmingham City Museum; Bristol City Museum; Cambridge University Museum; Leicester Museum; Pitt Rivers Museum at Oxford; Southampton Museum; Winchester Museum

Site	Comments	Principal Collections	Site	Comments	Principal Collections
Timsbury, Hants	Near Romsey and Dunbridge in Test Valley; generally similar material to that from those sites	Curtis Museum, Alton; Birmingham City Museum; Bristol City Museum; London Museum	Reculver and Bishop-stone, Kent: various find-spots	Pointed handaxes dominant in a mixed assemblage, some at least from gravels capping the modern sea cliffs	British Museum; Canterbury Royal Museum; Oxford (Ashmolean Museum)
Winslade, Hants: Swallick Farm	One of the finds reported by Ellaway and Willis in Crawford *et al.* (1922) and by Willis (1947) on high ground in north Hants. Pointed types clearly dominate a series of 40-50 handaxes	Willis Museum, Basingstoke	Ealing, West London: various find-spots	Pointed handaxes consistently dominant, especially small pointed types. From gravels beneath brickearth, where provenance is known, at various depths (Brown 1887; Wymer 1968: 260-8)	British Museum; London Museum
Rickmans-worth, Hertford-shire: Mill End	Pointed types dominate a mixed series, contrasting with the Group VII site at Croxley Green not far away (cf. Oakley 1947: 252)	British Museum; Cambridge University Museum; Oxford University Museum; Stroud Museum	West Drayton and Yiewsley area, West London	Well over a thousand handaxes from here, and Levalloisian artefacts in hundreds; the former apparently from gravel and the latter almost all from overlying brickearth. The two series are in different physical states. Pointed handaxes dominate at all the main pits, of which Eastwood's (later called Sabey's) and Boyer's (or Bowyer's) were most prolific (see Wymer 1968: 255-9)	British Museum; London Museum (especially); Cambridge University Museum; London University Institute of Archaeology
Bleak Down, Isle of Wight, mainly Vectis Stone Co.'s Pit	Pointed types dominate a mixed and derived assemblage	Carisbrooke Castle Museum, Isle of Wight			
New Hythe, Kent: Quarry in New Hythe Lane	Majority of pointed handaxes, with several large specimens, including ficrons. Strong Levalloisian element: not known whether associated with the handaxes, but some pieces at least are similar in patina and physical condition (see also pages 260-1 below, however)	Dartford Museum; Maidstone Museum	Thetford, Norfolk: area, including Red Hill	Red Hill is an old site, where abundant implements were found dispersed through a coarse sub-angular gravel, overlying chalk (Evans, Sir John 1897: 551-5). The	British Museum; British Museum (Natural History); Cambridge University Museum; Norwich

Site	Comments	Principal Collections
	nature of the gravel is unknown and there is no recent account of it. Pointed handaxes are dominant, often flaked in a bold and simple manner, though others show clear soft-hammer work. Many are made from tabular flint. Flakes were also present, and the gravel produced some mammalian remains. The occurrence is of more than average interest, and the site would be worth re-examination if it still exists	Castle Museum; Oxford (Ashmolean Museum)
Caversham, Oxford-shire: Toots Farm Pit	A large series (some hundreds) of handaxes and other artefacts from gravel at approximately the Boyn Hill Terrace height (Wymer 1968: 137-41). Well-made pointed and pyriform shapes are dominant, including ficrons and some fine flat handaxes with fully worked butts. Some confusion with other Caversham sites, however, in the extant collections	Reading Museum; Oxford University Museum
Salisbury, Wiltshire: Milford Hill	Pointed handaxes are dominant in a prolific but derived and probably mixed assemblage of a few hundred artefacts. The site has been known since the mid-nineteenth century	British Museum; Devizes Museum; Oxford (Ashmolean Museum); Salisbury Museum

LATE ACHEULIAN/MICOQUIAN

There are no additional site-names to add here to those mentioned when the affinities within Britain of the Wolvercote site were discussed in the previous chapter. However, the altogether broader view of the British material taken in the present chapter may have clarified the picture previously given of the Wolvercote industry and those like it, and of their context in the British sequence. In Table 13, it is the sole member of Group III, and was clearly distinct on the metrical and other analyses from Groups I and II. If the suggested dating (Ipswichian) is correct, then we can now see that other industries may approach Wolvercote in time (Stoke Newington or Caddington, for example, and certainly those attributed to the Mousterian of Acheulian Tradition: Great Pan Farm and Oldbury, of which the last-named looks likely to be even a little younger). This is not to imply precise contemporaneity, for a single interglacial (if that is what the Ipswichian is) is a long period of time and we simply cannot make correlations of such exactness at present. But it is at least clear that the industries of Wolvercote style are very different typologically and techno-logically from those which in Britain lie closest to them in time.

LEVALLOISIAN

At the close of Chapter 3 we left the Levalloisian side of the British Lower Palaeolithic with two apparent stages, based on the north Kent sequence, an earlier one with large bold flakes (Baker's Hole) and a later one with the flakes becoming smaller, neater and more blade-like (Ebbsfleet Channel and the Crayford brickearths). The ground covered in Chapter 4 did not alter this picture.

In the writer's *Gazetteer of the British Lower and Middle Palaeolithic*, minimum totals of 401 Levalloisian cores and 3,422 Levalloisian flakes are listed (1968b: vii), from around 320 separate find-spots (some confusion between different collectors' naming of particular sites renders an exact total of find-spots impossible); that is to say, roughly one in ten of all the British Lower and Middle Palaeolithic occurrences contains some trace of Levalloisian technique, even if only a single specimen. This accords well with our previous conclusion that 'Levalloisian' is the name of a technique, not of an archaeological 'culture': the technique was evidently well known and used by different groups as occasion demanded — and when raw material was sufficiently abundant, since it is highly uneconomic of flint. We are not therefore concerned here with making a complete catalogue of Levalloisian finds — that information can be extracted from the *Gazetteer* — but with

taking note of prolific Levalloisian occurrences (Map, Fig. 5:46), whether 'pure' or mixed with artefacts of other kinds.

The first thing that strikes one about the prolific Levalloisian sites in the list is that there are few convincing parallels for the Baker's Hole site. Certainly there are individual finds of large bold flakes with thick faceted striking platforms, and some series including quantities of such pieces in a derived state, but there is no other good *in situ* industry wholly consisting of them or even

5:46 Location map for the Levalloisian occurrences discussed in Chapter 5. Key to numbers on map: 1 Canterbury; 2 Ospringe; 3 Bapchild; 4 New Hythe; 5 Northfleet; 6 Purfleet; 7 Crayford; 8 Acton (including Creffield Road); 9 Ealing; 10 Southall; 11 Yiewsley/West Drayton; 12 Iver; 13 Bournemouth (area); 14 Caddington; 15 Brundon; 16 Ipswich; 17 Kempston; 18 Biddenham; 19 St Neots (Little Paxton); 20 Fenstanton; 21 Hemingford Grey; 22 Hartford; 23 Wyton; 24 St Ives; 25 Earith; 26 Peterborough; 27 Southacre

dominated by them. Baker's Hole is in many ways a unique site; the relatively early date suggested for it (inter-Wolstonian) may have something to do with this, but the abundance, high quality and large size of the flint nodules available there are probably more powerful factors. One of the closer industries to it, technologically, is perhaps that from the area of Yiewsley and West Drayton on the western edge of London (Fig. 5:47), though here (as throughout this section) the writer is giving opinions based on mere inspection of the material rather than on detailed metrical and statistical analyses.[13] At West Drayton there are certainly many blade-like Levalloisian flakes, but there are also plenty of oval or sub-oval ones, neatly made, with carefully faceted striking platforms and with the dorsal scars showing a convergent pattern rather than running longitudinally as is characteristic of the elongated flake-blades. The average size of the flakes, however, is much smaller than that of the Baker's Hole ones.

Wymer (1968: 255-8) has given a useful summary of the Palaeolithic finds from the West Drayton area, quoting *inter alia* the observations of J. Allen Brown (1887, 1896a). He is probably justified in regarding the stratigraphy over the whole area as consistent, with gravels overlain by a brickearth, which is likely originally to have been a continuous deposit. Some authorities lay stress on the occurrence of a chalky solifluction deposit at some of the pits between the gravel and the brickearth. The gravels may be at least in part a downstream continuation of the Lynch Hill deposit referred to earlier in this chapter, though they receive many names in the earlier literature, including Taplow Terrace, Upper Taplow Terrace, Iver Terrace and even Boyn Hill Terrace. We may feel reasonably confident that the essential stratigraphy of West Drayton and Yiewsley is continued directly eastward through Dawley to Acton and Ealing, and also westwards at least as far as Iver, but at Iver itself the brickearth is divisible, as we shall see.

The gravels in the West Drayton area have produced abundant handaxes, mostly somewhat abraded, but the Levalloisian artefacts (Fig. 5:47) are mostly very fresh and even unpatinated. A minority do show some rolling or abrasion, but the great majority are in a state suggesting that

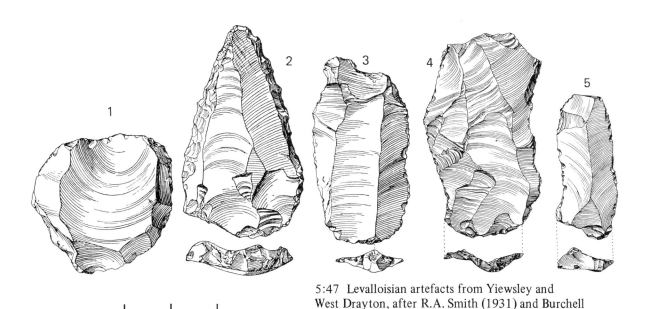

5:47 Levalloisian artefacts from Yiewsley and West Drayton, after R.A. Smith (1931) and Burchell (1934a): no. 1, struck core; no. 2, flake retouched to form a point; nos 3-5, flakes and flake-blade

they came from within the brickearth or perhaps from an old land surface below it but on top of the gravel. However, very few indeed have actual depths recorded. Even the old gravel pit names are somewhat confused and confusing. There were probably several separate and localized *in situ* Levalloisian 'floors', perhaps at differing depths, but there is nothing that can be done with the old collections except to generalize, and treat them as a loose single group. This is a pity, as there are a few signs of interesting technological idiosyncrasies: for example, several of the flakes from Boyer's Pit and Eastwood's Pit at Yiewsley have the bulbar swelling reduced by a single flat flake removal on the bulbar face, evidently designed to thin the butt end. In several flakes, the prepared striking platform consists of a single scar, running not vertically downwards like the usual facets, but horizontally; or sometimes there is a faceted platform with one of these horizontal scars and a number of vertical facets as well. There are also signs that even more interesting information might have been forthcoming from this area, notably the record by J.A. Brown (1889) — see also the summary by Wymer (1968: 261) — of the major part of a mammoth skeleton, at least partially articulated, found at Southall (Norwood Lane) associated with artefacts including at least one pointed Levalloisian flake-blade; the stratigraphic details suggest a position between the top of the basal gravel and the brickearth proper, analogous to the situation of the Levalloisian finds in Acton and the West Drayton area. Clearly this may have been a kill site, crying out for modern excavation methods, but as it is not even the bones survive.[14] To Brown, the pointed Levalloisian flake-blades of this area were clearly projectile points, and he noted amongst his finds deliberate thinning of their butt ends and the contriving on some of rudimentary basal tangs, these features being in his view devices to facilitate hafting. He may well have been right.

J.A. Brown's most important find, in terms of surviving material at least, was made in Creffield Road, Acton (1887; see also Wymer 1968: 265-7, quoting other references). Here he found three separate levels with artefacts, the lowest two, somewhat minor occurrences, were apparently in the upper part of the gravel, associated with 'black seams', while a third was on top of the gravel in the base of the sandy loam and brickearth which here overlies it. It was this upper level that contained the main material (Figs 5:48, 5:49), with a concentration which Brown reported as 'nearly 500 implements, worked flakes and waste fragments. . . . The whole of the specimens from Creffield Road are as sharp as when they were flaked off from the cores, and they have clearly never been removed from the spot where they were left by the Palaeolithic people who made them' (1887: 57). Brown, who was a shrewd observer, was quite certain that this find was a true and undisturbed 'floor'. His collection passed eventually to Dr Allen Sturge, and in R.A. Smith's catalogue of the Sturge Collection's British material (1931), no less than 850 specimens from the Creffield Road site are listed; some other collectors also acquired some. The small commercial excavation, in which the major floor occurred, covered an area of only 30 x 12 feet; two other small pits, respectively 20 and 6 feet away, produced comparatively few specimens, so the concentration was undoubtedly dense. Brown also indicated that he observed traces of similar floors in exposures in other parts of Acton and Ealing, but there does not seem to have been a major one among them (1887: 61).

No faunal remains were recovered from the Creffield Road site. As regards the industry, it does not give the impression of being a factory site in the manner of Baker's Hole, although the presence of cores and waste flakes suggests that

---

5:48 Levalloisian artefacts from Creffield Road, Acton: nos 1-5, various flakes and flake-blades after J. Allen Brown (1887), who lacked Worthington Smith's gifts as a draughtsman; nos 6-12, further flakes and flake-blades after R.A. Smith (1931) except no. 11, after Burchell (1934a); no. 13, handaxe, approaching the *bout coupé* form, after Smith (1931). Amongst the flakes and flake-blades, note nos 1, 6, and 9 as examples of the *pointe levallois typique*. Allen Brown was impressed by what he regarded as a prepared tang on no. 4, and there are protruberances at the butt end on some of the others also

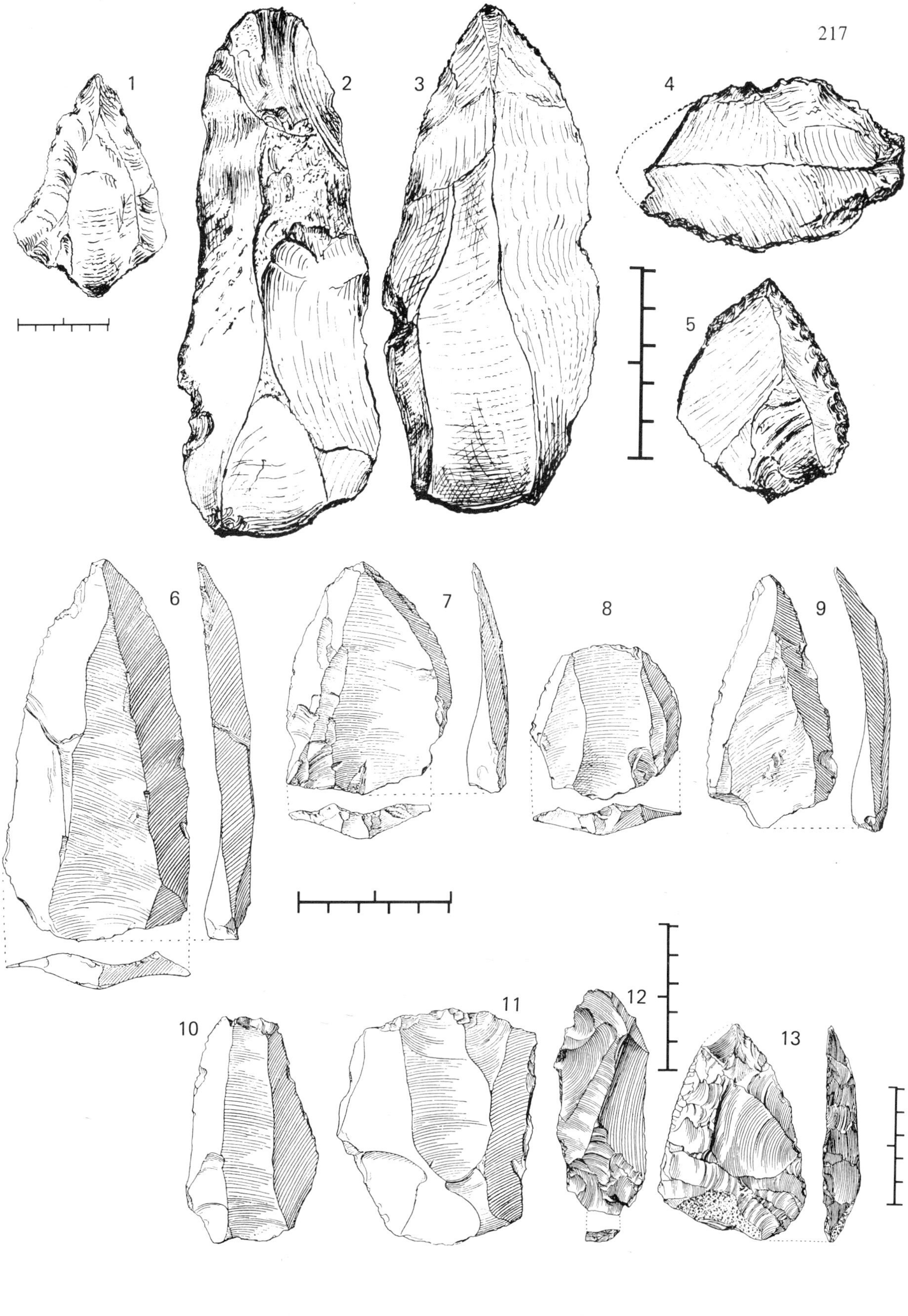
1
2
3
4
5
6
7
8
9
10
11
12
13

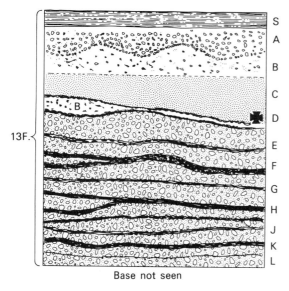

13F.

S – Surface soil
A – Agglomerated stones, 'Trail'
B – Brown brick earth
C – Sandy loam
D – Bleached pebbles etc., 'Floor'
    (over 400 worked flints found
    at this level)
E – Subangular gravel with
    seams of sand
F – Bleached pebbles, humus
    and black matter, (flakes)
G J L – Coarse gravel with seams of sand
  H K – Black seams

5:49 Section at Creffield Road, Acton, showing stratigraphic position of the Levalloisian site, as published by J. Allen Brown (1887)

flint knapping took place. Cores in fact are relatively few, although Brown was well aware of their significance. There has never been a published formal statistical analysis of the surviving Creffield Road artefacts, and it would be interesting to make one for purposes of comparison with certain north French sites, among others. The majority of the artefacts are Levalloisian flake-blades (Fig. 5:48) — flat, narrow, small or medium-sized elongated flakes, many of them naturally pointed but some actually retouched to a point. The dorsal preparatory scars usually run longitudinally, being struck from one or both ends of the core. Such an arrangement of dorsal scars creates longitudinal ridges on the core, usually two of them, parallel or convergent towards the distal end, and these ridges control the length and shape of the flake when the core is struck. The platforms are usually carefully prepared, and show several facets. Amongst the Levalloisian flake-blades of the Creffield Road site are several classic examples of the triangular-shaped type (Fig. 5:48) known as a *pointe levallois typique* (Bordes 1961: 18 and fig. 4). There is no conclusive evidence that these pieces were projectile points, but it is hard to imagine them as anything else. The *pointe levallois typique* appears frequently in Mousterian industries on the Continent (and indeed further afield), and is also certainly present in some Acheulian industries of Levallois facies. The present writer is not aware of any examples in Britain unequivocally associated with an Acheulian industry. We should also note particularly one handaxe from the Creffield Road site, apparently belonging to the same floor, which appears to belong to the *bout coupé* class. There is little doubt that at Creffield Road we are looking at a Middle Palaeolithic rather than a Lower Palaeolithic occurrence, technologically speaking, even if we cannot date it. Indeed, this version of Levalloisian technique is well on the way to the production of true blades, and in certain parts of the world the earliest Upper Palaeolithic industries are indeed based on blades removed from prismatic cores by a highly refined form of Levalloisian technique rather than by indirect percussion (i.e. the use of a 'punch'). Things had not gone that far at Creffield Road, but it remains an important site in the British sequence and one which deserves to be better known, notwithstanding the unsatisfactory nature of its discovery. The best collections are now at the British Museum and London Museum.

West of the West Drayton and Yiewsley area, beyond the Colne valley which cuts across the Thames deposits, there is an informative sequence to be gleaned from exposures at Iver, Buckinghamshire, with Levalloisian artefacts again involved (Fig. 5:50). Here we find two separate brickearths, overlying gravel of the 'Iver Terrace', which is capped by solifluction. This gravel is evidently a direct continuation of the Lynch Hill terrace, though usually called the Iver Terrace in the older

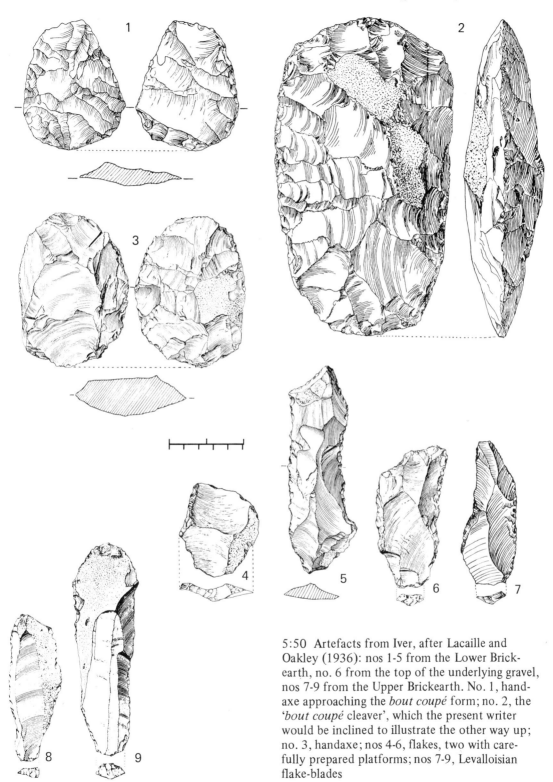

5:50 Artefacts from Iver, after Lacaille and
Oakley (1936): nos 1-5 from the Lower Brickearth, no. 6 from the top of the underlying gravel,
nos 7-9 from the Upper Brickearth. No. 1, handaxe approaching the *bout coupé* form; no. 2, the
'*bout coupé* cleaver', which the present writer
would be inclined to illustrate the other way up;
no. 3, handaxe; nos 4-6, flakes, two with carefully prepared platforms; nos 7-9, Levalloisian
flake-blades

literature, and it contains numerous handaxes of various kinds, all derived; with them are a few heavy oval Levalloisian flakes of the Baker's Hole kind. Of the two brickearths, the lower one is red and decalcified and the upper one is grey and slightly calcareous, but there is a sharp junction between them so that it is not a case of a single deposit with the different colours attributable merely to postdepositional alteration (Lacaille and Oakley 1936; Lacaille 1959; Wymer 1968: 251-5). The lower brickearth is thought to be of Ipswichian age and the upper one Devensian. Artefacts are not plentiful from either level and there are no true 'floors', but those from the lower brickearth include some Levalloisian flake-blades and small Levalloisian flakes with convergent dorsal scars, plus a few bifacial handaxes. Among the latter (Fig. 5:50, no. 1) is one good small cordiform handaxe approaching the *bout coupé* type and a large, flat, sub-rectangular form, which A.D. Lacaille called a '*bout coupé* cleaver' (Fig. 5:50, no. 2) and compared to certain north French pieces (Lacaille and Oakley 1936: 442-3). There is nothing else quite like it in England, but its shape is certainly like that of the classic *bout coupé* handaxes, even if it is twice as large as many of them. From the upper brickearth come a few typical Levalloisian flake-blades and no sign of handaxes. At Iver, then, we can actually see what we merely suspect in the West Drayton to Acton area, namely that the Levalloisian artefacts from the deposits younger than the gravel did occur at various depths, the industries persisting over a substantial period of time. This account of the Iver sequence is based on observations by Lacaille and others in a number of pits, notably Lavender's Pit (Mansion Lane), Purser's Pit (Richings Park), the Great Western Railway Pit, Mead's Bridge Pit and Reed's Pit.

The next area to be considered where there are some important Levalloisian occurrences is eastern England. In East Anglia proper Levalloisian artefacts are generally rather rare, but we cannot omit mention of Brundon, on the Suffolk/Essex border near Sudbury, or of Ipswich. At Brundon (Jordan's Pit), an important and interesting sequence was described by J.R. Moir and A.T. Hopwood (1939), whose account may be

summarized as follows (Table 17):

TABLE 17 : *The stratigraphic sequence at Jordan's Pit, Brundon, after Moir and Hopwood*

Strata and artefacts	Interpretation by Moir and Hopwood
Humus	(Modern and recent soil)
Unstratified sandy clay up to 8 feet thick where it fills hollows. *A few indeterminate flakes only*	deposited in glacial or at least periglacial conditions
Contorted reddish gravel, up to 5 feet thick in places	
Stratified yellowish gravel, up to 15 feet thick. *Numerous derived artefacts*	fluviatile aggradation
Stratum, up to 1 foot thick, of manganese-stained stones, practically devoid of matrix. *Fresh, unpatinated artefacts, numerous mammalian bones, freshwater and land mollusca. Some derived artefacts also*	remains of a land surface, subject to intermittent flooding
Grey unstratified clay with temperate mollusca, up to 2 feet thick	perhaps originally boulder clay material, but redeposited under interglacial conditions after lateral erosion by the river?
Coarse red gravel with manganese streaks, up to 3 feet thick	outwash during glacial retreat
Chalky boulder clay, up to 4 feet thick	a glacial moraine
Stratified chalky and sandy gravel, up to 8 feet thick in places	pro-glacial deposits of essentially morainic character?

These descriptions and interpretations really require modern checking, but at least there are clear indications of a cold-warm-cold sequence, even if the degree of continuity is uncertain and the boulder clay, if such it be, has not been clearly identified in terms of the East Anglian Pleistocene sequence. The fauna from the 'land surface' included, according to Hopwood, *Canis lupus*, *Ursus* sp. (identified as *Ursus spelaeus*), *Felis (Panthera) leo*, *Equus caballus*, *Rhinoceros* sp., *Cervus elaphus*, *Megaloceros giganteus*, *Bison priscus*, *Bos primigenius*, *Elephas (Palaeoloxodon) antiquus* and *Mammuthus primigenius*. If this somewhat mixed assemblage represents one interglacial, it would presumably be the Ipswichian as things stand at present. We may note too that among the mollusca of this level *Corbicula fluminalis* was quite common.

On the archaeological side the situation seems relatively simple, although there is a fair old mixture of artefacts (Fig. 5:51). Only one group of material is thought to be *in situ* – the unpatinated fresh pieces from the 'land surface'. These consist of neatly made Levalloisian flakes and flake-blades, which Moir compared specifically to the Crayford series discussed in Chapter 3, but perhaps the West Drayton-Yiewsley material would offer an even better comparison. The derived material, some of which came from the land surface, though most was in the yellow gravel, includes handaxes of many kinds and retouched flakes, some of which Moir compared to those of the 'classic flake industry' of High Lodge. In the present context, it is important to note that the derived material, whose condition indicates that it is older than the fresh unpatinated series, included several examples of Levalloisian flakes, and even some cores, of the larger Baker's Hole kind. Moir figured one such 'tortoise core', which he regarded as unsuccessfully struck, with a prominent but incomplete crack marking what might well have been the circumference of the flake, had it been

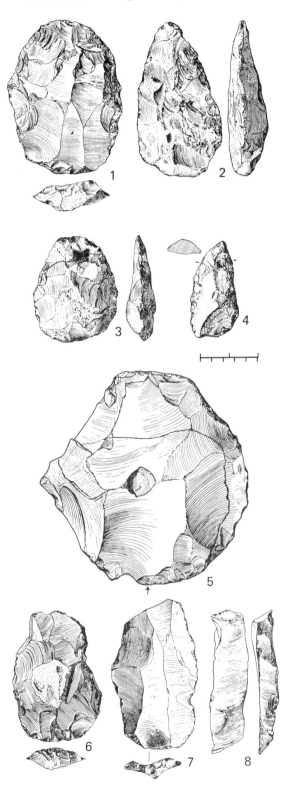

5:51 Artefacts from Brundon, after Moir and Hopwood (1939): no. 1, Levalloisian flake of 'Baker's Hole' type, from the land surface but abraded and derived; nos 2, 3, abraded handaxes, from the gravel; no. 4, flake-tool with cortex platform, abraded, from the gravel; no. 5, tortoise core, regarded by Moir as unsuccessfully struck (see pages 221-2), from the land surface but abraded and derived; nos 6-7, Levalloisian flakes, fresh and unpatinated, *in situ* on the land surface; no. 8, flake-blade (plain platform), fresh and unpatinated, *in situ* on the land surface

successfully removed from the core (Fig. 5:51, no. 5). To the present writer, this looks much more like a subsequent frost-crack — could the flake really have remained partially detached while the core underwent the abrasion it shows? This is a detail, however, and we can see that Moir was correct in regarding the finds from Brundon as generally confirming the Levalloisian sequence which we noted in the Northfleet area: an earlier phase with large, heavy cores and flakes, followed by one with smaller and neater oval flakes and a flake-blade element, in which the dorsal scars most often run 'longitudinally'. Indeed, nowhere in Britain do we see a convincing reversal of this situation: it looks very much like a simple techno-logical progression, and what the writer knows of the relevant Continental material seems to him to confirm it. The main Brundon collections are now at Ipswich Museum, but the artefacts were acquired at various times in various ways and are not easy to relate to the stratigraphy described above.

Some miles south and east of Brundon lies Ipswich, Suffolk, where Levalloisian artefacts are again common at certain sites. The most interest-ing and prolific are those recorded by J.R. Moir (1931) from the basal deposits of the Flood Plain Terrace in the Gipping-Orwell valley. This terrace, and the buried channel beneath it, yielded very many artefacts belonging to various different periods and industries — over 2,000 artefacts in all according to Moir (*op. cit.*, p. 187). We need not concern ourselves here in detail with Moir's claims of Upper Palaeolithic material, though there are some interesting pieces. However, from exposures in Hadleigh Road, Constantine Road, Sproughton Road and Bramford Road, he and others also obtained large quantities of what they regarded as Mousterian material. Bramford Road was easily the most prolific site, though the four may be taken together in view of the nature of the occur-rences. The water-table was usually encountered about four feet from the surface, and sections could rarely be observed. At Bramford Road the gravel was pumped up by suction from below the water-level and a fast-moving metal 'propeller' device broke up the material before it entered the mouth of the suction pipe. How efficient this contraption was seems open to doubt, since many

artefacts of substantial size came through unscathed to reach the next stage, rotary sieves, where the archaeologists could pick them out, and the suction pump was twice blocked by mammoth teeth. Quite a lot of bone came through safely, including two fragments of fossilized human long bones which Moir believed to be of Upper Pleistocene age. It would be an understatement to say that artefacts thus gathered lack strati-graphic precision, but we should not overlook an earlier report by Moir (1918) on observations made at Constantine Road, when a deep section was temporarily available and a 'floor of Combe Capelle age' was found *in situ* in peaty loam beneath a thick deposit of Flood Plain Terrace gravel, the implements and flakes being apparently associated with numerous reindeer bones, some of which were thought to have been artificially split. Moir notes (1931: 189) that some of the Bramford Road artefacts had traces of a similar peaty loam adhering to them when they emerged from the suction pump, and these too he classed as of 'Combe Capelle' type. This term, which implies comparison with a famous French Mousterian of Acheulian Tradition industry from the site of that name, can be taken when used in the 1930s to indicate the presence of handaxes of *bout coupé* and/or cordiform shape, accompanied (if it is a whole industry that is being referred to) by flake-tools and examples of Levalloisian technique. Moir proceeds to illustrate just such an assemblage (*op. cit.*, figs 8-16, examples reproduced here as Fig. 5:52), and quantities of such material survive from Bramford Road in the collections at Ipswich Museum and elsewhere.

The Constantine Road peaty loam level was at the base of the Flood Plain Terrace, but apparently above the gravel of the buried channel: Moir accordingly attributed all the 'Mousterian' material to this position on his composite diagrammatic sections for the whole area. It was his belief that most of the material was *in situ* and undisturbed in the peaty loam, since most is unabraded, but he allowed for disturbance of the 'floor' in some places in the course of deposition of the gravel which overlies it, and he accounted for the presence of a few abraded specimens in that way. On the basis of observations in another section at

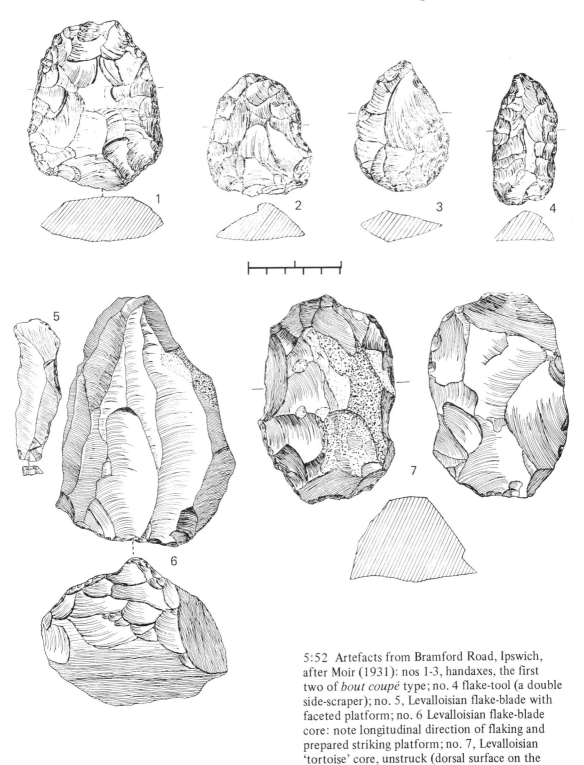

5:52 Artefacts from Bramford Road, Ipswich, after Moir (1931): nos 1-3, handaxes, the first two of *bout coupé* type; no. 4 flake-tool (a double side-scraper); no. 5, Levalloisian flake-blade with faceted platform; no. 6 Levalloisian flake-blade core: note longitudinal direction of flaking and prepared striking platform; no. 7, Levalloisian 'tortoise' core, unstruck (dorsal surface on the right)

Constantine Road, he attributed the most striking of his 'Upper Palaeolithic' implements, some of which he regarded as Solutrean, to a blue loam, probably only locally present, whose position was above the peaty loam which contained the 'Mousterian' artefacts but still below the main Flood Plain Gravel. At Bramford Road the suction pump brought up a few more 'Solutrean' pieces along with all the rest.

All of these observations by Moir would benefit greatly from modern checking under controlled conditions, and it is not likely that his interpretation of the relationship of the sequence described to what he regarded as 'Upper Chalky Boulder Clay' nearby, or his over-all reading of the chronology, would now be accepted. But his observations regarding the likely provenance of the assemblage with *bout coupé* handaxes and Levalloisian material may well have been correct, and if these artefacts were indeed associated with mammoth, reindeer and *Coelodonta antiquitatis*, then a Devensian age seems likely, presumably well into the glacial. Whether the horizon containing them was really younger than the buried channel, or whether the channel might after all prove to have been cut through it, could only emerge from new exposures; it has recently been shown (Wymer *et al.* 1975) that some of the deposits in the Gipping buried channel are of final Devensian and early Flandrian age (pollen zones III-IV). The presence of hominid bone fragments of possibly Devensian age adds extra interest to the whole situation. For purposes of our present discussion, then, here is another important occurrence in which Levalloisian artefacts are involved, very probably associated with *bout coupé* handaxes.

Next, still in eastern England, we can consider the finds from the Great Ouse Valley. A few of the sites are in Bedfordshire, near Bedford, e.g. Biddenham and Kempston, where several Levalloisian cores and flakes are included amongst the large mixed assemblages mentioned earlier in this chapter; most, however, are in Huntingdonshire, especially in the area of St Ives and St Neots, with some continuation downstream. There is one not infrequently quoted publication relating to these finds, by T.T. Paterson and C.F. Tebbutt (1947), relating especially to the finds from Little

Paxton near St Neots (pits in Paxton Park), and a few notes describing individual artefacts are tucked away here and there, e.g. by Tebbutt *et al.* (1927) and Garrood (1933). So far as dating is concerned, Paterson and Tebbutt showed clearly in their work at Little Paxton that the Levalloisian artefacts came from the lowest terrace of the Great Ouse, a few feet only above the present river, from a well-stratified fluviatile gravel with lenses of finer material, which also contained good faunal remains, notably mammoth, reindeer, rhinoceros and horse. The next older terrace in this area had quite a different fauna, with hippopotamus, giant deer and ox. There seems no doubt at all that the low terrace with the Levalloisian artefacts is of Devensian age, and, in the lower levels at least, earlier Devensian. The artefacts, however (Fig. 5:53), do not occur as a single industry in place; some are appreciably worn, and might antedate the terrace, while others are fresh and apparently contemporary. They include a few typical *bout coupé* handaxes and closely related forms, several Levalloisian flakes and flake-blades and perhaps a couple of hundred other flakes ranging from obvious handaxe trimmers to neatly made sidescrapers. The precise quantities are not known, because the publication does not give them and it is clear that not all the material reached museum collections; also, the terms in which Paterson and Tebbutt described the artefacts are obscure by comparison with those now in use.[15] The largest extant collections are now at Cambridge (University and Sedgwick Museums).

What does not appear from the report by Paterson and Tebbutt, nor indeed from the references to Little Paxton by later authors, is that similar material has come from the same Ouse terrace over several miles of the river's course in this area, notably at Earith (Colne Drove), Fenstanton (at least two gravel pits), Hartford (Allen's and Maddy's Pits), Hemingford Grey (Marsh Lane), St Ives (Meadow Lane Pits) and Wyton, plus a few other scattered find-spots. The bulk of these artefacts are or were in the Norris Museum at St Ives, but regrettably many were destroyed by enemy action during the Second World War.[16] There are several typical *bout coupé* handaxes amongst what survives (cf. list in the

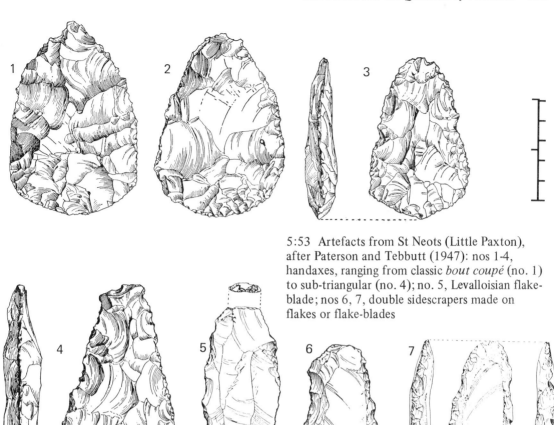

5:53 Artefacts from St Neots (Little Paxton), after Paterson and Tebbutt (1947): nos 1-4, handaxes, ranging from classic *bout coupé* (no. 1) to sub-triangular (no. 4); no. 5, Levalloisian flake-blade; nos 6, 7, double sidescrapers made on flakes or flake-blades

next chapter), and also Levalloisian flakes and flake-blades. There are records of mammoth and rhinoceros (*Coelodonta antiquitatis*) remains from some at least of the same pits. Most of the finds were not made *in situ*, since the gravel was worked below water-level; the artefacts and bones were picked up from gravel heaps in the pits. It seems clear however that only one low terrace deposit was involved, and that we may regard these other finds as confirming and strengthening the observations made at Little Paxton.

In passing we should note that further north in Huntingdonshire, and in Northamptonshire, in low level gravels of the River Nene, in the general area of Peterborough, Levalloisian artefacts have been

recorded as relatively frequent (cf. Posnansky 1958, 1963), but their stratigraphic provenances are rather obscure and only a small proportion of the totals claimed appear to survive in the extant collections (notably at Peterborough Museum). The general similarity between the Huntingdonshire sites in the Great Ouse Valley and the Ipswich occurrences described above are rather striking, both in the nature of the artefacts, the fauna from the containing deposits and indeed the low terrace deposits themselves and their suggested dating. It is sad that the similarities also extend to the shortcomings of the evidence in each case.

We must next turn to south-east England, in particular to north Kent and south Essex. North-west Kent has already contributed the basic sequence from which our whole discussion in this chapter has stemmed, including the Levalloisian of the Northfleet area, but there are other sites further east, unrelated to the Lower Thames: old finds, inevitably, but more neglected than they deserve in the recent literature. Levalloisian artefacts are relatively common in the Canterbury area, though there are no real 'Levalloisian sites' of the kind we have been discussing unless one takes seriously the tantalizingly brief reference by an anonymous author to the finds at Riverdale of a single very large unstruck tortoise core at the base of a gravel and a 'Levallois chipping site' in loam above it, directly beneath Roman foundations (*Antiquaries Journal* 1939: 317-18). A few miles west of Canterbury, at Ospringe, Faversham, a pit by the old Union Workhouse was apparently the source of nine elongated Levalloisian flakes, distinctly blade-like, which are now divided between the British Museum and the London Museum. Some are appreciably abraded, and their precise provenance remains obscure (Garraway Rice 1911), but they certainly look like a group. Most are retouched along one or both of their long edges, which is unusual. If some uncertainty must remain about their age, there is a much better occurrence not many miles west at Bapchild, described fifty years ago by H.G. Dines (1929).

Brickearth was dug at Bapchild in two pits, and a 'Coombe Rock deposit' (soliflucted gravel and chalk) was found to lie beneath it, capping the solid chalk or, in places, Tertiary Thanet Sand. Both the Coombe Rock and the brickearth contained artefacts in considerable quantities. From the Coombe Rock, principally at Smeed, Dean & Co.'s pit just west of Haywood Farm, came 'more than four hundred artefacts of Le Moustier type' (Dines, *op. cit.*, p. 12), while at a second pit about a quarter of a mile away to the east, the brickearth produced more than 200 artefacts, with a strong component of large blades, some retouched, plus flake implements and flakes. This brickearth industry has been regarded as vaguely Upper Palaeolithic, but a few at least of the flakes and blades have carefully faceted striking platforms – i.e. they were removed from prismatic cores by a highly developed kind of

Levalloisian technique. However, since they are undated, we will not consider them further here, beyond remarking that they are perhaps rather less Levalloisian, if one may put it that way, than the small group from Ospringe just mentioned, and that both sites might repay a new study if any of the key deposits remain: at least one might find out whether the industries were of Upper Pleistocene or of early Holocene age, since post-glacial industries with large blades and with use of Levallois-like technology do occur.

The Coombe Rock industry from Bapchild, however, is quite a different affair. Dines's use of the term 'Le Moustier' for it merely reflects the period at which he was writing; more specifically, he compared it to the Baker's Hole industry, and with some justification, since the flakes are typically large and oval or irregular in outline, with a convergent pattern of dorsal scars and thick faceted striking platforms. Many of the flakes were retouched, according to Dines, though some of the chipping of the edges may in fact be damage incurred when the Coombe Rock deposit was formed. There were no handaxes, although there was one 'core implement' (not illustrated in the article). There were four typical Levalloisian cores, one unstruck. Some supposed anvil blocks, shaped out of large flint nodules, were also recovered. In many ways the Bapchild industry (Fig. 5:54) probably offers the closest available comparison to the Baker's Hole find, though much less prolific, but at Bapchild there was no sign of a true floor under the Coombe Rock, and the periglacial phase represented by this deposit remains undated. No faunal remains were reported. An exact break-down of the industry is not possible, owing to the inadequate marking of such material from the two different Bapchild horizons as does survive in various museum collections, and to the fact that much of it evidently passed into private hands. Small quantities can however be seen at Maidstone Museum, the British Museum, the Geological Museum in South Kensington and the University Museum at Cambridge.

Lastly, in south-east England one site in Essex must be mentioned: Botany Pit at Purfleet, in south Essex, just west of Gray's Thurrock. Though the pit itself has existed for many years, serious archaeological excavations (directed by Mr A. Snelling) were not begun until the early 1960s (see Wymer 1968: 312-13; 318-19). As so often in Britain, the assemblage is interesting and the dating rather obscure. The principal deposit is a sheet of stratified sand and gravel, with a surface height close to 50 feet O.D. Between it and the underlying chalk some Coombe Rock and other signs of periglacial activity intervene. Although the modern Thames is less than a mile away to the south, there is an anticlinal chalk ridge between it and the Botany Pit gravel deposit, which in fact seems to be related to the Mar Dyke, now a small Thames tributary flowing generally south-westwards to join the main river close to Purfleet. The gravels are known to be banked against a steep northward-facing cliff in the chalk ridge, and they are apparently part of the filling of a channel, perhaps a former Mar Dyke course, which can be shown to have been cut through a higher sheet of gravel at about 95 to 100 feet O.D.

The artefacts found in the channel range from nearly fresh to moderately abraded, and while they certainly do not constitute an undisturbed occurrence, they probably came from a site or sites not very far away. Wymer mentions the important fact that the local chalk contains good quality flint and the occurrence and character of the artefacts are consistent with the suggestion that they are the debris of exploitation of that raw material. No doubt they found their way down the slope when the chalk cliff and the channel were formed, or in the periglacial phase represented by the Coombe Rock, and were redistributed and in some cases further abraded when the gravel of the channel filling was deposited, though the main concentration of them remained close to the buried chalk cliff and the edges of the channel. There is no proof that they belong only to a single exploitation of the chalk flint, and they could of course cover a long period of time. As for the nature of the assemblage, cores of various kinds are unusually frequent, while flakes run into thousands, but there are only a dozen handaxes. In making a somewhat informal classification of the material then available (British Museum, Snelling Collection) for purposes of the C.B.A.'s *Gazetteer*, the present writer recorded

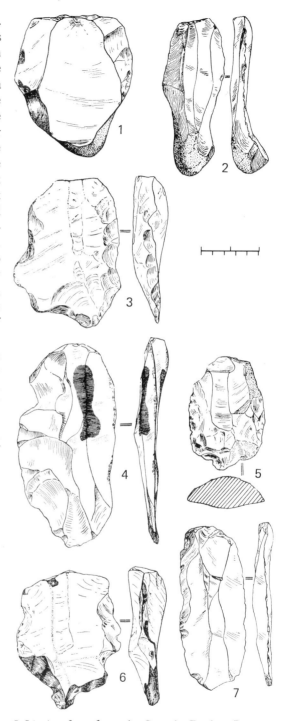

5:54 Artefacts from the Coombe Rock at Bapchild, after Dines (1929): no. 1, struck tortoise core; no. 2, plunging flake; nos 3-7, Levalloisian flakes

these totals (Table 18):

TABLE 18 : *Broad classifications of artefacts from Botany Pit, Purfleet*

Classification	Count	Percentage
Finished handaxes	12	0.31
Unfinished handaxes	2	0.05
Cores (non-Levalloisian)	175	4.56
Flakes (non-Levalloisian)		
(a) certainly or possibly retouched	1,005	26.19
(b) unretouched	2,419	63.04
Miscellaneous worked pieces	95	2.48
Levalloisian cores	98	2.55
Levalloisian flakes	31	0.81
Total	3,837	99.99

These figures should not be taken too seriously, but are probably accurate enough to reflect the character of the assemblage. The ordinary flakes are so numerous that the percentages of the other classes are tiny; however, ninety-eight Levalloisian cores from the same gravel pit can hardly be ignored in Britain! The non-Levalloisian cores include flat, globular, biconical and irregular shapes and are not dissimilar overall to the general run of Clactonian cores, though some certainly suggest better controlled flaking than that found at the classic Clactonian sites, in that they appear to have yielded more flakes before being abandoned because care was taken to preserve 'flakeable' angles. However, it is with the Levalloisian cores and flakes that we are principally concerned at present, and they are an interesting series, rather reminiscent of those from Caddington (see pages 191-5), with several showing signs of a 'reduced' Levalloisian technique — simplification of the preparatory stages, but still the removal of a big 'end-product' flake of predetermined shape and size. On the other hand, some of the cores, both struck and unstruck, are examples of classic Levalloisian technique, and this too was the case at Caddington. The same goes for the Purfleet Levalloisian flakes, of which the majority are unretouched: some are 'simplified', some are 'classic'. It should be emphasized that the des-

cription given here of the Purfleet material is based upon the writer's impressions rather than on a detailed study. It is interesting however to find Wymer, writing in 1968, suggesting that the Levalloisian element could be 'proto-Levalloisian' (*op. cit.*, p. 318), though wisely allowing that the abundance of raw material could account for the crudity of the industry — if, one might add, that is crudeness. It should be recorded finally that Mr Snelling obtained bones of elephant, red deer, horse and ox from the gravel containing the artefacts, but neither this fact nor the geological information given earlier really offers a firm dating for the artefacts.

Many more Levalloisian finds could be chronicled, but it is time to draw this section and this whole long chapter to a close. The conclusions about occurrences of Levalloisian technique in Britain may be summarized as follows.

(a) There are sites where the technique plays a minor part, or occasionally a less minor part, in essentially Acheulian industries — for example, Cuxton, Whitlingham, Bowman's Lodge or Caddington.

(b) There are industries which are dominantly, sometimes almost exclusively Levalloisian, such as Baker's Hole, Bapchild, Crayford, Creffield Road (Acton), and, doubtless, some of the West Drayton area finds if we had a clear picture of them.

(c) There are other industries where the Levalloisian technique is seen against a frankly Mousterian background, with *bout coupé* and cordiform handaxes and flake tools of Mousterian type. Of sites mentioned so far, examples of this kind are Oldbury, Pan Farm, the Ipswich Flood Plain Gravel sites and Little Paxton (taken with the nearby Ouse Valley occurrences). There are of course many tenuous associations between Levalloisian artefacts and single *bout coupé* handaxes: the lower brickearth at Iver has been mentioned above, and the Creffield Road site itself could count as an example. Many more instances will be listed in the next chapter. Such occurrences *may* very likely belong ultimately with this group, but they can hardly stand as primary members of it. The primary members must be those in which the balance between the 'Mousterian' elements and the 'Levalloisian' ones is even, or tipped in favour of the 'Mousterian' side. If it were not for the existence of the pure Levalloisian industries of (b), we might not have to worry about this balance, but as it is the writer has suggested already that 'pure' or almost 'pure' Levalloisian industries are a definite feature of the British Palaeolithic, even if a somewhat rare one; they may be linked to specific occurrences of abundant raw material of high quality. If that is so, one can only regard them as specialized industries, whose wider cultural contexts may not always be clear and are likely to vary in any case, as may the chronology.

(d) Then there are certainly or probably mixed assemblages, in which Levalloisian artefacts are frequent enough to deserve notice, or have special features that need to be recorded, but where their context cannot be clearly discerned. Botany Pit, Purfleet, is a good example; the gravel (as opposed to the 'land surface') at Brundon is another, and Biddenham (Bedfordshire) is a third. New Hythe, Kent (cf. page 212) illustrates the shortcomings of such occurrences — one may *suspect* that this site produced an Acheulian industry 'of Levallois facies', but one cannot prove the coherence of the assemblage. At Southacre, in Norfolk (cf. page 148-9), Levalloisian artefacts and handaxes occurred in an assemblage that also included material sometimes regarded as Clactonian. Are all these elements contemporary, or is it a mixture of periods with no difference in condition of the various artefacts? If they are contemporary, is this some 'survival of Clactonian technique', as has been argued by some writers, or are we simply seeing some specialized industry not precisely paralleled elsewhere (though the situation might be not dissimilar at Purfleet, perhaps)? The present writer has no intention of building hypotheses based upon such dubious occurrences, but he is simply not prepared, in a book of this scope, just to ignore *all* the mixed assemblages and the problems they pose. Others are at perfect liberty to do so if they wish.

(e) Even a superficial examination of the distribution of minor Levalloisian find-spots in Britain quickly reveals that it is patchy and uneven. So it might well be, if the technique is regarded as essentially linked to abundance of flint; but even so,

there are relatively well-populated areas and surprising blanks, which cannot easily be explained in that way. We have mentioned the Canterbury area as relatively rich in minor Levalloisian finds, and one might add the London area and the Bournemouth area in the same way, or parts of the Solent gravels (for example, around Warsash); on the other hand, Norfolk and Essex are examples of areas which seem curiously poor in Levalloisian finds. There is no obvious explanation for this situation, though it seems worth mentioning. One is always on the look-out for any evidence that might indicate territorial ranges of specific groups of people, but in the absence of proper chronological controls it would be grossly overstretching the data to suggest that we have such evidence in this case.

(f) Finally, there is the question of chronology and development within the period during which Levalloisian technique is current in Britain (probably from the late Hoxnian to the mid-Devensian). Nothing has been said in the present section to upset the basic sequence of Chapter 3, but quite a lot of information has been added. We can still see tenuous beginnings in a variable Middle Acheulian context, soon followed by the appearance of specialized Levalloisian industries. We have noted a few more instances of Levalloisian of the bold, heavy Baker's Hole kind, notably Bapchild and perhaps also the Brundon gravel, though their dating is not clear and it would be only on the basis of the north Kent sequence that we could call them 'Early Levalloisian'. We have seen several more good examples of the Levalloisian flake-blade industries of the Crayford/Ebbsfleet kind, sometimes predominantly blade-like (Creffield Road, Iver upper brickearth, Brundon 'land surface', etc.), and sometimes with a strong component of neatly made oval flakes, altogether more delicate than those of Baker's Hole (e.g. Yiewsley/West Drayton). These seem to be of Late Ipswichian to earlier Devensian age where dated. Ardent typologists will doubtless see here a Middle Levalloisian, in which the oval flakes appear as a development from the Baker's Hole stage, and a Late Levalloisian, in which they have vanished, but we lack the stratigraphic and chronological evidence necessary to assert that the two variants always occur in that order, and the writer is bound to advise against drawing a strong distinction between them in the present stage of knowledge. We have also added to the information of the basic sequence a number of associations of Levalloisian technique with *bout coupé* and cordiform handaxes, which seem to run into a Mousterian of Acheulian Tradition phase; some at least of these occurrences are of Devensian age (Ipswich, Little Paxton, Oldbury), but others are more likely to be Late Ipswichian (Iver lower brickearth, Great Pan Farm). Lastly, we have noted occurrences of an interesting 'reduced Levalloisian' technique at Caddington (probably of Ipswichian age) and at Purfleet (not well dated), of which we had no hint in the north Kent sequence; we have seen, however, no sign that this is 'proto-Levalloisian', as might well have been thought if typology of individual artefact classes were the only guide.

NOTES

1 The writer's *Gazetteer* was drawn up according to the county and other administrative boundaries then existing, and various changes have since taken place. National Grid References were given for all the sites of known location, and no information will have been destroyed by the changes, but users of the *Gazetteer* who need to make lists to fit the new administrative districts must take account of the old boundaries where necessary.

2 We may note that it is held to have been an extension of the Anglian ice-sheets, specifically, that pushed the Thames course southwards to something like its present position. If this is so, why should we get post-Anglian fluviatile deposits in a *Thames* channel at Clacton? Even if the basal gravel at the Golf Course site turns out to be inter-Anglian and thus perhaps older than the diversion of the Thames course, the overlying marl and the foreshore deposits previously studied are all still Hoxnian. The heavy minerals and lithology seem to demonstrate that the channel complex *is* part of a Thames-Medway drainage system. Could it be that after the diversion in the Finchley to Upminster section of its course the Thames still contrived for a while to flow past what is now Clacton, presumably turning sharply north or north-east somewhere east of Upminster and east, too, of Swanscombe? It does not seem possible to produce convincing evidence for such a course at present. But perhaps not many traces of it would be likely to survive in accessible places, i.e. they could now be covered by the sea.

3 Is it really a curiously low level? *If* the very same river were responsible for the Swanscombe Lower Gravels and the Clacton Channel filling, the gradient to link the two sites would only need to show a fall of one metre every 2.6 kilometres, since the sites are at least 70 kilometres apart (depending on how straight was the actual course of a river connecting them), according to figures given by Singer *et al.* (1973: 45). It is a little hard to envisage the British coastline's fluctuations over the Anglian-Hoxnian phase. How much of East Anglia was drowned by marine transgression during the Hoxnian, if the situation at Clacton was estuarine? In West Sussex, the evidence of raised beaches up to +130 feet O.D. at least in the Slindon area (between Arundel and Chichester) suggests that the present coastal plain there was deeply submerged at the Hoxnian maximum.

4 As regards the dating of the formation of the Ancient Channel deposits in the form in which we now see them: if one admits the technological status of the ovates as an indication of their age, as Wymer does (1961, 1968), one would suppose that the periglacial conditions envisaged were those of a Wolstonian stadial, presumably the last. This argument implies that an Anglian stadial would be too early for ovates of this kind to occur in the mixture of artefacts (and they are present at all levels), while if it had been a Devensian cold episode one would expect to find at least a few Levalloisian or Final Acheulian or even Mousterian artefacts present. Setting aside the Clactonian as something extra, one might perhaps be reminded of the mixture in the fluvio-glacial gravels of Warren Hill, discussed in the previous chapter, which was regarded as a Wolstonian deposit incorporating a mixture of evolved and early Acheulian. As it happens, though one would not of course wish to draw firm chronological conclusions, the ovate handaxes from Highlands Farm and Warren Hill (the fresh series) do bear a close resemblance to each other in points of morphological and technological detail (see Roe 1968a). At this

point of course we should piously remind ourselves of the dangers inherent in using artefact typology as a means of dating Pleistocene deposits, but it is an interesting exercise in speculation.

5   There are a few other British sites one might class with Grovelands and Southacre, but the evidence they provide is of poor quality. For example, there is Twydall in north Kent, near Gillingham, where a modern artificial causeway at Sharps Green was constructed of gravel brought from the nearby Twydall quarry — gravel which was later found to be extremely rich in Lower Palaeolithic artefacts (cf. Payne 1915; Roe 1968a: 21-2). The existing literature has little to say of Clactonian in this occurrence, but unpublished work a few years ago by A.G. Woodcock (pers. com.) showed that the causeway still exists and is still producing artefacts: he gathered over 700 in a few hours. Amongst these, the large majority are flakes and cores in the Clactonian manner, though some Acheulian handaxes and a few cleavers are also present. Both in this group of material, and in the old Twydall collections, there are many bold but well-retouched flake implements, worked on thick, heavy hard-hammer flakes with broad high-angle platforms. The design and execution of these pieces look rather above the level of the type-site Clactonian. Many of the artefacts are made from the same marbled north Kent flint which was so frequently used at Swanscombe. The primary flaking is certainly crude, and one often sees double or even multiple bulbs or cones of percussion, as one does at Clacton or in the Swanscombe Lower Gravels. It appears that none of the relevant Pleistocene deposits remains *in situ* at the old Twydall quarry, which was worked for its chalk rather than for the gravel above the chalk. The causeway probably contains the confused remnants of a fine Palaeolithic site with at least two major levels, but the damage was done over sixty years ago and that is why the occurrence is relegated here to a mere footnote.

6   This may well have happened, but one would feel happier with documentation of specific instances of it, preferably at each of the find-spots involved. It is one thing to use the obvious resorting of a gravel (as in the case of the Caversham Ancient Channel) to explain typological anomalies amongst its Palaeolithic contents, and quite another to invoke supposed resorting of a deposit because the typology looks wrong. The present writer does not

believe that the refined ovates with such features as 'tranchet finish' should be contemporary with a deposit of Anglian age in Britain, as 'Anglian' is at present understood — it would make a nonsense of the basic sequence if they were. But he is also aware of good evidence in other areas, particularly East Africa, for the manufacture of handaxes, just as refined, perhaps as much as two or three hundred thousand years before the Winter Hill terrace was formed, if the suggested dating for the Anglian in Chapter 2 is anywhere near correct — for example, some of the Olduvai Gorge Bed IV Acheulian industries.

7   Reid Moir, for once, was nearer the mark. He excavated at Hoxne and published reports (1926, 1935) in which he claimed that there were two separate horizons, 'Late Acheulian' and 'Early Mousterian' or 'Clacton III'. The latter is by no means a bad description of some aspects of the Upper Industry (cf. note 10 below). West and McBurney however specifically discounted his conclusions (1954: 135, 141) and they did not encounter the Upper Industry *in situ* in the area of their own excavation.

8   Richard Hubbard, then of the London University Institute of Archaeology, has recently argued ingeniously and rather persuasively (pers. com., unpublished as yet) that these sharpened stakes (Smith 1894: 268-9, 288-94) are much more likely to be the work of beavers. I am grateful to Mr Hubbard for permission to quote this suggestion. Masses of compacted fern material were found near them, with other wood and vegetable material not far away. Smith himself toyed with the idea that the masses of fern (*Osmunda regalis*) in particular 'represented litter, or the beds on which the savages of old had rested themselves' (*op. cit.*, p. 292). In one such mass of fern he found 'a keen edged Palaeolithic implement and a leg-bone of a horse' (*ibid.*).

9   The writer understands from John Wymer that none of the wood is worked, which is disappointing, as new information on Acheulian wooden artefacts would be very welcome. The wood at Hoxne is essentially a mass of driftwood which had accumulated as the lake became choked with sediments and vegetation and peat began to form.

10   A comment may be added here on the significance of these later Acheulian industries in France, according to views increasingly held amongst French prehistorians. They note the presence of handaxe industries, mostly of 'Rissian' age, in which flake-tools, finely

made, become increasingly important while handaxes gradually drop away to a minimal presence. Next, delete the handaxes altogether, and you are left with 'pre-Mousterian' industries. If there is a strong Levalloisian element present, such epi-Acheulian or pre-Mousterian industries can be thought of as ancestral to the Charentian 'Ferrassie' variant of the scheme proposed for the southern French Mousterian by M. Bourgon, F. Bordes and others (Bordes and Bourgon 1951; Bourgon 1957; Bordes 1961, 1968, etc); if the industries are not of Levallois facies, then they may be ancestral to the Charentian 'Quina' variant. There is also a Mousterian of Acheulian Tradition, whose roots are again firmly in the later Acheulian. These matters are more fully discussed in the next chapter. Thus, at Orgnac III, J. Combier (1967: 125-6) can regard the eight stratified Lower Palaeolithic levels as representing steady and continuous local evolution of this kind from an Upper Acheulian to a pre-Mousterian – a process of *'moustérianisation'*. H. de Lumley offers similar views in relation to some of the Rissian industries from his southern French sites (e.g. 1971: 355-6). In the north of France and in Britain, most of the sites are single-level or perhaps two-level ones, and the picture is less clear. But certainly, this general background should be kept in mind when one assesses the flake-tools from the Hoxne Upper Industry or from Stoke Newington, or from High Lodge (the classic flake industry).

11 The presence of material in particular museums was noted by the writer ten years and more ago; some exchange and redistribution of collections has inevitably taken place since then, not all of it known to him. Anyone following up the museum collections mentioned here or in Roe 1968a or 1968b must be ready to exercise a little patience and persistence. Well, why not? Persistence is a quality more or less essential to the pursuit of handaxes, anywhere, in any way. Reflect that the Acheulian people themselves also seem to have been a highly persistent lot, in their own fashion: they would probably have done admirable research work on the material culture of their predecessors, if they hadn't had more important matters to occupy them.

12 Thus Sturge (1912: 144) refers to '. . . the lower gravel at Dunbridge, in the Test Valley, which is one of the most markedly red gravels

known . . . the patinas on implements from this gravel vary widely, some not being red at all (I am of course not referring to the white implements from the upper gravel) . . .' Note especially the part at the end in brackets.

13 It would be interesting to study the British Levalloisian industries in such a way, and not hard to think of starting points: metrical analyses of shape, size and flatness of the flakes; size of striking platform; numbers of platform facets; numbers and orientations of primary dorsal scars; location and extent of retouch; sizes and shapes of cores, and various aspects of their preliminary preparation; etc., etc. It might be possible to pick out recurrent technological patterns amongst the industries.

14 One is reminded of Spurrell's find at Crayford of rather similar Levalloisian material in direct contact with a woolly rhinoceros jaw (see page 87).

15 Thus the handaxes are called 'Late Acheulian bouchers', for example. The authors seem to have had l'Abbé Breuil, at the height of his powers as a typologist, breathing down their necks. Paterson becomes drawn rather needlessly into a comparison between the Paxton assemblage and that from Elveden, which he had studied in an earlier paper in the same series (Paterson and Fagg 1940); the two occurrences do not really have much in common. On the final page, Paterson takes off completely, seeming rather to forget his co-author, but perhaps only he could have written '. . . and therefore I propose to call this the "Final Acheulian Levallois B, St Neots", the last stage of development of a compound culture resulting from the contact and reciprocal assimilation of Acheulian and Levalloisian elements during the Upper Pleistocene' (Paterson and Tebbutt 1947: 46). However, it is only too easy to disparage, when one has the advantage of thirty years' worth of hindsight by numerous colleagues.

16 It is a pleasure to record that the survival of the main information, and the present writer's awareness of it, are directly due to the contribution of information in the 1950s by local workers to the C.B.A.'s original 'Palaeolithic Survey', which gave birth to the *Gazetteer* compiled by the present writer. The main contributors in this case included Messrs Tebbutt, Garrood and Coote.

The Middle Palaeolithic   *Chapter 6*

The preceding discussion has already trespassed upon the ground properly belonging to this chapter. This took place mainly in the account of the later development of Levalloisian technique and also in the inclusion of two 'Mousterian of Acheulian Tradition' occurrences amongst the handaxe industries of Group VI. The writer does not regret these intrusions in the least, or apologize for them, because he has no wish to draw a sharp line or make an artificial division between the Lower and Middle Palaeolithic in Britain or indeed anywhere else. It is not really possible any longer to believe in some massive and rapid Mousterian take-over of Europe, linked to the explosive arrival on the scene of Neanderthal Man and bringing about the sudden demise of the Acheulian population. On the contrary, we can now observe a long period of overlap between the two, with Late Acheulian and Micoquian industries continuing into the early part of the Last Glacial in some areas, while several 'pre-Mousterian' or 'archaic Mousterian' sites of Riss/Saale age, and others of Riss-Würm/Eemian age are known. Besides, it has already been indicated that some Acheulian industries in which fine flake-tools were particularly important were probably influential in the development of certain facies of the Mousterian. As for populations, it is certainly true that there are many associations in Europe of *Homo sapiens neanderthalensis* with developed Mousterian industries, mainly of full Last Glacial age, while there is no certain evidence that Neanderthalers ever made a pure Acheulian industry. But why equate the cultural and technological evidence so inflexibly with the biological, when the evidence is so unequal? Many of the crucial industries lack associated hominid remains, while not all the important hominid finds that have been made more recently have yet been evaluated.[1]

So far as the nature of this gradual passage from Lower to Middle Palaeolithic is concerned, Britain has rather little solid information to contribute, partly no doubt because the human occupation of Britain must have been intermittent right through the Palaeolithic. And when we emerge from the transition period into the classic Mousterian of Last Glacial age, so well documented in southern France and elsewhere, we find the British evidence sparse and impoverished in the extreme. Since many of the best known Mousterian industries of the Continent belong to what is evidently a very cold period, on clear evidence derived from faunal and sedimentological studies, it seems reasonable enough to suppose that Britain offered too hostile an environment after the Early Devensian for anything but occasional and fleeting visits by hunters following the summer migrations of game herds. The British Mousterian is accordingly very restricted in quantity and it also has little of the rich variety of its French counterpart. But it does exist (*pace* Wymer 1968: 389), and we shall note its contents accordingly. However, to achieve any understanding of it we must first examine briefly the Continental background.

THE MOUSTERIAN IN EUROPE

Characteristically 'Mousterian' industries can be

found widely distributed over Western, Central and Eastern Europe and deep into the USSR. Occurrences are perhaps a little less frequent in the southernmost parts of Europe, i.e. the Iberian, Italian and Greek peninsulas, or perhaps they are merely less well known there. Away to the south and east of the Mediterranean, there are further rich and important areas of Middle Palaeolithic settlement, though we cannot go into details of them here. Not surprisingly, there is a great deal of variation between individual Mousterian industries over this vast area of the Old World. Yet a certain technological unity underlies it all, and there are surprisingly narrow limits to the over-all typological range. The common features include: (a) specialization in regular and standardized flake-tool forms, often finely made, different kinds of scrapers being particularly common; (b) a general rarity of bifacial tool forms, except in individual industries belonging to certain facies; (c) consistent methods of basic flake production for tool manu-facture, using 'prepared core' techniques, especially those based on 'disc cores'[2] and on Levalloisian cores (both the 'tortoise' and flake-blade types). There are other consistent features about the Mousterian, connected with economy and settle-ment – for example, the intensive use of caves wherever they were available, though open sites with artificial dwelling structures are also known. 'Cultural' features, if one may use the term, like care in disposal of the dead, may also be significant in this respect. Although formal burials remain rare overall by comparison with the number of Mousterian sites, yet they turn up in the Mousterian of widely scattered areas – Uzbekistan, Israel, Iraq, the Crimea, Italy, south-west France, for example – after having been quite unknown in the Lower Palaeolithic. The association of the Mousterian with Neanderthal Man in widely dispersed areas may also count as a unifying feature to some extent, though as already indicated we must not jump to the conclusion that only he made Mousterian industries or that he never made anything else.

There is, then, an underlying unity that makes it possible for us to refer to 'the Mousterian' over such a large area. The variability of Mousterian industries is perhaps an easier matter to describe

or at least to quantify, most of it inevitably depending on the classification of stone tools. One may fairly expect variation of both a chronological and a geographical nature. Is not an industry from an open site of the Russian steppe lands likely to differ from one found in a cave in the close lime-stone country of southern France? Is an industry of Late Riss age likely to be just the same technologically as one of the mid-Würm on the threshold of the Upper Palaeolithic, perhaps almost a hundred thousand years younger? Varia-bility of these kinds can indeed be seen, and is implied for example when some authors draw a distinction between 'West' and 'East' Mousterian (cf. McBurney 1950), or when our French col-leagues assign to particular industries such labels as 'Moustérien très évolué' or 'Moustérien de type Ferrassie archaïque'. However, many prehistorians now lay greater emphasis on other kinds of varia-tion, that which occurs between industries found in the same region and believed to be precisely or approximately contemporary – that is, in situations where geographical factors and time trends ought not to be admissible as causes of the observable differences. The classic case study for such local variability involves the Périgord region of south-west France. We must not here get too deeply drawn into this particular controversy, but some of the basic facts are important to us, and the clash of views has proved stimulating for Palaeolithic studies in general.

In south-west France, the work of M. Bourgon and especially of F. Bordes (referred to in note 10 in the preceding chapter) has defined several facies of Mousterian. The differences between them were originally expressed as shifts of emphasis and presences and absences over a standard list of care-fully defined Mousterian tool-types, together with the preferential use of particular flaking tech-niques. The differences were observed objectively and were carefully quantified for each Mousterian industry, the presence, absence and percentage value of each tool-type being noted, 'cumulative graphs' based on the results being drawn up (cf. Fig. 1:4a) and various typological and techno-logical indices being calculated. These various procedures have become standardized and welded together into the well-worn analytical method which has become known to its many users as the *'système Bordes'*. Whatever may be the personal reservations of individual analysts over attributions by their colleagues of particular tools to particular classes, there is no doubt that the system works, when operated by trained observers, at least to the extent of demonstrating that consistently different

TABLE 19 : *Mousterian variants in south-west France* (according to F. Bordes)

Mousterian facies	Some aspects of the tool-kit
Charentien (sensu lato) *group:*	
(a) *type Ferrassie*	Many side-scrapers (*racloirs*); few transverse scrapers; Levalloisian technique frequent
(b) *type Quina*	Many sidescrapers, including special 'Quina' forms; many transverse scrapers; Levalloisian technique rare
Moustérien à denticulés	Sidescrapers rare and poorly made; very high proportion of denticulate and notched flakes
Moustérien de Tradition Acheuléenne (often abbreviated to *MTA*)	
(a) *Type A*	Handaxes always present and sometimes frequent; backed knives, some denticulates and various scraper forms
(b) *Type B*	Handaxes fewer and less well made than in Type A. Many denticulates and backed knives; an important component of 'Upper Palaeolithic' tool-types: burins, awls, retouched blades, etc.
Moustérien typique	Moderate percentage of sidescrapers; a little of almost everything, in rather variable proportions

facies of Mousterian really do exist in south-west France. Bordes accordingly recognizes in the Périgord region the major variants shown in Table 19.

Only a first indication has been provided here of the differences between these variants, and more information can readily be gathered from the writings of Bordes (e.g. Bordes and de Sonneville-Bordes 1970; Mellars 1969, 1970) and many others. Probably enough information has been given however to indicate the reality and nature of the differences, and to show that an explanation of them is certainly required. Professor Bordes allows that within the MTA, Type B develops from Type A. His MTA Type B is a Middle Palaeolithic right on the threshold of Upper Palaeolithic status, and many prehistorians now accept the view, long held by Bordes and others, that in south-west France the basal Upper Palaeolithic (Lower Perigordian or Châtelperronian) develops locally directly out of the final Mousterian, without external influences. But for the other Mousterian variants, Bordes takes the view that they were essentially contemporary over a long period of time, being made by different cultures or tribes — ethnographically distinct groups, anyhow — who shared the same territory but kept their own identities and traditions, not much influencing each other. For other authors, particularly L.R. Binford (1973; Binford and Binford 1966), the observable differences between the stone tool industries are more likely to reflect functional considerations, i.e. the industries differ because the human groups who made them were carrying out quite different activities, whether in similar or different circumstances. Yet others, notably P.A. Mellars (1969, 1970), see at least some of the differences between the industries as reflecting consistent time-trends and regular stylistic differences. In the area under discussion, south-west France, the proponents of each of these views can argue their case in great detail because there are so many superb stratified sites available, with long successions of Mousterian occupation. Combe Grenal, with no less than fifty-five Mousterian levels, is merely the most remarkable. The interpretive controversy remains unsettled, and need not concern us too closely. The present writer has no doubt that each of the opposing camps (whose views are of course much oversimplified in the summary given here) has at least some right on its side, and that a distillation or blending of their opinions is required; also, an extensive programme of high magnification microwear analysis could perhaps solve some of the problems, though it has not been attempted yet.

For our purposes here it is perhaps more useful to note that when we pass beyond the Périgord and the immediately adjacent regions, we find that changes become necessary in the list of Mousterian facies set out above. Thus in *le Midi Méditerranéen*, H. de Lumley distinguishes more than a dozen different local versions of the *Moustérien typique* in the period Würm I-III, all of them *riches en racloirs*, let alone other kinds of *Moustérien typique*, and local versions of some of the other facies, such as *Charentien de type Ferrassie orientale*; MTA, on the other hand, is absent in the forms seen in the Périgord, though there are industries of Last Interglacial age which combine features of the Acheulian and the Mousterian (1969, 1971; for a summary, see 1971: 358-63). In the north of France, however (Bordes 1954; Tuffreau 1971a, 1976a, b, c; Callow 1976), MTA is relatively common, and some of it at least dates from very early in the Last Glaciation, the industries occurring at the base of the Younger Loess I — at Marcoing or le Tillet (*série café au lait*), for example. But by no means all of the Mousterian variants from the south-west are represented here, or indeed in Belgium, where cave sites have yielded a number of Mousterian industries including MTA and also some signs of 'East Mousterian' more in the manner of some of the German and Central European sites (Ulrix-Closset 1975).

The analysis of almost all the best published French Mousterian occurrences has proceeded according to the *système Bordes*, and some industries outside France have also been studied in this way, so that there is beginning to be a reasonable objective basis for assertions that such and such variants are present or absent in particular areas, always assuming that the different analysts have been reasonably consistent in their classifications over the basic type list.

BRITAIN IN THE MIDDLE PALAEOLITHIC

However, the *système Bordes* has not yet been formally used on British Mousterian occurrences. It is by nature best applicable to large unified samples from carefully excavated sites, and the British material is simply not of that quality, or even of suitable quantity, if it comes to that. We must therefore survey the British Middle Palaeolithic against the background of the brief summary just given of the Continental material, and we must do it informally. It appears that the British Mousterian proper consists almost entirely of MTA industries, or remnants of them, and that there is no sign at all of the elegant Charentian variants (Quina or Ferrassie) in their fully developed form, or of the much less elegant but equally interesting Denticulate Mousterian. Whether or not the Typical Mousterian may be represented in Britain is less clear, since that facies contains a considerable mixture of types, so that some of the stray finds could as well belong to the Typical Mousterian as to the MTA, we may suppose. It can, however, certainly be said that there is in Britain no large industry which certainly belongs to the Typical Mousterian as that term would be understood in France. Also, there is no 'East Mousterian' industry in Britain — just as well, perhaps, since Britain is at the extreme west end of Europe, though in fact there is no reason why human groups of eastern origin should not occasionally have made their way westward across the North European plain and so have come to Britain as indeed they seem to have come to Belgium.[3] The actual nature of the British Mousterian thus seems to be perfectly in keeping with that of the northern parts of France, though the occupation of Britain was evidently even more restricted in both quantity and variety. That is just what one would expect at this extreme edge of the Mousterian world. To the few British examples of actual MTA industries, we can add, under the heading of Middle Palaeolithic, the later British 'Levalloisian industries' already reviewed, at least one occurrence of 'proto-Mousterian' or archaic Mousterian, and a fairly long list of stray finds of typical *bout coupé* handaxes, most of them actually undated though arguably of Mousterian

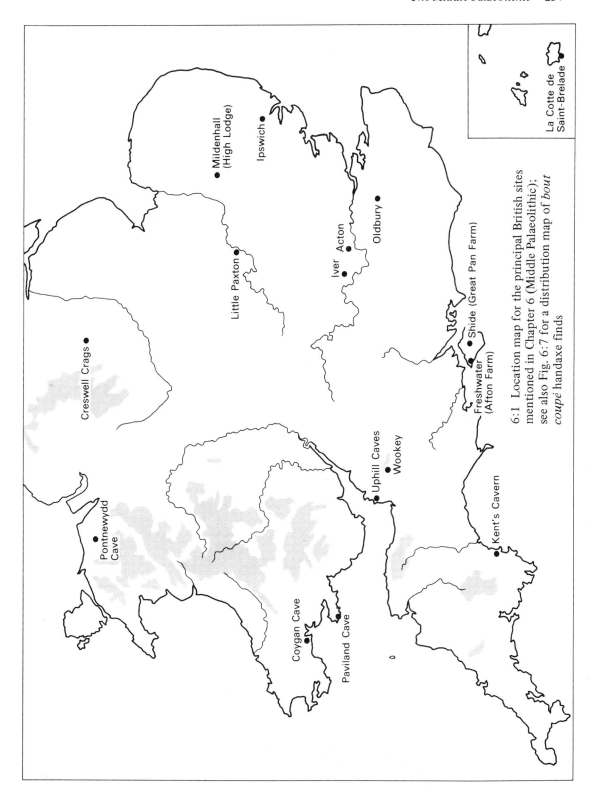

6:1 Location map for the principal British sites mentioned in Chapter 6 (Middle Palaeolithic); see also Fig. 6:7 for a distribution map of *bout coupé* handaxe finds

origin. Some of these British Middle Palaeolithic sites have already been considered in the preceding chapter, but a number of new names can be added. A location map for the main sites discussed is given in Fig. 6:1.

'Proto-' or 'Archaic' Mousterian

Under this heading, we are mainly concerned with the site of *High Lodge, Mildenhall*, Suffolk, already discussed on pages 188-9. It will be recalled that lake-margin sediments, apparently of Wolstonian Interstadial age, yielded two flake industries, a lower rather crude one and an upper one with elegant and finely made flake-tools (the 'classic flake industry of High Lodge'); above these came an ovate handaxe industry of our Group VII, in a soliflucted gravel. It will also be recalled that a definitive report on the two flake industries is still awaited, but even so the older accounts of the fine flake-tools from the younger of the two (Fig. 6:2) makes it clear that many of them resemble some of the best Charentian Mousterian scrapers, with the exception that most are made from flakes with plain striking platforms which do not seem to have been struck from prepared cores (disc or Levalloisian). This situation has led various Continental authors to refer to the High Lodge industry as 'proto-Mousterian' or even 'proto-Charentian'. The dating, inter-Wolstonian, is interesting, and probably corresponds broadly to some at least of the Continental 'Rissian' industries to which similar titles have been given. Examples of these include La Micoque, Dordogne, levels 3 and 4 (Bourgon 1957); Fontéchevade, Charente, Level E (Henri-Martin 1957); the Rissian levels at Baume Bonne, Baume des Peyrards and Grotte de Rigabe, all in Provence (de Lumley 1969a and see also summary in de Lumley 1971:353-6); Achenheim, Alsace, various horizons in the Older Loess complex (Wernert 1957); and perhaps also Grotte du Lazeret, Nice, Alpes Maritimes — some of the material from the Rissian levels as well as the 'pre-Mousterian' industry of Riss-Würm age (de Lumley 1969a, b). McBurney and Callow have also made some brief but useful comments on these lines (1971: 197-203); nor should we forget, in considering the affinities of the High Lodge

artefacts, the Upper Industry at Hoxne, or Stoke Newington, both discussed in the previous chapter. While no one would wish to imply that these occurrences are all precisely similar, and while distinctions have been drawn between 'Tayacian', 'proto-Quina' and 'proto-Ferrassie' industries amongst them, they have in common the presence of flake-tools very much in the Mousterian manner, relatively simple technology and surprisingly early dating. They certainly stand out from the typical Middle or later Acheulian industries with which they are broadly contemporary. The illustrated pieces from High Lodge (Fig. 6:2) should make these points clear. The High Lodge classic flake industry, then, may very well be one of those which contributed to the nature of the true Charentian, though the fully fledged version, which in France is of Würmian age, never came back to Britain. Of the unpublished older flake industry at High Lodge we can say nothing useful here, but its dating appears also to be inter-Wolstonian. Whether we should regard it as a Middle Palaeolithic occurrence is uncertain, and so is its significance; whether there might be any connection between it and the Clactonian-style part of such mixed occurrences as Grovelands, Southacre or Botany Pit, Purfleet, all mentioned in the previous chapter, remains a matter for speculation.

At this stage, mention must also be made of *La Cotte de Saint-Brelade*, Jersey, Channel Isles. This site has a long history of excavation beginning in the 1890s (Marett 1911a, b, 1916; Burdo 1960), and a long campaign is currently in progress by a team from Cambridge University directed by C.B.M. McBurney (Plate 32). A preliminary report (McBurney and Callow 1971) has appeared, giving

---

6:2 Flake tools from the 'classic flake industry' of High Lodge, Mildenhall, after R.A. Smith (1931). Note the high quality of the retouch, and that the platforms, where shown, are plain or only simply faceted. Nos 1-4, 13, scrapers with carefully made convex edges; nos 5-7, steeply retouched limaces or limace-like tools; nos 8, 9, 11, end-scrapers; no. 10, end-scraper and double side-scraper; nos 12, 14, double convergent sidescrapers

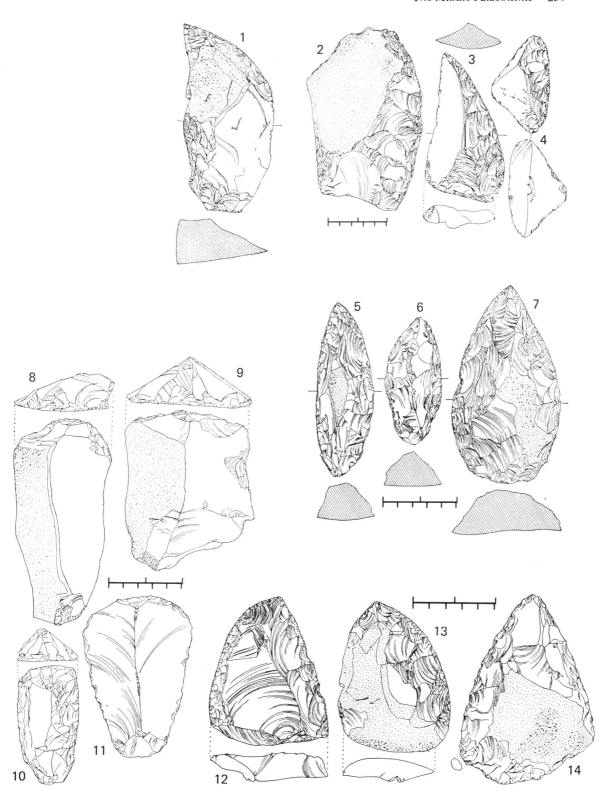

some useful information on McBurney's many seasons' work, and the site is a very rich and important one. Indeed, there are several times as many Mousterian artefacts from La Cotte as have ever been recorded from the whole of the rest of Britain together. There is also a complex and interesting stratigraphic succession, with various cave sediments, loesses and a raised beach at the base. In some levels animal bones have been preserved, though usually in a very fragile state, and these include two very remarkable heaps of mammoth and rhinoceros remains, while a number of human teeth attributed to *Homo sapiens neanderthalensis* were found as long ago as 1910. McBurney's work has radically altered and updated the conclusions of the earlier workers at the site and little can be said about the full archaeological sequence at La Cotte until more of his results have been published, but the present writer has another reason for devoting only limited space to such a major site: quite simply, it is far more a part of the French Palaeolithic than the British. Modern history and circumstances may have attached Jersey to Britain, but it is hard to see any valid link in the Upper Pleistocene: access can only have been from the French side during a time of lowered sea-level, and it follows that the human groups who made that journey were of western French origin. There is no reason to suppose that they ever set foot in what is now Britain, or that there should be much real connection between their industries and those of southern England. There is no certain indication that the temporary land bridge from France to the Channel Islands continued across the Channel itself to Britain.

We must, however, note a few of the facts which have been established at La Cotte. First, it is quite clear that the lower part of the sequence is of 'Rissian' age (in French terms) — broadly contemporary with High Lodge, we may assume. In the first place, access to Jersey would have had to be during a time of reduced sea-level, within a glacial complex, and second, these lower archaeological levels have been truncated by erosion forming a small cliff, at the base of which lies a raised beach at 8 metres O.D., of Last Interglacial age; that is to say, the archaeological levels in question must be *older* than the Last Interglacial.

Incidentally, there is no source of flint on Jersey itself, and the abundant flint used by the population at this time must have come from flint-bearing deposits now covered by the sea. McBurney has noted interesting changes in both the raw materials used and in the technology and typology of the industries of the post-Rissian levels, covering the period when the sea-level rose during the interglacial and Jersey became an island.

As for the lower levels themselves, it is hard to call the rich industries in them anything but Mousterian. Eleven separate superimposed concentrations of artefacts can be distinguished. A few handaxes certainly occur, and at least one flake cleaver, but the main body of material consists of flake-tools made on blanks of which a high proportion were obtained by use of prepared core technique, disc cores rather than Levalloisian cores. There are some unusual features, including a few pieces of a 'plano-convex' nature which would not be out of place in the East Mousterian, but we must await a proper analysis of the whole tool-kit before making formal comparisons. It is clear enough, however, that there is no substantial parallel in Britain for the La Cotte occurrence in technological terms, nor alas for its richness as a Mousterian site. High Lodge must count as the nearest, but there are certainly differences: we must not however forget that La Cotte is a cave site not far from the contemporary coast, while High Lodge was an inland open site on the shore of a lake. The resource situations must have differed considerably, and the human activities also. What the best French parallels for the Rissian levels at La Cotte may be is for others to say in due course, but the obvious candidates would include the sites mentioned during the discussion of High Lodge in this chapter.[4]

MTA in Britain

Two of the principal British MTA sites were discussed in the previous chapter — *Oldbury* and *Great Pan Farm* — because the writer used them in his study of the British handaxe groups (1967, 1968a). Other industries that we may ascribe to the Mousterian of Acheulian Tradition were mentioned or discussed in the account of the

Levalloisian, notably *Little Paxton* and *Ipswich* (*Bramford Road*). This ground need not be covered again, though we should recall the dating, which was probably Late Ipswichian at Pan Farm (Fig. 6:3) and earlier Devensian at the others. There are no other clear examples of prolific comparable sites in Britain, though the term 'industry' can just about be applied to a few, mainly in caves. There are also various isolated finds of typical *bout coupé* handaxes to be noted.

The most informative of the other Mousterian occurrences, then, are those from a few of the British caves, mainly old finds unfortunately. *Kent's Cavern*, Torquay, is (or was) probably the best of them. The superb but tragically ill-documented sequence from this cave system has

already been referred to several times and the archaic handaxe industry from it was discussed at some length in Chapter 3. The deposit now under consideration is the Loamy Cave Earth (A2), at the base of which, it will be recalled, some of the archaic implements were found, displaced from the B1 breccia along with some faunal remains and fragments of the breccia itself. According to Campbell and Sampson (1971: 23-4), Pengelly himself recorded about a thousand artefacts from this cave earth deposit; other workers also obtained material. In the cave earth Middle Palaeolithic artefacts occurred deep in the deposit, which has a maximum thickness of 30 feet where it fills deep hollows, and Earlier Upper Palaeolithic is found at a higher level, towards the top of the same deposit.

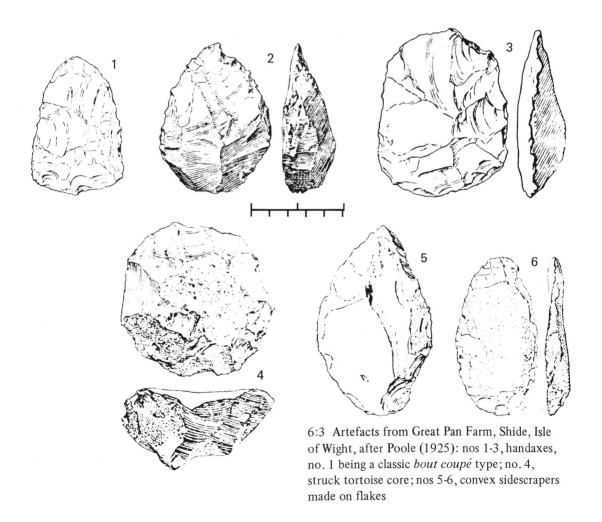

6:3 Artefacts from Great Pan Farm, Shide, Isle of Wight, after Poole (1925): nos 1-3, handaxes, no. 1 being a classic *bout coupé* type; no. 4, struck tortoise core; nos 5-6, convex sidescrapers made on flakes

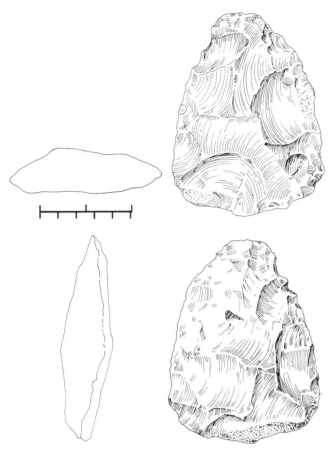

The loamy cave earth is overlain conformably by a stonier facies of cave earth (B2), in which a Later Upper Palaeolithic industry of very late Pleistocene age occurs. It seems possible that Pengelly's thousand or so artefacts from the loamy cave earth may include both the Mousterian and the Earlier Upper Palaeolithic, but Campbell (*op. cit.*) was only able to trace 33 of the former and 123 of the latter, so only about 15 per cent of Pengelly's original quantity survives and we cannot assume that we actually have more than a hint of the nature of the Mousterian industry. Campbell and Sampson list the following twenty-six finished implements amongst a sample of forty-five Mousterian artefacts which they classified, i.e. the thirty-three from the material obtained by Pengelly, plus a further twelve recovered by Ogilvie and others more than half a century later, whose provenance in the Mousterian levels seemed reliably established:

Handaxes (cordiform and *bout coupé* types)	5
Side-scrapers	7
Endscrapers or saws	2
Saws	3
Awls	7
Burin	1
Retouched flake fragment	1

They also noted various other pieces of Mousterian aspect, including three more handaxes, whose provenance was not satisfactorily enough known (*op. cit.*, p. 35). Two of the Kent's Cavern Mousterian handaxes are illustrated in Fig. 6:4. The fauna of the cave earth is predominantly cold,

6:4 Two Mousterian *bout coupé* handaxes from Kent's Cavern, Torquay, Devon, drawn for the author by Mrs D. Timms

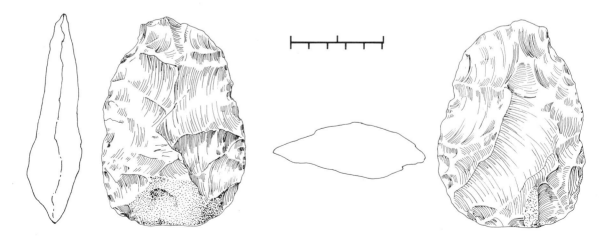

and of Devensian character, with mammoth, reindeer, bear and woolly rhinoceros, but how long a period the deposit represents, how far apart in time the Mousterian and Early Upper Palaeolithic occupations within it may lie, and whether there was more than a single horizon of either, are simply not known. In all the circumstances it would be both meaningless and misleading to set out the figures given above as percentages.

In passing at this point we should note that there also appears to have been Mousterian material at the famous *Windmill Cave, Brixham*, the site which was a test case in the mid-nineteenth-century debate on the antiquity of man (see Chapter 1). A fine *bout coupé* handaxe from here is now in Torquay Museum. Not all the original finds made by Pengelly appear to have survived, however.

The *Wookey Hole Caves* are in the Mendip Hills, Somerset: there are many caves in the Mendips, several of which have yielded Palaeolithic artefacts, notably those in the picturesque gorges of Cheddar, Burrington Combe and Wookey, all well known to tourists. It is the Later Upper Palaeolithic that is best represented overall; there is also some Earlier Upper Palaeolithic material, and Mousterian artefacts are the rarest. Wookey has produced the best of the latter, but there are also some more from one of the caves revealed in the sides of the *Uphill Quarry*, just south of Weston-super-Mare at the extreme west end of the Mendips.

At Wookey, the Mousterian artefacts come from two adjacent caves, known as the Hyaena Den and the Rhinoceros Hole, about 50 metres downstream from the famous Wookey Hole show cave. Tratman *et al.* (1971) have given a detailed account of the work done at the Hyaena Den intermittently over more than a century (from the 1850s). The deposits in this cave were unfortunately almost wholly cleaned out by Boyd Dawkins and other diggers in the nineteenth century; a patient and difficult campaign by Professor E.K. Tratman and members of the University of Bristol Spelaeological Society in 1966-70 failed to find more than a trace of *in situ* deposits, and no artefacts were obtained. Tratman, Donovan and Campbell have searched the litera-

ture and the extant collections and done all they can to collect evidence (*op. cit.*), but it is really only on typological grounds that they can suggest the presence at the site of at least one Mousterian level (Fig. 6:5) overlain by at least one Earlier Upper Palaeolithic one – though there is no reason to doubt this conclusion. Excellent faunal remains were obtained in the early days of research at the cave, and the bulk of the fauna is evidently of Devensian age, as one would expect, though traces of *Dicerorhinus hemitoechus* have been taken to indicate that the lowest deposits may have been laid down before the end of the Ipswichian. Pollen and sedimentary samples taken by J.B. Campbell from such undisturbed sections as were seen gave results which agreed with the faunal evidence. As for the Mousterian industry, Tratman and his co-authors concluded that there was evidence for the presence of eleven 'bifaces and related forms', plus various biface trimming flakes, but not all these artefacts now survive. There is no certainty that any flake-tools of Mousterian age were ever found. One of the bifaces (*op. cit.*, fig. 43, no. 5 shown here as Fig. 6:5, no. 1) may be counted as a typical *bout coupé* form, and the others that have survived all fall within the class of small ovates and cordiforms, well within the usual MTA range. At the nearby Rhinoceros Hole excavations have recently been carried out by the University of Bristol Spelaeological Society, for whose *Proceedings* the late Professor Tratman was preparing a report at the time of his death. Only one Middle Palaeolithic implement was found – a tiny but classic *bout coupé* handaxe, briefly mentioned by R.A. Harrison (1977). There were also three small waste flakes, all clearly handaxe trimmers, and a small blade-like flake that may not belong with them, especially since one typical Early Upper Palaeolithic artefact was also found. Professor Tratman reported (pers. com.) that the handaxe came from a deposit which may well be of Ipswichian age, and further details will no doubt be available in due course. Another Wookey cave, the Badger Hole, yielded some Early Upper Palaeolithic material but no Mousterian artefacts.

As regards *Uphill*, quarrying over a long period has revealed parts of several caves and fissures, no less than thirteen; R.A. Harrison has recently

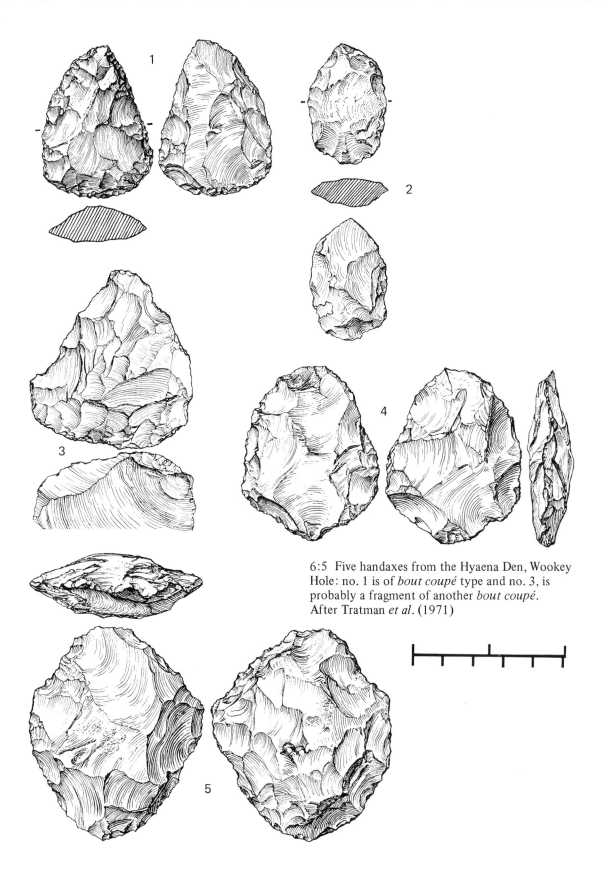

6:5 Five handaxes from the Hyaena Den, Wookey Hole: no. 1 is of *bout coupé* type and no. 3, is probably a fragment of another *bout coupé*. After Tratman *et al*. (1971)

gathered all the information he could about them into a useful summary report (1977) and has demonstrated clearly that both Middle and Upper Palaeolithic artefacts were present in one of them, his No. 8. Upper Pleistocene faunal remains were also recovered from this cave, and from some of the others, but the only archaeological material from the other Uphill caves seems to be post-Palaeolithic. The fauna of Uphill No. 8 is a typical Devensian assemblage, with mammoth, reindeer, woolly rhinoceros, bear, cave lion, spotted hyaena, horse, lemming and various other genera. Overall, as Harrison points out, it closely resembles the faunal assemblage from the Kent's Cavern Loamy Cave Earth A2. There seem to have been rather more than fifty stone artefacts of Palaeolithic age collected from Uphill at various times, apparently all from cave No. 8, including both implements and *débitage*: a few were destroyed at Bristol City Museum by enemy action during the Second World War, but most survive. Only the evidence of typology and technology enables us to distinguish the presence of two series, respectively Middle and Upper Palaeolithic; there are no useful details about the actual occupation horizons from which they came. Harrison attributes (*op. cit.*) the following to the Mousterian occupation of the cave: 1 small sub-triangular chert handaxe, approaching the *bout coupé* form and rather like some of the handaxes from the Hyaena Den at Wookey; 1 Mousterian point made unifacially on a large chert flake; 2 bifacially worked pieces, probably fragments of handaxes; 1 naturally-backed knife; 2 trimming flakes from handaxe manufacture; 3 miscellaneous retouched flakes, classifiable as scrapers (probably belonging to this group). Little can be made of such a sparse assemblage, but in their small size and general nature these artefacts seem to resemble those from Wookey well enough; indeed, one might be tempted to guess that Mousterian man visited the Mendips only once, and that briefly, were it not for the suggestion that the single handaxe from the Rhinoceros Hole is of Ipswichian age while the other two small series seem more likely to belong within the Devensian. However the precise provenances of all the old finds are not known with any proper degree of certainty. It is certainly worth

observing that the Mendip Mousterian handaxes are all small, and some of them bear evidence of reworking, as if flint and chert were in short supply for their makers who accordingly used the same implements for as long as possible.

Another group of caves of importance to the British Palaeolithic exists at *Creswell Crags* in Derbyshire; from here comes the name 'Creswellian', which has long been used for the principal facies of the British Later Upper Palaeolithic, dating from the close of the Devensian. The Creswell caves have also yielded a certain amount of Earlier Upper Palaeolithic material and a small amount of Mousterian, not to mention some Mesolithic and later period artefacts. Since the caves are obvious and easily accessible, it is hardly surprising that, like those of Wookey, they have a long history of excavation and research, not to mention plunder, much of it dating from the bad old days of the late nineteenth and early twentieth centuries. During this period large quantities of their fillings were dug away, with little care, by J. Magens Mello, Boyd Dawkins and others. The work of A.L. Armstrong, especially in the 1920s and 1930s, was of somewhat better quality, but is none too easy to assess from the published accounts of it or to reconcile with the surviving material. Attempts to salvage some information and to check and update the conclusions reached by those already mentioned have been made in the late 1950s, the 1960s and 1970s by C.B.M. McBurney, J.B. Campbell, S.N. Collcutt and a few others, but their achievements relate almost entirely to the Upper Palaeolithic and Mesolithic periods and so only marginally concern us here. The quantity, distribution and dating of the Mousterian of Creswell Crags thus remains extremely uncertain.

There are several caves at Creswell, the most important being Pin Hole, Church Hole, Robin Hood's Cave and Mother Grundy's Parlour. At one time or another, Mousterian material, or what sounds like it from the descriptions given, seems to have been claimed from all of these, but it can only be confirmed at *Pin Hole* (Plate 33a) and *Robin Hood's Cave*, so far as the present writer is personally aware. From Robin Hood's Cave, various artefacts of quartzite and ironstone, together with some rather dubious fragments of the same rocks, survive, notably at the British Museum and at Derby Museum. The status of most is doubtful, but there are at least two good small ovate handaxes (at Derby Museum) which are unlikely to be anything other than Mousterian, though certainly not of classic *bout coupé* form. In his excavations at this site in 1969, John Campbell (1969: 50) recovered a fragment of another generally similar handaxe, of flint this time, 'and other middle palaeolithic tools' from the spoil heap of one of the early excavations, where his own trench cut through it. P.A. Mellars illustrates a crudely made handaxe and a typical enough disc core from Robin Hood's Cave (1974: 63, Fig. 5, nos 4-5). As for Pin Hole, Armstrong dug here over many years and published various short accounts (e.g. 1931, 1933, 1939), which Zeuner has summarized (1958: 198-203), but there has never been a major monograph on the site. There was evidently a good sequence here, with Mousterian and two phases of Upper Palaeolithic (the usual Earlier and Later British variants). Armstrong claimed three stratigraphically distinct Mousterian horizons, of which the oldest was in a cave earth which he interpreted as formed in moderately warm conditions, possibly before the end of the Ipswichian, while the other two were evidently of Devensian age. This sounds all very well, but the finds were never described or even listed in proper detail, and the present writer has not himself seen them in any Museum collection (though that is not to say that they have not survived). Armstrong's terminology was also somewhat old-fashioned, and the upshot is that no clear statement of the Pin Hole Mousterian can be offered here. Armstrong referred to handaxes and rough flake-tools, and it certainly sounds as if Mousterian artefacts were present at the site. Subsequent authors seem to have accepted this, though they have not really elaborated it (e.g. Zeuner, *loc. cit.*; Mellars 1974: 65. The latter author also illustrates a Mousterian point from Pin Hole, his Fig. 5, no. 3).

There are also a few caves in Wales which have produced Middle Palaeolithic material, though once again few useful details are available. Two fine *bout coupé* handaxes were obtained in excava-

tions at the *Coygan Cave*, Laugharne, by C.B.M. McBurney, with other indications of Mousterian occupation, but this work remains unpublished beyond a passing mention by McBurney in Foster and Daniel (1965: 23) and a photograph of the two handaxes in the *Annual Report of the National Museum of Wales* for 1972-3 (facing p. 33; see also p. 16). The *Paviland Cave*, properly known as *Goat Hole Cavern*, in Gower, has produced some very interesting and important Upper Palaeolithic material, mostly a very long while ago, including Buckland's famous 'Red Lady' burial as long ago as 1823, and numerous artefacts obtained by W.J. Sollas early this century. One large retouched chert flake from here has been claimed as Middle Palaeolithic (Grimes 1939: 2-3; Lacaille 1954b), but even if this assessment is correct there does not appear to be a substantial Mousterian industry at this site, though one might have expected it to have been occupied by the group that reached the Coygan Cave. In passing, we may also note an apparent Mousterian point, made on a Levalloisian flake, which was a stray and isolated find at *Chepstow*, Gwent, recorded by Savory (1961). South Wales, then, should be included in the British Mousterian distribution, but no solid information is currently available about the dating or nature of the occupation.

Further north, at Cefn, near St Asaph, in Clwyd, the *Pontnewydd* (or *Bontnewydd*) *Cave* (Plate 33b) has been known and occasionally mentioned in the literature since the 1870s (Hughes 1874, 1887; Boyd Dawkins 1880). There is no detailed up to date account of the stratigraphy (see however Molleson 1976), but some at least of the original artefacts, including handaxes, have survived (Plate 34). There are various points of interest about this occurrence and new excavations were begun at the site in 1978 under the direction of Dr Stephen Green. First, the implements are mostly made of a local rock, a felstone, with only a little use of chert and this has certainly influenced their typology and lent an appearance of crudeness to their workmanship. There are no classic *bout coupé* forms, and the handaxes are squat, rather irregular and thick, being pyriform to cordiform in shape. They could be older than Mousterian if one were to argue typologically, of

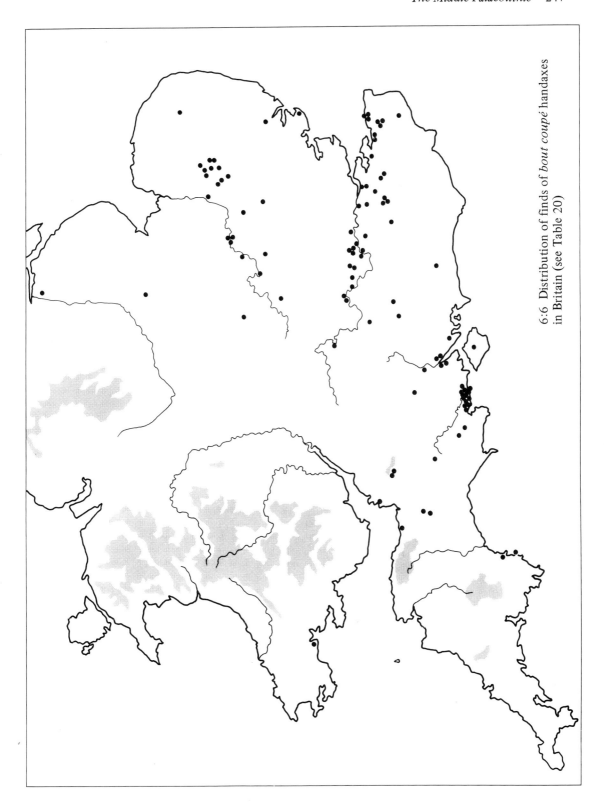

6:6 Distribution of finds of *bout coupé* handaxes in Britain (see Table 20)

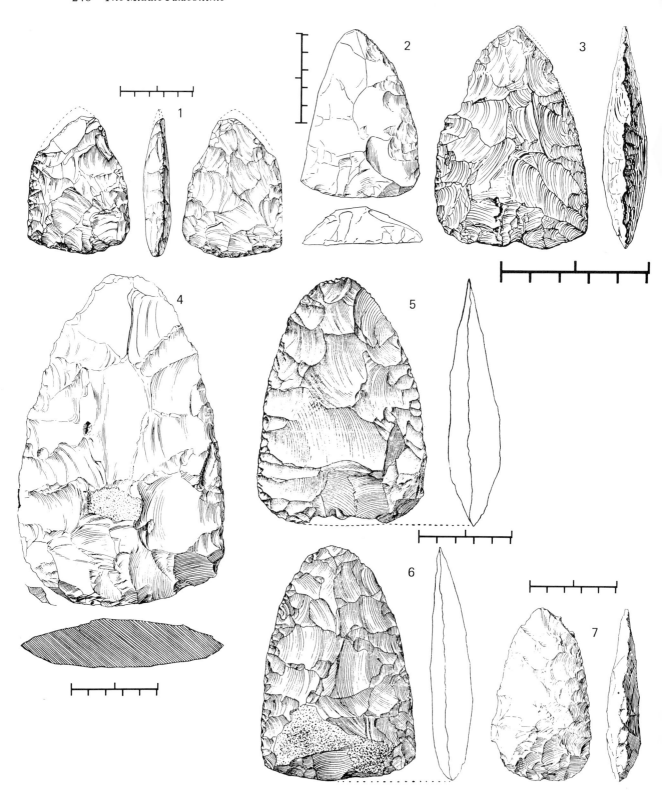

course. They would be somewhat isolated from the remaining distribution of the British Acheulian, but, to be fair, they are just as peripheral to the Mousterian distribution too. A heavy disc-like core of felstone is present – Mousterian-looking, certainly, though hardly conclusive in itself. Hughes (1887: 116 and Plate IX) lists and illustrates eight artefacts, which he describes as 'the principal types of implements found in Pontnewydd Cave': four felstone handaxes, the felstone core already mentioned, and a roughly retouched felstone 'scraper', plus a chert flake and a flint flake. The two latter might well be handaxe trimmers. The existence of other artefacts is implied in this and other of the early sources, but no definite and reliable total ever seems to have been given. The present writer, in the course of compiling his Palaeolithic Gazetteer, saw four handaxes, one core, nine retouched flakes, thirteen unretouched flakes and one Levalloisian flake from this site, most of which were at that time on loan for study at the Department of Archaeology in Cambridge. On balance, the Pontnewydd material seems perfectly acceptable as a small Middle Palaeolithic assemblage, presumably a local version of MTA influenced morphologically by its makers' dependence on the tough felstone as their main raw material. The industry's chronological position is vague. Faunal remains were fairly abundant, and included *Hippopotamus amphibius*, *Dicerorhinus hemitoechus* and *Elephas (Palaeodoxodon) antiquus*, as well as 'colder' species; it seems that an Ipswichian element is included. However, the bones are in a poor state, many being worn and abraded, quite apart from showing damage caused by carnivores. It seems highly doubtful that they are all contemporary

6:7 Some British *bout coupé* handaxes: 1, Marlow brickyard, after Wymer (1968); 2, Taplow, after R.A. Smith (1915b); 3, Sherborne Cemetery, after Arkell (1947); 4, Tilbury, after R.A. Smith (1915b); 5, Bournemouth (Castle Lane), after Calkin and Green (1949); 6, Bournemouth (Southbourne Broadway), *ibid*.; 7, Southampton (Rockstone Place), after R.A. Smith (1915b). For details, see Table 20

with the artefacts; if they are, however, we may recall a number of indications in this chapter and the previous one that MTA industries may have been present in Britain before the end of the Ipswichian (Great Pan Farm, Rhinoceros Hole, Iver Lower Brickearth, etc.). Lastly, we should note the reports that a single human molar tooth, large and evidently of rather archaic appearance, was recovered at Pontnewydd in the early days of the cave's exploration, though where it is now is regrettably not known (see Molleson 1976). Given the extreme rarity of Pleistocene hominid remains in Britain, and the possibility of an Ipswichian age for this specimen, the loss is a sad one. There is in fact no extant British hominid skeletal material at all of Middle Palaeolithic age, unless we count La Cotte de Saint-Brelade as part of the British Middle Palaeolithic. It certainly seems possible that the Pontnewydd cave, and any others in the area, might repay a new and careful research programme and the results of Dr Green's work will be eagerly awaited.

With Pontnewydd we end this account of cave occupations attributable to the British Middle Palaeolithic. Whether the Oldbury site in Kent was actually some kind of rock shelter at the time of its occupation in Middle Palaeolithic times seems undecided; certainly it is not one now, but the stony deposit which contained the artefacts may incorporate rock fragments that came from a contemporary overhang (cf. Collins and Collins 1970: 158, 174). However, we have not reached the end of the list of British Mousterian sites, because there are open sites to be considered. Some we have already mentioned, for example Bramford Road, Ipswich, Little Paxton, Dr Myra Shackley's finds on the south Hampshire coast, and the Pan Farm site in the Isle of Wight. In connection with the latter, it is perhaps worth mentioning a small and little known assemblage from a gravel pit at Afton Farm, Freshwater, Isle of Wight, now in the British Museum, which includes a couple of handaxes (not of *bout coupé* form but within the Mousterian range of ovate and cordiform shapes), five Levalloisian cores, two Levalloisian flakes and nineteen flake-tools or retouched flakes. Stone heaps at Freshwater, believed to have been brought from the same gravel pit, yielded five more Levalloisian flakes and eight more retouched flakes plus two other cores. This material is not dated, but its existence may make the Pan Farm site seem a little less out on its own in the island.

It was also suggested in the previous chapter that some of the 'pure' Levalloisian occurrences may have a relationship with the British MTA, especially those like Iver and Creffield Road, Acton, where there are possible associations with *bout coupé* handaxes. These industries are surely in any case technologically Middle Palaeolithic, even if they are not unequivocally Mousterian in the sense of matching up with one of the known French Mousterian variants. It seems very likely that they are functionally specialized tool-kits, possibly related to hunting activities (cf. Chapter 7), but it does not seem possible to prove this assertion at present.

The *bout coupé* handaxes, so often mentioned, really are in their classic forms highly distinctive, as the illustrations in this chapter should make clear. Not all Mousterian handaxes are so distinctive, either in Britain or on the Continent, and it would be idle to pretend that there is no overlap between them and the Acheulian ovate range. Not so the *bout coupé* type, and if that view is accepted it follows that any classic *bout coupé* handaxe can plausibly be regarded as belonging to the MTA, even if it is an isolated and undated find.[5] Some authors have indeed expressed this view directly or indirectly, either on their own account or following the opinions expressed in the present writer's doctoral thesis (1967); they have referred in general terms to the scatter of such finds over southern Britain, sometimes adding a selective distribution map to show some of the published occurrences (e.g. Collins and Collins 1970: 159-74; Tratman *et al*. 1971: 264-7). The writer doubts however whether many workers in this field realize the full extent of this scatter (Map, Fig. 6:6), knowledge of which really depends on a fair acquaintance with unpublished museum and private collections all over Britain, and it therefore seems to him worth giving here a comprehensive list of the *bout coupé* finds which he recorded in assembling material for his doctoral thesis, with a few examples added which have come to light (or

come to his notice) since then. There must surely be others which have passed unsung into museum or private collections over the past ten years, and there are many private collections which he did not examine, so no claim is made that the list is complete. This list is given in Table 20 at the end of the present chapter, for convenience. As a catalogue of finds of British *bout coupé* handaxes, it is the first published attempt, so far as the writer knows, to gather that particular information together in any detail, though D. and A. Collins (1970), E.K. Tratman *et al*. (1971), P. Mellars (1974) and M. Shackley (1975; 1977) have gone some way towards indicating the frequency and distribution of such finds, and the present writer included a substantial list in his Ph.D. thesis (1967) which has been revised and expanded to provide the corpus of information given here in Table 20. It seemed worth devoting this much space to the *bout coupé* finds simply because they are so distinctive (Figs. 6:7, 6:8) and really do appear to group together within a relatively short period of time, so far as the evidence goes; without them, our notions of the British Mousterian would be rather short of the mark. Also, they offer the chance of another valuable link with the work of our Continental colleagues in the field of palaeolithic studies. The information in this corpus should however be regarded as an informal presentation, which could form the basis for a worthwhile research topic, in the course of which it would need to be presented in an altogether tighter manner. A selection of British *bout coupé* handaxes is illustrated in Figs 6:7 and 6:8. The present writer has not even set metrical limits for the *bout coupé* form, nor followed up the signs that distinctive variants exist within it. The subtriangular version and the broad almost rectangular form are obvious examples, and probably represent the extremes, but between them the range may not be continuous.[6] A more exhaustive search of museum registers and archives might extract a few more precious details about provenances and associations: the present writer, with so many museums to visit, could not devote as much time to each as he would have liked. Similarly, there will be additional *bout coupé* specimens to list. More could be said, too, about the technology

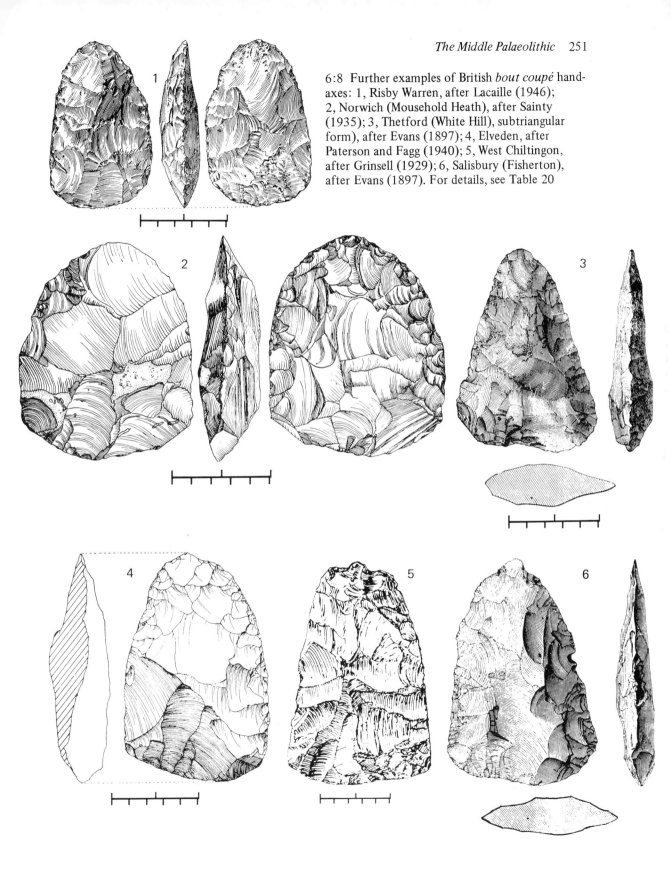

6:8 Further examples of British *bout coupé* hand-axes: 1, Risby Warren, after Lacaille (1946); 2, Norwich (Mousehold Heath), after Sainty (1935); 3, Thetford (White Hill), subtriangular form), after Evans (1897); 4, Elveden, after Paterson and Fagg (1940); 5, West Chiltingon, after Grinsell (1929); 6, Salisbury (Fisherton), after Evans (1897). For details, see Table 20

of these elegant handaxes: many possess neat 'tranchet' or similar finishes at the tip end, or have slightly twisted profiles, or show evidence of having been made from large flakes. Finally, the state of preservation of most of the *bout coupé* handaxes is excellent, and it may be that some of the unpatinated examples would yield microwear traces, if properly studied under high magnification. Which were the main working edges? To what use or uses were the implements put?

These matters await future research. What can be said meanwhile? Certain things stand out in the catalogue, vague though the information often is. These implements are clearly of relatively late date within the period with which we are concerned: apart from those from caves, they commonly occur in low terraces, in superficial deposits, in buried river channels or on the surface. The frequency of white or 'basket-work' patina reflects such environments, and so does the common occurrence of weathering. All this is in accord with such little evidence as there is for actual dating or for associated finds. It is no coincidence that, even with the stray finds, arguable examples of Middle Palaeolithic technology are often not far away, and this accords with the high technological standards of the *bout coupé* implements themselves. In short, it is the writer's firm opinion that these distinctive handaxes, regardless of the names that have been used for them in the earlier literature, are a record for us of the movements over southern Britain of Mousterian hunters and gatherers during, apparently, the close of the Ipswichian and the earlier parts of the Devensian. If this is so, then the over-all industry they represent must be an early version of the Mousterian of Acheulian Tradition, such as can also be seen in north France and perhaps (though less frequently) also in Germany and Belgium (Bosinski 1967, Ulrix-Closset 1975). Whether the increasing severity of the Last Glaciation in the north in due course drove the bearers of this industry out of Britain and so helped to provide the important much later version of MTA that can be seen in south-west France (cf. Mellars 1969) is not something that can be decided without a combined study of the British and Continental material, but it seems a tenable hypothesis for the moment.

Within Britain the *bout coupé* distribution is distinctly patchy (Fig. 6:6), with areas of relatively frequent finds, such as north Kent, south Hampshire, the central Great Ouse valley, and the London area, separated by blank areas. Within or near each concentration is to be found at least one substantial known or arguable Mousterian site: Oldbury, Acton, West Drayton, Little Paxton, Pan Farm, and so forth. In the furthermost areas to which they penetrated, the people who made these implements came (one might almost say 'at last') to such habitable caves as Britain can boast (Plate 33) — but when they did so, they also came to the limits of the distribution of abundant high quality flint and chert. Thus, in the Mendips, Devonshire, Derbyshire and Wales, the few Mousterian handaxes that survive are almost all poor and small specimens, which often show signs of reworking. Yet the occurrence of the classic *bout coupé* shapes amongst such material infallibly connects these sites with the stray finds of altogether finer-looking *bout coupé* handaxes in the very different terrain of central southern and southeastern England. The distribution of the occupied caves in itself demands migratory movements of people across southern Britain; of such movements, and doubtless too of more localized journeying around the principal sites, the stray *bout coupé* finds are striking evidence. Doubtless there are also handaxes of more generalized ovate or cordiform shape, and also stray Levalloisian flakes, in our collections, which these very same people also left behind, but for us these are less important because of their undoubted overlap, with Lower Palaeolithic technology and typology. The *bout coupé* handaxes, in the writer's opinion, have no such overlap.

If all this evidence is put together: the cave sites, the later Levalloisian sites, the Mousterian open sites like Great Pan Farm and Bramford Road, Ipswich, and the whole scatter of well over a hundred stray *bout coupé* finds, then the British Middle Palaeolithic begins at last to look like quite a tangible and even respectable episode. But it still remains impoverished, short-lived and indeed insignificant by Continental standards.

NOTES

1 Exactly what hominid types made which industries in the later Lower Palaeolithic and the Middle Palaeolithic, remains a vexed question. Without going into details, we may say that in Africa *Homo erectus* seems essentially a hand-axe maker; in south-east Asia, he is associated with non-Acheulian industries which have sometimes been described as belonging to a 'chopper-chopping-tool' or 'pebble tool' group. In Europe, the Heidelberg *Homo erectus* mandible had no associated artefacts, but recent discoveries at Bilzingsleben (DDR) are reported (Mania 1976) as showing *Homo erectus* remains associated with a remarkable, in part almost microlithic, industry of Holsteinian age (probably equivalent to our Hoxnian), with which it is hard to make comparisons before a detailed account is available. Some aspects of it may well come to be compared with the industry of Vértesszölös in Hungary (Kretzoi and Vértes 1965; Vértes 1965), where the hominid remains first reported as *Homo erectus* have since been reclassified by some authorities as *Homo sapiens palaeohungaricus*. On the other hand, the Swanscombe hominid, found with British Middle Acheulian artefacts and very probably (though not demonstrably) their maker, is also classed as *Homo sapiens*, and so is the hominid from Ehringsdorf, near Weimar, which occurred in an East Mousterian context of clearly Eemian age (Behm-Blancke 1960). Another important find from Petralona in Greece has not yet been reported in detail. There have also been some excellent discoveries recently in France, including those from Caune l'Arago (Tautavel), in the south-west, not far from the Pyrenees; the French, or some of them, are inclined to use the general term *Anténéanderthaliens* for their earlier hominids, and it will be some while before the status of the recent finds, in terms of the nomenclature used above, is generally agreed. Highly relevant to the present discussion would be the very recent find of hominid remains at Biâche-Saint-Vaast in northern France (in 1976), apparently associated with a prolific late Acheulian industry almost devoid of handaxes and rich in well-made flake-tools, but there is no information about the hominid at the time of writing (a report on the finds at Biâche, by A. Tuffreau, is in preparation). Time and the deliberations of experts may alter some of the assessments or assertions in this note, which does not set out to be comprehensive. The writer makes no claim to expertise in the highly specialized field of classifying fossil hominid remains, but it seems to him that there is beginning to be considerable and not unwelcome flexibility when it comes to correlating hominid types and Palaeolithic industries.

2 In this, the core is disc-shaped or hemispherical, and usable flakes are obtained from the flat upper surface, leaving a pattern of scars converging from the circumference towards the centre. Superficially this is not unlike the second stage of preparation of a Levalloisian 'tortoise core' (cf. pages 78-80), but in the latter case the flakes so removed are waste, while in the case of the disc core they are intended for use or retouch. The disc core technique is highly economical of flint, since, if proper attention is given to maintaining a flakeable angle right round the circumference, many usable flakes can be obtained before the core becomes too small to produce worthwhile ones; the tortoise core, it will be recalled, yields usually only one flake as end product. Flakes struck from a disc core show a relatively simple pattern of dorsal scars, and their striking platforms usually have only a few broad facets, unlike the multiple faceting of the typical Levalloisian platform (Fig. 3:9).

3 The 'East Mousterian' industries have various readily recognizable features (cf. McBurney 1950: 173-8), including, for example, a distinctive 'plano-convex' technique of retouch and the presence of a relatively high frequency, in many cases, of limace-like and leaf-shaped tools. At a few sites, notably Weimar-Ehringsdorf (Behm-Blancke 1960), there are East Mousterian industries which clearly date as early as the Eemian (Last Interglacial), so, in theory at least, groups using such tool-kits could have moved westward to Britain during the earlier Devensian, but there is no sign that they actually did so.

4 There is also a Mousterian occupation of Würmian age at La Cotte de Saint-Brelade in the upper series of deposits. Some impression of this can be gained from the earlier literature (e.g. Marett 1911a, 1911b: 203-9, 1916; Burdo 1960), but an up-to-date reassessment is required. Mousterian material is also known from another cave on Jersey, La Cotte à la Chèvre.

5 There is the risk of a circular argument here, of course. Those *bout coupé* handaxes which are dated all seem to be of late date — mostly Devensian, but with occasional late Ipswichian examples. Equally, there is no *bout coupé*

handaxe certainly belonging to a dated assemblage of artefacts of pre-Ipswichian date, and
none certainly forming part of any unequivocally Acheulian industry. So far, so good.
But the majority, as listed in this chapter, are
actually stray finds and undated, so that some
at least *could* presumably lie outside the time
range indicated by the dated finds, though the
present writer does not himself believe that this
is so, and the Continental evidence does not
seem to suggest it; there too, however, there are
undated occurrences. If we say of a British
stray find that it is a typical *bout coupé* handaxe and therefore it is of late date and MTA
origin, let it be clear that we do so only on the
basis of typology and technology — supported,
indeed, by a number of instances of such dating
and affinities for the type, but not backed by
certain and finite fact. This is a use that the
present writer is prepared to make of typology
and technology, but only on occasions when
the pieces concerned really do seem to be
distinctive. It is important therefore that the
list given in this chapter (Table 20) is firmly
based upon classic examples of the *bout coupé*
type. Dubious examples have either been
omitted altogether, or, if there are reasons for
mentioning them, the atypical features have
been noted. One must be prepared occasionally
to adopt such an approach, so that hypotheses
can be put forward. If future work demands
their replacement or modification, well and
good; they will have served their purpose.
Without them, how shall we bring order out
of chaos?

6 If the time range of the *bout coupé* handaxes
really is so short — though read note 5 again —
it is quite likely that only a few individual
makers were involved in producing the majority
of those which have survived. Is it too much to
hope that a detailed study of their technology
might yield hints of that situation?

APPENDIX

TABLE 20 : *British finds of* bout coupé *handaxes*

Site or find-spot	Details and source of information

BEDFORDSHIRE
Bedford
One sub-triangular *bout coupé* handaxe, now in
Wells Museum, Somerset. There are no further
details of the find-spot, but the implement is
marked as coming 'from Top Gravels' and has a
bluish-white patina

Site or find-spot	Details and source of information

Biggleswade: Gravel Pit
A fine large sub-triangular *bout coupé* handaxe is
now at the Cambridge University Museum, but
there are no further details of its discovery

BERKSHIRE
Sulhamstead Abbots: Abbots Pit
There is one *bout coupé* handaxe from here,
illustrated and referred to as Late Acheulian
'type N e/v' by Wymer (1968: 116 and Fig. 45,
no. 1). It is slightly twisted in profile and
somewhat abraded; the shape is not perfect, but
the implement seems to be a *bout coupé* rather
than an ovate. The pit where it was found is dug
mainly into gravel about 150 feet above the
present River Kennet. Wymer (*loc. cit.*) quotes
some earlier references

BUCKINGHAMSHIRE
Bourne End: New Road: 'Deesden'
One *bout coupé* handaxe, now in the Bucks
County Museum at Aylesbury, was found by Mr
G. Drewett while digging in his garden to construct
a septic tank. It is white-patinated and weathered,
and its profile has a suggestion of a twist. It is in
an entirely different condition from a rolled
roughly pointed handaxe which was found at the
same time. Wymer has recorded the find briefly
(1968: 213-14) and assigned the implement to his
type N
Fenny Stratford: Bow Brickhill Road
A typical *bout coupé* handaxe of broad shape
was found here in drainage digging in 1922, or
perhaps earlier, that being the date of its
presentation to the Bucks County Museum at
Aylesbury where it now is. It is slightly worn,
with a mottled patina on one face and no patina
on the other. It has been described and figured by
Miss L. Millard (1965). The tip end is somewhat
damaged
Iver: Mead's Bridge Pit (Fig. 5:50, no. 2)
One large '*bout coupé* cleaver' was found in the
lower (red) brickearth — see above, pages 218-20.
Several authors have mentioned or described it,
including Lacaille and Oakley (1936: 442-3 and
fig. 38). Note also their fig. 37, if checking this
reference: it shows a small cordiform handaxe not
very far from the *bout coupé* form, from the same
brickearth at Lavender's Pit, Mansion Lane, Iver;
note also the presence of Levalloisian artefacts in
this deposit
Marlow: Brickyard (Fig. 6:7, no. 1)
There are two classic *bout coupé* handaxes from
here, one now at the Bucks County Museum,

Site or find-spot	Details and source of information

Aylesbury, and one at the Oxford University Museum (Treacher Collection). In the latter collection there is also another handaxe with a well-made arch-like point, but with cortex at the butt end. In the Aylesbury collection there is a good retouched flake from a prepared core, arguably a disc core, which is perfectly well classifiable as a backed knife. Wymer summarizes these finds and illustrates the two pieces now at Aylesbury (1968: 212-13 and figs 25 (reproduced here as Fig. 6:7, no. 1) and 75). The pit was dug through brickearth into gravel of a very low terrace only a few feet above the present Thames floodplain. Though the artefacts mentioned are not demonstrably from a single occurrence, they are certainly suggestive that a good Mousterian site might have been located nearby

Taplow (Fig. 6:7, no. 2)
A fine sub-triangular *bout coupé* handaxe from here is now in the British Museum; its precise provenance is not known, but it is believed to come from brickearth. It has some bluish-white patina. The piece has been recorded by R.A. Smith (1915b: 38 and fig. 15). There is much Acheulian material from Taplow, mostly abraded, and mostly from the gravels; there is also some Levalloisian, but the relationship of this handaxe to the other artefacts is unknown

CAMBRIDGESHIRE
Burnt Fen
Various handaxes have come from here, most of them rolled, and there is no definite information about their provenance. There is one *bout coupé* handaxe, in altogether fresher condition; it is now in the Cambridge University Museum
Horningsea
A fine fresh *bout coupé* handaxe from here is in the Sedgwick Museum at Cambridge, but there are no details of its provenance
Linton
A fine and rather large white-patinated *bout coupé* handaxe from here is at Ipswich Museum; no further details of its provenance are known

DEVONSHIRE
Brixham: Windmill Cave
A *bout coupé* handaxe from here is preserved at the Torquay Natural History Society's Museum. Whether any others once existed is not known to the writer; some material seems to have been

destroyed in the Second World War
Torquay: Kent's Cavern (Fig. 6:4)
See description in this chapter. The writer himself has noted six surviving *bout coupé* handaxes from this site, some certainly (and all presumably) from the Mousterian level already discussed. They are now divided between the British Museum, the Torquay Natural History Society's Museum and the Geological Museum (South Kensington)

DORSET
Bere Regis: Gallows Hill
One damaged *bout coupé* handaxe was recorded by J.B. Calkin (1952), who called it Late Acheulian. It was picked up at about 240 feet O.D. in two pieces, recovered separately some little way apart. There is plateau gravel here, thinly capped with loam. The implement has some creamy white patina
Bournemouth: Boscombe
A fine typical *bout coupé* handaxe, slightly damaged at the tip end, was found in 1903 and is now in Brighton Museum with some other Boscombe material, but there is no information about its provenance or associations, if any
Bournemouth: Castle Lane, below Redbreast (Fig. 6:7, no. 5)
One of the most elegant and finely made of all the British *bout coupé* handaxes was attributed to a loamy deposit at this location and is now in the British Museum (Calkin Collection); it has been published by J.B. Calkin and J.F.N. Green (1949: 31-6). The implement was actually found in a lorry-load of loam being spread in 1931 at a new sports ground, but the source of the loam was traced with fair certainty. The implement is in fresh condition, with some blue and white patination. The loam was reckoned to be a hill wash overlying the 'Muscliff Delta' gravels of Green's local sequence; these gravels the authors attributed to a mild phase within the Last Glaciation
Bournemouth: East Common
A fine large *bout coupé* handaxe, of rather narrower shape than usual, fresh, with a whitish patina, is now at Liverpool Museum. No details of its exact provenance are known
Bournemouth: Ensbury Park: corner of Redhill Drive and Coombe Avenue
A sub-triangular *bout coupé* handaxe, with some relatively recent damage, was found 'by the roadside' here and is now at the Red House

Site or find-spot	Details and source of information	Site or find-spot	Details and source of information

Museum, Christchurch (Druitt Collection). No further information about it is recorded

Bournemouth: Hengistbury Head
A fine rather squat *bout coupé* handaxe was found 'on the beach at the east end of Hengistbury Head' in 1932, and is now in the Red House Museum, Christchurch. Its fresh condition suggests that it was not on the shore for long, so it seems likely that it fell from one of the deposits of Pleistocene age which can be seen in the cliff section here. A typical section of Hengistbury Head is included by Angela Mace in her paper on Upper Palaeolithic material from here (1959), and she also mentions that the cliff has receded 200 yards within the last century and is still receding fast (*op. cit.*, p. 236)

Bournemouth: Iford: Sheepwash
A probable *bout coupé* handaxe is preserved amongst miscellaneous handaxes from here at the Red House Museum, Christchurch (Druitt Collection). There are no details of its exact provenance

Bournemouth: Pokesdown: Fisherman's Walk
H. Druitt and others collected rather more than 40 Palaeolithic artefacts from here, including various types in various conditions; they are now at the Red House Museum, Christchurch, Birmingham City Museum and the Hunterian Museum, Glasgow. There is one *bout coupé* handaxe in the Christchurch series, rather less finely made than usual and very abraded. In the same series may be noted a Levalloisian core and two Levalloisian flakes, but there is no stratigraphic information and no indication that these artefacts were associated

Bournemouth: Southbourne: Broadway
(Fig. 6:7, no. 6)
Calkin and Green described and illustrated two handaxes from here (1949: 31-6 and figs 13 and 15). The first is a classic and fine *bout coupé* type, with recent damage at the base; it was found during sewer digging in 1925 at a depth of 12 feet or more, on sand at the base of gravel belonging to the bluff deposits between Green's Christchurch and Muscliff terraces. The second was found six years later, again in drainage digging, only 300 yards away, also beneath the bluff gravels, lying this time on clay. This second implement is asymmetrical but certainly approaches the *bout coupé* form and is similar in flaking technique to the first. It is in the British Museum, while the first is in the Red House Museum at Christchurch. Both are in fresh condition, and in the view of Calkin and Green should date to a mild phase in

the Last Glaciation

Bournemouth: Talbot Woods
A large and fine *bout coupé* handaxe, its tip removed by a recent break, was found by A.R. Mangin and is now in the British Museum (Calkin Collection). It is fresh, with slight 'basket work' patination and some iron staining. There is no detailed information about its provenance. Some 70 miscellaneous handaxes and a few other artefacts are preserved from Talbot Woods, mostly at the British Museum and the Red House Museum, Christchurch

Bournemouth: Winton: Green Road
One sub-triangular *bout coupé* handaxe is amongst miscellaneous Palaeolithic material from here in the Red House Museum, Christchurch (Druitt Collection). There are no useful details of the find. The series includes a couple of well-made flake-tools, which could certainly be Mousterian, but there is no indication of their actual age, provenance or associations

Christchurch
At Birmingham City Museum there is a small well-made *bout coupé* from Christchurch, somewhat abraded and white-patinated with a little iron staining. No details of its provenance are known

Christchurch: Purewell: Street Lane Pit
A good well-made *bout coupé* handaxe was found here, 4 feet down in 10 feet of stratified gravel, and is now in the British Museum (Calkin Collection). It is slightly abraded and has some 'basket work' and incipient white patina. No other Palaeolithic artefacts seem to be recorded from here

Christchurch: St Catherine's Hill
Over 50 Palaeolithic artefacts are known from here and the assemblage is certainly mixed. There is one small classic *bout coupé* handaxe, in fresh condition. Much of the other material is rolled or abraded, but it is interesting to note that the small proportion of fresh artefacts includes a fine Levalloisian flake and a limace-like flake-tool

Dewlish
In the Dorset County Museum at Dorchester, amongst about a dozen miscellaneous Lower Palaeolithic artefacts, mostly well rolled, is a white-patinated and weathered small *bout coupé* handaxe, with streaks of iron staining. No details of its provenance are known

Poole: West Howe
A rather poorly made, probable *bout coupé* type handaxe, slightly abraded, was noted by the writer amongst a miscellaneous collection of Palaeolithic

	Details and source of
Site or find-spot	*information*

artefacts from this locality in the Dorset County Museum at Dorchester. No details of its finding are recorded

Sherborne: The Cemetery (Fig. 6:7, no. 3)
A fine sub-triangular *bout coupé* handaxe was found here by grave diggers at or near the base of the 20-foot terrace of the River Yeo (Arkell 1947). Its surface shows some weathering and frost pitting, white patination and slight iron staining, but it does not appear to be rolled. It is now in the Dorset County Museum at Dorchester

DYFED

Laugharne: Coygan Cave
The two *bout coupé* handaxes found in an excavation by C.B.M. McBurney (unpublished) have already been mentioned. They are now in the National Museum of Wales at Cardiff

ESSEX

Tilbury: The Thames at Tilbury Dock (Fig. 6:7, no. 4)
A very large *bout coupé* handaxe was found here in dredging operations; it weighs about 27 ounces (*c.* 765 grams). It has been recorded and illustrated by R.A. Smith (e.g. 1926: 45-6). It is ochreous and slightly water-worn (as well it might be, from such a context); the deposits encountered in dredging here would inevitably be of late Pleistocene age, somewhere in the Devensian, though one cannot be more precise. An interesting comment is recorded in the *Proceedings of the Prehistoric Society of East Anglia*, VI: 143, in an account of a meeting on 12 June 1929, at which Reid Moir spoke on his Ipswich Mousterian finds and there was a discussion at which R.A. Smith was present: '. . . it was recalled that black, unrolled Mousterian handaxes had been dredged up from the Thames, near Tilbury . . .'. This particular implement being neither black nor unrolled, it sounds as if more material of the same kind may have been present here or not far away, but the present writer has no knowledge of what became of it

Walton-on-the-Naze
Much Palaeolithic material has been collected here at various times, mainly on the foreshore, much of it at Stone Point (Warren 1933: 9-10). It gives the impression of being a mixture, and it includes over 40 handaxes and about the same number of flakes and miscellaneous worked pieces (Cambridge University Museum; British Museum (Warren Collection); Colchester and Essex Museum; Bolton Museum). In the Bolton Museum series is a very

	Details and source of
Site or find-spot	*information*

small but typical *bout coupé* handaxe, much abraded; many of the pieces show beach abrasion of recent origin, so this is not significant. In passing, we may note a high proportion of refined ovate and cordiform shapes among the handaxes generally, and one struck Levalloisian core in the Cambridge series. There may have been a good Mousterian open site in this region, and it would be worth watching any new exposures of late Pleistocene deposits

HAMPSHIRE

Dunbridge
This site, which produced a prolific quantity of Acheulian material, has already been mentioned. The one fine *bout coupé* handaxe recorded from Dunbridge is now at the British Museum. It is sub-triangular and has a slightly twisted profile; it has a yellowish-white patina that differs from the other material, and its fresh condition also distinguishes it from the main bulk of the Dunbridge collections. No precise details of its finding are recorded, however

Fareham
Mr J.C. Draper of Fareham very kindly sent information about the following finds to the writer, and showed him the pieces. Two *bout coupé* handaxes were found in the garden of a house (40, Blackbrook Park Avenue) by Mr C.H. Briscoe. One is damaged at the tip, and has patchy white patina stained yellowish; the other is damaged at both ends, though enough of it remains to reveal that it is indeed a *bout coupé* form, and it is white-patinated with spots and streaks of rusty-looking iron stain. Both have indications of weathering. Also from Fareham, not far away (32 East Street) came a small white-patinated sub-triangular handaxe, which again has spots and streaks of iron staining; it was found on the surface by Mr Draper himself. While too roughly worked at the butt to count as a true *bout coupé* form, it is certainly not too dissimilar in general nature

Holybourne: Holybourne Down
Close to the scatter of Acheulian (Group VI) material already described in the previous chapter (see pages 183-4), a good rather small *bout coupé* handaxe was found on the surface, and is now in the Curtis Museum at Alton. In condition it is quite different from the other Holybourne Palaeolithic artefacts, being unworn and showing only a little white patination and intermittent iron staining

Site or find-spot	*Details and source of information*	Site or find-spot	*Details and source of information*

Southampton

A fine large *bout coupé* handaxe is in the British Museum, recorded as being a surface find but with no precise locality stated. It is slightly worn or weathered. Another, marked only 'Southampton' is in the Pitt Rivers Museum collection at Oxford (teaching collections in the Department of Ethnology and Prehistory). It has a damaged tip and a patchy white patina which is more pronounced on one face than the other

Southampton: Redbridge

A small, broad, almost rectangular *bout coupé* handaxe from here, white-patinated with some iron staining, is now in the Pitt Rivers Museum collection at Oxford (teaching collections of the Department of Ethnology and Prehistory). No details of its precise provenance are known. A cortex-covered depression rather mars one face, but the maker could not have removed it without reducing the implement to a minute size

Southampton: Rockstone Place: site of the Ordnance Survey Office (Fig. 6:7, no. 7)

A finely made narrow *bout coupé* handaxe from here, fresh but white-patinated, is at Winchester City Museum (Dale Collection); there is no stratigraphic information. A very rolled ovate handaxe from the same find-spot is at the British Museum, but the difference in condition makes any connection between the two unlikely. The *bout coupé* is mentioned and illustrated by R.A. Smith (1915b: 47-8 and fig. 27)

Southampton: Shirley

At Winchester City Museum (Dale Collection) there is a *bout coupé* handaxe from Shirley: no particular location is given for it, and there is only the not very helpful information that it was found at 100 feet O.D. It is in fresh condition, with white patination one side; the section is strikingly plano-convex, and the butt must count as rather roughly worked by the usual standards

HUNTINGDONSHIRE

Fenstanton

At the Norris Museum, St Ives, Hunts., there is a small fine *bout coupé* handaxe found at NGR TL 317700. It is in almost mint condition, with a slight suggestion of a twist in the profile view. Another *bout coupé* handaxe, in the same collection, came from even bedded sands and gravels of the Ouse in a pit at Fenstanton south of the Cambridge to Huntingdon Road at TL 307685: it is similar to the last, including the slight twist, but has a mainly cortical butt. A few flakes from this same pit, none of them very

informative, are preserved at the same Museum, and 20-30 artefacts from here are known to have been destroyed during the Second World War, though it is not known what they consisted of. Mammoth is recorded from the same gravels; see also the paragraphs about Levalloisian material in the Great Ouse Valley in the previous chapter (pages 224-6)

Hemingford Grey: Marsh Lane

The Norris Museum at St Ives has some 14 artefacts from here, including a fresh, squat, rather poorly made *bout coupé* handaxe, and a small irregular biface which is not dissimilar technologically, but lacks the typical shape. There is also a fine fresh flake with a carefully faceted platform, which is so thin that it might be a sophisticated handaxe trimming flake rather than Levalloisian. These all came from well-bedded gravels of a low Ouse terrace (cf. pages 224-6 above)

Little Paxton (Fig. 5:53)

The finds from the low-level Ouse gravels here have already been described (pages 224-6). At the Cambridge University Museum there are three handaxes which may be counted as true *bout coupé* forms, one being a rather unusual flat triangular one. All are of unpatinated black flint, and in fresh condition. There are five other handaxes which are technologically similar, and again very fresh, but do not have the true *bout coupé* shape. Many retouched and unretouched flakes, and some Levalloisian material also survive, the majority in this same collection but some also at the Sedgwick Museum in Cambridge and the Norris Museum at St Ives

St Ives: Meadow Lane

An area of gravel working here yielded Levalloisian artefacts, some handaxes and various flakes, from evenly bedded gravel of a low Ouse terrace (cf. pages 224-6 above); the gravel passes below present water-level and the artefacts were mostly found on gravel heaps in the pits. Remains of mammoth, woolly rhinoceros, reindeer, red deer and horse have been obtained from the same deposits. A good fresh *bout coupé* handaxe is amongst the material preserved at the Norris Museum, St Ives, and the Sedgwick Museum, Cambridge, has a tiny handaxe of sub-triangular to cordiform shape, which is very close to being a *bout coupé*

ISLE OF WIGHT

Shide: Great Pan Farm (Pan Pit)
(Fig. 6:3, nos. 1-3)

Site or find-spot	Details and source of information

This site produced a group of handaxes which the present writer studied metrically (1967, 1968), and it has already been discussed in Chapter 5. There is one classic *bout coupé* handaxe amongst the others and apparently of the same age, plus several others which come very close to the *bout coupé* form, an assessment with which Myra Shackley (1973) agrees. There are Levalloisian artefacts and good flake-tools in the same assemblage, which the present writer regards as belonging to the Mousterian of Acheulian Tradition; Dr Shackley has suggested that a Late Ipswichian date is likely. In so far as the writer has only traced about 50 handaxes out of the much larger amount of material that H.F. Poole (1925) collected and studied, there may well have been other examples of the *bout coupé* form originally. Poole illustrates the one surviving classic one (*op. cit.*, fig. 19)

KENT
Ash: Parsonage Farm
In the British Museum (Sturge Collection) there is a damaged, stained and very weathered broad *bout coupé* handaxe, found by Benjamin Harrison. Its condition suggests that it was a long-exposed surface find. It is marked 'Harrison Plate L', but the writer has not traced any record of it in a publication
Canterbury: St Stephen's Pit
There is a mixture of some 40 or so artefacts from this pit, where some 6 feet of brickearth overlay 12 to 14 feet of reddish gravel; the material is now rather scattered. There is one good small *bout coupé* handaxe at the British Museum (Ince Collection), a little damaged. This artefact is unusual for the pit in being white-patinated and, whether by coincidence or otherwise, the same collection has a broken white-patinated Levalloisian flake-blade from the same pit. Another Levalloisian flake-blade is at Plymouth Museum
Canterbury: Wallfield
A large and particularly fine triangular *bout coupé* handaxe from here is in the British Museum (Brent Collection); it is fresh and white-patinated, but damaged, two missing pieces having been 'restored' in plaster. There is no information about its finding
Canterbury: Wincheap
Sir John Evans (1897: 618) indicates that pits here, dug into gravel with a surface some 29 feet above the River Stour, produced many implements, but the present writer has only

encountered three artefacts actually marked as coming from Wincheap. One of them is a sub-triangular *bout coupé* handaxe, now at Maidstone Museum, to which it was presented in 1892 by John Marten. It is well made, with a slightly twisted profile, and the butt has some damage. The implement is white-patinated on one face and has 'basket work' patination on the other. No details of its occurrence are preserved
Elham: Dreals Farm and Standardhill Farm
A considerable number of handaxes and other artefacts have been picked up on the surface of the fields of these two adjacent farms. One brief report has been published (Tester 1952b), but much material has been found since then; some is in Canterbury Royal Museum and more is in private hands. Types are mixed, and not all the handaxes seen by the present writer seem to him to lie within the usual Mousterian range. Several are white-patinated. There are however two fine *bout coupé* handaxes at Canterbury Royal Museum, and these have hardly any patination on them at all. It is interesting that some Levalloisian flakes have also been found here (the artefacts have been collected on the surface of ploughed fields). Exact quantities are unknown, because a fair amount of material is known to be in private hands. There could well be one or more good sites here, perhaps both Lower and Middle Palaeolithic; this is a high ground occurrence in chalk country, rather reminiscent of the north Hampshire sites, including Holybourne, recorded by Willis (1947) and mentioned in the previous chapter
Erith
There is some confusion in the literature, and also in the marking of artefacts, between Erith and Crayford, since some of the famous 'Crayford Brickearth' Levalloisian finds actually lie in Erith, and others, which do not, have sometimes been attributed there. At the British Museum (Sturge Collection) there are two good *bout coupé* handaxes from Erith, though there are no details of their provenance and no firm indication that they actually belong with the Levalloisian finds from the area. One is much abraded, and the other hardly worn at all. In the same collection are two artefacts from the Thames at Erith: a handaxe, damaged at both ends, which was almost certainly a *bout coupé* type, and a Levalloisian flake. Both are substantially water-worn. Two more Levalloisian flakes from the Thames at Erith are in the London Museum. R.A. Smith (1931: 64, 124; figs 294-7) listed '11 Lower

Site or find-spot	Details and source of information	Site or find-spot	Details and source of information

Palaeolithic and 63 Le Moustier' artefacts from the river here as being in the Sturge Collection, but the present writer cannot confirm this from the material he has seen himself. Wymer (1968: 322) lists a little more relevant material: cordate handaxes and another Levalloisian flake

Faversham

A finely made and white-patinated *bout coupé* handaxe from Faversham is now at the Royal Museum, Canterbury, but there are no details of its provenance

Faversham: Copton in Preston

R.A. Smith recorded and illustrated (1915b: 37 and fig. 14) a somewhat lopsided but otherwise typical *bout coupé* handaxe from here. There are two refined ovates from Copton in Preston in the British Museum (Sturge Collection), but whether the three artefacts belong together or not is unknown

Herne Bay: Hampton

A fine broad *bout coupé* handaxe from Hampton, found by T.H. Powell, is in the British Museum (Trechmann Bequest). It is unabraded but somewhat lustrous. No useful details of the find are recorded

Hextable: Grounds of the Horticultural College

There are four handaxes from here, including two white-patinated *bout coupé* types, somewhat irregular in shape but quite acceptable, one in the London Museum and one in Dartford Museum. One is much weathered, with streaks of iron staining. The other two handaxes are both rolled and presumably older (a twisted ovate and one of pyriform shape). The condition of the *bout coupé* handaxes suggests that they spent some time on the surface; one of them was found in the making of a tennis court

Ightham

This was Benjamin Harrison's home village and artefacts collected by him in the area are abundant and widely dispersed, since he gave them away freely to his friends. A very small *bout coupé* handaxe, unworn but white-patinated, is in the British Museum (Lord Avebury Collection), without any useful data. It weighs only three ounces, and in size and shape resembles the Oldbury specimens, though it is unusually thick at the tip end

Ightham: Shode Valley: Heronshaw

A small and rather narrow *bout coupé* handaxe, found by Benjamin Harrison, is in the British Museum, marked as 'from excavation debris', whatever that may mean. It is weathered and has bluish and white patination and some relatively

recent damage affecting nearly half of its edge. A cordiform or nearly circular ovate handaxe from Heronshaw is or was in the Wellcome Prehistoric Collection (now transferred to the British Museum), according to information supplied to the present writer by the late A.D. Lacaille

Milton

Milton is now part of Gravesend. A neat small *bout coupé* handaxe, found by George Payne in the early 1880s, is now in the British Museum, with no details regarding its exact provenance. It is somewhat worn, presumably by weathering, and has some white and 'basket-work' patina, with slight iron staining

New Hythe

There is a very fine *bout coupé* handaxe from here in Maidstone Museum, unworn and unpatinated. No detailed information about its discovery is preserved. The question of its possible associations is tantalizing. There are numerous handaxes from New Hythe, many known to have come from the quarry in New Hythe Lane and one marked with the name 'Johnson's Pit'. Their condition is variable: many are fresh, but a few are considerably rolled. Some of the material is merely marked 'New Hythe'. It has already been noted that these handaxes are dominated by pointed types and that ficrons are included. But there is also a substantial quantity of Levalloisian artefacts, both cores and flakes, some from the 'quarry in New Hythe Lane' and others merely marked 'New Hythe'. Much of this Levalloisian material is in strikingly fresh condition, like the *bout coupé* handaxe. Just as significant (potentially if not demonstrably) is the presence of several well-retouched flakes, including some finely made scrapers and one elegant acute point; there are also three small hemispherical disc-like cores, which are again unworn. This New Hythe material, which also includes numerous waste flakes and handaxe trimming flakes (giving the assemblage a 'working site' appearance), is divided between the Maidstone and Dartford Museums, though a couple of Levalloisian flakes have found their way to Stroud Museum. The artefacts appear to have been collected at different times by various people, and the site does not seem to have been excavated or published. We therefore simply do not know how much of the material belongs together, or whether there were stratigraphically separate archaeological horizons, as one would expect from the material itself, but it is clear that there may well have been an important Middle Palaeolithic site here and it

Site or find-spot	*Details and source of information*

would be worth watching for fresh exposures. Raw material was evidently abundant and of good quality, and the artefacts are well made and often of large size

Newington

A small, narrow *bout coupé* handaxe, damaged, slightly worn and white-patinated, is now in the Geological Museum in South Kensington. It was 'found on a road near Newington Station'. Viewed in profile, it is somewhat plano-convex

Oldbury

The so-called Rockshelters site and its industry has already been described and discussed and the presence of Mousterian handaxes noted. Five may be classed as of *bout coupé* type, two of them being of particularly regular shape (cf. R.A. Smith 1926, Plate V, no. 1). Others in the industry have cordiform shapes near to the *bout coupé* form. The five *bout coupé* handaxes are with the Oldbury material at the British Museum; other handaxes from the site are at Maidstone Museum and Manchester City Museum. Both these collections have some other artefacts as well, but the main quantity of flake material is at the British Museum. Other artefacts were collected at various times on Oldbury Hill by Harrison and others, including derived Acheulian material from 'Medway gravels' banked against its lower slopes. Such artefacts are usually just marked 'Oldbury' or 'Oldbury Hill'. However, there are pieces amongst them which resemble the material from the actual 'Rockshelters' site, and these may well represent a scatter left by the latter's occupants. They include one more typical *bout coupé* handaxe, and five more which approach the classic form without quite attaining it; these are again all at the British Museum. There are other small ovate and cordiform shapes too, which might well be Mousterian in origin, but we shall never know for certain

Reculver

The gravels which cap the cliffs here, and the loam or brickearth which in places overlies them, have been the source of many Palaeolithic artefacts and known as such since well back into the nineteenth century. The material is certainly mixed, and many of the pieces have been found in cliff falls on the foreshore. The British Museum (Brent Collection) has a fine *bout coupé* handaxe of classic shape, found at Reculver as early as 1877; it is unpatinated and unrolled. Stored with it is a very fine white-patinated ovoid handaxe, technologically similar, but lacking the characteristic *bout coupé* butt shape. The

relationship between the two is unknown. The Reculver collections also include one or two fine flat sub-triangular handaxes which again may be Mousterian rather than Acheulian, but in the absence of stratigraphic evidence this remains a matter of opinion. Levalloisian flakes are also present; so are a few well-made flake-tools, and there is a small, hemispherical, rather disc-like core in the British Museum (Wellcome Collection). The Reculver artefacts are now widely scattered in museums in many parts of Britain

Reculver: Bishopstone

A large white-patinated and weathered *bout coupé* handaxe was found 'near The Haven' on 16 May 1866 by John Brent, and is now in the British Museum. There is no other information about the find

Snodland: Ham Hill: Clubb's Pit

Mr J.N. Carreck has kindly shown the writer three handaxes, found here in 1969 in deposits belonging to a buried channel of the River Medway. They have been mentioned in passing, without details, by Mitchell *et al.* (1973: 51, note 13). Two of them are classic *bout coupé* types, of rather large size, and the third, a smaller implement, is of generally similar shape. All are unpatinated and unworn; one is made of the 'marbled' flint known from several north Kent Palaeolithic sites, including Barnfield Pit, Swanscombe and Twydall. These implements were found by workmen at the pit, the two *bout coupé* handaxes at the screening plant and the other as a loose find, but there is no doubt that they came from the buried channel deposits and the workmen were able to attribute them to the lowest 5 feet of the gravels. Borings have shown that the buried channel descends as low as -23 feet O.D. not far from this exposure; its deposits have yielded remains of woolly rhinoceros, mammoth (of a late type), horse and red deer of large size. The gravels of the buried channel are apparently continuous with those of the Low Terrace of the Medway, and have been attributed to an early interstadial of the Devensian. The writer is most grateful to Mr Carreck for bringing these very interesting finds to his attention and for supplying the information on which this paragraph is based

LINCOLNSHIRE

Harlaxton

A badly damaged handaxe, which is surely the remains of a fine *bout coupé* type, was found in 1951 by Mr Richard How after deep ploughing in

Site or find-spot	*Details and source of information*	Site or find-spot	*Details and source of information*

light gravelly soil overlying glacial drift at NGR SK 880348. It has been split by frost action, leaving only about half of the original implement. Though not obviously rolled, it is certainly somewhat worn and has a creamy white patina. The find has been recorded by D.F. Petch (1961) and by J. May (1976: 26) and is now in Grantham Museum

Risby Warren (Fig. 6:8, no. 1)
A small, narrow, asymmetrical *bout coupé* handaxe from here is now in Scunthorpe Museum, and was recorded by its finder, H.E. Dudley (1949: 27-8), by A.D. Lacaille (1946), who regarded it however as a Middle Acheulian ovate derived from an older horizon which had yet to be found, and more recently by J. May (1976: 24-5). It is not so finely made as usual and is somewhat worn, probably by the action of blowing sand, since it lay in a thin clayey band at the base of wind-blown sand. The same horizon, or a very similar one, less than a hundred yards away, yielded a shouldered point believed to be of Upper Palaeolithic age. Dudley (*op. cit.*, pp. 29-35) mentions other Upper Palaeolithic artefacts from Risby Warren, found by A.L. Armstrong, but there was also Mesolithic material and there is a certain risk of confusion since the nature of the British Upper Palaeolithic was not clearly understood at the time. However, this does not affect the handaxe

LONDON AREA
Acton
A sub-triangular *bout coupé* handaxe from here is in the London Museum: it is unworn, though white-patinated, and recorded as coming from 'brickearth'. No precise location for the find is given

Acton: Creffield Road (Fig. 5:48, no. 13)
This site has already been described and discussed (pages 216-18). One sub-triangular *bout coupé* style handaxe, possibly unfinished, marked as coming from the 'workshop floor extensions', is now in the British Museum (Sturge Collection); see R.A. Smith (1931: 85, fig. 361). The piece has white patina, and this certainly agrees with some of the Levalloisian flakes and other artefacts (examples at both the British Museum and the London Museum), though others lack it. Paul Mellars (1974: 64, quoting also John Wymer) indicates that there are two *bout coupé* handaxes from the Creffield Road site, but the present writer cannot confirm this, the only other handaxe he has seen from here being a

rather crude rolled pointed one from the gravel below the main archaeological level. Wymer however does refer specifically to a 'flake handaxe' (1968: 268), having placed the *bout coupé* in his class N

Acton: The Priory
The British Museum (Sturge Collection) has a finely made *bout coupé* handaxe from here, white-patinated on one face. It was found 12 to 13 feet deep in fine gravel at about 45 to 50 feet O.D. according to J. Allen Brown, quoted by Wymer (1968: 268)

Hammersmith
The collections of the London Museum include a finely made small *bout coupé* handaxe, slightly rolled, which came from the River Thames, though it is not recorded under what circumstances

Hoxton
A *bout coupé* handaxe, moderately rolled, is in the British Museum (Sturge Collection). There is no information relating to its discovery

Isleworth
In the Manchester Museum there is a fairly large but entirely typical *bout coupé* handaxe, which was formerly in the collection of R.D. Darbishire. It is finely made and slightly rolled. No details of its exact provenance are recorded. R.A. Smith (1931: 126) lists a Le Moustier specimen from Isleworth in the Sturge Collection, but the present writer has not encountered it

West Drayton: Eastwoods Gravel Pit
The British Museum (Sturge Collection) has a good *bout coupé* handaxe from here, slightly weathered or worn, though not water rolled. It has 'basket-work' patina. The Levalloisian finds from this pit and area have already been noted (pages 215-16), but no stratigraphic information is preserved with this handaxe, so we cannot say firmly that it was associated with them. It does not however seem to have been in the gravel

Yiewsley
R.A. Smith (1915b: 36-7 and fig. 13) recorded and illustrated a *bout coupé* handaxe 'from one of the gravel pits at Yiewsley', though the present writer has not himself seen it. It had white-patination and the tip was damaged. There is no stratigraphic information and therefore no indication of definite association with the Levalloisian material from Yiewsley already described

NORFOLK
Norwich: Mousehold Heath (Fig. 6:8, no. 2)

Site or find-spot	*Details and source of information*

In the Norwich Castle Museum, there is a *bout coupé* handaxe from the Valley Drive Pit, somewhat plano-convex when viewed in profile, having white patina on one face and 'basket-work' patina on the other. It was recorded and illustrated as one of three 'Combe Capelle' handaxes from Norfolk by J.E. Sainty (1935), and came from Anglian outwash gravel which had been 'disturbed and rearranged by solifluxion' at some later date. The other two handaxes described in this article are not of the true *bout coupé* form
Thetford
There is much Palaeolithic material from the Thetford area of unspecified provenance, clearly of various ages. The series now at the British Museum (Natural History) includes one classic sub-triangular *bout coupé* handaxe, about which there is no stratigraphic information
Thetford: White Hill (Fig. 6:8, no. 3)
Sir John Evans (1872: 499-507) recorded and illustrated a fine flat sub-triangular *bout coupé* handaxe from the site which was known to him by this name, though the exact location of it is uncertain. He does not state the relationship of the implement to the gravel here, which he says yielded horse and mammoth remains. The implement closely resembles some of the fine triangular or sub-triangular handaxes from the base of the Younger Loess I in northern France (Bordes 1954). Such regularly triangular specimens as this are rather rare in Britain, but in France they seem closely connected with the broader shaped versions of the *bout coupé* type. This specimen has lost one corner at the base and has a thick white patina; it has also suffered substantial weathering, which has led to patches of decomposition or exfoliation of its surface, but these effects of time and exposure have not succeeded in masking the high quality of its workmanship. The implement, at one time in the Blackmore Collection at Salisbury Museum, is now in the Pitt Rivers collection at Oxford (teaching collections of the Department of Ethnology and Prehistory)
Weeting
One *bout coupé* handaxe from Weeting (no precise provenance) is in the Moyse's Hall Museum, Bury St Edmunds, without any useful stratigraphic information. At least its condition contrasts with that of the fairly abundant Lower Palaeolithic artefacts from the gravels of this region, and it looks more like a surface find: it has thick white patina and much frost pitting

Weeting: Grimes Graves
There is an inevitable element of doubt about any supposed Palaeolithic artefacts from Grimes Graves, because some of the roughouts, *débitage* and shaped tools associated with the later prehistoric flint mining activities strikingly resemble Palaeolithic types; for example, a version of Levalloisian technique seems to have been used to produce the flake blanks for the manufacture of discoidal knives. The site was for a long while believed (on purely typological grounds) to contain Palaeolithic levels. However, there is a very genuine-looking handaxe in the Acheulian manner at the Cambridge University Museum, recorded as being from Grimes Graves, and, more relevant here, Reginald Smith described and illustrated what appears to be a rather large *bout coupé* handaxe (1915b: 35-6 and fig. 12) which evidently satisfied him and which he specifically compared with the Tilbury specimen listed earlier. Certainly there are genuine *bout coupé* handaxes from this Breckland region included in the present list. No useful details of the implement's exact provenance were given, and it is only fair to add that 'celts' of later prehistoric age were certainly made at Grimes Graves, and Smith illustrates examples in this same article, which was a discussion of the evolution of the 'celt' form
West Tofts
A probable *bout coupé* handaxe from here, not seen by the present writer, is mentioned by R.A. Smith (1915b: 37) — that is to say, he illustrated some undoubted *bout coupé* handaxes (though he did not call them that) and then listed other examples of 'similar specimens', one being from West Tofts. Since the rest of the list consists of genuine *bout coupé* handaxes which the present writer has seen, it seems reasonable to accept his judgement on the West Tofts specimen. Three other handaxes are known from there, in fact, though none is another *bout coupé*

NORTHAMPTONSHIRE
Duston
A very small sub-triangular handaxe, with damaged edges but very probably a *bout coupé* type, is mentioned and illustrated by M. Posnansky (1963: 383 and fig. 1, no. 5); it is now in Northampton Museum. It is distinctly plano-convex in section. There are three other small handaxes from Duston, and a broken piece of another; two are known to have been surface finds. While not diagnostically Mousterian

Site or find-spot	Details and source of information

artefacts, they certainly seem within the Mousterian range

OXFORDSHIRE

Abingdon (Plate 35)

A fine unpatinated classic *bout coupé* handaxe was found in 1972 by a schoolboy, Nigel Scaysbrook; it was protruding from the bank of a small stream at a depth of 3 feet from the surface (NGR SU 482935). It is of black flint and shows only the slighest abrasion, though it was unfortunately broken and repaired subsequent to its discovery. The deposit which contained it is presumably an alluvium of late Pleistocene or post-Pleistocene age. The implement was kindly given by the finder to the Pitt Rivers Museum at Oxford (teaching collections of the Department of Ethnology and Prehistory). In passing, we might note that the same collection has a rather rough disc core, picked up by Mr G. Chaundy in his gravel pit at Radley, a mile or two away from Abingdon, though it was not found *in situ*. The gravels here belong to the Flood Plain Terrace of the Upper Thames, which is of Devensian age. This artefact should also be of Middle Palaeolithic age, but the period is evidently only sparsely represented in the Upper Thames area. The deposit which yielded the *bout coupé* handaxe at Abingdon seems likely to belong to the same Flood Plain Terrace or else to incorporate material derived from it

SOMERSET

Cheddon Fitzpaine: Priorswood Lane

A well-made *bout coupé* handaxe of Greensand chert, very abraded and having a whitish patina, is in the Somerset County Museum at Taunton Castle and has been recorded by W.A. Seaby (1950). It was found by Mr A. Bellamy at the side of a gravelled roadway. The source of the gravel was not traced, but it was not thought to have been brought from far away

Pitminster

A fine though rather abraded *bout coupé* handaxe of chert is in the Somerset County Museum at Taunton Castle, given in 1962 by Mr and Mrs Bradley

Weston-super-Mare: Uphill Quarry, cave no. 8

For the sake of completeness, the writer draws attention to the Mousterian artefacts from here listed in this chapter, since the one complete handaxe was a small sub-triangular one close to the *bout coupé* form

West Quantoxhead

A very worn and weathered *bout coupé* handaxe

Site or find-spot	Details and source of information

of chert, flat and well made, is in the Somerset County Museum at Taunton Castle. It is an old find, having been picked up 'on open ground considerably above the grounds of St Audries'. It is mentioned by W.A. Seaby (1950: 169)

Wookey (Fig. 6:5, no. 1)

Again for completeness' sake, we may recall the information given earlier in this chapter about MTA artefacts from the Hyaena Den and Rhinoceros Hole caves at Wookey. The former yielded one typical *bout coupé* handaxe amongst eleven 'bifaces and related forms', while the latter's only handaxe was a small but typical *bout coupé* form

SUFFOLK

Elveden (Fig. 6:8, no. 4)

The Acheulian site excavated by Paterson and Fagg has been discussed at some length in the previous chapter, where it was attributed to the writer's Group VI. The British Museum (Sturge Collection) has one *bout coupé* handaxe from Elveden, in fresh condition, with white patina on one face, and having a twisted profile. There is no precise record of its provenance, and it is not even marked as coming from the brickearth; there are very few occurrences of white patina amongst the other handaxes from the old brick pit itself, though it is not completely absent. This implement's presence in the Sturge Collection, which was bequeathed to the British Museum in 1919, indicates that it was one of the earlier finds at Elveden. There is a rather unsatisfactory illustration of it in the Sturge Collection publication (R.A. Smith 1931: 14-15 and fig. 100), in which it does not look like a *bout coupé* form at all; nor does the drawing really match the accompanying description 'subtriangular handaxe of exceptional quality . . . with sharp angle at one end of lower edge and thickened curve at the other, constituting a proto-celt.' A much better illustration was provided by Paterson and Fagg (1940: 13, fig. 9, reproduced here as Fig. 6:8, no. 4). However, the specimen itself survives and can be examined at the museum. It is true that the outline is not quite symmetrical

Eriswell

There is a fine, flat, typical *bout coupé* handaxe in sharp condition from here, now at Liverpool City Museum. No details of its provenance are preserved. There is a mixture of Palaeolithic material from the Eriswell area, much of it similarly unprovenanced

Site or find-spot	Details and source of information

Icklingham: Icklingham Warren
The Cambridge University Museum has a fine *bout coupé* handaxe of classic shape from here, white-patinated and weathered. Nothing is recorded about its discovery; it certainly looks like a surface find

Ipswich (Fig. 5:52, nos 1, 2)
Reid Moir's reports of Mousterian material from Bramford Road and other sites in the Gipping-Orwell Valley were discussed in the previous chapter and the presence of *bout coupé* handaxes mentioned. Here we may simply note that there are well over a hundred surviving handaxes from Bramford Road alone, with a strong element of broad ovate and cordiform plan-forms, and many which approach the flat-butted *bout coupé* shape. The present writer, in checking through and listing this material, accepted seven specimens as actually falling within the *bout coupé* range, some being good typical examples and some rather irregular. All of them are in the prolific Bramford Road collections at Ipswich Museum. It is interesting that three have white patina, since white patina is rare at the site; the only other white-patinated artefact in that series is a tiny cordiform handaxe which could readily be paralleled at many French MTA sites, whatever may be its actual origin. There is also a white-patinated Levalloisian flake in the Bramford Road series at the British Museum. The other four of the seven *bout coupé* handaxes share the bluish-black colouring and near absence of patina common to the main bulk of the assemblage, which also includes some hundreds of flakes and fragments amongst which several good Levalloisian flakes and flake-blades and many well-retouched flakes can be seen. But it must be stressed that the circumstances under which the material was collected make it entirely a matter of guesswork what is archaeologically associated with what

Mildenhall: High Lodge
This important site, with its sequence which includes a refined flake industry of possible 'proto-Mousterian' character has been discussed in this chapter and the previous one. To what has already been said may now be added the information that in the British Museum there is a *bout coupé* handaxe from High Lodge recorded as having come 'from undisturbed river drift gravel'. Exactly what this may mean is uncertain, since the sequence of deposits as noted above did not include any fluviatile gravel, though there was a solifluxion gravel overlying the lake sediments. Perhaps Mr Sieveking's forthcoming publication

will cast some light on this. We might deduce that at least the implement does not belong in the brickearth with the 'classic flake industry', which is perhaps as well if we regard that occurrence as of inter-Wolstonian age, since there is no sign that any other British *bout coupé* handaxe dates from before the Ipswichian and most of those for which there is any dating evidence seem to fall within the Devensian. The High Lodge *bout coupé*, which is slightly asymmetrical, is in very sharp condition. It appears to be an old find, and is presumably the one mentioned by R.A. Smith (1915b: 37). There is actually another *bout coupé* in Ipswich Museum marked as probably from High Lodge, but there seems to be no certainty that it is indeed from there; see also comment by R.A. Smith in Garraway Rice (1920)

Santon Downham
There are large numbers of handaxes from here, including some very refined ovate forms, though the stratigraphy of the deposits containing them is not well known. The British Museum has one *bout coupé* handaxe, stored with the other Santon Downham material in the Sturge Collection, noted and illustrated by R.A. Smith (1931: 46 and 49, fig. 244). It was found in 1868, and is white-patinated and weathered, which is quite a different state from that of almost all the rest of the collection, though there is one white-patinated, damaged and weathered ovate (*ibid.*, fig. 242). We may guess that these two artefacts came from a different situation from the rest, though this is not known for certain. Metrical analysis of the Santon Downham handaxes by the present writer placed them in the rather dubious Group IV

SURREY
Balham
The London Museum has a large typical *bout coupé* handaxe, somewhat abraded. Nothing is known of its provenance

Farnham: Firgrove
Liverpool City Museum has a very fresh *bout coupé* handaxe, somewhat less finely worked than usual at the butt. It was found 'up a side vein of clay'. The Firgrove gravel pit was on Terrace D of K.P. Oakley's (1939) Farnham sequence; few artefacts from this terrace are extant. Oakley records (*op. cit.*, 49-50) that few were found, but of them those in freshest condition were small cordiform handaxes with thin edges, some made from flakes, 'comparable with Levallois V types from the Somme'. That is virtually a contemporary description of the *bout coupé*

Site or find-spot	Details and source of information

type and its closest relatives. He illustrates (*op. cit.*, fig. 25 and Plate 1, no. 4, both taken from earlier publications by H. Bury) two such pieces from Terrace D, though he does not mention the pit; one is a *bout coupé* and the other is not so far off being one. Oakley suggested that Terrace D corresponded with 'the glacial phase with which the Upper Mousterian of the classic cave stations is generally associated'.

Limpsfield

Probably few readers will be aware of this name in connection with the Palaeolithic, but there are some interesting old finds from here which have not been followed up in recent times to the extent they deserve. Some hundreds of Palaeolithic artefacts in all were found, with two main concentrations. Much of the material came from the surface in each case, but some was also found *in situ*. The first locality was on the Common, at about 520 feet O.D., where a pit was dug into 'plateau gravel'. Some of the implements certainly occurred in this gravel, from 3 to 7 feet deep (Sir John Evans 1897: 610). The other locality was on the Greensand escarpment overlooking the Weald. Many implements were found here, between 450 and 590 feet O.D., on the surface or in brickearth at depths up to 5 feet (*ibid.*). The problems have been that relatively few artefacts out of the many said to have been found seemed to have survived, and that the marking of them has not always made clear which locality was involved. The writer, in assembling his own research material, noted that ovate forms were dominant, often very small and neat, with a high frequency of twisted forms. A small group of seven such handaxes, six of them twisted, in the British Museum, formerly in the collection of Sir Hercules Read, is typical enough. The writer suspected that an MTA element might be present, and we may note that several twisted handaxes occurred at Oldbury, whose geographical situation is not dissimilar, but there seemed little solid evidence on which to argue this view, and he did not know (and still does not know) what may be the maximum frequency of handaxes with twisted edges in Continental MTA industries. Besides, who is to say that all the Limpsfield handaxes belong together in time? Much of the material could be Acheulian. However, even since the writing of this chapter was begun, something new has turned up, in that some boxes of the largest original Limpsfield collection, that formed by A.M. Bell, have come to light in Oxford. While it will be some time before they can be examined

properly, the very first box opened was seen to contain two *bout coupé* handaxes from Limpsfield, in the same condition as the rest of the material. It thus looks as if the presence of MTA artefacts here will indeed become demonstrable, though how much more will be able to be said remains to be seen, including the question of postulating connections with Oldbury. But we may recall R.A. Smith's mention, in an early paper on high level palaeolithic finds, of 'flakes worked in the style of Le Moustier, but nearly all creamy white', from the Greensand escarpment site at Limpsfield (1917: 405). In this article, Smith quotes the main earlier references to Limpsfield. We cannot possibly here review all the surface finds from the high ground of West Kent, to the east of Limpsfield, collected by Harrison, Clinch and others (apart from the typical *bout coupé* handaxes already listed) but they are numerous. It seems likely to the writer that this was an area over which both Mousterian and Acheulian people in their time ranged widely, though they do not seem to have descended to the clay lands of the Weald below, which were doubtless thickly forested in warmer periods and unattractive to them at any time

Richmond

In the London Museum, there is a small very rolled *bout coupé* handaxe, which came from the Thames. Sir John Evans (1897: 588) records that G.F. Lawrence obtained one or more ovates from the Thames here, and a few other artefacts so marked survive

SUSSEX

West Chiltington: Woods Hill (Fig. 6:8, no. 5)
There is a rather large, nearly rectangular, *bout coupé* handaxe from here, now in Worthing Museum; it was recorded and figured by R. Garraway Rice (1920) and by L.V. Grinsell (1929: 181-2 and fig. 8). There is no information about its exact provenance and its rather axe-like shape might introduce an element of doubt about the age: however, its ochreous patination is unlike that of the local later prehistoric material. The present writer thought that it was certainly a *bout coupé* handaxe. In passing we may note that there is no other typical example from Sussex, but there are at least five other stray finds of handaxes which come very close to the *bout coupé* type (Holden and Roe 1974: 3-5, 7-8)

WILTSHIRE

Salisbury: Fisherton (Fig. 6:8, no. 6)
There is a superb fauna from the Fisherton

Site or find-spot	Details and source of information	Site or find-spot	Details and source of information

brickearths, famous since well back into the nineteenth century. The faunal assemblage is somewhat mixed in character, but has many cold-adapted species. Mammals, birds and molluscs are all well represented. Mammoth, reindeer, woolly rhinoceros and lemming are all present. As for artefacts, one fine sub-triangular *bout coupé* handaxe from Fisherton is at Salisbury Museum, recorded as having been found in loess or brickearth 'beneath the remains of a mammoth' in 1874. It is white-patinated and somewhat weathered, and very flat and well made. Sir John Evans figured and described the specimen (1897: 630) and also gave an account of the Fisherton deposits and their fauna, on which there is a good deal of other literature, earlier and later. He also mentioned another artefact, then also at Salisbury, though the writer has not seen it; it was only fragmentary, but the flint 'had assumed the same characters'. He does not say that it was another handaxe. There is a damaged and rolled handaxe from Fisherton, marked 'High Level', in the Ashmolean Museum at Oxford (Evans Collection), and two flakes from 'Higher Level Gravel' at Salisbury Museum, but there is no reason to connect any of these with the *bout coupé*.

Towards the Archaeology of the Period:

Some Conclusions, Interpretations and Speculations

Chapter 7

Is it not a sad thing that this should be the shortest chapter of the book and that it should have such a tentative title? We have fought through all this stuff about basic sequences, endured the long dusty road of typology and technology, stretched the evidence to its limits to establish relative chronology, invoked Continental parallels, applauded or despaired of colleagues long dead, striven to maintain a coherent thread of argument, and, undoubtedly, covered a great deal of ground. Now is the moment to draw it all together and write the prehistory of the British Lower and Middle Palaeolithic – and now is also the moment when the cornucopia of fact and opinion seems suddenly inclined to run dry. The writer is happy enough to deduce, infer and speculate, but he refuses firmly to manufacture facts with which to fill genuine gaps of knowledge. Those who feel it legitimate to do so should not find it too difficult to begin their work, for the basic ground has been covered for them and a mass of information provided. But the cynical might take the view, not without some reason, that the writer has warned them against the delusions of stone tool typology used on its own, and yet in the final analysis has offered them little else. So be it: after all, it was made clear at the very beginning of the first chapter that the task of producing an acceptable factual account of how men lived during this period in Britain was actually impossible. And yet ... doubtless it struck some human groups during the Lower Palaeolithic as impossible to reach Britain or to subsist there, but that did not prevent them from achieving it; maybe some of those

eccentricities which foreigners descry to-day in the British date back to the very beginning after all. We will not speculate on the antiquity of that traditional British warcry 'Come on, chaps'; let us simply utter it, and go down fighting in the cause of palaeoanthropology.

The problems at least are easy to state. We seek factual information about the economic and social life of early man in Britain, and we are confronted by inadequacies of the evidence, partly through the poor quality of past research and partly through the simple lack of survival of whole classes of vital data. Therefore we must deal mainly in generalities, and seek to attain only a rather simple level of understanding for the moment. The following sections of this chapter accordingly present the main archaeological conclusions reached in this book and attempt to look just a little way beyond them.

BRITAIN IN THE LOWER AND MIDDLE PALAEOLITHIC

Our area, now an island, or indeed a group of islands, was clearly at least in part a peninsula of mainland Europe during the Middle and Upper Pleistocene, though perhaps not permanently. The precise shape and extent of this British peninsula cannot be exactly stated, nor is it clear how often it may have been severed from, and rejoined to, Continental Europe as sea-level changes occurred. We must say 'at least in part a peninsula', since Ireland seems not to have been reached by man during the Pleistocene, and we may assume that some form of water barrier between Ireland and the rest of Britain existed at times when habitation would otherwise have been possible; also, the status of the present Scottish islands during the Pleistocene is not entirely clear, though these too were not reached by Palaeolithic man. The distribution of Lower and Middle Palaeolithic settlement is in fact mainly southerly and easterly, with the vast majority of the sites lying in England south of a line from the Bristol Channel to the Humber.

This distribution no doubt partly reflects the geographical position of the land connection to the Continent, but is also likely to have been influenced by the absence of good supplies of workable flint in northern and western Britain, and by the more rugged terrain there; also, except in the warmer periods, by climatic factors. It is not that Lower and Middle Palaeolithic man was unable to cope with such adverse circumstances, but one can see no reason why he should have bothered to put up with them when conditions in the south and east were so favourable. There is no sign that his numbers were ever great, so there would have been no population pressure to drive him far to the north or west, nor do we know of any specially attractive food resources that might have enticed him in those directions. It is worth commenting here that the initial peopling of Scotland seems to have been a Mesolithic event and that by that time pressure of population on habitable areas in the south may indeed have played a part. However, we must not forget the other side of the argument regarding British Lower and Middle Palaeolithic distribution, namely that it is precisely in the north and west of Britain that geological processes, especially those associated with glacial advances and retreats, are most likely to have destroyed or swept away any evidence of occupation that may have existed.

It has been stressed in this book that Britain lay right on the outer limit of Old World Palaeolithic settlement, and that it is accordingly a region to which people would have come only occasionally, at times when access was possible and conditions were favourable; it is not a major centre of continuous human development from which technological and economic ideas were dispersed in all directions. There are two obvious routes of access

to the British peninsula for early man; one from the south, from Atlantic Europe, via France, and the other from the east, across the north European lowlands, via Germany and the Low Countries. The archaeological record, viewed broadly, does give some cause for thinking that both routes were actually in operation at times. The Acheulian handaxe industries probably arrived by the Atlantic Europe route, immediately from France, though their ancestry can be regarded as ultimately African. We might however regard the Late Acheulian/Micoquian as more likely to have come in by the other route, in view of the good German parallels for our Wolvercote Channel industry, but there are some French examples too, so this is not certain. The Clactonian, for its part, is more likely to have reached Britain from the east rather than from the south, since typical Clactonian occurrences are rare (if they exist at all) in southern France and in Spain, while several examples of early industries with flakes, cores and choppers, and without handaxes, are certainly known in Central and Eastern Europe. It is in fact in Britain that the Clactonian is best seen, but even so it does not seem likely to have been of indigenous origin, for the geographical reasons already mentioned. As for the Middle Palaeolithic, it appears that our Mousterian industries came to Britain specifically from north France, and it is likely that they were with us for only a short period because of the climatic deterioration as the Devensian glaciation proceeded. In this case, the route from the east does not seem to have been active, since industries of the distinctive 'East Mousterian' kind are wholly absent. On the other hand, though it is not strictly our concern in this book, it looks very likely that the bearers of the British Earlier Upper Palaeolithic industries, with their distinctive leaf-point forms, came in by the eastern rather than the southern route a little later still in the Devensian, while the contribution from France to the British Upper Palaeolithic is minimal, surprisingly enough.

In this general situation the diversity of the British Lower Palaeolithic is not to be wondered at. People were arriving from different sources and staying for a while, but there was no permanent local population to absorb each new incursion and provide continuity. Rather, the story is one of stops and starts. Those who came should have thrived here during the more favourable climatic periods, and the admirable British chalk flint should have suited the stone tool makers. Doubtless it even exerted its own influence on the appearance of some of the lithic industries they produced, making possible for example the fine large Acheulian cleavers of the Middle Thames sites, the prodigal Levalloisian technique of Baker's Hole, or the elegant and precise flake-blades of Crayford or Creffield Road, Acton. If it is hard to find widespread close parallels on the Continent for some of the finest British industries, let us allow the possibility that there were distinctively British stone tool-kits, even if there was not a permanent British population. If the diversity of the industries still seems surprising, it is mainly the lack of clear dating for so many British sites that causes the picture to show bewildering variety rather than an orderly and predictable pattern of variation.

CHRONOLOGY

In Chapter 2, the British Pleistocene sequence was examined and summarized. The stages need not all be named again here, since they were set out in Tables 1-6. Their still tentative nature has been stressed, along with the certainty — rather than likelihood — that gaps exist in the record as it is at present expounded. The current system of Anglian-Hoxnian-Wolstonian-Ipswichian-Devensian is too simple, and there should be at least one more interglacial, to which some of the deposits at present ascribed to the Hoxnian or to the Ipswichian will ultimately prove to belong. There is also serious difficulty in correlating the British pre-Anglian sequence with its Continental equivalents, which suggests that gaps exist in this part too of the British record. Useful chronometric dating is still almost non-existent in the British Pleistocene until one reaches the middle and later parts of the Devensian, when radiocarbon dating can sometimes be used. Our knowledge of interstadials, except within the Devensian, remains pitifully weak. From the point of view of the archaeologist, these are all crucial problems when he tries to set about sorting out the internal British

Lower and Middle Palaeolithic sequence and correlating it with other areas. If all these matters were firmly in hand, the baleful influence of stone tool typology would be less strong, and one vital key to understanding the variability of the British industries would be in our possession.

Meanwhile, within the terminology we have followed, the indications are that the earliest Palaeolithic arrivals in Britain are of inter-Anglian or possibly late Cromerian date, and that they probably comprise separate 'Clactonian' and 'Early Acheulian' elements. Industries of both these kinds can also be seen in the Hoxnian, the Clactonian more or less unchanged, but the Acheulian technologically improved and attaining a 'Middle' rather than 'Early' status in this respect. It is arguable that there are a few signs of Levalloisian technique before the end of the Hoxnian. Within the Wolstonian complex there were clearly periods when Britain offered attractive opportunities for occupation, and the industries are diverse. Without being able to put them all in their correct order, we can see: numerous well-made Acheulian handaxe industries, presenting interesting morphological and technological variations; a few industries heavily dominated by bold use of the Levalloisian 'tortoise-core' technique; hints that non-Levalloisian flake industries, perhaps of 'epi-Clactonian' character, were sometimes made, though it is not clear whether they were entirely separate from other lithic traditions; and at least one industry classifiable as archaic Mousterian (High Lodge). The Ipswichian seems to have been a notably warm period at its optimum, and again there is varied occupation in Britain, in which can be distinguished: the last of the Middle Acheulian occurrences; a few distinctive late Acheulian/Micoquian handaxe industries, with good Continental parallels; industries specializing in Levalloisian technique, with the emphasis now changed from the heavier oval flakes struck from 'tortoise-cores' to elongated, blade-like ones struck from Levalloisian flake-blade cores: and the first occurrences of typical *bout coupé* handaxes, whose affinities evidently lie with the earliest Mousterian of Acheulian Tradition of northern France. In the colder Devensian period which follows, conditions were evidently mild enough at times to suit hunters of the 'cold' mammalian fauna (mammoth, woolly rhinoceros, reindeer, etc.). Such people used Middle Palaeolithic rather than Lower Palaeolithic technology, and the main industries or stray finds of this date can be attributed directly to the Mousterian of Acheulian Tradition, unless some prefer to give the title 'developed Levalloisian' to those occurrences amongst them where Levalloisian flake-blades are overwhelmingly dominant. Later in the Devensian come at least two main stages of Upper Palaeolithic occupation of Britain, but they lie outside the scope of this book: there is evidently no continuity or local transition from Middle to Upper Palaeolithic in Britain as there appears to be in certain other parts of the Old World.

This summary of the Palaeolithic industries of the various named stages of the British Pleistocene can be given only on the basis of extrapolation from the very few instances where good stratigraphic information has actually been obtained and local successions established, north Kent being the best region. The arguments about building up a basic sequence, and extending it to give this overall picture, form the core of this book, Chapters 3 to 5.

VARIABILITY IN THE LITHIC INDUSTRIES

To account satisfactorily for the differences between the contents of the general stages of the British Palaeolithic just mentioned, we may fairly invoke the passing of time on the one hand and the differing source areas of the various groups on the other. But these factors will hardly suffice to account for all the variability within these cultural stages. Such is the state of the evidence, however, that only in the case of the Middle Acheulian stage can the matter be properly discussed in any detail. As regards the Early Acheulian, the Clactonian, the Late Acheulian/Micoquian, the different facies of Levalloisian and the Mousterian of Britain, either the industries are too few or too impoverished to enable the amount of variation to be seen clearly, or else detailed analyses of stratigraphically reliable assemblages have not yet been made. But the Middle Acheulian material is in a somewhat better state, and in Chapter 5 a lengthy exposition

of the variants was offered, along with some discussion of their significance. Inevitably, since the Middle Acheulian stage extends from the late Hoxnian to the Ipswichian, the passing of time must be important and it is accordingly reasonable to look for at least some technological developments. But, in fact, no clear time-trends are apparent, and we cannot attribute their absence wholly to the weakness and ambiguity of the dating evidence. The writer's suggested Pointed and Ovate Traditions clearly overlap in time (Table 16). There certainly are technological differences between individual industries, like presence or absence of Levalloisian technique, frequent or infrequent use of 'tranchet finish', and so forth, but these may merely be stylistic details. Whether such features as the twisted cutting edges of some ovates and the twisted tips of some pointed handaxes are to be regarded as stylistic or functional, however, is not at present clear to the author; the elucidation of these points could certainly be sought by microwear analysis, if enough fresh specimens can be assembled.

The writer does however take the view that the acutely pointed types of handaxe on the one hand, and the flat, broad ended ovates with completely worked cutting edges, on the other, *must* reflect different functions. If this is so — and again a major microwear analysis programme is really required — then some particular functional significance must attach to the presence in Britain of whole industries with demonstrably (and indeed quantifiably) strong preferences for either pointed or ovate handaxe types. It is therefore important that we should consider not only the making of individual implements for specific purposes, but also the contriving of whole industries for particular group activities. Nor is this a simple question of pointed handaxes versus ovates, for there are many variations of emphasis within those two broad specializations. Thick-shafted ficrons, for example, are one distinctive pointed handaxe type which is not always present and may have had one particular use; the ovates, for their part, range from those with almost pointed tips to frankly square-ended forms. And there are all sorts of other implement types outside the pointed and ovate handaxe classes which should be significant, for example, the heavy, broad-ended, almost axe-like cleavers, which sometimes occur in Middle Acheulian industries, the most striking of them being markedly divergent or 'fan-shaped'. Surely these are likely to be implements with one specific function, rather than multi-purpose tools? It must also be recalled that there is much more than handaxes to any Acheulian industry, and that the quantity and nature of the formal flake-tools certainly vary from site to site. The writer does not feel that they have been adequately studied in Britain, neither by himself nor by anyone else, though a major drawback is that they were not always collected in the earlier days of British Palaeolithic archaeology, so that there are few really good samples. And apart from the formal flake-tools there are the 'utilized flakes' to be considered.

In short, it seems highly likely that there is a strong element of 'functional variation' in the British Middle Acheulian, superimposed on such differences as may arise from technological development as time passed, or from stylistic factors. It is all the more frustrating, therefore, that we find ourselves unable to spell out what kinds of industry go with what specific human activities. For this, we should need undisturbed sites with well-preserved industries, from a range of geographical situations (e.g. lakeside, riverside, uplands and lowlands), associated with clear evidence of the activities carried out (hunting, butchering, collecting of food or raw material, tool-making, domestic occupation of a base-camp and so forth), and preferably with evidence to show us what was the season of the year. There is no such corpus of evidence available. No single British site has yielded a complete set of the data required, and relatively few have yielded any such data at all. From what there is, we can only make deductions about human activities, and these are considered in the following sections. The evidence is so unevenly and thinly spread, however, that we cannot in all honesty use the conclusions to make a general interpretation of functional variability in the Middle Acheulian stage.

Functions of stone implements

Inevitably, as throughout this book, we are forced chiefly to consider the stone implements themselves and whatever information we can wring directly from them. As regards the handaxes, it is pleasing to be able to include at least a little factual information. In his highly important doctoral research, Lawrence H. Keeley, who worked at Oxford from 1972 to 1977 under the writer's supervision, was principally concerned with developing and testing methods and techniques of high-magnification microwear analysis, which he then applied to selected British Lower Palaeolithic material (1977). The majority of the artefacts he studied were retouched and unretouched flakes, the best of them from recent excavations directed by Professor Ronald Singer and Mr John Wymer: Clactonian from Clacton (the Golf Course site) and Acheulian from Hoxne. Very few handaxes were among the pieces examined, but Keeley did find typical microwear polishes on three. Two were from the Hoxne Lower Industry and one came from a small site discovered at South Woodford (London) in 1974 and excavated under the direction of Mr Terry Betts (report in preparation). In all three cases the polish was identifiable as the result of the implement's having been used for butchering and meat-cutting tasks (Plate 36a). The two Hoxne implements are both convex-sided forms with pointed tips (Fig 7:1): in one, the position of maximum breadth comes only slightly below the centre, while in the other it falls distinctly low, giving almost a broad cordiform shape. The South Woodford implement was also convex-sided, small, with a less acute but quite serviceable point at the tip end. It would be utterly wrong to jump from this evidence to the conclusion that handaxes in general, or even pointed convex-sided handaxes in general, were always meat knives and anyone who feels tempted to take that view should read *inter alia* the arguments of J.D. Clark and C.V. Haynes (1970) about the association of light duty flakes with butchery sites and the lack of positive evidence (in their view) that handaxes and cleavers were butchering tools. It is also worth noting that some of the flakes from the Lower Industry at Hoxne had also

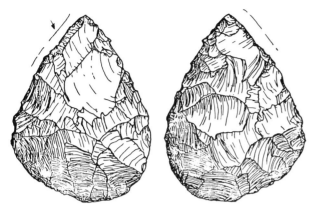

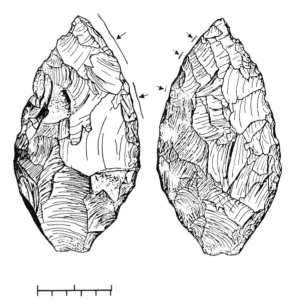

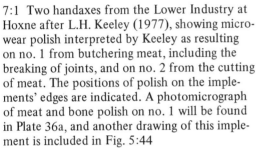

7:1 Two handaxes from the Lower Industry at Hoxne after L.H. Keeley (1977), showing micro-wear polish interpreted by Keeley as resulting on no. 1 from butchering meat, including the breaking of joints, and on no. 2 from the cutting of meat. The positions of polish on the implements' edges are indicated. A photomicrograph of meat and bone polish on no. 1 will be found in Plate 36a, and another drawing of this implement is included in Fig. 5:44

been used for the same kind of butchering tasks as the two handaxes. The message of Keeley's observation, apart from his identification of the uses of these particular implements, is that the problems of handaxe function (and hence of a major part of Acheulian variability) are *not* insoluble, provided enough handaxes of different kinds, from known contexts and in suitable condition, are forthcoming for study. Needless to say, there are already plans to build upon the foundation he has laid, and the writer is grateful to him for permission to report some of his work in this chapter meanwhile.

This is perhaps the place to mention one other remarkable observation about a British handaxe, recorded a great deal earlier, which is partly relevant to the problems of function if it can be taken at face value. Worthington Smith wrote in *Man the Primeval Savage*, about the butts of handaxes (1894: 221-2):

> It is certain that the butt-end of heavy pointed implements was frequently used for hammering: the results of repeated battering at the butt are not uncommon amongst certain classes of implements. I have an implement from Bedford which had the butt-end when first found wrapped round with herbaceous stems, probably rushes, as if for a protection for the hand. It was impossible to preserve the highly friable and dusty material, but the implement still retains traces of the rushes. . . .

He did not illustrate this piece, and the writer has never seen it, if it survives, but we have already seen that Smith was a careful observer. The association of the plant material and the implement may have been fortuitous, but if not it might cast light on how those handaxes (or indeed flakes) whose edges were sharp all round, were held in the hand for use when newly made. There is no definite evidence from anywhere in the world, so far as the writer knows, that Lower Palaeolithic handaxes were actually hafted. The morphology of the more robust forms seems to preclude it as a possibility in their case, but others look eminently haftable. However, one would need remarkable conditions of preservation, perhaps at a waterlogged site, if a hafted stone implement of this age were to survive intact. As for Smith's suggestion that heavy-butted handaxes were sometimes used as hammers, this view has been put forward by other authors too (e.g. Wymer in Ovey (ed.) 1964: 32-3). It is necessary of course to be sure that any areas of battering at the butt-end cannot have resulted merely from pressure against, or violent contact with, other stones at or after the time of deposition, before deciding that they represent utilization damage.

Another unsolved problem, relevant to explaining the functions of handaxes, lies in the fact that they commonly occur in vast numbers at a single site. We can see this in Britain in the Middle Gravels at Swanscombe, Furze Platt, Broom, Knowle Farm (Savernake), Warren Hill or Dunbridge, for example, but we do not get a very clear picture since these are all gravel pit finds with the artefacts not in a primary context. The excavations at Cuxton (see pages 168-70) perhaps give a better indication of the density of such handaxe concentrations (cf. also Plate 30), and anyone left in doubt has only to consider some of the African evidence: for example, the B5 floor at Kalambo Falls, Zambia; some of the occurrences at Isimila (Tanzania), Olorgesailie (Kenya), or Melka Kontouré (Ethiopia); or the HK site at Olduvai Gorge (Tanzania) – though this last is admittedly in a hill wash deposit. Even more prolific sites occur in South Africa – Cape Hangklip or Doornlagte, for example. Do these awe-inspiring spreads of artefacts – finished implements, not merely waste products – reflect density of population, or frequent visits by small groups to the same spot, or were the handaxes used only for very short periods and then cast aside with no thought of re-use or resharpening (if indeed the latter was even required), and no regret for all the care that had gone into their manufacture? But there seems to be no purely natural explanation that can account for *all* such concentrations, even if one can envisage occasions when heavy objects like handaxes, originally stratified at several different horizons in a fine-grained deposit, could 'migrate' to a common level under erosional conditions strong enough to remove the particles of the containing deposit but too weak to shift the large

artefacts. The famous 'Cat Walk' site at Olorgesailie (Plate 37a) features an impressive and apparently single spread of handaxes and other large artefacts, which are in fact demonstrably derived from two quite separate horizons which outcrop, as it were, in one sloping erosional surface. But what if they were now to be covered again gently by new sediments? However, such natural factors, and those which operate in active stream channels to bring together concentrations of sizeable stones (Plate 37b), cannot cover all the prolific Acheulian occurrences of this nature, and no ready explanation for them presents itself.

It is curious therefore that in this respect isolated finds of handaxes may even seem more informative – not when such single artefacts occur derived in a gravel, but when they are found in pristine state and quite by themselves in a brick-earth, a subaerial deposit or perhaps a cave sediment, for then they seem to declare themselves as lying where their users left them. If that is so, we may deduce that they were sometimes made to be carried abroad as tools or weapons and not accumulated at the home base for 'static' use only. That is interesting, since in many parts of Britain the wherewithal to make implements as and when they were needed must always have been ready to hand. Are we then to suppose that not everyone could or would make his own implements; that there were specialist knappers who provided the tools and weapons for others to carry? This might account for the extraordinarily close repetition of 'preferred' sizes and shapes of handaxes in some industries. In Britain, the *bout coupé* series discussed in Chapter 6 perhaps gives the best examples of these casually lost or discarded single implements, and maybe they are also as likely an example as any of specialist manufacture. But there are plenty of Middle Acheulian (and indeed Levalloisian) single finds in fresh condition too.

It would be pleasing if one could complete this speculative argument by suggesting that the massive concentrations of finished implements marked the places where specialist knappers plied their trade (and trade it could even have been in more than one sense), but if that were so we should also expect to find large quantities of flaking debris there, and that is just what is usually missing.

Certainly, however, there *are* examples of stone tool manufacturing sites, like Caddington, but at them finished implements are comparatively scarce, while debris abounds. The problem, alas, remains unsolved.

If we now leave the handaxes aside, there is a little that can be said about some other classes of artefacts. At Hoxne, in the Upper Industry, a special feature, as the work of Singer and Wymer showed, was the large quantity of fine convex sidescrapers made from large bold flakes. L.H. Keeley (1977), on the evidence of microwear polishes preserved on their edges, was able to show that some of them were certainly used to scrape hides (see also the report by Singer and others now in preparation). We may note that flake-tools generally similar to these are also present in quantity at Stoke Newington and at High Lodge (in the classic flake industry); both of these series should contain specimens suitable for microwear study, though none has yet been attempted. At High Lodge, no doubt, there will also be flake-tools of other formal kinds, with their own specific uses which ought to be identifiable by microwear analysis, though for the present they are not available for study. There are plenty of other Acheulian flake-tools in Britain, but they are not often preserved in large numbers from a single site, and too often they are in an abraded or heavily patinated state, which means that the microwear traces are gone or obscured.

We have also speculated a little about Levalloisian flakes in previous chapters and might usefully do so again here. First, the remarkable Baker's Hole industry may be recalled. This seems clearly to have been a site where large nodules of high quality raw material were exploited and Levalloisian technique was used on an unusual scale to obtain large oval or elongated flakes from them. We may count the cores and the minor flakes as waste and assume that the people took away what they wanted or could carry of the large Levalloisian flakes. Many imperfect ones, including plunging flakes, were certainly left behind. Now large Levalloisian flakes must have made very serviceable knife-like tools in themselves, with little or no further retouch, offering working edges not unlike those of a flat handaxe; others

could be retouched to form different kinds of flake-tools in much the same way as Mousterian man was to use Levalloisian flakes from time to time — in the Ferrassie facies of the Charentian variant, for example. If this was done in this case, it seems to have been done elsewhere than at the Baker's Hole working site, since formally retouched flakes are very rare there. There is one other possibility, namely that some of the larger flakes were actually used as blanks for the manufacture of bifacial handaxes. Definite evidence to support this suggestion is rather scarce, and the writer has already discussed the question of whether handaxes were present on the actual working floor (pages 82, 93). He did, however, note in the collection of the British Museum (Natural History) amongst the Baker's Hole material, one bifacially worked handaxe which preserves evidence of having been made from a Levalloisian flake; it is recorded as probably having come from the original floor. At Manchester Museum there is a similar piece, this time recorded only as from Northfleet, but stored with artefacts entirely typical of the Baker's Hole site. (Plenty of Baker's Hole material is marked simply 'Northfleet'.) At Manchester Museum there is also a large Levalloisian flake with flat retouch on the lower half of the bulbar surface, marked as from Bevan's Pit, Northfleet. In all these pieces, traces of the platforms survive as well as the typical dorsal scar patterns. We should also recall Spurrell's observations about the technology of the Baker's Hole artefacts (1883: 103), quoted above on page 92, in note 6 to Chapter 3. It is also worth mentioning here a German site, Reutersruh-bei-Ziegenhain, in Hessen (Luttropp and Bosinski 1971), where outcrops of a readily workable quartzite were exploited by the local Lower Palaeolithic population as well as by later groups. In the principal industry here, which can only be called Acheulian, there is a strong Levalloisian component, accompanied by a rather small quantity of handaxes, many of them broken or unfinished, and various flake-tools, as well as much manufacturing debris. It seems at least possible that the 'Early Levalloisian' of Baker's Hole, as we have called it, may actually be no more than an extreme Acheulian variant, a specialized activity site whose products were taken away to other places in north Kent, often in an unfinished state, where some of them were perhaps rendered unrecognizable by fully bifacial retouch. This suggestion must remain speculative, since the original Baker's Hole site was studied so long ago and nothing of it now remains, but it is worth keeping in mind. After all, Acheulian man in Britain was well aware of the Levalloisian technique, and at least a few examples of it come from the Middle Gravels at Swanscombe, accepted here as antedating Baker's Hole.

As for our 'Later Levalloisian', it is worth mentioning again here the fact that at both Crayford and Southall there were faunal remains in intimate association with Levalloisian artefacts of the blade-like variety (pages 87 and 216; see also Plate 24). The old and sketchy original accounts of these sites do not conflict with the notion that both occurrences may have been kill and/or butchery sites, involving a rhinoceros and a mammoth respectively. The Levalloisian flake-blade tools look for the most part very much like knives and projectile points, the latter including at some sites typical examples of the *pointe levallois typique* form, sometimes with the butt thinned as if for hafting (cf. pages 216-18). From Crayford and Creffield Road, Acton, and perhaps from one or two other sites which produced artefacts of this kind, there survive a few specimens which look fresh enough for microwear analysis. Meanwhile, we might adopt the hypothesis that Levalloisian industries of this kind include at least some variants related to hunting and butchering activities, perhaps at specific times of the year.

Let us not however forget that at Crayford there were also conjoinable groups of flakes (Plate 24), whose presence demonstrates that artefacts were made on the spot. We might envisage the kill being made by a relatively small group of hunters, and so far as the flint artefacts are concerned that part of the episode might be represented only by the projectile point types, though doubtless the hunters carried weapons made of other materials too — long wooden spears, perhaps, like the one from Lehringen in Saxony, and maybe also clubs. Once the animal was brought down and killed, and we do not know exactly how this was achieved (whether for example poisons may have been used

on the projectile points), then the hunters themselves, or maybe others who had been watching and waiting, would prepare fresh cutting implements and set about the business of butchery, doubtless watched by scavenging animals and birds from a respectful distance. And who were these hunters? If these are indeed again specialized toolkits, their users presumably made quite different artefacts on other occasions. Were they perhaps simply the same people who first brought the Mousterian of Acheulian Tradition to Britain? That could be the meaning of the occasional tenuous association, or mere proximity, of one or two *bout coupé* handaxes when we examine Levalloisian occurrences of this kind (cf. Chapters 5 and 6). The chronology, so far as it is known, would fit, and the hypothesis seems perfectly tenable in the absence of really clear evidence for or against it. Undoubtedly the MTA people passed across this terrain at about this time. Seasonal variation of activities, and hence of tool-kits, is a normal and indeed essential part of hunting and gathering economies. The Mousterian people of Europe frequently used the Levalloisian technique, especially where flint was abundant and of high quality. Maybe the only mental leap required is to use the name 'Mousterian of Acheulian Tradition' for those of the Levalloisian flake-blade industries where there is actually no clear evidence for handaxe manufacture at all.

These are the kind of factors one should keep in mind when it is asserted that the name 'Levalloisian' refers to the employment of a technique, not to a cultural tradition. If the hypotheses of these last few paragraphs are accepted, the 'pure Levalloisian' industries noted in the preceding chapters could all be taken back into the Acheulian or the Mousterian, under the heading of specific activity variants, which appear quite logical given the circumstances of Pleistocene Britain. All such names, including 'Acheulian' and 'Mousterian', are merely convenient labels and must never be used too rigidly. Perhaps it may even be admitted that in considering stone tool functions we have made a flexible and reasonable use of typology and found that it need not, after all, bind us in chains.

We have been dealing so far principally with the

more formal implement types, but it is in fact clear from the work of L.H. Keeley (already quoted) on the Clacton and Hoxne assemblages that, of the artefacts which bore the most informative microwear traces, the majority were not carefully shaped to formal patterns. Simple flakes and fragments, with only minor retouch or sometimes none at all, were frequently utilized, and they yielded evidence for use in a variety of tasks. Dr Keeley will be publishing his conclusions in full, but since we are here concerned with the functions of stone tools in the British Lower and Middle Palaeolithic, it seems appropriate to state briefly what kind of information he was able to obtain from Clacton and Hoxne[1] about human activities at those sites, from this uniquely direct evidence (Keeley 1977: chapters 5 and 7).

Clacton (Gravel and Marl at the Golf Course site; see pages 137-43 above for details and references). That flint-knapping took place at the site is attested by Keeley's discovery of the presence of conjoinable flakes. The microwear analysis of utilized pieces showed that wood was being worked (Plate 36b and Fig. 7:2) by sawing, scraping, boring, chopping (or adzing) and whittling (or planing); animal hides were being scraped and cut; carcases were being butchered, a process which included the cutting of meat; bone was also being worked. At a fairly simple level there was some correlation between the way in which artefacts were used and the angle and shape of their working edges. Retouch was primarily a matter of blunting or modifying edges on the selected piece of flint to make it easier to hold in use, rather than of creating specialized working edges. Flakes, shatter-pieces and cores were all used as tools, the last-named only rarely, however. The broad range of activities represented suggested to Keeley that the site was a general occupation area rather than a specialized activity camp.

Hoxne (the Upper and Lower Industries of Singer and Wymer; see pages 200-2 for details and references). Flint-knapping was carried out at the site, and it included handaxe manufacture, as the numerous typical waste-flakes show, many of them having been struck off with 'soft hammers'.

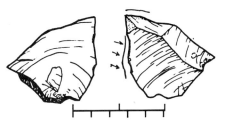

7:2 A flake from the marl at the Golf Course site at Clacton, showing microwear polish indicating use for whittling wood. The position of the polished area is indicated and a photomicrograph of the polish is shown in Plate 36b. Drawing after L.H. Keeley (1977)

Two of the handaxes from the Lower Industry, as we have already noted, were used for cutting meat (Plate 36a and Fig. 7:1). The rest of the tools include shaped and unshaped pieces, formally shaped ones being rather rare in the Lower Industry. There is some correlation between the angle and shape of their edges on the one hand, and the particular uses of the tools on the other. Rather more care was apparently taken than at Clacton over choosing the sizes and proportions of the flakes which were used. As at Clacton, retouch was sometimes used to blunt edges or projections to facilitate the holding of the tools by their users. The tasks carried out at the site, as revealed by the microwear analysis, do not differ greatly from those represented at Clacton: wood was variously whittled (or planed), chopped (or adzed), scraped, bored and split with wedges; hides were scraped and cut; meat was butchered; bone was chopped and bored; and plants of a non-woody nature, reeds perhaps, were cut. In the Upper Industry, which did not produce many artefacts in a suitable state for microwear analysis, some at least of the hide-scraping was done with boldly but elegantly made convex scrapers with fully retouched edges. One fascinating detail about the hide-cutting in the Lower Industry was revealed by the apparent superimposition on two pieces of a faint 'wood polish' over the basic 'hide polish' of the working edge, so placed that Keeley was able to interpret it as indicating that the hides were laid over a wooden support of some kind (probably just draped over a log) while the cutting was done, doubtless to facilitate the process (cf. also Keeley and Newcomer 1977: 60-1).

In considering this factual information about the uses of stone artefacts at Hoxne and Clacton, ordinary enough at a human level but remarkable in terms of Palaeolithic archaeology, we have passed at last from speculation about flint implements to facts, and from the pieces of classifiable worked stone to the people who shaped and used them with no thought of archaeological classification in their minds. We have also glimpsed the power and potential of this relatively new method of study, and we may see once more, only too clearly, exactly what kinds of objects and materials have perished for ever even from the few primary context sites. Where are the wooden objects that were shaped and the hides that were cut and scraped? What were the finished products used for? Many absurdly simple questions about ordinary human activities in the earlier Palaeolithic will always remain unanswered and we seem doomed to end up with an uneven mixture of general information interspersed on the one hand with blanks and on the other with points of minute detail relating to individual moments of remote prehistory — points like the wooden supports for hide-cutting at Hoxne or Worthington Smith's thirteen conjoined handaxe trimming flakes at Caddington (Fig. 5:43). But both the general information and the details should greatly increase as microwear studies proceed, and indeed we can hope to know much more about all the topics considered in this chapter within the next decade or so.

SETTLEMENT AND PALAEOANTHROPOLOGY

From variation in human activities as reflected by artefacts alone, we may proceed to consider the whole pattern of settlement in the Lower and Middle Palaeolithic of Britain. Drawing on the observations and theoretical approaches of many archaeologists, anthropologists and geographers, mainly over the past ten years, and considering the evidence from other regions, we may expect that the British populations during our period consisted of mobile bands, with a seasonal basis and rhythm

to their movements, as different food resources were exploited in turn, and stays of several days or sometimes of several weeks were made here and there. If we only had well-enough-preserved evidence, we would hope to be able to distinguish amongst our sites major base camps where the principal stops were made, and, disposed around them like satellites, the places where special activities were carried out as appropriate to that particular region and its resources. Sites of the latter kind would include kill sites, places where food was collected and places where raw materials of various kinds were acquired. We could hardly hope to make firm identifications of places where plant materials or wood were obtained or where fruits were gathered, since such activities leave few traces that are likely to survive for long periods, but at least the sites where stone was extracted and processed should be reasonably clear.[2] Between the major base camps we might expect to find minor sites marking ephemeral halts — overnight resting places when a journey was long, for example. And then there will be many find-spots of single implements, casual losses or abandonments of tools or weapons away from home during daily life. The major base camps themselves must actually count as temporary affairs, or 'semi-permanent' at the most, and they would vary in size and in density of occupation, since group size would have varied according to season and activity; for example, the women and children, and the very old, might not have made all of the seasonal moves. We might expect any winter settlements to be the largest and longest used, and any dwelling structures there would have needed to be more substantial, both for that reason and to withstand the colder conditions.

This is merely a general statement about the likely strategy of settlement in Palaeolithic Britain, and is not specific to any one of the human groups to which we have previously referred, but it is probably on the right lines for the whole of our period, and we need not go into greater detail; it takes slightly further some of the points already suggested in this chapter. We may also suppose that the bands would follow much the same cycle of movement for several successive years, so that we can look to find sites which suggest re-occupation; some of the 'brickearth' sites with several 'floors', or with artefacts dispersed through a substantial thickness of the sediments, might suggest this – Gaddesden Row, Caddington, Elveden or Foxhall Road, Ipswich, for example, in their various ways. But only in an ideal archaeological situation could we hope to check our general hypothesis in detail against actual surviving evidence; the difficulties are obvious. First, there is demonstrably a major palimpsest of different periods of Lower and Middle Palaeolithic occupation in Britain, each no doubt with its own nomadic settlement pattern of this kind, and we have far too little chronological and stratigraphic control when we try to sort out which occurrences belong with which; no one landscape and terrain survives intact, but only a jumble of fragments of successive landscapes in which most of the sites are disturbed or lost. It is not as if we were ethnographers observing present activity. Second, the European geographical situation may actually imply that southern Britain was not normally an integral territory in itself, but merely a part of one: that is to say, it is quite arguable, if these people were accustomed to cover long distances, that we do not see the full seasonal cycle of settlement at all in Britain. The winter camps might always have been back in what is now Continental Europe (except of course at any times when Britain might have been an occupied island). During the colder periods of the Pleistocene it is indeed highly likely that only summer hunting expeditions came to Britain, when anyone came at all. That could be true of all our Devensian Mousterian, for example. Direct evidence for seasonality at British Palaeolithic sites is unfortunately extremely scarce. One might make out a sketchy case for summer occupation at some sites,[3] but to argue any one of them, Lower or Middle Palaeolithic, as a specifically winter occupation seems impossible. However, in most cases there is no evidence at all.

Be that as it may, we can reasonably assert that the majority of the sites discussed in any detail in this book are likely to have been the temporary base camps of nomadic hunter-gatherers, often located near a stream channel or other water body such as a small lake; we have also noted a few special activity sites and plenty of isolated 'casual loss' finds. Baker's Hole, Caddington and Botany Pit, Purfleet, all furnished examples of special activity sites where stone was obtained and exploited for the manufacture of implements which were taken away; these places do not seem to have been living sites so much as working areas. To those names we can add the poorly known site of Frindsbury in north Kent, near Rochester, where a somewhat informal excavation (Cook and Killick 1924) uncovered several piles of collected flint nodules, debris of stone-working, and two handaxes only, to represent the end products of the operation and to give us a broad hint that the occurrence is an Acheulian one although it produced no dating evidence. The recently found site of Red Barns, Portchester, Hampshire (excavations by A.M. ApSimon and C. Gamble of Southampton University, who are preparing a report) is probably a similar occurrence, where nodules of chalk flint were exploited over a substantial stretch of foreshore associated with the 'hundred foot' raised shoreline that is a well-known feature of West Sussex and east Hampshire. We have also seen two probable kill or butchery sites, at Crayford and Southall, and it is sad that more do not survive in a more complete state. The principal faunal remains from John Waechter's excavations in the Swanscombe Lower Loam (Waechter *et al.* 1968, 1969, 1970, 1971) included some bones in an articulated state associated with artefacts, though it seems likely that he uncovered the outer scatter of material from a living site to which large joints of meat were brought, rather than a kill site; it is unfortunate that few of the artefacts were in a state to preserve microwear traces, even though the site had suffered minimal disturbance at the time when it became buried.

One class of site for which we seem to look in vain in the British Lower and Middle Palaeolithic is temporary coastal settlement specializing in the exploitation of marine resources. This may merely reflect the fact that our Pleistocene coastlines were in many areas quite different from those of today, and that such sites have been lost. There certainly are associations of artefacts with Pleistocene raised beaches, for example at several places in Sussex from Brighton westwards, notably at Slindon

(Calkin 1935; a new review of the sites in this area by A.G. Woodcock is in preparation), and in south Hampshire in the area studied by M.L. Shackley (1975), but primary context occurrences including food debris are not included. Though we have no reason to suspect that sophisticated fishing methods were practised in the Lower and Middle Palaeolithic, it would be surprising if the people wholly neglected shellfish as a source of food. Might there not have been a few British sites after the style of Terra Amata at Nice (de Lumley 1969b, 1975), though not necessarily of the same date, where annual summer visits were made to a coastal location and both fish and shell-fish formed part of the diet along with game obtained inland? It is only fair to remark, however, that such coastal sites are very rare throughout the Old World during the early periods and in Europe they do not become commonplace until the Mesolithic.

If we return from special activity sites to the main base camps, it is very clear that we lack a great deal of information about them. As they have come down to us, most have been badly disturbed and sometimes we have only the stone artefacts which we guess to have been transported together by natural agencies for a short distance. But in even the best examples – like the recently excavated sites at Hoxne or Clacton – there is no convincing trace of any artificial dwelling structure, or even of a formal hearth. Yet it is inconceivable that the numerous British open sites were without any form of shelter for their occupants during cold or inclement weather or even, come to that, by night. The oldest site at Olduvai Gorge, Tanzania, site DK in Bed I, dating from about 1.8 million years ago, shows clearly that the early hominid occupants, a pre-*Homo erectus* group, were capable of piling up lava blocks to make the base for a rudimentary, roughly circular, artificial shelter (M.D. Leakey 1971:24, plate 2 and fig. 7). Structures are known or have been claimed or deduced at various Lower Palaeolithic sites – for example Latamne in Syria (Clark, J.D. 1967, 1968), Terra Amata and Grotte du Lazaret in South France (de Lumley, 1969a, b, c, 1975), and perhaps Hunsgi and Chirki-on-Pravara in India (Corvinus 1970, 1973; Paddayya 1977). Middle Palaeolithic structures are also well

attested, with famous examples at Molodova, USSR, and Arcy-sur-Cure, Yonne, France, (Ivanova and Chernysh 1965; Klein 1973: 68-73; Leroi-Gourhan and Leroi-Gourhan 1964), to name only two. The use of fire also goes well back into the Lower Palaeolithic, though admittedly the evidence for it is not always well preserved on open sites. So these must count as important gaps in the British evidence, which it will be a task of future discovery to fill.[4]

Apart from the possibility of erecting light artificial structures, tents, windbreaks or simple huts, Palaeolithic man often made use of natural shelters: caves or rockshelters. But in Britain, as we have seen, he did not always have this option. In relation to the area of Palaeolithic settlement in Britain, the caves all lie on the northern and western edges. Rockshelters are rare anywhere in Britain, but their distribution is similar, with the exception of Oldbury in Kent, which may have been used in the Middle Palaeolithic. The point is simply that if people entered Britain via the south-east or east, they would have had to travel several days' journey into presumably unknown territory before they came to limestone country of the kind where caves occur, so they would have needed to use open sites and, no doubt, artificial shelter, long before they got there.[5] Given the distribution of the British caves, it is not so surprising that they do not seem to have been used as major bases for substantial groups of people; rather they appear to have given shelter only to small groups making occasional remote forays. Nevertheless, we can document both Acheulian and Mousterian cave occupation in Britain, as we have seen. It is interesting that two of our most important finds of early artefacts, those at Westbury-sub-Mendip and Kent's Cavern (the B1 breccia) come from cave sites (the Westbury site having been a cave at the time). It is during the long and variable Middle Acheulian period that there seems to have been no use at all of the British caves, which is rather curious; various Middle or Later Acheulian occupations of caves are known elsewhere including some in France.

Glynn Isaac has stressed on a number of occasions (e.g. in Isaac and McCown 1976: 483-514; see also Leakey and Lewin 1977) the importance of home bases to the early development of palaeo-lithic culture, along with the practice of food-sharing, the ability to make tools, and, after a while, the use of language. It is likely that the period which he was primarily discussing was wholly past before man first reached Britain, but it is certain that these same features, in a developed form, continued to be of the utmost importance to human society throughout the Middle and Upper Pleistocene, as indeed they still are. Amongst them, home bases are not the least important, which is why it is so regrettable that we cannot study examples of them in any detail in Britain. They should be able to tell us something of group size and of the level and perhaps the type of social organization, as well as casting yet more light on technology. Besides, they would be likely to contain items of domestic equipment in a domestic context, and maybe personal items too, such as decorative objects. It was (inevitably) Worthington Smith who, in a gravel pit at Bedford, found a remarkable cluster of specimens of the naturally perforated fossil *Coscinopora globularis* d'Orb, apparently showing artificial enlargement of the orifices, which he took to indicate that they had been 'used for personal ornaments as beads' (1894: 272-6). He also found a piece of (naturally) perforated shell nearby. These finds (Fig. 7:3 and Plate 38) occurred 'with unabraded implements and flakes, and carbonised vegetable remains'. Organic matter within some of the orifices he 'took to be the remains of part of the ligament on which the beads and perforated shell had been originally strung by their Palaeolithic owner' (*ibid*.). He even submitted some of the beads to analytical chemists, who confirmed the probable organic nature of the material in the orifices. Some of these possible beads survive, including a number at the Pitt Rivers Museum, Oxford, and they look not unconvincing (Plate 38), though the writer does not know with exactly what artefacts they were found. Shall we take Smith's interpretation at face value, or shall we just observe coldly that we have no good British evidence for the apparel or ornaments of earlier Palaeolithic man, and that these supposed beads are quite unproven? Either way, this is just the sort of evidence we could at least hope to find

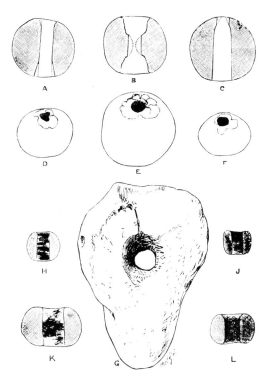

7:3 Worthington Smith's 'fossil beads': specimens of *Coscinopora globularis* d'Orb, with enlarged orifices and traces of black organic material, and a perforated piece of fossil shell found with them; see also Plate 38. As published by Smith (1894) (Natural size)

occasionally, if we had some primary context home base sites to examine.

Without them, the social organization of Lower and Middle Palaeolithic man in Britain must remain largely a matter of speculation, and the writer is not willing to venture much further along that road than this chapter has already taken him. But have we perhaps in these closing pages at least caught a glimpse of the people who made the stone artefacts? Can we say just enough in factual terms from the British evidence to indicate that the general suggestions made about the pattern and nature of settlement in our period are indeed likely to be true, and that it is now mainly a matter of filling in the details by new discovery? We have seen, alas, little more than shadows moving against a murky background, but maybe we can recognize them as shadows of people not so different from ourselves. How lightly they step, as they tread their obscure paths — and so they should, being concerned after all with their present and practical matters, and not with any foolhardy quest to disentangle the past.[6]

EPILOGUE

If this book has provided a working account of the present state of knowledge of the British Lower and Middle Palaeolithic, in a suitably wide context, if it has served as a reminder of half-forgotten past discoveries that are worth fresh consideration, and if it has suggested some problems worth solving in the future, then it has achieved its aims. Whether or not all its archaeological conclusions stand the test of time does not greatly matter, so long as knowledge moves forward; indeed, it would be much better if they were challenged and replaced quite quickly, so long as that meant that research in Britain was proceeding speedily and fruitfully and that new discoveries had been made to fill some of the gaps in the evidence which are at present such a barrier. Could this happen? While the balance of modern 'rescue archaeology' is quite naturally tipped in favour of the later archaeological periods, it is heartening to know that some of those in charge are deliberately taking note of the potential of rescue work for Palaeolithic studies.[7] New finds of undisturbed

primary context Palaeolithic sites, with good environmental and chronological evidence, are certainly the greatest single need, whether it be rescue or research archaeology that produces them. Let there be home bases and special activity sites of several different kinds, and when Heaven sends us these, may it send the accompanying stone artefacts without abrasion or patination, so that the fine work begun on microwear analysis may continue. But no one need think that British palaeolithic studies have ground to a halt until someone discovers a few new sites. Every conclusion reached in this book is really no more than a working hypothesis that needs checking and testing. The writer has suggested various old sites and old collections that need new examination. The task of making a detailed comparison of the British and Continental Lower and Middle Palaeolithic material has hardly been begun. Even the typological and technological analysis of existing stone artefacts still offers many research opportunities: but those who accept them will need to approach typology both objectively and flexibly. All these things are the province of Palaeolithic archaeologists, and there are other urgent tasks which are the parallel concern of Pleistocene geologists and biologists. Yes, there is much to be done, and good reason for thinking that much can be achieved. This is how things seem to the writer as the 1970s draw to their close. How will they look in ten years' time?

NOTES

1 The work at Hoxne and Clacton was carried out by a team from the University of Chicago, directed by Professor Ronald Singer and Mr John Wymer. Since the writer is here making use of information obtained directly by them, or by Dr Keeley from their material, it seems only fair to acknowledge the generous financial support, from various bodies, which made their very important work at these British sites possible: The U.S. National Science Foundation (Grants nos. GB 1658, GS 2907 and GS 41435), the U.S. Public Health Service (Grants GM 10113 and GRS RRO5367), the Wenner Gren Foundation for Anthropological Research, Inc., and the Louis Block Fund, Hinds Fund and

Abbott Memorial Fund of the University of Chicago.

2 As prehistory progresses through time, the diversity of special activity sites increases, and one can look, for example, for sacred sites or burial places. No convincing Lower Palaeolithic examples of these are known anywhere in the world yet, which is not of course to say that they never existed. The European and Asian Mousterian contains various examples of deliberate and careful burial of the dead, strongly suggestive of belief in life after death, but such burials do not appear to have been removed from the settlement area or placed in special locations; the first major cemetery sites

occur in the epi-Palaeolithic and Mesolithic of a few areas. The suggested 'special activities' of the British Lower and Middle Palaeolithic populations accordingly have a strong economic bias, and the list may do less than justice to the abilities and interests of the people. As ever, this is a question of surviving evidence.

3 How? Some faunal and floral remains can provide data. Deer antlers and teeth give useful seasonal evidence, and some marine and non-marine shells might also help, though for all such evidence one must be sure that it really is contemporary with the occupation, preferably occurring demonstrably as food debris. Plant remains are rather scarce on British Palaeolithic sites, but, for example, would there have been all that fern material at the Stoke Newington site (cf. pages 175, 231) in winter? Possibly it could have occurred or been collected as dry bracken but the other Stoke Newington plant remains recorded by Worthington Smith, like those from Hoxne quoted by him in his discussion (1894: 288-94), seem to indicate a spring to late summer seasonal range. Fish remains can sometimes be another source of seasonal information, but have not yet given useful data in Britain for our period; indeed, all the lines of evidence suggested here have yet to be used extensively and successfully on the British Palaeolithic. But one need not delve far in European Palaeolithic studies, in France or Germany for example, to see the potential of such evidence for determining seasonality: classic examples from the later Upper Palaeolithic include Stellmoor and Meiendorf near Hamburg (Rust 1937, 1943) and Pincevent in north France (Leroi-Gourhan and Brézillon 1972), or, from the Lower Palaeolithic, Terra Amata, Nice (de Lumley 1969b, 1975). Several other examples from elsewhere in the world could be added, and we must hope that British sites will produce similar conclusions in the future. Other kinds of evidence may sometimes be suggestive if not conclusive. Some of the lake-side settlements, Elveden, Foxhall Road, Ipswich, and perhaps High Lodge, for example, look as if they may have been situated close to the edges of lakes which were at a low summer level, the artefacts becoming sealed in by lake sediments afterwards, when the water-level rose again during the autumn to spring period. The occurrence of distinct occupation horizons at several levels in a brickearth might be interpreted in a similar way — repeated summer occupations, separated by winter and spring floodwater sedimentation — for example, at Gaddesden Row or in the Swanscombe Upper

Loam. Most of the sites of this kind would have been distinctly damp and inhospitable for winter occupation, one would think. Generally speaking, caves would seem likely to have made altogether better winter base camps. Yet in Britain the cave occupations all show distinctly low density — the Mousterian of the Mendip caves will serve as an example. Whether Kent's Cavern in Devon had some slightly larger assemblages is an open question, thanks to the long history of undocumented or poorly documented research, but even this site does not look like an intensively occupied winter headquarters. The same goes for Pin Hole Cave at Creswell Crags.

4 Perhaps Stoke Newington did produce some signs of a structure (cf. page 175), but the present writer finds Mr Hubbard's argument about beaver activity more convincing (page 231). As for fire, we must not forget the flecks of charcoal at Westbury-sub-Mendip or the signs of conflagration at Hoxne and Marks Tey — how did those fires start? But these occurrences are not like the finding of a carefully constructed hearth. For evidence that fire was used in the Middle Acheulian occupation at Swanscombe, see Oakley in Ovey 1964: 63-6. Fire was certainly used by the Middle Palaeolithic inhabitants of La Cotte de Saint-Brelade (McBurney and Callow 1971), for those who care to include it in the British Palaeolithic.

5 We might add that, except for any groups that arrived directly via Belgium, it was also presumably some days' journey from the last cave by the time they reached what is now Britain. Oldbury however is perhaps a hint that other rock shelters may have existed in the relatively soft sandstone outcrops of Kent and Sussex, and since have collapsed or been eroded away. Even if they did, the general point would remain valid.

6 There is of course one profound difference between them and us: they actually *know* the purpose of each item of their stone tool-kit and may therefore be regarded as having attained an intellectual Nirvana. On the other hand, they never had the chance to read this chapter.

7 The small Acheulian site recently found at South Woodford, mentioned earlier in this chapter, was discovered and excavated by the local Archaeological Unit as a rescue operation. Not everyone may realize that the great and remarkable Magdalenian open site at Pincevent, in northern France, came to light in commercial sand quarrying and was rescued for archaeological research by government intervention. The situation was similar at the important

south French Lower Palaeolithic site of Terra Amata, found when a block of flats was being erected. Are we making enough of the opportunities offered by commercial excavations in Britain, so far as the Palaeolithic is concerned?

Bibliography

ApSimon, A.M. (1969), 1919-1969: Fifty Years of Archaeological Research. The Spelaeological Society's contribution to Archaeology, *Proc. Univ. Bristol Spelaeological Soc.*, 12:1: 31-56.

Arkell, W.J. (1947), A palaeolith from Sherborne, *Proc. Dorset Natur. Hist. Archael. Soc.*, 68: 31-2.

Armstrong, A.L. (1931), Excavations in the Pin Hole Cave, Creswell Crags, *Proc. Prehist. Soc. E. Anglia*, 6: 330-4.

Armstrong, A.L. (1933), The Pin Hole Cave, Creswell Crags, *Trans. Hunter Archaeol. Soc.*, 4: 178.

Armstrong, A.L. (1939), Palaeolithic man in the North Midlands, *Mem. Proc. Manchester Lit. Phil. Soc.*, 83: 87-116.

Asher, J. (1922), A descriptive catalogue of stone implements in the Perth Museum, *Trans. Perthshire Soc. Natur. Sci.*, 8: 3.

Bada, J.L. (1972), The dating of fossil bones using the racemization of isoleucine, *Earth and Planetary Sci. Letters*, 15: 223-31.

Bada, J.L. and Helfman, P.M. (1975), Amino acid racemization dating of fossil bones, *World Archaeol.*, 7:2: 160-73.

Banham, P.H. (1968), A preliminary note on the Pleistocene stratigraphy of north-east Norfolk, *Proc. Geol. Ass. Lond.*, 79: 507-12.

Banham, P.H. (1971), Pleistocene beds at Corton, Suffolk, *Geol. Mag.*, 108: 281-5.

Banham, P.H. (1975), Glacitectonic structures: a general discussion with particular reference to the Contorted Drift of Norfolk, in *Ice Ages: Ancient and Modern*, eds A.E. Wright and F. Moseley, pp. 69-94 (*Geol. Journ.* Special Issue no. 6), Seel House Press, Liverpool.

Bartley, D.D. (1962), The stratigraphy and pollen analysis of lake deposits near Tadcaster, Yorkshire, *New Phytol.*, 61: 277-87.

Bar Yosef, O. (1975), Archaeological occurrences in the Middle Pleistocene of Israel in *After the Australopithecines: Stratigraphy, Ecology and Culture Change in the Middle Pleistocene*, eds K.W. Butzer and G. Ll. Isaac, pp. 571-604, Mouton, The Hague.

Beck, R.B., Funnell, B.M. and Lord, A.R. (1972), Correlation of Lower Pleistocene Crag at depth in Suffolk, *Geol. Mag.*, 109: 137-9.

Behm-Blancke, G. (1960), *Altsteinzeitliche Rastplätze im Travertingebiet von Taubach, Weimar, Ehringsdorf*, Hermann Böhlaus Nachfolger, Weimar (*Alt-Thüringen*, Band 4).

Bell, A.M. (1904), Implementiferous sections at Wolvercote (Oxfordshire), *Quart. Journ. Geol. Soc. Lond.*, 60: 120-32.

Bibby, G. (1957), *The Testimony of the Spade*, Collins, London.

Biberson, P. (1961), *Le Paléolithique inférieur du Maroc Atlantique*, Service des Antiquités du Maroc (Fasc. 17), Rabat.

Binford, L.R. (1972), *An Archeological Perspective*, Seminar Press, New York.

Binford, L.R. (1973), Interassemblage variability – the Mousterian and the 'functional' argument, in *The Explanation of Culture Change: Models in Prehistory*, ed. A.C. Renfrew, pp. 227-54, Duckworth, London.

Binford, L.R. and Binford, S.R. (1966), A preliminary analysis of functional variability in the Mousterian of Levallois facies, in *Recent Studies in Palaeoanthropology*, eds J.D. Clark and F.C. Howell, pp. 238-95, *American Anthropologist* special publication (68: 2: 2).

Birks, H.J.B. and Ransom, M.E. (1969), An interglacial peat at Fugla Ness, Shetland, *New Phytol.*, 68: 777-96.

Bishop, M.J. (1974), A preliminary report on

the Middle Pleistocene mammal bearing deposits of Westbury-sub-Mendip, Somerset, *Proc. Univ. Bristol Spelaeological Soc.*, 13:3: 301-18.

Bishop, M.J. (1975), Earliest record of man's presence in Britain, *Nature*, 273:5487: 95-7.

Bishop, W.W. (1958), The Pleistocene geology and geomorphology of three gaps in the Midland Jurassic Escarpment, *Phil. Trans. Roy. Soc. (Series B)*, 241: 255-306.

Bordaz, J. (1970), *Tools of the Old and New Stone Age*, Natural History Press, New York.

Bordes, F. (1950), Principes d'une méthode d'étude des techniques de débitage et de la typologie du Paléolithique ancien et moyen, *L'Anthropologie*, 54: 19-34.

Bordes, F. (1954), Les limons quaternaires du bassin de la Seine, *Archives de l'Institut de Paléontologie Humaine*, mém. 26, Masson, Paris.

Bordes, F. (1961), *Typologie du Paléolithique Ancien et Moyen*, Delmas, Bordeaux.

Bordes, F. (1968), *The Old Stone Age*, Weidenfeld & Nicolson, London.

Bordes, F. and Bourgon, M. (1951), Le complexe moustérien: Moustériens, Levalloisien et Tayacien, *L'Anthropologie*, 55: 1-23.

Bordes, F. and Fitte, P. (1953), L'atelier Commont, *L'Anthropologie*, 57: 1-45.

Bordes, F. and Sonneville-Bordes, D. de (1970), The significance of variability in Palaeolithic assemblages, *World Archaeol.*, 2: 61-73.

Bosinski, G. (1967), *Die mittelpaläolithischen Funde im Westlichen Mitteleuropa, Fundamenta*, Reihe A, Band 4, ed. H. Schwabedissen, Böhlau, Köln.

Bosinski, G. (1968), Zum Verhältnis von Jungacheuléen und Micoquien in Mitteleuropa, in *La Préhistoire: problèmes et tendances*, eds F. Bordes and D. de Sonneville-Bordes, pp. 77-86, C.N.R.S., Paris.

Boswell, P.G.H. and Moir, J.R. (1923), The Pleistocene deposits and their contained Palaeolithic flint implements at Foxhall Road, Ipswich, *J. Roy. Anthrop. Inst.*, 53: 229-62.

Bourgon, M. (1957), Les industries moustériennes et premoustériennes du Périgord, *Archives de l'Institut de Paléontologie Humaine*, mém. 27, Masson et Cie, Paris.

Bowen, D.Q. (1970), South-east and central South Wales, in *The Glaciations of Wales and Adjoining Regions*, ed. C.A. Lewis, pp. 197-227, Longmans, London.

Bowen, D.Q. (1978), *Quaternary Geology: a stratigraphic framework for multidisciplinary work*, Pergamon Press, Oxford.

Breuil, H. and Lantier, R. (1965), *The Men of the Old Stone Age (Palaeolithic and Mesolithic)* (translated from the French by B.B. Rafter), Harrap, London (original French publication by Payot (Paris) 1951).

Bristow, C.R. and Cox, F.C. (1973), The Gipping till: a reappraisal of East Anglian glacial stratigraphy, *J. Geol. Soc. Lond.*, 129: 1-37.

Brock, A. and Isaac, G.Ll. (1974), Palaeomagnetic stratigraphy and the chronology of hominid bearing deposits at East Rudolf, Kenya, *Nature*, 247: 344-8.

Brothwell, D.R. and Higgs, E.S. (eds) (1969), *Science in Archaeology: a survey of progress and research* (rev. and enlarged edn.), Thames & Hudson, London.

Brown, J.A. (1887), *Palaeolithic Man in North-west Middlesex. The evidence of his existence and the physical conditions under which he lived in Ealing and its neighbourhood, illustrated by the condition and culture presented by certain existing savages*, Macmillan, London.

Brown, J.A. (1889), On the discovery of *Elephas primigenius* associated with flint implements at Southall, *Proc. Geol. Ass. Lond.*, 10: 361-72.

Brown, J.A. (1896a), Excursion to Hanwell, Dawley and West Drayton, *Proc. Geol. Ass. Lond.*, 14: 118-20.

Brown, J.A. (1896b), Notes on the high-level river drift between Hanwell and Iver, *Proc. Geol. Ass. Lond.*, 14: 153-73.

Burchell, J.P.T. (1931), Early Neoanthropic Man and his relation to the Ice Age, *Proc. Prehist. Soc. E. Anglia*, 6: 253-303.

Burchell, J.P.T. (1933), The Northfleet 50 ft. Submergence later than the Coombe Rock of post-early Mousterian times, *Archaeologia*, 83: 67-91.

Burchell, J.P.T. (1934a), The Middle Mousterian Culture and its relation to the Coombe Rock of post-Early Mousterian times, *Antiq. Journ.*, 14: 33-9.

Burchell, J.P.T. (1934b), Fresh facts relating to the Boyn Hill Terrace of the Lower Thames Valley, *Antiq. Journ.*, 14: 163-6.

Burchell, J.P.T. (1936a), A final note on the Ebbsfleet Channel Series, *Geol. Mag.*, 73: 550-4.

Burchell, J.P.T. (1936b), Handaxes later than the Main Coombe-Rock of the Lower Thames Valley, *Antiq. Journ.*, 16: 260-4.

Burchell, J.P.T. (1954), Loessic deposits in the 50 foot terrace post-dating the Main Coombe Rock of Baker's Hole, Northfleet, Kent, *Proc. Geol. Ass. Lond.*, 65: 256-61.

Burchell, J.P.T., Moir, J.R. and Dixon, E.E.L.

(1929), Palaeolithic Man in north-west Ireland, *Prehist. Soc. E. Anglia Occ. Paper*, no. 1.

Burchell, J.P.T. and Moir, J.R. (1932), The evolution and distribution of the handaxe in north-east Ireland, *Proc. Prehist. Soc. E. Anglia*, 7: 18-34.

Burdo, C. (1960), *La Cotte de Saint-Brelade, Jersey, British Channel Islands. Excavation of a Pre-Mousterian horizon, 1950-58*, Société Jersiaise, St Helier, Jersey.

Burkitt, M.C. (1921), *Prehistory: a study of early cultures in Europe and the Mediterranean basin*, Cambridge University Press.

Burkitt, M.C. (1955), *The Old Stone Age: a study of Palaeolithic times* (3rd edn; first published 1933), Bowes & Bowes, London.

Burkitt, M.C., Paterson, T.T. and Mogridge, C.J. (1939), The Lower Palaeolithic industries near Warsash, Hampshire, *Proc. Prehist. Soc.*, 5: 39-50.

Bury, H. (1913), The gravel-beds of Farnham in relation to Palaeolithic man, *Proc. Geol. Ass. Lond.*, 24: 178-201.

Bury, H. (1916), The Palaeoliths of Farnham, *Proc. Geol. Ass. Lond.*, 27: 151-91.

Bury, H. (1923), Some aspects of the Hampshire Plateau Gravels, *Proc. Prehist. Soc. E. Anglia*, 4: 15-41.

Bury, H. (1935), The Farnham terraces and their sequence, *Proc. Prehist. Soc.*, 1: 60-9.

Butzer, K.W. (1971), *Environment and Archeology: an ecological approach to prehistory* (2nd edn), Aldine-Atherton, Chicago.

Butzer, K.W. and Isaac, G.Ll. (eds) (1975), *After the Australopithecines: stratigraphy, ecology and culture change in the Middle Pleistocene*, Mouton, The Hague.

Calkin, J.B. (1935), Implements from the higher raised beaches of Sussex, *Proc. Prehist. Soc. E. Anglia*, 7: 333-47.

Calkin, J.B. (1952), A late Acheulean hand-axe from Bere Regis, *Proc. Dorset Natur. Hist. Archaeol. Soc.*, 74: 102-3.

Calkin, J.B. and Green, J.F.N. (1949), Palaeoliths and terraces near Bournemouth, *Proc. Prehist. Soc.*, 15: 21-37.

Callow, P. (1976), 'The Lower and Middle Palaeolithic of Britain and adjacent areas of Europe', unpublished Ph.D. thesis, University of Cambridge.

Campbell, J.B. (1969), Excavations at Creswell Crags: a preliminary report, *Derbs. Archaeol. Journ.*, 89: 47-58.

Campbell, J.B. (1973), 'The Upper Palaeolithic of

Britain: a study of British Upper Palaeolithic material and its relation to environmental and chronological evidence', unpublished D. Phil. thesis, University of Oxford.

Campbell, J.B. (1977), *The Upper Palaeolithic of Britain: a study of man and nature in the late Ice Age* (2 vols), Clarendon Press, Oxford.

Campbell, J.B. and Sampson, C.G. (1971), A new analysis of Kent's Cavern, Devonshire, England, *University of Oregon Anthropological Papers*, no. 3.

Chandler, R.H. (1914), The Pleistocene deposits of Crayford, *Proc. Geol. Ass. Lond.*, 25: 61-71.

Chandler, R.H. (1916), The implements and cores of Crayford, *Proc. Prehist. Soc. E. Anglia*, 2: 240-8.

Chandler, R.H. (1930), On the Clactonian industry at Swanscombe, *Proc. Prehist. Soc. E. Anglia*, 6: 79-116.

Chandler, R.H. and Leach, A.L. (1912), On the Dartford Heath gravel and on a Palaeolithic implement factory, *Proc. Geol. Ass. Lond.*, 23: 102-11.

Charlesworth, J.K. (1957), *The Quaternary Era* (2 vols), Arnold, London.

Chartres, C.J. (1975), 'Soil development on the terraces of the River Kennet', unpublished Ph.D. thesis, University of Reading.

Cheetham, H. (1975), 'Late Quaternary palaeohydrology, with respect to the Kennet valley', unpublished Ph.D. thesis, University of Reading.

Chmielewski, W., Schild, R. and Więckowska, H. (1975), *Prahistoria ziem Polskich, Tom 1: Palaeolit i Mezolit*, Polska Akademia Nauk, Wroctaw, etc.

Clark, J.D. (1967), The Middle Acheulian occupation site at Latamne, Northern Syria (first paper), *Quaternaria*, 9: 1-68.

Clark, J.D. (1968), The Middle Acheulian occupation site at Latamne, Northern Syria (second paper), further escavations (*sic*) (1965): general results, definition and interpretation, *Quaternaria*, 10: 1-71.

Clark, J.D. (1969), *Kalambo Falls Prehistoric Site, I. The Geology, Palaeoecology and detailed Stratigraphy of the Excavations*, Cambridge University Press.

Clark, J.D. and Haynes, C.V. (1970), An elephant butchery site at Mwanganda's Village, Karonga, Malawi, and its relevance for Palaeolithic archaeology, *World Archaeol.*, 1:3: 390-411.

Clark, J.G.D. (1938), Early Man, *The Victoria History of the Counties of England: Cambridgeshire and the Isle of Ely*, I: 247-303.

Clark, J.G.D. (1952), *Prehistoric Europe: the economic basis*, Methuen, London.

Clark, J.G.D. (1954), *Excavations at Star Carr: an early Mesolithic site at Seamer, near Scarborough, Yorkshire*, Cambridge University Press.

Clarke, D.L. (1962), Matrix analysis and archaeology, with reference to British Beaker pottery, *Proc. Prehist. Soc.*, 28: 371-82.

Clarke, D.L. (1968), *Analytical Archaeology*, Methuen, London.

Clarke, D.L. (ed.), (1972), *Models in Archaeology*, Methuen, London.

Coles, J.M. (1968), Ancient Man in Europe, in *Studies in Ancient Europe: essays presented to Stuart Piggott*, eds J.M Coles and D.D.A. Simpson, pp. 17-44, Leicester University Press.

Coles, J.M. and Higgs, E.S. (1969), *The Archaeology of Early Man*, Faber & Faber, London.

Collins, D.M. (1969), Culture traditions and environment of Early Man, *Current Anthrop.*, 10:4: 267-316.

Collins, D.M. and Collins, A. (1970), Excavations at Oldbury in Kent: cultural evidence for Last Glacial occupation in Britain, *Bulletin of the Institute of Archaeology* (University of London), 8-9: 151-76.

Collins, D.M., Whitehouse, R., Henig, M. and Whitehouse, D. (1973), *Background to Archaeology: Britain in its European setting* (2nd edn), Cambridge University Press.

Combier, J. (1967), *Le Paléolithique de l'Ardèche dans son cadre paléoclimatique* (Publications de l'Institut de Préhistoire de l'Université de Bordeaux: Mém. 4), Delmas, Bordeaux.

Conway, B.W. (1968), Preliminary geological investigation of Boyn Hill terrace deposits at Barnfield Pit, Swanscombe, Kent, during 1968, *Proc. Roy. Anthrop. Inst.*, 1968: 59-61.

Cook, W.H. and Killick, J.R. (1924), On the discovery of a flint-working site of Palaeolithic date in the Medway Valley at Rochester, Kent, with notes on the drift stages of the Medway, *Proc. Prehist. Soc. E. Anglia*, 4: 133-49.

Coope, G.R. (1959), A Late Pleistocene insect fauna from Chelford, Cheshire, *Proc. Roy. Soc. Lond. (Series B)*, 151: 70-86.

Coope, G.R. (1961), On the study of glacial and interglacial insect faunas, *Proc. Linn. Soc. Lond.*, 172: 62-5.

Coope, G.R. (1962), A Pleistocene coleopterous fauna with Arctic affinities from Fladbury, Worcestershire, *Q. J. Geol. Soc. Lond.*, 118: 103-23.

Coope, G.R. (1965), Fossil insect faunas from late Quaternary deposits in Britain, *Adv. Sci.*, 21: 564-75.

Coope, G.R. (1970), Climatic interpretations of Late Weichselian coleoptera from the British Isles, *Rev. Géog. phys. Géol. dynam.*, 12:2: 149-55.

Coope, G.R., Shotton, F.W. and Strachan, I. (1961), A Late Pleistocene fauna and flora from Upton Warren, Worcestershire, *Phil. Trans. Roy. Soc. (Series B)*, 244: 379-421.

Coope, G.R. and Sands, C.H.S. (1966), Insect faunas of the last glaciation from the Tame Valley, Warwickshire, *Proc. Roy. Soc. Lond. (Series B)*, 165: 389-412.

Coope, G.R., Morgan, A. and Osborne, P.J. (1971), Fossil Coleoptera as indicators of climatic fluctuations during the Last Glaciation in Britain, *Palaeogeog. Palaeoclimatol. Palaeoecol.*, 10: 87-101.

Coppens, Y., Howell, F.C., Isaac, G.Ll. and Leakey, R.E.F. (eds) (1976), *Earliest Mᵣn and Environments in the Lake Rudolf Basin: Stratigraphy, palaeoecology and evolution*, University of Chicago Press (Prehistoric Archaeology and Ecology Series, eds K.W. Butzer and L.G. Freeman).

Corvinus, G.K. (1970), A report on the 1968-69 excavations at Chirki-on-Pravara, India, *Quaternaria*, 13: 169-76.

Corvinus, G.K. (1973), Excavations at an Acheulean site at Chirki-on-Pravara in India, in *South Asian Archaeology: papers from the First International Conference of South Asian Archaeologists held in the University of Cambridge*, ed. N. Hammond, pp. 13-28, Duckworth, London.

Cox, A. (1969), Geomagnetic Reversals, *Science*, 163: 237-46.

Cox, A. (1972), Geomagnetic reversals – their frequency, their origin and some problems of correlation, in *Calibration of Hominid Evolution: recent advances in isotopic and other dating methods applicable to the origin of man*, eds W.W. Bishop and J.A. Miller, pp. 93-106, Scottish Academic Press, Edinburgh.

Cox, A., Dalrymple, G.B. and Doell, R.R. (1967), Reversals of the Earth's magnetic field, *Scient. Am.*, 216:2: 44-54.

Crawford, O.G.S., Ellaway, J.R. and Willis, G.W. (1922), The antiquity of man in Hampshire, *Papers Proc. Hants. Field Club*, 9:2: 173-88.

Cunnington, W. and Cunnington, W.A. (1903), The palaeolithic implements and gravels of Knowle, Wilts., *Wilts. Archaeol. Mag.*, 33: 131-8.

Dalrymple, G.B. (1972), Potassium-argon dating of geomagnetic reversals and North American glaciations, in *Calibration of Hominid Evolution: recent advances in isotopic and other dating methods applicable to the origin of man*, eds W.W. Bishop and J.A. Miller, pp. 107-34, Scottish Academic Press, Edinburgh.

Daniel, G.E. (1943), *The Three Ages*, Cambridge University Press.

Daniel, G.E. (1950), *A Hundred Years of Archaeology*, Duckworth, London.

Daniel, G.E. (1962), *The Idea of Prehistory*, Watts (New Thinkers Library), London.

Daniel, G.E. (1967), *The Origins and Growth of Archaeology*, Penguin, Harmondsworth.

Daniel, G.E. (1975), *A Hundred and Fifty Years of Archaeology*, Duckworth, London.

Dawkins, W.B. (1874), *Cave Hunting: researches on the evidence of caves respecting the early inhabitants of Europe*, Macmillan, London.

Dawkins, W.B. (1880), *Early Man in Britain and his Place in the Tertiary Period*, Macmillan, London.

Day, M.H. (1977), *Guide to Fossil Man: a handbook of human palaeontology* (3rd edn), Cassell, London.

Dewey, H. (1932), The Palaeolithic deposits of the Lower Thames Valley, *Q. J. Geol. Soc. Lond.*, 88: 35-54.

Dewey, H. and Smith, R.A. (1924), Flints from the Sturry gravels, *Archaeologia*, 74: 117-36.

Dines, H.G. (1929), The flint industries of Bapchild, *Proc. Prehist. Soc. E. Anglia*, 6:1: 12-26.

Dines, H.G., King, W.B.R. and Oakley, K.P. (1938), A general account of the 100 foot terrace gravels of the Barnfield Pit, Swanscombe, *Journ. Roy. Anthrop. Inst.*, 68: 21-7.

Dixon, S.B. (1903), On the Palaeolithic flint implements from Knowle, Savernake Forest, *Wilts. Archaeol. Natur. Hist. Mag.*, 33: 139-44.

Doran, J.E. and Hodson, F.R. (1975), *Mathematics and Computers in Archaeology*, Edinburgh University Press.

Draper, J.C. (1951), Stone industries from Rainbow Bar, Hants., *Archaeol. News Letter*, 3:9: 147-9.

Dudley, H.E. (1949), *Early days in North-West Lincolnshire: a regional archaeology*, Caldicott, Scunthorpe.

Duigan, S.L. (1956), Interglacial plant remains from the Wolvercote Channel, Oxford, *Q. Jl. Geol. Soc. Lond.*, 112: 363-72.

Duigan, S.L. (1963), Pollen analyses of the Cromer Forest Bed Series in East Anglia, *Phil. Trans. Roy. Soc. (Series B)*, 246: 149-202.

Dyer, J.F. (1959), 'Middling for wrecks': extracts from the story of Worthington and Henrietta Smith, *Bedfordshire Archaeologist*, 2: 1-15.

Dyer, J.F. (1978), Worthington George Smith, in Worthington George Smith and other studies presented to Joyce Godber, *Bedfordshire Historical Record Society*, 57: 141-79.

Emiliani, C. (1955), Pleistocene temperatures, *Journ. Geol.*, 63: 149-58.

Emiliani, C. (1961), Cenozoic-climatic changes as indicated by the stratigraphy and chronology of deep-sea cores of *Globigerina*-ooze facies, *Ann. New York Acad. Sci.*, 95:1: 521-36.

Emiliani, C. (1966), Palaeotemperature analysis of Caribbean cores P 6304-8 and P 6304-9 and a generalized temperature curve for the last 425,000 years, *Journ. Geol.*, 74: 109-26.

Emiliani, C. (1969), The significance of deep-sea cores, in *Science in Archaeology: a survey of progress and research*, eds D.R. Brothwell and E.S. Higgs, (2nd edn, pp. 109-17), Thames & Hudson, London.

Emiliani, C. and Shackleton, N.J. (1974), The Brunhes epoch: isotopic palaeotemperatures and geochronology, *Science*, 183: 511-14.

Evans, Joan (1956), *A History of the Society of Antiquaries*, Oxford University Press, London.

Evans, J. (later Sir John) (1860), On the occurrence of flint implements in undisturbed beds of gravel, sand and clay, *Archaeologia*, 38: 280-307.

Evans, J. (later Sir John) (1872), *The Ancient Stone Implements, Weapons and Ornaments of Great Britain* (1st edn), Longmans, Green and Co., London.

Evans, Sir John (1897), *The Ancient Stone Implements, Weapons and Ornaments of Great Britain* (2nd edn, rev.), Longmans, Green and Co., London.

Evans, J.G. (1972), *Land Snails in Archaeology*, Seminar Press, London.

Evans, J.G. (1975), *The Environment of Early Man in the British Isles*, Elek, London.

Evans, P. (1971), Towards a Pleistocene time-scale, Part 2 of *The Phanerozoic Time-scale – a supplement*, Special Publication of the Geological Society of London, no. 5, pp. 123-356.

Flint, R.F. (1971), *Glacial and Quaternary Geology*, Wiley, New York.

Foster, I.Ll. and Daniel, G.E. (eds) (1965), *Prehistoric and Early Wales*, Routledge & Kegan Paul, London (Studies in Ancient History and Archaeology series, ed. F.T. Wainwright).

Franks, J.W. (1960), Interglacial deposits at Trafalgar Square, London, *New Phytol.*, 59: 145-52.

Frere, J. (1800), Flint weapons discovered at Hoxne in Suffolk, *Archaeologia*, 13: 204-5.

Freund, G. (1952), *Die Blattspitzen des Palaolithikums in Europa*, Quartär-Bibliothek, Band 1, Bonn.

Funnell, B.M. (1961), The Palaeogene and Early Pleistocene of Norfolk, *Trans. Norfolk Norwich Natur. Soc.*, 19: 340-64.

Gábori, M. (1976), *Les Civilizations du Paléolithique moyen entre les Alpes et l'Oural*, Akadémiai Kiadó, Budapest.

Garraway Rice, R. (1911), (contribution to discussion of R.A. Smith's paper on Baker's Hole), *Proc. Soc. Antiq.*, N.S., 23: 450.

Garraway Rice, R. (1920), Untitled report on an unusual palaeolithic implement and an unfinished neolith found at West Chiltington, with discussion, *Proc. Soc. Antiq.*, N.S., 32: 80-2.

Garrod, D.A.E. (1926), *The Upper Palaeolithic Age in Britain*, Clarendon Press, Oxford.

Garrod, D.A.E. and Bate, D.M.A. (1937), *The Stone Age of Mount Carmel: excavations at the Wady el-Mughara* (Volume I), Clarendon Press, Oxford.

Garrood, J.R. (1933), Palaeoliths from the Lower Ouse, *Antiq. Journ.*, 13: 313-15.

Gladfelter, B.G. (1975), Middle Pleistocene sedimentary sequences in East Anglia (United Kingdom), in *After the Australopithecines: stratigraphy, ecology and culture change in the Middle Pleistocene*, eds K.W. Butzer and G.Ll. Isaac, pp. 225-58, Mouton, The Hague.

Glass, B., Ericson, D.B., Heezen, B.C., Opdyke, N.D. and Glass, J.A. (1967), Geomagnetic reversals and Pleistocene chronology, *Nature*, 216: 437-42.

Graham, J. and Roe, D.A. (1970), Discrimination of British Lower and Middle Palaeolithic handaxe groups using canonical variates, *World Archaeol.*, 1:3: 321-42.

Green, J.F.N. (1946), The terraces of Bournemouth, Hants., *Proc. Geol. Ass. Lond.*, 57: 82-101.

Green, J.F.N. (1947), Some gravels and gravel-pits in Hampshire and Dorset, *Proc. Geol. Ass. Lond.*, 58: 128-43.

Grimes, W.F. (1939), *Guide to the Collection Illustrating the Prehistory of Wales*, National Museum of Wales, Cardiff.

Grinsell, L.V. (1929), The Lower and Middle Palaeolithic periods in Sussex, *Sussex Archaeol. Collect.*, 70: 173-82.

Hammen, T.C. van der, Maarleveld, G.C., Vogel, J.C. and Zagwijn, W.H. (1967), Stratigraphy, climatic succession and radiocarbon dating of the last glacial in the Netherlands, *Geologie en Mijnbouw*, 45: 79-95.

Hammen, T.C. van der, Wijmstra, T.A. and Zagwijn, W.H. (1971), The floral record of the Late Cenozoic of Europe, in *The Late Cenozoic Glacial Ages*, ed. K.K. Turekian, pp. 391-424, Yale University Press, New Haven.

Hare, F.K. (1947), The geomorphology of a part of the Middle Thames, *Proc. Geol. Ass. Lond.*, 58: 294-339.

Harrison, B. (1892), On certain Rude Implements from the North Downs (Note appended to paper by Sir Joseph Prestwich 1892, q.v.), *Journ. Anthrop. Inst.*, 21: 263-7.

Harrison, Sir Edward R. (1928), *Harrison of Ightham: a book about Benjamin Harrison, of Ightham, Kent, made up principally of extracts from his notebooks and correspondence*, Oxford University Press, London.

Harrison, R.A. (1977), The Uphill Quarry caves, Weston-super-Mare. A reappraisal, *Proc. Univ. Bristol Spelaeological Soc.*, 14: 3.

Hawkes, J. (1968), The proper study of mankind, *Antiquity*, 42: 168: 255-63.

Hay, R.L. (1976), *Geology of the Olduvai Gorge: a Study of sedimentation in a semiarid basin*, University of California Press, Berkeley, Los Angeles and London.

Hays, J.D., Saito, T., Opdyke, N.D. and Burckle, L.H. (1969), Plio-Pleistocene sediments of the Equatorial Pacific: their palaeomagnetic, biostratigraphic and climatic records, *Geol. Soc. Amer. Bull.*, 80: 1481-514.

Henri-Martin, G. (1957), La Grotte de Fontéchevade, I. Historique, fouilles, stratigraphie, archéologie, *Archives de l'Institut de Paléontologie Humaine*, mém. 28, Masson, Paris.

Higgs, E.S. and Vita-Finzi, C. (1970), Prehistoric economy in the Mount Carmel area of Palestine: site catchment analysis, *Proc. Prehist. Soc.*, 36, 1-37.

Hodder, I. and Orton, C. (1976), *Spatial Analysis in Archaeology* (New Studies in Archaeology, 1), Cambridge University Press.

Hodson, F.R. (1971), Numerical typology and prehistoric archaeology, in *Mathematics in the Archaeological and Historical Sciences*, eds F.R. Hodson, D.G. Kendall and P. Tautu, pp. 31-45, University Press, Edinburgh.

Holden, E.W. and Roe, D.A. (1974), The Ade Collection of flints and a Palaeolithic handaxe from Hassocks, *Sussex Archaeol. Collect.*, 112: 1-8.

Howells, W. (1972), *Evolution of the Genus Homo*, Addison-Wesley, London.

Hubbard, R.N.L.B. (1977), On the chronology of the Lower Palaeolithic in southern Britain, *Abstracts of the Xth INQUA Congress, Birmingham, 1977*, p. 216 (Typescript).

Hughes, T. McK. (1887), On the drifts of the Vale of Clwyd and their relation to the caves and cave deposits, *Q. Jl. Geol. Soc. Lond.*, 43: 73-120.

Hughes, T. McK. and Thomas, D.R. (1874), On the occurrence of felstone implements of the Le Moustier type in Pontnewydd cave, near Cefn, St. Asaph, *Journ. Anthrop. Inst.*, 3: 387-92.

Isaac, G. Ll. (1972a), Chronology and the tempo of cultural change during the Pleistocene, in *Calibration of Hominid Evolution: Recent Advances in Isotopic and Other Dating Methods Applicable to the Origin of Man*, eds W.W. Bishop and J.A. Miller, pp. 381-430, Scottish Academic Press, Edinburgh.

Isaac, G. Ll. (1972b), Early phases of human behaviour: models in Lower Palaeolithic archaeology, in *Models in Archaeology*, ed. D.L. Clarke, pp. 167-99, Methuen, London.

Isaac, G. Ll. and McCown, E.R. (eds) (1976), *Human Origins: Louis Leakey and the East African Evidence*, W.A. Benjamin Inc., Menlo Park, California.

Ivanova, I.K. and Chernysh, A.P. (1965), The Palaeolithic site of Molodova V on the Middle Dnestr (U.S.S.R.), *Quaternaria*, 7: 197-217.

Jessen, K., Andersen, S.T. and Farrington, A. (1959), The interglacial deposit near Gort, Co. Galway, Ireland, *Proc. R. Irish Acad. (Section B)*, 44: 205-60.

Jessup, R. (1964), *The Story of Archaeology in Britain*, Michael Joseph, London.

John, B.S. (1970), Pembrokeshire, in *The Glaciations of Wales and Adjoining Regions*, ed. C.A. Lewis, pp. 229-65, Longmans, London.

Keeley, L.H. (1974), Technique and methodology in microwear studies, *World Archaeol.*, 5: 323-36.

Keeley, L.H. (1977), 'An experimental study of microwear traces on selected British Palaeolithic implements', unpublished D. Phil. thesis, University of Oxford.

Keeley, L.H. and Newcomer, M.H. (1977), Microwear analysis of experimental flint tools: a test case, *Journ. Archaeol. Sci.*, 4: 29-62.

Kellaway, G.A., Redding, J.H., Shephard-Thorn, E.R. and Destombes, J-P. (1975), The Quaternary History of the English Channel, *Phil. Trans. Roy. Soc. (Series A)*, 279: 189-218.

Kelly, M.R. (1964), The Middle Pleistocene of North Birmingham, *Phil. Trans. Roy. Soc. (Series B)*, 247: 533-92.

Kelly, M.R. (1968), Floras of Middle and Upper Pleistocene age from Brandon, Warwickshire, *Phil. Trans. Roy. Soc. (Series B)*, 254: 401-15.

Kendall, H.G.O. (1906), Investigations at Knowle Farm Pit, *Wilts. Archaeol. Natur. Hist. Mag.*, 34: 299-307.

Kennard, A.S. (1944), The Crayford Brickearths, *Proc. Geol. Ass. Lond.*, 55: 121-69.

Kerney, M.P. (1959), An interglacial tufa near Hitchin, Hertfordshire, *Proc. Geol. Ass. Lond.*, 70: 322-37.

Kerney, M.P. (1963), Late-glacial deposits on the chalk of south-east England, *Phil. Trans. Roy. Soc. (Series B)*, 246: 203-54.

Kerney, M.P. (1971), Interglacial deposits in Barnfield Pit, Swanscombe, and their molluscan fauna, *Journ. Geol. Soc. Lond.*, 127: 69-86.

King, W.B.R. and Oakley, K.P. (1936), The Pleistocene Succession in the lower part of the Thames Valley, *Proc. Prehist. Soc.*, 2: 52-76.

King, W.B.R. and Oakley, K.P. (1949), Definition of the Pliocene-Pleistocene boundary, *Nature*, 163: 186.

Klein, R.G. (1973), *Ice-Age Hunters of the Ukraine*, University of Chicago Press.

Kleindienst, M.R. (1961), Variability within the Late Acheulian assemblage in eastern Africa, *S. Afr. Archaeol. Bull.*, 16 (62): 35-52.

Kleindienst, M.R. (1962), Components of the east African Acheulian assemblage: an analytical approach, *Actes du IVe Congrès panafricain de Préhistoire et de l'étude du Quaternaire* (eds G. Mortelmans and J. Nenquin), pp. 81-112, Musée Royal de l'Afrique Centrale, Tervuren.

Kolstrup, E. and Wijmstra, T.A. (1977), A palynological investigation of the Moershoofd, Hengelo and Denekamp Interstadials in the Netherlands, *Geologie en Mijnbouw*, 56:2, 85-102.

Kretzoi, M. and Vértes, L. (1965), Upper Biharian (Intermindel) Pebble-industry occupation site in Western Hungary, *Current Anthropology*, 6:1: 74-87.

Lacaille, A.D. (1939), The Palaeolithic contents of the gravels at East Burnham, Bucks, *Antiq. Journ.*, 19: 166-81.

Lacaille, A.D. (1940), The palaeoliths from the gravels of the Lower Boyn Hill Terrace around Maidenhead, *Antiq. Journ.*, 20: 245-71.

Lacaille, A.D. (1946), Some flint implements of

special interest from Lincolnshire, Hampshire and Middlesex, *Antiq. Journ.*, 26: 180-5.

Lacaille, A.D. (1954a), Palaeoliths from the lower reaches of the Bristol Avon, *Antiq. Journ.*, 34: 1-27.

Lacaille, A.D. (1954b), A hand-axe from Pen-y-Lan, Cardiff, *Antiq. Journ.*, 34: 64-7.

Lacaille, A.D. (1959), Palaeoliths from brickearth in south-east Buckinghamshire, *Records of Bucks.*, 16: 274-88.

Lacaille, A.D. (1960), On Palaeolithic choppers and cleavers (notes suggested by some Buckinghamshire examples), *Records of Bucks.*, 16: 5: 330-41.

Lacaille, A.D. (1961), The palaeoliths of Boyn Hill, Maidenhead, *Antiq. Journ.*, 41: 154-85.

Lacaille, A.D. and Oakley, K.P. (1936), The Palaeolithic sequence at Iver, Bucks., *Antiq. Journ.*, 16: 420-43.

Layard, N.F. (1903), A recent discovery of Palaeolithic implements in Ipswich, *Journ. Roy. Anthrop. Inst.*, 33: 41-3.

Layard, N.F. (1904), Further excavations on a Palaeolithic site in Ipswich, *Journ. Roy. Anthrop. Inst.*, 34: 306-10.

Layard, N.F. (1906), A winter's work on the Ipswich Palaeolithic site, *Journ. Roy. Anthrop. Inst.*, 36: 233-6.

Leakey, L.S.B. (1934), *Adam's Ancestors: an up-to-date outline of the Old Stone Age (Palaeolithic) and what is known about Man's origin and evolution* (1st edn; see also rev. 4th edn 1953), Methuen, London.

Leakey, M.D. (1971), *Olduvai Gorge, vol. 3: Excavations in Beds I and II, 1960-63*, Cambridge University Press.

Leakey, M.D. (1975), Cultural patterns in the Olduvai sequence, in *After the Australopithecines: stratigraphy, ecology and culture change in the Middle Pleistocene*, eds K.W. Butzer and G.Ll. Isaac, pp. 477-94, Mouton, The Hague.

Leakey, R.E.F. and Lewin, R. (1977), *Origins: what new discoveries reveal about the emergence of our species and its possible future*, Macdonald and Jane's, London.

Lee, R.B. and DeVore, I. (1968), *Man the Hunter*, Aldine-Atherton, Chicago.

Leroi-Gourhan, A. and Brézillon, M. (1972), *Fouilles de Pincevent: essai d'analyse ethnographique d'un habitat magdalénien (la section 36)*, VIIe supplément à *Gallia Préhistoire*, C.N.R.S., Paris.

Leroi-Gourhan, A. and Leroi-Gourhan, A. (1964), Chronologie des grottes d'Arcy-sur-Cure (Yonne), *Gallia Préhist.*, 7: 1-64.

Lord, A.R. (1969), A preliminary account of research boreholes at Stradbroke and Hoxne, Suffolk, *Bull. Geol. Soc. Norfolk*, 18: 13.

Lumley, H. de (H. de Lumley-Woodyear) (1969a), *Le Paléolithique inférieur et moyen du Midi méditerranéen dans son cadre géologique. Tome I: Ligurie-Provence*, C.N.R.S., Paris.

Lumley, H. de (1969b), A Palaeolithic camp at Nice, *Scient. Am.*, 220: 42-50.

Lumley, H. de (ed.) (1969c), Une cabane acheuléenne dans la grotte du Lazaret (Nice), *Mém. Soc. Préhist. Fr.*, no. 7, Paris.

Lumley, H. de (1971), *Le Paléolithique inférieur et moyen du Midi méditerranéen dans son cadre géologique. Tome II: Bas-Languedoc - Roussillon - Catalogne*, C.N.R.S., Paris.

Lumley, H. de (1975), Cultural evolution in France in its paleoecological setting during the Middle Pleistocene, in *After the Australopithecines: stratigraphy, ecology and culture change in the Middle Pleistocene*, eds K.W. Butzer and G.Ll. Isaac, pp. 745-808, Mouton, The Hague.

Luttropp, A. and Bosinski, G. (1971), *Der altsteinzeitliche Fundplatz Reutersruh bei Ziegenhain in Hessen (Fundamenta*, ed. H. Schwabedissen, Reihe A, Band 6), Böhlau Verlag, Köln.

McBurney, C.B.M. (1950), The geographical study of the older Palaeolithic stages in Europe, *Proc. Prehist. Soc.*, 16: 163-83.

McBurney, C.B.M. and Callow, P. (1971), The Cambridge excavations at La Cotte de Saint-Brelade, Jersey – a preliminary report, *Proc. Prehist. Soc.*, 37:2: 167-207.

Mace, A. (1959), The excavation of a Late Upper Palaeolithic open-site on Hengistbury Head, Christchurch, Hants., *Proc. Prehist. Soc.*, 25: 233-59.

Mania, D.L. (1976), Altpaläolithischer Rastplatz mit Hominidenresten aus dem mittelpleistozänen Travertin-Komplex von Bilzingsleben (D.D.R.), in *U.I.S.P.P. IXe Congrès (Nice, Sept. 1976): Colloque 9: Le peuplement anténéandertalien de l'Europe (Prétirage)*.

Marett, R.R. (1911a), Pleistocene Man in Jersey, *Archaeologia*, 61: 449-80.

Marett, R.R. (1911b), Further observations on Prehistoric Man in Jersey, *Archaeologia*, 63: 203-30.

Marett, R.R. (1916), The site, fauna and industry of La Cotte de Saint-Brelade, Jersey, *Archaeologia*, 67: 75-118.

Marr, J.E. (1926), The Pleistocene deposits of the lower part of the Great Ouse Basin, *Q. Jl. Geol. Soc. Lond.*, 82: 101-43.

Marr, J.E., Moir, J.R. and Smith, R.A. (1921), Excavations at High Lodge, Mildenhall, in 1920 A.D., *Proc. Prehist. Soc. E. Anglia*, 3: 353-79.

Marston, A.T. (1937), The Swanscombe Skull, *Journ. Roy. Anthrop. Inst.*, 67: 339-406.

Marston, A.T. (1942), Flint industries of the High Terrace at Swanscombe, *Proc. Geol. Ass. Lond.*, 53: 106.

May, J. (1976), *Prehistoric Lincolnshire (History of Lincolnshire*, vol. I, ed. J. Thirsk), History of Lincolnshire Committee, Lincoln.

Mellars, P.A. (1969), The chronology of Mousterian industries in the Périgord region of South West France, *Proc. Prehist. Soc.*, 35: 134-71.

Mellars, P.A. (1970), Some comments on the notion of 'functional variability' in stone-tool assemblages, *World Archaeol.*, 2:1: 74-89.

Mellars, P.A. (1974), The Palaeolithic and Mesolithic, in *British Prehistory: a new outline*, ed. A.C. Renfrew, pp. 41-99, 268-79, Duckworth, London.

Millard, L. (1965), Some palaeoliths from the Bletchley district, *Rec. Bucks.*, 17:5: 336-42.

Mitchell, G.F., Penny, L.F., Shotton, F.W. and West, R.G. (1973), *A Correlation of Quaternary Deposits in the British Isles*, Geol. Soc. Lond. (Special Report No. 4).

Moir, J.R. (1918), An Early Mousterian 'floor' discovered at Ipswich, *Man*, 18: no. 60: 98-100.

Moir, J.R. (1923), An early palaeolith from the glacial till at Sidestrand, Norfolk, *Antiq. Journ.*, 3: 135-7.

Moir, J.R. (1926), The silted-up lake of Hoxne and its contained flint implements, *Proc. Prehist. Soc. E. Anglia*, 5: 137-65.

Moir, J.R. (1927), *The Antiquity of Man in East Anglia*, Cambridge University Press.

Moir, J.R. (1931), Ancient Man in the Gipping-Orwell Valley, Suffolk, *Proc. Prehist. Soc. E. Anglia*, 6: 182-221.

Moir, J.R. (1932), The culture of Pliocene Man (Presidential Address for 1932), *Proc. Prehist. Soc. E. Anglia*, 7:1: 1-17.

Moir, J.R. (1935), Lower Palaeolithic Man at Hoxne, England, *Bull. Amer. Sch. Prehist. Res.*, 11: 43-53.

Moir, J.R. (1936), Ancient Man in Devon, part I, *Proc. Devon Archaeol. Exploration Soc.*, 2: 264-75.

Moir, J.R. and Hopwood, A.T. (1939), Excavations at Brundon, Suffolk (1935-1937), *Proc. Prehist. Soc.*, 5: 1-32.

Molleson, T. (1976), Remains of Pleistocene man in Paviland and Pontnewydd Caves, Wales,

Trans. Brit. Cave Res. Ass., 3:2: 112-16.

Montfrans, H.M. van (1971), *Palaeomagnetic Dating in the North Sea Basin*, Princo, Rotterdam.

Montfrans, H.M. van and Hospers, J. (1969), A preliminary report on the stratigraphical position of the Matuyama-Brunhes geomagnetic field reversal in the Quaternary sediments of the Netherlands, *Geologie en Mijnbouw*, 48: 565-71.

Morgan, A.V. (1973), The Pleistocene geology of the area north and west of Wolverhampton, Staffordshire, England, *Phil. Trans. Roy. Soc. (Series B)*, 265: 233-97.

Movius, H.L. (1942), *The Irish Stone Age: its chronology, development and relationships*, Cambridge University Press.

Movius, H.L. (1950), A wooden spear of Third Interglacial age from Lower Saxony, *South-western Jl. Anthrop.*, 6:2 139-42.

Müller-Beck, H-J. (1957), *Das obere Altpaläolithikum in Suddeutschland*, Bonn.

Müller-Karpe, H. (1965), *Handbuch der Vorgeschichte, Band I: Altsteinzeit*, C.H. Beck, München.

Murphy, B. (n.d.), A handaxe from Dun Aenghus, Inishmore, Aran Islands, Co. Galway, unpublished typescript.

Napier, J. (1971), *The roots of mankind*, Allen & Unwin, London.

Newcomer, M.H. (1971), Some quantitative experiments in handaxe manufacture, *World Archaeol.*, 3:1: 85-94.

Oakley, K.P. (1939), Part I: Geology and Palaeolithic Studies, in *A Survey of the Prehistory of the Farnham District (Surrey)*, prepared for the Surrey Archaeological Society, eds K.P. Oakley, W.F. Rankine and A.W.G. Lowther, pp. 3-58, Surrey Archaeological Society, Guildford.

Oakley, K.P. (1947), Early Man in Hertfordshire, *Trans. Herts. Natur. Hist. Soc.*, 22:5: 247-56.

Oakley, K.P. (1949), *Man the Toolmaker* (1st edn; 6th edn 1972), British Museum, London.

Oakley, K.P. (1964), *Frameworks for Dating Fossil Man* (1st edn), Weidenfeld & Nicolson, London.

Oakley, K.P. (1970), Pliocene Men, *Antiquity*, 44: 307-8.

Oakley, K.P. and Leakey, M.D. (1937), Report on excavations at Jaywick Sands, Essex (1934), with some observations on the Clactonian Industry, and on the fauna and geological significance of the Clacton Channel, *Proc. Prehist. Soc.*, 3:2: 217-60.

Oakley, K.P., Andrews, P., Keeley, L.H. and Clark, J.D. (1977), A reappraisal of the Clacton spearpoint, *Proc. Prehist. Soc.*, 43: 13-30.

Ohel, M.Y. (1977a), 'The Clactonian-Acheulian interface in Britain' (unpublished Ph.D. dissertation, University of Chicago Department of Anthropology).

Ohel, M.Y. (1977b), On the Clactonian: reexamined, redefined and reinterpreted, *Current Anthrop.*, 18:2: 329-31.

Ohel, M.Y. (1979), The Clactonian: an independent complex or an integral part of the Acheulian? *Current Anthrop.* 20:4: 685-744.

Opdyke, N.D. (1972), Palaeomagnetism of deep-sea cores, *Rev. Geophys. Space Phys.*, 10: 213-49.

Ovey, C.D. (ed.) (1964), *The Swanscombe Skull: a survey of research at a Pleistocene site*, Royal Anthropological Institute (Occasional Paper no. 20), London.

Paddayya, K. (1977), An Acheulian occupation site at Hunsgi, Peninsular India: a summary of the results of two seasons of excavation (1975-6), *World Archaeol.*, 8:3: 344-55.

Paterson, T.T. (1937), Studies on the Palaeolithic succession in England, no. I: the Barnham sequence, *Proc. Prehist. Soc.*, 3: 87-135.

Paterson, T.T. and Fagg, B.E.B. (1940), Studies on the Palaeolithic succession in England, no. II: the Upper Brecklandian Acheul (Elveden), *Proc. Prehist. Soc.*, 6: 1-29.

Paterson, T.T. and Tebbutt, C.F. (1947), Studies on the Palaeolithic succession in England, no. III: Palaeoliths from St. Neots, Huntingdonshire, *Proc. Prehist. Soc.*, 13: 37-46.

Payne, G. (1915), Researches and discoveries in Kent, 1912-1915, *Archaeol. Cantiana*, 31: 275-86.

Pengelly, W. (1865-1880), Manuscript notes and journal of work at Kent's Cavern, preserved at the Museum of the Torquay Natural History Society, Torquay, Devonshire, England (unpublished).

Pengelly, W. (on behalf of the Committee) (1873a), Ninth report of the Committee for exploring Kent's Cavern, Devonshire, *Br. Ass. Adv. Sci.: Rep. 1873*: 198-209.

Pengelly, W. (1873b), The Flint and Chert Implements found in Kent's Cavern, Torquay, Devonshire, *Br. Ass. Adv. Sci.: Rep. 1873*: 209-14.

Petch, D.F. (1961), Archaeological notes for 1961, *Lincs. Archit. Archaeol. Soc. Rep. Pap.*, 9: 1-25.

Peyrony, D. (1931), La Micoque et ses diverses industries, *15e Congrès Inst. d'Anth. et d'Arch. Préh.*, 435.

Peyrony, D. (1938), La Micoque. Les fouilles

recentes. Leur signification, *Bull. Soc. Préhist. Franç.*, 35: 257-88.

Pickering, R. (1957), The Pleistocene geology of the south Birmingham area, *Q. Jl. Geol. Soc. Lond.*, 113: 223-37.

Pike, K. and Godwin, H. (1953), The interglacial at Clacton-on-Sea, Essex, *Q. Jl. Geol. Soc. Lond.*, 108: 261-72.

Pilbeam, D. (1972), *The Ascent of Man: an introduction to human evolution*, Macmillan, New York.

Poole, H.F. (1925), Palaeoliths from Great Pan Farm, Isle of Wight, *Pap. Proc. Hants. Field Club.*, 9: 305-19.

Posnansky, M. (1958), A Levalloisian implement from Lake Welbeck, Nottinghamshire, *Antiq. Journ.*, 38: 85-7.

Posnansky, M. (1963), The Lower and Middle Palaeolithic industries of the English East Midlands, *Proc. Prehist. Soc.*, 29: 357-94.

Prestwich, J. (1872), Report on the Exploration of Brixham Cave, conducted by a Committee of the Geological Society, and under the immediate superintendence and record of Wm. Pengelly, Esq., F.R.S., aided by a local Committee; with descriptions of the organic remains by G. Busk, Esq., F.R.S., and of the flint implements by John Evans, Esq., F.R.S., *Proc. Roy. Soc.*, 20:137: 514-24.

Prestwich, J. (1889), On the occurrence of Palaeolithic flint implements in the neighbourhood of Ightham, Kent, their distribution and probable age, *Q. Jl. Geol. Soc. Lond.*, 47:2: 270-97.

Prestwich, J. (1892), On the Primitive characters of the flint implements of the chalk plateau of Kent, with reference to the question of their Glacial or pre-Glacial age (with notes by Messrs. B. Harrison and De Barri Crawshay), *Journ. Anthrop. Inst.*, 21: 246-62.

Roe, D.A. (1964), The British Lower and Middle Palaeolithic: some problems, methods of study and preliminary results, *Proc. Prehist. Soc.*, 30: 245-67.

Roe, D.A. (1967), 'A study of handaxe groups of the British Lower and Middle Palaeolithic periods, using methods of metrical and statistical analysis, with a gazetteer of British Lower and Middle Palaeolithic sites', unpublished Ph.D. thesis, University of Cambridge.

Roe, D.A. (1968a), British Lower and Middle Palaeolithic handaxe groups, *Proc. Prehist. Soc.*, 34: 1-82.

Roe, D.A. (1968b), *A Gazetteer of British Lower and Middle Palaeolithic Sites*, Council for British Archaeology (Research Report no. 8), London.

Roe, D.A. (1970), *Prehistory: an Introduction*, Macmillan, London.

Roe, D.A. (1974), Palaeolithic artefacts from the River Avon terraces near Bristol, *Proc. Univ. Bristol Spelaeological Soc.*, 13:3: 319-26.

Roe, D.A. (1975), Some Hampshire and Dorset handaxes and the question of 'Early Acheulian' in Britain, *Proc. Prehist. Soc.*, 41: 1-9.

Roe, D.A. (1976), Typology and the trouble with handaxes, in *Problems in Economic and Social Archaeology*, eds G. de G. Sieveking, I.H. Longworth and K.E. Wilson, pp. 61-70, Duckworth, London.

Rust, A. (1937), *Das altsteinzeitliche Rentierjägerlager Meiendorf*, Wachholtz, Neumünster.

Rust, A. (1943), *Die alt- und mittelsteinzeitlichen Funde von Stellmoor*, Wachholtz, Neumünster.

Rust, A. (1950), *Die Höhlenfunde von Jabrud (Syrien)*, Wachholtz, Neumünster.

Sainty, J.E. (1927), An Acheulian Palaeolithic workshop site at Whitlingham, *Proc. Prehist. Soc. E. Anglia*, 5: 177-213.

Sainty, J.E. (1933), Some Norfolk Palaeolithic discoveries, *Proc. Prehist. Soc. E. Anglia*, 7:2: 171-7.

Sainty, J.E. (1935), Three Combe-Capelle handaxes from Norfolk, *Proc. Prehist. Soc.*, 1: 98-100.

Sainty, J.E. (1951), The Geology of Norfolk, *Trans. Norfolk Norwich Natur. Soc.*, 17:3: 149-85.

Sainty, J.E. and Watson, A.Q. (1944), Palaeolithic implements from Southacre, *Norfolk Archaeol.*, (Norfolk and Norwich Archaeol. Soc.), 28: 183-6.

Sampson, C.G. (ed.) (1978), *Paleoecology and archaeology of an Acheulian site at Caddington, England*, Dept. of Anthropology, Southern Methodist University, Dallas.

Sandford, K.S. (1924), The river gravels of the Oxford district, *Q. Jl. Geol. Soc. Lond.*, 80: 113-79.

Sandford, K.S. (1926), Pleistocene deposits, in *The Geology of the Country around Oxford* (2nd edn), eds T.I. Pocock and J. Pringle, pp. 104-72 (Memoirs of the Geological Survey, England: explanation of special Oxford sheet), HMSO, London.

Sandford, K.S. (1939), The Quaternary Geology of Oxfordshire, with reference to Palaeolithic Man, in *Victoria County History of Oxfordshire*, vol. 1, pp. 223-38.

Savory, H.N. (1961), Levalloisian flake implement from Chepstow (Mon.), *Bulletin of the Board of Celtic Studies*, 19:3: 250-2.

Seaby, W.A. (1950), Palaeolithic hand-axe from Cheddon Fitzpaine, *Proc. Somerset. Archaeol. Natur. Hist. Soc.*, 94: 168-9.

Sealy, K.R. (1955), The terraces of the Salisbury Avon, *Geog. Journ.*, 121: 350-6.

Sealy, K.R. and Sealy, C.E. (1956), The terraces of the Middle Thames, *Proc. Geol. Ass. Lond.*, 67: 369-92.

Semenov, S.A. (1964), *Prehistoric Technology: an experimental study of the oldest tools and artefacts from traces of manufacture and wear* (translated by M.W. Thompson), Cory, Adams & Mackay, London.

Semenov, S.A. (1970), Forms and functions of the oldest stone tools, *Quartär*, 21: 1-20.

Shackleton, N.J. (1967), Oxygen isotope analyses and Pleistocene temperatures re-assessed, *Nature*, 215: 15-17.

Shackleton, N.J. (1968), Depth of pelagic foraminifera and isotopic changes in Pleistocene oceans, *Nature*, 218: 79-80.

Shackleton, N.J. (1975), The stratigraphic record of deep-sea cores and its implications for the assessment of glacials, interglacials, stadials and interstadials in the mid-Pleistocene, in *After the Australopithecines: stratigraphy, ecology and culture change in the Middle Pleistocene*, eds K.W. Butzer and G. Ll. Isaac, pp. 1-24, Mouton, The Hague.

Shackleton, N.J. (1977), The oxygen isotope stratigraphic record of the Late Pleistocene, *Phil. Trans. Roy. Soc. (Series B)*, 280: 169-82.

Shackleton, N.J. and Opdyke, N.D. (1973), Oxygen isotope and palaeomagnetic stratigraphy of Equatorial Pacific core V28-238, *Quat. Res.*, 3: 39-55.

Shackleton, N.J. and Opdyke, N.D. (1976), Oxygen-isotope and palaeomagnetic stratigraphy of Pacific core V28-239: Late Pliocene to Latest Pleistocene, *Geol. Soc. Am. Mem.*, 145: 449-64.

Shackleton, N.J. and Turner, C. (1967), Correlation between marine and terrestrial Pleistocene successions, *Nature*, 216: 5120: 1079-82.

Shackley, M.L. (1973), A contextual study of the Mousterian industry from Great Pan Farm, Newport, Isle of Wight, *Proc. I.W. Natur. Hist. Archaeol. Soc.*, 6:8: 542-54.

Shackley, M.L. (1975), 'A study of the Mousterian of Acheulian Tradition industries of Southern England', unpublished Ph.D. thesis, University of Southampton.

Shackley, M.L. (1977), The *bout coupé* handaxe as a typological marker for the British Mousterian industries, in *Stone Tools as Cultural Markers: change, evolution and complexity*, ed. R.V.S. Wright, Canberra, Australian Institute of Aboriginal Studies, *Prehistory and Material Culture Series*, no. 12.

Shepherd, W. (1972), *Flint: its origin, properties and uses*, Faber & Faber, London.

Shotton, F.W. (1953), Pleistocene deposits of the area between Coventry, Rugby and Leamington and their bearing on the topographic development of the Midlands, *Phil. Trans. Roy. Soc. (Series B)*, 237: 209-60.

Shotton, F.W. (1965), Movements of insect populations in the British Pleistocene, *Geol. Soc. Am. Spec. Pap.*, 84: 17-33.

Shotton, F.W. (1968), The Pleistocene succession around Brandon, Warwickshire, *Phil. Trans. Roy. Soc. (Series B)*, 254: 387-400.

Shotton, F.W. (1976), Amplification of the Wolstonian stage of the British Pleistocene, *Geol. Mag.*, 113:3: 241-50.

Shotton, F.W. (ed.) (1977), *British Quaternary Studies: recent advances*, Clarendon Press, Oxford.

Sieveking, G. de G. (1968), High Lodge industry, *Nature*, 220: 1065-6.

Simpson, I.M. and West, R.G. (1958), On the stratigraphy and palaeobotany of a late-Pleistocene organic deposit at Chelford, Cheshire, *New Phytol.*, 57: 239-50.

Singer, R., Wymer, J.J., Gladfelter, B.G. and Wolff, R.G. (1973), Excavation of the Clactonian Industry at the Golf Course, Clacton-on-Sea, Essex, *Proc. Prehist. Soc.*, 39: 6-74.

Singer, R. and Wymer, J.J. (1976), The sequence of Acheulian industries at Hoxne, Suffolk, in *U.I.S.P.P. IXe Congrès (Nice, Sept. 1976): Colloque X: L'évolution de l'Acheuléen en Europe (prétirage)*: 14-30.

Smith, F. (1909), *The Stone Ages in North Britain and Ireland*, Blackie, London.

Smith, F. (1926), *Palaeolithic Man and the Cambridge Gravels*, Heffer, Cambridge.

Smith, R.A. (1911), A palaeolithic industry at Northfleet, Kent, *Archaeologia*, 62: 515-32.

Smith, R.A. (1915a), High level finds in the Upper Thames Valley, *Proc. Prehist. Soc. E. Anglia*, 2: 99-107.

Smith, R.A. (1915b), Origin of the Neolithic celt, *Archaeologia*, 67: 27-48.

Smith, R.A. (1917), Plateau deposits and implements, *Proc. Prehist. Soc. E. Anglia*, 2: 392-408.

Smith, R.A. (1921), Implements from Plateau Brickearth at Ipswich, *Proc. Geol. Ass. Lond.*, 32: 1-16.

Smith, R.A. (1926), *A Guide to Antiquities of the Stone Age in the Department of British and Mediaeval Antiquities* (3rd edn), British Museum, London.

Smith, R.A. (1931), *The Sturge Collection: An illustrated selection of flints from Britain bequeathed in 1919 by William Allen Sturge, M.V.O., M.D., F.R.C.P.*, British Museum, London.

Smith, R.A. (1933), Implements from high level gravel near Canterbury, *Proc. Prehist. Soc. E. Anglia*, 7:2: 165-70.

Smith, R.A. and Dewey, H. (1913), Stratification at Swanscombe, *Archaeologia*, 64: 177-204.

Smith, R.A. and Dewey, H. (1914), The High Terrace of the Thames: report on excavations made on behalf of the British Museum and H.M. Geological Survey in 1913, *Archaeologia*, 65: 187-212.

Smith, R.A. and Dewey, H. (1915), Researches at Rickmansworth: report on excavations made in 1914 on behalf of the British Museum, *Archaeologia*, 66: 195-224.

Smith, W.G. (1894), *Man the Primeval Savage: his haunts and relics from the hill-tops of Bedfordshire to Blackwall*, Stanford, London.

Smith, W.G. (1916), Notes on the Palaeolithic floor near Caddington, *Archaeologia*, 67:49-74.

Sollas, W.J. (1905), *The Age of the Earth and other Geological Studies*, T. Fisher Unwin, London.

Sollas, W.J. (1911), *Ancient Hunters and their Modern Representatives* (1st edn), Macmillan, London.

Solomon, J.D. (1932), On the heavy mineral assemblages of the Great Chalky Boulder-clay and Cannon-shot gravels of East Anglia, and their significance, *Geol. Mag.*, 69: 314-20.

Solomon, J.D. (1933), The implementiferous gravels of Warren Hill, *Journ. Roy. Anthrop. Inst.*, 63: 101-10.

Sommé, J. and Tuffreau, A. (1976), Les formations quaternaires et les industries de la Pointe-aux-Oies (Wimereux, Pas-de-Calais), in *U.I.S.P.P. IXe Congrès (Nice, Sept. 1976): Livret-guide de l'excursion A.10: Nord-ouest de la France (Bassin de la Seine, Bassin de la Somme et Nord)*, pp. 168-71.

Sparks, B.W. (1961), The ecological interpretation of Quaternary non-marine mollusca, *Proc. Linn. Soc.*, 172: 71-80.

Sparks, B.W. (1969), Non-marine mollusca and archaeology, in *Science in Archaeology* (2nd edn) eds D.R. Brothwell and E.S. Higgs, pp. 395-406, Thames & Hudson, London.

Sparks, B.W., West, R.G., Williams, R.B.G. and Ransom, M.E. (1969), Hoxnian interglacial deposits near Hatfield, Herts, *Proc. Geol. Ass. Lond.*, 80: 243-67.

Sparks, B.W. and West, R.G. (1959), The palaeoecology of the interglacial deposits at Histon Road, Cambridge, *Eiszeitälter und Gegenwart*, 10: 123-43.

Sparks, B.W. and West, R.G. (1964), The interglacial deposits at Stutton, Suffolk, *Proc. Geol. Ass. Lond.*, 74: 419-32.

Sparks, B.W. and West, R.G. (1967), A note on the interglacial deposit at Bobbitshole, near Ipswich, *Trans. Suffolk Natur. Soc.*, 13: 390-2.

Sparks, B.W. and West, R.G. (1968), Interglacial deposits at Wortwell, Norfolk, *Geol. Mag.*, 105: 471-81.

Sparks. B.W. and West, R.G. (1970), Late Pleistocene deposits at Wretton, Norfolk: I, Ipswichian interglacial deposits, *Phil. Trans. Roy. Soc. (Series B)*, 258: 1-30.

Sparks, B.W. and West, R.G. (1972), *The Ice Age in Britain*, Methuen, London.

Spurrell, F.C.J. (1880), On the discovery of the place where Palaeolithic implements were made at Crayford, *Q. Jl. Geol. Soc. Lond.*, 36: 544-8.

Spurrell, F.C.J. (1883), Palaeolithic implements found in West Kent, *Archaeol. Cantiana*, 15: 89-103.

Spurrell, F.C.J. (1884), On some Palaeolithic knapping tools and modes of using them, *Journ. Anthrop. Inst.*, 13: 109-18.

Stekelis, M. (1966), *Archaeological excavations at 'Ubeidiya, 1960-1963*, Israel Academy of Sciences and Humanities, Jerusalem.

Stekelis, M., Bar-Yosef, O. and Schick, T. (1969), *Archaeological Excavations at 'Ubediya, 1964-1966*, Israel Academy of Sciences and Humanities, Jerusalem.

Stevens, L.A. (1960), The interglacial of the Nar Valley, Norfolk, *Q. Jl. Geol. Soc. Lond.*, 115: 291-315.

Straw, A. (1973), The glacial geomorphology of central and north Norfolk, *E. Midlands Geog.*, 5:7:39: 333-54.

Sturge, W.A. (1911), Early Man: Palaeolithic Age, in *The Victoria History of the Counties of England: Suffolk*, vol. I, ed. W. Page, pp. 235-48, Constable, London.

Sturge, W.A. (1912), The patina of flint implements, *Proc. Prehist. Soc. E. Anglia*, 1: 140-57.

Sutcliffe, A.J. (1975), A hazard in the interpretation of glacial-interglacial sequences, *Quaternary Newsletter*, 17 (Nov. 1975): 1-3.

Sutcliffe, A.J. (1976), The British glacial-interglacial sequence, *Quaternary Newsletter*, 18 (Feb. 1976): 1-7.

Swanscombe Committee (1938), Report on the Swanscombe Skull, *Journ. Roy. Anthrop. Inst.*, 68: 17-98.

Szabo, B.J. and Collins, D.M. (1975), Ages of fossil bones from British interglacial sites, *Nature*, 254: 680-2.

Tebbutt, C.F., Marr, J.E. and Burkitt, M.C. (1927), Palaeolithic industries from the Great Ouse Gravels at and near St. Neots, *Proc. Prehist. Soc. E. Anglia*, 5: 166-73.

Tester, P.J. (1951), Palaeolithic flint implements from the Bowman's Lodge Gravel Pit, Dartford Heath, *Archaeol. Cantiana*, 63: 122-34.

Tester, P.J. (1952a), Early use of the Levallois technique in the Palaeolithic succession of the Thames Valley, *Arch. News Letter*, 4:8: 118-19.

Tester, P.J. (1952b), Surface palaeoliths from Standardhill Farm, near Elham, *Archaeol. Cantiana*, 65: 85-9.

Tester, P.J. (1958), An Acheulian site at Orpington, *Archaeol. Cantiana*, 72: 194-7.

Tester, P.J. (1965), An Acheulian site at Cuxton, *Archaeol. Cantiana*, 80: 30-60.

Tester, P.J. (1976), Further consideration of the Bowman's Lodge industry, *Archaeol. Cantiana*, 91: 29-39.

Thomas, M.F. (1961), River terraces and drainage development in the Reading area, *Proc. Geol. Ass. Lond.*, 72: 415-36.

Timms, P. (1974), *Flint Implements of the Old Stone Age*, Shire Publications, Aylesbury.

Tobias, P.V. (1967), *The Cranium and Maxillary dentition of* Australopithecus (Zinjanthropus) boisei, (*Olduvai Gorge*, vol. 2, ed. L.S.B. Leakey), Cambridge University Press.

Tomlinson, M.E. (1963), The Pleistocene chronology of the Midlands, *Proc. Geol. Ass. Lond.*, 74: 187-202.

Tratman, E.K., Donovan, D.T. and Campbell, J.B. (1971), The Hyaena Den (Wookey Hole), Mendip Hills, Somerset, *Proc. Univ. Bristol Spelaeological Soc.*, 12:3: 245-79.

Treacher, M.S., Arkell, W.J. and Oakley, K.P. (1948), On the ancient channel between Caversham and Henley, Oxfordshire, and its contained flint implements, *Proc. Prehist. Soc.*, 14: 126-54.

Tringham, R., Cooper, G., Odell, G., Voytek, B. and Whitman, A. (1974), Experimentation in the formation of edge damage: a new approach to lithic analysis, *Journal of Field Archaeology*, 1: 171-96.

Tuffreau, A. (1971a), *Quelques aspects du Paléolithique ancien et moyen dans le Nord de la France* (Bullétin de la Société de Préhistoire du Nord, numéro spécial no. 8), Amiens.

Tuffreau, A. (1971b), Quelques observations sur le Paléolithique de la Pointe-aux-Oies à Wimereux (Pas-de-Calais), *Bull. Soc. Préhist. Fr.*, 68: Études et Travaux, fasc. 2: 496-504.

Tuffreau, A. (1972), Observations complémentaires sur le Paléolithique de la Pointe-aux-Oies à Wimereux (Pas-de-Calais), *Septentrion: Rev. Archéol.*, 1: 6-9.

Tuffreau, A. (1976a), Les civilisations du Paléolithique moyen dans la région parisienne et en Normandie, in *La Préhistoire française, 1.2: Civilisations paléolithiques et mésolithiques*, ed. H. de Lumley, pp. 1098-104, CNRS, Paris.

Tuffreau, A. (1976b), Les civilisations du Paléolithique moyen dans le Bassin de la Somme et en Picardie, in *La Préhistoire française, 1.2: Civilisations paléolithiques et mésolithiques*, ed. H. de Lumley, pp. 1105-9, CNRS, Paris.

Tuffreau, A. (1976c), Les civilisations du Paléolithique moyen en Artois et dans le Cambresis, in *La Préhistoire française, 1:2. Civilisations paléolithiques et mésolithiques*, ed. H. de Lumley, pp. 1110-14, CNRS, Paris.

Turner, C. (1968), A Lowestoftian Late-glacial flora from the Pleistocene deposits at Hoxne, Suffolk, *New Phytol*, 67: 327-32.

Turner, C. (1970), The Middle Pleistocene deposits at Marks Tey, Essex, *Phil. Trans. Roy. Soc. (Series B)*, 257: 373-440.

Turner, C. (1975), The correlation and duration of Middle Pleistocene interglacial periods in Northwest Europe, in *After the Australopithecines: stratigraphy, ecology and culture change in the Middle Pleistocene*, eds K.W. Butzer and G.Ll. Isaac, pp. 259-308, Mouton, The Hague.

Turner, C. and Kerney, M.P. (1971), A note on the age of the freshwater beds of the Clacton Channel, *Journ. Geol. Soc. Lond.*, 127: 87-93.

Turner, C. and West, R.G. (1968), The subdivision and zonation of interglacial periods, *Eiszeitalter und Gegenwart*, 19: 93-101.

Ulrix-Closset, M. (1975), *Le paléolithique moyen dans le bassin mosan en Belgique* (Bibliothèque de la Faculté de Philosophie et Lettres de l'Université de Liège, Publications Exceptionelles no. 3). Éditions Universa, Wetteren.

Underwood, W. (1913), a discovery of Pleistocene bones and flint implements in a gravel pit at Dovercourt, Essex, *Proc. Prehist. Soc. E. Anglia*, 1: 360-8.

Valoch, K. (ed.) (1976), *Les premières industries de l'Europe* (UISPP IXe Congrès (Nice, Sept. 1976): Colloque VIII, prétirage).

Vértes, L. (1965), Typology of the Buda Industry, a pebble-tool industry from the Hungarian Lower Palaeolithic, *Quaternaria*, 7: 185-96.

Villa, P. (1977), Sols et niveaux d'habitat du Paléolithique inférieur en Europe et au Proche Orient, *Quaternaria*, 19: 107-34.

Vogel, J.C. and Hammen, T.C. van der (1967), The Denekamp and Paudorf interstadials, *Geologie en Mijnbouw*, 46: 187-94.

Vulliamy, C.E. (1925), *Our Prehistoric Forerunners*, Bodley Head, London.

Waechter, J. d'A. (1968), Swanscombe 1968, *Proc. Roy. Anthrop. Inst.*, 1968: 53-8.

Waechter, J. d'A. (1973), The Late Middle Acheulian industries in the Swanscombe area, in *Archaeological Theory and Practice*, ed. D.E. Strong, pp. 67-86, Seminar Press, London and New York.

Waechter, J. d'A., Newcomer, M.H. and Conway, B.W. (1969), Swanscombe 1969, *Proc. Roy. Anthrop. Inst.*, 1969: 83-94.

Waechter, J. d'A., Newcomer, M.H. and Conway, B.W. (1970), Swanscombe 1970, *Proc. Roy. Anthrop. Inst.*, 1970: 43-64.

Waechter, J. d'A., Hubbard, R.N.L.B. and Conway, B.W. (1971), Swanscombe 1971, *Proc. Roy. Anthrop. Inst.*, 1971: 73-85.

Warren, S.H. (1911), Palaeolithic wooden spear from Clacton, *Q. Jl. Geol. Soc. Lond.*, 67: cxix.

Warren, S.H. (1922), The Mesvinian industry of Clacton-on-Sea, *Proc. Prehist. Soc. E. Anglia*, 3: 597-602.

Warren, S.H. (1923), Sub-soil pressure flaking, *Proc. Geol. Ass. Lond.*, 34: 153-75.

Warren, S.H. (1924), The Elephant-Bed of Clacton-on-Sea, *Essex Naturalist*, 21: 32-40.

Warren, S.H. (1933), The Palaeolithic industries of the Clacton and Dovercourt districts, *Essex Naturalist*, 24: 1-29.

Warren, S.H. (1951), The Clactonian flint industry: a new interpretation, *Proc. Geol. Ass. Lond.*, 62: 107-35.

Warren, S.H. (1955), The Clacton (Essex) Channel deposits, *Q. Jl. Geol. Soc. Lond.*, 111: 287-307.

Warren, S.H. (1958), The Clacton flint industry: a supplementary note, *Proc. Geol. Ass. Lond.*, 69: 123-9.

Warren, S.H., Reid, C., Reid, E.M., Groves, J., Andrews, C.W., Hinton, M.A.C., Withers, T.H., Kennard, A.S. and Woodward, B.B. (1923), The *Elephas antiquus* bed of Clacton-on-Sea (Essex) and its flora and fauna, *Q. Jl. Geol. Soc. Lond.*, 79: 606-34.

Warren, S.H., Piggott, S., Clark, J.G.D., Burkitt, M.C., Godwin, H. and Godwin, M.E. (1936), Archaeology of the submerged land-surface of the Essex coast, *Proc. Prehist. Soc.*, 2: 178-210.

Watson, W. (1950), *Flint Implements: an account of Stone Age techniques and cultures*, British Museum, London. (N.B. There are numerous later editions of this book, including revision by G. de G. Sieveking.)

Wernert, P. (1957), *Stratigraphie paléontologique et préhistorique des sédiments quaternaires d'Alsace Achenheim*, Service de la Carte Géologique d'Alsace et de Lorraine (*Mémoires* no. 14), Strasbourg.

West, R.G. (1956), The Quaternary deposits at Hoxne, Suffolk, *Phil. Trans. Roy. Soc. (Series B)*, 239: 265-356.

West, R.G. (1957), Interglacial deposits at Bobbitshole, Ipswich, *Phil. Trans. Roy. Soc. (Series B)*, 241: 1-31.

West, R.G. (1961a), The glacial and interglacial deposits of Norfolk, *Trans. Norfolk Norwich Natur. Soc.*, 19: 365-75.

West, R.G. (1961b), Vegetational history of the Early Pleistocene of the Royal Society borehole at Ludham, Norfolk, *Proc. Roy. Soc. (Series B)*, 155: 437-53.

West, R.G. (1969), Pollen analyses from interglacial deposits at Aveley and Grays, Essex, *Proc. Geol. Ass. Lond.*, 80: 271-82.

West, R.G. (1977), *Pleistocene Geology and Biology, with especial reference to the British Isles* (second edition, revised), Longmans, London.

West, R.G., Dickson, C.A., Catt, J.A., Weir, A.H. and Sparks, B.W. (1974), Late Pleistocene deposits at Wretton, Norfolk. II. Devensian deposits, *Phil. Trans. Roy. Soc. (Series B)*, 267: 337-420.

West, R.G., Lambert, C.A. and Sparks, B.W. (1964), Interglacial deposits at Ilford, Essex, *Phil. Trans. Roy. Soc. (Series B)*, 247: 185-212.

West, R.G. and McBurney, C.B.M. (1954), The Quaternary deposits at Hoxne, Suffolk and their archaeology, *Proc. Prehist. Soc.*, 20:2: 131-54.

West, R.G. and Sparks, B.W. (1960), Coastal interglacial deposits of the English Channel, *Phil. Trans. Roy. Soc. (Series B)*, 243: 95-133.

West, R.G. and Wilson, D.G. (1966), Cromer Forest Bed Series, *Nature*, 209: 497-8.

Wetzel, R. (1958), *Die Bocksteinschmiede. I Teil.*, Müller & Gräff, Stuttgart.

Wetzel, R. and Bosinski, G. (1969), *Die Bocksteinschmiede im Lonetal*, 2 vols (Veröffentlichungen des Staatlichen Amtes für Denkmalpflege Stuttgart: Reihe A, Vor- und Frühgeschichte, Heft 15), Müller &

Gräff, Stuttgart.

Willis, G.W. (1947), Hampshire palaeoliths and the Clay-with-flints, *Pap. Proc. Hants. Field Club*, 16:3: 253-6.

Windle, B.C.A. (1904), *Remains of the Prehistoric Age in England*, Methuen, London.

Woodward, H.B. (1907), *The History of the Geological Society of London*, Geological Society, London.

Wooldridge, S.W. (1957), Some aspects of the physiography of the Thames Valley in relation to the Ice Age and Early Man, *Proc. Prehist. Soc.*, 23: 1-19.

Wooldridge, S.W. (1960), The Pleistocene succession in the London Basin, *Proc. Geol. Ass. Lond.*, 71: 113-29.

Wright, W.B. (1937), *The Quaternary Ice Age*, Macmillan, London.

Wymer, J.J. (1957), A Clactonian flint industry at Little Thurrock, Grays, Essex, *Proc. Geol. Ass. Lond.*, 68: 159-77.

Wymer, J.J. (1961), The Lower Palaeolithic succession in the Thames Valley and the date of the ancient channel between Caversham and Henley, *Proc. Prehist. Soc.*, 27: 1-27.

Wymer, J.J. (1964), Excavations at Barnfield Pit, 1955-60, in *The Swanscombe Skull: a survey of research at a Pleistocene site*, ed. C.D. Ovey, pp. 19-60, Royal Anthropological Institute (Occasional Paper no. 20), London.

Wymer, J.J. (1968), *Lower Palaeolithic Archaeology in Britain as represented by the Thames Valley*, John Baker, London.

Wymer, J.J. (1974), Clactonian and Acheulian Industries in Britain: their chronology and significance, *Proc. Geol. Ass. Lond.*, 85: 3: 391-421.

Wymer, J.J., Jacobi, R.M. and Rose, J. (1975), Late Devensian and Early Flandrian barbed points from Sproughton, Suffolk, *Proc. Prehist. Soc.*, 41: 235-41.

Wymer, J.J. and Singer, R. (1970), The first season of excavation at Clacton-on-Sea, Essex, England: a brief report, *World Archaeol.*, 2: 12-16.

Wymer, J.J. and Straw, A. (1977), Handaxes from beneath glacial till at Welton-le-Wold, Lincolnshire, and the distribution of palaeoliths in Britain, *Proc. Prehist. Soc.*, 43: 355-60.

Zagwijn, W.H., Montfrans, H.M. van and Zandstra, J.G. (1971), Subdivision of the 'Cromerian' in the Netherlands: pollen analysis, paleomagnetism, sedimentary petrology, *Geologie en Mijnbouw*, 50: 41-58.

Zeuner, F.E. (1958), *Dating the Past*, Methuen, London.

Zeuner, F.E. (1959), *The Pleistocene Period*, Hutchinson, London.

Zuckerman, S., ed. (1973), Concepts of Human Evolution, *Symposium Zool. Soc. Lond.*, 33.

Summary

THE LOWER AND MIDDLE PALAEOLITHIC PERIODS IN BRITAIN

1 Background to a study of the Old Stone Age in Britain, pages 1-33

The Palaeolithic is the most difficult of the prehistoric periods to study in Britain, because of the grave lack of undisturbed sites and the extreme scarcity of evidence other than stone artefacts. Our knowledge of the British Pleistocene sequence also remains incomplete, and chronometric dates are very hard to establish in the absence of Pleistocene volcanic activity. During the Pleistocene, Britain lay at the northwest extremity of Old World human distribution; it was sometimes an island and sometimes a peninsula, intermittently reachable by major routes from the east and the south, and was certainly not continuously inhabited. It is essential to study the British Palaeolithic sequence in its full European and Old World context, rather than in isolation. The earliest British industries probably fall in the time-range 500,000-250,000 years ago, which implies a late start by comparison with areas such as East Africa, and all the British Palaeolithic material is therefore likely to be of Middle or Upper Pleistocene age. There are more than 3,000 find-spots of Lower and Middle Palaeolithic artefacts in Britain, but very few have produced good environmental, chronological or palaeo-anthropological evidence. Unravelling the story of the Pleistocene and the Palaeolithic is a task for many different specialists within the general field of Quaternary Research. An account is given of the development of Palaeolithic and Quaternary studies in Britain over the past hundred and fifty years or more, with an assessment of current research trends and interests. Previous attempts to describe the whole, or major parts, of the British Palaeolithic are briefly discussed and it is noted that a comprehensive account of the British Lower and Middle Palaeolithic is still needed.

2 The Pleistocene Background, pages 34-64

The nature of glacial, periglacial, interglacial and interstadial conditions is outlined, and the kinds of evidence by which each is represented are listed. The Pleistocene sequence in Britain is then described, with reference to various key sites and sections, including West Runton (Norfolk), Corton (Suffolk), Hoxne (Suffolk), Marks Tey (Essex) and several others. The principal stages of the British Pleistocene relevant to this book are (in chronological order): the Cromerian interglacial, Anglian glaciation, Hoxnian interglacial, Wolstonian glaciation, Ipswichian interglacial and Devensian glaciation. Some of these are likely to be more complex than can be clearly seen at present, and there may well be one or two major gaps in the sequence which these names provide. Better and more complete Pleistocene sequences are available from Continental Europe and in the isotopic temperature curves obtained from various deep-sea cores. Attempts at correlation between the deep-sea cores and the British terrestrial sequence suggest that the latter leaves much to be desired. Only within the Devensian are interstadials seen at all clearly in Britain, though they must have existed in the Wolstonian and Anglian. Tentative chronometric ages are suggested for the named British Pleistocene stages, though direct factual evidence to support them is extremely sparse for periods earlier than the Devensian.

3 The search for a basic Lower Palaeolithic sequence, pages 65-93

The task of describing the archaeological evidence might be approached in various ways. The author decided to use sites in North Kent as a basic sequence, because only here do a variety of Palaeolithic industries occur in a sequence of Pleistocene deposits whose order can be demonstrated geologically. The principal sites are the famous Swanscombe gravel pits (particularly Barnfield Pit and Ricksons Pit) and the nearby occurrences at Northfleet: the classic Baker's Hole site and certain exposures in the so-called Ebbsfleet Channel. Finds from the brickearths at Crayford, only a few miles away, can also be taken into account. The combination of these sites gives a clear local archaeological sequence, with Clactonian followed by well-made Acheulian industries, after which come industries with a striking emphasis on the use of Levalloisian technique, at first to produce large bold flakes and afterwards fine elongated flake-blades. There are signs that hand-axe manufacture continued at least sporadically in this part of North Kent while these 'Levalloisian' industries were current. The establishment of this basic sequence makes it possible to ask certain questions, the answers to which are considered in the next two chapters. Do other stages or industries exist elsewhere in Britain to expand this sequence? Are there sites elsewhere in Britain whose industries compare well with those from North Kent? Can it be said that there are in the British Lower Palaeolithic *contemporary* industries which differ from each other substantially, or are the differing industries always also different from each other in age, as seems to be the case in the North Kent sequence? – i.e., can we detect 'horizontal' as well as 'vertical' variation amongst British Lower Palaeolithic industries?

4   *Expanding the basic sequence, pages 94-130*

It is clear that industries do occur elsewhere in Britain which are earlier than any in the Swanscombe-Northfleet-Crayford area sequence. Westbury-sub-Mendip (Somerset) and Kent's Cavern (Devon) have both yielded artefacts associated with faunal remains of Late Cromerian or (more probably) inter-Anglian age. The artefacts from the former site are not diagnostic of any particular industry, but those from the latter include typical handaxes of archaic appearance. The writer accordingly argues for the existence of a British Earlier Acheulian stage, and suggests that certain other industries belong to it, though they are not themselves well dated. Of these, the most important are Fordwich (Kent), Farnham Terrace A (Surrey) and the worn series from Warren Hill, Mildenhall (Suffolk). If this view is accepted, it becomes appropriate to call the Swanscombe handaxe industries 'Middle Acheulian'. There is

also evidence for a younger Acheulian stage than that represented in the Swanscombe Middle Gravels and Upper Loam: a 'Final Acheulian/ Micoquian' stage, with elegant pointed plano-convex handaxes which compare well with those from certain German and French sites, dating from the end of the Last Interglacial and the start of the Last Glaciation. The Wolvercote Channel (Oxfordshire) occurrence is the most important one, and at this site the implements were associated with an interglacial fauna, which the author suggests is Ipswichian rather than Hoxnian.

5   *More sites, and the question of variation, pages 131-232*

The distribution of British Lower Palaeolithic sites is outlined and discussed. Then the main stages so far distinguished are recapitulated, with the addition of important sites from other parts of Britain. It is noted that the Clactonian may have been present in Britain before the end of the Anglian glaciation. There are few pure Clactonian sites in Britain, and most of them seem to be of Hoxnian age; it seems possible, however, from a small number of sites that the Clactonian tradition continued in a technologically improved form after the Hoxnian. These impressions of the Clactonian would accord reasonably well with what is known of the occurrence in certain parts of Continental Europe of flake industries older than the Mousterian in its typical forms.

A few more possible Earlier Acheulian sites are mentioned. The Middle Acheulian of Britain is then discussed at length, with reference to all the most important sites. The writer summarizes, updates and extends his own previous work on the British handaxe industries, giving a selection of the results of his metrical analyses. A pattern of Traditions, Groups and Sub-Groups can be distinguished amongst the best of the British sites, and a number of attributions to certain parts of it can be made, with more or less confidence, on typological and technological grounds, from the large quantity of mixed and undated British sites. When such dating evidence as there is from the good sites is considered, it can be seen that the suggested Pointed and Ovate Traditions (the groups of industries dominated respectively by pointed and ovate handaxe types) certainly overlap in time to a considerable extent. It follows therefore that the order of occurrence seen at Barnfield Pit, Swanscombe, where a 'pointed' handaxe industry in the Middle Gravels preceded an 'ovate' one in the Upper Loam, does *not* hold good for Britain in general. There are no obvious regional variants in the British Acheulian. It can be seen that the 'Middle Acheulian' in Britain is a long and variable stage; the causes of the observable variations are by no means clear, but it is likely that differing human activities were an important factor. The later part of the 'Middle Acheulian' stage may even overlap in time with the Final Acheulian/Micoquian episode already discussed.

The account of the use of Levalloisian technique in Britain, begun in Chapter 3, is now continued and expanded. Summary accounts are given of several more important sites, in West London, East Anglia, the Great Ouse Valley (in Bedfordshire and Huntingdonshire), Northeast Kent and South Essex. There is no 'Levalloisian Culture' in Britain, as was once believed: apart from industries consisting almost exclusively of Levalloisian artefacts, there are Acheulian industries which employ the Levallois technique in varying degrees, and others in which use of the Levallois technique is associated with the occurrence of typically Mousterian artefacts. A few mixed assemblages, in which Levalloisian technique features, are mentioned, where there are factors of particular significance, and there are two interesting and prolific occurrences in which a simplified or 'reduced' Levalloisian technique is found. The distribution of find-spots of Levalloisian artefacts in Britain is uneven, suggesting that the technique was perhaps used on a local basis, depending at least partly on the availability of suitable raw material in sufficient quantity. Use of Levalloisian technique in one form or another during the Palaeolithic extends in Britain from the late Hoxnian until the middle Devensian; so far as it is concerned, the order of events noted in the North Kent basic sequence is generally confirmed in other areas, but the information available in North Kent also receives some amplification.

6   The Middle Palaeolithic, pages 233-67

Some of the Levalloisian industries already discussed must be counted as Middle Palaeolithic; in view of the discontinuity of occupation in Britain, we do not see either a clear interface between Lower and Middle Palaeolithic or a gradual local transition from one to the other. The Continental Mousterian is briefly considered, as essential background to the study of the British material. The only Continental variant of the fully developed Mousterian which can clearly be seen in Britain is the Mousterian of Acheulian Tradition (MTA), though there are probably some examples of 'archaic Mousterian' industries of Wolstonian age, notably at High Lodge, Mildenhall (Suffolk),

which are not without Continental parallels. The only British Mousterian site with really abundant material is La Cotte de Saint-Brelade, Jersey (Channel Islands), though the writer takes the view that it is better regarded as belonging to the Mousterian occupation of Western France than to that of Britain, notwithstanding its considerable importance. There are MTA occupations at various British caves in the North Midlands, in the South-West and in Wales, and these are described. It is notable that the British caves are all situated on the periphery of the area populated by man during the Lower and Middle Palaeolithic, and none appears to have been intensively occupied or frequently visited. There is however a considerable if patchy distribution of typical Mousterian *bout coupé* handaxes over Southern and Eastern Britain, most being isolated finds in open situations. These distinctive implements, of which a comprehensive list is given for the first time, lie outside the morphological range of Acheulian handaxes, in the writer's view, and, where there is any dating evidence for individual examples, it suggests a Devensian or very occasionally a late Ipswichian age. They fit well into the context of the North French MTA of that period, and the writer regards them as evidence for movements across and within southern Britain by Mousterian groups coming from North France and perhaps also Belgium and Germany. A few more substantial MTA open sites are also known in Britain, such as Bramford Road, Ipswich (Suffolk), or Great Pan Farm, Shide (Isle of Wight), and these are briefly described.

7   Towards the archaeology of the period: some conclusions, interpretations and speculations, pages 268-84

The conclusions reached about the sequence of Lower and Middle Palaeolithic industries, and the place of Britain in the European Palaeolithic, are recapitulated. Their probable chronology is summarized and the shortcomings of the present British Pleistocene sequence again emphasized. It is difficult to attempt an account of the palaeoanthropology of the British Lower and Middle Palaeolithic, when the evidence is so poor. Only for the Middle Acheulian stage is it worth discussing the question of variability of contemporary industries, and here it seems likely that functional variation is important. However, the precise functions of implements are hard to determine throughout the Palaeolithic, Acheulian handaxes being a classic example. Microwear analysis (using high magnification) is the most promising line of research and some important first results, obtained by L.H. Keeley, are summarized, with particular reference to the sites of Clacton and Hoxne. Other points relevant to the problems of implement function are discussed. It seems possible that the large oval Levalloisian flakes may sometimes have been blanks for handaxe manufacture; Baker's Hole might accordingly be regarded as an extreme variant within the Acheulian. In the later Levalloisian 'flake-blade' industries, many of the pieces seem likely to have been projectile points and knives, and two of the sites, though discovered in the nineteenth century and poorly reported, appear to have been kill or butchery sites — the only British examples. It is suggested that these 'flake-blade Levalloisian' occurrences may be variant industries belonging to the British MTA, specialized for hunting and butchering activities at open sites.

No clear evidence for artificial dwelling structures exists in the British Lower and Middle Palaeolithic, although good examples occur elsewhere in the world. Little can be said about seasonal movements of hunter-gatherer groups, from the existing evidence, or about 'permanent' or 'temporary' camps. The writer suggests, however, that much of the Palaeolithic occupation of Britain may have consisted of summer hunting visits, the winter base camps being in what is now western Continental Europe. This looks particularly likely to be true for the British Mousterian of Devensian age; no site looks like a winter base camp at all, and winter conditions in Britain at this time may have been somewhat unpleasant. The diagnosis of specialized activity sites in the British Lower and Middle Palaeolithic is also very difficult, with the exception of the two kill or butchery sites already mentioned and a number of locations where the main activities were certainly obtaining stone and manufacturing implements. Little or nothing can be said of the size of human groups in Britain during this period, or of social organization or domestic equipment. There is one possible case of ornamental items (stone beads) having been discovered. Better socio-economic data will not be forthcoming until new, well-preserved, primary context sites are discovered in Britain and examined under modern conditions. Such sites may well exist.

Résumé

LE PALÉOLITHIQUE INFÉRIEUR ET MOYEN EN GRANDE BRETAGNE

1 Le cadre fondamental de l'étude de l'Age de la Pierre Taillée en Grande Bretagne, pages 1-33

Le Paléolithique est la période préhistorique la plus difficile à étudier en Grande Bretagne, à cause de la pénurie de gisements en place et de l'extrême rareté de documents autres que les objets de pierre. Notre connaissance de la succession pléistocène britannique demeure également incomplète et les datations chronométriques sont fort difficiles à établir à défaut d'activité volcanique à cette époque. Pendant le Pléistocène, la Grande Bretagne se situait à l'extrémité nord-ouest de la répartition humaine dans l'Ancien Monde; c'était tantôt une île, tantôt une péninsule, irrégulièrement accessible par les grandes routes de l'Est et du Sud, certainement un pays qui n'était habité que d'une façon intermittente. Il est essentiel d'étudier la succession pléistocène britannique dans le cadre intégral de l'Europe et de l'Ancien Monde, plutôt que d'une manière hors contexte. Les industries britanniques les plus anciennes se situent vraisemblablement dans la période 500.000-250.000 BP, ce qui implique un début tardif par rapport aux régions telles que l'Afrique orientale. Il est donc probable que la totalité des documents paléolithiques de la Grande Bretagne date du Pléistocène moyen ou supérieur. Il existe plus de 3.000 endroits où l'on a trouvé des outils du Paléolithique inférieur et moyen, mais très rares sont ceux qui ont livré des données certaines sur l'aspect environnemental, chronologique ou paléo-anthropologique. Eclairer l'histoire du Pléistocène et du Paléolithique est une tâche pour de nombreux spécialistes des différents sujets qui constituent le domaine général de la recherche du Quaternaire. Le développement de l'étude du Paléolithique et du Quaternaire en Grande Bretagne pendant au moins les dernières cent cinquante années est présenté ici, ainsi qu'une évaluation des tendances et des intérêts actuels qui animent la recherche. Sont brièvement discutés les essais antérieurs de description de l'ensemble, ou de majeures parties, du Paléolithique britannique. On constate qu'un exposé compréhensif du Paléolithique inférieur et moyen fait toujours défaut.

2 La succession pléistocène, pages 34-64

Les caractères des régimes glaciaire, périglaciaire, interglaciaire et interstadiaire sont esquissés et les différents types de documents représentatifs de chaque régime sont catalogués. La succession pléistocène en Grande Bretagne est ensuite décrite par rapport aux différents sites et sections clefs: West Runton (Norfolk), Corton (Suffolk), Hoxne (Suffolk), Marks Tey (Essex) et quelques autres. Les principales phases du Pléistocène britannique intéressant cet ouvrage sont, par ordre chronologique, les suivantes: l'Interglaciaire cromérien, la Glaciation anglienne, l'Interglaciaire hoxnien, la Glaciation wolstonienne, l'Interglaciaire ipswichien et la Glaciation devensienne. Il est probable que quelques unes de ces phases soient plus complexes que ne l'indiquerait notre appréciation actuelle, toujours floue, et il est fort possible qu'il y ait une ou plusieurs lacunes importantes dans la succession que fournit cette nomenclature. L'Europe continentale offre des successions pléistocène plus distinctes et plus complètes et il en est de même pour les courbes de température isotopique obtenues par des carottages des fonds océaniques. Des tentatives de corrélation entre ces carottes et la succession terrestre britannique suggèrent que cette dernière laisse beaucoup à désirer. La Glaciation devensienne est la seule qui ait des interstadiaires tant soit peu repérables, bien qu'ils aient pu exister pendant les Glaciations wolstonienne et anglienne. Nous suggérons des âges chronométriques pour les phases types du Pléistocène britannique, quoique les documents directs et matériels, nécessaires pour appuyer ces datations, soient extrêmement clairesemés dans les périodes antérieures à la Glaciation devensienne.

3   A la recherche d'une séquence de base pour le Paléolithique inférieur, pages 65-93

Décrire les documents archéologiques peut être abordé de plusieurs manières. Nous avons décidé d'utiliser des gisements du nord du département de Kent pour établir la séquence de base. En effet, c'est le seul endroit où se trouvent diverses industries paléolithiques incluses dans une succession de dépôts pléistocènes, dont l'ordre peut être démontré géologiquement. Les gisements principaux comprennent les célèbres gravières de Swanscombe (particulièrement Barnfield Pit et Ricksons Pit), les sites voisins de Northfleet, le gisement classique de Baker's Hole et certaines coupes de l'endroit dit 'Ebbsfleet Channel'. Des trouvailles provenant des terres à briques de Crayford, distant seulement de quelques kilomètres, peuvent également servir. La combinaison de ces gisements donne une séquence archéologique locale claire: le Clactonien, suivi par des industries acheuléennes bien finies, puis des industries avec une tendance frappante pour la technique Levallois, tout d'abord dans la production de grands éclats robustes et plus tard dans la fabrication de beaux éclats-lames allongés. La production de bifaces semble avoir continué, au moins sporadiquement, dans cette région du nord de Kent pendant le développement des industries 'levalloisiennes'. L'établissement de cette séquence de base rend possibles certaines questions, dont les solutions seront considérées dans les deux chapitres suivants. Existe-t-il ailleurs en Grande Bretagne d'autres stades ou industries qui développeraient cette séquence? Existe-t-il ailleurs en Grande Bretagne des sites dont les industries seraient nettement comparables à celles du nord de Kent? Peut-on dire qu'il y ait dans le Paléolithique inférieur de la Grande Bretagne des industries contemporaines qui diffèrent substantiellement les unes des autres? Alternativement, les industries différentes sont-elles toujours d'âges différents, comme semble être le cas dans la séquence du nord de Kent? C'est-à-dire, peut-on découvrir, parmi les industries du Paléolithique inférieur en Grande Bretagne, des variations dans l'espace aussi bien que dans le temps?

4   Le développement de la séquence de base, pages 94-130

Il est clair qu'il existe ailleurs en Grande Bretagne des industries plus anciennes qu'aucune de la séquence de Swanscombe-Northfleet-Crayford. Westbury-sub-Mendip (Somerset) et Kent's Cavern (Devon) ont tous deux fourni des outils associés à des restes de faune qui datent de la fin de l'Interglaciaire cromérien ou, plus probablement, d'une période inter-anglienne. Les objets provenant de ce premier gisement ne sont diagnostiques d'aucune industrie particulière, mais ceux du deuxième comprennent des bifaces typiques, d'aspect archaïque. En conséquence, nous soutenons l'existence en Grande Bretagne d'un stade Acheuléen inférieur et nous suggérons que certaines autres industries lui appartiennent, bien qu'elles ne soient pas elles-mêmes bien datées. Parmi celles-ci, les plus importantes sont Fordwich (Kent), Farnham Terrace A (Surrey) et la série roulée de Warren Hill, Mildenhall (Suffolk). Si l'on accepte cette opinion, il convient d'appeler les industries à bifaces de Swanscombe 'Acheuléen moyen'. De même, il y a évidence pour un stade acheuléen, postérieur à celui représenté dans les graviers moyens (Middle Gravels) et les limons supérieurs (Upper Loam) de Swanscombe: stade 'Acheuléen final/Micoquien', avec d'élégants bifaces pointus, de section plano-convexe, comparables à ceux de certains sites allemands et français datés de la fin du dernier interglaciaire et du début de la dernière glaciation. Le site de Wolvercote Channel (Oxfordshire) est le plus important, les outils étant associés à une faune interglaciaire, que nous pensons être ipswichienne plutôt que hoxnienne.

5   D'autres gisements et la question de variation, pages 131-232

La distribution de sites britanniques du Paléolithique inférieur est esquissée et discutée. Ensuite, les stades principaux déterminés ci-dessus sont récapitulés et d'autres gisements ailleurs en Grande Bretagne sont ajoutés. Il est à noter que le Clactonien a pu être présent en Grande Bretagne avant la fin de la Glaciation anglienne. Il n'y a que de rares sites du Clactonien pur en Grande Bretagne et la plupart semblent dater de l'Interglaciaire hoxnien. Cependant, à juger par un petit nombre de gisements, il se peut que la tradition clactonienne ait continué après l'Interglaciaire hoxnien, sous une forme technologiquement élaborée. Cette idée sur le Clactonien s'accorderait assez bien à ce que l'on sait de l'occurrence, dans certaines régions de l'Europe continentale, des industries à éclats, plus anciennes que le Moustérien sous ses formes classiques.

Quelques autres sites que l'on peut, peut-être, rapporter à l'Acheuléen inférieur sont mentionnés. Ensuite, l'Acheuléen moyen de la Grande Bretagne est discuté en détail, en nous référant aux sites les plus importants. Nous résumons, révisons et développons nos propres recherches antérieures sur les industries à bifaces de la Grande Bretagne, en offrant une sélection des résultats de nos analyses morphométriques. Un tableau de Traditions, de Groups et de Sous-Groups peut être distingué parmi les meilleurs gisements britanniques. Pour des raisons de typologie et de technologie, on peut attribuer à certaines parties de ce tableau, avec plus ou moins d'assurance, un nombre de documents provenant des maints gisements britanniques qui contiennent des outillages mélangés et non datés. Quand on considère les quelques éléments de datation que l'on possède pour les meilleurs gisements, on voit clairement que deux des traditions proposées, celle où dominent les bifaces pointus (Pointed Tradition) et celle où dominent les bifaces ovales (Ovate Tradition), se chevauchent considérablement dans le temps. Il s'ensuit que l'ordre d'apparition constaté à Barnfield Pit, Swanscombe (une industrie à bifaces 'pointus', située dans les graviers moyens, succédée par une industrie à formes 'ovales', située dans les limons supérieurs), n'est point un ordre valable pour la Grande Bretagne en général. Il n'existe pas de variantes régionales évidentes dans l'Acheuléen britannique. On peut constater que 'l'Acheuléen moyen' en Grande Bretagne constitue un stade, long et variable. Les causes des variations observées ne sont pas du tout claires, mais il est probable que des activités humaines différentes constituent un élément important. Il est même possible que la dernière partie du stade 'Acheuléen moyen' empiète sur la période du stade Acheuléen final/Micoquien, déjà discuté.

La description de l'utilisation de la technique Levallois en Grande Bretagne, commencée dans le chapitre 3, est ici continuée et élargie. Plusieurs autres sites importants sont brièvement décrits, à l'ouest de Londres, dans l'East Anglia, dans la vallée de la Great Ouse (Bedfordshire et Huntingdonshire), au nord-est de Kent et au sud d'Essex. Il n'y a pas de 'Culture levalloisienne' en Grande Bretagne, comme on le croyait autrefois: outre les industries comprenant presque exclusivement des outils levalloisiens, il y a des industries acheuléennes, qui font un usage variable de la technique Levallois et d'autres industries, où la technique Levallois est associée à des outils typiquement moustériens. Quelques ensembles mélangés, où figure la technique Levallois, sont indiqués quand il s'agit de particularités significa-

tives et il y a deux cas intéressants d'outillages prolifiques où l'on trouve une technique Levallois simplifiée ou 'réduite'. La répartition des trouvailles d'outils levalloisiens en Grande Bretagne est inégale, ce qui suggère que la technique était peut-être utilisée à l'échelle locale, dépendant, au moins partiellement, de la disponibilité de la matière première convenable. L'emploi pendant le Paléolithique de la technique Levallois, sous une forme ou sous une autre, s'étend en Grande Bretagne de la partie finale de l'Interglaciaire hoxnien jusqu'au milieu de la Glaciation devensienne. Dans la mesure où cette technique est pertinente, l'ordre d'événements noté dans la séquence de base du nord de Kent est généralement confirmé dans d'autres régions, mais les données relevées dans les gisements du nord de Kent sont également quelque peu amplifiées.

6 *Le Paléolithique moyen, pages 233-67*

Quelques unes des industries levalloisiennes déjà discutées doivent être reconnues comme faisant partie du Paléolithique moyen. Considérant la discontinuité d'occupation de la Grande Bretagne, nous ne voyons ni limite nette entre le Paléolithique inférieur et moyen, ni transition locale progressive de l'un à l'autre. Le Moustérien continental est brièvement considéré, comme cadre essentiel à l'étude des documents britanniques. La seule variante continentale du Moustérien développé que l'on distingue sans difficulté en Grande Bretagne est le MTA, bien qu'il soit probable qu'il existe quelques exemples d'industries du 'Moustérien archaïque' d'âge wolstonien, notamment à High Lodge, Mildenhall (Suffolk), industries qui ne sont pas sans parallèles continentaux. Le seul gisement moustérien de la Grande Bretagne qui ait fourni des documents réellement abondants est la Cotte de Saint-Brelade, Jersey (Iles de la Manche), bien que nous considérions que cette industrie serait mieux classée parmi les phénomènes d'occupation moustérienne de l'Ouest de la France, plutôt que rapportée à celle de la Grande Bretagne, malgré son importance considérable. Nous décrivons des occupations MTA dans plusieurs grottes britanniques au nord des Midlands, dans le Sud-Ouest et au Pays de Galles. Il est à noter que les grottes britanniques sont toutes situées à la périphérie de la région peuplée par l'homme pendant le Paléolithique inférieur et moyen et qu'aucune de ces grottes ne semble avoir été habitée intensément ou fréquemment. D'autrepart, il y a une répartition considérable, bien qu'inégale, de bifaces typiquement moustériens de la forme dite 'bout coupé', qui recouvre le Sud et l'Est de la Grande Bretagne, pour la plupart, des trouvailles isolées provenant de sites de plein air. Ces outils distinctifs, dont une liste compréhensive est donnée pour la première fois, se trouvent, à notre avis, en dehors du champs de variations morphologiques des bifaces acheuléens et, quand il existe des indications chronologiques pour des exemplaires individuelles, celles-ci suggèrent un âge devensien ou, très rarement, ipswichien tardif. Ces bifaces cadrent bien dans le contexte du MTA de cette période dans le Nord de la France et nous les considérons comme preuve des traversées et des déplacements à l'intérieur du Sud de la Grande Bretagne, mouvements entrepris par des groupes moustériens venus du Nord de la France et peut-être aussi de la Belgique et de l'Allemagne. Quelques sites de plein air plus substantiels, référables au MTA, sont connus en Grande Bretagne, tels que Bramford Road, Ipswich (Suffolk), ou Great Pan Farm, Shide (Ile de Wight); ceux-ci sont brièvement décrits.

7   *Pour une meilleure connaissance de l'archéologie de la période: quelques conclusions, interprétations et conjectures, pages 268-84*

Nous récapitulons les conclusions données au sujet de la séquence d'industries du Paléolithique inférieur et moyen, ainsi que de la place des documents britanniques dans le Paléolithique européen. La chronologie probable de ces industries est résumée et les défauts de la succession pléistocène, telle qu'elle est actuellement perçue en Grande Bretagne, sont de nouveau soulignés. Il est difficile d'aborder un exposé de la paléo-anthropologie du Paléolithique inférieur et moyen de la Grande Bretagne, lorsque les documents sont si pauvres. Le stade Acheuléen moyen est le seul que mérite une discussion de la question de variabilité d'industries contemporaines et il est alors vraisemblable que la variation de fonction soit importante. Cependant, les fonctions précises d'outils sont difficiles à déterminer pendant tout le Paléolithique, les bifaces acheuléens étant un exemple classique. L'analyse des traces d'usure (à fort grossissement sous microscope) constitue la voie de recherche la plus prometteuse. Quelques résultats préliminaires importants, obtenus par L.H. Keeley, sont résumés, en nous référant en particulier aux gisements de Clacton et de Hoxne. Nous discutons d'autres détails relatifs aux problèmes des fonctions d'outils. Il semble possible que les grands éclats levalloisiens ovales aient parfois pu être des pièces supports, des 'flans', pour la fabrication des bifaces. Donc, on

pourrait considérer Baker's Hole comme une variante extrême à l'intérieur de l'Acheuléen. Dans les industries postérieures, à éclats-lames levalloisiens, beaucoup de pièces semblent avoir été des armatures de projectile et des couteaux. Deux de ces gisements, bien qu'ayant été découverts au dix-neuvième siècle et mal publiés, semblent avoir été des lieux de chasse ou de dépeçage et sont les seuls exemples britanniques connus. Nous suggérons que les occurrences d'éclats-lames levalloisiens peuvent constituer des industries variantes appartenant au MTA britannique, spécialisées dans des activités de chasse et de dépeçage dans les sites de plein air.

Nulle évidence claire de constructions d'habitation n'existe dans le Paléolithique inférieur et moyen en Grande Bretagne, quoique de bons exemples se rencontrent ailleurs dans le monde. Il y a peu de choses à dire, à en juger par les documents existants, au sujet des déplacements saisonniers des groupes de chasse/cueillette, pas plus que des campements 'permanents' ou 'temporaires'. Nous suggérons, néanmoins, qu'en majeure partie, l'occupation paléolithique de la Grande Bretagne se soit constituée de visites de chasse pendant l'été, les campements de base d'hiver étant dans les régions formant actuellement l'Ouest de l'Europe continentale. Cette proposition semble particulièrement probable pour le Moustérien britannique d'âge devensien; aucun gisement ne ressemble en rien à un campement de base occupé pendant l'hiver. En effet, les conditions hivernales en Grande Bretagne à cette époque ont dû être quelque peu désagréables. La diagnose de sites d'activités spécialisées pendant le Paléolithique inférieur et moyen de la Grande Bretagne est également fort difficile, à l'exception des deux lieux de chasse ou de dépeçage déjà mentionnés et d'un certain nombre de sites où les activités primaires étaient certainement l'acquisition de pierre et la fabrication d'outils. Il n'y a pratiquement rien à dire au sujet de l'importance des groupes humains en Grande Bretagne pendant cette période, pas plus que sur l'organisation sociale ou sur l'équipement domestique. Il existe un seul cas possible de découverte d'objets ornementaux: des perles de pierre. De meilleures données socio-économiques n'apparaîtront qu'après l'examen, dans des conditions modernes, de nouveaux gisements britanniques, bien préservés et en contexte primaire. De tels gisements pourraient bien exister.

(Translation of the English summary by Mr and Mrs S.N. Collcutt)

Zusammenfassung

DIE ALT- UND MITTELPALÄOLITHISCHEN PERIODEN BRITANNIENS

1 Voraussetzungen für eine Untersuchung der britischen Altsteinzeit, Seiten 1-33

Unter den prähistorischen Perioden Britanniens ist das Paläolithikum am schwierigsten zu erhellen. Dafür sind der erhebliche Mangel an ungestörten Stationen und die extreme Seltenheit von anderen Spuren als Steinartefakten verantwortlich. Auch unsere Kenntnisse der britischen Pleistozän-Abfolge sind noch unvollständig, und wegen des Fehlens pleistozäner Vulkantätigkeit können chronometrische Daten nur sehr schwer festgelegt werden. Während des Pleistozäns lag Britannien am nordwestlichen Rand der altweltlichen Verbreitung des Menschen. Es war manchmal eine Insel, gelegentlich eine Halbinsel und dann zeitweilig über ausgeprägte Fernrouten von Süd und Ost erreichbar. Es war aber sicher nicht ununterbrochen bewohnt. Dabei bleibt bedeutsam, dass die Abfolge des britischen Paläolithikums vollständig im europäischen und altweltlichen Zusammenhang und nicht als isoliertes Geschehen untersucht wird. Die frühesten britischen Industrien gehören wahrscheinlich in den Zeitraum zwischen 500 000 und 200 000 Jahren vor heute. Im Vergleich mit anderen Regionen, wie etwa derjenigen Ost-Afrikas, bedeutet dies einen verhältnismässig späten Beginn, und das gesamte britische paläolithische Material besitzt daher wohl ein mittel- oder jungpleistozänes Alter. In Britannien gibt es mehr als 3 000 Fundpunkte alt- und mittelpaläolithischer Artefakte. Aber nur sehr wenige haben gute ökologische, chronologische oder paläoanthropologische Belege erbracht. Die Entwirrung der Ereignisse des Pleistozäns und des Paläolithikums ist eine Aufgabe für zahlreiche unterschiedliche Spezialisten innerhalb des allgemeinen Faches der Quartärforschung. Zusammen mit der Abschätzung der gegenwärtigen Forschungstendenzen und -interessen wird ein Bericht über die letzten 150 oder etwas mehr Jahre der quartären und Paläolithischen Forschung in Britannien vorgelegt. Es werden frühere Versuche, das gesamte britische paläolithikum — oder grössere Teile davon — zu beschreiben, erörtert, und es wird dabei festgestellt, dass eine zusammenfassende Darstellung des britischen Alt- und Mittelpaläolithikums noch fehlt.

2 Die Pleistozäne Abfolge, Seiten 34-64

Zunächst wird die Natur der glazialen, periglazialen und interstadialen Verhältnisse umschrieben und danach die Art der Belege, durch die sie im einzelnen nachgewiesen sind, aufgelistet. Ferner wird die Pleistozänabfolge in Britannien aufgezeigt und zwar unter Verweis auf die verschiedenen Schlüsselstationen und -profile, einschliesslich von West Runton (Norfolk), Corton (Suffolk), Hoxne (Suffolk), Marks Tey (Essex) und verschiedener anderer. Die für dieses Buch wichtigen Hauptstufen des britischen Pleistozäns sind (in chronologischer Folge): Cromerian Interglazial, Anglian Glazial, Hoxnian Interglazial, Wolstonian Glazial, Ipswichian Interglazial und Devensian Glazial. Einige von diesen sind wahrscheinlich komplexer als gegenwärtig deutlich erkannt werden kann, und es könnte gut eine oder sogar mehrer Lücken innerhalb der durch diese Namen belegten Abfolge geben. Bessere und vollständigere Pleistozänabfolgen sind auf dem europäischen Kontinent und in den Isotop-Temperaturkurven aus verschiedenen Tiefseebohrkernen verfügbar. Versuche der Korrelation zwischen Tiefseebohrkernen und der britischen terrestrischen Abfolge deuten an, dass letztere viele Probleme offen lässt. Nur innerhalb des Devensian sind Interstadiale überhaupt klar erkennbar, obwohl sie auch im Wolstonian und Anglian existiert haben müssen. Für die aufgezählten Pleistozänstufen werden vorläufige chronometrische Altersangaben zur Diskussion gestellt, auch wenn tatsächliche Belege für deren Absicherung in den Perioden vor dem Devensian äusserst selten bleiben.

3   *Die Suche nach einer grundlegenden altpaläolithischen Abfolge, Seiten 65-93*

Die Aufgabe, archäologische Belege zu beschreiben, kann auf verschiedene Weise angegangen werden. Der Autor entschied sich dazu, Stationen im nördlichen Kent als grundlegende Abfolge zu benutzen, da nur hier mehrere paläolithische Industrien in einer Sequenz von Pleistozänablagerungen vorkommen, deren stratigraphische Anordnung geologisch demonstriert werden kann. Die Hauptstationen sind die berühmten Kiesgruben von Swanscombe (vor allem die Barnfield-Grube und Ricksons-Grube), sowie die benachbarten Vorkommen von Northfleet: die klassische Station Baker's Hole und einige bestimmte Aufschlüsse im sogenannten Ebbsfleet-Kanal. Auch Funde aus den nur einige Meilen entfernten Ziegelerden von Crayford können angeführt werden. Die Kombination dieser Stationen ergibt eine klare lokale archäologische Abfolge mit Clactonian, das von gutgearbeiteten Acheul-Industrien gefolgt wird. Danach tauchen Industrien mit auffälliger Betonung des Gebrauchs der Levallois-Technik auf, zunächst um damit grosse, schwere und später um feinere längliche Abschlag-Klingen herzustellen. Es gibt Anzeichen dafür, dass sich wenigstens die Herstellung von Faustkeilen sporadisch in diesem Teil von Kent fortsetzte, als diese Levallois-Industrien geläufig waren. Die Erstellung dieser Grundabfolge ermöglicht, einige Fragen, deren Beantwortung in den nächsten beiden Kapiteln erwogen werden soll. Gibt es in Britannien andere Stufen oder Industrien, die diese Abfolge ausweiten lässt? Bestehen anderswo in Britannien Stationen, deren Industrien mit jenen aus Kent gut übereinstimmen? Kann behauptet werden, dass es im britischen Altpaläolithikum *gleichzeitige* Industrien gibt, die sich voneinander deutlich unterscheiden, oder sind die unterschiedlichen Industrien auch in ihrem Alter voneinander getrennt, wie dies in der Abfolge von Nord Kent der Fall zu sein scheint? – d.h.: können wir innerhalb der britischen altpaläolithischen Industrien sowohl 'horizontale' wie 'vertikale' Variationen erfassen?

4   *Die Ausweitung der grundlegenden Abfolge, Seiten 94-130*

Es ist klar, dass es anderswo in Britannien Indus-trien gibt, die früher anzusetzen sind als diejenigen in der Swanscombe-Northfleet-Crayford-Abfolge. Sowohl Westbury-sub-Mendip (Somerset) wie Kent's Cavern (Devon) haben Artefakte in Verbindung mit Faunenresten aus dem späten Cromerian oder (wahrscheinlicher) Inter-Anglian-Alter erbracht. Die Artefakte der erstgenannten Station sind für keine bestimmte Industrie kennzeichnend, aber jene der zweiten enthalten Faustkeile mit archaischem Erscheinungsbild. Der Autor plädiert daher für die Existenz eines britischen Früh-Acheul und schlägt die Zugehörigkeit einiger anderer Industrien dazu vor, obwohl diese in sich selbst nicht gut datiert sind. Die bedeutendsten von ihnen sind: Fordwich (Kent), Farnham Terrace A (Surrey) und die abgerollten Serien von Warren Hill, Mildenhall (Suffolk). Wenn diese Vorstellung auf Zustimmung stösst, wird es sinnvoll, die Faustkeil-Industrien von Swanscombe als 'Mittel-Acheul' zu bezeichnen. Es gibt ebenfalls Belege für eine Acheul-Stufe, die jünger ist als jene, die im Mittleren Schotter und Oberen Lehm von Swanscombe vertreten ist: eine 'End-Acheul/Micoque'-Stufe mit eleganten spitzen plano-konvexen Faustkeilen, die gut jenen aus einigen deutschen und französischen Stationen entsprechen und in das Ende des letzten Interglazials und den Beginn des letzten Glazials zu datieren sind. Das Vorkommen von Wolvercote Channel (Oxfordshire) ist das wichtigste der hierher gehörenden Stationen, und dort waren die Geräte mit einer interglazialen Fauna verbunden, für die der Autor eher eine Stellung im Ipswichian als im Hoxnian vorschlägt.

5   *Weitere Stationen und die Frage der Variation, Seiten 131-232*

Die Verteilung der britischen altpaläolithischen Stationen wird umrissen und diskutiert. Anschliessend werden unter Einbeziehung wichtiger Stationen aus anderen Teilen Britanniens die bisher ausgeschiedenen Hauptstufen zusammenfassend dargestellt. Es wird festgehalten, dass das Clactonian in Britannien vor dem Ende der Anglian-Vereisung vorhanden gewesen sein dürfte. Es gibt wenige reine Clacton-Stationen in Britannien, und die meisten von ihnen scheinen ein Hoxnian-Alter zu besitzen. Dennoch wäre es nach Ausweis einer kleinen Anzahl von Stationen möglich, dass die Clacton-Tradition in einer technologisch verbesserten Form nach dem Hoxnian andauerte. Dieser Eindruck würde recht gut mit dem übereinstimmen, was in einigen Teilen des kontinentalen Europas von Abschlagindustrien bekannt ist, die älter als das Moustérien in seiner typischen Form sind.

Einige weitere Früh-Acheul-Stationen werden erwähnt. Anschliessend wird das Mittel-Acheul von Britannien unter Hinweis auf alle wichtigen Stationen eingehend diskutiert. Der Schreibende fasst seine eigene bisherige Arbeit über die britischen Faustkeil-Industrien zusammen und ergänzt sie auf den neuesten Stand. Ein System von Traditionen, Gruppen und Untergruppen lässt sich innerhalb der besten britischen Stationen unterscheiden. Aus der grossen Menge von vermischten und undatierten britischen Stationen kann aus typologischen und technologischen Gründen mit mehr oder weniger Zuverlässigkeit eine Anzahl von Zuordnungen zu bestimmten Bereichen dieses Systems vorgenommen werden. Wenn der Datierungsnachweis, der von geeigneten Stationen ableitbar ist, berücksichtigt wird, dann ist verständlich, dass die vorgeschlagenen 'Spitzen-' (Pointed) und 'Oval-' (Ovate) 'Traditionen' (jene Gruppen von Industrien, in denen jeweils spitze oder ovale Faustkeil-Typen vorherrschen) sich zeitlich in beachtlichem Umfang überlappen. Es folgert daher, dass die Sequenz des Auftretens, wie sie in der Barnfield-Grube, Swanscombe, zu beobachten ist, wo eine 'spitze' Faustkeil-Industrie in den Mittleren Schottern einer 'ovalen' im Lehm voranging, *nicht* für Britannien im allgemeinen gilt. Es gibt keine klar erkennbaren lokalen Varianten innerhalb des britischen Acheulian. Deutlich wird aber, dass das Mittel-Acheul in Britannien eine lang andauernde und variable Stufe ist. Der Grund für diesen erkennbaren Unterschied ist noch keineswegs klar. Aber es ist wahrscheinlich, dass menschliche Aktivitäten in ihrem Wechsel ein bedeutsamer Faktor waren. Der spätere Abschnitt der 'Mittel-Acheul'-Stufe könnte sich zeitlich sogar mit der schon diskutierten End-Acheul/Micoque-Episode überlappen.

Die im Kapitel 3 begonnene Schilderung der Levallois-Technik in ihrem Gebrauch in Britannien wird fortgesetzt und ergänzt. Zusammenfassende Darstellungen werden für einige wichtigere Stationen gegeben: in West London, East Anglia, im Great Ouse Tal (in Bedfordshire und Hunting-donshire), in Nordost-Kent und Süd-Essex. Es existiert keine Levallois-Kultur in Britannien, wie man einst glaubte. Neben Industrien, die fast ausschliesslich aus Levallois-Artefakten bestehen, gibt es Acheul-Industrien, die die Levallois-Technik in wechselndem Umfang einsetzen, und andere, in denen der Gebrauch der Levallois-Technik mit dem Vorkommen typischer Moustier-Artefakte verbunden ist. Einige gemischte Inventare, in denen die Levallois-Technik auftritt, werden erwähnt. Dort gibt es Faktoren von besonderer Bedeutung und zwei interessante und auffallende Vorkommen, in denen eine vereinfachte oder 'reduzierte' Levallois-Technik zu finden ist. Die Verteilung der Fundpunkte mit Levallois-Artefakten in Britannien ist unausgeglichen, so dass der Eindruck entsteht, als ob die Technik möglicherweise in Abhängigkeit von einer lokalen Basis angewandt wurde, wenigstens teilweise in Zusammenhang von der Verfügbarkeit geeigneten Rohmaterials in ausreichender Menge. Die Anwendung der Levallois-Technik erstreckt sich in Britannien vom späten Hoxnian bis in das mittlere Devensian in der einen oder anderen Form innerhalb des Paläolithikums. In dieser Beziehung wird der Ablauf der Ereignisse, wie sie in der Grundabfolge von Nord Kent festgehalten ist, in anderen Regionen im allgemeinen bestätigt. Aber die in Nord Kent verfügbaren Informationen erfahren zugleich eine Ausweitung.

6 *Das Mittelpaläolithikum, Seiten 233-67*

Einige der bereits diskutierten Levallois-Industrien müssen dem Mittelpaläolithikum zugerechnet werden. Im Hinblick auf die Diskontinuität der Besiedlung in Britannien sehen wir weder eine klare Trennung zwischen Alt- und Mittelpaläolithikum noch einen allmählichen lokalen Übergang von dem einen zum anderen. Das kontinentale Moustérien wird kurz als wichtiger Hintergrund für das Studium des britischen Materials betrachtet. Die einzige kontinentale Variante des vollentwickelten Moustérien, die deutlich in Britannien erkennbar ist, stellt das Moustérien mit Acheul-Tradition dar (MTA), obwohl es wahrscheinlich auch einige Beispiele 'archaischer Moustier-' Industrien von Wolstonian-Alter gibt, vor allem in High Lodge, Mildenhall (Suffolk), die nicht ohne kontinentale Parallelen sind. Die einzige Moustier-Station mit wirklich umfangreichem Material ist La Cotte de Saint Brelade, Jersey (Channel Islands), wenn auch der Autor die Ansicht vertritt, dass sie eher zur Moustier-Besiedlung Frankreichs zugehörig anzusehen ist als zu der Britanniens, ohne Rücksicht auf ihre beachtliche Bedeutung. Es gibt MTA-Besiedlungen in verschiedenen britischen Höhlen der nördlichen Midlands, im Südwesten und Wales, die beschrieben werden. Auffallend ist, dass alle britischen Höhlen am Rande des Gebietes liegen, das vom Menschen im Alt- und Mittelpaläolithikum bevölkert wurde. Keine einzige scheint intensiver besiedelt oder häufiger besucht worden zu sein. Dagegen gibt es eine beachtliche, wenn auch lückenhafte Verteilung typischer Moustier-Faustkeile vom Typus *bout coupé* im gesamten Süden und Osten Britanniens, meist Einzelfunde im Freiland. Diese charakteristischen Geräte, von denen zum ersten Mal eine umfassende

Liste publiziert wird, liegen nach Ansicht des Autors ausserhalb der Variationsbreite der Acheul-Faustkeile. Wo es irgendwelche Datierungshinweise für Einzelstücke gibt, deuten sie auf einen Ansatz im Devensian oder sehr gelegentlich auch im späten Ipswichian hin. Sie passen gut in den Zusammenhang des nordfranzösischen MTA dieser Periode, und der Autor betrachtet sie daher als Nachweis für Bewegungen durch und innerhalb des südlichen Britanniens, die von Nordfrankreich und vielleicht auch Belgien und Deutschland ausgehen. Einige weitere klare MTA-Freilandstationen sind aus Britannien gleichfalls bekannt, wie Bramford Road, Ipswich (Suffolk), oder Great Pan Farm, Shide (Isle of Wight) und diese werden kurz beschrieben.

7   Als Annäherung an eine Archäologie der Periode: einige Schlüsse, Interpretationen und Spekulationen, Seiten 268-84

Die erreichten Schlüsse über die Abfolge der alt- und mittelpaläolithischen Industrien und die Stellung Britanniens im europäischen Paläolithikum werden rekapituliert. Die wahrscheinliche Chronologie wird zusammenfassend dargestellt, und die Mängel der gegenwärtigen britischen Pleistozän-Gliederung werden erneut hervorgehoben. Es ist schwierig, eine versuchsweise Bilanz der Palaeoanthropologie des britischen Alt- und Mittelpaläolithikums zu ziehen, da die Belege so wenig umfangreich sind. Nur für die Stufe des Mittel-Acheul ist die Erörterung der Frage nach der Variabilität der gleichzeitigen Industrien lohnend, und es scheint einleuchtend, dass die funktionellen Differenzen bedeutsam sind. Allerdings ist es im Paläolithikum schwierig, die genaue Funktion von Geräten zu bestimmen. Dabei bilden die Acheul-Faustkeile ein klassisches Beispiel. Die Analyse der Feinabnutzung ist (unter Benutzung starker Vergrösserung) die erfolgversprechendste Forschungsrichtung in diesem Bereich, und einige wichtige, von L.H. Keeley erarbeitete erste Resultate werden unter besonderer Berücksichtigung der Stationen von Clacton und Hoxne zusammenfassend dargestellt. Andere Gesichtspunkte, die für das Problem der Gerätefunktion wichtig sind, werden diskutiert. Es scheint möglich, dass die grossen Levallois-Abschläge gelegentlich Vorprodukte für die Faustkeilherstellung sind: Baker's Hole kann daher

als eine extreme Variante innerhalb des Acheul angesehen werden. In den späteren 'Abschlag-Klingen'-Levallois-Industrien müssen viele der Stücke Geschoss-Spitzen oder Messer gewesen sein. Zwei dieser Stationen, obwohl während des 19. Jahrhunderts entdeckt und schlecht veröffentlicht, scheinen Tötungs- order Zerlegungsplätze dargestellt zu haben. Dies sind die einzigen britischen Beispiele. Es wird erwogen, ob diese 'Abschlag-Klingen-Levallois'-Vorkommen, die zum britischen MTA gehören, auf Jagd- und Zerlegungsaktivitäten spezialisierte Industrievarianten in Freilandstationen sein könnten.

Es existieren keine klaren Belege für die Existenz artefizieller Behausungsstrukturen innerhalb des britischen Alt- und Mittelpaläolithikums, obwohl es gute Beispiele anderswo gibt. Wenig kann über die saisonalen Bewegungen von Jäger-Sammler Gruppen oder über 'ständige' oder 'kurzfristige' Lager gesagt werden. Der Autor macht allerdings den Vorschlag, erhebliche Teile der paläolithischen Aufenthalte in Britannien als sommerliche Jagdbesuche anzusehen, während sich die Winterlager dort befanden, wo heute das kontinentale Westeuropa existiert. Das trifft besonders für das britische Moustérien von Devensian-Alter zu. Keine einzige Station sieht wie ein Winter-Basislager aus, und die Winterverhältnisse dürften während dieser Zeit in Britannien etwas unangenehm gewesen sein. Der Nachweis von Stationen mit spezialisierten Aktivitäten ist im britischen Alt- und Mittelpaläolithikum ebenfalls sehr schwierig. Eine Ausnahme bilden die beiden bereits erwähnten Tötungs- und Zerlegungsplätze, sowie eine Anzahl von Lokalitäten, wo die Hauptaktivitäten sicher in der Gewinnung von Stein und der Produktion von Geräten bestanden. Wenig oder nichts kann über die Grösse menschlicher Gruppen während dieser Zeit oder ihre soziale Organisation und die allgemeine Ausstattung in Britannien gesagt werden. In einem einzigen Fall besteht die Möglichkeit, dass Schmuck (Steinperlen) entdeckt wurde. Bessere sozioökonomische Daten werden erst verfügbar sein, wenn neue, gut erhaltene Stationen in primärer Lagerung in Britannien entdeckt und mit modernen Methoden untersucht werden. Derartige Stationen könnten durchaus vorhanden sein.

(Translation of the English summary by
H. Müller-Beck)

Index

1 Flint-knapping waste: this view of Peter R. Jones at work on the experimental replication of prehistoric flint implements gives some idea of the quantities of knapping debris quickly produced

2 Some characteristic microwear polishes on flint, produced experimentally by L. H. Keeley (scale × 200 approx.): (a) wood polish produced by whittling; (b) bone polish produced by scraping; (c) polish from scraping greased dry hide; (d) polish from cutting meat. Some microwear polishes on archaeological specimens are shown in Plate 36

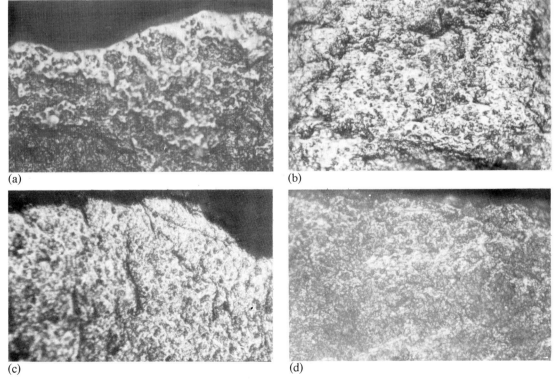

(a)

(b)

(c)

(d)

(a)

3 Kent's Cavern, Torquay: (a) an early photograph of the cave entrance: the figure furthest from the camera is believed to be William Pengelly; (b) work in progress inside the cave in 1925 by members of the Torquay Natural History Society: from left, Dr Tebbs, Rev. Shooter, Miss Dick, Miss Webb, Mr Ogilvie, Mr Rogers and a workman

(b)

(a)

(b)

(c)

(d)

4 (a) Sir John Evans (1823–1908), from a photograph
taken in 1871; (b) Worthington G. Smith
(1835–1917); (c) A. D. Lacaille (1894–1975), from a
photograph taken in 1933; (d) Benjamin Harrison
(1837–1921) at work on one of his eolith sites in the
Ightham area

5 Some mementoes of Benjamin Harrison: background, one of his beautiful watercolour drawings of eoliths from a site near Maplescombe, Kent (in the author's possession); foreground, five eoliths (Pitt Rivers Museum, Oxford), showing the usual natural chipping of the edges. The one in the centre has been derisively ornamented by Worthington Smith to make it 'human' after Harrison had sent it to him for an opinion

6 A raised beach. The famous section at Black Rock, Brighton, showing a somewhat degraded Pleistocene chalk cliff (right), with the old beach at its foot (bottom left of photograph, above the modern wall). The old cliff and beach have been buried beneath massive deposits of Coombe Rock (soliflucted chalky material), which can clearly be seen to have sludged down over the old cliff. The section is exposed in a modern cliff face running almost at right angles to the buried Pleistocene cliff

7 Wave-cut platform at Reighton, near Filey, Yorkshire, exposing boulder clay (till), consisting of fine sediments incorporating various erratic rock fragments

8 Glacially sculptured landscape in the English Lake District, west of Derwentwater, including a fine corrie (upper centre) and characteristically sharp ridges between valleys which once contained valley glaciers

9 Cast of an ice-wedge in the Upper Series at Hoxne, cf. Plate 13

(b)

(a)

10 Cliff sections at West Runton, Norfolk, the Cromerian type site (cf. Fig. 2:2 and Table 2): (a) estuarine silts and gravel (lower half of photograph), overlain by Anglian till (upper half). (b) The cliffs at West Runton in 1977: parts of the classic exposures are somewhat overgrown, but the dark, peaty Cromerian deposits can clearly be seen at the base of the cliff, with overlying chalky Anglian till in the cliff face (top right)

11 Cliff section at Corton, Suffolk, complete with eager geologists. The sequence present here includes deposits of the Cromer Forest Bed Series, just above the sea wall, overlain by a succession of Anglian deposits: decalcified Cromer Till, Corton Sands and Lowestoft Till (cf. Table 3 and Fig. 2:3)

(a)

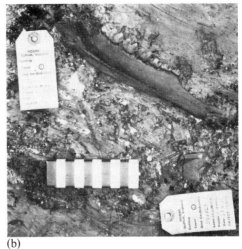

(b)

12 The sequence at Hoxne: (a) the peaty detritus mud, Stratum D of West, at the top of the interglacial lake sediments, is shown at the base of a cutting in the excavations of 1972 (the dark layer just above the standing water). The Hoxne Lower Industry lay on its surface. Above are reworked lake deposits, overlain by fluviatile silt and chalky gravels with cool microfauna. (b) Close association of faunal remains and arte-facts in the Lower Industry: a fine deer mandible with teeth (to right of the upper label) and a struck flake in mint fresh condition (just above the lower label)

(a)

(b)

13 The sequence at Hoxne (continued): (a) general view of work in progress on the Upper Series in 1971; (b) section through part of the Upper Series in 1971. The floor of the trench exposes the top of the fluviatile silt and chalky gravel also seen in 12 (a); above comes flood plain silt; the Hoxne Upper Industry was found within it and on its surface. It is overlain by a band of coarse gravel with many derived artefacts, representing torrential flooding of the river valley probably under periglacial con-ditions. Above the gravel are laminated sands and silts, with occasional ice-wedge casts, one of which can be seen in the side section just above the ranging pole (see also Plate 9)

14 The fragments of the Swanscombe hominid skull (occipital view)

15 Barnfield Pit, Swanscombe in the 1930s: a view taken about the time of the discovery of the first skull fragments

16 The sequence at Barnfield Pit, Swanscombe: Lower Gravel, overlain by Lower Loam

17 The sequence at Barnfield Pit, Swanscombe: the Lower Loam, with the darker weathered horizon capping it (at and above the top of the ranging pole). A little of the Lower Middle Gravel can be seen above the top of the cutting

18 *above, left* Barnfield Pit, Swanscombe: the 'midden' level at the base of the Lower Loam, with various vertebrate remains denoted by letters. Amongst them, note an antler of *Dama* attached to a skull fragment (0); another antler (H); a skull of *Ursus* (M); a rhinoceros molar tooth (K); and an acetabulum of *Bos* or *Bison* (W)

19 *above, right* The sequence at Barnfield Pit, Swanscombe: the Middle Gravels, with Lower Middle Gravel at the base, overlain by Upper Middle Gravel, here consisting mainly of cross-bedded sands. The flame-like structures at the extreme top result from modern soil-creep. The Swanscombe hominid skull fragments (Plate 14) were found elsewhere in the pit just above the junction of the Lower Middle and Upper Middle Gravels

20 The sequence at Barnfield Pit, Swanscombe: Upper Loam overlain by Upper Gravel (a solifluction deposit, top of photograph)

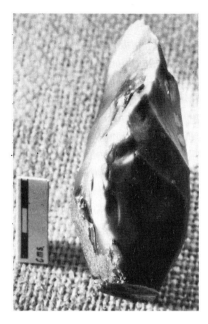

21 Twisted cutting edge in the profile view of a handaxe. The implement, from Hitchin, Herts, is now in the Pitt Rivers Museum at Oxford

22 Levalloisian artefacts from Baker's Hole, Northfleet: a classic struck tortoise core and Levalloisian flake in the foreground, with more Levalloisian flakes behind. Scale: the core is 184mm long, along the axis of the main flake removal, and 153mm broad

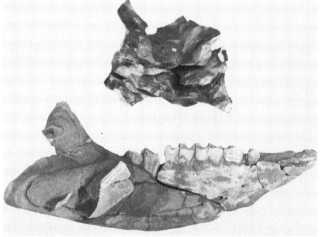

23 Levalloisian flake-blades from Crayford, Kent, now in the collection of Dartford Museum. All are from the Lower Brickearth at Furner's Pit and were found in the period 1908–10

24 Some of Spurrell's finds from Crayford: above, a group of conjoined flakes, in fresh condition; below, the famous rhinoceros jaw and some flint flakes found in contact with it

25 *above, left and right* Westbury-sub-Mendip: two views of the precipitously situated Pleistocene deposits, indicating their general nature and the problems involved in excavating them

(a)

(b)

26 Handaxes from the Wolvercote Channel industry. (a) Six of the implements, showing characteristic shapes; the 'convex' face is upwards in each case; (b) closer view of both faces of the handaxe shown at bottom left in (a), to illustrate the typical 'plano-convex' style of manufacture: flat face on the left, ridged convex face on the right. The implements are all from the collection of the Pitt Rivers Museum, Oxford

27 The Golf Course site, Clacton-on-Sea: area excavation in 1970, exposing the top of the gravel in the West Cutting after removal of the marl. The infilled crack is a periglacial feature postdating the marl

28 A typical section at Furze Platt (Cannoncourt Farm Pit), from a photograph by A. D. Lacaille, c. 1939: poorly stratified gravel with sand lenses, disturbed by solifluction at the top and overlain by a variable thickness of stony loam or brickearth

29 Four fine implements (two handaxes and two cleavers) from Furze Platt, now in the Treacher Collection, University Museum, Oxford

30 *above* Artefacts *in situ* at Cuxton during the excavations of 1963. The four arte- facts shown lie within an area about two feet long and a few inches wide. Note the abundant presence of large flint nodules in the gravel. Brecciated chalk can be seen in the floor of the trench

31 Two views of the main excavation site at Caddington, Bedfordshire, in 1970, giving some idea of the extent of the opera- tion which failed to locate Worthington Smith's floor. Some brickearth is visible in the sections, but no archaeological horizon was present

32 Excavations in progress at the Mousterian site of La Cotte de Saint-Brelade, Jersey, in 1961; Professor C. B. M. McBurney is in the foreground. The sections are cut in the upper levels of the sequence: some loess and thick deposits of ash and occupation debris can be seen centre left

33 Two British caves: (a) *below, left* Pin Hole, Creswell Crags, 1960; (b) *below* Pontnewydd Cave, Clwyd, during the 1978 excavations; the entrance is blocked by a modern wall

(a)

(b)

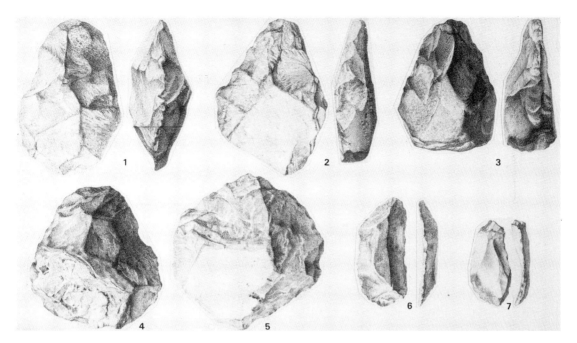

34 Artefacts from the Pontnewydd Cave, as illustrated by McKenny Hughes (1887): nos 1-4 handaxes; no. 5, disc core; nos 6,7, retouched flakes (half size)

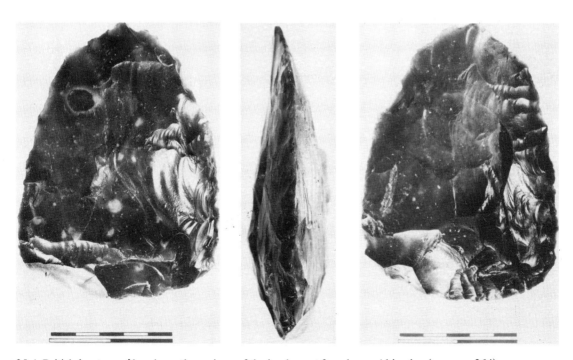

35 A British *bout coupé* handaxe: three views of the implement found near Abingdon (see page 264)

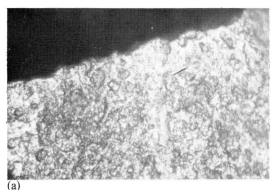 

(a)   (b)

36 Microwear polishes on British Lower Palaeolithic artefacts, scale × 200 (see Figs 7:1, 7:2, and cf. Plate 2): (a) meat and bone polish on a handaxe from the Lower Industry at Hoxne; (b) wood polish on a flake from the marl at the Golf Course site at Clacton

(a)   (b)

37 Occurrences of handaxes and other artefacts at two famous Kenyan sites: (a) the Catwalk Site at Olorgesailie: two black arrows on the rear slope indicate the two separate land surfaces from which the artefacts have been derived by erosion; (b) artefacts (including handaxes of black obsidian) in a stream channel at Kariandusi

38 Naturally perforated fossils (*Coscinopora globularis* d'Orb) found by Worthington Smith in a gravel pit near Bedford and interpreted by him as having been used as personal ornaments or beads (see also Fig. 7:3). A few are shown threaded on a modern leather thong